Ninth Edition

Psychology for Living

Adjustment, Growth, and Behavior Today

Karen Grover Duffy

Eastwood Atwater

PEARSON

Prentice
Hall

UPPER SADDLE RIVER, NJ 07458

Library of Congress Cataloging-in-Publication Data

Duffy, Karen Grover.
    Psychology for living : adjustment, growth, and behavior today/Karen Grover Duffy
    and Eastwood Atwater. —9th ed.
       p. cm.
    Includes bibliographical references and indexes.
    ISBN-13: 978-0-13-222447-5
    ISBN-10: 0-13-222447-X
    1. Conduct of life—Textbooks. I. Atwater, Eastwood, 1925- II. Title.

BF335.A88 2007
158—dc22   2007008541

Editorial Director: Leah Jewell
Executive Editor: Jeff Marshall
Project Manager: LeeAnn Doherty
Editorial Assistant: Jennifer Puma
Senior Marketing Manager: Jeannette Moyer
Marketing Assistant: Laura Kennedy
Production Liaison: Marianne Peters-Riordan
Manufacturing Buyer: Sherry Lewis
Cover Art Director: Jayne Conte
Cover Design: Bruce Kenselaar
Cover Illustration/Photo: Sergio Baradat/Stock Illustration Source, Inc.
Director, Image Resource Center: Melinda Patelli
Manager, Rights and Permissions: Zina Arabia
Manager, Visual Research: Beth Brenzel
Manager, Cover Visual Research & Permissions: Karen Sanatar
Image Permission Coordinator: Nancy Seise
Photo Researcher: Teri Stratford
Composition/Full-Service Project Management: GGS Book Services/Chitra Ganesan
Printer/Binder: Edwards Brothers
Cover Printer: Lehigh Lithographers

Credits and acknowledgments borrowed from other sources and reproduced, with permission, in this textbook appear on appropriate page within text.

Pearson Education LTD.   Pearson Education North Asia Ltd
Pearson Education Singapore, Pte. Ltd   Pearson Educación de Mexico, S.A. de C.V.
Pearson Education, Canada, Ltd   Pearson Education Malaysia, Pte. Ltd
Pearson Education–Japan   Pearson Education, Upper Saddle River, New Jersey
Pearson Education Australia PTY, Limited

10 9 8 7 6 5 4 3 2 1
ISBN-13: 978-0-13-222447-5
ISBN-10:   0-13-222447-X

*Dedicated to Anastasia
Nicholaevna, Alexandra
Feodorovna, and Natalia
Musikantov, for giving me such
sheer delight*

Rose Ikinya

Brief Contents

Tel. (908)222-9455.

1 Self-Direction in a Changing World   1

2 The Journey Begins—Childhood   25

3 Affirmative Aging—Adulthood   57

4 Seeking Selfhood   82

5 Toward Better Health   105

6 Taking Charge   139

7 Managing Motives and Emotions   163

8 Making and Keeping Friends   193

9 Leader or Follower?   221

10 At Work and Play   252

11 Sexuality   280

12 Love and Commitment   312

13 Stress!   343

14 Understanding Mental Disorders   369

15 If You Go for Help   401

16 Good Grief and Death   430

Contents

Preface   xix

How to Study   xxiii

About the Author   xxviii

PART 1 INTRODUCTION

CHAPTER 1

SELF-DIRECTION IN A CHANGING WORLD   **1**

Social Change   **3**

    Living in a Technological World 3   Living with Other
Social Changes 6   How Certain Is Our Future? 7

The Challenge of Self-Direction   **9**

    Self-Direction and Society 9   The Ambiguity of Personal
Freedom 10   Taking Charge of Our Lives 11   Living in
Today's Individualistic Society 14

Themes of Personal Growth   **15**

    Living with Contradictions and Uncertainty 15   Continuity
and Change 16   The Experience of Personal
Growth 17   Beyond Individualism 18

    SUMMARY 21   SELF-TEST 22   EXERCISES 23   QUESTIONS FOR
SELF-REFLECTION 23   FOR FURTHER INFORMATION 24

PART 2 BECOMING

CHAPTER 2

THE JOURNEY BEGINS—CHILDHOOD   25

Perspectives on Child Development   27

The Biological Perspective on Child Development   27

Nature Versus Nurture—An Old Debate 27   A Newer
Approach 30   Applying It to Yourself 30

The Psychodynamic Perspective on Child Development   31

Development of Personality 31   The Structure of
Personality 33   Modifications 35   Applying It
to Yourself 35

The Social-Cognitive Perspective on Child Development   37

Social Learning Theories 37   Recent Additions: Cognition
and Behavior 39   Applying It to Yourself 40

The Humanistic Perspective on Child Development   41

The Phenomenal Self 41   Self-Actualization 43
Applying It to Yourself 44

Developmental Challenges in Childhood   46

Temperament 46   Self-Recognition and Self-Concept 48
Attachment 49   Applying It to Yourself 51

Conclusion   51

SUMMARY 51   SELF-TEST 53   EXERCISES 54   QUESTIONS FOR
SELF-REFLECTION 55   FOR FURTHER INFORMATION 55

CHAPTER 3

AFFIRMATIVE AGING—ADULTHOOD   57

Adult Development   58

Decisions, Decisions, Decisions—Early Adulthood   61

Leaving Home 61   Choosing a Career 62
Establishing Close Relationships 63   Starting a Family 63

Same Old, Same Old?—Middle Adulthood   65

Midlife Transition or Midlife Crisis? 65   Physical and
Cognitive Changes 66   Possible Career Changes 67
Sexual Changes 68

Aging Gracefully—Late Adulthood   **70**

Physical and Cognitive Changes 71   Personal
and Social Adjustment 73   Retirement 75
Successful Aging 76

Summary 77   Answers to Aging Quiz 78   Self-Test 78
Exercises 79   Questions for Self-Reflection 80
For Further Information 80

PART 3 BETTER THAN EVER

CHAPTER 4

SEEKING SELFHOOD   82

What Is Self-Concept?   **83**

Self-Image 84   Ideal Self 85   Multiple Selves 86

Core Characteristics of Self-Concept   **88**

Self-Consistency 89   Self-Esteem 90
Self-Enhancement and Self-Verification 93

The Self-Concept and Personal Growth   **94**

The Self You'd Like to Be 95   Our Social Selves 95
Learning from Criticism 97   Greater Self-Direction 98

Summary 100   Scoring Key for the Self-Image
and Ideal-Self Exercise 101   Self-Test 102
Exercises 103   Questions for Self-Reflection 103
For Further Information 104

CHAPTER 5

TOWARD BETTER HEALTH   105

Body Image   **107**

How We Feel About Our Bodies 107
Our Ideal Body 109

Psychological Factors and Physical Illness   **109**

The Immune System 110   Personality 110
Lifestyle Choices 112   Environmental Issues 121

Coping with Illness   **122**

Noticing and Interpreting Symptoms 122
Seeking Help 123   Adhering to Treatment 125

Promoting Wellness   **126**

Taking Charge of Your Own Health 128   Eating
Sensibly 129   Getting Enough Sleep 130   Keeping
Physically Fit 132   Finding Social Support 133

SUMMARY 134   SELF-TEST 135   EXERCISES 136   QUESTIONS
FOR SELF-REFLECTION 137   FOR FURTHER INFORMATION 137

CHAPTER 6

TAKING CHARGE   **139**

Mastery and Personal Control   **140**

Perceived Control 141   Consequences of Perceived
Control 143   Misperception and Maladjustment 146
Learned Optimism 147

Personal Resolve and Decision Making   **149**

The Process of Decision Making 150   Making Better
Decisions 153

Decisions and Personal Growth   **155**

Identifying the Basic Decisions in Your Life 155   Making
New Decisions 156   Some Practical Applications 157

SUMMARY 158   SELF-TEST 159   EXERCISES 160
QUESTIONS FOR SELF-REFLECTION 161   FOR FURTHER INFORMATION 161

CHAPTER 7

MANAGING MOTIVES AND EMOTIONS   **163**

Understanding Motivation   **164**

Understanding Your Needs 165   Differences
Between You and Others 167   Everyone's Basic
Needs 167   Psychosocial Motives 168
Personal Motivation 172

Understanding Emotions   **173**

What Are Emotions? 173   Experiencing
Emotions 175   Expressing Emotions 177
Managing Emotions 178   Special Emotions 180

SUMMARY 187   SCORING KEY 188   SELF-TEST 189
EXERCISES 190   QUESTIONS FOR SELF-REFLECTION 191
FOR FURTHER INFORMATION 191

PART 4 BEING SOCIAL

CHAPTER 8

MAKING AND KEEPING FRIENDS — **193**

Meeting People — **195**
Are First Impressions Most Important? 196
Mistaken Impressions 202   Shyness 205

Keeping Friends — **208**
Friendships Are Precious 208   When Friends Get
Together 208   Self-Disclosure—Those Little Secrets 209
Same-Sex, Opposite-Sex Friends 211   Staying Friends 213
Loneliness 213

SUMMARY 216   SELF-TEST 217   EXERCISES 218   QUESTIONS FOR
SELF-REFLECTION 219   FOR FURTHER INFORMATION 219

CHAPTER 9

LEADER OR FOLLOWER? — **221**

Kinds of Groups — **223**
Favored Groups—Primary Groups 223
Bigger Than Both of Us—Secondary Groups 224
What Goes Wrong at Rock Concerts?—Collectives 224
"Us" Versus "Them"—In-Groups and Out-Groups 224

How Do Groups Form? — **226**

Why Join a Group? — **227**

What Goes On in Groups? — **229**
What Did You Say?—Communication Patterns 229
You Want Me to Do What?—Social Influence 231
Let the Other Guy Do It—Social Loafing 235
All in Favor Say "Aye"—Group Polarization 235

Are Leaders Made or Born? — **236**
The Great Man Theory 236   Situational
Explanations of Leadership 237   Contingency
Theory 237   Contemporary Theories 239
Gender and Leadership 240   Culture and Leadership 241

When Groups Go Wrong — **241**
The Fiasco of Groupthink 242   A Little Shove
Goes a Long Way—Group Conflict 243

SUMMARY 247   SELF-TEST 248   EXERCISES 249   QUESTIONS
FOR SELF-REFLECTION 250   FOR FURTHER INFORMATION 250

CHAPTER 10

AT WORK AND PLAY   252

Choosing Your Career   254

Taking Stock of Yourself 254   Identifying Compatible
Careers 256   Arriving at Your Career Decision 258
Preparing for Your Career 259

Your Career Outlook   262

Forecasting Your Career's Growth 262
Changing Jobs or Careers 263

Contemporary Issues in the World of Work   265

Job Satisfaction 265   Technology and Work 266
Diversity in the Workplace 268

Leisure Time   271

What Is Leisure? 272   Work and Leisure 273
Using Leisure Positively 273

SUMMARY 275   SELF-TEST 276   EXERCISES 277   QUESTIONS
FOR SELF-REFLECTION 278   FOR FURTHER INFORMATION 279

PART 5 BEING INTIMATE

CHAPTER 11

SEXUALITY   280

Men and Women   281

Changing Views of Sexuality 281   Sexual Communication 284
Initiating and Refusing Sex 287

Sexual Responsiveness   287

The Sexual Response Cycle 288   Individual
Differences 290   Love and Sex 294

Practical Issues   295

Sexual Dysfunctions 295   Contraception 298
Sexually Transmitted Diseases 298   Sexual Victimization 303

SUMMARY 307   SELF-TEST 308   EXERCISES 309
QUESTIONS FOR SELF-REFLECTION 310   FOR FURTHER INFORMATION 310

CHAPTER 12

LOVE AND COMMITMENT   **312**

Love and Intimacy   **314**

The Ingredients of Love 314   Love and Close
Relationships 319

Commitment   **323**

Cohabitation 323   Marriage and Other
Committed Relationships 324

Adjusting to Intimate Relationships   **328**

Sharing Responsibilities 329   Communication
and Conflict 330   Making the Relationship Better 330
Sexuality 331   Changes Over Time 332

Divorce and Its Consequences   **333**

The Divorce Experience 334   Single-Parent
Families 334   Remarriage 336

SUMMARY 337   SCORING KEY FOR THE MARITAL MYTHS QUIZ 338
SELF-TEST 339   EXERCISES 340   QUESTIONS FOR SELF-REFLECTION 341
FOR FURTHER INFORMATION 341

PART 6 FACING CHALLENGES

CHAPTER 13

STRESS!   **343**

Oh No!—Understanding Stress   **344**

Conceptualizing Stress 345   Stress and You 348

Yikes!—Reactions to Stress   **349**

Physiological Stress Reactions 351   Psychological
Stress Reactions 353   How Do You
React to Stress? 354

Phew!—Managing Stress   **359**

Modifying Your Environment 359
Altering Your Lifestyle 361   Using
Stress for Personal Growth 364

SUMMARY 364   SELF-TEST 365   EXERCISES 366
QUESTIONS FOR SELF-REFLECTION 367
FOR FURTHER INFORMATION 367

CHAPTER 14

UNDERSTANDING MENTAL DISORDERS   369

Psychological Disorders   371

What Are Psychological Disorders? 372
How Common Are Psychological Disorders? 374
How Are Disorders Classified? 377

Anxiety Disorders: The Most Common Disorder   378

Generalized Anxiety Disorder 378   Phobias: Fear
of Something That Won't Really Hurt 380
Obsessive-Compulsive Disorder: The Doubting
Disease 381   Trauma and Disaster 382

Mood Disorders   383

What Is Depression? 383   Suicide: Who and
Why? 386   What Is Bipolar Disorder? 387

Other Common Disorders   388

Do You Have an Eating Disorder? 388   What
Are Personality Disorders? 391   Schizophrenia—
The Enigmatic Disorder 392

SUMMARY 396   SELF-TEST 397   EXERCISES 398   QUESTIONS
FOR SELF-REFLECTION 399   FOR FURTHER INFORMATION 400

CHAPTER 15

IF YOU GO FOR HELP   401

Insight Therapies—The Talking Cure   405

Psychoanalysis 405   The Person-Centered
Approach 406   A Variety of Approaches 408

Cognitive-Behavioral Therapies   409

Behavioral Therapies 409   Cognitive
Therapies 411   Status of Psychotherapy Today 411

Other Approaches to Treatment   413

Family, Couples, and Relationship Therapy 414
Biomedical Therapies 415   Community-Based Services 418

How Well Does Therapy Work?   420

Finding Help   422

SUMMARY 425   SELF-TEST 426   EXERCISES 427
QUESTIONS FOR SELF-REFLECTION 428   FOR FURTHER INFORMATION 428

CHAPTER 16

GOOD GRIEF AND DEATH 430

Death and Dying 431

Risks of Dying 432   Awareness of Death 435
Near-Death Experiences 436   The Experience of Dying 437

Bereavement and Grief 438

Grief Work 439   Unresolved Grief 440   Good Grief 441

Life and Death in Perspective 442

The Right to Die 443   A Natural Death 446   Funerals
and Other Services 449   Death and Growth 449

SUMMARY 450   SELF-TEST 451   EXERCISES 452   QUESTIONS
FOR SELF-REFLECTION 453   FOR FURTHER INFORMATION 453

Answers to the Self-Tests 455

Glossary 457

References 465

Photo Acknowledgments 493

Name Index 495

Subject Index 511

Preface

This book is intended for those who are interested in applying psychological insights and principles to their own lives as a way of achieving a better understanding of themselves *and* of living more effectively. To this end, I have included material from the major perspectives of psychology, including the psychodynamic, cognitive-behavioral, and humanistic viewpoints. Since a well-rounded text cuts across several branches of psychology, I have included contributions from clinical, personality, social, and developmental psychology, as well as from the important fields of cognitive, biological, and health psychology. Throughout the book, I've presented differing views on the same issue, along with questions that are designed to stimulate readers' critical thinking. My aim is to increase readers' understanding as well as their knowledge about personal adjustment, in order that they may continue learning on their own.

Major features of this ninth edition are explained in the following sections.

ORGANIZATION

In this edition some chapters have been retitled to reflect a more personalized tone. Please note if you are a former reader of this book: The chapters still stand alone; that is, you can read them out of order and still understand all of the material even though you have not read a preceding chapter.

The introductory chapter on self-direction and social change remains at the beginning, of course. The second large unit is about development or the state of "becoming." The chapters on childhood and adulthood can be found here. The third large unit pertains to the individual in the present or in a state of "being." Here you will find the chapters on self-concept, health, personal control, and decision making, as well as on emotion and motivation.

The next large unit is about the social side of adjustment and growth. Here are located the chapters on friends, groups (leaders and followers), and work and leisure. This unit is followed by an apt unit about closer intimate relationships. This short unit contains two chapters, one each on sexuality and on committed or intimate relationships.

Finally, any book about personal growth and adjustment would be incomplete without including material on the challenges each of us faces. The last unit contains chapters on stress, mental disorders, therapy, and death and dying. Please let me know how you feel about this organization, and remember that the chapters are self-contained so can easily be read in any order you wish. I can be reached at duffy@geneseo.edu.

NEW CONTENT

I have made some changes to the content of the book to reflect changes in the field of psychology in addition to world events. First, there are nearly 800 new references as well as new glossary terms. Second, you will also find new or additional information on the following topics:

- Technology and how it is shrinking our world
- The threat of terrorism and how it has changed the way we live and cope
- Changes in American attitudes toward such things as free speech
- Expanded critique of the concepts of individual and collective societies
- Environmental psychology and how the environment is changing and affecting each of us
- Population changes related to many topics as evidenced by the latest census
- The status of America's children and what the future holds for them
- Changes in the American family and how they affect the individual members
- The effects of the baby boomers as they enter late adulthood
- Gender similarities and differences, especially as related to education, career choice, leadership, and so on
- Information on self-complexity and discussion of pluses and minuses of promoting self-esteem
- Updated information on Viagra and other such medications
- Thoughtful analysis of the lack of health care for ethnic and racial minorities
- Information on the newly published food pyramid
- Charismatic and transformational leadership and group behavior
- Additional information on intrinsic and extrinsic motivation
- Cultural effects on nonverbal communication (and miscommunication)
- More information on sexual orientation
- Further information on child pornography and sexual assault
- Additional coverage of stress with special attention on terror and trauma
- Inclusion of material on the allostatic concept of stress and its effects
- Stigma as it relates to mental disorders as well as the prevalence of various disorders
- Alternative forms of therapy such as art therapy and acupuncture

LEARNING AIDS

Several features have been included to assist the student in making the best use of this book:

- A How to Study section at the beginning of the book provides suggestions for studying and taking tests.
- Chapter outlines at the beginning of each chapter give students an overview of what will be covered.

- Learning objectives identify what students are expected to attain in regard to knowledge, understanding, and application.
- Terms that may be new to students are boldfaced and are followed by an italicized definition that is repeated in the glossary. Each time the term is used, regardless of the chapter, it is highlighted so that no matter in what order the chapters are read, the term will be familiar to the reader.
- Special-interest boxes, figures, and tables contain interesting and important material supplemental to the text.
- A glossary at the end of the book defines key, boldfaced terms in the text.
- End-of-chapter summaries, arranged by major headings, help the reader to grasp the main points of the chapter.
- Self-tests, consisting of 10 multiple-choice questions, help students to assess their understanding of the material covered.

APPLICATIONS

- Cases intertwined throughout the chapter reify the information for readers. These are *real* cases based on Dr. Atwater's (founding author of this text) or my experiences. The cases have been fictionalized and modified to protect the identity of the people in them.
- One or two self-scoring inventories in each chapter enable students to apply the concepts and principles covered in the text. These inventories are designed by me, so please note that they have no scientifically derived validity or reliability. They are merely meant to be tools for self-exploration and self-understanding and should be interpreted as such.
- End-of-chapter exercises heighten the student's involvement in the material.
- Questions for self-reflection encourage students to relate the material in the text to themselves.

FOR FURTHER INFORMATION

A special feature at the end of each chapter is a list of ways to explore topics electronically or in print. One of the points the text establishes is that we have moved into a technological information age. Therefore, World Wide Web sites are listed at the end of the chapter along with recommended additional readings. These web sites and additional readings are provided with a brief description of their contents and are intended for those who wish to pursue a given topic in greater depth.

INSTRUCTOR'S MANUAL

A separately bound Instructor's Manual is also available. Each chapter in the learning aids section includes a chapter overview, class activities, discussion questions, lecture suggestions, and audiovisual resources. For each chapter in the test item section, there are representative multiple-choice questions, essay questions, short-answer questions, and true-false items.

ACKNOWLEDGMENTS

Many thanks to Dr. Eastwood Atwater for providing me with the opportunity to take over this well-established book. While he is no longer with us, I hope that he would approve of my continued efforts at producing the same high-quality book he wrote. Thanks also to Tim Tomczak for his contributions to Chapter 2; I hope to be able to turn this book over to him in the future. Tim also worked on the *Instructor's Manual*, including the test bank, for which I am very grateful. Many thanks to the professors who adopted past editions and provided feedback to me. I really DO appreciate your comments and take them to heart. Thank you to Sherri Tkachuk who patiently typed hundreds of new references (and to the professors who taught her APA style). Special thanks goes to Jeff Marshall and his staff at Prentice Hall. Jeff is patient but gently prodding, just the type of editor I need and appreciate. Thanks also go to LeeAnn for patiently shepherding this project through the production process. To my friends and family, a big thank you for nudging me along when I got discouraged about getting this and other books completed, especially given the vicissitudes of daily life and the distracting tug at my heart strings of the sun, moon, stars, and my critters who needed petting.

Many thanks to the following reviewers for their insightful comments and helpful suggestions:

Jennifer Pisarik
Middlesex Community College

Valerie S. Smead
Western Illinois University

Jamalat Daoud
Ball State University

Benjamin Landman
Alamance Community College

Debra Rowe
Oakland Community College

Kathrin Milbury
York Technical College

How to Study

Students give many excuses about why they haven't done well on a test. Occasionally, they will admit outright, "I just didn't study." But more often they will say, "I really studied for that test. I can't understand why I did so poorly." A common problem is waiting until the last minute to study. But in many instances, students just don't know how to study. Whether or not you fall into this category, chances are you could improve your studying habits by applying one of the following time-honored methods of studying.

THE PQ4R METHOD

The PQ4R method gets its name from the six overlapping stages for studying material such as textbook chapters—preview, question, read, reflect, recite, and review.★ Extensive experience has shown that this method can improve your understanding and memory, and thus your test performance.

PREVIEW

It's a good idea to look over the chapter as a whole before you begin it. When you read a novel, you usually start at the beginning and read straight through so as not to spoil the surprise ending. But with concepts and factual material, it's just the opposite. Here, it's important to get an idea of the material as a whole so you can put the details in context as you read.

- First, look over the table of contents.
- Next, skim through the chapter, looking at the headings and subheadings.
- Then, read the chapter summary.
- Finally, decide how much you want to read at a sitting.

★E. L. Thomas and H. A. Robinson, *Improving memory in every class: A sourcebook for teachers* (Boston: Allyn & Bacon, 1972).

QUESTION

Once you've looked over the chapter, you may be curious about the material. A helpful technique is to ask yourself questions about the material. Then read the chapter with the aim of finding the answers to your questions. One way to do this is to turn each bold-faced heading and subheading into a question. For example, the first major heading and subheadings in Chapter 1 on self-direction are

- Social Change
- Living in a Technological World
- Living with Other Social Changes
- How Certain Is Our Future?

Now use these headings and subheadings to think up some questions. Here are some examples: What is social change? I know I live in a technological world, but how does that relate to social change and self-direction? What are some of the other social changes that I have witnessed? With terror alerts and other dramatic changes, just how certain is my future? Your use of such questions may prove even more effective if you jot them down, and then, as you read, write down your answers.

READ

Make it a point to understand what you're reading, digesting the material in one section before proceeding to the next. Skimming through material without comprehending it leads to superficial understanding at best, but more often, to downright confusion. In contrast, when you take the time to understand what you read, you'll also retain it better. If you're not clear about the meaning of a word, check the glossary of terms at the end of the book. If you can't find the word in the glossary, look it up in one of the better dictionaries such as *Webster's New World Dictionary*. Also, feel free to make explanatory notes to yourself in the margins of the pages of your textbook.

REFLECT

A good way to improve your understanding of something is to pause periodically and reflect on it. Ask yourself: Do I really understand this material? Could I explain it to someone else? If the answer is no, reread the material.

It's also helpful to mark or underline key passages in the chapter. This makes you an active participant in reading and provides you with key passages to review for tests. Some students prefer to mark or underline as they read. Others prefer to read through the material and then go back and highlight the most important points. Experts prefer the latter approach, because we usually have a better idea of the key passages after we've read through the material. Here are some suggestions for marking or underlining:

- Read through each section before marking or underlining.
- Mark only key passages or ideas.
- Use a marker or pen. Pencil often smears.

RECITE

Perhaps you've had this experience: You look up someone's telephone number, but no sooner have you closed the phone book than you've forgotten the number. You reopen the book and find the number again. But this time as you close the book, you repeat the number to yourself, either silently or audibly. You're improving your memory through recitation—the act of repeating or speaking aloud. Recitation improves your memory in several ways. First, by focusing your attention on the page a bit longer, you can encode the material better, thereby ensuring accurate storage of the material. Repeated practice may also help you to retrieve the material when you need it.

There are several ways to use recitation. First, the act of reflection, or asking questions about the material, mentioned earlier, is itself a form of recitation. Second, you may also recite by closing the book and mentally recalling what you've just read. A third way is to recite aloud, either by discussing the material with a classmate or by sharing your reactions or asking questions about it in class. A fourth way is to make a written outline of what you've read. I highly recommend this method because it forces you to select the main ideas in the material. Occasionally, students attempt to escape the thinking process by simply copying down the headings and subheadings, including little else. Others include too much detail, which becomes distracting. Instead, be selective. You should be able to outline an entire chapter of this book in just several written pages, depending, of course, on how large you write. The entire process of selecting the major ideas and writing them down is an excellent form of recitation. It also provides you with a handy guide to review for the test.

The amount of time spent on recitation depends on the material covered. When you're trying to remember isolated bits of information, like names or numbers, up to 80 percent of your time should be spent in recitation. But when you're learning ideas or concepts that are highly meaningful and well organized, perhaps you would spend only 20 percent of your time in recitation. Personal experience will help you to determine which method of recitation works best for you.

REVIEW

When you're ready to review, reread the summary at the end of the chapter to give yourself a sense of the material as a whole. Then look back over the material in the chapter, paying special attention to the key ideas you've marked or underlined under each heading and subheading. If you've made a written outline of the chapter, review this, too. Ideally, you should review the material periodically, to offset the rapid decline in retention once you've learned something. It's recommended that you review the material within 24 hours of the initial reading, and then again 72 hours later. After this, it's a good idea to review the material about once a week until you're tested on it.

When you're ready, do the self-test at the end of each chapter. Then check your responses against the list of correct answers provided in the back of this book. When you miss a question, it's important to go back and look up the correct answer. Otherwise, you may make the same mistake again. You may observe that the order of test items parallels the sequence of material in the chapter, thus facilitating your use of the self-test for study purposes.

WHERE AND WHEN TO STUDY

Once the semester is under way, you're ready to plan your study schedule. Consider your class schedule, the workload in each course, and other commitments, such as a part-time job or family responsibilities. Be realistic. Don't try to study too much material at one time.

First, it's important to find a place to study that is free from distractions. Then use this place only for studying. In this way, you'll develop a set of associations that will strengthen your study habits. One of the worst places to study is on your bed. The bed is associated with fatigue; thus, you may find yourself falling asleep rather than studying. When you find yourself daydreaming or worrying about something else, take a short break and return when you're ready to study. When you finish studying, leave this place. By consistently doing so, you'll associate this place with studying and feel more like studying only there.

It's also important to set aside particular times for study. You may wish to study for a given block of time and quit at the end of this period regardless of how much you've read. Or you may want to study until you've covered a certain amount of material. Either way, it's best to study in reasonable blocks of time, about 1 to 3 hours. After a long stretch you may have difficulty concentrating on the material at hand. That's why it's a good idea to take a short break at least once an hour, or even on the half-hour when you're covering very difficult material. Also, you might select other things you enjoy doing and make them contingent on completing your study goal for a given time slot. For instance, if you'd like to call a friend or watch television, do your studying first. Then make your call or watch TV as a reward to yourself.

Above all, don't procrastinate. Distribute your study times realistically so you don't try to absorb too much material at a time. For instance, if you must cover four chapters in this book for a test, plan to read no more than one chapter in a given time slot. Spacing out your study time cuts down on boredom and fatigue and also allows your memory time to consolidate the material. Your mind may continue absorbing the material in the intervals between study periods. This is especially important to keep in mind when you're learning complex or difficult material.

TAKING TESTS

When taking a test, stay calm and reasonably relaxed. By keeping your anxiety at a mild to moderate level, you minimize its interference with your thinking process. If you encounter a question that makes you especially anxious, note this on the question sheet. Then proceed to do the remaining questions before returning to tackle the difficult question(s). Realizing that you've completed most of the test helps you to concentrate on the more difficult items.

Regardless of the type of test, take time to read the questions carefully. Make certain you understand what the instructor is asking. Don't read things into a question, making it more complicated than it is. If the item looks particularly confusing, raise your hand and ask the instructor to rephrase the item. Be sure also to read every single choice for multiple-choice questions before selecting the correct one.

Before answering an essay question, take a few moments to jot down a brief outline on the back of a page. This helps to keep your thoughts on the subject while you write. If your test includes both multiple-choice and essay questions, first outline the essay question. Then complete the multiple-choice questions before writing out the essay answer.

After you've read a multiple-choice question and selected an answer, it's best to reread the question to make certain your answer matches the question. This helps to avoid simple "forgetting" mistakes, because material stays in our short-term memory for only about 30 seconds. By the time you've decided on the correct answer, chances are you've forgotten the exact wording of the question. Consequently, it's helpful to reread the question before marking your answer. This time, read the answer choices in reverse order.

Learn to eliminate incorrect answers before settling on the correct one. For instance, if there are four possible answers, eliminate the two that are the least plausible. With only two remaining answers to choose from, you have a 50–50 chance of selecting the correct one. Answers containing words like *always*, *never*, *only*, *must*, and *totally* often imply sweeping assertions and can usually be eliminated early on.

Should you ever change your answer? It all depends. If you have studied reasonably well and feel good about your answer, stick with it. If you have strong doubts about an answer, however, especially if you're not well informed on the subject, it might pay to reconsider. At the same time, a lot depends on the individual. In going over tests with students, we've found that anxious, impulsive students may initially choose an incorrect answer and would benefit from taking another look at their answer. On the other hand, students who lack self-confidence will often change a correct answer to an incorrect one because they distrust their own abilities. As a result, we suggest keeping track of the answers you change. Then go over each test, recording the number of answers you changed from wrong to right, and vice versa. Take this information into consideration throughout future test taking.

Finally, there are other ways you can learn from your test results. If your instructor goes over the test in class, make it a point to attend that day. Find out what you missed and, equally important, why. Were the questions different from what you expected, requiring, say, the understanding of concepts rather than factual information? If you didn't do well on an essay test, ask your instructor how you can do better next time. Try not to waste time making excuses or blaming your instructor or yourself. Find out what you need to do in order to improve your test performance next time. Then modify your study habits and test taking accordingly. Good luck!

About the Author

Karen Duffy is a Distinguished Service Professor–emerita, at the State University of New York College at Geneseo. She received her Ph.D. in social and personality psychology from Michigan State University. Dr. Duffy served as a family mediator for the New York Unified Court System. She has also served on the executive committee and as the chief instructor for the training institute for the New York State Employee Assistance Program (EAP), as well as on the board of directors for a shelter for domestic violence and on an educational committee for a family planning agency. She has consulted to a variety of work settings on stress management, EAPs, and other work issues. She is a member of the American Psychological Society. Dr. Duffy has written several other books, including *Community Mediation: A Handbook for Practitioners and Researchers* and *Community Psychology*. She also edits several hard-copy and web-based annual editions for another publisher, on topics including psychology of personality, social psychology, introductory psychology, and adjustment. She has held two Fulbright Fellowships to St. Petersburg State University, St. Petersburg, Russia. While in Russia, she worked with AIDS International, several children's shelters, and other community agencies. More recently, she completed a humanitarian aid trip to Mongolia.

CHAPTER 1

Self-Direction in a Changing World

SOCIAL CHANGE
Living in a Technological World
Living with Other Social Changes
How Certain Is Our Future?

THE CHALLENGE OF SELF-DIRECTION
Self-Direction and Society
The Ambiguity of Personal
    Freedom
Taking Charge of Our Lives
Living in Today's Individualistic
    Society

THEMES OF PERSONAL GROWTH
Living with Contradictions and
    Uncertainty
Continuity and Change
The Experience of Personal
    Growth
Beyond Individualism

SUMMARY
SELF-TEST
EXERCISES
QUESTIONS FOR SELF-REFLECTION
FOR FURTHER INFORMATION

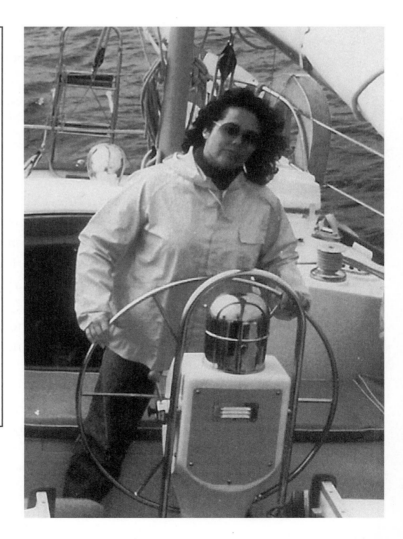

Change has always been an important part of our American way of life. To understand the impact of change, let's meet two college students, Zachary and Karen, related by blood but separated by 100 years. Zachary is a freshman in college in the late 1800s. He is among the privileged few to attend college, mostly because his family is sufficiently well off to send him to school. Zachary travels to college by train, passing through miles of farmland and forests along the way. He keeps in touch with his family by letters. Zachary hopes to be a physician, an occupation pretty much closed to women in the 1800s. A few women do attend Zachary's college but major in home economics, teacher education, and more traditional female majors. Zachary lives at a boardinghouse for male college students. He takes his meals there but studies at the library, where he reads by gaslight. There are no computers or other technology such as photocopiers in the library. Zachary goes to the librarian to find what he needs. He hand-copies everything and also writes papers by hand. No one, absolutely no one, is using a mobile phone in Zachary's library.

Karen, Zachary's great-granddaughter, is a first-year college student of the twenty-first century. Since her parents' divorce, she has lived with her mother and sister. She is able to attend college mostly because of financial aid from private lenders and the government. Karen travels back and forth to college by plane several times a year, passing over the megalopolis on the East Coast spread out over several hundred miles. To keep in touch with her family, she has only to pick up her walk-talkie enabled phone or send an electronic message via computer. Electricity lights up the room in which Karen reads and powers the computer she uses for term papers and correspondence. She is very glad that the computer checks her spelling and grammar. Karen lives in a coed dormitory. Also, she is accustomed to mingling with students from different ethnic and racial groups on campus, and about half of them are women. In Karen's dining hall, genetically engineered tomatoes are occasionally served along with chicken and beef that have been infused with flavor enhancers. Karen uses the library as Zachary did, but she is fortunate to have an electronic card catalog, photocopiers, electronic article downloads, and access to the information highway known as the World Wide Web. Karen hopes to be a physician, as did Zachary. She, however, wants to specialize in gynecology, something Zachary would never dream of. Zachary planned to be a general practitioner who would visit the homes of his patients. Zachary knew some patients could not give him money, so he would take produce, wool, or other products in payment. Karen, on the other hand, wants a posh office, working hours from 9 a.m. to 5 p.m., and an answering service so she can enjoy her private life. She knows she will set up her financial accounting system to accept credit cards, not eggs and bacon.

SOCIAL CHANGE

Living in a Technological World

Both Zachary and Karen have lived in periods of rapid social change. **Social changes** are *changes in social patterns and institutions in society*. Social change can occur in any time period and be planned in advance or totally unplanned (Duffy & Wong, 2003). Planned changes are those created and engineered by humans, for example, building a new housing development wired for the most current technology. Unplanned changes are created by nature or by social accident, such as tsunamis and hurricanes or unexpected shifts in the population of a country.

In Zachary's lifetime, America slowly transformed from an agrarian society to an urban one, and numerous inventions made transportation, farming, and manufacturing better and easier. Shortly, America was transformed from a frontier society to an industrial giant. Karen, in turn, takes technological change for granted. She believes that medical advances will soon have a cure for many life-threatening illnesses, including AIDS and cancer. She worries that the shortages of fossil fuels in addition to increased pollution are changing the world she knows. Meanwhile, she has learned that spiraling social change is normal and inevitable, though she occasionally wonders what lies ahead. Karen knows that social change is not always planned or positive.

All of us now realize that the galloping rate of technological, scientific, and social change occurs worldwide and has far-reaching (global) effects. Social change seems to be a pervasive condition of our time (Duffy & Wong, 2003), and technology has expanded interconnectedness of peoples and increased awareness of a common, global humanity

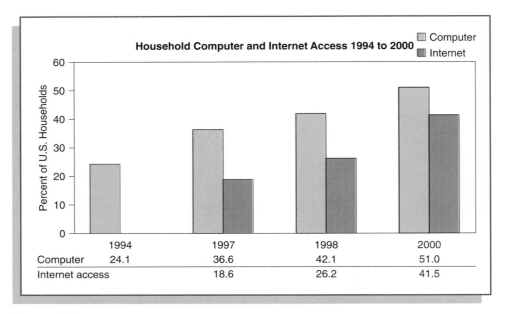

FIGURE 1–1

Household computer and Internet access in the United States: 1984 to 2000.
SOURCE: NTIA and ESA, U.S. Department of Commerce, using: U.S. Bureau of the Census Population Survey supplements, www.ntia.doc.gov.

(Stepinsky, 2005). Figure 1–1 reveals the steep increase in computer and Internet use in American households. Technology makes relationships among people more fluid, flexible, and portable and has freed us from the constraints of being in only one place. Technology connects us to more people more of the time; it also equips us to live both at home and work, blurring the boundaries between them (Jackson, 2005). Technology, in fact, may be the most powerful engine of change in today's world (Sood & Tellis, 2005). People in almost every country are growing up in a world of greater interdependence because of technology. The revolution in communication, in particular, is re-creating the world in the image of a "global village," in which every aspect of life—every thought, act, and institution—is being reconsidered in light of what is happening to people in other parts of the world (Alterman, 1999). In fact, there are some scientists who claim that, especially for those of us who use the World Wide Web, there are only six degrees of separation between us and anyone else in the world (Wright, 2002).

Another fact that might interest you as an educated person is the rate at which knowledge grows. In the 1980s and 1990s, every 7 or 8 years, the stockpile of information doubled. More recently, between 2000 and 2002—a mere 2-year span—the amount of known information in the world doubled (Discover, 2003). Much of the growth in knowledge is attributed to new technologies. Table 1–1 identifies some of the specific ways the information revolution has altered lives and businesses around the world. The more economically developed nations such as Germany and the United States as Karen knows them are experiencing massive social changes of their own. Although people recognize the fact of change, they often disagree on the direction (better or worse) in which we're headed. Some assume that the world as we know it will last indefinitely and that all the changes around us will not shake the familiar social, economic, and political structures that hold our society together (Moen & Roehling, 2005). A larger proportion of people, however, fed by a steady diet of bad news about crime, economic problems, world

---

TABLE 1–1

THE SOCIAL/CULTURAL DIMENSION OF THE INFORMATION REVOLUTION: HOW THE WORLD HAS CHANGED

- More information flowing among people and countries with less obstruction and fewer delays
- Information flowing *regardless* of distance
- Increased opportunities for economic cooperation across borders
- Greater opportunities for businesses and individuals to profit globally
- The erosion or difficulty of censorship in certain countries with a history of censorship
- People being inundated with vast quantities of information
- The democratization of information [e.g., people voicing their opinions more freely (e.g., blogging)]
- Greater awareness of prosperity and poverty in our own country or elsewhere in the world
- A growing information gap between wealthy and poor individuals and nations

SOURCE: Alterman, J. (1999). *The social/cultural dimension of the information revolution.* Washington, DC: Retrieved January 10, 2006 from CIA.gov/nic/pdf_gif_research/html/cf154.chap6.html.

---

crises, the threats of terrorism, natural disasters, and possible nuclear destruction, have adopted a bleaker view (Huddy, Khatib, & Capelos, 2002).

Many forms of employment will be affected by automation and computerized systems. The increasing need for technical solutions places a premium on intellectual and technical knowledge. In turn, educated, middle-class workers will make up a larger proportion of the workforce in comparison to blue-collar workers. One problem related to increasing people's knowledge and use of technology, however, is that *some people fear technology. Such fear is called* **technophobia** (Duffy & Wong, 2003). For example, some people are apprehensive about using computers because they fear they will break the computers, make costly errors, or look stupid. Marginalized individuals who are not well educated, are poor, elderly, disabled, Hispanic or African American (Karavides, Lim, & Katsikas, 2005; Mehra, Merkel, & Bishop, 2004; National Science Foundation, 2003; Wasserman & Richmond-Abbott, 2005), or live in rural areas (U.S. Department of Commerce, 2002) are least likely to use technology. Except for women whose frequency of use of technology has recently become more similar to men's (Wasserman & Richmond-Abbott, 2005) but whose anxiety about technology is higher than men's (Zeidner & Matthews, 2005), those individuals who are already less powerful use technology least; they are perhaps the very individuals who could benefit from knowledge about technology in order to improve their social and economic conditions (Mehra et al., 2004).

These technological changes along with scientific discoveries are moving Americans away from manufacturing and industry to service-oriented and technological employment. To demonstrate just how far technology has come, turn to Table 1–2, which documents some facts and figures related to science and technology. Wherever we can in this book, we will look at technology and how it affects our daily lives. Besides increased use of technology, do you know of any other changes in our new postindustrial society? What are they and which are the most evident to you? How do you think these changes will affect the continued evolution of our society?

The notion of a technological society is not without its critics. For instance, in the United States, some individuals are opposed to the idea of increased centralization and government control, as in domestic spying made easier via technology. Also, critics note that some features of a postindustrial, technological society are not so different from or better than those of industrialized societies. Such problems as employee alienation,

---

TABLE 1–2

HOW TECHNOLOGICAL HAVE WE BECOME?

- The typical American home also contains some 40 computing devices, from electric toothbrushes to bread makers to cordless phones and microwaves.
- The rate of growth of Internet use is currently 2 million new users per month.
- One in four Americans has two or more computers.
- Almost 50 percent of Americans use e-mail.
- One-third of Americans use the Internet to search for product and service information.
- The Internet is now used to find information more often than books, newspapers, television, and radio (in that order).
- Among Internet users, 40 percent make online purchases.
- By 2010 there will be 10,000 microsensors for every person on the planet.
- Wireless communication will grow to a more than $300 billion industry.
- Not surprisingly, 90 percent of American adults report being moderately or very interested in new inventions and new technology.

---

social and economic inequality, racism, and poverty are still with us. Then, too, some individuals feel that projections of postindustrial trends assume an overly optimistic view of the future. High government deficits, inflation, unemployment, energy shortages, and the prospect of more terrorism suggest that we do not have unlimited horizons any more than do Third World countries. As a result, a more pessimistic view of the future for advanced societies has emerged recently, which strongly encourages us to reevaluate our growth-oriented priorities and instead to conserve and alter our lifestyles. Otherwise, the world in the twenty-first century will be more crowded, more polluted, less stable, and more vulnerable to disruptions.

Living with Other Social Changes

Although both Karen and Zachary were affected by new technologies in their lifetimes, Zachary by the cotton gin and Karen by the World Wide Web, the technological changes Karen is experiencing are quite different. The changes in Zachary's lifetime were developments mostly in the areas of industry and agriculture, whereas many of those in Karen's lifetime pertain to communication. Thus, despite surges in the world population, the world seems much smaller to Karen than it did to Zachary. Karen can zip a letter to a college friend who resides in Ireland. Karen can view the news about Iraq, Russia, Peru, and Kenya on television or even on her mobile phone. Karen also hears about the cloning of animals and stem cell research, which interests her immensely because it relates to medicine. Karen can visit the supermarket and watch the scanned price of each item rapidly appear. Karen can take digital photos with her mobile phone, edit them, and zap them in an instant to multiple friends. Zachary had no such abilities or knowledge. In Zachary's day, word traveled via itinerate workers such as doctors and blacksmiths or by rural dwellers visiting town to obtain provisions they could not grow or make themselves.

What other changes can we expect in the global village some now call our world? One additional change will be continued population expansion and attendant worries about the health of our environment, including sufficient water and arable land, increased pollution, poverty, unemployment, and a plethora of other problems. The world population stands at over 6½ billion, with almost 150 new people born every minute. Furthermore, pollution as well as exhaustion of natural resources are problems

Americans are now more likely to support First Amendment freedoms, such as freedom of expression, than they were in the recent past.

for all countries and contributed to by our increasing population. To provide you with an idea of just how polluted our environment is, see Table 1–3.

As mentioned above, another dramatic change will be the increase in the diversity of the population in the United States. Table 1–4 documents some of these historic changes. An increasing number of immigrants from various regions of the world are entering this country. They bring a wealth of cultural ideas, languages, and customs. Accommodating these individuals will not be easy, in particular because some Americans are closed-minded and rather ignorant of or insensitive to other cultures. Because of increasing **cultural diversity** in this country, that is, *the increase in the number of cultures,* this book offers information about various racial and ethnic groups in America and how they uniquely cope with problems of adjustment. Where possible, information about other countries and cultures is also introduced. Similarly, we will also include valuable information on men and women.

How Certain Is Our Future?

How each of us understands the changes and trends in today's world is somewhat like the proverbial question of whether we perceive a partly filled glass as half empty or half full. Pessimists tend to see the glass as half empty; optimists see it as half full. Social

TABLE 1–3

HOW POLLUTED IS OUR WORLD?

Pollution Facts and Figures

- Within the next 15 years, one of every five biological species will die out and thus be unknown to your grandchildren.
- More than 98 percent of the streams in the lower 48 states are degraded enough to be unworthy of federal designation as wild or scenic rivers.
- Despite the Clean Water Act, 218 million Americans live within 10 miles of polluted water.
- Cars, trucks, and buses are the biggest source of cancer-causing air pollution, spewing more than 12 billion pounds of toxic chemicals each year.
- The world's leading scientists project that during our children's lifetimes, global warming will raise the average temperature of the planet by up to 11 degrees Fahrenheit.
- 5.3 million metric tons of sewage sludge are produced each year in the United States.
- According to the American College of Allergists, 50 percent of all illness is aggravated or caused by polluted indoor air.

What Can We Do to Reduce Pollution?—Recycle and Reuse

- Recycling prevents the emission of many greenhouse gases and water pollutants, saves energy, supplies valuable raw materials to industry, creates jobs, reduces the need for landfills, and conserves resources for our children's future.
- Recycling of one aluminum can save enough energy to run a TV for 3 hours.
- Recycling of each ton of paper saves 17 trees and 7,000 gallons of water.
- Recycling every plastic bottle would keep 2 billion tons of plastic out of landfills.
- Over a ton of resources is saved for every ton of glass recycled—1,330 pounds of sand, 433 pounds of soda ash, 433 pounds of limestone, and 151 pounds of feldspar.

TABLE 1–4

CHANGES IN OUR POPULATION

As you can determine from this table, the percentage of the population made up by minorities as identified by the U.S. Census Bureau is increasing.

Population	1990—% of total	2004—% of total
White	75.6	67.4
Black or African American	11.7	12.2
Hispanic★	9.0	14.2
Asian	2.8	4.2
American Indian or Alaska Native	0.7	0.8
Race other than above	0.1	5.2
Two or more races	Not available	1.9

★Hispanics are the fastest-growing segment of our population.
SOURCES: U.S. Census Bureau, Census 2000, Summary File, Tables PL1 and PL2, http://www.census.gov/main/www/cen2000.html, and U.S. Census Bureau American Community Survey Data Profile Highlights (2004), http://quickfacts.census.gov/qfd/states/00000.html.

forecasters, who speculate on the long-term future, admit that we live in uncertain times—both good and bad times. They nevertheless project a fairly optimistic future. Although they do not necessarily agree on what the future holds for us, they typically see it as promising.

Social forecasters view many of the problems of our time as the growing pains of success rather than the harbingers of doom. While the problems of overcrowding, economic inequality, environmental pollution, scarcity of resources, and poverty cannot be dismissed, such issues perhaps should be seen as temporary phenomena with which society must deal rather than the inevitable foreshadowing of the end of civilization. For example, results of a survey in June of 2004 (Anonymous, 2004) indicated that Americans are now more likely to support First Amendment freedoms (e.g., freedom of speech) than they were immediately after the terrorist attacks of September 11, 2001. Societies can and do rebound from problems that at the time appear to be insurmountable.

THE CHALLENGE OF SELF-DIRECTION

Self-Direction and Society

These rapid social changes and the growing importance of information and access to technology heighten the challenge of **self-direction**, which is *the need to learn more about ourselves and our world as a means of directing our lives more effectively*. Self-direction helps us respond to many life events—such as technological advances—as either a threat or a challenge. For example, like Karen, the young woman you met in the opening vignette, some individuals find using computers to be exciting and challenging; they purposely seek them out and try to learn more about them. Others view computers as a threat or complain about having to use them.

Another issue is that the world is seemingly changing and shrinking, in large part due to the technological changes discussed earlier. Given this, there are bound to be cultural clashes, disputes, and sometimes out-and-out warfare. On a daily basis, people from one society are bound to conflict with or misunderstand others from a different society. Here's an example. Park, Lee, & Song (2005) studied SPAM (electronic advertising)

People from collective societies take others' needs into account more than do people from individualistic societies. Many Asian societies are collective in nature.

sent to American and Korean citizens. The Korean SPAMs included apologies for the unsolicited advertising; the American ones did not. Koreans, therefore, might well think Americans rude for any unsolicited American advertisements they receive.

The study of culture, then, is extremely important to our understanding of one another; thus, you should begin to better understand cultural difference. To that end, one commonly used system for classifying cultures is via the orientation taken toward the individual in that culture. **Individualistic societies**, referred to throughout this text, are *societies in which individual gain is appreciated more than general societal gain*. Individualistic societies are sometimes referred to as *independent* cultures, where the sense of self is developed based on privately held attitudes, preferences, and judgments (Kitayama & Uchida, 2005). Another term for individualistic culture is *individual-level* culture (Matsumoto, 2003). Individualistic societies can be contrasted to **collectivist societies**, *in which collective or societal gain is cherished over individual advancement*. Collectivist societies are also known as *interdependent* societies, where the sense of self is based on attitudes, preferences, and judgments held by others (Kitayama & Uchida, 2005). Another way to refer to collectivistic cultures is as *consensual-level* (or *group-level*) cultures (Matsumoto).

In contrast to contemporary America, many Eastern and Asian cultures remain collectivist societies. Some contemporary scientists argue, however, that the contrasts are not as sharp between individualistic and collectivistic societies as once thought (Oishi, Hahn, Schimmack, Radhakrishan, Dzokoto, & Ahadi, 2005; Oyserman, Coon, & Kemmelmeier, 2002). In the same vein, it is important to remember that any label applied to a culture cannot and does not capture the individual variations that exist within that culture (Matsumoto, 2003). For example, there is culture-level consensus in the United States about the value of egalitarianism, but in reality, life for many Americans is not very egalitarian (Matsumoto). A case in point is that most of-age Americans are entitled to vote, including the elderly in nursing homes, but often residents of nursing homes do not vote if no one makes voting or going to a polling place easy for them.

You may well be familiar with individualistic societies but may be unfamiliar with collective societies if you are living in the United States. Describing his childhood in a collectivist society, Joseph Lemasolai Lekuton, born Maasai in Kenya, said about his childhood in this nomadic society, "In my tribe, the village is you, and you are the village. . . . Everyone older than you will tell you what to do. And you never defy their orders" (Court, 2003, p. 5). As adults, in mainstream American culture, we enjoy personal freedom, independence from others, and take greater pride in personal achievements than do people in collectivist cultures. By the same token, we as Americans may be more vulnerable to insecurity, confusion, and loneliness. Rest assured that there are many other dimensions along which societies and cultures vary (Nair, 2001), for example, masculine–feminine and respect for authority figures. You will read about them in other chapters of this book.

This brings us to another issue related to self-direction—freedom. Americans assume that freedom is a wonderful thing, but is it?

The Ambiguity of Personal Freedom

Nobody has written more eloquently about the ambiguity of human freedom than Erich Fromm (1963), the distinguished psychoanalyst. His experience of growing up in Germany during the Nazi regime and his subsequent move to the United States gave him tremendous insight into the problems of totalitarianism and human freedom. One of Fromm's basic ideas is that human freedom has a twofold meaning for people in the modern world: (1) the freedom "from" traditional authorities such as the state and (2) the freedom "for" actualizing one's individual destiny. Fromm holds that although people in advanced societies have been freed from the bonds of preindividualistic society, which gave them both security and limitations, they have not gained freedom in the positive sense of realizing their individual selves. That is, they have not found an outlet for the optimal expression of their intellectual, emotional, and social potential. We have freedom to direct our lives—from the details of daily life to the more crucial choices such as our careers. But at times, the challenge of self-direction makes us feel more anxious, insecure, and isolated. Fromm contends that such isolation is so unbearable that many people are inclined to escape from the burden of freedom into new dependencies, such as looking to experts and the government for assistance or conforming to the crowd. In our modern society, people are also becoming dependent on the Internet for assistance, for example, for health-related information (U.S. Department of Commerce, 2002).

The ambiguity of human freedom is especially evident when making important life choices, for example, *who* we want to be and *how* we want to live our lives. We may find ourselves becoming anxious and "freezing up" in the face of important decisions. Another common coping strategy is drifting. Instead of choosing how to live, people simply drift along, either by living according to the status quo or by dropping out, becoming people whose lives are guided by no ties, codes, traditions, or major purposes. Another strategy is based on shared decision making, as in committee work, marriage, and family life, and assumed agreements among friends. Instead of really making a decision, people just talk until something happens. They presume a consensus, often never questioning it. But if things turn out badly, no one feels responsible: Each merely goes along. Another frequently used strategy for making choices is based on an appeal to some type of authority—an expert, a movement, a religion, the government, or some institution. Although individuals may experience a tension between their loyalty and their personal conscience, they find innumerable ways to justify either alternative.

Truly autonomous people rely on none of these strategies. Some psychologists call such autonomous, optimal people "self-actualized" individuals. (Self-actualization is described in more detail in the next chapter on child development.) Autonomous or **self-actualized** individuals *accept responsibility for their lives and carefully scrutinize the alternatives available to them. They also keep their eyes open and have the courage to admit when they are wrong and need to change.* For example, many Russian writers working under communist rule in Soviet times, such as Alexander Solzhenitsyn, are examples of truly autonomous persons who made one decisive choice after another in order to maintain their personal integrity. They often made these decisions in the face of overwhelming criticism and the threat of punishment from their oppressive governments.

Taking Charge of Our Lives

Today, many people the world over are pursuing a similar odyssey of freedom. Much of the dissatisfaction that occurs in other countries reflects people's desire for the greater freedom and economic opportunity they see in the more economically advanced societies. Many of the people who immigrate to the United States seek the very freedoms we take for granted—freedom of speech and freedom of movement, for instance.

Surveys indicate that the majority of Americans feel they have more freedom and control over their lives than their parents did. As for the two individuals in our opening vignette, Karen probably experiences more freedom (e.g., mobility) than did Zachary, as well as more control (e.g., more laws). Most people today feel their parents' lives we~~

hemmed in by all kinds of social, educational, and economic constraints that they themselves have escaped. For example, most of today's middle-aged Americans did not face the Great Depression and World War II, which delimited their parents' options. They believe they have more options in the important areas of education, work, sex, marriage, family, friends, travel, possessions, where to live, and how to live.

Before you proceed further, make an honest assessment of whether you are actively taking charge of your life by completing the survey in Activity 1–1.

ACTIVITY 1–1

Do You Take Charge of Your Life?

INSTRUCTIONS: *For each statement below, circle T if the statement is generally true of you; circle F if the statement generally is not true of you.*

1. I enjoy being interconnected to others—both friends and family members.   T   F

2. Sometimes I have difficulty making the choices that make the most sense for my life.   T   F

3. I have many options from which to select in terms of my education, career, social circle, etc.   T   F

4. My friends are better than I am at making efficient and sound decisions.   T   F

5. I get a great deal of satisfaction out of helping others less fortunate than I.   T   F

6. If I have a choice, I much prefer to do the safe rather than the risky thing.   T   F

7. I strongly feel that a promise is a promise and should not be broken.   T   F

8. Difficult decisions daunt me because I have little confidence in my decisional abilities.   T   F

9. No matter where I am (e.g., at work or at college), I accept my responsibilities.   T   F

10. Sometimes I call in sick when I am healthy because I do not want to work or study.   T   F

11. I'd invest my money in a risky but challenging venture.   T   F

12. During times of stress, I feel as if my life is out of control.   T   F

13. I am fully aware of who, where, and what I am as well as my personal goals.   T   F

14. I am disturbed that some charities call me for donations and   T   F
invade my privacy.

15. When and if I ever borrow money, I make sure that I pay   T   F
it back.

16. I do not like it when others expect me to be the one to   T   F
choose our leisure activity.

SCORING: These items are intended as a self-assessment to stimulate you to think about how much you take charge of or direct your life. The even-numbered items are phrased in a negative direction, so if you answered "F" (false), you may have a "take-charge" attitude or exercise self-direction. The odd-numbered items are phrased such that a "T" (true) indicates agreement with an item demonstrating that you probably have self-direction.

Total number of _____ "Fs" for even numbered items _____

+ Total number of _____ "Ts" for odd-numbered items _____
_____

= Grand total for self-determination _____

The higher your grand total, the more self-direction you likely have. Now return to the regular reading with your score in mind. Pay attention to how and in what areas of self-direction you can improve.

Freedom, however, has its downside. Exercising our positive freedom means facing up to the necessity of decision making in our lives, especially the life choices that shape our destinies. At the same time, the fear of making the wrong decision in front of others is so great that many youths speak of "keeping my options open," living in an "extended holding pattern," and being "leery of commitment." Much of this reaction is understandable in light of the uncertainties of our times; however, research has demonstrated that individuals extrinsically motivated by financial success, an appealing appearance, or social recognition have lower vitality and lower self-actualizing potential and report more physical (health) symptoms than individuals who are more intrinsically or internally inspired. Intrinsically motivated, autonomous individuals appear to be healthier, more self-accepting, and more community-minded (Kasser & Ryan, 1996) as well as better adjusted and less distressed (Baker, 2004).

Taking charge of our lives means that we *can and must choose for ourselves*, that is, be self-directed. A lack of decisiveness, by default, becomes its own decision. Also, we must make choices in a timely fashion so that our choices do not fall short of the ideal. On the other hand, it is fortunate that not all decisions are cast in stone. We can and often do change many decisions as we grow and mature. Meanwhile, the realization that our decisions are only as good as the information they are based on reminds us again of the value of continuous learning and critical thinking.

Acting on our *positive* freedom also means *assuming responsibility for our choices*, without blaming others or fate for what happens to us. In fact, those who are self-actualized or internally directed experience less interpersonal distress (Baker, 2004) and more interpersonal closeness (Sheffield, Carey, Patenaude, & Lambert, 1995), perhaps because they are less likely to blame others. Interestingly, self-actualization correlates with **altruism**, or *the desire to help others at cost to the helper* (Sharma & Rosha, 1992).

Admittedly, we had no choice about being thrust into the world, but we have a great deal of choice in the manner in which we live. However, we often hear people say things such as "I can't help it because that's the way I am" or "Naturally I'm this way because of the way I grew up." These people fail to realize that free choice and responsibility go hand in hand. As a constant reminder of this fact, Viktor Frankl (1978) suggested that the Statue of Liberty on the East Coast be supplemented by the Statue of Responsibility on the West Coast.

Self-realization also involves taking calculated risks and making commitments in spite of uncertainty. Where would the world be without the risks taken by, for example, Thomas Edison, Mikhail Gorbachev, and Bill Gates? Personal growth involves stepping into unfamiliar and potentially risky situations, thereby leaving us more vulnerable to hurt and disappointment. Perfectionists are especially prone *not* to take risks and to be satisfied with low levels of actualization. Self-actualizers are more tolerant of failure (Flett, Hewitt, Blankstein, & Mosher, 1991). With regard to these issues, it is important to ask yourself the following questions: How self-directed are you? How does perfectionism interfere with your taking risks? How actualized are you? How open are you to new experiences?

The decision to grow or actualize our potential often has to be made in spite of risks and therefore requires courage. This is the "courage to be," that is, the courage to affirm ourselves and our possibilities in spite of risks. On the other hand, we run a risk whenever we avoid growing. Each time we pass up an opportunity to develop a new skill or when we value security over challenge, we run the risk of becoming stagnant or succumbing to boredom. When we habitually suppress or deny the inherent growth tendency of humans, we risk becoming maladaptive, sometimes in obvious ways, sometimes in subtle ways, sometimes immediately, or sometimes later in life. Fortunately, higher education and continual learning, mechanisms for growth that you as well as Zachary and Karen are taking advantage of, helps individuals self-actualize (Barnes & Srinivas, 1993; MacKay & Kuh, 1994). One of the fathers of humanistic psychology Abraham Maslow (1968) once observed that many of the characteristic disorders of our time such as the "stunted person," the "amoral person," or the "apathetic person" result from the fundamental failure to grow.

Living in Today's Individualistic Society

Interestingly, the times in which we live afford us a more supportive environment because of the technological advances that bring friends and family on the other side of the continent "closer" to us. Just as important, though, is the increased number of hazards in our social and physical environments: We meet more people, some of whom are highly critical of us and judgmental; we become bewildered by the increasing number of available consumer choices; and we worry about the proliferation of hazards in our environment, from threats of weapons of mass destruction to pandemics such as Avian Bird Flu and AIDS. These, in turn, heighten the challenge of self-direction.

The cumulative impact of these social changes has given rise to newer social values and newer rules by which people live in comparison to those of Zachary's generation. Generally, these changes mean greater interest in shaping the environment to meet our needs (i.e., increased personal control) rather than society's needs and goals. It may appear true that many people are preoccupied with themselves today. Especially to our international visitors, Americans appear to be rather self-absorbed in some ways.

There is often great impatience in Americans to satisfy one's own goals. Individuals scoff when told they need to "pay your dues" through hard work to achieve success in a career or happiness in a marriage. They want success and happiness NOW. Or to paraphrase the more self-centered seekers, "I want it all—right now!" The "future" orientation of earlier generations like Zachary's—with the assumption that things need to get better for future generations—appears to have been superseded by a "now" orientation, by living solely in the present, where the collective future is merely a lurking shadow in the back of our minds.

Still another change is the greater assertiveness of individuals, who seem more concerned with their personal rights than with social responsibilities. As a result, more individuals today appear to be relentlessly pursuing their own interests and goals, at the risk of violating the rights of others. When conflicts of interest do arise, individuals are less willing to deny themselves anything to accommodate or compromise with others, as if adhering to some new moral principle—"I have a duty to myself, not to you or society." Road rage is an apt example of obstinately pursuing one's own needs at the expense of others. Luckily, Zachary never experienced road rage, but Karen has.

THEMES OF PERSONAL GROWTH

Living with Contradictions and Uncertainty

Each of us faces the challenge of reconciling old rules with new rules and old values with new values. Many of us feel we must honor the old values of hard work, frugality, and moderation to complete an education and secure our careers and, thus, the means to enjoy the new values associated with personal pleasure and freedom (Moen & Roehling, 2005). In many ways these two sets of values contradict each other, making it difficult to reconcile them. For example, we know we must work to support our families, but we also want to drive an expensive convertible car and experience the thrill of the wind blowing through our hair—a symbol of independence and freedom. This task of reconciling the old and the new is hard enough for reasonably well-educated and well-informed individuals. It is even more confusing and upsetting to the less educated, who anticipate more dramatic and negative social changes than do college-educated people.

Those of us who seek guidance about personal growth from popular self-help books, television shows that entertain more than they educate, and movements that blend pop psychology with quasi-religious thought do not always fare well. Many of these sources oversimplify the process of personal and social change, generating grossly unrealistic and disappointing results. In contrast, a good textbook on scientific psychology can provide sound principles of personal development and growth as well as guidance related to self-direction and social responsibility. Throughout this book we attempt to show how the principles and findings of contemporary psychology can help us better understand ourselves and others and, thus, to cope more effectively with our environment and fulfill more of our potential.

This statement does not mean that personal growth can be achieved by simply reading a book on the subject. Neither does mere exposure to scientific knowledge or interesting examples guarantee that you will use the information. For instance, despite evidence that cigarette smoking is hazardous to one's health and despite the fact that most individuals who smoke acknowledge that they know smoking is harmful, cigarettes are widely used in our society. Modern psychology can provide dependable information about ourselves and our world, but the mastery and effective use of this knowledge is up to you.

Now, let's look further at some other issues related to seeking self-direction.

Continuity and Change

A key issue for psychologists and the public alike is the extent to which people change over a lifetime. Do our personalities really change, or do they remain stable? Or do we simply and naturally mellow with age? Do we change in fits and starts or gradually? What makes us change—many small experiences or cataclysmic events?

A generation ago psychologists and the public assumed that genes and early experiences were the decisive influences on development, so that once we reached adulthood we tended to remain the same. Then, during the 1960s and 1970s, new findings as well as social trends suggested that people tend to continue growing throughout their adult lives. Today, professionals acknowledge that *both continuity and change* are important to development.

Robert McCrae and Paul Costa (1994; 2003) have discovered some evidence for the stability of personality throughout the life span. The highest degree of stability was found in the domain of introversion–extroversion, which reflects gregariousness, warmth, and assertiveness. There is almost as much stability in the area of "neuroticism," which includes such traits as depression and hostility. Thus, individuals who were expressive and outgoing in their teens are apt to remain that way in adulthood; those who were inhibited and shy in their teens tend to remain inhibited and shy. Similarly, **longitudinal studies**, *which follow the same individuals over a long time period*, indicate only slight decreases over the course of adulthood in anxiety, hostility, and impulsiveness.

Psychologists supporting the stability thesis state that even when individuals do change because of personal maturation or life experiences, the unique differences among people remain. This means that a rather impulsive 20-year-old like Karen may be a bit less impulsive by the time she is 55, but she is still likely to be more impulsive than her age-mates at any given time. In addition, as people grow older, the stability of their personalities becomes more evident. Thus, there is more stability of personality from 30 to 40 than there is from 20 to 30 years of age (Pfaffenberger, 2005). Part of the reason for increased stability with age is that we tend to select and stay in environments and marry people that help sustain our traits (Caspi & Herbener, 1990).

Other researchers, while acknowledging the importance of stability, emphasize the variability or change that occurs with development (Pfaffenberger, 2005). They point out that *only certain traits* have been shown to be relatively stable, most notably introversion–extroversion, anxiety, and depression. These researchers suggest that people are more likely to change in other respects, especially self-esteem, sense of personal mastery or control over their environment, and values. The emphasis on the potential for change has been embraced by those who want to foster change, from weight watchers to social watchers, all of whom stress openness to change throughout the course of adulthood.

The tension between continuity and change is found not only in academic debates but also in each of us. How much personal growth or change in a desirable direction we want depends greatly on the different priorities we assign to stability or change, that is, how much we want to change and how differently we want to live our lives. Thus, people with traditional values tend to exhibit a high degree of stability in their lives unless something happens to make them change. The events most likely to change deeply ingrained patterns are usually quite dramatic, such as an unwanted divorce, the death of a child, failure in one's career, or witnessing a traumatic event. In these cases, individuals may become motivated to make marked changes in their outlook and personality. In contrast, those who put more value on personal growth may continue changing to a greater extent throughout their lives unless they become stuck at a particular developmental milestone. For instance, a coal miner who spends 10 hours a day under the earth for 30 years may have little opportunity for personal growth. You, on the other hand, probably have ample opportunities to experience change and personal growth.

The Experience of Personal Growth

To believe we can change is one thing. To *pursue and actively achieve personal change* is something else, because the experience of change can be unsettling. Think about all the times you have vowed to lose weight but didn't, or vowed to quit smoking cigarettes and failed. These are but small instances of attempts to change.

Like all patterns of development, our inner experience of growth tends to be uneven, with spurts and plateaus. We may be willing to try out something new one minute and retreat to the familiar the next. Because we experience our inner world more as a continuous flow of ideas, feelings, and meanings, we are more apt to realize that we've grown *in retrospect* than while we're in the midst of a particular growth cycle.

The experience of growth tends to follow a three-phase cycle. Typically, it begins with (1) acknowledging some change within ourselves or our surroundings, which evokes (2) a sense of dissonance or dissatisfaction within, which in turn leads us to (3) reorganizing our experience in some way, such as adopting a new attitude toward ourselves or others.

1. Acknowledging change.   Growth usually begins with the acknowledgment of change. Actually, changes occur all the time, but we're not always aware of them. A constant awareness of change would be too disrupting. Instead, we strive to construct an image of ourselves and our world that pictures reality as under our control and more stable than it really is. As a result, we become more acutely aware of changes at some moments than at others. Sometimes, we become aware of change rather suddenly, for example, by receiving an unexpected compliment or criticism. Times of uncertainty and decision making also remind us that more changes will be forthcoming, for example, when we are wrestling with the choice of which college major or career to select. Taking on new responsibilities, such as a new marriage, parenthood, or a promotion at work, forces us to acknowledge change, too. Karen's graduation from college and her entry into medical school will force her to acknowledge change. Disappointments and failures, such as being fired from a job without warning, also force us to acknowledge change. Karen might not land the prestigious medical residency she wants, thus again compelling her to acknowledge change. The common denominator in all these experiences is the realization that things are different from what they were—or what we believed or expected they would be.

2. A sense of dissonance or dissatisfaction.   Whether or not the awareness of change leads to growth depends on how we react. Sometimes we may respond to change defensively, with little awareness of our real feelings, as when Karen dismissed her failure to land a residency at a large, prestigious hospital by saying, "I really didn't want it anyway." Because she was denying her feelings about the change, she was minimizing the possibility for growth. In contrast, when someone feels disappointment, he or she actually may be aroused or motivated to seek further change. When Karen did not get her first-choice residency, she eventually sought out another prestigious one, located closer to her new fiancé's residence. To her delight, she was immediately accepted. Thus, the growth cycle can often be triggered by disappointment and failure as well as by success.

This phase of growth (dissonance) is inevitably accompanied by a certain degree of anxiety and discomfort. When our motive for growth proceeds out of a sense of challenge or mastery, we may be more stimulated and less apprehensive about the outcome, as when Zachary, Karen's ancestor, decided to break in his own horse—out of a need for accomplishment but with some trepidation—rather than let his older brother do it as was usual. But when our motive springs from profound dissatisfaction with ourselves, our feelings tend to be more agonizing. Either way, the old saying "How can something that feels so bad be so good?" reminds us that these unsettling feelings are more often than not a necessary part of achieving some desired goal.

3. Reorganizing our experience. In conventional terms, reorganizing is often defined as acquiring new ideas and then altering our attitudes, behaviors, and values in response. In some instances, such as the discovery that most students like Karen, Zachary, and you feel anxious about examinations, additional insight may alter our understanding of ourselves or others. We may become aware of our own largely unconscious processes, such as realizing that our chronic sense of anxiety during tests masks an undue fear of criticism and failure. Or we may adopt a new attitude toward another person, becoming more willing to listen to someone's criticism because we know that the person wants to help rather than hurt us. Growth may also take the form of new self-perceptions, such as increased self-acceptance and confidence from an achievement like earning a medical degree. The main point is that each inner adjustment or change we make affects the whole of our experience, so that growth consists of the continuous reorganization of that experience.

We're more apt to have positive, gratifying feelings at this point than in the earlier stages. We're also more likely to understand how we've grown. As existentialist philosopher Søren Kierkegaard once said, "Life is necessarily understood in a backward direction, but it must be lived in a forward direction." Perhaps you have looked back at a very trying time in your life that eventually led to growth and said to yourself, "Now I realize what was happening in my life."

Beyond Individualism

There exists in America a language of individualism that limits the way people think. For example, we celebrate "independence" on July 4. Many Americans today act independently of any cultural or social influence, being responsible to the self alone. As a result, we are becoming less committed to the common purposes of society, unlike collectivist societies or earlier periods of American life—say, in Zachary's lifetime—in which self-orientation was held in check by strong ties to the family, church, and community. But now that these ties are weakening, people are putting aside the public concerns that are necessary for the survival of a free and caring society. We are, however, still very good at "coming together" with others in times of crisis. Witness how the whole nation pulled together when the World Trade Center and Pentagon

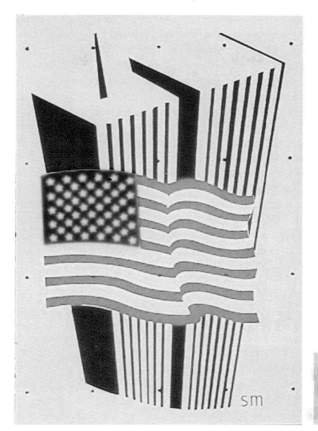

Despite being an individualistic culture, Americans frequently come together in times of crisis such as during the terrorist attacks of September 11th or during natural disasters.

were bombed or when Hurricane Katrina decimated the Gulf Coast. Petty differences, regional competitiveness, and attitudinal conflicts typically were set aside, at least for the time being.

The contradiction between the lone individual and the necessary social context of life is repeatedly expressed in various American attitudes, but we often fail to realize the contradictions in our views. How can you personally expect a bright financial future despite a mounting national deficit, unemployment, and national poverty? How realistic is it to expect a happy family life while faced with a rising divorce rate and the difficulties of being a working parent?

A major reassessment of the search for self-fulfillment may be giving rise to a more recent and realistic view of life and personal fulfillment. Millions of Americans are discovering, often through such painful experiences as terrorist attacks, that preoccupation with their own personal needs is not a direct path to fulfillment. Americans are learning that they cannot disregard the rest of the world. The heart of this new outlook is the realization that *personal fulfillment can be achieved only in relation to others*—through a web of shared meanings that transcend the isolated individual. Personal fulfillment in the deeper sense requires commitments that endure over long periods of time and perhaps require self-sacrifice. These may include commitments to loved ones, family, friends, career, ideas, beliefs, social causes, nature, places, or adventures—depending on the individual and his or her values. The term *commitment* shifts the focus away from unduly individualistic notions of the self, either self-denial or self-fulfillment, toward the more inclusive "self connected to others." Almost all of our activity occurs in relationships, groups, and community, structured by institutions and interpreted by cultural meaning. The isolated, unencumbered self is but an abstraction. Even the positive aspects of our individualism are dependent in countless ways on a social context that sustains us even when we are not fully aware of it. Activity 1–2 is designed to help you discover the extent of your own individualism in our interdependent world. When you have finished the activity, ask yourself if you need to be more interconnected with your community and the rest of the world.

As we've seen, human fulfillment is more complex than popularly thought and requires a better balance between the claims of self and society. A one-sided or self-interested approach to life does not promote extensive personal growth. Every realm of life requires a constant striving to achieve that balance of give-and-take between others and ourselves that ensures a truly satisfying life. Throughout this book we'll explore the major areas of personal growth and behavior.

ACTIVITY 1–2

HOW INDIVIDUALISTIC ARE YOU?

Psychologists have figured out some very clever ways to research people's behaviors and attitudes without directly asking or observing them. Once a person is approached by a psychologist, the study and data can become contaminated. For example, if you knew I wanted to know about your individualism, you might try to guess the answers to my questions rather than give me an honest assessment of your individualistic tendencies.

Psychological scientists, then, turn to indirect methods. One indirect method is the **archival method**, *where scientists examine existing data such as historical documents that were fashioned before anyone knew they would be the subject of study.* You have created many such historical documents that have never been studied. Go back to your e-mail account, your diary, letters you have written to your friends and family, or some other written document developed by you. Count how many times pronouns related to yourself such as *I*, *my*, *me*, *mine*, etc. occur and how many time pronouns such as *you* or *we* or *they* (or pronouns indicating that you were taking into account another's feelings, needs, or desires) occur.

PRONOUNS RELATED TO SELF _____

PRONOUNS RELATED TO OTHERS _____

Which type of pronouns prevailed? Are pronouns indicating the importance of others more predominant or are pronouns related to you more predominant? In terms of individualism and social connectedness, what do your results suggest about you?

SUMMARY

SOCIAL CHANGE

We began the chapter by describing how rapid technological and social changes are having far-reaching effects throughout the world. The revolution in communication, in particular, is giving rise to a global outlook in which people in many countries are influenced by what they see happening in other countries.

Economically developed nations, such as the United States, are moving into a postindustrial era in which the service industries are becoming dominant and there is a premium on intellectual and technical knowledge. Similarly, the information age drives us to create, process, and distribute information in different ways and with a wider variety of people. Social forecasters admit we live in uncertain times, but they tend to have an optimistic view of the future. The biggest challenge is how to prepare people to live and work in the new information society that demands high-tech skills and more education.

THE CHALLENGE OF SELF-DIRECTION

Living in a rapidly changing society poses an even greater challenge to the self-direction of individuals than was the case in the past. As Fromm reminds us, we have been more successful in achieving freedom "from" traditional authorities than in using this freedom "for" actualizing our individual destinies. The challenge of self-direction is so great that we tend to escape from it by looking to the experts for decisions on important choices or conforming to the crowd or simply drifting. In contrast, taking charge of our lives means facing up to the importance of decision making, taking calculated risks for the sake of growth, and assuming full responsibility for our lives.

The new rules in today's individualistic societies accentuate the challenge of self-direction. As a result, people are increasingly questioning the old rules that emphasize social conformity and self-denial. Instead, individuals are busily pursuing their individual rights and, in varying degrees, self-fulfillment. A major change is that people want and expect more out of life in return for their efforts.

THEMES OF PERSONAL GROWTH

The search for self-fulfillment creates a predicament for the individual as well as the nation, challenging us to reconcile old and new values. People looking to self-help books for advice tend to find an oversimplified idea of self-fulfillment, leading to unrealistic expectations that end in disappointment. In contrast, the field of psychology offers sound principles and tested knowledge that may help to achieve realistic self-direction and growth.

According to psychology, the tendencies toward both continuity and change are present in each of us. How much you and others change depends greatly on the different priorities we assign to stability or change. At the same time, we live in an era in which personal growth occurs more widely than before.

The subjective experience of growth involves a three-phase cycle: (1) the acknowledgment of change within ourselves or our environment, (2) a sense of dissonance or dissatisfaction within, which in turn leads to (3) reorganizing our experience in some way, such as adopting a new attitude toward ourselves or others. Critics claim that the self-fulfillment movement encourages people to become unduly self-centered and individualistic and thus to withdraw from the social involvement necessary for a democratic society. Today, however, a major reassessment of the self-fulfillment movement is under way, giving rise to a more realistic view of life and personal fulfillment. The core of this new approach is the call for a realignment of the claims of self and society so that personal fulfillment can be realized only in relation to others—through a web of shared meanings that transcend the isolated individual.

SELF-TEST

1. Early American society can be described as
   a. ruggedly individualistic.
   b. agrarian and collective.
   c. self-directed.
   d. materialistic.

2. Who suffers most from technophobia?
   a. mid-level managers.
   b. white-collar workers.
   c. children.
   d. minorities and women.

3. An individualistic society
   a. is consensual.
   b. looks upon social gain as important.
   c. is exemplified by American culture.
   d. is the same as a collectivist society.

4. Which group is increasing fastest in the United States?
   a. Hispanics.
   b. African Americans.
   c. Asians.
   d. Whites.

5. The "old rules" governing Americans were based on self-denial and
   a. hard work.
   b. a "now" orientation.
   c. personal fulfillment.
   d. individual rights.

6. Which of the following characteristics is the least likely to change throughout adulthood?
   a. extroversion.
   b. anxiety.
   c. depression.
   d. neuroticism.

7. A subjective experience of growth begins with
   a. a sense of dissonance.
   b. acknowledging change.
   c. a commitment to change.
   d. reorganizing experiences.

8. The second stage of personal growth is
   a. a sense of dissonance.
   b. acknowledging change.
   c. a commitment to change.
   d. reorganizing our experiences.

9. Modern, mainstream American society is typified by
   a. less attention to societal needs.
   b. a need for relatedness.
   c. personal inability to make decisions.
   d. slower rates of social change than in the past.

10. The contemporary reassessment of the self-fulfillment movement suggests that personal fulfillment can be realized only
    a. by educated people.
    b. during middle or late adulthood.
    c. in relation to others.
    d. by perfectionistic people.

EXERCISES

1. *Social change.* What two or three societal changes are having the greatest impact on your life? Write a page or so about how your life is affected by these changes. For example, think about how a computer has altered your academic, business, and personal life.

2. *Change as a challenge or threat.* Select some change that has occurred in your environment recently, such as a new professor or layoffs at work. Then write a page or so describing how you feel about this change, especially whether you see it as a challenge or a threat.

3. *Identify your level of interdependence.* Identify at least one important aspect of your life, such as a job, a friendship, or marriage. Then describe in a few paragraphs how much you're prepared to give to this relationship and how much you expect in return. To what extent is your interdependence based on the old rules or the new rules of self-fulfillment?

4. *How important is self-fulfillment to you?* Think about what you do that is fulfilling. What are your life goals? Are they other-centered or self-centered? What do you do to actively meet these goals?

5. *Self-fulfillment and personal and social involvement.* Select some area of your life that has been very gratifying to you (an accomplishment, relationship, etc.) and describe the extent to which your sense of fulfillment depended on involvement with others.

QUESTIONS FOR SELF-REFLECTION

1. Are you more optimistic about your own personal future than that of our society or the world?

2. Are you so concerned about keeping your options open that you may suffer from the inability to make decisions? Are you too perfectionistic?

3. How much control do you feel you have over your life? Are you a self-directed person?

4. Would you agree that many of the ground rules in our society have changed from one century to the next? How so?

5. Have you met people who act as if there are no rules—that anything goes? What are such people like?

6. How important are self-fulfillment values to you?

7. Do you expect more out of life than your parents did?

8. To what extent are you experiencing and reconciling the old and new values described in this book?

9. Can you remember a difficult time in your life and, in retrospect, realize it was a time of growth?

10. Would you agree that personal fulfillment is achieved mostly in and through our relationships with others?

FOR FURTHER INFORMATION

RECOMMENDED READINGS

BUFFONE, G. (2003). *The myth of tomorrow: Seven essential keys for living the life you want today.* New York: McGraw-Hill. People often postpone doing what they really want or need to do until something dramatic happens in their lives. This book seeks to expand people's sense of choice and freedom.

HALL, B. J. (2004). *Among cultures: The challenge of communication.* Belmont, CA: Wadsworth. The author, a communication expert, explores issues of cross-cultural communication, including how world views differ from culture to culture and thus create misunderstanding.

JOHNSON, D. W. (2005). *Reaching out: Interpersonal effectiveness and self-actualization.* Upper Saddle River, NJ: Prentice Hall. An expert on group behavior and interpersonal relationships examines the relevancy of other people to the concept of self-actualization and vice versa.

KEYES, C. L. M., & HALDT, J. (Eds.). (2003). *Flourishing: Positive psychology and the life well-lived.* Washington, DC: American Psychological Association. What makes life worthwhile? What makes us healthy, productive, and happy? The book examines these issues related to positive psychology.

MOEN, P., & ROEHLING, P. (2004). *The career mystique: Cracks in the American Dream.* Lanham, MD: Rowman & Littlefield. The authors review the American dream of hard work and frugality turning into success. Given the changing world and the many uncertainties of modern life, the authors claim that today the dream is a myth.

RYCHLAK, J. F. (2003). *The human image in postmodern America.* Washington, DC: American Psychological Association. Many of the processes posited by American psychology to explain human behavior fail to take into account free will, the love of freedom, and other qualities that make us human. The book helps the reader understand what it really means to be human; then and only then can we resolve the pressing issues of our times.

WEB SITES AND THE INTERNET

http://www.apa.org/psychnet/   A site designed to provide lots of information about psychology on a wide range of topics.

http://www.culturalstudies.net   A location where popular American culture in its ever-changing forms is tracked. There are links to other cultural studies sites.

http://www.cpsr.org   A site supported by computer professionals concerned about the responsible use of technology in society.

http://www.wfs.org   Interested in the future or what the world will look like in several years? This site has predictions and other information that will appeal to you.

http://www.sierraclub.org   America's oldest, largest, and most influential grassroots environmental organization.

CHAPTER 2

The Journey Begins—Childhood

PERSPECTIVES ON CHILD DEVELOPMENT

THE BIOLOGICAL PERSPECTIVE ON CHILD DEVELOPMENT
Nature Versus Nurture—An Old Debate
A Newer Approach
Applying It to Yourself

THE PSYCHODYNAMIC PERSPECTIVE ON CHILD DEVELOPMENT
Development of Personality
The Structure of Personality
Modifications
Applying It to Yourself

THE SOCIAL-COGNITIVE PERSPECTIVE ON CHILD DEVELOPMENT
Social Learning Theories
Recent Additions: Cognition and Behavior
Applying It to Yourself

THE HUMANISTIC PERSPECTIVE ON CHILD DEVELOPMENT
The Phenomenal Self
Self-Actualization
Applying It to Yourself

DEVELOPMENTAL CHALLENGES IN CHILDHOOD
Temperament

Self-Recognition and Self-Concept
Attachment
Applying It to Yourself

CONCLUSION

SUMMARY
SELF-TEST
EXERCISES
QUESTIONS FOR SELF-REFLECTION
FOR FURTHER INFORMATION

Ken had led a rather normal, middle-class childhood. By junior high school he was popular, good-looking, and athletic. At 15 years old, he developed a keen interest in being a lawyer like his mother, although his father urged him to be a college professor like him. Ken, however, wanted "the fast track" and to make "big bucks" as he put it. He graduated from a prestigious private college in the Northeast. After college, Ken continued on to law school and finished second in his class. From law school, Ken joined a large law firm. Although he knew he was at the bottom of the partnership hierarchy, Ken had designs on eventually becoming a partner in one of the old, respected firms or ultimately founding his own firm. This meant that he had to make several moves in terms of jobs, but Ken remained undaunted in his quest for prestige. Despite the fact that Ken was enthusiastically moving ahead with his career plans, he felt a sense of loneliness that led him to his first and only real girlfriend, Audra, a young woman who was a lawyer in the firm for which Ken worked. Audra knew about Ken's drive, and she admired that in him. She, too, was determined that she would be a successful lawyer. They both dreamed of founding their own law firm. Because of their career plans, neither of them wanted children.

When the hard-working, driven Ken was 49 years old, he came home one day and announced to Audra that he was thoroughly disenchanted with his career and his life. Just before this moment, he had been working hard on an important case with a more senior partner. The law firm lost the case, and the senior partner blamed Ken (or at least Ken thought so). As Ken unfolded his angst to the astonished and surprised Audra, he made clear that the stress, the unpredictability of the practice of law, and the long hours were killing him. He longed for a quieter, less frenetic life, or, as he expressed it, a "saner" life. He begged Audra to move to Oregon with him. He said that he had been reading a magazine for wine enthusiasts and had seen a winery for sale. He wanted the two of them to buy the winery and live on-site.

PERSPECTIVES ON CHILD DEVELOPMENT

Psychologists approach development from different viewpoints or perspectives. Although there are dozens of different theories of development, most of them generally can be grouped into four basic types: the biological, psychodynamic or psychoanalytic, social-cognitive (including behavioral), and humanistic perspectives. Each perspective emphasizes certain aspects of development, but no one perspective provides the complete picture or "truth." **Development** can be defined as *the relatively enduring changes in people's capacities and behavior as they grow older because of biological growth processes and people's interaction with their environment, including their social environment.* Attempting to prove which view of development is more correct, especially on issues that admit to no simple test of truth, is rather fruitless. Instead, it's more helpful to learn the best that each perspective has to offer (Slater, Hocking, & Loose, 2003). What each view offers us is an optimal range of explanations about development. That is, each perspective explains some aspects of personal development especially well, while minimizing, if not neglecting, others.

Let us first discuss, however, why childhood is so important. Many psychologists liken human development to the building of a house. Childhood is the foundation upon which the remainder of development rests, just as the house's foundation is the support for the rest of the home—the floors, walls, roof, and so forth. If the foundation is weak, the future of the house is in jeopardy as problems such as cracks in the walls or sticky windows develop when the foundation sags. If the foundation of the house is sound, however, the house may well withstand duress such as floods and high winds. If not, it can certainly be easily rebuilt. Many perspectives on development take this same tack—that a healthy childhood can create resiliency that helps the person overcome problems later in life. Before proceeding further, look at Box 2–1, which presents some interesting and often startling statistics about childhood in America. Ask yourself whether today's children have a solid foundation on which to develop into happy and healthy adults.

THE BIOLOGICAL PERSPECTIVE ON CHILD DEVELOPMENT

Nature Versus Nurture—An Old Debate

Today, the rapid increase in knowledge about brain functioning and **genes** (*the biochemical units by which characteristics are inherited*) provides scientific evidence for a biological basis for some aspects of development. For example, extensive comparisons of

Box 2–1

AMERICA'S CHILDREN: WILL THEY MAKE IT?

This chapter primarily discusses the social and personality development of children, rather than of adults. Most of the perspectives presented suggest that children need a positive start—physically and psychologically—in order to become well-adjusted adults. Here are some revealing statistics—both positive and negative—about America's children. Decide for yourself whether you think today's children have a good start on a happy and productive life:

AMERICAN FAMILIES

- The number of children in the United States is projected to increase to 77.2 million by 2020. In 2004, 68 percent of our children lived with two parents. Of the 25 million who live with only one parent, one-third will never see their father over the course of the year.

- Nearly one-third of American children are born out of wedlock.

CHILDREN'S HEALTH

- Over 12 percent of pregnant women smoke. Smoking is detrimental to the unborn child.

- Several federal agencies estimate that about five children die of maltreatment (abuse and neglect) every day in the United States.

- Fifty-eight million children (82 percent of the total) enjoy excellent or very good health; 2 percent are in fair or poor health.

- Almost one-third of all 12th-graders report having five or more alcoholic drinks per week.

EDUCATION

- Recently, about one-quarter of American schoolchildren attended school without missing a day. Six percent of school-age children missed more than 10 days of school due to illness or injury.

- The overall high school completion rate for young adults recently has declined to about 85 percent.

- The number of children 5 to 7 years of age who spoke a language other than English and who had difficulty speaking English has increased to over 2.5 million.

- Boys earn 70 percent of the Ds and Fs teachers assign. Boys make up two-thirds of the students labeled "learning disabled."

identical twins, whether reared together or apart, have shown evidence of genetic influences on aspects of human growth such as intelligence and personality. For instance, Ken, the lawyer in the chapter opening, had a twin brother Paul. In grade school, when their intelligence was tested, both boys scored within three points of each other. Each of them liked sports and competitive activities. As adults, Ken and Paul had similar hairstyles, mustaches, and aviator-style glasses. They also had slightly crooked smiles that made strangers a bit hesitant when they first interacted with the twins. Each twin made his living as a white-collar professional; Ken was a lawyer while Paul became a college professor like their father. Interestingly, both twins liked the same wine, chardonnay, so Ken eagerly approached his brother to ask if Paul would like to be a joint partner in the winery. Paul rebuked Ken with a resounding "no," which was a complete surprise to Ken, who thought that they were alike on almost every aspect of personality, interests, and style.

Some psychologists argue that biology influences almost all of our personal qualities and development (e.g., Pinker, 2002), whereas other psychologists argue that environment counts more than biology in determining the direction of our development (e.g., Buller, 2005; Rose, 2000). The first group of psychologists would argue that Ken

Proponents of the biological perspective suggest that identical twins ought to behave similarly because of their common genetic makeup.

and Paul ought to be very much alike as indicated by their scores on intelligence tests; the second group would predict that depending on the environments to which they were exposed, they might be different especially if the environments are different. For example, the second group of psychologists might predict that Paul would not follow Ken into the wine business. Biological aspects of development include evolution, heredity, the influence of hormones on behavior, and aspects of the nervous system related to behavior. In most arguments about development, heredity comes to the forefront as the most important biological determinant of who we are and how we develop. Environment, on the other hand, includes our social and cultural environments (e.g., friends and family), learning environments (e.g., schools), and physical environments.

In reality, although the exact proportions remain unknown, both environmental and biological aspects contribute to our development. Genetic influences probably account for 25 to 75 percent of the differences in some characteristics among the general population (Bouchard, Lykken, McGue, Segal, & Tellegen, 1990; Harris, 1998; Plomin & Rende, 1991; Scarr, 1987), while the environment likely contributes 25 and up to 75 percent of the differences among people. The specific percentage attributed to **heredity** (*the transmission of traits from parents to offspring*) varies greatly among different traits, among different individuals, and even among different research projects examining a particular characteristic. The same can be said of the influence of the environment. Biology is not thought to be completely responsible for any single trait, and neither is environment considered completely responsible for a particular attribute. Some theorists believe that when biology plays a large role, environment may well play a much smaller role. When environment plays a large role, biology may play a lesser role. And sometimes, the two play equally important roles.

Let us return to biology, though. Powerful genetic factors have been cited for a wide range of characteristics, including alcoholism, depression, and phobias. The evidence, however, seems strongest for such characteristics as intelligence, sociability, emotionality, and activity level (Bouchard et al., 1990; Plomin & Rende, 1991). Along related lines of thinking, in Darwinian or evolutionary theory (from which evolutionary psychology originates), when a characteristic is inherited, it also probably is adaptive (Goode, 2000); that is, it helps us cope with our physical and social world and thus aids our survival. Perhaps the Darwinian concept of evolution (a biological concept) helps to explain why characteristics such as intelligence, sociability, and activity level appear partly or largely inherited, in that they enhance our adaptability or adjustment to our environment. That is, the more intelligent a person is, the greater the chances for survival.

But important questions remain about the roles of biology (nature) versus environment (nurture). If each child in a family receives a different combination of genes, why do children in the same family seem so similar, yet different at other times? Perhaps different children even within the same family seek out environments that are suited to their unique dispositions? It is also possible that each child in a family experiences the same home environment somewhat differently no matter what the genetic disposition, enabling the environment to play a major role. Perhaps each child's unique experience (or perception of experience) exerts a substantial influence on development no matter what the genetic underpinnings? The arguments continue about why, how much, and by what means biology versus environment influences each person's development (Mandler, 2001; Rutter, 2002; Watt, 2004).

A Newer Approach

The debate about what counts more—**nature or nurture**—is *the debate over the importance of heredity versus environment* (Howe, 2001; Mandler, 2001; Watt, 2004). Perhaps it makes more sense to speak of the nature-nurture issue as nature *via* (through) nurture or nature *wedded to* nurture rather than nature *versus* nurture. Development may well be a product of both inherited or biological factors *and* environment or learning. For example, how much or how little of our genetic potential we realize may depend greatly on our interaction with the environment, especially our selection and reaction to particular environments. Instead of arguing, then, that Ken and Paul *must be the same* because they are identical twins or instead of arguing that *they are different* because they parted company in early adulthood (i.e., each selected a different environment), scientists ought to be examining *the overlap and interaction* between the two *as well as the differences* between the two. Although Paul and Ken share the same genes and perhaps the potential to respond in the same way, Paul has not yet experienced the stress of the boss's scorn as has Ken. Paul has no one like Audra to give him emotional support. For Ken, the winery appears to be a viable and less stressful career move, while to Paul it spells disaster because it is too risky for him when he has steady work. On the other hand, for individuals hardier and more resilient than Ken and Paul, job stress may well be perceived as a challenge rather than as a stressor.

Applying It to Yourself

According to the **biological perspective**, *many of our personal attributes and much of our personal development may be attributable to genetic and other biological influences.* But since most of us spend our formative years in a family with a common pool of genes and a common environment, it is difficult to tell how much a given characteristic reflects our heredity and how much it reflects our environment or training. The specific characteristic is important. As we've seen, characteristics like intelligence and sociability may have a marked genetic influence. Even these characteristics are determined not so much by a single gene as by a complex combination of genes that gives rise to a range of potential responses. How much or how little of our potential we develop, however, depends largely on our interaction with the environment. For instance, a first-born girl might earn high grades and go on to become a physician. Her younger sister, who is equally smart but impatient about waiting to start her career, may choose a paramedical career as an emergency medical technician. The schooling required is less demanding and time-consuming and therefore may appeal to her impatient tendencies. While both sisters may continue to get similar scores on the same intelligence test, they have different perceptions about their futures.

Have you ever considered the dominant traits in your family tree? At the next family gathering, observe your relatives for a while. You might observe that a favorite uncle or aunt exhibits the same warmth and sociability that you do. You might wonder why you are more similar to this more distant relative than to your siblings on this trait. The answer may be heredity; you may simply share more genes with this person than with your brothers and sisters. Suppose something like depression runs in your family. Do you wonder how much at risk you are for developing depression? Even though genetic factors are likely to account for a predisposition to this disorder, they do not, in themselves, necessarily determine its appearance. Other influences, such as increased levels of anxiety, may also be involved in triggering the disorder. We will discuss depression and other disorders elsewhere in the book.

THE PSYCHODYNAMIC PERSPECTIVE ON CHILD DEVELOPMENT

Psychodynamic theory consists of a *group of related theories that view personality and behavior in terms of the dynamics, or interactions, of driving forces of personality and development such as desires, anxieties, conflicts, and defenses.* According to this viewpoint, individuals are inevitably caught in the clash between conflicting forces of life, such as between impulses and inhibitions or between individuals and society. For the child, the conflict occurs between the child's own desires and the demands of parents and society. Although different psychodynamic theories emphasize different aspects of development, most psychodynamic theorists agree that basic dynamics include conflict between two opposing forces: anxiety (which results from the clash between desires and inhibitions) and defenses against the desires that arouse anxiety. Since Sigmund Freud's ideas provide the core concepts for this perspective, much of the discussion will be devoted to his ideas.

Development of Personality

Since Freud regarded **libido**, or *psychic energy related to sexuality*, as fundamental, he interpreted development on the basis of the *sequential process* of **psychosexual stages**. In each stage, *the child seeks to gratify the drive for pleasure in the various body zones: the mouth, the anus, and the genitals. The manner in which children handle the conflict between their impulses and environmental restrictions is decisive for development.* Too little or too much gratification at a certain stage may result in **fixation**, *by which the person becomes emotionally fixed at a particular anxiety-ridden stage and continues to act out symbolically the wishes that were overly inhibited or indulged.*

The **oral stage** *occurs during the first year of life, during which the mouth becomes the primary means of gratification.* Although infants must suck milk from the breast (or bottle) to survive, their mouths soon become a means to satisfying pleasurable and, to some extent, aggressive impulses. Thus, the various ways infants achieve gratification through sucking lay the foundations for later adult development. Fixation at this stage may result in a passive personality associated with addictive eating, smoking, or drinking or in sarcasm in a person who is always criticizing everyone else's ideas without offering any of his or her own.

The **anal stage** *occurs during the second year of life, when the child's major source of physical pleasure becomes the releasing or retaining of feces.* Caught between pleasurable urges and parental demands, the child may experience considerable anxiety and conflict. Fixation in the early phase of this stage may result in adult tendencies toward disorderly, messy behavior. By contrast, fixation in the later phase of this stage would give rise to the stubborn, compulsively orderly personality in adulthood. The **phallic stage**, *which extends from the third to the fifth or sixth year, is the period in which the child experiences sensual pleasure through handling of his or her genitals.* Again, too little or too much gratification sets the stage for later difficulties, such as the individual who feels guilty about his or her sexuality or engages in sex to reduce anxiety. The phallic stage is especially important because of the occurrence of the Oedipus complex for boys and the Electra complex for girls during this period. In Greek legend, King Oedipus unwittingly kills a man who turns out to be his father and marries a woman he later discovers is his mother. And Electra, the legendary daughter of King Agamemnon, longs for him after his death and plots revenge on his killers—her mother and her mother's lover. Freud would have found interesting that Audra was a bit like Ken's mother in that she was tall, had dark hair, possessed a warm personality, and was very intelligent, but not particularly affectionate.

According to Freud, children during the **Oedipal (or Electra) complex** *are sexually attracted to the opposite-sex parent and envy the same-sex parent.* Freud, in other words, pointed out that both fathers and mothers are important to child development. Research today suggests that fathers are as important to child development as are mothers, who earlier were thought to be more influential (Rohner, 1998; *Today's Issues*, 1998). To read more about the impact of both fathers and mothers on their children, turn to Box 2–2. The conflict at this stage arouses considerable anxiety in children of both sexes, though in due time it is resolved as spontaneously as it emerged. Instead of trying to possess the opposite-sex parent and risk losing the love of the same-sex parent, the child settles for identification with the same-sex parent. In so doing, children incorporate that parent's sexual orientation, mannerisms, and values. Furthermore, the resolution of the Oedipus or Electra conflict (i.e., complex) results in the formation of the superego, about which you will read shortly. Examples of people who suffer from unresolved Oedipal conflicts are the male Don Juan, who "loves 'em and leaves 'em" without ever getting close to his partners, and the actively seductive female who paradoxically feels guilty about sex.

The **latency period** *takes place between about 5 years and 12 years of age. During this time the child's interests turn away from sexual satisfactions. Early sexual feelings are forgotten and sexual urges lie relatively dormant.* Paul and Ken as boys were typical examples of the latency stage. Neither had any interest in the opposite sex; in fact, they both thought that girls were silly and that any contact with girls would give them "cooties." The next stage, the **genital stage**, *begins with the onset of puberty and sexual maturation, from about 12 years of age on. In this period the individual's sexual interests are reawakened and focus on gratification through genital or sexual activity.* The well-adjusted adult experiences genital strivings so that he or she is capable of genuine love and adult sexual satisfaction. Ken, for example, outgrew his resistance to girls and as a young man was very happy to have

Box 2–2

Recognizing the Importance of Fathers

Psychologists have long recognized the significant impact parents have on their children (e.g., Collins, Maccoby, Steinberg, Hetherington, & Bornstein, 2000). For generations, however, researchers mainly focused on mothers, resulting in a lack of reliable information about the role fathers play in their children's lives (Stolz, Barber, & Olsen, 2005). Collecting information on fathers could help parents, social service agencies, and government policy makers meet the needs of children and families. Without such information, the stereotype of fathers remains that of a clueless dad stumped by his eye-rolling and sometimes sarcastic offspring (Dickinson, 2002).

Statistics support that fathers are very important in the lives of their children. More than 2 million children in the United States are raised primarily by their fathers, and fathers now provide three-fourths of the day-to-day child care that mothers provide; this is contrary to the stereotype of modern American fathers providing little care for their children (Abrams & Lamb, 2002). Additionally and contrary to popular opinion, most unmarried fathers in their twenties and thirties maintain close contact with at least one of their children (*Today's Issues*, 1998).

Researchers are therefore finding that fathers are significant in their child's development (e.g., Stolz et al., 2005):

- When fathers are involved in their children's schooling, the children complete more years of school and have higher wages as adults than children whose fathers were uninvolved.

- When both the mother and the father are present in the family, the children have fewer behavioral problems and earn better math and reading scores in school.

- When no father is present in a son's life, the son is more likely to become a father as a teenager and to live apart from his children.

- When fathers are present and have warm relationships with their daughters, the daughters are less likely to engage in early sexual activities.

- The more sons and daughters report feeling supported by their fathers, the more likely they are to show initiative in engaging in prosocial activities outside the home.

Fathers indeed make a difference; thus, researchers are pushing for more research on fatherhood. In the meantime, all parents—whether fathers or mothers—need to do the best parenting job they can in order to raise well-adjusted, healthy children. A few parents (as well as some observers of parental behavior) may well guess that there are many "bad" parents. The National Mental Health Information Center (2003), however, suggests that this is a myth. There are *no* dysfunctional families, the Center suggests; there are only distressed and under supported families.

---

found Audra. Most adult problems with sex derive from fixations at the earlier oral, anal, or phallic stages. Some examples of such fixations are people who are cynical about sex and enter into lustful relationships as ends in themselves or those who withdraw from all sexual relationships.

The Structure of Personality

Freud held that the structure of personality develops as the stages unfold and consists of three interacting concepts or processes: the id, the ego, and the superego (see Figure 2–1). Because each has different goals, their interaction often takes the form of conflict. The **id** is *the unconscious reservoir of psychic energy for the overall personality and the source of later development when the ego and superego appear.* All the drives that make up the id are derived from the two primal instincts: the "life," or sex, instinct and the "death," or aggressive, instinct.

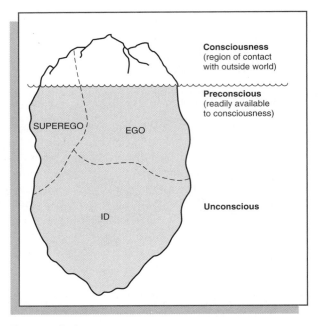

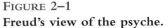

FIGURE 2–1
Freud's view of the psyche.

Freud regarded the sex drive as the major source of psychic energy, affecting the entire person, including the need for affection, love of family and friends, the urge toward creativity, and erotic behavior. The id operates entirely on the pleasure principle, taking no account of reason, reality, or morality. The **pleasure principle** *means that our actions are guided by the seeking of gratification or pleasure.*

The **ego** is *a direct outgrowth of the id and functions as a manager of personality, enabling the individual to cope with the conflicting demands of the id, the superego, and society.* Accordingly, the ego operates on the basis of the **reality principle**, *with the primary concern being the individual's well-being.* When a desire from the id bids for expression, the ego looks for a potential means of gratifying the desire in a socially satisfying way. The ego anticipates the consequences of such action and then either acts accordingly or delays gratification. For example, Ken always wanted to be wealthy (a very id-like desire), but he knew that only a socially acceptable means for obtaining wealth would assure his future. This was one of the driving forces behind his desire to go to law school.

The **superego** is *that part of the personality which has been shaped by the moral standards of society as transmitted by the parents.* It is roughly equivalent to "conscience" or to our moral compass, though much of it remains unconscious. As such, the superego takes no more account of reality than does the id and, instead, operates in accordance with the **principle of perfection**, *which motivates the person to be moral and perfect.* Thus, the effects of the superego on the individual tend to be harsh and punitive, or hypermoral. Much of the repression of unacceptable impulses is carried out by the superego directly or by the ego at the urging of the superego. Ken, for example, often thought about cheating on his college exams so as to achieve good grades, but his superego was sufficiently strong that he knew not to cheat.

The id, ego, and superego are not entities or even parts of the mind. They are best seen as metaphors or names that Freud gave to highly complex psychological processes that make up our mental life.

Modifications

Many of Freud's followers were original thinkers in their own right who revised and expanded his views. Although post-Freudian thought developed in many different directions, two trends are especially significant. First, there has been a greater emphasis on the ego, with Freud's daughter, Anna, heading up the movement. Many of the later psychodynamic thinkers de-emphasized sex, the unconscious, and the deterministic aspects of Freud's views. Instead, they stressed the goals and self-directed aspects of development. Carl Jung, for instance, held that the purpose of insight is not simply to gain rational control over the id and the source of psychic energy. The purpose is to help the individual discover and develop his or her wholeness and uniqueness. A second trend in the revision of Freud's thinking has been a more positive emphasis on the individual's social interactions. Freud had interpreted the child's social interactions in relation to the forces of the id. On the other hand, Erik Erikson, a psychologist showcased in Box 2–3, altered Freud's theory not only to address more developmental stages but also to emphasize *social rather than intrapsychic events* (Slater et al., 2003). These revisions of Freud's thought have enriched the psychodynamic perspective and brought it closer to the other branches of psychology, with their emphasis on social influences.

Applying It to Yourself

In the psychodynamic perspective, each of us is driven by motives, needs, and conflicts we're not fully aware of. Accordingly, at times we're beset by ambivalence and indecision, such as whether we really want to remain in a given relationship or job or not. For example, one of the questions most commonly asked of psychologists is "Can you love and hate the same person?" Most psychodynamic therapists would say "yes" because of the unconscious and conflicting urges inherent in human nature.

However, much of the way we cope with life and relate to others depends on how we've grown up. That is, each of us tends to act out of our psychic character in our adult personality. This aspect, in turn, has evolved through a developmental process in which early experiences have had a significant bearing on our present or adult functioning, especially if our childhood experiences were marked by trauma or maladaptive relationships.

At the same time, it's normal to have "problems." Even Freud had them, being afflicted by migraine headaches, nicotine addiction, and a variety of other symptoms he himself labeled "neurotic" (Jones, 1953). But the various symptoms of maladjustment, whether Freud's or ours, share a common feature: The individual's ego and coping defenses are weakened, making that person vulnerable to further maladjustment. In extreme cases, the individual's defenses break down, overwhelming the ego with impulses and anxiety, leading to serious psychological disorders.

Optimal adjustment comes from strengthening the ego and its orientation to reality, that is, learning to live in the world as it is rather than fantasizing about life as it could be. Essentially, this consists of increasing our self-understanding and self-mastery

Box 2–3

ERIKSON'S EIGHT STAGES OF PSYCHOSOCIAL DEVELOPMENT

Erik Erikson has widened the potential application of psychodynamic theory by transforming Freud's psychosexual theory of development into a more inclusive view of personality development. Whereas Freud focused on the child's psychosexual development with the family, Erikson takes into account the individual's psychosocial relationships within the larger society. And whereas Freud's stages covered only the years between birth and puberty, Erikson's stages extend throughout adulthood into old age. Each of the eight psychosocial stages is presented as a polarity, with a positive ability to be achieved along with a related threat or vulnerability. Personality development is sequential, with one's overall personality composed of the strengths and weaknesses acquired during each of the following stages:

1. *Trust versus mistrust.* If children's physical and emotional needs are met in the first year of life, they learn to trust people around them. If not, they become anxious and mistrustful of their environment.

2. *Autonomy versus doubt and shame.* As parents encourage children to walk, talk, and do things for themselves through the second and third years of life, the children will develop age-appropriate autonomy. But if the parents are coercive or overprotective, children will experience self-doubt and feel ashamed of themselves.

3. *Initiative versus guilt.* During the fourth and fifth years of development, children readily roam about and make new friends. If such efforts are supported by the parents, children will enjoy exploring their environment. If such actions are unduly restricted or punished, however, children may become passive and guilt-ridden about taking the initiative.

4. *Industry versus inferiority.* From about 6 to 11 years of age, children enjoy developing various abilities at home, school, and play. The more competent they become in dealing with their environment, the better they feel about themselves as persons. Undue frustration and failure evoke the sense of inferiority or worthlessness.

5. *Identity versus role confusion.* Throughout adolescence, roughly 12 to 18 years of age, individuals are busily redefining their identities in ways that incorporate the various changes occurring in their bodies, minds, and sexual development. The more successful they are in this task, the stronger their sense of personal identity. The more difficulty experienced, the more confusion adolescents feel about who they are and what they may become.

6. *Intimacy versus isolation.* As family ties are loosened during early adulthood, individuals need to form satisfying, close relationships with peers of both sexes. The inability to establish satisfying relationships with friends, including a lover or spouse, results in a painful sense of isolation or loneliness.

7. *Generativity versus stagnation.* By middle age, individuals are especially ready to develop generativity—the ability to look beyond one's self, family, and job and to contribute to the welfare of others. The person who succeeds in doing so may continue being productive and happy. The person who doesn't tends to become self-absorbed.

8. *Integrity versus despair.* In late adulthood, individuals tend to look back upon their lives as a whole. To the extent they have achieved a satisfying life, they will feel happy with themselves in old age. But if they feel that their life has been disappointing and a failure, despair will be the result.

SOURCE: Erikson, E.H. (1963). *Childhood and society* (2nd ed.). New York: W. W. Norton.

so that we can make meaningful accommodations between our deepest needs and desires and, on the other hand, the social demands made of us. Our goal should be to maximize the satisfaction of our needs while minimizing guilt, self-defeating tendencies, and harm to others and society. As a result, Freud observed that if we are able "to love and to work"—to establish satisfying relationships and find meaningful work—we are indeed fortunate.

THE SOCIAL-COGNITIVE PERSPECTIVE ON CHILD DEVELOPMENT

The **social–cognitive perspective** *is a broad term that includes behavioral and social learning theories* as well as **cognitive psychology**. *This perspective often assumes that learning and behavior involve higher-level cognitive functions or thinking.* The early behavioral psychologists relied on scientific laboratory methods to observe behavior. As such, they focused on how behavior is learned; hence, the terms *learning theory* and *behaviorism* are often associated with their approach. **Learning theory** *is the systematic statement of learning principles that explain* **learning**, *which is a relatively permanent change in behavior;* **behaviorism** (also known as behavior analysis) *is an objective science that studies external behaviors.* Most learning theorists, following the pioneering efforts of Ivan Pavlov, John Watson, and B. F. Skinner, focused on the mechanics of behavior, especially the importance of reinforcement, in a way that excluded (Lenderking, 2005; Slater et al., 2003) human consciousness. **Reinforcement** *is the addition of something that increases the likelihood of a behavior.* (For example, if a child cleans his room, the parents might hug or praise the child.) Many of the early findings of learning theory and behaviorism were based on animal studies and dealt with the more elementary types of learning and behavior rather than consciousness and cognition (Baars, 2003).

In recent years, behavioral research has shifted to complex human behaviors and real-life problems. Learning concepts are being expanded and integrated with ideas and findings in other areas of psychology—especially cognitive psychology. As a result, there is more emphasis on the interaction between individuals and their environment, as well as on how their elaborate cognitive abilities affect learning and behavior (Hohwy, 2004; Zimmerman & Schunk, 2003). Such cognitive abilities include but are not limited to thinking, problem solving, decision making, and interpretation of events.

Social Learning Theories

More recently, Albert Bandura (1986; Zimmerman & Schunk, 2003) and others have demonstrated that much of what we know and do, especially as children, is acquired through the process of **observational learning**. This is *a process in which we learn by observing events and other people, or "models," without any direct reward or reinforcement.* Such learning depends on four components: attention, retention, reproduction, and motivation. In other words, we must *pay attention* to what is going on around us, *retain* what we learn, *be motivated* to perform what we learn, and therefore *reproduce* the same behavior that we observed in others. Such learning is often combined with direct reinforcement (or "reward") to enhance learning. As a concrete example of this, let us again examine Ken's decision to leave the practice of law. What is interesting from the social learning perspective is that another lawyer in Ken's firm had left the firm a year earlier due to a stress-related illness. When Ken inquired, he discovered that the man did not return to the practice of law even after he recovered. Instead, the man moved to Vermont where he opened a craft mart that sold the creations of local artists. He related to his incredulous friends how very happy he now was. Perhaps this individual provided a model for Ken.

Bandura (1973) has paid special attention to how aggressive behavior may be acquired through observational learning (Slater et al., 2003). In one study, he compared overly aggressive boys who were in trouble with the law with better-adjusted boys. He found that their home environments could explain much of the aggressive boys' behaviors. More specifically, he found that the fathers of overly aggressive boys were more rejecting of their sons, so that their sons became less dependent on them and spent less time with them. Parents of overly aggressive boys were also more likely to use harsh, physical punishment, so their sons were more apt to imitate their parents' aggressive behavior than their verbal warnings to the contrary. These parents also tended to encourage their sons in aggressive behavior, such as standing up for their rights or leading with their fists. To learn more about the effects of physical punishment, read Box 2–4 on spanking. Parents of the better-adjusted boys showed more accepting attitudes toward their sons, explained their discipline and demands, and were less likely to use physical punishment. As a result, these boys tended to develop inner control over their aggression, that is, an adequate conscience and a sense of guilt, so that they kept their aggressive behavior well within the bounds of the law.

Of course, Bandura's work on observational learning also means that he has come out strongly against media violence. Bandura and others in the social-cognitive camp

---

Box 2–4

SPANKING: DOES IT WORK?

Spanking tends to be fairly prevalent among American parents and their children. In America, it is an acknowledged and widespread method of aversive control of children's behavior. A 1999 study found that 94 percent of American parents spank their toddlers (Straus & Stewart, 1999). A pertinent question therefore arises: "Is spanking a good idea?" In other words, does spanking eliminate or lessen the undesirable behavior of the child, or does spanking actually make undesirable behavior worse? Think about this: When parents use spanking as a means for punishing their child's aggression, are they modeling the very same behavior they hope to eliminate in their children?

Most experts on learning and behavior strongly suggest that spanking should not be used (Owen, 2004; Payne, 2004; Slade & Wissow, 2004), although some argue that mild spanking or punishment may be effective (Kazdin & Benjet, 2003). The reasoning is that spanking invariably *does not work to lessen* the undesirable behavior. New studies, in fact, show that spanking instead *increases other undesirable behaviors* (Straus, 2001). Let's look at a sample study. Simons, Lin, and Gordon (1998) examined another link between parental spanking and the consequences for their children's behavior. Using over 100 boys, the researchers tracked how much spanking the parents administered and its eventual effect

on dating violence committed by the boys. The researchers concluded that the more the boys were physically punished, the more likely they were, years later, to report hitting or shoving a girl whom they were dating.

Researchers have found that the only positive outcome of spanking a child is rapid compliance with the parent's request to cease the undesired behavior (Gershoff, 2002; Kazdin & Benjet, 2003; Owen, 2004). As much as spanking seems efficient, psychologists far prefer that parents find some other means for managing the behaviors of their children (e.g., time-outs, removal of privileges), because the long-term consequences of spanking, as noted, are simply too serious. Instead of (punishing negative behaviors in children, parents) should use other methods, say psychologists. One of the most preferred alternatives is to reward or reinforce positive behaviors of a child, such as praising a child for good grades at school, rather than punishing a child for poor academic performance. The notion is that a child cannot be both naughty and nice at the same time. If parental reinforcement of positive behaviors increases the likelihood of other positive behaviors, soon the child will be producing far more desirable than undesirable behaviors. The message is clear, then. Avoid spanking; praise constructive behaviors for a better-behaved, less aggressive child.

TABLE 2–1

HOW PREVALENT IS MEDIA VIOLENCE AND WHAT ARE ITS POSSIBLE CONSEQUENCES?

1. American children between 2 and 18 years of age are exposed to an average of 6 hours and 32 minutes of various media each day. Media include, but are not limited to, television, radio, music, computers, video games, etc.

2. The average young person will see 200,000 acts of violence portrayed in the media by the age of 18.

3. Over 60 percent of media programs show some type of interpersonal violence.

4. Only 68 percent of parents report using television rating systems to determine and monitor program violence.

5. Of 3,500 studies on the effects of media violence, only 18 showed no link between exposure to media violence and actual aggressiveness of children.

6. When teachers and parents help children lower their media usage, children use media less often, approximately 30 percent less.

7. When children interact with media less, verbal and physical aggression decrease by about 25 percent.

8. Gun violence is now a leading killer of children and adolescents. Each year, 3,500 youths are murdered and more than 150,000 youths are arrested for violent crimes.

---

contend that violence in films, television, video games, and other media not only de-sensitize us to violence but also induce violence in children and adults (Brown & Hamilton-Giachritsis, 2005; Gavin, 2005; Kieffer, 2005; Kirsh, 2006). Unfortunately, the level of televised and other media aggression in our society remains high. For evidence of this, see Table 2–1.

In the social-cognitive tradition, once a given characteristic or behavior has been learned, as Bandura observed, it is not necessarily expressed uniformly in all situations. For example, not all aggressive children are aggressive in all situations. A lot depends on the extent to which the behavior is valued or rewarded in various situations. For instance, whereas Ken and Paul's parents might have encouraged physical aggressiveness while sparring in the gym, they would not have been tolerated it as a response to their younger sister's crying. Current behavior is therefore best understood in terms of the interaction between a child's past learning and the demands of the present situation. In fact, behavior is often shaped more by the requirements of the particular situation we happen to be in at the moment than by some unconscious dynamic, according to the social-cognitive theorists. Thus, the same child may act aggressively in sports, compliantly in the classroom, and democratically when socializing with friends.

Recent Additions: Cognition and Behavior

In recent years, psychologists have begun exploring the impact of cognition on behavior. Essentially, **cognition** has to do with *the processing of information, and it involves a variety of processes such as selective attention, information gathering, memory, and motivation.* Psychologists are studying cognition as a means of understanding those processes that mediate between the environment and the individual's behaviors. They believe that the impact of a stimulus depends on more than its objective physical characteristics. It also depends on environmental or contextual clues such as *how* it is presented and *the meaning* it has for the child. In other words, many contemporary learning theorists recognize that the total stimulus complex or environment and its interpretation, and not just some single isolated stimulus, influence behavior.

The recognition that cognitive variables intervene between our behavior and the environment means that we are active, complex beings and that a host of complicating factors affects our behavior (Hohwy, 2004). Bandura (1986) refers to the mutual interaction between the various components of learning as "reciprocal determinism." That is, the internal personal-cognitive variables, environmental influences, and behaviors all operate as interlocking determinants of one another. For example, our eating habits are influenced by our family's eating habits (environmental factors), which are also influenced by our past personal preferences (a cognitive factor)—no navy blue eggs please! All these influences are mutual. Consequently, if we should learn more about nutrition (a personal-cognitive factor), this would affect which types of restaurants we would seek (an environmental factor), which in turn would shape our present eating patterns (or behavior). Such a view gives us a richer, more realistic understanding of human existence than earlier learning theories.

More recently, Bandura (1997; Zimmerman & Schunk, 2003) has added another important concept to his theoretical notions, self-efficacy. **Self-efficacy** is *the belief in one's capacity to organize and execute the courses of action required to produce given attainments.* Ken, the lawyer in the opening sketch, can once again be used as an example. When Ken first sprang his idea of moving to Oregon on Audra, he argued persuasively and confidently that both of them could easily make the career change. Ken was confident that they both had the intelligence and stamina to make the winery succeed even though neither of them had any experience as vintners. We would assume, then, that Ken was high in self-efficacy.

Our overall functioning is enhanced by high self-efficacy (Bandura, 1997; Wiedenfeld et al., 1990). Self-efficacy as a cognitive process affects our achievement, our physical and mental health, our career development, and even our voting behavior. Self-efficacy is an important concept to understand and thus is discussed elsewhere in the book.

Applying It to Yourself

According to the social-cognitive perspective, much of a child's personality and behavior patterns have been acquired through interaction with the environment, especially the significant people in their lives (Zimmerman & Schunk, 2003). Although past experience may affect present functioning, it need not determine the whole of life. That is, through the learning process many of the same mechanisms that are involved in childhood can be used to improve adult adjustment. For instance, a teen who acquired the smoking habit by imitating parents or peers may, by the same token, give up this habit as an adult when sufficiently motivated and encouraged by positive role models at work.

Unlike the psychodynamic or Freudian view, which holds that we act in "character," social-cognitive learning theorists emphasize the importance of the environment and the present situation. Thus, children often act the way they do because of specific influences in their immediate environment, whether at school or at home. As such, maladaptive behavior is often more attributable to inadequate circumstances and faulty learning than deficiencies in a child's psychological makeup. Conversely, the possibility of change involves seeking out a more positive or promising environment, such as a new job or career, as Ken planned, as well as learning new skills, such as winemaking. Also, when judging children, it's important to take into consideration their circumstances at the time rather than blaming their motives—unconscious or otherwise.

Optimal adjustment consists of maximizing our competencies and coping skills, along with improving interactions with our environment. Problems and conflicts, whether intrapsychic or interpersonal, need not be considered inevitable. Instead, problems and conflicts may be dealt with through a lifelong learning process. Thus, changes in our personality and behavior not only are possible but actually occur fairly continuously throughout a lifetime, not just in childhood, especially in an environment conducive to growth. Accordingly, it's best to see ourselves as active creatures with a tremendous capacity to learn, especially when we make full use of our "minds" (cognitions) and continue to increase our range of problem-solving and relationship-enhancing skills (Baars, 2003; Hohwy, 2004).

THE HUMANISTIC PERSPECTIVE ON CHILD DEVELOPMENT

Although the psychodynamic and social-cognitive perspectives differ in many respects, they agree on one point, namely, that human behavior can be broken down into small components. More specifically, both approaches seek to identify the specific causes of human behavior. For instance, because Ken was having difficulty getting along with his boss at work, both psychodynamic and behavioral theorists would reduce his problem to special causal factors, such as conflicts at home or childhood learning experiences. In contrast, psychologists in the humanistic perspective claim that these other approaches leave out much of what makes human existence distinctive, such as the meaning and richness of subjective experience, the holistic characteristics of experience, and our capacity to willfully choose and determine behaviors and thoughts for ourselves (Lenderking, 2005). They might interpret Ken's desire to leave the practice of law and buy a vineyard as his desire for more personal growth.

During the 1950s and 1960s, when many thinkers became concerned about modern technology's threat (e.g., the nuclear bomb) to human values, humanistic psychology achieved national prominence as the **third force in psychology**, an *alternative to the deterministic outlook of psychodynamic and behavioral psychology* (Giorgi, 2005). **Humanistic psychology** consists of *a group of related theories and therapies that emphasize the values of human freedom and the uniqueness of the individual* (Slater et al., 2003).

Humanistic psychologists, thus, have called our attention to the constructive side of psychology. Individuals are now being viewed in the light of their potential for health and fulfillment as well as in terms of their vulnerabilities and maladjustments. Interestingly, in line with this, a relatively new theme in psychology has emerged—**positive psychology**. Positive psychology is *an umbrella term for the study of positive emotions, positive character traits, and enabling institutions* (Seligman, Steen, Park, & Peterson, 2005).

The Phenomenal Self

Two of the main ideas in the humanistic perspective are the phenomenal self and self-actualization. The term *phenomenon* here refers to that which is apparent to or perceived by the senses—in short, reality as experienced by the individual. Carl Rogers (1980), a leading humanistic psychologist, emphasized that it is this "perceived reality," rather than absolute reality, that is the basis of behavior. Essentially, human behavior is the goal-directed attempt by individuals to satisfy needs as they experience or perceive them. In other words, how a child sees and interprets events in the environment determines how the child reacts to them.

A key concept in Rogers's theory of personality is the **phenomenal self**, or *the individual's overall self-concept available to awareness*. Rogers assumed the existence of an actualizing tendency at the biological level—a human's tendency to develop and fulfill the self. In the course of actualizing, the individual engages in a valuing (evaluation) process. Experiences that are perceived as enhancing are valued positively and sought after (e.g., buying a vineyard); those that are perceived as blocking fulfillment are valued negatively and avoided (e.g., practicing law). The degree to which individuals trust this valuing process depends in a large measure on their self-concept, especially the self-image derived from one's experience with significant others (such as parents) during the formative years of childhood. Thus, just as psychoanalysts such as Freud recognized the importance of childhood, so, too, do the humanistic theorists.

As children become aware of themselves, they automatically develop a need for **positive regard** or *acceptance by others*. Parental acceptance often comes with strings attached, however, and the child incorporates these "conditions of worth" into his or her self-concept. For example, a mother might say, "Kenny, if you would stop fighting with your little sister, Mommy would love you more." From then on, these extraneous valuing processes compete with the child's own valuing process. If the conditions of worth are few and reasonable, the child engages in a variety of experiences and, in cooperation with the valuing process, can judge independently which are enhancing and which are not. If the conditions of self-worth placed upon the child by the parents are many and severely limiting, however, they serve to screen out or prevent much of the child's experience, whereby the self distorts and denies much of its overall experience.

The resulting tension between the self-concept and the child's valuing tendency is the major source of maladjustment. The basic problem is the discrepancy between our human tendency to value experiences on the basis of what is good or desirable to fulfill

Humanistic psychologists propose that conditions of worth placed on children by their parents stunt the children's personal growth.

basic needs ("I need a change," said Ken) and the self's tendency to value experiences selectively ("What? Give up law?" asked Audra), screening out experiences that don't conform to conditions of worth set by parents or by society. In fact, research has shown that when a major discrepancy exists between what we would like to be and who we really are, depression results (e.g., Neff, 2003). In the context of child development, humanistic psychologists like Rogers believe that children reared in supportive environments are more creative, perhaps because they can be more fully functioning in these environments. These ideas about supportive environments and psychological growth will be explained in greater detail in the chapters on self-concept and on therapy.

Ken, for example, grew up feeling he had to be successful to be accepted by his parents. As a result, he spent many years denying his anger toward his parents as well as the need to relax and be himself. When Ken first told Audra about his desire to leave the practice of law and to move to Oregon, she asked him first to consider counseling. He agreed. After he had discovered in therapy his buried anger toward his parents, he said, "So much hurt and anger came out of me that I never really knew existed. I continued to feel this way until one night I was sitting and thinking and I realized that I had been trying to find the real me, not the one my parents wanted me to be, for a long time." Here, Ken's denial of his own thoughts and feelings had become so strong that self-alienation was thwarting his own growth. Interestingly, even after Ken finished his counseling, he still wanted to move to Oregon and give up the practice of law.

Self-Actualization

Still another idea in the humanistic perspective is the concept of **self-actualization**, *the process of fulfilling our inborn potential*. The term *self-actualization* is usually associated with Abraham Maslow, who gave it its fullest explanation (Hanley & Abell, 2002; Slater et al., 2003). Maslow, like Rogers, assumed the existence of an inborn actualizing tendency in the individual. Each child and adult has an inherent need to actualize his or her potentialities. However, in Maslow's conceptualization, the core of growth operates in relation to a hierarchy of needs. Only as the individual's most basic needs are met do the higher growth needs become a potent force in motivation. As long as the individual's needs of hunger, safety, and human companionship remain *un*satisfied, the person's existence is governed mostly by deficiency motivation. Once these needs are relatively satisfied, the individual becomes more aware of growth motivation and of the desire to fulfill needs such as autonomy and creativity. Development, especially of our self-actualizing potential, continues throughout childhood *and* adulthood (Reiss & Havercamp, 2005).

Ken, for example, had little to worry about in terms of his physical and safety needs. He also felt that he belonged in society and that he and Audra belonged together. However, as he became aware that these needs had been satisfied, he felt a strong need to "find himself," as he said, to know himself better. It was through self-realization that he understood the high level of distress and unhappiness he was experiencing in the law profession. Ken was fortunate in this respect; it can otherwise take an entire lifetime for growth needs to unfold, so that self-actualization is more of a lifelong process than a readily attainable goal.

Maslow (1971) held that certain people have reached a healthier, more optimal level of functioning than the average person. He called them *self-actualizing* people and held that studying them may teach us much about our potential for growth. Such people are relatively free from major psychological problems and have made the best possible use of their talents and strengths. Compared to the average person, self-actualizing people have certain characteristics in common, such as a continued freshness of appreciation of everyday realities; greater acceptance of themselves and others; high creativity, though not necessarily in the arts; and high resistance to conformity. However, Maslow made it clear that self-actualizing people are not perfect; they remain vulnerable to some of the same concerns and problems that plague everyone. At times they can be boring, irritating, or depressed. Essentially, self-actualizing people are like the rest of us but without the inhibited capabilities so characteristic of the average person.

If self-actualization is indeed a positive process, we should seek out means by which to become more actualized. Activity 2–1 contains a questionnaire designed to assess how much you are moving toward your self-actualization.

Our inner core of growth needs may be relatively weak and undeveloped, making it easily stifled by discouraging circumstances. Many people fail to actualize themselves because of the lack of supportive circumstances. However, countless people have been significantly creative despite deprived circumstances, and Maslow acknowledged that it is something of a mystery why affluence releases some people for growth while stunting others. As a result, Maslow suggested that a favorable environment is not enough to ensure growth. Individuals must also have an intense desire to grow, to offset the fear and resistance to growth.

All things considered, Maslow envisioned personal development as a struggle between growth-fostering forces and growth-discouraging forces, such as fear of the unfamiliar. He felt that our society discourages growth by overvaluing safety and physical comfort, as, for example, overly protective parents do. Instead, he suggested that we should minimize the attractions of security and maximize its dangers, such as boredom and stagnation. At the same time, he felt we should emphasize the attractiveness of growth while minimizing its dangers. Maslow (1968) repeatedly emphasized that "growth is, in itself, a rewarding and exciting process, thereby overcoming much of our resistance to self-actualization" (p. 30).

Applying It to Yourself

Humanistic psychologists encourage us to see ourselves in terms of our positive potential, or what we can become. As such, they are more concerned with our personal growth than with sheer survival. Problems and conflicts are neither necessary nor inevitable. When these occur, it's apt to be because of our restrictive self-images, faulty choices, or an unsupportive environment. We may improve ourselves by changing the way we see ourselves and achieving more of the potential control we have over our lives. For example, they would see Ken's choice of being an attorney as restricted by his parents' wishes, and his own choice of becoming a winemaker as being more self-directed. Such changes occur more readily in an environment conducive to growth, whether a challenging job or a happy marriage, not simply in psychotherapy.

Because of the high value placed on the individual, adjustment is rarely interpreted in terms of conventional conformity to society. In fact, much of the maladjustment in life occurs because we live as if there were no inherent potential for something better. In terms of Rogers's phenomenal self, we risk becoming maladjusted when we accept our limited, defensive self as the inevitable state of existence rather than achieving greater self-acceptance and self-direction. In terms of May's human freedom, many of our difficulties come from the refusal to face up to the important choices in our lives, if only by default. And in terms of Maslow's concept of self-actualization, a good part of our maladjustment comes from settling for a conventional life based on security and boredom rather than on the more challenging choices that foster growth.

ACTIVITY 2–1

ARE YOU BECOMING MORE SELF-ACTUALIZED?

The following questionnaire is based on Abraham Maslow's work. It was specifically devised for this book so has no scientifically researched validity or reliability. Please complete this survey and use the results as a guide rather than as fact in determining how far you have progressed on the road to self-actualization.

Each statement is followed by a scale of 1 (disagree) to 7 (agree). Please mark the extent of your agreement by circling the appropriate number.

1. I experience life fully in the present moment rather than dwelling on the past or worrying about the future.

    Disagree   1   2   3   4   5   6   7   Agree

2. I make choices that will enhance my growth by taking reasonable risks that will develop my potential rather than keep me safe and secure.

    Disagree   1   2   3   4   5   6   7   Agree

3. I listen to my own needs and reactions rather than let others influence me.

    Disagree   1   2   3   4   5   6   7   Agree

4. I am honest with myself and with other people.

    Disagree   1   2   3   4   5   6   7   Agree

5. I strive to do my best in accomplishing tangible goals in everyday life.

    Disagree   1   2   3   4   5   6   7   Agree

6. I am assertive in expressing my needs, ideas, and values.

    Disagree   1   2   3   4   5   6   7   Agree

7. I recognize and live by the inspiration of special moments or peak experiences in which I feel especially close to fulfilling my potential.

    Disagree   1   2   3   4   5   6   7   Agree

8. I relish new experiences and new knowledge.

    Disagree   1   2   3   4   5   6   7   Agree

9. I can identify my defenses and am willing to put them aside in order to revise my expectations, ideas, and values.

    Disagree   1   2   3   4   5   6   7   Agree

10. I commit to concerns and causes outside of myself because I recognize that self-actualization comes as a by-product of unique experiences.

    Disagree   1   2   3   4   5   6   7   Agree

11. I remember that self-actualization is a lifelong process; it is never fully achieved.

    Disagree   1   2   3   4   5   6   7   Agree

12. I trust my own experiences to be my guides in life.

    Disagree   1   2   3   4   5   6   7   Agree

Now add up your scores. The higher the score, the more you may have progressed toward optimal being or self-actualization. Find topics (questionnaire items with low scores) that might need more work. Also, keep in mind that few people are truly self-actualized. Actualization is a process, not a final end state.

SOURCE: Based on Maslow, A. H. (1971). *The farther reaches of human nature*. New York: Viking.

Optimal adjustment is achieved by making choices that will enhance growth and by taking reasonable risks that will develop our potential. However, we must remember that self-actualization is a lifelong process (Reiss & Havercamp, 2005), rather than an end state, that is only imperfectly realized in anyone's experience. Most people find growth experiences inherently gratifying, despite their imperfections. For instance, Maslow himself had an unhappy childhood; felt his ideas of self-actualizing people were not fully appreciated; and suffered from chronic fatigue, which only later in life was diagnosed as a form of hypoglycemia.

DEVELOPMENTAL CHALLENGES IN CHILDHOOD

As you can see, various theorists tend to emphasize different aspects of personality, development, and adjustment. Regardless of these specific theoretical perspectives, psychologists have documented several constructs and have highlighted certain developmental milestones that serve as the foundation of an individual's personality and development.

Temperament

One foundational component of personality is temperament. **Temperament** is defined as *an individual's characteristic pattern of emotional response and behavioral reactivity to situations and stressors*. When we describe an individual as "easy-going," "laid-back," or "intense," we basically are describing that individual's temperament. For example, do Ken and Paul seem to you to have the same emotional and behavioral patterns or different patterns?

Just as Freud proposed, an individual's early life is very important. Temperament provides an example, as it is apparent early in life—even at birth! In a landmark study published in 1968, Chess, Thomas, and Birch observed and documented temperamental differences in 133 infants. The temperament of the majority of these infants could be categorized in one of three ways: 40 percent were described as "easy"—these children were happy and cheerful for the most part, had very regular biological rhythms, and they adapted to new situations well; 10 percent were described as "difficult"—irritable in their responses, unpredictable with regard to their eating and sleep habits, and intense in terms of their emotional expression; 15 percent were categorized as "slow-to-warm"—in novel situations, slow-to-warm children appear to be cautious and restrained, but as they "warm up" they become more open and playful in their responses. The remaining 35 percent of the infants in the sample could not be categorized neatly. Their temperamental patterns seemed to consist of various combinations of the three primary patterns observed (Thomas & Chess, 1977, 1984).

The consensus among researchers is that temperament seems to be inborn, strongly based in our biology and surprisingly consistent over time—even through adulthood (Thomas & Chess, 1997, 1984). The notion of a biological element accounting for temperament is consistent with the biological perspective as presented earlier. Chess and Thomas tracked the original 133 infants into adulthood and found that individuals' temperaments, for the most part, remained consistent through the years. Other researchers, using measures derived from Chess and Thomas's original findings, have found that a child's temperament at age three is highly correlated with personality in young adulthood. Accordingly, Ken and Paul ought to have the same temperaments because they are twins.

Many psychologists believe that a child's temperament (e.g. difficult or easy) may be inborn.

In another long-term study, Caspi and Silva (1995) used three temperamental dimensions, Lack of Control, Sluggishness, and Approach, which resemble Chess and Thomas's original temperamental styles. A sample of over 800 three-year-olds were categorized by trained observers as exhibiting one of five behavioral styles that represented various combinations of these temperamental dimensions. Children with an *Undercontrolled style* had a difficult time sitting still and were emotionally reactive; those with an *Inhibited style* were shy in new settings, were emotionally reactive to changes in the environment, and also had a difficult time sitting still; *Confident children* actively explored the environment and engaged in responsive social exchanges with the researchers; *Reserved children* displayed shyness but were not emotionally reactive to changes in the environment; and children who displayed a *Well-Adjusted behavioral style* were socially reserved or outgoing, depending on what the interaction with the rater demanded, and were confident in solving problems.

When these children were 18 years of age, they were given parts of the Multidimensional Personality Questionnaire, a self-report measure that is designed to assess various personality characteristics. The relationship between their early temperamental style and personality traits measured at 18 was remarkable. For example, children identified as *Inhibited* at age 3, often described themselves as restrained and nonassertive as adults; they preferred to engage in "safe" activities rather than "dangerous" ones and rarely reported behaving impulsively. *Reserved* children at age 3 were likely to be 18-years-olds who reported being indecisive and less forceful in social situations much of the time. And *Well-Adjusted* children at age 18 continued to display the socially responsive and controlled behavior they displayed at age 3 (Caspi & Silva, 1995). In a follow-up study, Newman, Caspi, Moffitt, and Silva (1997), using the same group a few years later, found that the type of temperamental style identified at age 3 often predicted the quality of the individual's interpersonal functioning at home, work, and with friends and romantic partners at age 21, with Undercontrolled children reporting poor social adjustment and more interpersonal conflict later in life.

So, if you are the type of person who is fairly laid-back and easy-going and things don't upset you too much, it is more than likely as a baby you had an easy temperament. If you are the type of person who gets agitated and is restless for the most part, as a baby you may have had a difficult temperament. If you are the type of person who is shy and inhibited but become more outgoing after you relax in a situation, it is likely you were a slow-to-warm baby.

Temperament is not necessarily the sum total of who you are and how you adjust—most certainly the experiences that we have and the interactions we have with others throughout our lifetimes affect our personality in a number of ways. Because of their unique life experiences, Ken and Paul may indeed be different. But based on the fact that temperamental patterns can be observed in infants, we can say that temperament serves as one of the building blocks for our social and emotional functioning.

Self-Recognition and Self-Concept

Humanistic psychologists such as Rogers and Maslow made apparent the importance of the self-concept to personal growth and adjustment. (Chapter 4 of this book is dedicated exclusively to the all-important issues of self-concept, self-image, and self-esteem.) Here we will discuss only the development of these constructs. The development of a sense of self (or self-concept) is contingent on a *child's ability to differentiate him- or herself from others in the social environment*, or what is termed **self-recognition**. Of course, this differentiation is made possible by the natural progression of neurological and cognitive development. But when does an infant develop the ability to recognize himself?

In an ingenious study, Michael Lewis and Jeanne Brooks-Gunn (1979) utilized the "rouge test," now more commonly referred to as the "surprise-mark" test to estimate the age at which children are able to recognize themselves. They asked mothers to gently and inconspicuously smudge a dab of rouge on their infants' noses and place their babies in front of a mirror. The researchers observed that infants between the ages of 18 and 24 months reliably touched their noses in a seeming attempt to rub off the strange marks! Infants younger than 18 months, although capable of touching their noses, rarely did so. Lewis and Brooks-Gunn came to the conclusion that this difference was due to the fact that children between 18 and 24 months of age have developed the capacity to recognize themselves, whereas younger children have not.

Other researchers (Nielsen, Suddendorf, & Slaughter, 2006) placed stickers on toddlers' legs in a variation on the rouge test and discovered that even when sitting in a high chair with a tray obstructing their view, children between 18 and 24 months reliably attempt to remove the sticker from their legs when they see themselves in a mirror, indicating that self-recognition at this age extends beyond the face. Interestingly, the rouge test findings have been replicated in a cross-cultural study (Priel & deSchonen, 1986), and children with mental retardation and other developmental disabilities also display evidence of self-recognition as evidenced by the rouge test only when they achieve a mental age of 18 to 20 months (Hill & Tomlin, 1981).

Lewis (1997) noted that toddlers start to use first-person pronouns like "I" and "me" around 20 to 24 months—another indication of self-awareness at this interval in a child's life. Ken and Paul both learned to use first-person pronouns within a week of each other at about the age of 2 years. Lewis and Ramsay (2004) studied infants at 15, 18, and 24 months and discovered that as the tendency to touch their noses in the rouge test increased at each age cutoff, so did their tendency to use personal pronouns. Once a child can distinguish him- or herself from the others in the social environment, the stage is set for the development of self-concept. In answer to the question "Who are you?" most preschool-aged children define themselves by their physical characteristics ("I have brown hair") or by what they own ("I have a tricycle") (Keller, Ford, & Meacham, 1978). Self-concept during the preschool years is colored by the concrete, tangible characteristics that define a child's impressions of self. As a child progresses through the school years into adolescence, behavior-based characteristics and physical attributes gradually are replaced by more reflective, abstract, psychologically based qualities in self-descriptions (Damon & Hart, 1988).

Sense of self is a very important aspect of personal and social functioning. With the development of self-recognition between the ages of 18 and 24 months, the stage is set for the acquisition of self-concept, self-esteem, and related constructs like self-efficacy, all of which guide us as we navigate the social world throughout our lives.

Attachment

The close emotional relationships we have with others in our social environment, or our attachments to these individuals, color our social lives. **Attachment** is often defined as *a close, emotional tie with another person*. Throughout our lives we develop attachments to various individuals—parents, grandparents, siblings, friends, boyfriends, girlfriends, spouses (Cassidy, 1999). Ken and Paul, because they are twins, bonded to each other more than to the primary caregiver—something, you will recall, that inspired Freud to develop the idea of the Oedipal conflict. Back in the 1960s and 1970s, when research on attachment burgeoned, the primary caregiver in most children's lives was the mother and, thus, most research examined the relationship between mother and child.

It is believed that the attachment one develops with the primary caregiver is strongly based on biology. For human infants, who are particularly vulnerable from an evolutionary standpoint, attachment has survival value (Bowlby, 1969, 1973), as suggested by psychologists proponing the biological perspective. Although there may be a genetic basis for attachment, the quality of that attachment is very much determined by the early interaction one has with the primary caregiver, much as Freud, Rogers, and other important psychologists theorized. And as we will see in Chapter 12, there is a significant connection between the quality of the attachment between caregiver and child and the attachments the individual forms as an adult with others (Hazan & Shaver, 1987).

How is attachment with the primary caregiver studied? Back in the 1970s, Mary Ainsworth and her colleagues developed an experimental procedure now referred to as the "Strange Situation." The procedure involves observing the interactions between mother, child, and stranger in an unfamiliar playroom filled with novel toys. The quality of the attachment is gauged by how readily the child explores the room, how the child responds to the stranger entering the room, how the child reacts when the mother leaves the room, and how the child responds when mother returns.

After observing hundreds of mothers and infants, Ainsworth and her colleagues (1978) found the quality of a child's attachment to a caregiver could be categorized in one of three ways. Most children displayed *secure* attachments. They were very comfortable exploring the new environment and interacting with the stranger as long as mom was present. When mom was coached to leave the room, these children became very distressed and sought out mom's comfort when she returned. In Ainsworth's thinking, mom is a secure base from which these children can explore the physical and social world. Some children in Ainsworth's sample displayed an *anxious-ambivalent* attachment. As the label implies, these children were very anxious in the new environment and in interacting with the stranger, even in the presence of the mother. They became upset when mom left the room, but weren't necessarily comforted when she returned. Another portion of the sample displayed what was termed an *avoidant* attachment. These children did not often interact with their mothers, nor were they distressed when mother left the room. The latter two attachment patterns have been collectively labeled "insecure" attachment patterns.

Additional research has verified that a variety of positive cognitive and social characteristics seem to be related to and may develop as a result of secure attachment, just as theorized by Carl Rogers and the other Humanists. Securely attached toddlers generally display more positive emotions like joy, whereas insecurely attached toddlers often display more negative emotions such as anger, fear, and distress (Kochanska, 2001). Children with secure attachments have larger vocabularies than same-aged peers with insecure attachments (Meins, 1998), and they are more sociable (Elicker, Eglund, & Sroufe, 1992). And securely attached children tend to have closer, more stable friendships at ages 10–12 (Schneider, Atkinson, & Tardif, 2001).

It only makes sense that early interactions with our caregivers help set the stage for our interactions with others later in life. As mentioned, in a study detailed more closely in Chapter 12, Cindy Hazan and Phil Shaver (1987) questioned adults about the quality of their attachments and the nature of their relationships with others as adults and found that security of attachment in childhood often predicted security in individuals' adult relationships.

Applying It to Yourself

Are you an easy-going person or are you generally suspicious of others until you get to know them? When you look in the mirror what do you see? If you were to describe yourself, what qualities would you identify as characteristic of you? Are you happy with the person you are or do you have different ideas regarding who you want to be? Are you secure in your relationships with friends and lovers, or do you sometimes feel betrayed or suspicious of their actions or intentions? The answers to these questions all have their roots in some of the major concepts examined in early childhood by developmental psychologists.

CONCLUSION

As you can well see, there exist many theories or perspectives on development, but no one perspective is perfect (Slater et al., 2003). There are many forces—our genetic predispositions, for example, as well as the attachments we have with our primary caregivers—that shape us as we grow and mature. Each theory suggests different ideas about how, why, and when we grow or change. Can we conclude that one theory is better than another? Now that you are familiar with some of these theories and the various aspects of development, you can decide for yourself whether you think one theory better characterizes human development than another. Perhaps the conclusion that you draw is that one theory best explains your own personal growth but cannot explain your friend's level of adjustment. Or perhaps you might conclude that one theory seems to best describe general human growth and development. Everyone reading this book may well settle on a different answer.

SUMMARY

PERSPECTIVES ON CHILD DEVELOPMENT

Psychologists approach development, adjustment, and growth from differing perspectives, each of which offers an optimal range of explanations rather than a comprehensive truth. Thus, by examining the distinctive contributions of all four major perspectives, we may attain a more inclusive, balanced understanding of personality and behavior. The four major perspectives are biological, psychodynamic (or psychoanalytic), social-cognitive, and humanistic.

THE BIOLOGICAL PERSPECTIVE ON CHILD DEVELOPMENT

Extensive studies of twins and others have shown that genetic influences may account for between 25 percent and 50 percent of the differences in personal characteristics among the general population. At the same time, the extent of the way we develop depends greatly on the interaction with our environment. As a result, we should speak of nature *via* or *through* nurture or perhaps nature *and* nurture rather than nature *versus* nurture.

THE PSYCHODYNAMIC PERSPECTIVE ON CHILD DEVELOPMENT

According to the psychodynamic view, we develop in a sequential process, and the manner in which the child handles the characteristic developmental conflicts has a decisive influence on adult development. Individuals are also inevitably caught up in the interplay between conflicting forces of life, such as our unconscious drives and the ego's defenses, as well as the tension between the individual and society. The ego is the managerial part of the psyche that enables the individual to cope with the conflicting demands of the id, the superego, and society. Since the ego, the id, and the superego are often in conflict, individuals commonly experience anxiety as well as the various ego defense mechanisms that reduce it. Many of Freud's followers have de-emphasized sex and the unconscious and given greater emphasis to the managerial functions of the ego as well as to interpersonal relationships. In the psychodynamic view, optimal adjustment consists of increasing the individual's self-mastery and the attendant orientation to reality.

THE SOCIAL-COGNITIVE PERSPECTIVE ON CHILD DEVELOPMENT

Learning theorists de-emphasize the biological basis of behavior and instead focus on how behavior is learned through interaction with the environment. They contend that most of our personality and behavior is acquired through such processes as observational learning, with or without direct reinforcement (or reward). Furthermore, their recognition of cognitive variables that intervene between the environment and our behavior suggests that learning is affected by more complex factors than an isolated stimulus, as was the belief in early behavioral theory. Bandura has characterized the mutual interaction among the various components of learning—personal-cognitive variables, environment, and behavior—as reciprocal determinism. In this view, humans have a tremendous capacity to learn and change, especially when they make full use of their minds and maximize their competencies in dealing with the environment. Self-efficacy is one means for accomplishing growth and change.

THE HUMANISTIC PERSPECTIVE ON CHILD DEVELOPMENT

Humanistic psychologists emphasize the holistic characteristics of human experiences, such as human freedom and self-actualization. Rogers's theory of the phenomenal self stresses the importance of perceived reality, especially the way individuals perceive and experience themselves in relation to their environment. In May's view, we begin to live authentically only as we affirm our inherent human freedom and take responsibility for our lives. Both Maslow and Rogers hold that each person has an inherent need to actualize his or her potentialities but that self-actualization is more of a lifelong process that enhances the meaning of life rather than being a readily attainable goal.

DEVELOPMENTAL CHALLENGES IN CHILDHOOD

Developmental psychologists study many factors emerging in childhood that set the stage for later personality and social functioning. Temperament, described as a person's characteristic reactivity, is apparent at birth and is remarkably consistent throughout a person's life. Self-recognition, critical to the development of self-concept, emerges at around 18 months. Self-concept in young children is based on their concrete personal characteristics, but as a child develops cognitively, psychological attributes tend to color self-characterization. And the quality of our early attachment to our caregiver tends to frame the ways we relate to significant others later in our lives.

SELF-TEST

1. According to research, which one of the following traits is most strongly affected by genetic influences?
   a. intelligence.
   b. frugality.
   c. impulsiveness.
   d. shrewdness.

2. The part of the psyche that operates entirely on the pleasure principle is the
   a. ego.
   b. id.
   c. superego.
   d. ego ideal.

3. According to Freud, the emotional alarm signal that warns the ego of danger is
   a. anxiety.
   b. the superego.
   c. the id.
   d. repression.

4. The process by which people may acquire new behaviors without any direct reinforcement is called
   a. self-actualization.
   b. observational learning.
   c. the conditioned response.
   d. operant learning.

5. Which one of the following signifies the idea that we are in charge of our own actions to attain goals?
   a. self-efficacy.
   b. human freedom.
   c. ego.
   d. self-actualization.

6. Bandura's research demonstrates that we should be very concerned about children's imitation of
   a. adults eating the wrong diet.
   b. adult misconduct.
   c. media violence.
   d. other people's religious attitudes.

7. From the social-cognitive perspective, optimal adjustment is achieved through maximizing the individual's
   a. management of inner conflicts.
   b. self-actualizing drive.
   c. competencies and coping skills.
   d. self-esteem.

8. Carl Rogers holds that human behavior is determined primarily by
   a. perceived reality.
   b. social reinforcers.
   c. ego defenses.
   d. biological drives.

9. According to Maslow, self-actualization
   a. is rarely experienced after middle age.
   b. occurs among half of the population.
   c. is a lifelong process.
   d. is an achievable goal for many.

10. A(n) _____ child is reticent at first and then becomes more open to others.
   a. difficult.   c. easy.
   b. slow to warm up.   d. all three equally.

EXERCISES

1. *Which of Erikson's stages are you in?* Write approximately a page explaining how well you're mastering the appropriate developmental task for your stage, according to Erikson's theory. How important do you consider this task for someone at your stage of life? If possible, comment on how your past development affects your experience in the present stage of development.

2. *The importance of other people in your life.* Describe several of the important people, including your parents, who have most influenced your past development. What are these people like? What effect did they have on your development? To what extent has your personality been shaped by them? To what extent do you think your development was determined by inheritance?

3. *Self-actualization.* Take the survey in the chapter about self-actualization. How actualized are you? What factors frustrate your actualizing potential? In which areas are you the most fully actualized? In which areas is further growth most and least likely?

4. *Barriers to personal growth.* Each of the four major perspectives covered in this chapter offers a different view of the barriers to personal growth. The biological view reminds us of the importance of heredity to our temperament, for example; the psychodynamic view stresses unconscious conflicts and fixations; the social learning view emphasizes faulty models, environments, and maladaptive behavior; and the humanistic view highlights the importance of restricted self-concepts and self-actualization. Write a paragraph or so explaining how each of these views may help to account for the barriers to your own personal growth.

5. *Human freedom.* Select a specific but recent situation in which you exercised your human freedom or free will in the face of restricted circumstances. Then write a page or so about your experience. How much do you agree or disagree with the view expressed by May and Rogers, that is, that we possess an inner freedom of choice over and above the available options in our environment?

6. *Which major perspective most reflects your views?* Select one of the four major perspectives that is most compatible with your own thoughts on adjustment and development. Then write a page or so explaining why you prefer this viewpoint. To what extent are you receptive to viewpoints different from your own? Would you agree that no one perspective possesses the whole truth?

7. *Career changes.* You may find yourself thinking as Ken did—that a career change might be good. Or perhaps you selected one major in college and are thinking about changing. What other information do you need to know before you settle on the change? How can you collect this information? Once these tasks are done, is there anything else you might want to do or think about before you make the change? What would dissuade you from changing? Would the change result in growth? If you chose not to change, would it mean that you are avoiding self-actualization?

8. *Early experiences.* How would you characterize your early life? Were you securely attached to your primary caregiver? Did you have a difficult or easy temperament? Do you recall when you were first able to differentiate yourself from others? How have these early experiences carried through to affect your personality and adjustment now?

QUESTIONS FOR SELF-REFLECTION

1. Why is it important to take a perspectival approach to the study of development?

2. Given what you now know about development, do America's children stand a reasonably good chance of being happy and well adjusted?

3. Are there personal characteristics that seem to run in your family tree?

4. Do you agree with Freud that personality is like a submerged iceberg—with only the tip surfacing in awareness?

5. Do you sometimes experience ambivalence—being pulled in opposite directions simultaneously? What can you do to cope better when this happens?

6. Do you believe that much of the inconsistency in people's behavior can be explained by situational factors?

7. When psychologists label their perspective "cognitive," what does this term mean to you?

8. How would you explain the differences between Bandura's social learning view and Rogers's humanistic view?

9. Do you think parents ought to use spanking? If not, what might prove better?

10. Are you as convinced as Rogers that we have within ourselves vast resources for self-understanding and growth?

11. Would you agree that self-actualization is always "in progress" rather than something ultimately completed?

12. Why do you think people aren't more fully self-actualized?

13. Why is it that not everyone is securely attached? Do you think that if caregivers knew more about adjustment and child development, the world would be a different place? How so?

FOR FURTHER INFORMATION

RECOMMENDED READINGS

BERK, L. (2005). *Child development.* Boston: Allyn and Bacon. Berk reviews normal child development. This book includes more cross-cultural information than the usual child development text.

CRAIN, W. (2004). *Theories of development*. Upper Saddle River, NJ: Prentice Hall. This book introduces the read to various theories of development and provides fairly extensive critiques of each theory.

DUNLAP, L. L. (2002). *What all children need: Theory and application*. Lanham, MD: University Press of America. Dunlap discusses important aspects of what children need, including experiencing love and being valued. She also discusses building positive self-esteem and teaching children how to value themselves.

KOHN, A. (2005). *Unconditional parenting: Moving from rewards and punishment to love and reason*. New York: Atria. Kohn discusses modes of parenting and relationships between parents and children. His book is sprinkled with anecdotes with which most parents can identify.

GARBARINO, J. (2006). *Why girls are growing more violent and what we can do about it*. New York: Penguin Press. An important book about why American girls turn to violence and other antisocial behaviors. This book is a follow-up to Garbarino's book on the same topic but with regard to boys.

WEB SITES AND THE INTERNET

http://www.parentingivillage.com/ A site dedicated to helping parents in all domains of child rearing. Chat rooms are also available so that parents can share their thoughts and concerns with other parents.

http://www.nhgri.nih.gov/ The web site for the human genome project, which is trying to document all of the genes on human chromosomes. This site also contains information on the policy, medical, and ethical considerations of trying to understand more about human genetics.

http://www.positiveparenting.com/ A web site that has the main goal of making parenting a positive experience, for example, other ways to discipline children besides spanking.

http://www.esrb.org/ A web site that assists parents and others by rating web sites and video games for appropriateness for children.

http://www.apa.org/ppo/issues/snichd.html The American Psychological Association's main page for links to information on children, developmental psychology, and other relevant topics.

CHAPTER **3**

Affirmative Aging—Adulthood

ADULT DEVELOPMENT

DECISIONS, DECISIONS, DECISIONS—EARLY ADULTHOOD
Leaving Home
Choosing a Career
Establishing Close Relationships
Starting a Family

SAME OLD, SAME OLD?—MIDDLE ADULTHOOD
Midlife Transition or Midlife Crisis?
Physical and Cognitive Changes
Possible Career Changes
Sexual Changes

AGING GRACEFULLY—LATE ADULTHOOD
Physical and Cognitive Changes
Personal and Social Adjustment
Retirement
Successful Aging

SUMMARY
ANSWERS TO AGING QUIZ
SELF-TEST
EXERCISES
QUESTIONS FOR SELF-REFLECTION
FOR FURTHER INFORMATION

Learning Objectives

After completing this chapter, you should be able to

1. Describe various emotional and social aspects of leaving home in young adulthood.
2. Explain the importance of a secure sense of identity to the forming of close relationships.
3. Explain Erikson's concept of the midlife developmental task of generativity versus stagnation.
4. Describe the characteristic physical and cognitive changes accompanying late adulthood.
5. Identify different paths to successful aging.
6. Discuss differences between men and women with regard to the process of aging.
7. Describe how individuals cope with retirement.

Zena sat on the edge of her bed. She felt stiff this morning and did not know why. She thought, "The funny thing about aging is the way it sneaks up on you. One minute you're 30 or 40. Before you know it, you're 64, like I am." She continued her thoughts as she rubbed her sore, stiff hands. "I don't feel 64, but my birthdays betray me. So do my grandkids and my slightly arthritic hands," she thought.

Zena continued to think of herself as someone in her late 40s, though she was reminded otherwise each time she looked in the mirror. It usually came as a surprise when her body rebelled. She didn't feel older, except in those rash moments when she overexerted herself, such as walking too quickly up a steep hill, or when she awoke to morning hand stiffness. As had Zena at times in her life, virtually all of us have been hit with the admonishment "Act your age." "But what if your chronological age isn't the age you feel?" Zena wondered as she sat on her bed.

ADULT DEVELOPMENT

Defined, **development** means that *our capabilities and behaviors continue to change as we grow older not only because of biological growth processes but also because of our understanding of and interactions with our environment.* New tasks, different challenges, and new sources of happiness and frustration mark each new period of our lives in adulthood. The process of personal growth, therefore, continues throughout our life span, as you will see in this

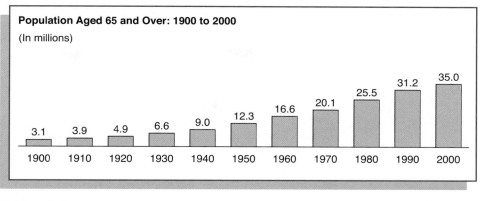

FIGURE 3–1

Population aged 65 and over: 1900 to 2000. NOTE: The reference population for these data is the U.S. population.
SOURCES: 1900 to 1940, 1970, and 1980, U.S. Bureau of the Census, 1983, Table 42; 1950, U.S. Bureau of the Census, 1953, Table 38; 1960, U.S. Bureau of the Census, 1964, *Table 155; 1990,* U.S. Bureau of the Census, *1991, Table QT-PI; 2000, U.S. Census Bureau, 2001, Table PCT12. For full citations, see references at end of chapter.*

chapter. Zena, then, was older but not old. The segment of the population known as "old" has been growing dramatically in recent years due to healthier lifestyles and medical advances. Figure 3–1 illustrates the dramatic rise in the number of older people through the year 2000. Ask yourself, "Is our society ready?"

Adulthood can be defined *as the period of life from physical maturity on, consisting of a sequence of physical and psychosocial changes throughout early, middle, and late adulthood.* A central theme of adult development concerns continuity and change (Giarrusso, Mabry, & Bengston, 2001). On the one hand, some studies have shown that the individual's personality remains relatively consistent throughout adult life (Hamarat, Thompson, Steele, Matheny, & Simons, 2002; McCrae & Costa, 2003). For example, people who have been relatively successful in their earlier stages of development also seem to cope well with the critical stages of adult life, such as marriage, parenthood, and retirement. On the other hand, there is mounting evidence that personality changes with age. For example, older people score higher on characteristics such as conscientiousness, agreeableness, and adherence to social norms but score lower on social vitality (Helson, Kwan, John, & Jones, 2002).

Why these contradictions about change and continuity? People are dynamic organisms who continue striving to master their environment; thus, they change and grow as they get older (Pfaffenberger, 2005). Perhaps more than ever before, people are deliberately trying to change themselves, so that with age and experience they have greater coping skills and self-mastery. On the other hand, once in a while people like to feel settled and connected to the familiar. Older people, for example, much prefer to stay in their own homes rather than move to assisted living or move in with their children (Administration on Aging, 2005). As Carl Rogers (1980), one of the pioneers of information on personal growth, grew older, he became convinced that the phrase "older but still growing" is a more apt description of adult development than the conventional cliché "growing old." Zena, our gracefully aging woman in the opening vignette, would heartily agree.

Another theme of adult development concerns the emergent individuality or uniqueness that often comes with maturity. Up through adolescence, much of our development is associated with **age-related changes**—*changes that occur at a given age,* such as puberty and high school graduation. In contrast, adult development depends more on **non-age-related changes**, or *events and influences that are unique to each of us and may occur at any age or not at all*, such as divorce or the decision to change careers. Also with advancing age, individual differences in development become more pronounced. For example, Zena met her former classmates later in life at a high school reunion and discovered that they were even more different from one another at 35 or 40 than they were at 18. With age, we all develop our own individual identities to a greater extent, feel more confidence in ourselves, and can achieve greater personal control and mastery over our lives (Pfaffenberger, 2005).

Because of the increased importance of individual differences with age, some social scientists prefer to discuss adulthood without regard to any stages at all. However, the self-perceptions and social circumstances of a 25-year-old are likely to differ from those of a 45-year-old, and both are likely to differ from those of a 65-year-old (The Federal Executive Institute and Management Development Centers, 2006). Consequently, as is customary, we'll examine adult adjustment and growth in terms of three broad stages: early, middle, and late adulthood. Keep in mind that the age boundaries between these stages are fuzzy and that people differ considerably in their own individual patterns of development. Before you read further, take the quiz in Activity 3–1 to examine how much knowledge you possess about the aging process.

ACTIVITY 3–1

How Much Do You Know About Aging?

Write either "true" or "false" by each of the following statements. Then check your responses with the answers at the end of this chapter.

_____ 1. All five senses tend to decline in old age.

_____ 2. People lose about one-third of their brain cells or neurons by late adulthood.

_____ 3. Drivers over 65 years of age have fewer traffic accidents per person than those under 30.

_____ 4. Most older people are pretty much alike.

_____ 5. Older adults become less susceptible to short-term illnesses, such as the common cold.

_____ 6. Recognition memory declines sharply with old age.

_____ 7. Reaction time generally becomes slower with age.

_____ 8. About one-fourth of those over 65 live in nursing homes.

_____ 9. People become more fearful of death as they grow older.

_____ 10. Widows outnumber widowers about three to one.

The answers can be found at the end of the chapter.

DECISIONS, DECISIONS, DECISIONS—EARLY ADULTHOOD

In their classic longitudinal study of adult development, Levinson, Darrow, Klein, Levinson, and McKee (1978) discovered what parents and young people themselves have long suspected, namely, that the transition to adulthood is more complex and strung out than ordinarily understood (Strom & Strom, 2005). In their view, **early adulthood** begins with an "early adult transition," *roughly from the late teens or early 20s and lasting well into a person's 30s.* The major developmental tasks of this period are leaving home, choosing and preparing for a career, establishing close relationships like friendship and significant others, and starting a family of one's own. Because the decisions young people make will affect them for 50 years or more, this transition can be stressful (Lindgren, 2002a).

Leaving Home

One developmental task in early adulthood concerns seeing ourselves as autonomous adults separate from our families of origin. Because the separation from our families is never complete, it may be more accurate to understand leaving home in terms of the transformation of emotional ties between young persons and their families that takes place during this period. The external aspects include moving out of the family home, becoming less dependent financially on our parents, and entering new roles and responsibilities. The internal aspects include increasing differentiation of ourselves from parents along with more autonomous decision making. It is this psychosocial transition that is essential for entering adulthood. Some youths may run away from an unhappy home at an early age but take a long time before growing up emotionally. Choosing to achieve self-sufficiency in other ways, others, mostly because of a lengthy education, may remain home well into their 20s (Strom & Strom, 2005). In both cases, it is the "symbolic" leaving from home that is so crucial to attaining emotional autonomy.

Difficulties coping at this stage may reflect problems in separating from home and from the dynamics of the family itself. Separation troubles can take many forms, including drug addiction, delinquent behavior, emotional disturbances, paralyzing apathy, or suicide. In the case of Zena's second son, his separation problems showed up in problems with his grades at college. Zena was consoled, however, by the fact that her friend Olga's son expressed his angst at college by using illicit drugs. In many instances, young people have difficulty leaving home because of their parents' unwillingness to "let go." Such parents may complain of a young person's problems at school or with drugs while deriving an unconscious satisfaction from knowing they are still needed as parents. Young people themselves also experience conflicts over leaving home. On the one hand, they may feel impatient and resentful toward their parents for their attempts to control them, but on the other hand, they may also feel anxious about their ability to be successful on their own.

At the same time, a curious thing has been happening in the last decade. Like birds flying back to the nest, more young adults are moving in with their parents after years of absence from home (Strom & Strom, 2005). The increase in "nesters," as some professionals call them, is partly due to the increase of this age group in our society and to economic situations. For example, Zena's only daughter Jonelle, moved back with Zena after her divorce to "regroup," as Jonelle called it. Demographers estimate today that up to 5 percent of American grandparents are raising their grandchildren (U.S. Bureau of

A developmental task for young adults involves leaving their childhood home.

the Census, 2001). An even larger percentage of elderly have grown children with their own young children living with them. It is often difficult for young people to maintain their own apartments or homes because housing prices generally continue to increase, and many young people are having a hard time finding a suitable job.

As you might expect, there are pros and cons to such an arrangement (Strom & Strom, 2005). The increased food bills are sometimes incredible, though some young people pay board to offset these expenses. Also, parents may find it natural to ask, "Where were you last night?" as Zena asked of Jonelle, who as an adult deeply resented this questioning. However, individuals and their parents often find that this is a satisfying time for sharing and strengthening their ties before a son or daughter leaves home again, usually for good.

Choosing a Career

A major developmental task during this period is the choice of a career, along with the appropriate preparation for it. In choosing a career, young adults must strike a balance between two somewhat contradictory tasks. One task is to explore the possibilities in the adult world, keeping their options open. The other task is to create a stable life structure with the aim of making something of themselves. Young adults often agonize over the important decisions they must make at this stage, whether they are making the right choice, and if not, how difficult it will be to change. If you experience some distress about career options as you progress through college, this is perfectly normal, to an extent. Decisions, decisions, decisions.

Careers and financial security have become more important considerations for many of today's young adults compared to their parents. This development can be seen in the marked shift in values among college students in the past few decades (Dey, Astin, & Korn, 1991). For instance, in 1967 more than 80 percent of entering college students felt that developing a "meaningful philosophy of life" was a major life goal, and less than half that number felt that "being well off financially" was equally important. However, nearly 40 years later these values have become reversed. Many students now plan to major in biology (for medical school), business, or economics, almost double the number several decades ago. Also, fewer students major in the humanities and social sciences. As a result, many young adults decide to delay or to give up starting a family for the benefit of their careers because they want to start earning a good salary and building their careers as soon as possible. In fact, the goal of earning a good salary has been demonstrated to be essential in selecting an academic major (Montmarquette, Cannings, & Mahseredjian, 2002). However, not everyone fits this pattern.

Establishing Close Relationships

A major developmental task during the period of early or young adulthood is forming close relationships with one's peers. Developmental psychologist Erik Erikson (1974), who is also introduced in Chapter 2, contends that young adults' success in this venture depends largely on how well they have resolved the earlier issue of identity exploration in adolescence. Individuals who are unsure of themselves or what they want to be may be so fearful of losing themselves in a close relationship that they enter into only superficial, dependent, or unstable relationships. Those with more self-assurance and clearer life goals are freer to engage in the emotional give-and-take of a close, committed relationship.

How well two people get along as a couple also depends largely on their emotional involvement and commitment to the relationship. For most couples, there is at least one partner who is primarily committed to the relationship. That person, who is more emotionally involved, is also the more vulnerable and unhappy partner. Furthermore, relationships with uneven emotional involvement are not only less satisfying, they are also less stable. You will read more about close relationships in Chapter 12.

Starting a Family

Early adulthood is usually the time for starting a family. However, couples are giving more thought to whether they want children and if so, when to have them. One result is more voluntary childlessness. Few couples resolve this issue directly. Usually, couples decide to postpone having children until they eventually make the postponement permanent. Those who decide to have children tend to wait longer before doing so than did couples during the 1950s. When Zena and her husband married in their early 20s, they decided they wanted children right away and that Zena would delay her education and her career until the youngest began school. Today, many couples do not have their first child until they are in their late 20s or early 30s.

A disadvantage common to having children at any age is the conflict between balancing careers and child rearing. Because so many mothers work, society has had to offer alternative arrangements to in-home care, such as day care centers. Sandra Scarr (1998, 2004), a leading child development specialist, suggests that the *quality* of child care is more important than whether mothers work or provide child care. Scarr defines **quality care** as *care provided by a warm, supportive adult in a safe, healthy, and stimulating environment.* This type of environment best engenders trust and supports the child's physical, emotional, social, and intellectual development.

For Zena and her husband, having children was not a question. Married couples in those days were expected to have children—ideally, a boy and a girl, with the boy born first. Today, having children may affect a couple's marriage in several ways. On the positive side, many couples report that having children makes them feel more responsible and adult. They also report increased satisfaction in sharing affection and experiences with their children, which enhances their sense of purpose in life. On the minus side, taking care of small children is an added stress on the marriage (Puterbaugh, 2005), leaving less time for the parents to do things on their own. Even without children, there can be a great deal of marital stress as individuals question their marriages and their relationships to their mates. For working couples, the stress increases; the couple may wish to spend lots of quality time with their children but cannot. Studies show that today's parents have 22 fewer hours a week to spend with their children (Kornblush, 2003). Many people have children before they realize how children can alter parents'

Another developmental task of young adulthood is starting a family.

lifestyles, sleep habits, and other matters of daily life. You might want to volunteer to babysit a young child or visit a nursery school if you do not yet have experience with young children and are thinking about having a family.

SAME OLD, SAME OLD?—MIDDLE ADULTHOOD

Sometime between the late 30s and mid-40s, people make the transition from early adulthood to middle adulthood, often called midlife by many developmental psychologists. **Middle adulthood** may be defined as *that era between the late 30s and the 60s that is generally characterized by fulfillment of career and family goals*. Both men and women begin to see themselves differently, with new opportunities and tasks as well as new limitations. These individuals are going through the midlife transition. Today's middle-aged adults do not see themselves as old, whereas in earlier times, middle age *was* old age, when people were expected to die. A large contemporary study, however, conducted by the American Association for Retired Persons found that middle-aged Americans nowadays identify more with younger adults than with the elderly (Elias, 2002). As a matter of fact, an intriguing and oft-repeated research finding is that adults of all ages tend to see themselves as younger than they really are (Furstenberg, 2002).

Midlife Transition or Midlife Crisis?

Essentially, the **midlife transition** is *a period of personal evaluation that comes sometimes with the realization that one's life is about half over*. The individual gradually pays less attention to the "time since birth" and starts thinking more in terms of "time I have left." Some people at this age may hide some of the more obvious changes of age or compensate by trying harder to appear young. For example, Americans spend several billion dollars each year on cosmetic surgery in an attempt to obtain a more youthful or pleasing appearance; others may accuse them of having a "midlife crisis." It is sometimes difficult for middle-aged individuals to ignore other fundamental changes. For one thing, their parents retire, become ill, and die during these years. More of their friends and acquaintances are also lost through death, with death from all causes rising sharply at this time of life. Their children grow up and leave home, and middle-aged parents feel more aware of the mistakes they have made raising their children. For Zena, these middle adult years were particularly trying times; not only did her mother die, but her father was infirm, and her beloved husband died from cancer.

When Zena cared for her husband and her father, she found what other middle-aged adult children discover: that there is a crisis in caregiving in America (Carbonell, 2003; Conway-Giustra, Crowley, & Gorin, 2002). Zena found little other help when her parents and her husband needed almost constant attention and assistance. Her grown children left for college and subsequently started their own lives and families, so could not assist her. In addition, her adult children frequently called and asked Zena if "Grandma" could babysit. The midlife transition, then, can become an uncomfortable time for some people. This need not be so, as recent research has discovered. Box 3–1 examines well-being in adulthood with information that may surprise you, because it indicates middle-aged people and older adults are remarkably happy.

Box 3–1

WELL-BEING THROUGHOUT ADULTHOOD

Many people believe that life will become less satisfying as they move away from their 20s and 30s. They view midlife as an unstable period and old age as the worst of times. This negative image of aging, however, is at odds with some of the research on older people. Aging research is focusing more and more on successful aging. Along this line, longitudinal research has found that life satisfaction tends to peak at about 65 years of age (Mroczek & Spiro, 2005). Despite the fact that health declines with age (Ross, 2005), other factors contribute to happiness in middle and early old age. Compared to younger adults, individuals at these older ages experience more autonomy in their lives and also feel that they are more likely to be doing their duty (e.g. voting or helping others). Thus, they experience a greater sense of well-being than younger adults (Sheldon, Kasser, Houser-Marko, Jones, & Turban, 2005). Additionally, older individuals are more likely than younger adults to experience memories of personal growth (e.g., successfully addressing challenges) (Bauer, McAdams, & Sakaeda, 2005). At the same time, well-being across the life span may be partly due to age-related emotional differences. Mather and Carstensen (2005) note that as people age, they experience more emotion regulation. They find themselves less often experiencing negative emotions and more often experiencing positive emotions than do younger people. Other factors also influence successful adaptation to aging. They include life course factors such as marital stability, religiosity, and health (Crosnoe & Elder, 2002).

In Erikson's (1968) theory of development (see also Chapter 2), the main life task at this stage is achieving a sense of generativity, which involves becoming less self-absorbed and more caring about others and future generations. The realization that life is half over prompts people to ask what they would like to do with the rest of their lives. Such self-questioning may lead to changes in their careers, marriages, or personal relationships (Helson & Soto, 2005; Lindgren, 2002b). It often leads individuals to take up new interests or become active in community or national affairs as a way of making their world a better place in which to live. Zena thought to herself, "It's a time for becoming aware of the 'opposite,' unrealized side of my personality." For example, a hard-driving businessperson like Zena's husband may take more of an interest in helping others, or a middle-aged homemaker may go back to school to refresh her skills as a laboratory technician. Middle age, then, is a time for shifting gears and developing new interests and values. Research has shown that developing multiple interests is a great buffer against mental and physical illness in adults (Pfaffenberger, 2006).

Physical and Cognitive Changes

The most obvious signs of middle age are certain physical changes in appearance. People tend to gain weight around the waist, especially after 40 (Ziebland, Robertson, Jay, & Neil, 2002)—with women worrying most about their bodies (Saucier, 2004)—and head hair may turn gray. Men's hairlines may begin to recede around their upper temples and make them wonder if they are going bald. All these changes reflect a gradual slowing down in the overall physical system, which can result in less physical energy and stamina. People typically get tired more easily and take more time to bounce back from fatigue or illness.

There is actually some improvement in general health in the sense that middle-aged adults get fewer colds, allergies, or minor illnesses, and they may experience fewer accidents. But they become more susceptible to chronic and serious illnesses, such as diabetes, heart attacks, strokes, and cancer. Recall that Zena's husband died of cancer in midlife. As a result, there is increasing concern over health and sometimes more attention placed on keeping fit (Crowley, 1999; Malmberg, Miilunpalo, Pasanen, Vuori, & Oja, 2005). In fact, much research shows that greater overall activity level is related to greater happiness, function, and reduced mortality rate in adulthood. Even mild involvement in less strenuous activities, such as reading, can result in increased happiness, perhaps because it engages us in life (Menec, 2003).

Cognitive abilities may also change, depending on the person and the prior level of cognitive activity (Wilson et al., 2005). Starting around the age of 50, people begin to differ more and more from one another in terms of their intellectual capacity. In other words, some cognitive capabilities decrease (Hedge, Borman, & Lammlein, 2006), but at different rates. And some cognitive capacities seem to drop while others remain steady or might actually rise. If any decline occurs, one of the first abilities to diminish is the ability to make sense of spatial relationships. Spatial ability helps us navigate through three-dimensional space; it allows us to remember where we parked our cars at the airport or how to drive to the shopping mall. Another ability that may decline is abstract reasoning. This is the ability that helps us solve the following puzzle: Apple is to pear as dog is to which of the following: (1) movie, (2) tree, (3) moon, (4) cat. In midlife, the ability to remember things after some delay might also decline. Another ability that slowly declines is processing speed; older people generally take longer to learn and remember (Herbert, 1999). *A debilitating cognitive disorder that may, in fact, begin to develop in midlife but is often associated with old age* is **Alzheimer's disease**. More information on this baffling disorder is available in Box 3–2.

Possible Career Changes

How people's work is affected by the midlife transition depends on many factors, such as their earlier successes and failures, satisfaction on the job, changing abilities, and unfulfilled aspirations. Women sometimes may react to their midlife transitions differently than men, depending largely on whether their primary involvement has been in a career or the home. Professional women who have considered having children may realize that the biological clock is running down, and they may decide to have a child at this age. Single-mother adoptions also tend to increase. The common pattern is seen among women who married in their 20s, as Zena did. Their children are in school, and their husbands are working longer hours. Having spent much of their married lives caring for their husbands and children, these women often feel the need to fulfill themselves in other ways. Many women return to school at this age, take a job outside the home, or do both simultaneously.

Zena married soon after leaving high school and enjoyed being a wife and mother. But as her three children approached college age, she began rethinking what she wanted to do with her life. Initially, she joined a paramedic team and began taking one premedical course each semester at the local community college. She quickly gained confidence in her ability to do the work and decided to fulfill her ambition to become a nurse. By the time her youngest son graduated from college, Zena had received her 4-year degree and become a registered nurse. "I feel lucky," she said upon landing her first job. "My husband has been supportive all the way. And I really enjoy nursing."

Box 3–2

ALZHEIMER'S DISEASE: WILL YOU BE A VICTIM?

Alzheimer's disease, a term that often strikes fear in our hearts, was not well known 100 years ago. Why? People simply did not live long enough for the disease to manifest itself.

Between now and 2050, the number of people with Alzheimer's will increase from an estimated 4 million up to 14 million, as the baby boomers enter the age of highest risk of the disease (Alzheimer's Association, 2006c). Three million of these elderly live at home and are dependent on family caregivers. The caregivers, who are often adult children, find difficult the constant caring for a loved one who is confused, has trouble remembering the simplest of things such as whether to eat meat with a spoon or a fork, and whose behavior is often unpredictable. (Caregiving is discussed in more detail in Chapter 16 on grief and death.)

Alzheimer's, at first blush, appears to be a degenerative brain disease of only the elderly. New research is shedding light on earlier memory problems that may forebode Alzheimer's disease. Scientists have found that they can sometimes predict who in midlife is at risk for Alzheimer's. A new diagnosis, **mild cognitive impairment (MCI)**, *has been identified in a subgroup of people who have memory problems during the course of normal aging but are otherwise healthy and functional* (Alzheimer's Association, 2006a). When studied longitudinally (i.e., followed over a span of several years), such individuals develop Alzheimer's at a much higher rate than people in the general population. In MCI people have more trouble, for example, with the "tip of the tongue phenomenon," where information is at first difficult to recall but is eventually remembered by those without MCI. In other words, MCI sufferers have difficulty with everyday memory searches. An MCI diagnosis also hinges on problems with memory for tasks that involve a sequence of steps, such as the steps taken in baking a cake. MCI sufferers have more problems remembering things in a series than those with normal middle-aged memories.

Why would anyone want to know in advance that she or he might potentially develop this very disabling disease? Because help is on the horizon. Scientists appear to be on the brink of discovering much-needed treatments and even a preventive vaccine for Alzheimer's disease. One promising treatment involves the use of an enzyme that would block brain cell degeneration caused by Alzheimer's. The vaccine, which thus far has been tested with some success in humans and monkeys, might eventually immunize people if serious side effects are not found (Alzheimer's Association, 2006b).

Sexual Changes

The biological and psychological changes that accompany the loss of reproduction contribute to the midlife transition in both sexes. Although these changes can pose new anxieties for men and women, they can present new opportunities for personal growth.

The most significant physical change in women is **menopause**, or *cessation of monthly menstrual cycles*, which signals the loss of childbearing capacity. Menopause in women is also sometimes called *the climacteric.* Menopause tends to occur sometime between 45 and 55 years of age in American women. The physical effects vary from a certain degree of atrophy in the uterus, vagina, and breasts to a variety of other changes such as hot flashes. Some women find menopause mostly a negative experience, with adverse effects on their appearance and their physical, emotional, and sexual lives. Other women feel little or none of these effects. Some positive changes also occur during this period, thus evening out the quality of life between pre- and postmenopausal women (Özkan, Alatas, & Zencir, 2005). The lessened fear of pregnancy often leads to increased sexual responsiveness for many women. Other events of middle adulthood, such as changes in the marriage relationship, freedom from child-care responsibilities, and return to work outside the home, can be more important to women than the physical changes. Unlike Zena, middle-aged women today have the opportunity to address menopausal changes with hormone supplements, usually a combination of estrogen and progesterone. This treatment is not without controversy because of such possible side effects as increased risk of certain cancers and heart disease. Differences in the use of these drugs also exist, with African American and Hispanic women less likely to use replacement hormone therapy than White women (Elias, 1999a).

Although men are not subject to menopause, they do go through a male **climacteric**, defined technically as *the loss of reproductive capacity*. In men, the climacteric is accompanied by a gradual reduction in fertile sperm, a diminution of testosterone, and reduced sexual vigor, sometimes with increasing impotency in some men. However, men tend to reach their climacteric 5 to 10 years later than women reach menopause and do so in a much more gradual way, with fewer physiological consequences. The drug Viagra for men has added an interesting element to the aging male's sexuality, as revealed in Box 3–3.

Box 3–3

THAT LITTLE BLUE PILL . . .

Who would think a little blue pill would make such a big splash? The mass media tell us that there is a flourishing illegal trade in this supposedly magical sex cure and that people, both men and women, are flocking over the Mexican border to procure this blue aphrodisiac, this sexual enhancer, without a prescription.

Viagra (generically known as sildenafil), the little blue pill described here, was introduced in 1998 as a treatment for **male impotence** or **erectile inhibition**. This disorder is defined in the chapter on sexuality as *inability to experience an erection*. Scientists estimate that 52 percent of the men between the ages of 40 and 70 years old may suffer from erectile dysfunction (Cappelleri, Bell, Althof, Siegel, & Stecher, 2006). Within months of the introduction of Viagra, sales reached 4.5 million prescriptions a month, breaking the all-time record for all new drug sales. It was quickly followed in the intimacy products market by Cialis (generically named Tadofil) and Levitra (Vardenafil) (Harder, 2005).

Collectively, these drugs are known as PDE5 inhibitors. They work by blocking an enzyme that impedes blood flow to the penis and which, in turn, impedes erection (Harder, 2005). Diminished blood flow is the most common cause of erectile inhibition (Stock, 1999). Many studies to date demonstrate that these drugs successfully treat erectile dysfunction (e.g., Cappelleri, Bell, Althof, Siegel, & Stecher, 2006; Rosen, Shabsigh, Kuritzky, Wang, & Sides, 2006). The drug itself does not cause erection.

These drugs do not work for every man; they don't take effect immediately either and have some unwelcome side effects, such as a flushed face and, worse, sudden blindness (Harder, 2005). That is one reason why a doctor's prescription is really important. There are other causes of sexual dysfunction for both men and women. Depression and some of the medications used to treat high blood pressure, diabetes, prostate cancer, and other factors affect general and sexual health. That is why a regular physician's checkup is also important.

The true psychological and societal value of such drugs may be that they

- bring sexual dysfunction into the open.

- motivate more men to see physicians for physical exams.

- prompt researchers to search for a comparable sexual enhancer for women.

In the meantime, research on these drugs continues. Because they function as vasodilators, they may prove effective as treatments for a wide range of other health problems related to the circulatory system. Viagra has already been reborn as Revatio, a drug used to treat certain lung diseases (Sternberg, 2005). Other studies are attempting to examine whether the PDE5 inhibitors can successfully treat Raynaud's syndrome, diabetes-induced kidney problems, heart failure, and certain complications of pregnancy (Harder, 2005).

Men and women who take these changes in stride often find their lives even more sat-isfying than before, including the sexual aspects of their lives. For one thing, the changes and anxieties of this period may make each individual more aware of the need for a spouse and the security of marriage. In fact, at middle age and older, men and women's friends and family are very important to their quality of life (Jaccoby, 1999). Perhaps nothing helps a man or woman through this stage as much as an understand-ing and supportive partner (Spotts et al., 2005). Actually, there is a rise in marital happiness among many couples as they age, with individuals in their late 40s and 50s reporting levels of marital happiness surpassing couples in their 20s (Bookwala & Jacobs, 2004).

AGING GRACEFULLY—LATE ADULTHOOD

What is it like to be old? Zena was just beginning to find out. If you are a traditionally aged college student, this might be hard to imagine. Research has found that when young adults use stereotypes of the old, their stereotypes are quite negative (Levy, 2001; Pecchioni & Croghan, 2002). Some authors, furthermore, declare that American society actually fears aging; greeting cards, jokes, the mass media poke fun at the elderly. One reason perhaps is that we dread our own old age and anticipated dependency on others (Pipher, 2002).

If you are daring, you might do what Patricia Brown (1985) did. With the help of a theatrical makeup artist, she transformed herself into an 85-year-old woman. She altered the shape and texture of her face with a mask and makeup and tinted her hair gray. She inserted clouded lenses into her eyes; taped her fingers together; and swathed herself in splints, bandages, and corsets to restrict her body move-ments. Then off and on for the next 3 years she experienced life as a person would in late adulthood. Significantly, age stereotypes sometimes translate into age dis-crimination; the number of age-bias suits has surged in recent years (Nicholson, 2003).

Late adulthood is *the final stage of adult development, from the mid-60s to death, and is characterized by adjustment to changing health, income, and social roles.* Zena discovered that old people don't fit well into our society. Bottle caps are too hard to get off, and the print on medicine labels is so small older people can't read it. Older adults frequently report usability problems (Fisk & Rogers, 2002) that can cause them actual harm, especially if related to health care.

Discriminatory experiences have led gerontologists to coin the term **ageism**, which refers to *negative attitudes toward and treatment of older Americans.* Ageism can be seen in the readiness with which people attribute all sorts of negative qualities to the elderly, mostly because of their age. For example, many younger people assume that the typical older person is helpless and infirm and resides in a nursing home, despite the fact that over 95 percent of older adults are not in need of custodial care. Another symptom of ageism is that the elderly are often **infantilized** or *treated like infants, as, for example, when other adults speak to them in baby talk.* Such instances of ageism perpetuate stereotypes—false generalizations—about the elderly, thereby restricting their opportunities, under-mining their personal dignity, and alienating them from the larger society. We need to become more sensitive to ageism because as the largest cohort group, the baby boomers, moves through historic time (Teichert, 2002), the elderly American population will continue to grow.

Let's look at some statistics on the aging of America. Today, more than 30 million men and women are 65 years of age or older. By the year 2050, there will be nearly 82 million Americans 65 or older (Gavzer, 2000). The "graying of America" will alter every aspect of society—business, education, government spending, housing, medical care, and leisure. We need to develop a better understanding of the aging process and what it's like to grow old. Likewise, our society needs to be better prepared for this aging population with expanded services for the elderly.

Physical and Cognitive Changes

The literature on aging has identified two distinct groups of elderly: one group aged 65 to 74, known as *the young elderly*, and another group aged 75 and beyond, known as *the old elderly*. At age 64, Zena is about to become one of the young elderly. These two groups differ psychologically and physically. Many of the young elderly are free of infirmity, whereas those in the old elderly experience more disability.

By **aging**, psychologists mean *a decline in the biological processes that comes with advancing years, increases the risk of illness and death, and is usually accompanied by appropriate psychosocial change*. Aging can involve a progressive slowing down of bodily processes. With age, the skin often wrinkles and becomes thinner, the hair grays, there is a reduction in sharpness of vision and hearing (Wingfield, Tun, & McCoy, 2005), and the reflexes slow down (Brown, 1991). Some older people eat less because their sense of taste diminishes, they exercise less, and they have less physical energy for life. They also sleep less restfully, though they spend more time in bed compensating for this lack of sleep. The old elderly sometimes have more trouble maintaining their sense of balance. Deaths from falls occur twice as frequently as deaths from other accidents. Deaths from high blood pressure, cancer, and heart disease are also more common among the old elderly. These changes, however, do not necessarily have to result in disability, especially in the young elderly and those older elderly who continue to exercise and adopt healthy lifestyles (Fries, 2002; Kolata, 2002).

Fortunately for Zena and others like her, with improved understanding of aging and of the importance of good health care and supportive environments, we are discovering that older people can remain in reasonably good health (*Harvard Health Letter*, 2002) and function better at the same age than their parents and grandparents did. We're also learning that many of the negative changes associated with aging are due to stress, disease, and lifestyle rather than to the aging process itself. Box 3–4 discusses ways we can approach aging as healthy individuals.

Cognitive functions can also continue to be affected by the aging process (Wingfield et al., 2005), though rarely to the extent that justifies the stereotype of the absent-minded old person. In fact, scientists now know that cognitive decline in late life is *not* inevitable, as nonscientists often assume (Wright, Kunz-Ebrecht, Iliffe, Foese, & Steptoe, 2005). **Fluid intelligence**, *the ability to process new information based on perceptual skills and memory*, is most affected by aging of the nervous system and does decline somewhat in middle age and more sharply in late adulthood (Phillips, 2005). As a result, older people may exhibit slower mental reactions and are often less adept at processing new information. But **crystallized intelligence**, *the ability to use accumulated knowledge to make judgments and solve problems*, often remains the same and in many instances can improve with age.

It is also thought that individuals can maintain their creativity well into late adulthood, depending on their type of work. Artists hit their peak in their 40s, scientists

Box 3–4

HEALTHY AGING

For traditionally aged college students, old age may seem far away. For less traditional students, old age may be approaching. Each of us can start NOW practicing healthy techniques that can ensure a healthier old age. The sooner we start, the longer our life is likely to be and the better the quality of our health as we age.

- Exercise, exercise, exercise. Study after study shows the benefits even for the very old. Exercise lowers the risk of heart attacks, results in fewer hip fractures, and promotes better mental health.

- Stop smoking. No matter how long you have smoked, when you stop your health improves. Avoid the use of drugs (other than medications), and if you drink alcohol, drink only in moderation.

- Eat well. In the chapter on health, the food pyramid is reviewed. Refer to this pyramid daily. Avoiding sugars

and fats also improves overall health and helps ward off diabetes and arteriosclerosis.

- Avoid stress. This is easier said than done in today's modern world. If stress is overtaking your life, refer to the chapter on stress and stress management.

- Develop and maintain outside interests.

- See a physician regularly. Some of the infirmities of aging are silent, such as high blood pressure. Preventive checkups earlier in life can ensure healthier aging later in life.

- Find and maintain a social support system. Social support for the elderly increases their morale, buffers the effects of the loss of loved ones, and enhances their self-esteem.

maintain their creativity well into their 60s, and those in the humanities (e.g., historians and philosophers) may show a steady increase in creativity through their 70s. For example, Benjamin Franklin invented the bifocal lens at age 78, and actress Jessica Tandy won acting awards well into her 80s. More recently, actors Judi Dench and Peter O'Toole continue winning awards into their 70s. It may be that any decreased creativity ordinarily seen among older people is due more to their restricted environments than to aging. About 16 percent of America's elderly have some mobility limitations, especially elderly women, who are more prone to osteoarthritis than men. Such limitations restrict the types of environments in which the elderly find themselves.

Box 3–5 showcases other individuals who seemed at their peak of achievement in their old age.

Many adult children and grandchildren worry about an aging relative's memory. They wonder, "Is Gramma going to remember to turn the stove off when she uses it?" Generally, people older than 60 and *without dementia* show somewhat poorer overall memory performance than young, healthy individuals (Maruff & Darby, 2006). However, there exist several different types of memory, for example, temporal memory. **Temporal memory** *relates to remembering things related to time*, such as the order of their occurrence or which event occurred more recently. Temporal memory is typically diminished in older adults as compared to younger adults (Hartman & Warren, 2005). However, not all types of memory diminish with age. For example, Grühn, Smith, and Baltes (2005) as well as Carstensen and Mikels (2005) found that there is no difference between young adults and older adults for memory of positively framed material. On a practical level, Castel (2005) found that aged adults and young adults recall price ranges and realistic prices equally well. Thus, the type of material being recalled, strategies used for recall, and type of memory called upon can affect whether there are age-related

Box 3–5

A FEW OF THE LATE, GREAT ACHIEVERS

Sophocles wrote *Oedipus Rex* when he was 70 and *Electra* when he was 90.

Michelangelo began work on St. Peter's Basilica at age 70.

Anna Mary Robertson ("Grandma") Moses took up painting as a hobby at 76 and later staged 15 one-woman shows throughout Europe.

Pablo Picasso married for the second time at 77 and completed three series of drawings between 85 and 90.

Laura Ingalls Wilder didn't publish her first book until age 65 and wrote some of her best children's stories during her 70s.

Benjamin Franklin helped to write the Declaration of Independence at age 70 and was named chief executive of the state of Pennsylvania at 79.

Mother Teresa continued her missionary work around the clock, helping less fortunate people throughout the world, until her death at age 87.

Artur Rubinstein gave one of his greatest piano performances at New York's Carnegie Hall at age 89.

Golda Meir was named prime minister of Israel at age 71 and held that office for 5 years.

Mahatma Gandhi led India's opposition to British rule when he was 77.

Frank Lloyd Wright completed New York's Guggenheim Museum at 89 and continued teaching until his death.

memory differences. Perhaps the most important point is that memory need not necessarily decline with age.

Personal and Social Adjustment

If the elderly are resilient and motivated rather than bitter and passive, aging is more successful. Those people with positive attitudes toward aging also live longer (Levy, Slade, Kunkel, & Kasl, 2002). Erikson (1963) suggested that integrity also brings successful aging (recall his developmental theory from Chapter 2). For example, the elderly who concentrate on what they *can* do rather than on what they cannot do age more gracefully and experience less anxiety about aging.

One of the most important ingredients of successful aging is the ability to maintain an **internal locus of control** such that *an individual believes that something within him- or herself controls life events* or, basically, such that a person possesses a sense of autonomy, as discussed in Chapter 6. When the elderly feel that they have control over their fates, they tend to live longer, healthier lives (Zarit, Pearlin, & Schaie, 2003). Due to losses that older individuals experience, in Zena's case the loss of her husband, the death of her parents, and the maturity of her children who left home to be on their own, the elderly sometimes perceive less control than younger adults. Older adults who cope with loss of control by maintaining or enhancing their competencies (Schulz & Heckhausen, 1996) or by shifting the subjective importance of their personal goals (Brandstadter & Rothermund, 1994) adjust better to the aging process.

An important area of psychosocial change and therefore control involves living arrangements for the elderly. The young elderly, those individuals from 65 to 74 years of age, are more likely to live at home, be in better health, and be more financially comfortable than the old elderly. As mentioned earlier, many elderly prefer to stay in their own homes, but a small number of older people find they are unable to care for themselves. These individuals generally are the frail or old elderly. Contrary to stereotypes, however, only a small portion of these individuals (4.5 percent) reside in nursing homes (Administration on Aging, 2005). Zena, as she faces her 65th birthday, is pleased that she is able to live in the same charming home that she shared with her husband and her children. She is somewhat typical in that about twice as many older women as men live alone (Administration on Aging, 2005). Conversely and logically, more than twice as many men as women live with their spouses (Administration on Aging, 2005).

By the age of 85, only about one-half of all the old elderly live alone. Unfortunately, a significant proportion of the old are at or below the poverty level, making any living arrangement difficult. Poverty is a special problem for elderly women (Administration on Aging, 2005), especially elderly women of color. A much smaller proportion of old elderly lives with others, such as with a grown child, because of a desire for independence (i.e., autonomy or control) and privacy not found in facilities for the elderly. Other older people live near a grown child who visits frequently. In some instances, as mentioned earlier, elderly parents can assist their children with childcare, and the latter can help their parents with finances and emotional support in times of illness.

Social support is important to the happiness and survival of the elderly. Research demonstrates that, just like other age groups, the elderly can be educated to use the Internet to maintain contact with distant friends and family.

Because most married women will outlive their husbands, there are more widows like Zena than widowers among the elderly. Half of the women in the United States are widowed by their early 60s, and 80 percent by their early 70s. Among those over 65, widows outnumber widowers three to one. Women tend to adjust to the loss of their spouse more readily than men. Although, as mentioned earlier, older men are usually better off financially than older women, they tend to have more difficulty coping with routine household tasks, are lonelier, and are less happy than widows and older women. People who have remained single throughout their lives often feel more satisfied in late adulthood than do widows or widowers the same age, possibly because they have chosen a single lifestyle and have become better adjusted to it.

Friendships are very important to the elderly and influence their survival (Giles, Glonek, Luszcz, & Andrews 2005). Women often have an easier time making and keeping friends in their old age, partly because of the way they have been socialized and partly because of the disproportionate number of older women. Yet with the reduction of social contacts at this age, friends become even more important to both sexes. People who continue to live in the same neighborhood as they get older, an increasingly frequent phenomenon, may keep in touch with their friends from the past. Other friends may be deceased, so the social networks of the old elderly are smaller but just as close as those of younger people (Lang & Carstensen, 1994). Those who move elsewhere must make new friends. In both instances, friends can play as important a role as family members in preventing loneliness and disengagement from life among the elderly (Greenberg & Springen, 2001). This is perhaps why some people prefer to live in a retirement home or assisted living community, often in the Sunbelt of the South or Southwest. One such living facility found a unique but very modern method for keeping their elderly residents in contact with friends and family, no matter how distant.

Retirement

The retirement experience, which varies considerably from one person to another, usually depends on several factors (Hershey, Jacobs-Lawson, & Neukam, 2002). Generally, the more voluntary the retirement, the better the adjustment. Second, reasonably good health is also an important predictor for a satisfying retirement as well as for age of retirement; some people's retirements are related to poor health. Third, an adequate income is also very important at this age. It is the "perceived adequacy" of one's income rather than actual income that is the most crucial factor. Many seniors plan on living on Social Security after retirement, but the retirement age to receive this income is slowly rising. Social Security alone is generally not sufficient for the retired to maintain a reasonable standard of living (Moreau, 2002). Although retired people usually have a reduced income, they also have fewer major expenses such as mortgage payments or union dues, so their incomes may be sufficient for their present lifestyle. Zena, for example, was glad that she, her husband, and ultimately her husband's life insurance had paid off their mortgage when she was in her 50s. Those who have insufficient income after retirement are likely to continue to work somewhere; in fact, a "need for money" is the leading reason people continue to work after retirement from their primary jobs (Novelli, 2006). People from upper-level careers generally report a more favorable retirement experience, partly because they have ample income (Furstenberg, 2002).

Research on retirement demonstrates that retirees have the same levels of self-esteem as those who continue to work, and retirees are generally as well adjusted as nonretirees (Drentea, 2002); if anything, research demonstrates that retirement improves mental health (Mein, Martikainen, Hemingway, Stansfeld, & Marmot, 2003). Other factors that influence the decision to retire or continue to work include the need to be a caregiver, especially for women (Dentinger & Clarkberg, 2002), and whether the spouse will also retire (Pienta & Hayward, 2002). In retirement, volunteer work is the "work" most favored by retirees (Carey & Ward, 2000), especially those who have sufficient funds.

Successful Aging

Which person does a better job of growing old gracefully—the individual who continues to work actively as a lawyer and keeps up an active social life or the person who retires to a rocking chair on the porch? Gerontologists who favor the activity theory of aging suggest that the more active a person remains, the more satisfied and better adjusted that person is likely to be, regardless of age. Those who adhere to the disengagement theory of aging point out individuals tend to disengage from society with advancing age, with psychological disengagement usually preceding social withdrawal by about 10 years. Zena, for example, was content sometimes to sit in a chair, read, and listen to music. She also enjoyed doing volunteer work at her former place of employment, the community hospital. She was both active and disengaged, depending on the day.

As Zena's retirement demonstrates, there is no single way to age successfully, and different people adapt to old age in their own way. In her now classic research, Bernice Neugarten (1986) found that people tend to select a style of aging that best suits their personality, needs, and interests. Thus, an energetic, hard-working person will continue to tackle new projects, whereas a more contemplative person will probably do more reading. Neugarten found that some older people tend to benefit from activity more than others. For example, although those with a well-integrated personality generally adjusted better to old age regardless of how active they were, the less well-integrated exhibited better adjustment with higher levels of activity.

It's also important for individuals to feel an inner satisfaction with their lives as they grow older. Recall that in Erikson's theory (1968), the developmental task of older people is to establish a sense of integrity—a sense that one's life as a whole has been meaningful and satisfying. Those who have experienced a great deal of frustration and suffering may have more misgivings than satisfactions, experiencing despair and depression. Actually, people ordinarily experience both ego integrity and despair, but the healthier the person, the more self-acceptance and personal satisfaction will prevail.

Older people also obtain a sense of their lives as a whole by engaging in the **life review**, *a naturally occurring process of self-review prompted by the realization that life is approaching an end*. Although such a process can lead to wisdom and serenity, it may also evoke some negative feelings, such as regret, anger, guilt, or depression, or obsessional rumination about negative past events such as illness (Kraaij, Pruymboom, & Garnefski, 2002). The process consists of **reminiscence**—*thinking about oneself and reconsideration of past events and their meanings*. Some older people prefer to reminisce in private, whereas others may enjoy doing it more publicly, such as by making a family tree or telling their children and grandchildren about the significant aspects of their lives and family history. Such reminiscing serves to give them a final perspective of their lives while leaving a record of the past to their family and friends.

SUMMARY

ADULT DEVELOPMENT

We began by pointing out that human development is now viewed as a lifelong process that includes psychological growth as well as biological changes, so that individuals tend to acquire greater coping skills and individuality with age and experience. Although we've followed the common practice of describing adult development in terms of three broad stages—early, middle, and late adulthood—the age boundaries are often fuzzy, and individual patterns of development vary considerably within each stage.

DECISIONS, DECISIONS, DECISIONS—EARLY ADULTHOOD

The transition to adulthood from adolescence is more complex and prolonged than is ordinarily understood, especially now that lengthy education often postpones financial independence. Leaving home involves achieving emotional and psychological independence as well as moving out of the family home; going away to college is a natural transition for many people at this age. Close relationships are an important consideration for men and women at this age, and couples in which both partners put their relationship first seem happiest. Couples are giving more thought to whether they want children and, if so, when to have them. Many couples are waiting until their late 20s or early 30s to have their first child.

SAME OLD, SAME OLD?—MIDDLE ADULTHOOD

Sometime in between the late 30s and the mid-40s, people experience the midlife transition, a time of personal evaluation that comes with the realization that life is half over. This does not necessarily mean a midlife crisis. The most obvious signs of middle age are certain physical changes such as graying hair and perhaps slower mental reactions. Midlife sometimes brings changes in careers for both sexes, with both women and men changing jobs or careers to fulfill their aspirations and many traditional women taking a job outside the home or returning to school. The biological and psychological changes that accompany the loss of reproductive abilities pose both new anxieties and new opportunities for both sexes, and men and women may experience a new stability in their marriages as they enter their 50s.

AGING GRACEFULLY—LATE ADULTHOOD

The literature on aging recognizes the young elderly and the old elderly, with the old elderly being more infirm and less active. As people grow older, their physical functions progressively slow down. Crystallized intelligence, or those cognitive functions that depend mostly on learning, may continue to improve with age. There may also be some memory problems but only certain types of memory are affected. People's basic adaptive abilities tend to remain remarkably stable throughout adulthood. Satisfaction in retirement depends on a variety of factors, such as one's attitude toward retirement, health, income, and involvement in meaningful activities such as volunteer work. There is no single best way to age successfully, however, and each individual adapts to old age in his or her own way. Aging is an individualized process. Successful aging depends on one's social network, maintaining a sense of control, and positive reminiscing.

Answers to Aging Quiz

1. True. Various aspects of hearing, vision, and touch decline in old age. In many cases, taste and smell also become less sensitive.

2. False. People lose very few of their neurons. The loss starts at about the age of 30 rather than in later adulthood.

3. True. Aged drivers have fewer accidents than those under 30 but more accidents than middle-aged people.

4. False. There are at least as many, if not more, differences among older individuals as among people at other age levels.

5. True. Because of the accumulation of antigens, older people suffer less from short-term ailments such as the common cold. However, the weakening of the immune system makes them more susceptible to life-threatening ailments, such as cancer and pneumonia.

6. False. Recognition memory shows little or no decline with age, in contrast to the marked decline in recall memory.

7. True. Slower reaction time is one of the best-documented facts about older people.

8. False. Less than 5 percent of the population over 65 lives in a nursing home during a given year.

9. False. Although older people become more aware of death, they tend to have less fear of it than other age groups.

10. True. There are more widows than widowers.

Self-Test

1. Which of the following is typically an age-related change?
    a. a career change.
    c. leaving home.
    b. having one's first child.
    d. the climacteric.

2. Which of the following is a developmental task of young adulthood?
    a. leaving home.
    c. finding a romantic partner.
    b. choosing a career.
    d. all of the above.

3. Compared to couples in the past, married couples are
    a. starting their families later.
    b. having more children.
    c. more likely to include a working husband and a stay-at-home wife.
    d. more desirous of girl than boy babies.

4. According to Erikson, the main developmental task of middle-aged people is
    a. identity versus confusion.
    c. intimacy versus isolation.
    b. generativity versus stagnation.
    d. integrity versus despair.

5. The most obvious signs of middle age are
   a. more colds and allergies.
   b. significant memory losses.
   c. fewer chronic illnesses.
   d. changes in physical appearance.

6. The correct term for the reduction in fertile sperm and lessened sexual vigor among middle-aged men is
   a. the climacteric.
   b. impotence.
   c. male menopause.
   d. sexual senility.

7. Stereotyping of the elderly is known as
   a. ageism.
   b. infantilization.
   c. climacterosis.
   d. generationism.

8. By 65 years of age,
   a. half the men live alone.
   b. most women live alone.
   c. half the women are widowed.
   d. one-fourth of the men are divorced.

9. What factors are most important in determining how people will adjust to retirement?
   a. health status.
   b. whether retirement was voluntary.
   c. income status.
   d. all of these are important.

10. What has happened to the number of age-discrimination cases?
   a. They have decreased over time.
   b. They have increased, but only for men.
   c. Overall, they have increased.
   d. There has been no change.

EXERCISES

1. *How have you grown as an adult?* Write a brief paragraph describing your personal development since adolescence. In what ways has your personality changed or remained the same? Comment on the factors that have contributed to your personal growth, such as success at school, disappointment in love, or new responsibilities at work.

2. *Leaving home.* Describe your experience with leaving home. If you're already living on your own, how peaceful or stormy was your departure? If you're still living at home or are away at college part of the year, how well are you coming to terms with this developmental task? How helpful are your parents in this matter?

3. *Mentors.* List all the people who have influenced your development from your high school years and up. Have any of these people served as your mentor, that is, encouraged or sponsored your career? What effect has this person had on your career? Would you recommend mentors for others? Do you think there are sex differences in the likelihood of being mentored?

4. *The midlife transition.* If you're going through the midlife transition or have completed this stage, write a page or so describing your experience. If you are not middle-aged, write about what you think the experience will be like. To what extent has this been, or do you think this will be, a stressful time or crisis for you?

5. *Widows and widowers.* Select an older person you know well who has outlived his or her spouse, including yourself if this applies to you, and comment on how well this person has adjusted to living alone. What has been the most difficult adjustment? Has the experience of loss also brought about personal growth?

6. *Successful aging.* Select someone in your family who has reached late adulthood, such as an aunt, uncle, or grandparent. Or perhaps this applies to you. Then comment on how successfully the person has aged. To what extent has the person kept active or become disengaged from his or her environment? Has this person also grown old in his or her own distinctive way? How has your relationship with this person affected your understanding of aging?

QUESTIONS FOR SELF-REFLECTION

1. In what ways have you mellowed with age and experience?

2. Would you agree that leaving home involves more than moving out of the family home?

3. What were your parents like at your age?

4. At what stage of adulthood are you now? Does this differ from your perceived favorite age?

5. Are you aware that the midlife transition doesn't have to be a crisis? What characteristics of middle age make others assume that the transition is really a crisis?

6. Do you realize that people in middle and late adulthood are more active for their age than in the past? How are they more active?

7. Why do older people report feeling younger than they really are?

8. What kind of older people were you familiar with as a child? Did these experiences fashion your stereotypes of the elderly? If not, what did fashion your anticipated trajectory into old age?

9. What would you like to do when you retire? Why?

10. Do you think that our personal traits become more pronounced with age?

11. What do you think it would be like to live in a nursing home?

FOR FURTHER INFORMATION

RECOMMENDED READINGS

FOGG, N. P., HARRINGTON, P., & HARRINGTON, T. (2004). *College majors handbook with real career paths and payoffs: The actual jobs, earnings, and trends for graduates of 60 college majors.* Indianapolis, IN: Jist Publishing. The title of this book says it all; it is a compendium of useful information about how to match yourself with majors and careers.

FREEMAN, C. (2005). *Creating magic at midlife: 101 questions and answers to reinvent your work, relationships and life!* Santa Barbara, CA: Philogenesis. Written by a clinical social worker, this book helps any middle-aged individual understand that only half of life has been lived. The second half can be just as wonderful and productive as the first half.

HARVEY, J. H., & WEBER, A. L. (2002). *Odyssey of the heart: Close relationships in the 21st century.* Mahwah, NJ: Lawrence Erlbaum. This book provides research on how, why, and when close relationships develop in both hetero- and homosexual relationships. The book also examines issues such as the conflict between work and family, whether to have children, why divorce occurs, whether cohabitation is a good idea, etc.

LEMME, B. H. (2005). *Development in adulthood.* Boston: Allyn & Bacon. An excellent, general, multidisciplinary text on adulthood, including information on diversity, development, culture, cohort effects, economics, and more.

NOVAK, M. (2005). *Issues in aging.* Boston: Allyn & Bacon. This book of readings is written for those who are aging as well as those who work with or care for them. The book also discusses what the burgeoning aging population means for American society.

WEB SITES AND THE INTERNET

http://www.employmentguide.com/   A rich source of information on careers, internships, networking, resume development, and other useful information for job seekers.

http://www.alzheimers.org/   This is the web site for information on Alzheimer's disease with good information for patients and families about this disabling disease.

http://www.caregiving.com/   The site for finding out about elder care. A good place to find information for those caring for a frail elderly family member.

http://www.aarp.org/   The web site for the largest advocacy group for the elderly, the American Association for Retired Persons. Contains information on the association's advocacy programs, information on retirement and aging, and government lobbying on behalf of our aging population.

http://www.ncoa.org/   This is the web site of the National Council on Aging, a site replete with information about growing older and advocacy for the elderly.

CHAPTER 4

Seeking Selfhood

WHAT IS SELF-CONCEPT?
Self-Image
Ideal Self
Multiple Selves

CORE CHARACTERISTICS OF SELF-CONCEPT
Self-Consistency
Self-Esteem
Self-Enhancement and
    Self Verification

THE SELF-CONCEPT AND PERSONAL GROWTH
The Self You'd Like to Be
Our Social Selves
Learning from Criticism
Greater Self-Direction

SUMMARY
SCORING KEY FOR THE SELF-IMAGE AND IDEAL-SELF EXERCISE
SELF-TEST
EXERCISES
QUESTIONS FOR SELF-REFLECTION
FOR FURTHER INFORMATION

Shandra was shopping with a friend. She stopped to admire the clothes in a shop window. "Let's go in," suggested her friend. They entered the store and browsed for a few minutes. Then Shandra tried on a pair of jeans. Looking at herself in the mirror, she noticed her hair was in disarray. She instinctively straightened it so that it appeared more the way she wanted it to look. She then noticed that she must have gained 10 or 15 pounds and that her usual size was too tight. She knew she couldn't lose that much weight in a few minutes, so she tried various ways of reconciling her appearance in the mirror with her self-image. She first asked her friend how she looked in the jeans, and her friend replied, "Not bad, but they may be a little tight around your rear end." She then tried on a larger size, but the very idea bothered her. She decided to put off buying ner weight-loss program. One thing is clear from Shandra's shopping spreew clothes to avoid looking at herself in the mirror. She was also inspired to resume he—the discrepancy between self-concept and the image in the mirror has a powerful influence on behavior.

WHAT IS SELF-CONCEPT?

Essentially, the **self-concept** is *the overall image or awareness we have of ourselves. It includes all those perceptions of "I" and "me," together with the feelings, beliefs, and values associated with them.* As such, the self-concept is actually a complex concept made up "of" a multiplicity of selves, even though we habitually refer to it in the singular. Ordinarily, we take our self-concept for granted, as when we are engaged in an activity at work or play. At other times, we are very much aware of ourselves, as when we're making an important decision, taking on a heavy responsibility, or are feeling embarrassed. We also may become acutely self-conscious whenever we experience a discrepancy between our self-image and the way we appear to others. In all of these instances, the self-concept exerts a powerful influence, affecting the way we perceive, judge, and behave.

The self-concept provides you, Shandra, and others with a personal identity or sense of who we are. "The self is arguably the largest and most accessible structure in the cognitive system. It encompasses virtually every facet of one's experience . . . and it is never more than a stranger's glance from being activated" (Vallacher, Nowak, Froehlich, & Rockloff, 2002, p. 370). Even though situations and people around us change, our self-concept reassures us that we are basically the same person we were yesterday. In other words, there is coherence or consistency to our thoughts and actions (Bigler, Neimeyer, & Brown, 2001; Nail, Misak, & Davis, 2004). Our self-image sometimes appears more real to us than our bodies, and it governs the way we experience our bodies. Our sense of identity is so important that we typically resist anyone or anything that threatens it (Greve & Wentura, 2003; Mezulis, Abramson, Hyde, & Hankin, 2004) or feel ego-shocked (Campbell, Baumeister, Dhavale, & Tice, 2003). Even the fear of death itself may not be a fear of suffering or of the unknown so much as it is the deep fear that our personal identity will be dissolved (Pyszczynski & Cox, 2004)—which is inconceivable to us.

Research on how we incorporate information about ourselves into our self-concept suggests just this, that we actively manage our self-concept such that we try to maintain a positive view of ourselves (Greve & Wentura, 2003; Mezulis et al., 2004). We typically seek positive information about ourselves from our friends and families and from our performance at work or in school or elsewhere. Shandra was pleased, for example, that her friend said the jeans almost fit and looked good on her. When confronted with ambiguous information, we generally choose to interpret it in the most positive way we can (Greve & Wentura, 2003; Sedikides & Koole, 2004). In other words, psychologists would contend that most people adopt a self-serving attributional bias. **Attribution** is *the process of attributing or ascribing the cause of some event.* We can make *internal* attributions to the self or *external* attributions to the environment. With regard to ourselves, we commonly choose self-serving attributions. **Self-serving attributions** are *those that glorify the self or conceive of the self as causing the good outcomes that come our way.* For example, we often take personal credit for our successes but blame external causes for our failures. Take Shandra, for example. She blamed her recent overeating on difficult examinations and unreasonable professors; otherwise, she thought she had pretty good self-control where food was concerned.

How many selves we choose to distinguish within our overall self-concept varies by the individual and with age (Bybee & Wells, 2003). At a general level, however, it is common to identify

- **body image**, *the awareness of my body*
- the **self-image**, *the self I see myself to be*
- the **ideal self**, *the self I'd like to be*
- the **social self**, *the ways I feel others see me*

Because body image is discussed in Chapter 5, on the body and health, let's begin here by looking at the self-image and the ideal self. We'll examine the importance of our social selves in a later section of this chapter.

Self-Image

Self-image, as noted, is *the way you see yourself.* It is the self you think you are. It is made up of highly personal self-images. Because it is so private, each of us is an expert on our self-image—however realistic or unrealistic our perception may be.

Our self-image is made up of the many self-perceptions we have acquired growing up, especially in our formative or early years. It is mostly influenced by the way we are seen and treated by significant others, especially by our parents or romantic partners. When we were young and impressionable, we tended to internalize what they thought of us—their judgments and expectations—and regarded ourselves accordingly. For example, Keery, Boutelle, van den Berg, and Thompson (2005) studied the impact of teasing by family members on middle school children. Not surprisingly, teasing from mothers and fathers predicted low self-esteem and depression.

Imagine a mother who resents having to take care of her children and constantly yells, "Don't do that, Stupid!" "What's wrong with you?" "You're going to be the death of me yet." Can you imagine how her children would feel about themselves after years of repeated exposure to such remarks? Would you be surprised to learn that they were troublemakers at home and at school? On the other hand, Shandra, a young African American woman, grew up in a supportive family who instilled in her a sense of pride, especially about her African American heritage. Her parents also taught Shandra that the way to a better life was through education, good grades, and excellent interpersonal skills.

We tend to revise our self-images through experience with others, especially with our friends, lovers, teachers, and spouses, but even a stranger's rejection can hurt now and then (Murray, 2005). One of Shandra's friends suffered from a low opinion of herself, partly because of overly critical parents. With time, though, she began seeing herself in a new way. Through doing more things on her own and sharing opinions and special moments with her friends, she began appreciating her good points and acquired a more positive view of herself. She even got to the point of being able to shrug off her parents' sarcastic remarks, much to her parents' amazement.

Ideal Self

Remember that the self-concept is complex. Another aspect of self is the ideal self. The **ideal self** is *the self you would like to be, including your aspirations, moral ideals, and values.* According to the psychoanalytic view, we are not fully aware of our ideal self because we have acquired much of it by identifying with parental demands and societal prohibitions during the formative years of childhood. Accordingly, many of the "shoulds" and "should nots" of our conscience represent unconscious and unrealistic demands that may keep us from growing. An example is Shandra's college classmate, a perfectionist who felt he must make all to please his parents rather than to satisfy himself.

Ordinarily, as we grow up, it's best to reexamine the shoulds and oughts we've assimilated from our parents and others during our formative years. Why? Because if our ideal self is quite different from how others see us, the result is **social anxiety**, or *extreme shyness that can interfere with daily life* (Sanchez-Bernardos & Sanz, 1992). With experience and maturity, our aspirations should increasingly represent self-chosen goals and values (i.e., self-directedness) that express in a healthy, adult way what we've come to expect of *ourselves.* Consequently, our ideal self may serve as an incentive for us to do our best, as with Shandra's other classmate who puts forth her best effort in the hope of entering medical school rather than simply pleasing her parents. If we fail to live up to our ideal self, as can be the case, it is healthy to feel we have a choice either to redouble our efforts to achieve our aspirations or to modify them in the direction of more fruitful goals. Ordinarily, we think of having to change our self-image and behavior to better match our ideals. In those instances when our aspirations prove to be excessive or unrealistic, it may be more appropriate for us to modify our ideal self as a way of furthering our growth and self-esteem.

How would you characterize your own ideal self? Do you tend to be idealistic and rather hard on yourself when you fall short of your aims? Or are you more down-to-earth and practical-minded, shrugging off disappointments with yourself and giving it another try? To check on your perceptions, you might do the exercise on self-image and ideal self in Activity 4–1, which is based on the work of Carl Rogers, about whom you'll soon learn more.

Multiple Selves

Actually, the overall self-concept, as indicated earlier, is an organized cluster of selves, so it would be more accurate to speak of our multiple selves (Bargh, McKenna, & Fitzsimons, 2002) or **self-complexity** (McConnell et al., 2005). Self-complexity is *the extent to which one's self-concept is comprised of many differentiated self-aspects.* As such, the self-concept includes hundreds, perhaps thousands, of self-perceptions with varying degrees of clarity and intensity that we have acquired over a lifetime. For example, Shandra's self-concept included her gender role, her body image, her racial identity, her concept of herself as a student, her attitudes and values and whether they were respected by society, and many other components. Psychologists also know that some individuals have more complex and differentiated selves than do others (Bigler et al., 2001).

Development of multiple selves is related to our participation in various social roles and social situations.

ACTIVITY 4–1

SELF-IMAGE AND IDEAL SELF

This is an exercise to measure the correspondence between your self-image and ideal self. Reproduce the box containing items A through P. Then cut out the 16 cards or rectangles as indicated by the lines and put them on a table or desk in random order.

First, you're to get a profile of your self-image, or the self you see yourself to be. To do so, arrange the cards in a line, either from top to bottom or left to right. At one end, place the statement that you think describes you best. Then arrange the remaining cards in order, ranging from the next most true and so forth to the least true at the end. Then record the rank number of each item in the column labeled "self." For instance, if you placed card A in the eighth position, write "8" next to card A.

Next, repeat this procedure in regard to your ideal self. That is, arrange the cards in the order that describes the self you'd like to be, ranging from the card that you wish were most true of you at one end to that which is least true of your ideal self at the other end. When you've completed your rankings, record the order of the items or cards in the column labeled "ideal."

When you finish ranking the cards and recording the numbers, consult the scoring key at the end of the chapter.

I'm a likable person A	I have sex appeal I
I'm rather self-centered at times B	I'm an anxious person J
I'm physically attractive C	I have above-average intelligence K
I have a strong need for approval D	I'm shy in groups L
I'm usually a hard worker E	I have a good sense of humor M
I daydream too much F	I'm sometimes dishonest N
I can be assertive when necessary G	I have a good disposition O
I often feel discouraged H	I gossip a lot P

Item	Self	Ideal	Differences
A			
B			
C			
D			
E			
F			
G			
H			
I			
J			
K			
L			
M			
N			
O			
P			
		Sum of differences	

Psychologists now possess evidence that these multiple aspects of self vary greatly from culture to culture (Choi & Choi, 2002; Markus & Kitayama, 2003). For example, self-constructs of the Japanese often include a familial (family-oriented) self as well as a spiritual self, neither of which may play a prominent part in the self-constructs of White Americans (Miller, 1999). And research shows that Koreans tolerate inconsistencies in the self-concept better than Americans (Choi & Choi, 2002). Much of the diversity of the self reflects our social and cultural roles, so that even the normally happy person wears "many masks," as we'll discuss later in this chapter. Much recent research, however, has demonstrated that there is one fairly universal aspect of self, the tendency to evaluate oneself favorably, known as *self-enhancement*, which will be discussed shortly (e.g., Mezulis et al., 2004; Schmitt & Allik, 2005; Sedikides, Gaertner, & Vevea, 2005).

At the same time, there are many other self-perceptions that are less clearly associated with social roles. Some self-images arise from the experience of our own bodies. Others reflect needs, interests, traits, and habits acquired through experience, and these self-images may be integrated within our overall self-concept in varying degrees. For instance, Shandra was ordinarily an easy-going person. Then one day she discovered a friend had misinterpreted her intentions and bad-mouthed her to others. Shandra became angry and told her friend how she felt. A couple of hours later, after an apology from her friend, she appeared calm again. Her friend thought, "She certainly is moody!" But when you stop and think, it's not that Shandra had changed so much as that she had simply expressed different aspects of herself at different times. We seldom like to think of ourselves as made up of different parts or selves. Even if we acknowledge this fact in theory, we tend to forget it in practice. Making due allowance for the diversity of selves—in both ourselves and others—may help to account for some of the inconsistency in human behavior. It may also help to avoid the endless circle of blame and guilt that undermines good relationships.

Our various selves usually do exhibit a certain consistency or organizing pattern as a whole (Stone, 2003; Nail et al., 2004); we refer to them collectively as the self-concept. It should be clear, however, that the self-concept is more of a hypothesis or theory to explain how these selves function or "glue" our experiences, behaviors, and feelings together. People with a fragmented, incoherent view of themselves—such as the severely emotionally disordered—are often unsure of who they are and may behave in a highly inconsistent manner. In extreme cases, as with multiple personality disorders, individuals alternate between two or more distinct personalities, each with its own name, habits, memories, and behaviors. In contrast, those of us who have achieved a more desirable integration of our various selves may feel a clearer sense of personal identity and behave in a somewhat more consistent manner—"somewhat" because, as we've just described, even the healthiest person's psychic makeup includes a considerable degree of inconsistency. Indeed, self-clarity is related to well-being and adjustment (Bigler et al., 2001).

CORE CHARACTERISTICS OF SELF-CONCEPT

Critics of the notion of self-concept complain that traditional psychology regards the self-concept as a straitjacket that once acquired during our formative years resists further efforts at change. A more appropriate approach, they contend, would be to view the self-concept as a loosely fitting garment that is continually being altered with experience.

Actually, there is some truth to both views. In this section, we'll focus on the core tendency of the self-concept to maintain and perpetuate itself. In the next section, we'll look at some of the major ways our self-concepts can and do change.

Once established, the core of the self-concept generally exhibits a high degree of stability, as seen in the consistent ways we perceive ourselves over time. Rather peripheral aspects of the self can, and often do, change rather quickly. For example, the core of the self, which comprises those aspects of ourselves we regard as very important to us, tends to perpetuate itself. Shandra, for example, was very proud of a concept dear to her heart—her African American heritage—and little could shake her pride in her racial identity. On the other hand, Shandra never thought of herself as graceful or believed gracefulness was particularly important. However, in college she took a ballet class and found herself the best in the class and actually enjoyed ballet. She eventually came to think of herself as more graceful. Essentially, the self-concept functions as a filter through which everything we see or hear passes (Christensen, Wood, & Barrett, 2003). It thereby exerts a selective influence on our experience, so that we typically tend to perceive, judge, and act in ways that are consistent with our self-concept.

Self-Consistency

This characteristic tendency toward self-clarity (Bigler et al., 2001) is known as **self-consistency** (*our tendency to perceive our experiences in a manner consistent with our self-concept*). Significant others have a great effect on our self-concept and our self-consistency because of what Carl Rogers called **conditions of worth**, *where instead of growing up in an atmosphere of unconditional acceptance, most of us feel we are loved and accepted only if we meet certain expectations and approvals.* Shandra's parents, for example, never commented on her gracefulness. Other students in the ballet class felt their instructor's scrutiny more sharply because their parents frequently commented on their clumsiness.

To return to self-consistency, experiences that are consistent with our self-concept tend to be perceived accurately and admitted fully into our conscious awareness. These self-perceptions make up the core of our self-concept. Experiences that are *not* consistent with both our sensory experiences and our self-concept are perceived more selectively and sometimes inaccurately. Such experiences are either distorted or kept from awareness, according to Carl Rogers. For example, Shandra was influenced by the stereotyped gender roles in our society and believed women generally to be less adept at math than men. Each time she worked with numbers, she therefore thought she would perform poorly. She readily assimilated experiences of failure because they were consistent with her existing self-concept. When she performed well on a math quiz, she thought her good grade was just a fluke.

Experiences that are not consistent with our learned self-concept might be perceived as too threatening and, consequently, may not be accurately perceived or labeled and may be kept from awareness, either in part or in whole. Here, denial is roughly comparable to the Freudian concept of repression and refers to an unconscious exclusion of experience because of the threat associated with it.

Suppose Shandra, who believed she was no good at math, was required to take two semesters of math as part of her major studies. She began the course with a determination to do well, accompanied by a fear that she wouldn't. At first, she worked hard and even discovered to her surprise that she enjoyed the precision of mathematical thinking. Then she received her grade on her first test—an 86! "My doing OK in math?" she wondered. "How can this be? Maybe the instructor made a mistake in grading the papers.

Maybe he likes me or feels sorry for me. It's probably dumb luck. It won't happen again." Like the rest of us, she would probably rely on a variety of such self-justifying mechanisms to make this experience acceptable to her existing self-concept. In doing so she would also deny her actual experience of success and thereby fail to discover her personal potential for math. However, suppose she completed both semesters of math with B⁺s. Chances are she would gradually revise her self-concept in a way that reflected her real ability in math, thereby incorporating aspects of herself previously denied.

Modern research has shown that we actually use defensive mechanisms, one of which is called **self-immunization**, *which involves trivializing threatening information, such as failure, by making the behavior seem less important* (Greve & Wentura, 2003). One of Shandra's friends failed both math tests and waved off her failure by saying, "I'm going into fashion design; I don't need math for that." Another self-defense is **mnemonic neglect** or *poor recall (or forgetting) of negative feedback that is inconsistent with core aspects of the self-concept* (Sedikides & Koole, 2004). Two years later, the same friend graduated and sought a job as a clothing buyer for a well-known department store. When asked about her math ability during her job interview, the friend said it was excellent. Shandra later reminded her that she failed two math tests, to which the friend replied, "What are you talking about? I didn't even take math in college!"

Self-Esteem

One of the most important aspects of the self-concept is our **self-esteem**—*the personal evaluation of ourselves and the resulting feelings of worth associated with our self-concept*. Self-esteem is affected by a variety of influences, ranging from significant childhood experiences to our own standards or ideal self and beyond to our general culture (Markus & Kitayama, 2003). Individuals with high self-esteem, such as Shandra, appear to be raised by parents who were supportive (Park, Crocker, & Mickelson, 2004), expressed a lot of affection, and established firm but reasonable rules—all of which foster high self-esteem. Individuals with low self-esteem usually were brought up by parents who relied on parenting styles that were overly strict, overly permissive, or inconsistent.

Our self-esteem is also influenced by success and failure, although there is often a low correspondence between people's self-views and their actual performance (Dunning, Heath, & Suls, 2004). Psychologists once thought that a backlog of stored success enhanced self-esteem and repeated failure undermined it. For example, it was once thought that praising children for their successes or achievements would make children think they were intelligent and, thus, give them more confidence. However, recent and important research has demonstrated this is not quite true. Praising children for their *efforts* rather than for their intelligence results in children's desire for more challenges. Children obsessed with their own intelligence are afraid to take risks, which may trigger maladaptive achievement patterns (Dweck, 1999).

At the same time, the impact of a particular achievement often depends on the process of comparison with a reference group (Leary, 1999) or on fear of social rejection by one's own group (Sommer & Baumeister, 2002). For example, Shandra may have felt good about her ballet performance after earning the highest grade in her class. In contrast, her friend Josie, who got an equally high grade in the same class, may feel less favorable about her performance because she compared her grade with a group of ballet students in a more advanced class. *The process of using others to compare ourselves to in order to understand who we are relative to them* is known as **social comparison**. Thus, individuals with similar talents and success may vary in their self-esteem, depending on

Self-esteem is often influenced by our successes and failures during life's challenges.

to whom they compare themselves. Table 4–1 will help you identify some of the signs of high and low self-esteem in yourself.

Although people customarily speak of self-esteem as a single entity—global esteem—our self-esteem also includes many compartmentalized or situation-specific aspects, which vary according to circumstances. For instance, another of Shandra's friends, Mark, enjoyed a great deal of self-confidence while playing tennis but lacked confidence in his writing skills in English composition. Another acquaintance, Thalia, felt satisfied with her school-work, but her contentment varied somewhat from one subject to another. At the same time, Thalia suffered from low self-esteem in regard to her weight. Thus, our overall self-esteem is more complex than ordinarily portrayed and fluctuates somewhat depending on our experiences (Crocker & Wolfe, 2001).

Self-esteem exerts a powerful influence on people's expectations and their judgments about themselves and others as well as on their behavior (Dunning et al., 2004). The self-esteem movement, spawned by Carl Rogers and Abraham Maslow, has pushed itself to the forefront of the American psyche and the scientific literature. Leading psychologists such as Jennifer Crocker and Roy Baumeister have attempted to sort through the literature to make sense out of just what high and low self-esteem does and does not mean for individuals. These psychologists conclude that high self-esteem is both a blessing and a curse.

It is a blessing in that high self-esteem correlates with better academic performance (although the direction of the correlation is unclear). Baumeister et al. (2003; 2005) contend that good grades might cause high esteem *or* high esteem might cause better school performance. The same can be said of the relationship between high self-esteem and job performance (Baumeister et al., 2003; 2005); there is a modest, positive relationship but, again, the cause remains unknown. There is also a complicated link between self-esteem and interpersonal relationships. For example, for different reasons,

TABLE 4–1
HIGH AND LOW SELF-ESTEEM

Signs of High Self-Esteem Do you . . .	Signs of Low Self-Esteem Do you . . .
like your appearance when you see yourself in the mirror?	avoid viewing yourself in the mirror?
feel comfortable with yourself most of the time?	feel discontented with yourself most of the time?
savor your accomplishments?	brag excessively or apologize about your achievements?
regard your failures as opportunities to learn?	make excuses for your failures?
express your opinions readily?	withhold your views, especially if asked?
listen to what others say, even if you disagree?	try to convince others of your views?
accept compliments graciously?	reject compliments or qualify them?
give credit to others when it's due?	envy others and put them down by sarcasm or gossip?
make realistic demands on yourself?	expect too much or too little of yourself?
give and receive affection generously?	withhold your affection out of fear of being hurt?

both high and low esteem can lead to relationship breakups. People with high esteem often exit bad relationships. On the other hand, people with low esteem often find themselves in an unhappy relationship, but, again, the cause is not clear. Perhaps low esteem causes negative responses from partners or perhaps negative responses from partners cause low self-esteem. High self-esteem is also a blessing because people with high self-esteem perform better in groups and are likelier to persist in the face of failure than people with low self-esteem (Baumeister et al., 2005). The strongest positive finding about self-esteem, though, is that people with high self-esteem are happier (or less depressed) than those with low self-esteem.

The downside of high self-esteem as reported by Baumeister and his associates (2003) is that high self-esteem can also be related to antisocial behaviors such as cheating on tests and annoying or interrupting others. Bullies, for example, often possess overly inflated self-esteem. Another downside is that there is little evidence to show that high self-esteem creates better health for the individual. For example, high esteem does not prevent or inhibit cigarette smoking, alcohol or drug abuse, or premarital sexual behavior.

In addition, Jennifer Crocker and her colleagues contend that *how* people strive for self-esteem is more important than *whether* esteem is high or low (Crocker & Park, 2004a). More specifically, "The pursuit of self-esteem does not depend on whether one's attempt to help actually demonstrates helpfulness or boosts self-esteem, but rather on whether one's intention in helping others is to raise self-esteem by demonstrating one's helpfulness" (Crocker & Park, 2004b, p. 431). *How* people pursue or intend to use self-esteem can be damaging. Why?

- Pursuing self-esteem results in mistakes, failures, threats, and other negative consequences that cause anxiety.
- Anxiety inhibits learning, especially from feedback designed to help the esteem-seeker.
- Autonomy or choice is influenced negatively, too. When people in hot pursuit of self-esteem feel they have no choice but to persist, they experience pressure and tension.
- Pursuing self-esteem also negatively impacts relationships because it focuses the pursuer on the self rather than on others who also want attention.

In the end, seeking self-esteem may cause distress in many areas and consequently affect one's physical and mental health in harmful ways. Crocker et al. suggest that the "cure" for questing for self-esteem is to turn from self-directedness to other-directedness, that is, seeking goals that are beneficial to others as much as or more than to the self (Crocker & Knight, 2005).

Other psychologists agree in principle that the unabashed pursuit of self-esteem is problematic, but they disagree about the proposed solution. Pyszczynski and Cox (2004) add that pursuing a self-directed or self-determined life, as urged in Chapter 1, may be a solution as good or better than that proposed by Jenny Crocker and her associates. Seeking self-created standards rather than pursuing self-esteem reduces defensiveness and other negative consequences associated with striving for self-esteem. Shandra, for example, admired Dr. Martin Luther King, a fellow African American, because he based his pursuit of racial equality not on what he wanted for himself, but on principles he wished for everyone in our society. Pyszczynski and Cox, in differing with Crocker and Park (2004a), state

> Self-determined standards of value are those that are thoroughly integrated with one's core sense of self . . . are derived from the diverse array of cultural influences . . . [and] are the result of extensive integrative processing rather than simply introjected or "swallowed whole" with little consideration of how they fit with other aspects of one's system of means and value [p. 428].

The debates over how important self-esteem is, whether its pursuit is good for the individual, and how individuals should satisfy the need for self-esteem will undoubtedly continue for years in the psychological literature.

Self-Enhancement and Self-Verification

We receive a great deal of information about how people see us through our interactions with them (Leary, 1999). As a matter of fact, we often make deliberate attempts to elicit such information, whether through actions or direct questioning. Scientists have proposed different theories concerning the actual kind of reaction or feedback we solicit from others (Gilovich & Savitsky, 1999). According to **self-enhancement theory**, *people will try to get positive feedback that affirms their own ideas about their positive qualities.* Most people prefer and seek out positive feedback about themselves, but mostly for those attributes that they themselves view as positive, primarily because positive self-views are generally adaptive (Taylor & Brown, 1994). Along the same line of thinking, people's autobiographical memory induces them to perceive themselves as better and better over time (e.g., Ross & Wilson, 2003).

In contrast, in accordance with **self-verification theory**, *people want to preserve their own images (both positive and negative) of themselves and therefore elicit feedback that verifies or confirms their own self-perceptions.* Thus, self-verification is important to us, in that it gives us a sense of stability or consistency in an unpredictable world. Also, such confirmation is vital to social interaction because if others see us as we see ourselves, they will have a better idea of how to treat us, what to expect of us, and so forth. In sum, people generally prefer to hear opinions that are positive but also supportive of their own views of themselves.

Is this true for women and minorities, two less powerful groups in our society? In other words, is Shandra, a young African American woman, typical because she has high esteem or atypical? Let's look at gender roles and self-esteem first. A **gender role** *is a social and cultural expectation about what is appropriate for males and females.* Masculine traits initially appear more valued by American society (Sanchez & Crocker, 2005), for example, the traits of independence, decisiveness, and emotional stability. However, research on gender and esteem has not borne out that men necessarily have higher self-esteem than women. Sanchez and Crocker (2005) suggest that although gender ideals differ for men and women and although the gender ideal for men is more culturally valued in our society, being invested in an ideal imposed by society may itself be harmful. Basing self-worth on external sources (such as social standards) is more related to negative psychological outcomes than basing self-worth on more internal aspects of self, such as being a virtuous person. Sanchez and Crocker's research, in fact, confirmed just this. Investment in gender ideals negatively affected self-esteem not just for men and women but for several racial and ethnic groups as well. There are some documented sex differences, however. Women report engaging more in self-reflection than men do (Rudman & Goodwin, 2004). Similarly, women, especially Western women, possess greater **self-clarity**, *which is the extent to which one's individual self-beliefs are clearly and confidently defined, internally consistent, and stable* (Csank & Conway, 2004). Overall, though, the bulk of the research shows that men's and women's self-esteem levels are not necessarily different (Pierson & Glaeser, 2002).

Can the same be said for racial and ethnic minorities? Is their esteem as high as that of White Americans? Based on their research, Twenge and Crocker (2000) say "yes"; self-esteem of minorities is just as high as or higher than that of Whites. The reason is that just as other individuals do, minorities also use some self-protective mechanisms for maintaining self-esteem (Major, Kaiser, & McCoy, 2003). For example, members of **minority groups** (*groups that are relatively small in number or have less power as compared to majority groups*) often compare themselves to each other rather than to the White majority. In addition, many minority-group members attribute negative feedback and failure to prejudice and discrimination against their group rather than to personal failure (Major et al.).

However, other recent research has suggested that people repeatedly perceiving themselves to be or actually being the victims of discrimination and prejudice cannot avoid having their psychological adjustment or self-concept negatively impacted (Cassidy, O'Connor, Howe, & Warden, 2004). Likewise, the relationship between prejudice and self-concept may be more complex than thought. For example, the relationship between perceived discrimination and self-esteem may well vary across ethnic groups, with individuals from some groups more negatively affected by prejudice than are other groups.

THE SELF-CONCEPT AND PERSONAL GROWTH

As mentioned earlier, your self-concept continues to change as you mature and develop. Indeed, there is growing recognition that the cluster of selves comprising the self-concept can and does change to a greater extent than previously realized. Self-esteem, for example, is relatively high in childhood, drops during adolescence (particularly for girls), rises gradually throughout adulthood, and then declines in old age (Robins & Trzesniewski, 2005). These developmental trends appear to hold regardless of ethnicity.

Much of the change in our self-concept occurs with experience, but a great deal of change in our self-image comes from adapting to different people and situations (Sanchez & Crocker, 2005). Job changes, new friends, and modifications in responsibilities, like marriage and parenting, all affect the way we see ourselves. Although we retain a stable core of self, the many self-perceptions that make up our overall self-concept are in a state of flux or change and are more readily influenced by current experience than previously thought. In this section, we'll explore how our self-concepts change as a result of our personal aspirations, changing roles and behaviors, criticism from others, and greater self-direction.

The Self You'd Like to Be

Buying and trying self-help manuals and cassettes and attending workshops, Americans spend millions of dollars every year in the hope of improving themselves. Shandra recognized this and decided that instead of buying books or joining Weight Watchers, she would lose weight in a way that would make her happy. She continued her ballet classes and in a year, without dieting, lost 10 pounds.

One promising approach to self-improvement consists of visualizing the person you'd like to become—the thin self, the confident self, or the rich self (Zampelli, 2000). **Visualization**, also known as **guided imagery**, is *a procedure that helps a person shut off the outside world and bypass the censor we call the brain, enabling the person to see, experience, and learn from an intuitive, feeling, unconscious nature* (Leviton & Leviton, 2004). Visualization has successfully been used in health psychology to enhance the comfort of people undergoing chemotherapy to treat cancer (Roffe, Schmidt, & Ernst, 2005); some psychotherapists believe that it can be utilized for psychological discomfort as well (Grocke, 2005). Visualizing your "possible selves," including the desired as well as the feared selves, helps you not only to attain goals but also to cope more effectively with the present. Visualizing our possible selves may also help us to cope with present life difficulties. A major implication is that we can create new images of ourselves, and this ability, in turn, may help us to handle our present lives more effectively. Each of us varies in how we think of our possible selves. Some have clear-cut images of what they might be (i.e., *self-clarity*); others have ideas and feelings that are only dimly envisioned. To help realize your aim of self-improvement, you might elaborate the self or selves you'd like to be. Imagine as vividly as possible how you'll look, how you'll feel, and how you'll act. It also helps to create an image of any feared self, that is, the self that would result if you don't succeed. Think of the failed attempts to lose weight, the mediocre performances in school and at work, and the disappointments in love. Then visualize a better you, a you created from using different strategies to overcome failure. Self-change is difficult (Polivy & Herman, 2000) but not impossible. In each instance, vivid mental images of our possible selves may help us to become the person we'd like to be, especially when accompanied by the appropriate efforts. Activity 4–2 will help you think more about the person you would like to be.

Our Social Selves

As stated repeatedly above, one of the most common ways our self-concept changes is through our interactions with people, including their perceptions of and reactions toward us. The term **social selves** refers to *the impressions we think others have of us*. It is the way we *think* they view us, which may not be an accurate representation of their actual views. Nevertheless, our *perception* of how others view us, in turn, greatly influences the way we see ourselves.

We have as many different social selves as there are distinct groups of persons about whose opinion we care, observed William James (1890/1950) and restated more recently by Crocker and Wolfe (2001). As a result, we see ourselves somewhat differently with each person we meet. With a stranger, we may be guarded and unsure of ourselves, at least until we get to know what kind of person we're dealing with. A bossy, critical employer may make us feel anxious and inferior, but a close friend who admires and compliments us makes us feel confident and affectionate. It's not that we're being two-faced or untrue to ourselves. Rather, each of these people brings out a different aspect of self. Realizing this fact, we might make a greater effort to seek out people who bring

---

ACTIVITY 4–2

VISUALIZE THE PERSON YOU'D LIKE TO BE

Select a quiet place where you can relax and have a few minutes to yourself. Then close your eyes and imagine, as vividly as possible, the kind of person you'd like to become.

How would you look?
What would you be wearing?
How would you feel?
Would you be happy, serious, or relaxed?
What would you be doing?
Where would you be?

You might repeat this exercise every night before you go to sleep—say, for a week. Do you notice any difference in yourself?

---

out the best in us. For example, of all her professors, Shandra knew and liked best her ballet instructor, who strongly encouraged her budding dance talent.

We can make errors, though, when we assess feedback about ourselves from others. For example, Libby, Eibach, and Gilovich (2005) have demonstrated a "spotlight effect" in which we overestimate how salient our own behaviors, appearance, and emotions are to others. In other words, we think the spotlight shines more brightly on us than it really does. Additionally, Gilovich and Savitsky (1999) empirically determined that because their own self-recriminations are so harsh, most individuals expect others to judge them *more harshly* than they really do.

The way we see ourselves is also vitally affected by the way we behave in different roles and situations. Often, the way we see ourselves leads us to act in a given manner.

Individuals critical of us can induce defensiveness while individuals supportive of us can enhance our self-esteem. Our social environments, therefore, should be thoughtfully selected.

Equally often, we act in a certain way, and that action, in turn, changes the way we perceive ourselves and the way others see us. As a result, countless qualities—obedience, assertiveness, competitiveness, compassion, ambition, self-worth, and happiness—change remarkably with a change in our circumstances. For instance, our jobs affect us more than we affect our jobs. Many aspects of work, such as routinization, the complexity of tasks, advancement, fringe benefits, and peers, significantly change our self-image, self-worth, job commitment, and moral standards. Thus, many qualities attributed to the self-concept are keyed to what we *do* rather than to our inner notions of what we are.

The realization that our sense of self is affected by social and cultural influences heightens the importance of our social roles and social relationships (Miller, 1999; Srivastava & Beer, 2005). Once we have chosen to associate with certain friends, select a lover or marriage partner, or attend a given school or job, the people involved help to shape the way we see ourselves. Because of this we need to ask, "Are there overly critical people who devalue us?" We probably should avoid them. "Are there others who see the best in us?" Perhaps we should seek them out more often. In both instances, we can change the way we see ourselves by modifying the social influences on our lives. It would be foolish to think we can change everything about ourselves in this way or that we can always avoid negative people. But the notion of fluid, changing social selves reminds us that we have more possibilities for change and personal growth than we may be using.

Learning from Criticism

How do you feel when you are criticized? Do you feel angry and rejected? Do you feel resentful, even when you're in the wrong? For most people, the answer to these questions is yes. When people have been asked to finish the statement "When I am criticized . . . ," typical responses include "I get upset," "I resent it," "I feel she doesn't love me anymore," and "I wonder when the ax will fall." Sound familiar? All too often, as these comments suggest, people feel that criticism is a personal attack that they must defend themselves against at all costs. As a result, they waste a lot of energy worrying about criticism, justifying themselves, and going to great lengths to avoid it.

Accepting criticism can become a valuable means of personal growth. For example, when asked to complete the statement cited earlier, some people make more positive responses. For example, Shandra said to her friend, "Criticism tells me where the other person is coming from, how that person sees me, and what he or she expects of me." Shandra's close friend thought that she had gained too much weight for ballet; however, once Shandra realized how good she was at ballet, she viewed losing weight as a challenge rather than as something that prohibited her from doing well in the class. Another example involves an experienced executive who said, "Your critics can tell you where you're going wrong before your friends can." And a woman Shandra knew once told her, "When I'm criticized, I try to figure out what the other person is trying to tell me, especially how I can improve my performance." All these people have learned the valuable art of taking criticism constructively.

You should perhaps view criticism as a valuable source of new information to be evaluated objectively. Each time you're criticized, you don't necessarily have to rush out and change something about yourself. Instead, criticism should be taken as a cue that *may* require action. Even then, you must look beyond the surface of the criticism and ask yourself, "What is this person trying to tell me, and is this person sincere?" Ask yourself too, "How important is this criticism?" The more important the information is to you, the more likely you'll need to do something about it.

Consider also how many times a specific criticism is offered. If several people offer the same criticism for the same behavior, there's a good chance that the criticism is valid and should be acted on. Then, too, you must assess the source of criticism. People often feel they're being criticized unfairly, especially if the other person is under a lot of stress. The more qualified the person is to judge you, the more you should take criticism to heart. Even criticism spoken in frustration or anger may need to be heeded, but take into account the exaggerated emotion of the messenger.

Weigh the pros and cons of acting on a criticism. You should decide whether the benefits that come from acting on the criticism balance or outweigh the effort involved. For example, students who do poorly on tests may wonder whether it's worthwhile to follow the teacher's suggestion to get help in reading comprehension and note-taking skills. On the other hand, if they continue to get low grades, their career goals may be in jeopardy.

Put the emotional energy aroused by criticism to work for you, not against you. Emotional arousal tends to interfere with your ability to perform well, lowering your self-confidence as well. Instead, when criticized, try to stay calm. Relax physically. Remind yourself that nobody is trying to hurt you. What this person is saying may be helpful. Then use your emotions as a source of energy to make the necessary changes. For example, whenever Shandra did something her boyfriend, Brad, disliked, he would yell, "That's stupid. How dumb can you be?" Shandra became upset and ignored his accusations as a way of justifying her actions. Gradually, Shandra learned to remain calm in the face of Brad's emotional outbursts. She would calmly ask, "What is it you're objecting to?" or "How would you suggest handling this?" Responding in kind, Brad learned to give more specific criticisms in a gentler tone of voice, which Shandra found more helpful.

Finally, take positive steps to put the needed changes into action. Don't waste energy defending yourself. Instead, listen carefully to what is being said. Ask for more information. Ask the person for suggested solutions to the criticism. You might ask for this information indirectly, such as, "If you were in my place, what would you do?" Or you might ask, more directly, "What would you like me to do?" People usually criticize something we're doing. But it often comes across as a personal attack because many people do not know how to give criticism constructively. So if someone says, "You're rude and inconsiderate," ask, "In what ways have I been inconsiderate? How would you suggest I behave?" In this way, you'll focus on something tangible that you can do, which in due time may lead to the desired changes in your self-image and reputation.

Greater Self-Direction

Learning how to listen to others so that we'll grow and benefit from their criticism is difficult enough. Learning to listen to ourselves and be true to our own deepest desires and goals can be even more challenging, especially in a world full of people—parents, peers, politicians, and advertisers, among countless others—intent on making us into somebody else. Carl Rogers (1961) once observed that beneath the bewildering complexity of problems presented by his clients in therapy—the trouble with grades or an employer or indecision about an unsatisfying marriage—lies one central search. Underneath it all, each person, knowingly or unknowingly, is asking, "Who am I, really? How can I get in touch with this real self, underlying all my surface behavior? How can I become myself?" (p. 108).

Rogers (1980) found that in the process of becoming a person, especially in psychotherapy, the individual's experience of growth follows a general pattern. The early stages of self-revision are usually characterized by a movement away from internalizing others' criticisms and consequent distorted self-perceptions acquired while growing up. Individuals are busily sorting out aspects of themselves acquired under social pressure or the desire to be accepted. Some self-perceptions are affirmed and strengthened; others are modified or rejected. This process may explain the typical negativism of adolescents and young adults in the stage of leaving home.

This stage also accounts for the prevalence of complaints and self-disparagement so often seen in the early phases of psychotherapy. For example, Pam, a woman in her early 30s, told her therapist how she had tried to be a good wife by giving in to her husband and how discouraging it had been. Although she had tried to meet his demands, each time he would make yet another, until it became an endless series of demands. In the process Pam had become overly submissive and resentful toward her husband. She had also built up a great deal of self-hatred. "I don't like myself this way," Pam said. "How can you have any self-respect when you're always giving in to someone? Yet I've always felt this is the way you have to be if you want to be loved. But I just can't live this way any longer." The disdain in her voice made it clear that Pam had already begun moving away from a self-image designed to please other people.

The later stages of self-actualization are characterized by greater self-direction and self-acceptance. Individuals become more open to and trusting of their own experience. For example, Shandra soon decided to sign up for jazz and then modern dancing, both of which led her to declare a dance minor at college. As people come to accept themselves more fully, they may be more accepting of others. Shandra found with time that her criticism of others' dancing gave way to generosity as she remembered her first clumsy steps in her ballet class. Most important, as individuals strive to discover themselves, they become more willing to accept themselves as *a process of becoming*.

More specifically, individuals become *more open* to their own experiences. They become *more aware of and comfortable* with the complexity of their feelings. For example, they can experience love and disdain toward the same person. Or they may feel excited and fearful about their new job. In both instances, they become more trusting of their own experience and find it a suitable source for discovering the most satisfying behavior in each immediate situation. A young woman like Shandra considering marriage may ask herself about her boyfriend, "Is this the man I want as my partner in love?" As long as she feels she must justify the decision of marriage, she may see only the good qualities in her prospective mate. Greater openness to her experience would indicate that he has faults as well. The more open the young woman is to the full range of her feelings, the more she can weigh all the pros and cons of such a choice. A mistaken choice might be made, but because there is greater openness to her experience, a quicker correction can also be made. The important point is that she is choosing out of the richness of her own experience rather than out of a sense of obligation or from seeking the approval of others. Activity 4–3 provides some activities that you can complete to help you appreciate your own openness to experience and complexities.

Second, as individuals accept themselves more fully, they often become more accepting of others. This is a reversal of **self-alienation**, which occurs *when we fail to acknowledge or accept certain aspects of ourselves. We then feel these qualities are foreign to us and we project them onto others, whom we then dislike.* Thus, the man who, while denying his own dependency needs, appears to be strong and self-sufficient may feel contempt for men who allow themselves to be taken care of when weak or ill. In contrast, a man who through therapy or a loving relationship recognizes within himself the existence of dependency needs alongside those of adequacy and self-confidence may be more accepting of men who exhibit their need for others. Affirming the complexity of feelings and needs within himself, he can appreciate a wider variety of people as well as the inconsistency they display in different situations. Finally, there is a greater willingness to affirm oneself as *being in a process of becoming*. People enter therapy hoping to achieve some fixed state in which their problems will be resolved such that they will be more successful in their careers or their

Activity 4–3

Self-Affirming Activities

Instructions: *Do one or more of the following activities. When you have a low point in your self-image, pull out the activity and your answers and reread them.*

- Name five of your strengths.
- List five things you admire about yourself.
- What are your five greatest achievements in life so far?
- Describe five ways you can reward yourself for accomplishments.
- Explain five ways you can make yourself laugh.
- What are five things you can do for someone else to make them feel good?
- List five things you do to treat yourself well.
- What five activities have you recently engaged in that gave you joy?

Source: Adapted from The Center for Mental Health Services/United States Department of Health and Human Services—Substance Abuse and Mental Health Services Administration. (2003). *Building self-esteem: A self-help guide*. Found at www.mentalhealth.org/publications/alloubs/SMA-3715/.

marriages will be more satisfying. It is usually a sign of progress when clients drop such fixed goals and accept a more satisfying realization that they are not a fixed entity but in a process of becoming. They come to appreciate that change is the one true constant in life. People who are actualizing themselves to a high degree learn to live more in the present moment. They enjoy the richness and complexity, even the inconsistency, of life as it is, using their aspirations more as guideposts than as fixed points.

As you can see, personal growth may be unsettling at times. It involves moving away from some of the familiar self-images acquired during your formative years. And it involves seeing yourself in new ways, especially as a more self-directed person. Because each of us has different values and goals, there is no detailed guide to assure us that we are doing the right thing. Understanding the general pattern of growth, as suggested in the preceding pages, may be helpful. Feedback from others may serve as a useful mirror. Increased self-awareness also may be helpful up to a point. *It is optimal rather than constant or excessive awareness that is desirable.* Most important of all, learn to trust yourself. Be open to your own experience. And remember, "The good life is a process, not a state of being. It is a direction, not a destination" (Rogers, 1961, p. 186).

SUMMARY

What Is the Self-Concept?

Essentially, the self-concept is the overall image or awareness we have of ourselves. It includes all those perceptions of "I" and "me," together with the feelings, beliefs, and values associated with them. Although the self-concept itself does not do anything, it exerts a tremendous influence on the way we think and act as a whole. Actually, the overall self-concept is an organized cluster of many selves (self-complexity), helping to explain why we do not always act consistently. Commonly, we identify our body image (how we perceive and feel about our body), the self-image (the self we see ourselves to be), the ideal self (the self we'd like to be), and our social selves (the way we feel others see us).

CORE CHARACTERISTICS OF THE SELF-CONCEPT

One of the core characteristics of the self-concept is its stability over time. Once developed, the self-concept tends to maintain and perpetuate itself as it is. It serves as a filter through which we view our experiences, so that experiences that are not consistent with the self-concept are apt to be distorted or kept out of awareness. The tendency to think and act in a self-consistent manner is also strengthened by our self-esteem—the personal evaluation of ourselves and the resulting feelings of worth associated with the self-concept. Largely because of the self's influence, people generally prefer to hear opinions that support their own views of themselves. Today's psychologists, however, are busy debating whether individuals indeed should pursue high self-esteem, with many psychologists suggesting that this practice is detrimental to the individual.

THE SELF-CONCEPT AND PERSONAL GROWTH

Although we retain a stable core of self, the many selves that make up our overall self-concept (self-complexity) are in a state of flux and are more readily influenced by current experience than previously thought; that is, our self-concept tends to change with personal growth.

We described how visualizing our future possible selves not only helps us to attain them but also aids in our present life adjustment. Also, our social selves—the impressions we think others have of us—may be improved by changing our social roles, circumstances, and the people with whom we associate. Furthermore, we may use personal criticism for growth by putting the energy it arouses to work for us rather than against us, thus using it as an opportunity to learn about ourselves and put the needed changes into action. Ultimately, personal growth involves moving away from negative reflected appraisals from others that distort self-perceptions acquired while growing up and moving toward greater self-acceptance and self-direction. Then we become more open to our own experiences and willing to affirm ourselves in a process of becoming.

SCORING KEY FOR THE SELF-IMAGE AND IDEAL-SELF EXERCISE

To find the correspondence between your self-image and your ideal self, note the difference in the rank for each card. For example, on card A if you ranked your self-image as 8 and your ideal self as 2, the difference would be 6. For each card, record the *absolute* difference between numbers without regard to pluses or minuses. Then total the numbers in the column of differences. A score in the range of 50 would be about average. A difference lower than 30 indicates a high correspondence between your self-image and your ideal self. A score of more than 80 indicates a rather low correspondence between your self-image and ideal self. A high score doesn't necessarily mean that you have problems, however. Remember, this is a self-activity, not a valid test, so use your results to do some self-reflection and personal growth.

SELF-TEST

1. Which of the following includes all those perceptions of "I" and "me," together with the feelings, beliefs, and values associated with them?
   a. superego.
   b. self-concept.
   c. ideal self.
   d. body image.

2. The self-image is the
   a. self I'd like to be.
   b. self as I think others see me.
   c. self I see myself to be.
   d. image I have of my body.

3. Our ideal self should be
   a. modified when unduly high.
   b. unattainable in principle.
   c. the same as our self-image.
   d. rarely if ever compromised or changed.

4. Experiences that are consistent with our self-concept but are not confirmed by our "gut" reactions are
   a. admitted fully into our awareness.
   b. accurately perceived and labeled.
   c. creatively altered.
   d. perceived in a distorted manner.

5. Leading psychologists now believe that the pursuit of high self-esteem
   a. is a good idea.
   b. may be detrimental to the individual.
   c. enhances our self-esteem.
   d. does little to alter self-esteem.

6. According to self-enhancement theory, we welcome positive feedback about
   a. all our qualities.
   b. our positive qualities.
   c. our negative qualities.
   d. anything.

7. Who typically has low self-esteem?
   a. women compared to men.
   b. minorities compared to the White majority.
   c. children with parents who consistently criticize.
   d. all of the above.

8. The social self refers to
   a. how we perceive other people.
   b. the way we think others see us.
   c. how well we get along with others.
   d. the way others see us.

9. The most helpful way of handling personal criticism is to regard it as something that
   a. needs immediate action.
   b. reflects others' faults.
   c. necessitates self-defense.
   d. may require action.

10. During the later stages of personal growth and therapy, people have a heightened sense of
    a. self-direction.
    b. fixed personal goals.
    c. self-criticalness.
    d. future orientation.

1. *Self-image.* This is the self you perceive yourself to be. Using a full 8 1/2- by 11-inch page, draw two concentric circles (a circle within a circle)—the inner circle representing the core of your self-concept and the outer circle the more flexible, changeable selves. Within the inner circle list six to eight of your most enduring aspects (traits). In the outer circle list a similar number of aspects of yourself that are more dependent on changing roles and circumstances. How would you describe your overall self-image?

2. *The self you'd like to be.* Among the various possible selves you'd like to be, including any feared self, select one specific image. Visualize it in specific terms as vividly as possible. Write down how you'd look, how you'd feel, and how you'd act. If possible, you might spend several minutes a day for a week daydreaming about your possible self. How did this affect your present self-image and adjustment?

3. *Self-esteem.* Our sense of personal worth fluctuates somewhat from one situation to another. Think of several situations or occasions in which you usually feel good about yourself and exhibit a lot of self-confidence. Then think of several situations in which you feel unsure of yourself and inferior. Can you identify the people or demands that make you feel good or bad about yourself? What are some practical steps you can take to improve your self-esteem?

4. *Identifying your social selves.* We have many social selves, William James observed, because there are many people whose opinions we value. Select five or six people you associate with regularly. Then identify which aspects of yourself are most readily expressed when you're with these people. Jot down some of the shared interests, typical activities, and your feelings and attitudes toward each person. Would you agree that you feel and behave somewhat differently with different people?

5. *How well do you take criticism*? Select an instance when someone criticized you and describe your experience in a page or so. Did you interpret the person's remarks as a personal attack? Or did you try to look beyond the surface of the criticism to what the person was trying to tell you? Looking back, to what extent was this a positive learning experience for you? Jot down some suggestions that will help you to benefit from personal criticism in the future.

6. *Self and ideal.* If you did the self-image and ideal-self exercise in Activity 4–1, write a page or two commenting on the specific items on which you scored the highest discrepancies between your self-image and ideal self. How would you account for this score? Are you doing anything about lessening the gap?

1. How would you describe your self-image?

2. Which aspects of your self-concept would you like to change?

3. Do you basically like yourself?

4. Are you more self-confident in some situations than in others?

5. Are you aware of how others see you?

6. When you've accepted something within yourself, are you more accepting of it in others?

7. How well do you take personal criticism?

8. What do you say when complimented by others?

9. Are you aware that self-actualization is a direction rather than a destination?

10. Do you tend to trust your own experiences?

FOR FURTHER INFORMATION

RECOMMENDED READINGS

MCGRAW, P. (2003). *Self matters: Creating your life from the inside out.* New York: Simon & Schuster/Free Press. Popular media psychologist Phil McGraw discusses how you created your own life via defining moments and critical choices. Using this and other information, he helps you define a "new" you.

MYSS, C. (2002). *Self-esteem: Your fundamental power.* Burton, MI: Sun Angel/Sounds True, Inc. Myss helps the reader discover how self-esteem developed in childhood and why it is important to build a sense of esteem for oneself.

SCHIRALDI, G., FANNING, P., & McKAY, M. (2001). *The self-esteem workbook.* Oakland, CA: New Harbinger Publications. Surprisingly, even though much is known about self-esteem, little is done to actually help an individual raise it. This is a workbook for those folks hoping to feel better about themselves.

SCHMIDT, J. J. (2005). *Social and cultural foundations of counseling and human services: Multiple influences on self-concept development.* Boston: Allyn & Bacon. This book takes a multicultural approach (collective and individualistic) to understanding how self-identity develops.

TESSER, A., FELSON, R. B., & SULS, J. M. (Eds.). (2000). *Psychological perspectives on self and identity.* Washington, DC: American Psychological Association. A scientific book about self-concept and related concepts.

WEB SITES AND THE INTERNET

http://www.selfgrowth.com/topics.html Interested in higher self-esteem, in fact, higher everything? This site provides much information about self-improvement and personal growth.

http://www.Mentalhelp.net A site where you can find all kinds of information on the self, such as changing our self-attitudes, the relationship of low self-esteem to depression, and so forth. Search on the word *self*.

http://www.Oxygen.com A site that sells itself as a woman's view of the world; when women realize that their views are shared, they experience more power and esteem. The site has articles on coping, family, health, and other topics.

http://www.myshoes.com My Shoes is a support group in cyberspace hosted by a clinical psychologist for multiracial children, adolescents, and adults who grapple with the racial identity issue.

http://www.pridelinks.com A web site for gays and lesbians or those interested in the issue of homosexuality, with multiple links and multiple topics, for example, links on health and social supports.

CHAPTER 5

Toward Better Health

BODY IMAGE
How We Feel About Our Bodies
Our Ideal Body

PSYCHOLOGICAL FACTORS AND PHYSICAL ILLNESS
The Immune System
Personality
Lifestyle Choices
Environmental Issues

COPING WITH ILLNESS
Noticing and Interpreting
    Symptoms
Seeking Help
Adhering to Treatment

PROMOTING WELLNESS
Taking Charge of Your Own
    Health
Eating Sensibly
Getting Enough Sleep
Keeping Physically Fit
Finding Social Support

SUMMARY
SELF-TEST
EXERCISES
QUESTIONS FOR SELF-REFLECTION
FOR FURTHER INFORMATION

Learning Objectives

After completing this chapter, you should be able to

1. Discuss the relationship between body image and psychological well-being.
2. Discuss the major health hazards: obesity, smoking, and alcohol and drug abuse.
3. Describe the three stages of decision making in seeking medical care.
4. Understand why patients do not always comply with medical advice.
5. List several factors related to taking charge of your health.
6. Describe the food pyramid.
7. Explain what makes a personal fitness program effective.
8. Discuss the role of social support in wellness.

Amanda, in her mid-30s, works at a large department store as an artist and designer. She designs some of the art for the store's newspaper and catalog advertising. She also decorates the windows and creates many of the in-store displays. When she is at her desk at work, she drinks one cup of coffee after another. It seems she is always behind deadline, so for lunch she grabs a candy bar and soda pop on the run. When she finally goes home to her apartment, she is too tired to fix herself a decent meal. Instead, she sits with a glass of wine, a bag of taco chips, and some nacho dip. When the wine glass empties, she has another one or two glasses of wine. As a result, Amanda is overweight though not yet obese. She wears baggy clothes to disguise her plump and expanding figure, an interesting situation given that she works in the fashion industry. Complaining she doesn't have time to do so, she rarely exercises. Amanda also smokes about a pack of cigarettes a day, a habit she developed in college while sitting in the art student lounge. She thought the other students looked sophisticated when they smoked, so she began.

Amanda is not now sick and, in fact, feels healthy enough so that she rarely complains of her health to others. But how healthy is she? Chances are she could be much healthier. The problem basically lies in Amanda's lifestyle—fast, frenzied, and unhealthy. Because Amanda is overweight from her faulty eating and exercise habits, she has a poor body image. It doesn't help that she sometimes has to interact with rail-thin runway models. Also, she lacks awareness of what her sedentary and stressful lifestyle is doing to her. She subscribes as well to the mistaken notion, more subconscious than conscious, that "not being sick" means she is "well."

Clearly, Amanda never completed a health psychology class; otherwise, she might lead a healthier life. **Health psychology,** *a subfield of psychology that is concerned with how psychological and social factors affect health, wellness, and illness,* pertains to much of what follows.

BODY IMAGE

Not unlike Amanda, many people lack a clear image of their bodies and do not take very good care of themselves. You'd think we would have a fairly accurate picture of our own bodies. After all, who is more familiar with your body than you? Each day, we spend an unaccountable amount of time bathing, touching, and grooming ourselves. Naturally, we acquire a great deal of information about our bodies in other ways, for example, feedback from others such as our doctors and families. But we have blind spots just as Amanda does, so our body image approximates rather than coincides with reality. To commence our discussion of body image, compare your actual weight with your ideal weight by using the chart in Figure 5–1. The chart also includes information on BMI, a topic addressed later in the unit on obesity. Assess whether you are underweight, overweight, or at ideal weight. Now think about how you feel about any discrepancy between your actual and your ideal weight.

A major barrier to reconciling this discrepancy is **depersonalization** or **unembodiment**—*the sense of not being intimately attached to one's body*. Workers like Amanda come home so tired that they spend hours passively watching television, rarely moving their bodies except to feed themselves out of boredom or shake their foot to keep it from going to sleep. Because of our urban, technological way of life, by the time we've reached college age, about three-fourths of us have some type of physical defect that has resulted from unembodiment and disuse or misuse of our bodies. Conversely, when elderly people are taught how to breathe, sit, stand, and walk properly, many of the "symptoms" of aging, such as a stooped walk, disappear.

How We Feel About Our Bodies

Traditionally, **body image** refers to *the mental image we form of our own bodies*. As disclosed in the chapter on self (Chapter 4), body image is a part of our self-concept. Recently, however, the term *body image* has been expanded to include how we feel about our bodies as well as how satisfied or dissatisfied we are with our bodies. Because our society—especially the media—puts so much emphasis on physical appearance, we might expect that many people would be dissatisfied with their bodies. Psychologists often accuse Hollywood celebrities, fashion models, and well-known athletes of influencing our personal body image. Magazine covers, TV ads, and films bombard us with images that reflect the standard but often unattainable ideal of a beautiful body for each sex. Individuals who don't fit media images tend to have negative feelings about themselves, making it difficult for them to accept themselves as they are (Brody, 2002) and perhaps leading to eating disorders. Teasing by others and parental attitudes are also powerful influences on body image (Abramovitz, 2002).

Research indeed bears this out. The American Academy of Pediatrics (2006) reports that multiple studies indicate girls of all ages worry about their weight. Park (2005) and Clay, Vignoles, and Dittmar (2005) found that beauty and fashion magazines directly influence the drive for thinness in women. Tiggeman (2005) also notes that watching

Are you a healthy weight?

Locate your height in the left-most column and read across the row for that height to your weight. Follow the column of the weight up to the top row that lists the BMI. BMI of 18.5–24.9 is the healthy weight range, BMI of 25–29.9 is the overweight range, and BMI of 30 and above is in the obese range.

BMI	19	20	21	22	23	24	25	26	27	28	29	30	31	22	23	24	25
Height							Weight in Pounds										
4'10"	97	96	100	105	110	115	119	124	129	134	138	143	148	153	158	162	167
4'11"	94	99	104	109	114	119	124	128	133	138	143	148	153	158	163	168	173
5'	97	102	107	112	118	123	128	133	138	143	148	153	158	163	168	174	179
5'1"	100	106	111	116	122	127	132	137	143	148	153	158	164	169	174	180	185
5'2"	104	100	115	120	126	131	136	142	147	153	158	164	169	175	180	186	191
5'3"	107	113	118	124	130	135	141	146	152	158	163	169	175	180	186	194	197
5'4"	110	116	122	128	134	140	145	150	157	163	168	174	180	186	192	197	204
5'5"	114	120	126	132	138	144	150	156	162	168	174	180	186	192	198	204	210
5'6"	118	124	130	136	142	148	155	161	167	173	179	186	192	198	204	210	216
5'7"	121	127	134	140	146	153	159	166	172	178	185	191	198	204	211	217	223
5'8"	125	131	138	144	151	158	164	171	177	184	190	197	203	210	216	223	230
5'9"	128	135	142	149	155	162	169	176	182	189	196	203	209	216	223	230	236
5'10"	132	139	146	153	160	167	174	181	188	195	202	209	216	222	229	226	243
5'11"	136	143	150	157	165	172	179	186	193	200	208	215	222	229	236	243	250
6'	140	147	154	162	169	177	184	191	199	206	213	221	228	235	242	250	258
6'1"	144	151	159	166	174	182	189	197	204	212	219	227	235	242	250	257	265
6'2"	148	155	163	171	179	186	194	202	210	218	225	233	241	249	256	264	272
6'3"	152	160	168	176	184	192	200	208	216	232	232	240	248	256	264	272	279
Healthy Weight							Overweight					Obese					

FIGURE 5–1

Are you a healthy weight?

SOURCE: Dietary Guidelines for Americans 2005, Washington, DC: Department of Health and Human services and Department of Agriculture. www.healthierus.gov/dietaryguidelines.

soap operas provides a stimulus for body dissatisfaction. Spurgas (2005) found similar results for women of all races and ethnicities.

Men are affected by media portrayals, too (Tiggeman, 2005), although the idealized body for men is V-shaped with large torso and smaller hips (Tiggeman, 2004) rather than thin. Moreover, most studies indicate that dissatisfaction is not as strong in men as it is in women (Tiggeman, 2004). Perhaps the reason is that the media have less impact on men (Green & Pritchard, 2003). Research has found that dimensions such as age and family pressure predict body dissatisfaction in men. Similarly, men are sensitive to specific depictions of the male body in the media. For example, many men are highly critical of images of men that are too feminine or sexual (Elliott & Elliott, 2005), probably because these portrayals hint at homosexuality and pique homophobia. Heterosexual men are not alone in their dissatisfaction with their bodies; gay men may also exhibit high levels of body dissatisfaction (Kaminski, Chapman, Haynes, & Own, 2005).

A literature review of body image across the adult life span (Tiggemann, 2004) found that body dissatisfaction, although it becomes less important over time, nonetheless remains relatively stable across a lifetime, a surprising finding in that we might expect it to increase with age. As people age, they tend to gain weight, develop wrinkles, and report changes in their hair color and thickness—all of which might actually increase body dissatisfaction.

Overall, the closer to the ideal body we are, the less pressure we feel to change. On the other hand, those who are obviously different—the overweight and the physically disabled—may feel more pressure to change or hide the disliked parts of their bodies, just as Amanda did in her baggy clothes.

Our Ideal Body

The satisfaction with our bodies is greatly influenced by our image of the *ideal* body, an integral part of our overall body image. Specifically, our **ideal body** is *the body we would like to have*. Our ideal body, in turn, is greatly influenced by the particular body ideals prevalent in our culture. For example, in Jamaican society, plumpness is desirable, so although foreign media are available, the desire for plumpness is strong enough to counteract foreign preoccupation with thinness (Smith & Cogswell, 1994).

Every society throughout history has had somewhat different ideals of beauty (Brody, 2002), but at no time in the past has there been such an intense barrage of media attention telling Americans how we should look. As mentioned, for Whites, the ideal man is tall, large, muscular, energetic, and V-shaped. The ideal White woman is slim as well as shapely, smooth-skinned, young, glamorous, and often blonde. These images do not hold true for all people, however. Hispanics, for example, are even more likely than African Americans or Whites to consider themselves overweight (Centers for Disease Control and Prevention, 2001).

Each of us needs to construct a personal body ideal that is not too different from those in our culture but is revised to accommodate our own particular shape and features. The **body ideal** is *our [own] image of the ideal body*. This need becomes especially important with increasing age, so that our body ideal will allow us to see ourselves as reasonably attractive persons at each stage of life.

Perceptions of what the opposite sex finds ideal or attractive differ substantially from what the opposite sex *actually* finds attractive. This is especially true for women's perceptions of what men want. Women believe that men prefer thin or bony women while men actually do *not* prefer such women (Bergstron, Neighbors, & Lewis, 2004). Men are more in tune with what women actually find attractive in a man's physique.

PSYCHOLOGICAL FACTORS AND PHYSICAL ILLNESS

Physicians and mental health professionals today pay greater attention to the mutual interactions of the mind and body than they did in the past. There's compelling evidence that organic factors—genes, the brain, and **neurotransmitters** (*chemical substances that transmit neural impulses*)—contribute to psychological disorders such as schizophrenia, major depression, and manic depression (bipolar disorder). And conversely, there is substantial research indicating that psychological factors influence our susceptibility and resistance to physical illnesses (Lemonick, 2003a). Although traditional efforts attempt to link specific diseases to single causes, such as genes, germs, and emotions, much of contemporary research assumes a **systems theory** perspective. In this view, *human existence is made up of various subsystems and is itself an integral part of larger systems.* Thus, to understand health and illness we must consider how these biological, psychological, and social factors interact, for example, as in the study of stress-related illnesses.

In the following section we'll examine stress-related illnesses to see how psychological factors such as negative emotions and stress make us susceptible to physical illnesses. The emphasis until recently has been on such negative factors. Newer research, however, indicates that positive affectivity or emotion also influences longevity and health (Cohen & Pressman, in *Current Directions in Psychological Science*, June 2006, in press). For now, you will learn how stress affects the immune system and, in turn, how we may strengthen our resistance to stress. You will also read about three of the most common lifestyle hazards associated with stress and illness: obesity, cigarette smoking, and substance abuse such as alcohol and drug abuse.

The Immune System

Amanda had had a serious case of mononucleosis in college so her immune system had been damaged. The **immune system** is *a complex surveillance system, including the brain and various blood cells, that defends our bodies by identifying and destroying various foreign invaders.* Amanda likened herself to the proverbial canary in the coal mine. If there was a stomach flu or a cold going around, she was always first to catch it; then and only then would her friends become aware of the latest illness. Although Amanda's immune system was impaired, other individuals and, we hope, you possess more robust immune systems.

In emphasizing the link between psychological factors such as stress and physical illnesses, it is important that we do not exceed the boundary between science and capricious thinking. In fact, the exact linking mechanisms remain unknown (*Harvard Health Letter*, 2002), although cortisol (Sher, 2004), a hormone, and proinflammatory cytokines (immune system proteins that incite inflammation) (Robles, Glaser, & Kiecolt-Glaser, 2005) have been implicated. Thus, stress might not *cause* illness directly. Rather, stress may tend to weaken the immune system, thereby making us more vulnerable to illness. How does this happen?

First, in times of distress, psychological processes such as depression can prevent us from taking positive health-related measures such as eating well. Second, research has demonstrated that in stressful situations, the body's immune system functions less well (Glaser, 2005; Oxington, 2005; Segerstrom & Miller, 2004). For instance, stress lowers the body's resistance to a variety of physical ailments (*Harvard Health Letter*, 2002), ranging from herpes viruses to upper respiratory infections. One study, for example, demonstrated that unhappily married women had lower numbers of certain immune system cells than women in happier marriages (*Harvard Health Letter*, 2002).

Personality

There is increasing evidence suggesting that we can bolster our resistance to stress and illness by harnessing the powers of the mind—our thoughts, attitudes, and emotions. Psychologists recognize the importance of five personality traits in their descriptions of individuals' personalities; the traits are *openness to experience* (being open-minded about novelty), *conscientiousness* (diligence), *agreeableness* (being good-natured), *extroversion* (being friendly), and *emotional stability* (high or low anxiety and rational or irrational). Goodwin and Engstron (2002) enlisted a representative sample of American adults and measured them on their self-perceived health. Using the five traits, the researchers found that openness to experience, extroversion, and conscientiousness were associated with perceptions of good health; emotional instability was associated with perceptions of poor health. These particular findings have been replicated by others (Raynor, Wing, & Phelan, 2007). The same findings also held true for individuals with self-reported medical conditions.

Another personality factor that pertains to our ability to resist illness is self-efficacy, described more fully elsewhere in this book. **Self-efficacy** is *the belief in one's capabilities to organize and execute actions required to produce given attainments* (Bandura, 1997). With regard to health behaviors, self-efficacy is that trait that enables us to adopt healthy and therefore preventive behaviors such as physical exercise or to adhere to programs designed to eliminate unhealthy habits such as smoking. Individuals high in self-efficacy are more likely to adopt healthy lifestyles and to be able to stick to their regimens when attempting to eliminate unhealthy behaviors (Lippke & Ziegelmann, 2006). People see little point in trying to change if they do not believe they can succeed. Just exactly how does self-efficacy function in relationship to health?

- First, a sense of efficacy can activate a wide range of biological processes that mediate human health and disease processes. For example, exposure to stressors along with the ability to control them or a sense of efficacy about ability to control them often results in few to no adverse physical effects.

- Second, people's beliefs that they can motivate themselves and regulate their own behavior play a crucial role in whether they even consider changing detrimental health habits or pursuing rehabilitative activities (Bandura, 1997). In other words, *individuals with high self-efficacy are more likely to stick to a healthy diet.* To illustrate, Williams and Bond (2002) demonstrated that self-efficacy is a strong predictor of whether diabetics adhere to their special diets and exercise.

- Third, the onus for healthy lifestyles does not reside solely with individuals. With regard to self-efficacy, people are exposed to a variety of health-related messages from the media. From the media, people can glean information about how to regulate their behavior and to engage in preventive behaviors. Compared with threatening messages, public health messages that elicit positive emotions make people feel more efficacious and optimistic about the benefits of healthy practices. In a study by Williams, Clarke, and Borland (2001), women with greater self-efficacy who were mailed a brochure were more likely to do self breast exams.

- Finally, adherence to healthy lifestyles or to rehabilitation programs once they are commenced also can be problematic. Lippke & Ziegelmann (2006) found that those high in self-efficacy are more likely to stick with such programs, and Bebetsos, Chroni, and Theodorakis (2002) demonstrated that self-efficacy is related to students' maintaining a healthy diet.

How can individuals develop or promote high self-efficacy? According to Albert Bandura (1997), the leading theorist on such matters, individuals must learn to monitor their own behaviors, especially the ones they wish to change. They must set short-range, attainable goals to motivate and direct their own efforts and enlist positive social support from others to help them sustain the efforts needed to succeed. Modeling after successful others also benefits those embarking on healthier lifestyles. Interestingly, self-efficacy appears to function similarly across cultures with regard to promoting healthy behaviors (Luszczynska, Scholtz, & Scwarzer, 2005).

We must guard against emphasizing personality as responsible for our health to such an extent that people are made to feel guilty when they become sick or fail to get well. As mentioned earlier, a multitude of other factors contribute to our physical and mental well-being. Another important factor is lifestyle, which we will discuss next.

Lifestyle Choices

Lifestyle kills more Americans than any other single factor. This cannot be said about citizens of other countries where environmental hazards, disease, war, and starvation account for more deaths. Lifestyle change, then, can be extremely effective in maintaining good health (Wing & Raynor, 2006). Three major health hazards that are directly associated with lifestyle and that can be controlled (though many people have difficulty doing so) are obesity, smoking, and alcohol and drug abuse. Thus, we will explore them further.

Obesity is *an excessive amount of body fat, usually defined as exceeding the desirable weight for one's height, build, and age.* Recall our earlier discussion of body image and American media. Nowhere is thinness more desirable than in mainstream American society, yet paradoxically, nowhere is obesity more prevalent, probably because food is so available here compared to other countries. Likewise, Americans live a pretty fast-paced life, so they often turn to snacks and fast foods, which are unusually laden with empty calories (Horgen, 2005). Amanda, the young adult from the opening story, was overweight because of her habit of binging on snacks from vending machines.

Earlier in the chapter you were introduced to the height and weight table to help you identify whether you are overweight. Another measure introduced earlier is BMI or **Body Mass Index**, which is *a measure of total body fat calculated from knowing an individual's*

Tobacco abuse continues to be a major health hazard in the United States.

height and weight. You can estimate your BMI by multiplying your total weight times 703 and dividing by your height squared (National Institutes of Health, 2000). BMI combined with waist circumference can be a good indicator of who is gaining or carrying too much weight. Men with a circumference greater than 40 inches and women with a circumference greater than 35 inches are considered at risk for health problems related to obesity. Using these measures, sadly, only 35 percent of all Americans have a healthy BMI (Eckel, 2005), whereas 64 percent of Americans are overweight or outright obese (National Health and Nutrition Examination Survey). Being overweight or obese is not just a problem for adults either; these health problems in children and adolescents have recently increased threefold (Eckel). High blood pressure, diabetes, stroke, sleep disorders, cancer, and liver and gall bladder diseases are but a few of the complications of weighing too much, and each year, more than 300,000 deaths are linked to obesity in the United States (Mayo Clinic, 2005). The more overweight people are, the greater their risk. In general, obese individuals have a 50 to 100 percent increased risk of death from all causes, compared with normal-weight individuals. Amanda is therefore headed down the road for early death.

Obesity probably results from an interaction of physiological and psychological factors. We all know overweight people who eat moderately but remain fat and thin people who eat heartily but remain slender. Although apparently some people are born to carry more fat, a lot of obesity results from overeating and insufficient exercise. There is also a variety of psychological and social factors associated with obesity. For instance, obese people tend to be more responsive to external cues, such as the visibility, availability, and smell of food, rather than to the internal cues of hunger. Some individuals also eat more food when with others, especially others who are fast eaters—so be careful with whom you dine!

People who want to lose weight must somehow help their bodies to use up more calories than they consume. The two basic ways to do so are to (1) change your diet so that you eat less, especially fewer foods high in fat, and (2) exercise more. The benefits of crash diets are generally short-lived. To make matters worse, strict dieting tends to lower the rate of metabolism, so even though you count calories carefully, you will still not lose weight. It's preferable to follow a reasonable diet aimed at a more modest weight loss—say, 1 pound a week—over a longer period of time, combined with regular exercise. Perhaps you've heard the myth that exercise is self-defeating because it makes you want to

---

TABLE 5–1

TIPS FOR STICKING TO YOUR EXERCISE PROGRAM

1. Adopt a specific plan and write it down.
2. Keep setting realistic goals as you go along, and remind yourself of them often.
3. Keep a log to record your progress and make sure to keep it up-to-date.
4. Include weight and/or percent body fat measures in your log. Extra pounds can easily creep back.
5. Upgrade your fitness program as you progress.
6. Enlist the support and company of your family and friends.
7. Update others on your successes.
8. Avoid injuries by pacing yourself and including a warm-up and cool-down period as part of every workout.
9. Reward yourself periodically for a job well done!

SOURCE: www.fitness.gov/exerciseweight.html.

eat more. Actually, exercise not only burns up calories but also increases your metabolic rate, so that even when active people are not exercising, their bodies are burning up calories faster. Exercise during and after dieting is an important predictor of successful long-term weight loss (Wing & Raynor, 2006). And small lifestyle changes, such as watching less television, are also related to maintaining weight loss (Raynor et al., 2006). Unfortunately, only 22 percent of American adults get the recommended regular physical activity. The recommendation is five times a week for at least 30 minutes of vigorous activity such as brisk walking (National Institute of Diabetes and Digestive and Kidney Diseases, 2000). Table 5–1 provides some tips for you on how to stick to an exercise program.

Self-efficacy also plays an important role, such that individuals who acquire a greater sense of self-control over their eating and exercise habits can successfully manage their weight long after the completion of dieting and treatment programs. Finally, weight-loss programs are a big business in America and will probably continue to grow as Americans' girths grow. If you are thinking of joining such a program, make sure that the program meets the guidelines established by the federal government in Box 5–1.

Tobacco abuse continues to be a major health hazard (Ostbyte & Taylor, 2004). **Tobacco abuse** is *the abuse of tobacco to such an extent that heart, respiratory, and other health-related problems develop.* An estimated 44.5 million adults in the United States smoke cigarettes even though this single behavior will result in death or disability for half of the regular smokers (National Center for Chronic Disease Prevention and Health Promotion, 2005). Tobacco use remains the leading *preventable* cause of death in the United States as well as one of the most expensive habits, increasing health-care costs manifold (Centers for Disease Control and Prevention, 2002d; Ostbyte & Taylor, 2004). There is compelling

Box 5–1

SELECTING A WEIGHT-LOSS PROGRAM

A responsible and safe weight-loss program should be able to document for you the following five features:

1. *The diet should be safe.* It should include all of the Recommended Daily Allowances (RDAs) for vitamins, minerals, and protein.

2. *The weight-loss program should be directed toward a slow, steady weight loss* unless your doctor feels your health condition would benefit from more rapid weight loss.

3. *Check for health problems before starting.* If you plan to lose more than 15 to 20 pounds, suspect or know you have any health problems, or take medication on a regular basis, you should be evaluated by your doctor before beginning your weight-loss program.

4. *The program should include plans for weight maintenance after the weight-loss phase is over.* It is of little benefit to

lose a large amount of weight only to regain it. Weight maintenance is the most difficult part of controlling weight and is not consistently implemented in weight-loss programs. The program you select should include help in permanently changing your dietary habits and level of physical activity, to alter a lifestyle that may have contributed to weight gain in the past.

5. *Know how much it might cost.* A commercial weight-loss program should provide a detailed statement of fees and costs of additional items such as dietary supplements.

SOURCE: Adapted from "Choosing a safe and successful weight-loss program." National Institute of Diabetes & Digestive & Kidney Diseases, 1998. www.niddk.nih.gov/nutrit/pubs/choose.

evidence that cigarette smoking is a major factor in heart disease, lung cancer, emphysema, and other fatal illnesses. In addition, smoking contributes to many forms of cancer, including cancers of the mouth, larynx, bladder, and pancreas (e.g., Ostbyte & Taylor, 2004). Smokers who also drink alcohol magnify their risks of cancer even more because it enhances the carcinogenic effect of tobacco at certain sites of the body, such as the esophagus, mouth, and larynx.

Greater awareness of the health hazards of smoking and chewing tobacco has prompted some people to give up the habit. Today, 21.6 percent of U.S. adults—over 45 million people—are current smokers. That's down from 22.5 percent in 2002 and 22.8 percent in 2001 (National Center for Chronic Disease Prevention and Health Promotion, 2005). At the same time, these gains should not blind us to the fact that a large number of children and adolescents smoke (23.6 percent) and a large number of young adults smoke (23.8 percent). That means that a large portion of children living today will die prematurely because of the decision they made to smoke (Centers for Disease Control and Prevention, 2002d). Not surprisingly, tobacco companies are under fire from the public and health officials for this increase. On a second front, many authorities are disturbed that smoking rates are even higher in other countries, many of which have citizens who cannot afford to smoke and who have inadequate health care as it is.

Smoking is a difficult habit to break, but the benefits of smoking cessation are substantial (Ostbyte & Taylor, 2004). However, even conservative estimates imply that half or more of those who quit smoking eventually resume the habit. In addition to the psychological dependence on the smoking habit, nicotine is considered to be physically addictive. Consequently, smokers build a tolerance to nicotine and need to smoke a larger number of cigarettes or ones with higher nicotine content to get the same effect. The average smoker smokes 20 to 30 cigarettes a day—one cigarette about every 30 to 40 minutes. And because the biological half-life of nicotine in humans is about 20 to 30 minutes, habitual smokers keep their systems primed with nicotine during most of their waking hours. Not surprisingly, withdrawal from habitual smoking and nicotine produces a variety of symptoms, including nervousness, headaches, dizziness, fatigue, insomnia, sweating, cramps, tremors, and heart palpitations. Many famous and well-educated people sadly have been addicted to tobacco. They, too, have found the habit terribly difficult to stop. Box 5–2 is about just such a famous person.

Box 5–2

An Interesting Case of Nicotine Addiction

After a prominent physician was told that his heart arrhythmia was aggravated by his heavy smoking, up to 20 cigars a day, he decided to stop smoking. In fact, he had smoked so much that clients claimed they could smell a lighted cigar even when he wasn't smoking. The odor hovered on the curtains, furniture, and his clothes. Later, describing the agony of not being able to smoke as "beyond human power to bear," he resumed smoking, though on a somewhat more moderate basis (Jones, 1953). Eventually, he developed cancer of the jaw and mouth, which also was associated with his smoking. However, despite 33 operations for cancer and the construction of an artificial jaw, this physician continued to smoke until his death at the age of 83. His efforts to stop smoking and the suffering he endured from cancer make him a tragic example of nicotine addiction. His name was Sigmund Freud.

Box 5–3

TIPS FOR QUITTING

FIVE KEYS FOR QUITTING

Studies have shown that these five steps will help you quit and quit for good. You have the best chances of quitting if you use them together.

1. *Get Ready*

   • Set a quit date.

   • Change your environment.

      1. Get rid of ALL cigarettes and ashtrays in your home, car, and place of work.

      2. Don't let people smoke in your home.

   • Review your past attempts to quit. Think about what worked and what did not.

   • Once you quit, don't smoke—NOT EVEN A PUFF!

2. *Get Support and Encouragement.* Studies have shown that you have a better chance of being successful if you have help. You can get support in many ways:

   • Tell your family, friends, and coworkers that you are going to quit and want their support. Ask them not to smoke around you or leave cigarettes out.

   • Talk to your health care provider (for example, doctor, dentist, nurse, pharmacist, psychologist, or smoking counselor).

3. *Learn New Skills and Behaviors*

   • Try to distract yourself from urges to smoke. Talk to someone, go for a walk, or get busy with a task.

   • When you first try to quit, change your routine. Use a different route to work. Drink tea instead of coffee. Eat breakfast in a different place.

   • Do something to reduce your stress. Take a hot bath, exercise, or read a book.

   • Plan something enjoyable to do every day.

   • Drink a lot of water and other fluids.

4. *Get Medication and Use It Correctly.* Medications can help you stop smoking and lessen the urge to smoke. These double your chance of quitting. The U.S. Food and Drug Administration (FDA) has approved five medications to help you quit smoking:

   • Ask your health care provider for advice and carefully read the information on the package.

   • If you are pregnant or trying to become pregnant, nursing, under age 18, smoking fewer than 10 cigarettes per day, or have a medical condition, talk to your doctor or other health care provider before taking medications.

5. *Be Prepared for Relapse or Difficult Situations.* Most relapses occur within the first 3 months after quitting. Don't be discouraged if you start smoking again. Remember, most people try several times before they finally quit. Here are some difficult situations to watch for:

   • Alcohol. Avoid drinking alcohol. Drinking lowers your chances of success.

   • Other Smokers. Being around smoking can make you want to smoke.

   • Weight Gain. Many smokers will gain weight when they quit, usually less than 10 pounds. Eat a healthy diet and stay active.

   • Bad Mood or Depression. There are a lot of ways to improve your mood other than smoking.

If you are having problems with any of these situations, talk to your doctor or other health care provider.

SOURCE: Adapted from the Centers for Disease Control and Prevention's "You can quit smoking consumer guide" (www.cdc.gov/tobacco/quit/can quit.htm).

There are many approaches to reducing **nicotine addiction** or to reducing *the difficulty of quitting smoking when smoking has become habitual*. In recent years, many people have begun using the "patch," which, when attached to one's arm, releases nicotine into the body, thereby reducing the physical craving for a smoke. In addition, a variety of psychological and behavioral methods is available. One approach is monitoring stimulus control, in which smokers become aware of the stimuli and the situations that trigger their smoking. Then they develop alternative behaviors. For instance, Amanda usually lit a cigarette whenever she talked on the telephone or ate spicy food. A friend suggested that she begin holding a glass of water in her right hand while on the phone and chewing gum after spicy food, thereby breaking the associations between the telephone and smoking and spicy food and cigarettes. Generally, when trying to convince yourself or someone else to quit, it's better to emphasize the *positive* aspects of not smoking, such as the desire to take charge of one's life and to maintain physical fitness, rather than the fear of illness. Although most smokers who give up smoking resume the habit within 6 months to a year, former smokers may increase their chance of success through the support of friends, spouses, or support groups (Thomas et al., 2005). Also, vigorous exercise helps smokers quit and stay smoke free (Marcus, 1999). Then too, with sufficient motivation, many smokers may give up the habit without any formal program. If you want to quit or help someone else quit, see Box 5–3 for more tips on how to quit.

    Alcohol and drug abuse continues to be a major health hazard for many people. Such abuse may be defined as *the misuse or dependence on a psychoactive substance like alcohol*. Three-fourths of American men and almost two-thirds of women drink alcoholic beverages, but not all of them develop alcoholism. Alcoholism may be hereditary, in part, so is often found recurring in family trees (McGue, 1999). Approximately one-third of both sexes are light drinkers, but at least 1 out of 10 adults is a heavy drinker; the proportion being higher among men, especially those 18 to 25 years old. Activity 5–1 can help you assess whether you are a heavy drinker.

ACTIVITY 5–1

ARE YOU DRINKING TOO MUCH?

INSTRUCTIONS: *Indicate the strength of your agreement on a scale of 1 to 7 for the following statements by circling the appropriate number under the statement.*

1.   I drink alcohol (or use drugs) heavily after a confrontation or argument or because of emotional pain.

     Strongly disagree   1   2   3   4   5   6   7   Strongly agree

2.   I need more and more alcohol (or more and more drugs) to get the same effect.

     Strongly disagree   1   2   3   4   5   6   7   Strongly agree

3. I often remember starting out, beginning to drink, and then drinking more, but that's all I remember.

Strongly disagree   1   2   3   4   5   6   7   Strongly agree

4. I often blackout or don't remember what happened when I was drinking (or using drugs).

Strongly disagree   1   2   3   4   5   6   7   Strongly agree

5. Not remembering what I was doing when I was drinking causes me alarm to the point of switching drinks, switching jobs, and switching promises to myself.

Strongly disagree   1   2   3   4   5   6   7   Strongly agree

6. My friends have told me that I lose control when I drink too much alcohol.

Strongly disagree   1   2   3   4   5   6   7   Strongly agree

7. I realize that others are talking about my drinking (or drugging) too much.

Strongly disagree   1   2   3   4   5   6   7   Strongly agree

8. My hands shake in the morning and/or I feel hung over after I have been drinking (or drugging).

Strongly disagree   1   2   3   4   5   6   7   Strongly agree

9. People seem extremely irritated with me because of my drinking (or drug use).

Strongly disagree   1   2   3   4   5   6   7   Strongly agree

10. I often drink more than I eat.

Strongly disagree   1   2   3   4   5   6   7   Strongly agree

SCORING: Add up all your points for each statement. The higher the total score, the more likely it is that you have an alcohol (or drug) abuse problem. If you believe that you do have a problem, find professional help as soon as possible.

SOURCE: Adapted from "Moving forward with your life! Leaving alcohol and other drugs behind." U.S. Department of Health and Human Services, National Clearinghouse for Alcohol and Drug Information. http://www.health.org/govpubs/PHD626/.

Alcohol use constitutes a major health hazard in many ways. Nearly two-thirds of the drivers in fatal traffic accidents have been drinking. Automobile accidents involving alcohol are a leading cause of death among youths. Furthermore, people with alcohol-related ailments fill half of all hospital beds in America. In addition, chronic heavy drinking is often accompanied by poor nutrition and results in serious damage to many parts of the body, such as the liver, with at least one of every five chronic heavy drinkers developing cirrhosis of the liver.

Although alcohol remains the drug of choice for a large segment of the population, we should not overlook the abuse of prescription or over-the-counter drugs. Overdosing on barbiturates has become a common means of committing suicide. People who attempt to stop taking barbiturates, or sleeping pills, often experience a rebound effect that disturbs their sleep. This rebound effect is common with many drugs, including alcohol. For example, Amanda sometimes found herself awakening several hours into a deep sleep on each night that she consumed two or more glasses of wine. As many as half of all insomniacs have drug-induced insomnia. An excessive or prolonged use of tranquilizers, especially among the elderly, may damage the respiratory system, kidneys, and liver. Furthermore, combining alcohol with drugs tends to multiply the effect of the drug, sometimes with fatal results. The use of illegal or street drugs poses special problems. There is no control over the strength or purity of the drug, who takes them, who makes them, or the dosage. Furthermore, the tendency to use greater amounts of the mood-altering drugs over time to offset tolerance increases the health hazard.

People who develop problems with drugs exhibit a familiar sequential pattern. Box 5–4 reveals more about this pattern.

Individuals who become *dependent on a drug like alcohol or marijuana exhibit characteristic symptoms* of the **psychoactive substance dependence disorder**. Such individuals display an impaired control of and continued use of the substance despite adverse consequences. The symptoms of the dependence syndrome include, but are not limited to, the physiological symptoms of tolerance and withdrawal. In addition, symptoms must have persisted for at least 1 month or have occurred repeatedly over a longer period of time, as in binge drinking. Individuals may also display differing degrees of drug dependence—mild, moderate, or severe.

Although many programs are available for treating drug abuse, some have a relatively high failure rate. Individuals may not be ready for the complete change in lifestyle demanded by the program, often because of denial on their part, or they may become bored and frustrated with the program or the lifestyle changes demanded by it. A large proportion of people who enter drug treatment drop out in the first few weeks only to reenter the program at a later date, though relapse remains the rule rather than the exception. **Relapse** means *a return to a previous behavior or state*—in this case, a return to drinking alcohol or using drugs. The prevalence of relapse has led some cognitive-behavioral therapists to develop relapse-prevention training, which generally is incorporated into the treatment program. Substance abusers are taught how to cope with high-risk situations—for example, coming into contact with acquaintances who are still addicted—and to prevent small lapses from becoming full-blown relapses. Individuals are encouraged to view lapses as temporary setbacks that they can learn from and avoid in the future. Amanda, for example, went to a smoking cessation program and learned that she should avoid going to dinner with her friends who smoked. She was also taught to think, "Okay, I had a slip. But that doesn't mean I'm all through. I can get back on track."

Box 5–4

DRUG USE: WHEN DOES DRUG USE START? HOW DOES IT PROCEED?

WHAT ARE THE HIGHEST RISK PERIODS FOR DRUG ABUSE AMONG YOUTH?

Research has shown that the key risk periods for drug abuse are during major transitions in children's lives. The first big transition for children is when they leave the security of the family and enter school. Later, when they advance from elementary school to middle school, they often experience new academic and social situations, such as learning to get along with a wider group of peers. It is at this stage—early adolescence—that children are likely to encounter drugs for the first time.

When they enter high school, adolescents face additional social, emotional, and educational challenges. At the same time, they may be exposed to greater availability of drugs, drug abusers, and social activities involving drugs. These challenges can increase the risk that they will abuse alcohol, tobacco, and other substances.

When young adults leave home for college or work and are on their own for the first time, their risk for drug and alcohol abuse is very high. Consequently, young adult interventions are needed as well.

Because risks appear at every life transition, prevention planners need to choose programs that strengthen protective factors at each stage of development.

WHEN AND HOW DOES DRUG ABUSE START AND PROGRESS?

Studies such as the National Survey on Drug Use and Health, formally called the National Household Survey on Drug Abuse, reported by the Substance Abuse and Mental Health Services Administration, indicate that some children are already abusing drugs at age 12 or 13, which likely means that some begin even earlier. Early abuse often includes such substances as tobacco, alcohol, inhalants, marijuana, and prescription drugs such as sleeping pills and anti-anxiety medicines. If drug abuse persists into later adolescence, abusers typically become more heavily involved with marijuana and then advance to other drugs, while continuing their abuse of tobacco and alcohol. Studies have also shown that abuse of drugs in late childhood and early adolescence is associated with greater drug involvement. It is important to note that most youth, however, do not progress to abusing other drugs.

Scientists have proposed various explanations of why some individuals become involved with drugs and then escalate to abuse. One explanation points to a biological cause, such as having a family history of drug or alcohol abuse. Another explanation is that abusing drugs can lead to affiliation with drug-abusing peers, which, in turn, exposes the individual to other drugs.

Researchers have found that youth who rapidly increase their substance abuse have high levels of risk factors with low levels of protective factors. Gender, race, and geographic location can also play a role in how and when children begin abusing drugs.

Preventive interventions can provide skills and support to high-risk youth to enhance levels of protective factors and prevent escalation to drug abuse.

SOURCE: National Institute on Drug Abuse. (2006). *Preventing drug abuse among children and adolescents*. http://www.nida.nih.gov/Prevention/prevopen.html.

The best programs prevent substance abuse altogether by teaching parents to take a proactive role in their child's development and understanding of substance abuse (Haggerty, Kosterman, Catalano, & Hawkins, 1999). Additionally, for college students, a group at high risk for alcoholism and use of illicit substances, simple web-based assessments over time can help to prevent such abuse (American Psychological Society, 1999). Similarly, making students aware that the average college student does not get drunk every weekend (e.g., sharing social norms) may also reduce the level of alcohol consumption on college campuses (Haines, Barker, & Rice, 2003).

Environmental Issues

Various environments in which we find ourselves are more or less conducive to health problems. You may well be thinking that environmental pollutants or contaminants are one of the major sources for health-related problems. You are correct. About 25 percent of Americans live where the standards for air quality are not met (National Center for Health Statistics, 2002). It has long been known that living near polluting industries can affect one's *physical* health; Downey and Willigen (2005) also discovered that living near polluting industries also affects *mental* health.

Social and psychological environments can be just as toxic (Evans & Stecker, 2004). Messages about the popularity of drugs have become a common part of children's lives. Thompson (2005) found that 95 percent of all films depict the use of some unhealthy substance (e.g., cigarettes, alcohol, or drugs), but most do not depict the negative consequences of use. In addition, Sargent, Willis, Stoolmiller, Gibson, and Gibbons (2006), studying alcohol use in motion pictures, found a significant effect of exposure to alcohol use in movies on early onset teen drinking. They suggested that this type of environmental risk factor is easily modifiable by eliminating scenes of alcohol and drug use from the media. Conversely, the mass media could play a role in protecting children from drugs by portraying them as unglamorous, dangerous, and socially unacceptable (Weiner, Panton, & Weber, 1999).

As a second example of a toxic environment, let's turn back to Amanda's life. Amanda became very distressed when her boss bellowed at her one day that she was always behind schedule. The very next day, though, her employer acted as if nothing had been wrong the previous day. "What does this mean?" asked Amanda. "What could I have done differently?" Before Amanda could answer these questions, though, she was sick with a stress cold.

Living near pollution can affect one's physical and mental health.

Let's analyze Amanda's situation. One reason the event was stressful to Amanda is that she felt she had done nothing to prompt her supervisor's ire. In other words, the situation was out of Amanda's control or was *uncontrollable*. Amanda hoped that maybe her boss had just had an upsetting morning at home and that the anger had nothing to do with her job performance. Amanda had seen her supervisor have these little tantrums before but could not predict when they would occur. *Unpredictability* is another aspect of the environment that is distressing to us (Evans & Stecker, 2004). If we can predict when a negative or otherwise stressful event will occur, we can brace for it, prepare for it. Not knowing when the tantrums were coming was distressing for Amanda.

Another feature of environments that is not conducive to wellness is *ambiguity*. Recall that Amanda's boss acted angry one minute and as if nothing had happened the next. This situation is very ambiguous, again leaving Amanda wondering if she really was the cause of the outburst or if it was caused by a problem at her boss's home. Ambiguity, then, also creates distress.

A final problem of stress that originates in the environment is that often the distress is *unresolvable*; that is, there is little the distressed individual can do to settle the issue or reduce the distress. Let's hope that this was not the case for Amanda; perhaps she can speak to her supervisor and come to some understanding about how to avoid incurring her supervisor's wrath in the future. In order to cope better, it is best if we avoid situations that are uncontrollable, unpredictable, ambiguous, or unresolvable. If such situations are unavoidable, as often is the case, the next best thing we can do is cope effectively with them. Coping is discussed in the next section and elsewhere in this book.

COPING WITH ILLNESS

Every so often each of us has a minor health problem, such as a stress cold, which we usually treat with a variety of over-the-counter remedies like aspirin, antihistamines, and stomach medicine. However, if the problem persists, especially when it interferes with our everyday lives, we begin to consider seeing a doctor. Whether we are aware of it or not, such experiences set in motion a decision-making process that includes three stages:

(1) *Noticing and interpreting* the seriousness of our symptoms

(2) *Seeking professional help* when needed

(3) *Adhering to the prescribed treatment*

In this section, we'll look at how people react to symptoms and illnesses at each of these three stages.

Noticing and Interpreting Symptoms

Even healthy young adults like Amanda may experience a variety of symptoms, including nasal congestion, sore muscles, stiff joints, headaches, racing heart, dizziness, and constipation or diarrhea. Each of us differs somewhat in the tendency to label our body aches and pains as symptoms of an illness. *People who habitually complain of unfounded ailments or exhibit an undue fear of illness* are often called **hypochondriacs**. On the other hand, some people tend to underreport their physical symptoms. These people are often **extroverts**, *people who tend to be warm, outgoing, and involved in life*, so much so that they don't have time to complain of or notice their ailments. Each person's sense of well-being is a function of both of these traits, the relative strength of each tendency determining how we perceive and interpret our inner state. Individuals high in hypochondriasis report two or three times as many symptoms as the better-adjusted people. Conversely, those high in extroversion generally report fewer ailments.

Psychologists have also identified other coping strategies related to health concerns. One strategy is **avoidance**. In this pattern, *the individual minimizes or denies that there are any symptoms to notice.* Such individuals are believed to cope well with short-term stressors. On the other hand, some individuals actively confront stressors. These individuals use **confrontation** to *note symptoms of an illness are present.* One other means for coping with bad health news is through **downward comparison**. Individuals who choose to do this *compare their own situation to others who are worse off.* For example, Amanda smoked about a pack of cigarettes a day but found herself comparing this habit to that of Virginia, a coworker who smoked almost two packs a day.

There are other personal characteristics that determine typical coping styles related to health behaviors. One is the *culture* in which we were reared; the other is gender. With regard to culture, pain signifies different things in different cultures. In the United States, many visits to doctors are prompted by the experience of pain (Turk, 1994). In some cultures, individuals attend to the intensity of pain, whereas in other cultures individuals respond to what they think the pain signifies. Thus, in the latter cultures, minor pain could still signal something serious.

With regard to gender, differences exist in death and illness rates between men and women, some of which are attributable to lifestyle, with others attributable to what is deemed socially appropriate for men and women. In North America, women live longer than men, perhaps because men are more likely to die in, for example, car accidents and homicides. Men are generally exposed to more dangerous work environments (e.g., mines). On the other hand, women experience more symptoms and have more physical ailments than men (Matud, 2004). Women, then, have longer lives but higher illness rates. Why remains a mystery. One answer lies in the fact that women simply may be more likely to report symptoms to a health care provider than are men (Banks, 2001; Leventhal, 1994). Additionally, men are less likely to discuss their fears about health with a professional and also are more likely to visit their health care provider later in the course of an illness, in part because of their fears (Banks).

Seeking Help

About the only time it's easy to decide whether or not to see a doctor is when our symptoms become extreme. At the same time, the decision to seek professional help also depends on many other factors. For instance, if people believe their symptoms have a psychological rather than a physical cause, they are more reluctant to go for help. Also, if their complaints—such as hemorrhoids or unplanned pregnancy—are embarrassing to talk about, they may resist treatment. Individuals are also less likely to visit a physician if the ailment seems virus-related or involves the upper half of the body. If people believe the benefits of going to the doctor are not worth the time, trouble, and cost of a visit, especially if the visit is not covered by medical insurance, they may hold back. Furthermore, the dread of a devastating or fateful diagnosis might delay seeking help.

Men and women differ in their readiness to see a doctor (Galdas, Cheater, & Marshall, 2005; Mansfield, Addis, & Courtenay, 2005). Men seek help less often; on average, they go 2 or more years without seeing a doctor, a situation that may put them at risk for more fatalities than women (Mansfield, Addis, & Courtenay, 2005). Women generally are more sensitive to changes in their bodies and to pain and, thus, visit physicians more often than men (Berkley, 1997). Yet men have higher rates of hypertension, ulcers, heart attacks, and cancer and, as mentioned earlier, significantly shorter life expectancies. One possible explanation is that men are more preoccupied with the external world and are less attentive to their bodies. Or perhaps men are more reluctant to seek professional help because it implies a "weakness" on their part.

Some of the most glaring differences in help-seeking occur between racial or ethnic minorities and Whites. One of the problems of these minority groups, which are more prone to certain health problems, is lack of health insurance. Large percentages of African Americans, Asians, Latinos, Pacific Islanders, and Native Americans lack health insurance or other means to pay for health care (Administration on Aging, 2006). Perceived prejudice may also keep these individuals from finding care, but prejudice and discrimination may also be the culprits creating increased stress and thus causing some of the health-related problems in the first place (Carlson & Chamberlain, 2004).

Let's look also at general cultural differences in seeking health care. In the United States, citizens expect to visit a doctor in a professional-looking office or in a pristine and large hospital. Not so in rural India. Individuals there are more likely to seek medical help if the medical center resembles an Indian village, with separate huts housing the lab, surgical suite, pharmacy, and wards (Perry, 2005). In Nepal, where adequate health care is lacking, people are more likely to use health care services if they are endorsed by some of the most important people in their society—grandmothers (Kluger, 2005). In Somalia, the roads are so terrible due to droughts, wars, and lack of care, patients cannot traverse them. Therefore, the nonprofit Save the Children Fund has bought small motorcycles so that health care workers can go to the patients (Kluger, Brunton, & Robinson, 2005).

In deciding whether to go to a doctor, we risk making two kinds of basic mistakes:

(1) We may go too quickly or too often because we overinterpret the seriousness of our physical ailments.

(2) We may ignore the symptoms of diseases that should be treated at once.

Examples are a fever that is not obviously associated with a cold or stuffy nose; signs of internal bleeding such as blood in the sputum, vomit, or bowel movement; a persistent abdominal pain, especially when it is in one spot and associated with nausea; and a stiff neck that is not associated with any physical strain or injury. At the same time, many diseases are without symptoms at certain points in the course of the illness. Hypertension, diabetes, tuberculosis, heart disease, and anemia, among others, may present few or no symptoms initially.

People who are in poor health report the most dissatisfaction with their health care. One reason may be that their physicians curtail social conversations with them and cut right to the medical dialogues (Hall, Roter, & Milburn, 1999) and ask more questions than patients (Ohtaki, Ohtaki, & Fetters, 2003). It should come as no surprise, then, that patients' and physicians' perceptions of how well physicians explain medical information differ (Hagihara, Odamaki, Nobutomo, & Tarumi, 2006) and that such encounters are often unproductive (*Harvard Health Letter*, July 2004).

Research has demonstrated that the type of physician we see also affects our desire to communicate with that physician. Female doctors spend more time with their patients, allow their patients to talk more so that more communication is exchanged, and explain medical terminology better than male doctors (*Harvard Health Letter*, May 2001).

Other research has uncovered that some individuals possess negative stereotypes of modern doctors and that such individuals are less likely to seek treatment and less likely to adhere to treatments (Bogart, Bird, Walt, Delahanty, & Figler, 2004), which brings us to our next topic, adherence to treatment.

Adhering to Treatment

Adherence to treatment regimens is *the degree to which a person's behavior (e.g., taking medications, attending treatment sessions, etc.) coincides with medical or health advice* (Raynor et al., 2007). Surprisingly, as many as one-half of all adult patients do not follow or complete the doctor's prescribed treatment (Osterberg & Blaschke, 2005). For example, Amanda had a sore throat, and before she had finished her medication, the soreness was gone. Thus, Amanda discontinued her medication early and to her dismay, the soreness and hoarseness returned. People may fail to follow the instructions given with the medicine; discontinue the medication too soon, as did Amanda; or ignore admonitions to adopt a healthier lifestyle. Interestingly, the patient's personality, gender, and socio-economic status do not seem to predict accurately who will and will not adhere to treatment plans. Patient characteristics do interact with several other factors to influence compliance. These other factors include, but are not limited to, the nature of the illness (e.g., HIV versus diabetes), patient depression (Raynor et al.), and the treatment regimen (e.g., medication versus exercise) (Christensen & Johnson, 2002).

People may fail to adhere to the prescribed treatment for many other reasons. A common reason for failure to adhere is dissatisfaction with the physician (Hall et al., 1999; *Harvard Health Letter*, July 2004). Patients who have a warm relationship with their doctor and are involved in planning the treatment are more apt to comply with the doctor's orders (Rall, Peskoff, & Byrne, 1994). Another reason patients do not follow the treatment plan is that many of them do not sufficiently understand the nature of their illness or the doctor's instructions. By contrast, when the desired treatment is explained in everyday language with easy-to-follow written instructions, patients are much more likely to comply. Patients' beliefs about a medication also influence adherence, with individuals who worry about drug dependence or long-term side effects least likely to take the medication as prescribed (Horne & Weinman, 1999). Overall, patients' reluctance to take medicine appears most related to their fear of medication and their preference to take as little medicine as possible (Pound et al., 2005).

The way the information is presented is important, too. Information can be presented or framed in *negative* (about potential losses or costs) or *positive* ways (about potential gains) (*Harvard Health Letter*, October 2004; Moxey, O'Connell, McGettigan, & Henry, 2003; Rothman & Salovey, 1997). A negatively framed message would be something like this: "If you don't stop smoking, Amanda, you are likely to die at a young age." A positively framed message is "Amanda, if you stop smoking, you'll feel better and live longer." Some scientists believe that positively framed messages from medical practitioners are best for promoting *preventive* behaviors such as sticking to a healthy diet, whereas negatively framed messages are best for facilitating *detection* behaviors such as noticing pain (Rothman & Salovey, 1997; van Assema, Martens, Ruiter, & Brug, 2001). Recent research on the framing of health messages indicates that the situation is more complicated than the mere type of frame—negative or positive. Factors such as involvement of the patient in a particular medical issue are also important (Donovan & Jalleh, 2000). An example would be pregnant women being more involved than nonpregnant women when listening to a message about the importance of infant immunizations.

PROMOTING WELLNESS

Until recently, people in the health care field made little distinction between people who were "not sick" and those who were "healthy" (Friedman, 2005). For all practical purposes, wellness was the absence of sickness. Amanda was one of these believers. She considered herself healthy despite her unhealthy lifestyle. However, in recent years there has been a growing realization that health is considerably more than the absence of a minor or major illness. Enlightened individuals today believe that **wellness** means *the positive ideal of health in which one strives to maintain and improve one's health*. To be healthy is to have the full use of one's body and mind and, despite an occasional bout of illness, to be alert, energetic, and happy to be alive even in old age. As a result, health practitioners and the public alike are beginning to think more in terms of optimum health and wellness.

Optimum health is not something you can get from your doctor, guru, lover, health food store, or wonder supplement. Positive health is something that comes mostly through your *own* efforts, aided by good genes and regular medical care. By viewing your everyday well-being in terms of the positive ideal of health, instead of merely the absence of illness, you may function better and live more enthusiastically than you would have otherwise. Activity 5–2 will help you rate your current health habits.

ACTIVITY 5–2

How Do Your Health Habits Rate?

INSTRUCTIONS: *Circle the appropriate number after each of the following statements and add up the numbers to get a total score for each section. Then check the norms at the end to determine what your score means.*

Eating habits: Almost always   Sometimes   Almost never

1. I eat a variety of foods each day, such as fruits and vegetables, whole-grain breads and cereals, lean meats, dairy products, dry peas and beans, and nuts and seeds.

            4   1   0

2. I limit the amount of fat, saturated fat, and cholesterol I eat (including fat on meats, eggs, butter, cream, shortenings, and organ meats such as liver).

            2   1   0

3. I limit the amount of salt I eat by cooking with only small amounts, not adding salt at the table, and avoiding salty snacks.

            2   1   0

4. I avoid eating too much sugar (especially frequent snacks of sticky candy or soft drinks).

            2   1   0

Eating habits score: _____

Exercise/fitness: Almost always   Sometimes   Almost never

1.   I maintain a desired weight, avoiding overweight and underweight.

           3   1   0

2.   I do vigorous exercises for 15 to 30 minutes at least three times a week (examples include running, swimming, and brisk walking).

           3   1   0

3.   I do exercises that enhance my muscle tone for 15 to 30 minutes at least three times a week (examples include yoga and calisthenics).

           2   1   0

4.   I use part of my leisure time participating in individual, family, or team activities that increase my level of fitness (such as gardening, bowling, golf, and baseball).

           2   1   0

Exercise/fitness score: _____

Alcohol and drugs: Almost always   Sometimes   Almost never

1.   I avoid drinking alcoholic beverages or I drink no more than one or two drinks a day.

           4   1   0

2.   I avoid using alcohol or other drugs (especially illegal drugs) as a way of handling stressful situations or the problems in my life.

           2   1   0

3.   I am careful not to drink alcohol when taking certain medicines (for example, medicine for sleeping, pain, colds, and allergies).

           2   1   0

4.   I read and follow the label directions when using prescribed and over-the-counter drugs.

           2   1   0

Alcohol and drugs score: _____

What your scores mean:

9–10 Excellent   6–8 Good   3–5 Mediocre   0–2 Poor

SOURCE: Adapted from U.S. Department of Health and Human Services, Public Health Service. (1981). *Health style: A self-test* (PHS 81-50155). Washington, DC: Author.

Taking Charge of Your Own Health

As Americans become better educated and enjoy greater freedom of choice, generally we want to exercise greater personal control over our own health and health care. When seeing the doctor, we don't want to be told to do this or that. Instead, we want to know the evidence and reasoning involved so we can make an informed choice. We also want solid information, without getting bogged down in a lot of technical details. As would you and Amanda, most Americans would like to live a longer life but want to enjoy it along the way. Taking the best possible care of ourselves shouldn't have to mean putting everything we enjoy on the "forbidden list." When we are ill, we want to be able to ask the right questions and evaluate the answers. When a medical decision needs to be made, we expect to be a partner in making it; thus, physician behavior can have an impact on a patient's health (Hall et al., 1999; *Harvard Health Letter*, October 2004, 2006).

Key factors in assuming greater personal responsibility for your own health include the following:

- Understanding how your body works
- Knowing how the body and mind interact
- Managing stress effectively
- Developing healthy eating and exercise habits
- Monitoring your health
- Getting periodic medical checkups
- Keeping your own medical records
- Knowing the health risks related to your family history
- Being aware of health hazards in your lifestyle, workplace, and environment
- Being an active participant in your own health care

Each individual or family should have one or more appropriate resources to be used as a guide to self-care and medical matters. Such books contain a great deal of valuable information about the body's functioning, eating and exercise habits for staying well, home health care for minor problems, and how to asses if medical help is needed. The use of the self-diagnosis symptom charts in the American Medical Association's *Family Medical Guide* is especially helpful in determining when to seek medical assistance.

Individuals can and should take charge of their lifestyles, such as their diets, to ensure better health and a longer life.

Taking charge of your own health generally involves basic changes in how you relate to the medical establishment. In traditional practice, individuals are expected to assume the "good" patient role—being cooperative, undemanding, and unquestioning. Such docile behavior often has a detrimental side effect. Patients are anxious and depressed when they have little control over their treatment. Research demonstrates that patients are more likely to adhere to treatment plans when they feel they have control or decision-making power over what happens to them medically (McDonald-Miszczak, Maki, & Gould, 2000). Furthermore, because most patients are often cooperative, doctors underestimate patients' desire for information. On the other hand, people who go to the opposite extreme and adopt a "bad" patient role—complaining and demanding a lot from their doctors—may not fare much better because their aggressive behavior usually alienates medical personnel.

Instead, individuals should become *active* participants in their health care in a *collaborative* way, by cooperating with doctors but not surrendering their own rights (*Harvard Health Letter*, 2006). The aim is to establish a working alliance between doctor and patient, with both working together for the good of the patient. Patients need to know that most doctors are willing to inform them of their medical condition and their options for treatment but that they are expected to take the initiative in asking questions. And doctors need to realize that patients who are informed of their medical problems and given an active role in deciding their course of treatment are more likely to monitor their progress and adhere to the prescribed treatment.

Eating Sensibly

An integral part of a health-producing routine is practicing good health habits such as sensible patterns of eating and drinking, keeping physically fit, getting adequate rest, and visiting a physician regularly. Because more people "kill themselves" with a knife and fork than by any other means, one of the best ways to promote good health is to eat sensibly. Unfortunately, Amanda is not a very good role model. Eating sensibly involves eating a *reasonable* amount of *healthy* food. The amount of food is often measured in **calories**—*a measurement of energy produced by food when oxidized, or "burned," in the body.* The number of calories needed each day depends on such factors as age, sex, size, and rate of metabolism. A woman in her early 20s with a desk job needs about 2,000 calories a day; a woman with a more active life needs about 2,200 calories. A man with a desk job uses about 2,500 calories; one with a fairly active job, such as a carpenter, needs about 2,800 calories. Men and women who are in strenuous jobs or in athletic training may need anywhere from 3,000 to 4,000 calories a day. Sticking to calorie counts is not easy given that high-calorie, fast-food restaurants are everywhere and portion sizes on American tables and in restaurants are increasing. Although results are mixed on studies of aging and calorie consumption in humans, some studies demonstrate that calorie restriction postpones age-related declines (Lofshult, 2006) and delays the onset of late-life diseases such as cancer and heart disease (Spindler, 2001).

A well-balanced diet includes adequate amounts of various groups of substances: proteins, carbohydrates, certain fats, vitamins, minerals, and fibers. Individuals vary in their nutritional needs because of factors such as their size, age, sex, and level of physical activity. A handy guide to eating a balanced diet is the new food guide pyramid (see www.MyPyramid.gov) issued by the United States Department of Agriculture. The pyramid puts greater emphasis on grains as found in cereal and bread, vegetables, and fruits and less emphasis on foods containing fats and sugar (see Figure 5–2).

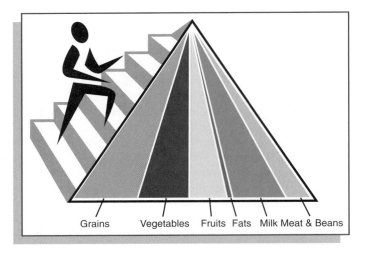

Grains   Vegetables   Fruits   Fats   Milk   Meat & Beans

FIGURE 5–2
My pyramid
Go to mypyramid.gov to create a personally customized pyramid for you.
SOURCE: www.mypyramid.gov

The new pyramid, as depicted here, is just a general representation of good nutrition. By **nutrition**, experts generally mean *a proper, balanced diet that promotes health*. The strength of the new pyramid is that you can *customize* it for your age, sex, and lifestyle by going to the web site and indicating your personal characteristics (U.S. Department of Agriculture, 2005). The results will reveal exactly how many servings of or how much of each food group you should consume. Most overweight people have poor nutrition in that they consume too many carbohydrates in the form of high-sugar foods such as donuts and high-fat food such as fast-food French fries. A more desirable diet includes generous amounts of vegetables and fruits, which provide nutrition and energy as well as fiber. Dairy products and meat, along with other protein-laden foods, are needed in fewer servings per day and are used for energy and the growth and repair of body tissue.

Getting Enough Sleep

When Amanda was in college, she sometimes stayed up all night to study for a major exam. Now that she is older and arriving home late, she also stays up late in an attempt to hear the latest gossip on talk shows. Have you ever stayed up all night? Perhaps, as Amanda does, you've missed several consecutive nights of sleep. The effects of sleep deprivation vary from one person to another. Deprived of sleep, most people make greater errors on routine tasks and experience increased drowsiness, a stronger desire to sleep, and a tendency to fall asleep easily. When they finally fall asleep, chances are they'll sleep a few hours longer than usual, but extra hours of sleep won't make up the total sleep time lost.

Our sleep/wake cycles typically follow a biochemical clock designed to help us conserve energy. Reestablishing our natural sleep cycle is more important than trying to make up all the hours of lost sleep. Although we can accommodate ourselves to a variety of changes such as shift work, jet lag, and all-night study sessions, these adjustments take a toll on our bodies as well as our sense of well-being. How much sleep do you need? Does it vary from other individuals' needs? The average person sleeps about 7 hours each night, but the need for sleep again varies from one person to another. You're probably getting enough sleep if you

(1) wake up spontaneously;

(2) feel well rested;

(3) don't have to struggle through periods of sleepiness during the day.

Perhaps you have difficulty sleeping. Box 5–5 provides tips for falling asleep faster and better.

We also need to dream, though the amount of dream time diminishes as we get older. Young adults such as Amanda spend about one-fourth of their total sleep time in dreams. Many people enjoy trying to analyze their dreams, but do dreams really have meaning? The experts disagree. Most of us are familiar with Freud's wish-fulfillment theory in which dreams are regarded as expressions of our repressed impulses or conflicts. More recent and controversial neurological theories hold that dreams are mostly the result of the spontaneous activity of neurons in the brain and that dreams have little or no psychological meaning. Another theory, cognitive theory, holds that dreams are related to the processes of thinking, learning, and memory. According to this theory, the more we learn during the day, the more we need to dream at night, which may help to explain the student's familiar complaint of never having enough sleep (Neimark, 1999). A final theory suggests that our dreams are guided by our emotional states (Hartmann, 1999).

Box 5–5

CAN'T GET TO SLEEP?

Most of us have trouble falling asleep occasionally. For some, especially older adults, it's a recurring problem. Although there is no magical solution to this age-old complaint, following are some suggestions:

- Go to bed and get up at about the same time each day. Make sure you're allowing enough time for sleep.

- Relax before bedtime. Listen to music or practice yoga. But avoid strenuous exercise.

- Keep your bedroom conducive to sleep. Make sure it's quiet and dark and at a suitable temperature.

- Avoid alcohol and sleeping pills. Although these may put you to sleep sooner, they interfere with your normal sleep cycle.

- Take a lukewarm bath before bed. Hot or cold showers tend to be too stimulating. Sleep is induced when the body's core temperature falls, so you can artificially induce this by taking a warm bath.

- When you're having trouble falling asleep, count sheep or think of something pleasant that will distract you from worrying.

- Take some honey, which releases serotonin, the biochemical that induces sleep and relaxation.

- Don't stay awake fretting that sleeplessness will harm your health.

- If your home remedies don't work, seek professional help at a sleep center.

Keeping Physically Fit

What comes to mind when you think of fitness? **Physical fitness** *is our ability to function efficiently and effectively, including both health-related and skill-related fitness components.* Do you imagine some muscular person lifting weights? Or do you think of people jogging or running along the road? Whatever you imagine, chances are that it represents only part of what is necessary for overall physical fitness. Actually, physical fitness is the *entire* human organism's ability to function efficiently and effectively and therefore to increase life expectancy. Despite common knowledge that exercise is healthful, 30 percent of the adult population is not active at all (Centers for Disease Control and Prevention, 2005). Moreover, although many people have enthusiastically embarked on vigorous exercise programs at one time or another, most do not sustain their participation.

The body responds to physical activity in ways that have important positive effects on the muscular, skeletal, cardiovascular, respiratory, and endocrine systems. These changes are consistent with a number of health benefits, including a reduced risk of premature mortality and reduced risks of coronary heart disease, hypertension, colon cancer, and diabetes mellitus. Regular participation in physical activity also appears to reduce depression and anxiety (Crone, Smith, & Gough, 2005), improve mood, and enhance ability to perform daily tasks throughout the life span (Centers for Disease Control and Prevention, 2005). Physical fitness also provides us with a sense of mastery, helps us overcome sad moods, and can even help fend off some forms of cancer (Fischer, 1999). Fitness also reduces feelings of depression and anxiety (Centers for Disease Control and Prevention, 2004).

The risks associated with physical activity must also be considered. The most common health problems that have been associated with physical activity are injuries, which can occur with excessive amounts of activity or with suddenly beginning an activity for which the body is not conditioned. Much more serious associated health problems (e.g., heart attack) are rarer, occurring primarily among sedentary people with advanced coronary disease who engage in strenuous activity to which they are unaccustomed. Sedentary people, especially those with preexisting health conditions, who wish to increase their physical activity should check with their physician first and gradually build up to the desired level of activity (National Center for Chronic Disease Prevention and Health Promotion, 1999). Table 5–2 shows some of the calories you can burn doing everyday activities, many of which you may enjoy doing. There are few reasons to be completely inactive!

In selecting your personal exercise program, you may find it helpful to observe the following points:

1. Identify your personal physical fitness needs.   A good way to do so is to consult someone in the physical education department of your college or a specialist in one of the physical fitness centers in your community.

2. Select personalized physical exercises to make exercise more enjoyable. Choose physical activities that are related to your interests, needs, and personality. If you are a sociable person, consider a group activity such as volleyball. Choose an activity that feels good to you, regardless of what others do.

3. Vary your activities.   By varying your activities you can include ones that will develop different aspects of physical fitness. This variation also helps to keep exercise interesting and enjoyable. Usually, changes in the weather and the seasons along with availability of facilities suggest some variation in your exercise program.

TABLE 5–2	
EXAMPLES OF MODERATE AMOUNTS OF ACTIVITY THAT WILL HELP YOU STAY FIT	
Common Chores	**Sporting Activities**
Washing and waxing a car for 45–60 minutes	Playing volleyball for 45–60 minutes
Washing windows or floors for 45–60 minutes	Playing touch football for 45 minutes
Gardening for 30–45 minutes	Walking 1 3/4 miles in 35 minute (20 min/mile)
Wheeling self in wheelchair 30–40 minutes	Basketball (shooting baskets) 30 minutes
Pushing a stroller 1 1/2 miles in 30 minutes	Bicycling 5 miles in 30 minutes
Raking leaves for 30 minutes	Dancing fast (social) for 30 minutes
Walking 2 miles in 30 minutes (15 min/mile)	Water aerobics for 30 minutes
Shoveling snow for 15 minutes	Swimming laps for 20 minutes
Stairwalking for 15 minutes	Basketball (playing game) for 15–20 minutes
	Bicycling 4 miles in 15 minutes
	Jumping rope for 15 minutes
	Running 1 1/2 miles in 15 minutes (10 min/mile)

SOURCE: Department of Health and Human Services. (2006). *Guide to physical activity.* http://www.nhlbi.nih.gov/health/public/heart/obesity/lose_wt/phy_act.htm.

4. Exercise regularly.   It's best to set aside a time and place for your exercise activities, making exercise part of your daily routine. It's also important to perform your exercises to a level that will promote optimal fitness, usually a minimum of 20 to 30 minutes three times a week. For people who are unable to set aside 30 minutes for physical activity, shorter episodes are clearly better than none (National Center for Chronic Disease Prevention and Health Promotion, 1999).

5. Periodically evaluate and modify your routine.   As time passes, your needs and interests change. Shifts in your work schedule and family responsibilities may also dictate a change in your exercise program. Then, too, your age and overall level of stress should be kept in mind. Listen to your body. Assess how you feel.

Physical fitness is a vital part of the sense of wholeness mentioned earlier, but from all that you have read, it should also be clear that your overall well-being includes other considerations, such as eating habits, work schedules, lifestyles, awareness of health hazards and stress, personal attitudes, and morale.

Finding Social Support

One other means by which we can remain healthy is to *affiliate with others such as friends and family to find comfort and advice,* in other words to seek **social support**. Individuals like Amanda who are sociable are generally healthier than those who are not. Said another way, individuals who have sturdy social support networks are healthier (Jorm, 2005). For example, elderly people with good social support networks report better health (Krause, 2006), and persons suffering from severe brain trauma rehabilitate better with good social support (Tomberg, Toomela, Pulver, & Tikk, 2005). On the contrary, individuals who are socially isolated are at greater risk for health problems than those who are socially engaged. Some caution is needed here, though, because socializing and seeking social support is not for everyone. Some research demonstrates that individuals who were securely attached as children cope effectively via social support but those who experienced other forms of attachment may be uncomfortable seeking social support as adults (Bachman & Bippus, 2005). Attachment styles are discussed in some detail in the chapter on love and commitment.

SUMMARY

BODY IMAGE

Although Americans may be healthy and fit, they are not necessarily satisfied with their looks. Weight is a major factor, and about one-half of men and women are dissatisfied with their weight. Many Americans are dissatisfied with their bodies because their weight is at odds with the prevailing ideal of slimness in our society as promoted by our media. A somewhat higher proportion of women than men are dissatisfied with their looks, largely because our society encourages women to hold themselves to a stricter standard of thinness than men.

PSYCHOLOGICAL FACTORS AND PHYSICAL ILLNESS

The growing acceptance of mind-body unity suggests that psychological factors may play a significant role in almost any physical ailment, not just in the traditional psychosomatic illnesses. The detrimental effects of stress tend to weaken our immune system, thereby making us more susceptible to illness. At the same time, there is increasing evidence that we may bolster our resistance to stress and illness by harnessing the powers of the mind—our thoughts, attitudes, emotions, and sense of control.

Other major health hazards are related to lifestyle and include obesity, cigarette smoking, and alcohol and drug abuse. Obesity and being overweight, affecting over half of all Americans, are associated with an increased risk of illness and death from a variety of causes, including diabetes, high blood pressure, and coronary heart disease.

Many Americans smoke cigarettes. Cigarette smoking is a major factor in heart disease, lung cancer, and emphysema and may be one entry point to illicit drug use. Three-fourths of American adult men and two-thirds of women drink alcoholic beverages. Automobile accidents involving alcohol are still a leading cause of death among youths, and people with alcohol-related ailments fill half of the occupied beds in American hospitals.

COPING WITH ILLNESS

In evaluating the seriousness of our body complaints, we tend to rely on a decision-making process with three stages: (1) noticing and interpreting symptoms, (2) seeking professional help when needed, and (3) adhering to the prescribed treatment. Depending on culture, ethnicity, race, and gender, individuals differ in their tendency to label body aches and pains as symptoms of serious illness and subsequently seek help. Though men are generally more reluctant than women to do so, people are more likely to see a doctor when they have severe, disabling symptoms rather than minor ones, especially in the lower half of the body. As many as half of those who get professional help do not complete the prescribed treatment for a variety of reasons.

PROMOTING WELLNESS

There is an increased emphasis on optimal health and wellness rather than simply the absence of illness. To be healthy is to have the full use of one's body and mind, despite an occasional bout of illness—and to be alert, energetic, and happy to be alive even in old age. An important factor in the pursuit of positive health is the willingness to take charge of our own health, including greater personal responsibility and more collaboration with health care professionals in all matters pertaining to health.

An integral part of producing a healthy lifestyle is practicing good health habits. Eating sensibly involves both the amount and the kind of food we eat, including a balanced diet that provides the necessary nutrition and calories for someone of our age, size, and lifestyle. Keeping physically fit usually involves following a personalized exercise program especially suited to our interests and needs. Social contact and support is also healthy for most people. The pursuit of wellness, though it is rarely fully achieved, may enable each of us to function better than we would have otherwise.

SELF-TEST

1. In terms of body image, the greatest proportion of men and women feel the most dissatisfied with their
   a. face.
   b. upper torso.
   c. mid-torso.
   d. arm and thigh flab.

2. A positive body image is strongly associated with
   a. higher self-esteem.
   b. height.
   c. higher intelligence.
   d. sexual interest in the opposite sex.

3. The prevalence of obesity among American adults tends to rise with higher
   a. education.
   b. age.
   c. socioeconomic status.
   d. income.

4. At least one of every five chronic heavy drinkers of alcohol develops
   a. diabetes.
   b. heart attack.
   c. throat cancer.
   d. cirrhosis of the liver.

5. People most likely to label their physical symptoms as an illness are high in
   a. hypochondriasis.
   b. self-esteem.
   c. extroversion.
   d. sensation seeking.

6. About half of the people who discover they have an illness
   a. die within 3 months.
   b. seek professional help for it.
   c. become depressed over their condition.
   d. complete the prescribed treatment for it.

7. Assuming greater responsibility for your health involves
   a. getting periodic checkups.
   b. using only name-brand drugs.
   c. being a good patient by not asking doctors too many questions.
   d. All of these are responsible behaviors.

8. People with high blood cholesterol tend to eat a lot of food with
   a. carbohydrates.   c. fats.
   b. proteins.   d. fiber.

9. The recommended amount of exercise for a healthy adult is
   a. 10 minutes a day.
   b. 1 hour every day.
   c. 30 minutes three to five times a week.
   d. Healthy adults do not need to exercise.

10. Finding social support
   a. has no effect on health.   c. has negative effects on health.
   b. has little effect on health.   d. usually has positive effects on health.

EXERCISES

1. *Examine yourself in a mirror.* Undress and look at yourself in a full-length mirror. First, move up to the mirror and examine your face closely. What do you most notice about your face? Then step back and examine your entire body. Turn around slowly, looking at yourself from each side and then at your rear. Which aspects of your body do you like the most? Are there parts of your body you have difficulty accepting? All things considered, how satisfied are you with your body?

2. *Do you practice good eating habits?* Describe your eating habits in terms of the calories consumed each day and a balanced diet. If you're not sure how many calories you consume, keep a daily count for at least 3 days and take an average. How does your calorie count compare to the average for someone like yourself as indicated in the text? Do you also choose foods from each of the major food areas as described in the chapter?

3. *Describe your personal exercise habits.* How much exercise do you get in the course of your daily activities? Would you agree that everyone needs to be physically active on a regular basis? If you have a personalized exercise program, describe it in a paragraph or two.

4. *Identify your biggest health hazard.* Are you guilty of one of the common health hazards, such as overeating, poor nutrition, smoking, drinking, or drug abuse? If so, what are you doing about it? Try eliminating this hazard for 5 consecutive days and see if you feel better about yourself and your health. Better yet, try to eliminate it over the long term.

5. *Do you suffer from a chronic ailment?* Do you have to cope with some type of chronic or recurring condition, such as an allergy, asthma, arthritis, hypertension, diabetes, migraine headaches, or ulcers? How well are you managing such ailments? Are you aware of the psychosocial factors that may influence your ailments, such as environmental stress and your emotions? What are you doing to improve your condition? Does this ailment affect your self-esteem?

6. *How much control do you exercise over your health?* Do you believe you can minimize your chances of getting sick by practicing good nutrition, regular exercise, positive attitudes, and stress management? Or do you feel that coming down with a cold or the flu is mostly a matter of luck?

7. *Do you adhere to prescribed treatments?* When you are placed on a treatment regimen, do you follow doctor's orders? If not, why not? Once you have assessed your reasons for noncompliance, determine whether they are legitimate or not.

QUESTIONS FOR SELF-REFLECTION

1. Which part of your body or face has been the most difficult for you to accept?

2. Do you take care of your body?

3. What aspect of your eating habits would you most like to change?

4. Do you enjoy regular, vigorous physical exercise? If not, why not? How could you alter the latter situation?

5. What is your worst health hazard?

6. If you're a smoker, how many times have you tried to quit? What is it that keeps you from quitting permanently?

7. Are you aware that the use of alcohol easily becomes a health hazard? Be honest; do you have a drug or alcohol problem?

8. Do you often find that a cold or flu was preceded by a period of intense emotional stress?

9. Would you agree that a healthy body and a sound mind go together?

10. Were you securely attached as a child? Do you find that you prefer social support or would you rather cope with your problems alone?

FOR FURTHER INFORMATION

RECOMMENDED READINGS

American Medical Association. (2004). *Family medical guide.* Hoboken, NJ: Wiley. A book with up-to-date health care advice from the top association for American physicians.

GREGSON, D., & EFRAN, J. S. (2002). *The Tao of sobriety: Helping you to recover from alcohol and drug addiction.* New York: Thomas Dunne. A classic that helps individuals recognize when they suffer from addiction and abuse as well as how they can tackle these issues.

HIRKOWITZ, M., SMITH, P. B., & DEMENT, W. C. (2004). *Sleep disorders for dummies.* For Dummies. Hoboken, NJ: Wiley. The average person's guide to recognizing and overcoming sleep disorders.

HOEGER, W. W. K., & HOEGER, S. A. (2007). *Fitness and wellness.* Belmont, CA: Wadsworth. A comprehensive fitness and wellness book that also comes with ancillaries such as a log book and a personalized health profile.

SARAFINO, E. P. (2005). *Health psychology: Biopsychosocial perspectives.* Hoboken, NJ: Wiley. A textbook in the zeitgeist field of health psychology, which forms the basis for much of this chapter.

WEB SITES AND THE INTERNET

http://www.nlm.nih.gov/medlineplus/wellnessandlifestyle.html A government web site for links to wellness and health-related information on a plethora of topics, which are listed alphabetically.

http://www.firstpath.com   The site provides valuable diet and fitness tips. It claims to help balance body, mind and soul.

http://www.healthfinder.gov   A site provided by the government that you can utilize to find information prepared by health agencies under various health topics.

http://www.cdc.gov   The official site for the Centers for Disease Control and Prevention. There is a wealth of information on all types of health concerns as well as links to other sites related to health and wellness.

http://www.seekwellness.com   This site provides lots of tips on all types of health and wellness issues such as fitness, weight control, sexuality, and nutrition.

CHAPTER 6

Taking Charge

MASTERY AND PERSONAL CONTROL
Perceived Control
Consequences of Perceived
    Control
Misperception and Maladjustment
Learned Optimism

PERSONAL RESOLVE AND DECISION
MAKING
The Process of Decision Making
Making Better Decisions

DECISIONS AND PERSONAL GROWTH
Identifying the Basic Decisions in
    Your Life
Making New Decisions
Some Practical Applications

SUMMARY
SELF-TEST
EXERCISES
QUESTIONS FOR SELF-REFLECTION
FOR FURTHER INFORMATION

Stan, a 46-year-old married student, was facing an important choice. It seems he had lost his job as a foreman in a steel plant during the past year. Then, after months of unsuccessful job hunting and agonizing over his future, Stan had decided to enroll in college to become an engineer. He worked as a handyman part-time to pay the family bills. Recently and unexpectedly, Stan's former employer called and offered him a chance to return to work. "It's a tempting offer," Stan said to himself. "But I'm not sure I want to go back." Stan acknowledged that by taking back his old job he would be able to support his wife and two small children more adequately. "But then I'd always worry about when the next layoff was coming," he thought. At the same time, Stan was under great stress attending school full-time; he was having a difficult time paying bills, and he was constantly tired. Nor was there any assurance he would get a good job as an engineer once he got his degree.

MASTERY AND PERSONAL CONTROL

As you can see, Stan is caught in a major life dilemma. His case illustrates two important concepts in this chapter—personal control and decision making. Like Stan, if we perceive that a goal is attainable, we usually take charge (seek control) and surge into action. In other words, we feel some sense of control or personal mastery over our lives. When we are doubtful that a goal is attainable, we are less likely to feel we have control and less likely to undertake the actions necessary to achieve the goal (Jackson, Weiss, Lundquist, & Soderlind, 2002). Thus, we have to make both large and small decisions in our lives, based in part on whether we perceive we have mastery and control over various events.

Stan, like many of us, is striving to attain a greater degree of self-mastery, or, as psychologists have labeled it, personal control, over his life. **Personal control** means *the achieved amount of control we have over our lives; this term is often synonymous with perceived control.* Stan resents being at the mercy of a large corporation and having a job that is so vulnerable to the ups and downs of the economy. He realizes that acquiring greater mastery over his life means facing up to important life choices. It's not simply a matter of whether to accept his old job or to remain in school, as hard a choice as this is. It goes deeper than that. Such decisions also involve important value choices in regard to what he wants out of life, what he's willing to settle for, and how hard he's willing to work to get what he wants. It's no surprise that this has been a trying time in Stan's life, with many sleepless nights and numerous heart-to-heart talks with his wife, who supports his decision to attend college. You may be interested to know that eventually Stan refused the offer of his old job and continued his education.

Stan's experience reminds us of the importance of personal control and of the crucial role of decision making in our lives. We'll begin the chapter by exploring the topic of personal control and its implications for personal adjustment and growth. Then we'll devote the rest of the chapter to the process of decision making, including how we can improve our decision-making skills to facilitate our personal growth.

Personal control has become a very important issue today for many reasons. First, our lives, just as is Stan's, are increasingly shaped by large, impersonal bureaucracies, such as the government and business corporations; they often have more impact on the economy than we do and thus on our personal lives. Then, too, there is greater awareness that our lives are at the mercy of events or conditions beyond our immediate control, such as economic recession, terrorism, or hurricanes. At the same time, the civil rights movement and the other movements that have followed in its wake have taught us that individuals *can* gain greater mastery over their lives by active participation in the democratic process, like participating in demonstrations and boycotts or promoting certain pieces of legislation. In a democratic society that nourishes independence and freedom of choice, it is well to remember that each of us has considerable power to shape our destinies through personal decisions, such as the choosing of a career, deciding where to live, and finding a marriage partner, as well as through changing our lifestyles and values.

Perceived Control

The aspect of personal control that has received the most attention from psychologists, primarily because it is the most accessible to empirical investigation (Double, 2004), is **perceived control**—*the belief that we can influence the occurrence of events in our environment that affect our lives.* In other words, we sometimes feel or like to feel that we have control over fate, even if we really do not. Perceived control is very important because it appears to be the one type of control that accounts for our motivation to behave in a certain fashion (Jewell & Kidwell, 2005). For example, Stan *perceived* that a better education would give him more control over his destiny, although this was not a certainty.

An important related concept to perceived control is **locus of control**, which means *the source from which an individual believes control over life events originates—either within the person or with something outside of the person.* Perceived control is similar to a concept introduced elsewhere in this book (Ajzen, 2002; Judge, Erez, Bono, & Thoreson, 2002),

self-efficacy, *belief in one's capabilities to organize and execute the courses of action required to produce given attainments* (Bandura, 1997).

Psychologists have identified two sources of perceived control (Zuckerman, Knee, Kieffer, & Gagne, 2004). One is an **internal locus of control**, *in which the individual believes he or she has control over life events*. Stan exemplifies a person with an internal sense of control. He believed that if he studied hard and obtained his degree, he and his family would have a better future. The other source of control is **external locus of control**, *in which the individual believes that something outside of him- or herself, such as other individuals, fate, or various external situations, controls life events*. One of Stan's engineering classmates exemplifies this type of control, especially after she did not do well in her first engineering course. She believed that no matter how hard she studied, she would never end up with an engineering degree because of the stigma held by certain professors against women in the engineering field.

A large body of research indicates that perception of control is related to various beneficial outcomes, such as improved well-being, better performance on various tasks, and better coping with adversity (Zuckerman et al., 2004). For example, individuals with an internalized locus of causality or control are more likely to maintain physical fitness routines (Chatzisarantis, Hagger, Biddle, & Karageorghis, 2002) and better cope with trauma (Frazier, Steward, & Mortensen, 2004). Similarly, individuals with an internal locus of control cope better with pain (Vallerand, Hasenau, Templin, & Collins-Bohler, 2005) and with bereavement (Ong, Bergeman, & Bisconti, 2005). On the other hand, Griffin, Fuhrer Stansfeld, and Marmot (2002) replicated much research that shows individuals who believe in external control or low personal control are more prone to depression and anxiety.

Internalized control, however, is very "American" (O'Connor & Shimizu, 2002; Yamaguchi, Gelfand, Ohashi, & Zemba, 2005). We might expect that in Eastern or Asian cultures, which are more collective and interdependent rather than individualistic, an internal locus of control is not as appreciated or expected. For instance, Liu and Yussen (2005) found that Chinese students were far more likely than American students to attribute school success to luck, probably because of differences in religion, school feedback, and life philosophy. Likewise, Yamaguchi et al. found that Japanese individuals have an exaggerated sense of collective (group) control as compared to Americans, who possess an exaggerated sense of individual or personal control.

Other differences in locus of control exist. Men have a greater sense of internal control than women, especially when older men and women are compared (Ross & Mirowsky, 2002). Husbands report feeling more mastery (control) than do wives (Cassidy & Davies, 2003). People in developing countries perceive more externalized control than members of industrialized societies (Matsumoto, 2000). Individuals from Western cultures may prefer and have more experience with primary control, whereas individuals reared in Asian cultures may prefer and experience secondary control. **Primary control** *refers to actions directed at attempting to change the world to fit one's needs and desires*; **secondary control** *involves the individual utilizing processes directed at making him- or herself fit into the world better* (Ashman, Shiomura, & Levy, 2006). Some research also indicates age differences in primary and secondary control, with older individuals more likely to use secondary control strategies (Ashman et al.). Given such differences, research reveals that for most people, optimal adjustment is achieved *when the amount of actual control matches the desired need for control* (Conway, Vickers, & French, 1992).

Research also demonstrates that individuals high in external control can learn to develop a sense of internal locus of control if internal control is deemed best. Cone and

Owens (1991) enrolled freshmen at risk for failing or dropping out of college in a study skills and adjustment course. At the end of the semester, these students' grade point averages were compared to students who were also at risk but who were not enrolled in the special course. Compared to students not in the class, the students who were registered had higher grades and had shifted to more internalized loci of control. Manger, Eikeland, and Asbjornsen (2002) dipped lower into the age pool and retrained children with an external locus of control to develop more perceived internal control.

How much control would you say you have over your personal life? To check on your perception, complete the personal control survey in Activity 6–1.

Consequences of Perceived Control

Research has shown that the presence or absence of perceived control or self-mastery has important consequences in our lives, over and above the actual control available to us in a given situation. When we believe we can affect actual outcomes in our lives, choose among them, cope with the consequences, and understand them, we behave in a significantly different way than when we don't hold this belief (Jackson, Weiss, et al., 2002; Jewell & Kidwell, 2005). One such difference is in level of persistence on a task. Stan, for example, sincerely believed that *if he studied hard* he *would* earn a college degree that would eventually garner his family and him a better standard of living. Thus, Stan studied hard in college and persisted at his studies even though now and then he was discouraged by a below-average grade.

People who possess a high degree of perceived control tend to exhibit certain characteristics (Zuckerman et al., 2004). First and foremost, they are likely to seek knowledge and information about the events that affect their lives. Feeling they are in control of their lives, they make greater efforts to acquire information about themselves and their environment. For instance, when facing surgery or a serious illness, patients with a high degree of perceived control are especially likely to seek information about their condition, to ask questions of the doctors and nurses, and to make use of the resources available to them. This is one of the most consistent findings in studies of

People high in perceived control are more likely to take steps that maximize their health and well being, such as avoiding talking on a cell phone while driving.

ACTIVITY 6–1

HOW MUCH SELF-CONTROL DO YOU HAVE?

INSTRUCTIONS: *This survey is designed to inspire you to think about how much perceived control you have. For each statement below, circle T for "true" or F for "false" as the statement applies to you.*

T   F   **1.** I like to put off decisions as long as I can because situations affecting the decision might change without warning.

T   F   **2.** The amount of time I study is unrelated to my grades and whether I leave a favorable impression on my professors.

T   F   **3.** Some people are just born lucky; others are not so lucky and in fact seem to be jinxed.

T   F   **4.** If people like you, they like you. If they don't, they don't, so there is little point in trying to woo them as friends.

T   F   **5.** My health is a matter of how many sick people I am around or whether there is a surge of illness in the community.

T   F   **6.** Whether I take care of it or not, something is bound to go wrong at my home once in a while.

T   F   **7.** People are born good or bad and rarely change over their life span.

T   F   **8.** Even if I am in good shape, factors outside of me, such as the weather and others' competitiveness, keep me from performing well in competitive events.

T   F   **9.** I am rather superstitious; I believe in bad omens (such as black cats) and good-luck charms (such as four-leaf clovers).

T   F   **10.** There are so many bad drivers on the road that I am bound to be involved in a car accident sooner or later.

T   F   **11.** If I carefully consider my options for major decisions, I know I can make the correct decision.

T   F   **12.** When my friends and I disagree, I know that we will still be friends because I can argue my points in a reasonable manner.

T   F   **13.** If people just keep trying, eventually good things will happen for them.

T   F   **14.** When I am shopping for a hard-to-find item, my persistence typically pays off and I find what I need.

T   F   **15.** I believe I have good judgment and that in hard times my common sense will prevail.

T   F   **16.** I am a firm believer in American resilience; we can overcome negative events such as terrorist attacks.

T   F   **17.** There are times when I feel really angry when things go wrong, but I know I can control my temper and make things better.

T   F   **18.** When I meet a stranger, I feel that I can befriend this person if I so desire.

T   F   **19.** If a crisis occurred, I would be fine because I have the wherewithal to overcome it.

T   F   **20.** If I found myself at a job that was stressful or unappealing, I would take measures to find another and perhaps better job.

SCORING: This scale was designed for this book to encourage you to examine your level of perceived control over your life. Items 1–10 were phrased in the negative, indicating low perceived control. Items 11–20 were phrased in the affirmative, indicating higher levels of perceived control. Fill in the blanks below to determine your perceived level of control.

Total "Fs" or falses for items 1–10 _____

Total "Ts" or trues for items 11–20 _____

Grand Total = _____

INTERPRETATION: The higher your grand total, the more you feel you take charge of your own life. With the highest possible score being 20, a score of 1–5 suggests that you perceive little or no control over your life; a score of 6–10 indicates that you have some doubts that you possess control; a score of 11–15 signifies you believe you have reasonable control; and a score of 16–20 may demonstrate that you perceive high levels of control over your life. Remember that this scale is designed solely to stimulate some thought about your own life. If you scored on the low end (i.e., low perceived control), you might think about how you can increase actual or perceived control over your life by using some of the ideas in this chapter. If you scored at the very high end, consider whether you suffer from the illusion of control.

perceived control. Second, people high in perceived control are likely to attribute responsibility to themselves and to their abilities and efforts rather than to luck or the environment, at least in regard to desirable outcomes. When Stan received high grades in college, he readily attributed them to his hard work and intelligence. Third, people high in perceived control are resistant to social influence and are more likely to take part in social action that helps others. Stan, for example, ignored his brother's chuckles when teased about returning to college only to "ogle the young coeds." Stan instead found time to volunteer at the Special Olympics held each year on the college campus. And finally, individuals high in perceived control such as Stan are strongly achievement-oriented. They appear to work harder at intellectual and performance tasks, and their efforts are rewarded with better grades than those with less perceived control.

As you might expect, there is a strong positive relationship between perceived mastery or self-control and personal adjustment (Jackson, Weiss, et al., 2002; Zuckerman et al., 2004). In American society, individuals high in perceived control tend to be less anxious, better adjusted, and less likely to be classified with psychiatric labels than those with less perceived control. Perhaps the active, self-reliant qualities of those high in mastery lead to the kinds of successes that promote adjustment and growth. Or it may be that believing that one is in charge of one's destiny results in less anxiety and better adjustment.

People high in perceived control also use more effective strategies for coping with stress (Zuckerman et al., 2004). For example, individuals high in perceived mastery tend to use positive coping strategies, such as making a plan of action and sticking to it, taking one step at a time, or getting professional help and doing what is recommended (e.g., Cooper, Okamura, & McNeil, 1995). In contrast, people low in perceived control are more apt to use maladaptive strategies, such as wishing the problem would go away; blaming themselves; and seeking relief through overreacting, drinking, or abusing drugs (Blum, 1998). In the long run, the use of more effective coping strategies promotes better adjustment and growth (e.g., Aspinwall & Taylor, 1992; Zuckerman et al.).

People high in perceived control also are more likely to take steps that will maximize their health and well-being and minimize the risk of illness (Zuckerman et al., 2004). Heth and Somer (2002) report that people with high mastery awareness perceive they have less stress and better health; such individuals also think in ways that enable them to manage environmental demands in more effective ways. These individuals are especially apt to seek information about health maintenance, engage in preventive health practices, adopt more positive attitudes about physical exercise, and participate in physical exercise more regularly. Stan, for example, realized that his college studies and his part-time job were creating stress, so he often went for what he called "stress management walks" when he came home from his day's classes.

People who believe they are in charge of their lives are likely to refrain from or give up the habit of smoking, to successfully complete weight-reduction programs, and to cooperate with prescribed treatment for medical problems. In regard to substance abuse, perceived self-control is a reliable predictor of who will complete the program and who will drop out. High perceived control also helps to predict who will succeed in overcoming eating disorders and successfully recover from the trauma of heart attacks. Finally, people who feel empowered in their personal lives also demonstrate a relatively high level of happiness or subjective well-being (Klonowicz, 2001).

Misperception and Maladjustment

Unfortunately, the misperception of personal control usually tends to have negative consequences. For instance, some individuals habitually believe they have even less control over their lives than they really do (Gilbert, Brown, Pinel, & Wilson, 2000), and thus they prematurely surrender potential self-mastery available to them. Others, even in the same situation, may go to the opposite extreme: Believing they exercise greater control than they actually do, they set themselves up for frustration and eventual disappointment (Seligman, 1994). In both cases, as you will see, such mistaken beliefs about personal control lead to maladaptive behavior (Zuckerman et al., 2004).

When people repeatedly encounter bad outcomes regardless of what they do, such as losing a job because of company layoffs, they tend to experience a diminished sense of personal control, thereby attributing too little control to themselves. Suppose that no matter how hard Stan studied when he first entered college, he failed every test. Stan might come to think that he could not succeed in college no matter what he did.

Martin Seligman (1981), who has studied this problem extensively, refers to this phenomenon as **learned helplessness**—*a maladaptive passivity that frequently follows an individual's experience with uncontrollable events.* In a series of now classic studies, Seligman exposed animals to a sequence of uncontrollable shocks. Then, 24 hours later, the animals were tested in a "shuttle box." Animals could "turn off" the shocks by moving from one end of the box to another, that is, by shuttling. Most animals learned how to shuttle with little difficulty. However, animals previously exposed to uncontrollable shocks failed to learn how to escape. They just sat there passively absorbing the shocks. They had *learned to be helpless.* In contrast, animals exposed to similar shocks they could control had no trouble learning how to escape.

Seligman (1988) points out that learned helplessness also occurs among people. Studies have shown that a host of psychological and physical difficulties follow a series of negative events outside a person's control, like unemployment, accidents, illnesses, death of a spouse, terrorism, and victimization. However, uncontrollable events in themselves do not necessarily produce learned helplessness. The crucial matter consists of *how* people explain these events. To the extent they offer a permanent ("It's going to last forever"), universal ("This screws up everything"), and internal ("It's me") explanation for bad events, people tend to surrender control over their lives prematurely and respond poorly to such events when they occur. Accordingly, learned helplessness is associated with a variety of ills, including depression, academic failure, bureaucratic apathy, and premature death.

At the other extreme are people who believe they exercise more control over their lives than they actually do. In some cases, people exaggerate the degree of control they possess when outcomes are positive. Such overestimates of personal control tend to be fairly commonplace (Thompson, 1999; Yamaguchi et al., 2005). People often take more credit for good outcomes than they probably deserve, perhaps as a way of enhancing their self-regard. In other cases, people subscribe to the **illusion of control**, *believing they exert control over what is really a chance-determined event*—such as winning a lottery. From where does this overestimation come? Situational factors such as the familiarity of the situation and past successes influence overestimation. Likewise, personal factors such as a depressed mood or, as mentioned, living in a collective society also affect the illusion of control.

It is probably wise to recognize what we can and cannot effectively change or control (Seligman, 1994). When we want to change or break our bad habits, such as cigarette smoking, experts suggest that we focus on long-term negative consequences and minimize short-term rewards. In other words, we should take a rather futuristic orientation (Chapman, 1999).

Learned Optimism

A helpful way of achieving optimal but realistic perceived control can be seen in what Martin Seligman (1992) calls **learned optimism**, defined as *a learned way of explaining both good and bad life events that in turn enhances our perceived control and adaptive responses to them.* Optimism relates to control in that the greater control people perceive over future events, the greater their optimism (Klein & Helwig-Larson, 2002; Ratelle, Vallerand, Chantal, & Provencher, 2004). Optimism is another personal dimension that has been linked to good adjustment (Jackson, Weiss, et al., 2002; Ratelle et al.). Optimism is related to better problem solving under stress (Amirkhan, Risinger, & Swickert, 1995), ego resiliency (Klohnen, 1996), better physical health

(Cerrato, 2001; Chang, 1996; Matthews, Raikkonen, Sutton-Tyrell, & Kuller, 2004), active coping and seeking of social support when appropriate (Aspinwall & Taylor, 1992), and overall psychological well-being (Bood, Archer, & Norlander, 2004; Scheier & Carver, 1993; Ratelle et al.).

As mentioned earlier, Seligman, along with other cognitive theorists, holds that it is not life events in themselves that overwhelm us. Rather, it is our beliefs and interpretations of them and, in turn, our subsequent responses that most affect our lives. Consequently, in learned optimism, the emphasis is on *interpreting life events in a reasonably accurate way* to enhance our perceived control and, thus, our adaptive responses. This goal is accomplished primarily by modifying our explanatory style, that is, the way we explain life events to ourselves (Jackson, Weiss, et al., 2002). The term *learned* precedes the word *optimism* because optimism can be learned. Parents can teach their children optimism by instructing them in problem-solving skills and adaptive coping skills and by modeling optimistic thinking for their children (Jackson, Pratt, Hunsberger, & Pancer, 2005; Scheier & Carver, 1993).

The three main categories of explanatory style are *permanence* (How long will the event last?), *pervasiveness* (How much does it affect me?), and *personalization* (How much at fault am I?). However, there are two polar meanings within each category, one meaning being preferable to the other, depending on whether you are dealing with a negative or positive life event. For instance, suppose Stan's best friend hasn't returned his phone calls all day, which is understandably a negative event. If Stan interpreted this situation as something that is permanent ("I guess he isn't ever going to call back"), pervasive ("Well, there goes my whole day"), and personal ("No wonder he doesn't call back, I'm so selfish and inconsiderate"), Stan would tend to feel depressed all day. However, if this situation were viewed differently, it might not bother Stan, for example, if he interpreted the same event as temporary ("He may be especially busy today"), specific ("Not having my phone call returned doesn't make or break my entire day"), and external ("Not returning my calls probably has more to do with his schedule than his attitude toward me").

In contrast, the preferred way of explaining positive or good events is the opposite of that used for negative events. You interpret positive events in terms of that which is permanent, universal, and internal, that is, more attributable to your own efforts than to circumstances. For instance, suppose Stan did exceptionally well on an essay exam. Regarding his performance as temporary ("It was my lucky day"), specific ("It happened to be an easy test, nothing more"), and external ("The professor liked me") would tend to undermine Stan's self-confidence by attributing his success mostly to circumstances. However, if Stan regarded his success as permanent ("I always study hard"), universal ("A good essay is one of the many things I do well"), and internal ("I think and write well"), his self-esteem would be enhanced and he would perceive control by giving himself sufficient credit for his success.

Although there are clear benefits to learned optimism, there is also a danger, namely, whether or not changing beliefs about failure from internal to external ("It wasn't my fault . . . it was bad luck") will undermine personal responsibility. As a result, Seligman (1992) does not advocate changing beliefs from internal to external in a wholesale manner, although there is one condition under which it is best to do so, namely, depression. When people become depressed, they tend to assume more responsibility, or more accurately, self-blame, for bad events than is warranted (Peterson & Vaidya, 2001). Thus, if people are to change, the internal dimension is less crucial than that of permanence. If you believe the cause of your trouble is permanent, such as the lack of intelligence or talent, you will not act to change it. But if you believe the cause is temporary, such as too little effort or a bad mood, you can act to effect a change. Similarly, surface problems are easier to change than in-depth problems (Seligman, 1994).

Furthermore, Seligman (1992) emphasizes that learned optimism is not an absolute, unconditional optimism to be blindly applied to all situations. Instead, it is a flexible optimism that is more appropriate in some situations than in others. An optimistic explanatory style tends to be appropriate in the following situations:

- If you're in a situation that involves achievement, such as writing a paper, getting a promotion, or winning a game, it helps to be optimistic. If you're concerned about how you will feel, that is, about keeping up your morale or fighting off discouragement and depression, emphasize the positive.

- If you're under chronic stress and your physical health is an issue, an optimistic outlook becomes crucial.

- If you want to lead, inspire others, or gain people's confidence, it's better to use optimism. However, there are also times when optimism is not appropriate.

- If your goal involves planning for a risky and uncertain future, do not use optimism.

- If your goal is to counsel others whose future is dim, do not use optimism initially.

- If you want to appear sympathetic to people's troubles, do not start with optimism, although, once confidence and empathy are established, optimism may help.

The basic guideline for choosing optimism or not is to ask what *the cost of failure* is in the particular situation. When the cost of failure is high, optimism is probably the wrong strategy, for example, the partygoer deciding to drive home after drinking too much. When the cost of failure is low, optimism is more appropriate, for example, the sales agent who decides to make one more call at the risk of only losing a little bit of personal time.

PERSONAL RESOLVE AND DECISION MAKING

As you just learned, a major means of exercising personal control or self-mastery is through the decisions we make—the basic life choices as well as everyday decisions. From the moment we awake until we go to sleep at night, we must make decisions or choices between various options (Luce, 2005). Modern life is awash in choices that force us to make decisions (Rosenthal, 2005; Schwartz, 2004). Fortunately, many of our day-to-day decisions, such as when to get up and what to eat for breakfast, are made with little effort, mostly because of our habits and daily routines. It is mainly when we encounter a new and serious problem or face an important life choice, as did Stan when he had to decide between his old job and college, that we become acutely aware of the need to make a decision (Schwartz). Then we may become so overwhelmed by the alternatives or so caught up in the mental anguish of considering the consequences of our choice that we put off making the decision (Anderson, 2003). Worse still, we may make a hasty decision to "get it over with," thereby increasing the risk of a poor decision. In both instances, we lose sight of the overall process of making decisions we can live with.

In this section you will learn about the process of decision making along with valuable aids for making sound decisions and acting on them. **Decision making** is *the process of gathering information about relevant alternatives and making an appropriate choice.*

The Process of Decision Making

Psychologists have formulated a system for making *wise* decisions—the kind of decisions we can live with. They recommend that we proceed systematically through several stages:

1. Rise to the challenge.   This stage involves your recognizing a problem or challenge for what it is, guarding against such hazards as oversimplifying a complex problem. Key question: "What are the risks of doing nothing, not changing, or not deciding?"

2. Search for alternatives.   This stage requires you to have an attitude of openness and flexibility, with a concern for information about all possible alternatives, obvious or not. Key question: "Have I considered all the alternatives?"

3. Evaluate the alternatives.   You should next evaluate all the options with regard to their practicality and consequences. Here you weigh various risks, costs, and possible gains. Key question: "Which is the best alternative?"

4. Make a commitment.   Ordinarily, it's best for you to choose the alternative that gives you maximum benefits at minimum costs. Yet there's the danger of acting impulsively to "get it over with." Key question: "When do I implement the best alternative and let others know my decision?" After due consideration, you should be able to *act on your decision* at this stage.

5. Assess your decision.   After you have acted on your decision, you can learn about your decision-making ability by assessing the quality, results, and consequences of your decision. Because every decision involves some risk, it is important that you do not overreact with disappointment, criticism, and self-blame. The danger here is often changing your mind prematurely or defensively justifying your choice, thus shutting out valuable feedback. Key questions: "Are the risks serious if I don't change? Are they more serious if I do change?"

A critical element in your decision-making process, especially in the earlier stages, is vigorous information processing; in other words, seeking information is crucial to deliberate decision making (Hogarth, 2005). That is, you need to seek out sources of information, take time to know and understand them, and talk to people who are in a position to help. Gathering information takes time and energy, disrupting routines and building tension and conflict, all of which can be unpleasant (Luce, 2005; Schwartz, 2004). Consequently, most of us do not seek sufficient information, although we are more willing to look for new information when we expect the benefits of a decision to outweigh the costs. In our fast-paced society, Americans sometimes expect snap judgments and quick action and chide those who are slow or deliberate when making decisions. Interestingly, research shows that individuals who appear to procrastinate in decision making actually are more systematic and seek more information before they make a decision (Ferrari & Dovidio, 2000). Procrastination in the form of thoughtfulness is not bad.

It is also easy to use shortcuts in your decision making, especially when you are in a hurry, busy, or tired. Some people, for example, turn to the media (World Wide Web, television, or newspapers) to gather information. The Internet, indeed, has become the number-one source for health information for consumers (Morahan-Martin, 2004). The danger of this seemingly efficient method is that the media may offer an unrepresentative view of the world (Anastasio, Rose, & Chapman, 1999; Hajjar, Gable, Jenkinson, Kane, & Riley, 2005). The media, therefore, can cause you to make mistakes in your

An important and expected aspect of decision-making is post-decisional regret; after making a decision, you may feel that "the grass is greener on the other side of the fence."

gathering and assessing of information. A better idea is to turn to a variety of sources that might offer a mixture of professional information (Anastasio et al.), thus resulting in your making more realistic and informed decisions.

Unfortunately, in making important life choices, such as that of a career, many of us tend to underestimate the benefits of information gathering and therefore pay a high price for not doing it. There's nothing more agonizing than discovering a better choice after you've already committed to a less desirable course of action—right? Fortunately for Stan, before he paid his first semester of tuition, a major expense for him, he visited the college's career development center to examine his career projections over the next decade. These projections estimated the number of jobs in various fields and forecasted future salaries. Armed with this information, Stan was firmly convinced he had made the right decision to enroll in college and study engineering.

Another element in decision making of which to be mindful is **postdecisional regret**, *the regret that can be experienced shortly after we have finally made a particularly difficult choice or decision.* It is quite normal after you have made a decision to feel that you may have made an incorrect or poor decision and to experience regret (Connolly & Zeelenberg, 2002; Roese & Summerville, 2005). We all tend to suffer from the "grass is greener on the other side of the fence" phenomenon, but mostly *after* we make a decision. You're not alone if you experience regret. Some of the top life-choice decisions about which Americans experience regret are: education careers, romance, and parenting (Roese & Summerville).

Regret about decision making may have at least three contributory components:

(1) That the outcome is poorer than expected (perhaps because the unchosen alternative really was better)

(2) Self-blame for having made a bad decision (Connolly & Zeelenberg, 2002; Gilbert, Morewedge, Risen, & Wilson, 2004; Roese & Summerville, 2005)

(3) Missed opportunities, especially when the missed opportunity was a near miss (Roese & Summerville)

We sometimes anticipate regret or other negative emotion *before* the decision (Luce, 2005) but we are all quite familiar with postdecisional regret from our past mistakes (Crawford, McConnell, Lewis, & Sherman, 2002; van Dijk & Zeelenberg, 2005). Moreover, our *actions* tend to generate more regret in the short term while our *inaction* produces more regret in the long run (Gilovich & Medvec, 1995). Similarly, people usually feel more regret because of inaction than from action (Feldman, Miyamoto, & Loftus, 1999). Knowing these parameters may help you avoid or cope better with postdecisional regret when it happens to you.

Psychologists alternatively call *this uncomfortable feeling of regret* **cognitive dissonance**. Most people can live with dissonance and regret, especially if they have carefully planned the decision or are well adjusted. Eventually, the dissonance goes away as we discover that we really did make a good decision or that the unselected alternatives really are less desirable. For Stan, the support of his wife confirmed for him that staying in college rather than returning to his old job was wise. Postdecisional dissonance or regret did not last a long time for Stan.

There are other processes that essentially take decision making out of our hands. When this happens, we again feel uncomfortable, because, as mentioned, we like to have control over our own decisions and our own actions. One manipulative strategy that others use to influence our decision making is known as reactance by social psychologists. **Reactance** *is an oppositional response that occurs when our personal freedom is restricted*. Reactance occurs when others limit our personal freedom by getting us to do what they want us to do rather than what we want. Said another way, reactance is our response to attempts to constrain our freely chosen behaviors (Donnell, Thomas, & Buboltz, 2001). In other words, we lose some control over our decision making. Box 6–1 reveals more about this social psychological process.

Box 6–1

REACTANCE

Reactance is a negative reaction to efforts by others to limit our personal freedom. Others limit our freedom by getting us to behave or decide things in accord with their wishes rather than our wishes. For example, while out driving, you may decide that it is a nice, sunny spring day and that you are not in a hurry. Another car suddenly zooms up behind you and tailgates you. This other driver is nudging you to go faster against your wishes. Although you were previously content to drive at the moderate speed you had selected before the tailgating, you might now decide to drive even more slowly in reaction to this other driver's insistence that you go faster.

Try this little demonstration of reactance. Buy a small bag of potato chips and try to give it to a stranger. The stranger will probably refuse. Perhaps the stranger wanted some chips just before you made the offer, but now you have limited the stranger's ability to decide for him- or herself whether chips are wanted. On the other hand, leave the unopened chips on a table as if an unfortunate diner accidentally left them behind. The chips, which appear to be waiting for their rightful owner, will probably quickly disappear because they are not supposed to be taken by anyone else.

Reactance can make us want things we did not previously want and avoid things that we really do want. When was the last time reactance altered your decision or sense of control?

Making Better Decisions

Keep in mind that your purpose in making a decision is to bring about desired results and avoid undesirable ones. In this sense, only you can define what constitutes a "good" or "bad" decision. At the same time, your personal issues, such as your attitudes, values, and tolerance for ambiguity, can complicate decision making. With such factors in mind, you can improve your decision-making skills by following these suggestions:

- *Use sounder judgment.* Judgment, the raw material of decision making, involves drawing inferences from data. Many decisions are doomed from the start because of poor judgment, often involving the human tendency to simplify complex matters into familiar ideas, especially stereotypes. Replace simplistic, intuitive strategies with the more empirical probability orientation that guides scientists, asking yourself such questions as these: What are the facts? How representative are they? What do the alternatives look like? How much is due to situational and chance factors? Sounder judgments may lead to better decisions. Recall that Stan turned to employment projections before he decided to go to college.

- *Draw up a balance sheet.* This step consists of listing the various advantages and disadvantages of each course of action. A sample balance sheet in Table 6–1 represents Stan's situation before he made his decision. Students like Stan as well as adults of all ages have found that the balance sheet procedure helps them to make a comprehensive appraisal of a situation requiring a decision and promotes contingency planning, that is, figuring out what to do if something in the minus column materializes. People who use this procedure are more likely to stick to their decisions and express fewer regrets about the options not taken.

- *Clarify your values and objectives.* Many conflicts arise from confusion over the values that guided the decision rather than rejection of the conflicting alternatives. Because values are neither "good" nor "bad" in themselves, this step requires a personal examination. Once you have clarified your values, they can be translated into tangible objectives that guide your decisions. For example, often vacillating in their decisions, students are sometimes torn between the need to study, work,

TABLE 6–1		
STAN'S BALANCE SHEET: ATTENDING COLLEGE		
Projected Consequences	**Positive Anticipations**	**Negative Anticipations**
Tangible gains and losses for me	1. Better job prospects 2. Better income 3. More challenging career	1. Hard courses 2. Financial difficulties 3. Need to start over in new job and career
Tangible gains and losses	1. Family proud of me 2. Substantial emotional support from family 3. Positive role model for my children	1. Fewer toys and clothes for children 2. Wife will need to work and care for children—more stress for her
Self-approval or disapproval	1. Confidence in mastering challenge 2. Pride in new opportunities	1. Lingering doubts about my academic abilities
Social approval or disapproval	1. Admiration from others for making a midlife change	1. Will be unemployed and perhaps stigmatized due to this

socialize, and play. Those who have made a clear choice about what they hope to gain from college will be more likely to resolve their daily decisions effectively.

• *Accept reasonable results.* Nothing is as devastating to decision making as the wish for an "ideal" solution. People with perfectionist tendencies are especially susceptible, because constant striving for perfection guarantees failure. It is usually wiser for you to accept the most reasonable results under the circumstances. Among the methods of combating perfectionism, should it be characteristic of you, are recognizing the advantages and disadvantages of perfectionism and comparing how perfectly you did something with how much you enjoyed it. For example, you may feel that you didn't play tennis very well, but you enjoyed the game nevertheless because of the exercise and companionship.

• *Make the best of faulty decisions.* Despite your best efforts, not every decision will turn out to be a wise one. Some common reasons are limitations in circumstances, unforeseen events, and the difficulty of anticipating how differently you'll view things 5, 10, even 20 years down the road. Many people waste time berating themselves or trying to justify their poor decisions. It may be wiser to realize that more often than not they made the best decision possible under the circumstances. It's better to learn from your mistakes and, whenever possible, to modify

When we voluntarily participate in an activity, we enjoy it more than when we are forced to engage in it.

Box 6–2

Did You Know That...

- Half the people who make New Year's resolutions give up within 3 months? Nearly one-quarter give up the first week?

- Those who put their resolutions in writing or reveal them openly are more likely to achieve them?

- Indecisive people who exercise regularly for a few months become more decisive during this period?

- It's easier to choose between two desirable outcomes, such as attaining better health or more money, than

between two undesirable ones, such as being ill or poor?

- Our decisions are affected by whether the outcome is presented positively or negatively; for example, more people elect to have surgery when told they have a 90 percent chance of living than when told they have a 10 percent chance of dying?

- When we freely choose an activity, we become more involved in it and enjoy it more than when we feel it is something "expected" of us?

your decisions to achieve a more desirable result. If all else fails, take heart in the fact that no one makes perfect decisions. Box 6–2 provides some interesting facts about successful as well as failed decision making.

DECISIONS AND PERSONAL GROWTH

Decisions are especially crucial in regard to personal growth, including overcoming problem behaviors. All too often, people become stuck in self-defeating behaviors because they've never made a decision to change their ways. Change may be resisted because of the inertia of past habits (Anderson, 2003; Blum, 1998), psychological laziness, or simply fear. When confronted with the need for change, people sometimes become defensive and resist, although they may promise to change if threatened with the loss of their jobs or their family's love. However, many of those who enter psychotherapy or a treatment program drop out prematurely, mostly because they haven't made a firm decision to change. For instance, while talking with a classmate who works with alcoholics and people who are drug dependent, Stan asked at what point in the program clients began making significant progress. "It's hard to say," the classmate responded, "because so much depends on when a person makes up his or her mind to change. In fact, we won't even admit people into our program until they have made some sort of commitment to change."

Identifying the Basic Decisions in Your Life

A good beginning point is to examine the basic decisions underlying our everyday behavior, especially problem behaviors such as habitual procrastination or drinking too much alcohol. Although we may be aware that our behavior is a reaction to people and situations, on closer examination we may find that we have consciously chosen to act in a certain way. Once a decision is made, we usually organize life and perceptions around it, so that we understand everything that happens to us in a certain way. Some practical examples illustrate that point.

Take Stan's wife, Susan, as an example. Before Stan decided that he wanted to return to college, Susan was unsure what she wanted to do. After high school and before marriage, she had gone to secretarial school and had worked as a secretary until she met Stan and had their first child. For the next 10 years Susan talked, but only talked, about returning for a college degree. Have you ever wondered why people procrastinate or fail to put forth their best efforts on important matters? Often such behavior is the outgrowth of a basic life choice to protect oneself from failure or hurt, though the individual may not be aware of it. Perhaps Susan was afraid that she would not succeed in college, but once Stan decided to return to college and give up his job, she had no choice. She had to return to secretarial work to help supplement the family income. College, for now, was out of the question for her. Another example was the young man who waited until the end of August to apply for admission to the same college attended by Stan. In both instances, these individuals have a face-saving excuse if they fail—"I was too late." Somewhere in the dim past, each has made a basic decision to play it safe because of a fear of failure or of getting hurt. Only when they change that decision will they put forth their best efforts and have a greater chance of success. Much negative behavior, such as rebelliousness and defiance, is also the result of a basic life decision, though again not necessarily in the person's awareness. For example, Stan's neighbor's son, Bobby, left home in his late teens because of constant fights with his father, whom he considered overly strict. Nevertheless, even after leaving home, Bobby was still known to be "touchy" and "hard to get along with," even by his friends. He was always doing the opposite of what people expected of him, often with disappointing results. Bobby had made a choice in opposition to what he deemed as coercive parental authority: He had decided "No!" Until this rebellion, he was an appendage of his parents. But after rebelling, he felt more in charge of his life. This should not surprise us, because the defiance of the young child or adolescent is often the initial step toward autonomy. However, as long as Bobby remained stuck in this initial but negative stage of independence, his life was destined to be controlled more by what he was *against* than what he was *for*.

Making New Decisions

It is only when a *wish* to change leads to a *decision to change* that we can *really change and grow*. For example, many smokers know about the negative health effects of their smoking habit. They say things such as "I'd like to stop smoking" and "I hope to give it up soon" and "I plan to cut down on my smoking" or "I know it's bad for my family and me." Until they *really decide* to stop smoking and learn how to implement that decision, nothing happens or they try and fail.

So far we have assumed that people will automatically decide to change for the better, but this is not always the case. In some instances, people may become so overwhelmed with the anxiety and risks of change or fear post-decisional regret so much that they decide to remain the way they are, however unsatisfying or painful that may be (Anderson, 2003). Nor can someone be forced into growth, especially by therapists who are militant about people living up to their human potential. However well intentioned such therapists may be, they can make the same mistakes that parents and spouses are prone to make—namely, trying to tell someone else what he or she *ought* to decide. Rather, the therapist's task should be to help the client to discover first what he or she wants to do and then help the client make a personal decision to do it. As most of us have discovered, once you know what you want to do and really decide to do it, you're well on your way. Use Figure 6–1 to help you make your next few important decisions

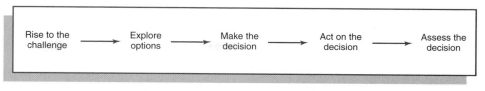

FIGURE 6–1
Steps in making effective decisions.

so that you can learn from them. In fact, copy it and carry it in your wallet if you like! Bring it out and use it when making important decisions.

Some Practical Applications

One of the most common examples of decision making is decision by default—taking the path of least resistance, taking the most familiar path, or taking no action at all (Anderson, 2003; Chapman, 1999). Putting things off, whether temporarily or indefinitely, while itself a decision (Anderson, 2003), nonetheless is a poor decision. A young man whom Stan knew as his teaching assistant in one of his classes was just such an example. This young man was having considerable difficulty completing his doctoral dissertation, partly because of writer's block and partly because of conflicts with his adviser. The young man became so frustrated that he simply turned his efforts elsewhere. He took the part-time teaching assistant job at the university ("while I finish my degree") and spent more time jogging ("to take my mind off my problems"). Several years later, when asked how his degree program was progressing, he said he had finally "decided" to give it up. Actually, he had made that decision earlier on, hadn't he? The failure to make a positive decision often is itself a decision with fateful consequences.

Overcoming negative, self-defeating behavior usually involves making a positive decision at a basic level of motivation. For example, when Stan's sister, Janet, was 24, she was bothered by depression and a poor relationship with her work supervisor. She reported to Stan that she had spent much time at work complaining and had been especially critical of her boss, often without any apparent reason. During some subsequent counseling, Janet discovered that earlier in her life she had learned to suppress her anger for fear of parental disapproval. She had become a passive "good little girl" but resented those on whom she remained dependent. Gradually, she learned to take more initiative, to show her anger more directly, but as an expression of her feelings rather than as judgmental remarks that might put others on the defensive. As Janet became more assertive, she felt less depressed and enjoyed a more satisfying relationship with those in authority. As did Stan, she returned to school, but for a master's degree in hospital administration, and later assumed a supervisory position at a prestigious health clinic.

Sometimes it is wise to make a decision that counters or reverses an earlier commitment that has led to undesirable consequences. For example, Stan's brother-in-law was a 45-year-old lawyer who married the daughter of the senior partner in his firm. He admitted to having married out of "mixed motives." That is, although he had been genuinely attracted to his wife, he had also hoped that his "connections" would enhance his career. He soon discovered that conflicts with his father-in-law complicated his life both at work *and* at home. Consultation with a specialist about his asthma attacks, which seemed worse during joint vacations at his in-laws' summer home, suggested that the attacks were brought on by emotional conflicts concerning his in-laws. Gradually, Stan's brother-in-law realized that it had not been a good idea to marry the boss's daughter, so eventually he decided to start his own firm rather than divorce his wife. Although he went through a few lean years, he soon had a flourishing law practice and was much happier in his marriage as well. Failure to make such a courageous decision often results in feelings such as being trapped in one's career, developing drinking problems, or engaging in extramarital affairs and other self-defeating behaviors.

Sometimes dramatic changes involve group, not individual, decision making, as is made clear in the later chapter on leaders and groups. In one instance at a company where Stan had worked as a young adult, the quality of work had gotten so bad that the company was considering simply closing several divisions. As a final attempt at saving Stan's division, the high-level managers suggested that department supervisors inform the involved workers of the situation and ask for their input. They discovered that the workers themselves were well aware of their poor work, although they justified it as the result of poor working conditions and bad management. So as to keep their jobs, the employees wanted to improve the situation just as much as the company did. A group decision was reached to save the plant, involving concessions from both management and labor. During a 6-month probationary period, a new policy was adopted involving workers' suggestions to improve production, to improve treatment of workers, and to make the work more meaningful. Each team of workers followed a product through to its finish and became responsible for the acceptance of the final product. The improvement in productivity and quality of work was so dramatic that the plant not only survived but also became a model for the rest of the plants in the parent company.

SUMMARY

MASTERY AND PERSONAL CONTROL

We began by discussing the importance of personal control in our lives. Two forms of control are particularly important—internal (person-centered) locus of control and external (situation-centered) locus of control. Emphasis in the literature has been placed on attaining greater perceived control—the belief that we can influence the occurrence of events in our environment that determine our lives. People who underestimate the control they have over their lives sometimes exhibit learned helplessness; those who exaggerate their personal control often exhibit the illusion of control. In both cases, the misperception of control leads to maladaptive behavior. In contrast, people who are high in realistically perceived control tend to be less anxious and better adjusted. A way to achieve optimal perceived control is through what Martin Seligman calls learned optimism—interpreting life events in a reasonably accurate way that enhances our perceived control and, thus, our adaptive response to events.

PERSONAL RESOLVE AND DECISION MAKING

A major way of exercising personal control is through our life choices and everyday decisions. Guidelines for making sound decisions include five stages: Accept the challenge, search for alternatives, evaluate the alternatives, make a commitment, and follow through with the decision. We may improve our decision-making skills by better judgment, the balance sheet procedure, clarifying our objectives, accepting reasonable results, and making the best of a poor decision. Also, we must repeatedly reaffirm our choice to change, abandoning perfectionism, accepting an occasional failure, picking ourselves up, and continuing our commitment to personal growth.

DECISIONS AND PERSONAL GROWTH

We can promote personal growth by seeing our problems in terms of past decisions, examining the consequences of such decisions, and then choosing a more satisfying alternative. In this way, we learn to view our problems and unfulfilled potential more in terms of our decisions than as the result of events and circumstances that simply happen or are beyond our control. However, it's only when a wish to change leads to a personal decision to change that our personal lives begin to improve.

SELF-TEST

1. The belief that you can influence events in your environment that affect your life is known as
   a. perceived control.
   b. external control.
   c. the illusion of control.
   d. a psychological delusion.

2. The maladaptive passivity that frequently follows people's experience with uncontrollable events is called
   a. the Type A syndrome.
   b. learned helplessness.
   c. the illusion of control.
   d. vacillation.

3. People who exhibit high perceived control tend to
   a. exhibit high anxiety.
   b. make only average grades in school.
   c. attribute their successes to good luck.
   d. use effective strategies for coping with stress.

4. Explaining negative events in temporary, specific, and external terms is a way of increasing which outlook?
   a. learned helplessness.
   b. the self-fulfilling prophecy.
   c. learned optimism.
   d. external locus of control.

5. The first stage of decision making is to
   a. evaluate the alternatives.
   b. make a commitment.
   c. accept the challenge.
   d. search for alternatives.

6. The final stage of the decision-making process consists of
   a. following through with your decision.
   b. making a commitment.
   c. evaluating your decision.
   d. accepting the challenge.

7. When we feel our personal freedom has been restricted, we experience
   a. reactance.
   b. resilience.
   c. neurosis.
   d. learned pessimism.

8. A common phenomenon after a decision has been made is the experience of a feeling of
   a. external control.
   b. elation.
   c. pessimism.
   d. regret.

9. Therapists who are helping clients change should
   a. tell the client what to do.
   b. provide lots of structure to assist client's decision making.
   c. help clients discover what they want to do.
   d. tell clients what they want to hear.

10. Which statement about resolutions and decision making is true?
    a. Ninety percent of us keep our New Year's resolutions.
    b. It is easier to choose between two desirable than two undesirable outcomes.
    c. Putting resolutions in writing doesn't work.
    d. All of these statements are true.

EXERCISES

1. *Personal control.* To what extent do you believe you can influence the occurrence of events in your environment that affect your life? In a page or so, discuss the degree of personal control you have over your life, emphasizing perceived control, or the belief you can control your life. How does your belief affect specific aspects of your life, such as your goals, work, intimate relationships, fitness, and health?

2. *Understanding bad outcomes.* Select a negative event that has happened to you over which you had little control, such as losing your job because of a layoff at work. Then explain this event in terms of the three categories of causal explanation discussed in the chapter, that is, permanence, pervasiveness, and personalization. To what extent do you now understand this event in temporary, specific, and external terms?

3. *Stages in decision making.* Review the five stages of decision making discussed in the chapter. Select an important decision you're about to make or one you've already made. Then analyze it in terms of the five stages of the decision-making process. How well did you follow these five stages? What do you find to be the most difficult part of making decisions?

4. *Aids in making decisions.* Reread the section on aids (such as the balance sheet method) to making sounder decisions. Then select one of the poorer decisions you've made and review this decision in light of these aids. What do you think you need to do to make better decisions in the future?

5. *Decision making and personal growth.* Select some aspect of your life, such as a habit or problem behavior, that you would like to change. Do you consider the problem behavior to be partly the result of some other decisions you've made? Have you made a deliberate decision to change your behavior, or do you merely wish to change? What do you need to do to really make the change?

QUESTIONS FOR SELF-REFLECTION

1. How much control do you believe you have over your life?

2. Are you inclined to underestimate your level of personal control?

3. Or do you suffer from the illusion of control?

4. When there appears to be no choice in a situation, what do you do?

5. How do you go about making important decisions?

6. Do you often "decide" things by not deciding?

7. Are you willing to take calculated risks?

8. What was the best decision you ever made? Why was your decision process successful?

9. What was your worst decision? What would you do differently now?

10. Is the grass always greener on the other side of the fence for you? Why do you think this is so?

11. How much truth is there in the saying that "life is what happens to us while we're making other plans"?

12. Is your life too full of choices? Do your choices frequently inspire regret in you?

FOR FURTHER INFORMATION

RECOMMENDED READINGS

BANDURA, A. (1997). *Self-efficacy: The exercise of control.* New York: W. H. Freeman. The leading authority on self-agency writes about its development and uses.

DAWES, R. M., & HASTIE, R. (2001). *Rational choice in an uncertain world: The psychology of judgment and decision-making.* Thousand Oaks, CA: Sage. This research-based psychology book discusses what scientists say about the steps in higher-quality decisions and how to make them.

HENDERSON, D. R., & HOOPER, C. L. (2005). *Making great decisions in business and in life.* Chicago, IL: Chicago Park Press. A well-received book on how to make better decisions no matter what the venue.

RACHLIN, H. (2004). *The science of self-control.* Cambridge, MA: Harvard University Press. A behaviorist writes about how difficult self-control is and why and then offers advice on how to improve it.

SMITH, H. W. (2002). *What matters most? The power of living with your values.* New York: Simon & Schuster. People hold important personal values but in many cases do not act on them. There is a disconnect between what they do and what they think and feel. This practical book gives advice about clarifying your values and then living accordingly.

WEB SITES AND THE INTERNET

http://www.mapnp.org/library/prsn_prd/decision.htm   A site designed by an expert who guides you through step-by-step decision-making.

http://encarta.msn.com/encnet/refpages/RefArticle.aspx?refid=761566271#endads   A site about freedoms and liberties that we take for granted. The site also provides a historic overview of freedom and raises contemporary issues related to freedom and liberty.

http://www.macses.ucsf.edu/Research/Psychosocial/notebook/control.html   A location with lots of information about personal control: what it is, how it is measured, and its relationship to our health, socioeconomic status, beliefs, and so forth.

http://www.doitnow.org/pages/163.html   This site discusses how to overcome peer pressure and instead be in charge of making our own choices.

http://mentalhelp.net/psyhelp/chap4/   A subdivision of a well-known site on psychological information, this site helps you understand why you behave as you do by examining such aspects of behavior as procrastination, self-control, and managing difficult behaviors such as loss of control or relapse.

CHAPTER 7

Managing Motives and Emotions

UNDERSTANDING MOTIVATION
Understanding Your Needs
Differences Between You and
    Others
Everyone's Basic Needs
Psychosocial Motives
Personal Motivation

UNDERSTANDING EMOTIONS
What Are Emotions?
Experiencing Emotions
Expressing Emotions
Managing Emotions
Special Emotions

SUMMARY
SCORING KEY
SELF-TEST
EXERCISES
QUESTIONS FOR SELF-REFLECTION
FOR FURTHER INFORMATION

Du is one of those students never to be forgotten. A pleasant and rather slender young man, he sat in the rear of the classroom next to the door. He was cheery, articulate, and eager to learn. He spoke up in class whenever possible. He was well liked by his peers and professors alike. Everyone who knew him realized that golf was Du's "reason for being" as he often declared. Du hoped to make it as a professional golfer one day, but "just in case," he said, "I'm attending a community college to obtain an education if my golf career never pays off."

Du's parents were immigrants and were none too happy about his plans to play sports. Instead, they wanted Du to become a doctor—a dream they held for him from the day they left their homeland. While Du's Asian culture taught him to respect his parents, he could not help but be disappointed that they did not share his enthusiasm for golf. His parents, on the other hand, carefully monitored his grades and his academic progress, although their language limitations often kept them from fully understanding how their son was performing. On the other hand, because of Du's passion for golf, his parents always knew how well he played and where his team finished in the intercollegiate rankings.

UNDERSTANDING MOTIVATION

Most of us can sympathize with Du. Sometimes we do the task at hand, especially when it will bring us closer to some desired goal, such as becoming a professional golfer. At other times, we may feel little or no motivation for what we're supposed to do. We procrastinate, we make excuses, and we waste precious time. Not surprisingly, many people, such as parents, teachers, and managers in the workplace, are interested in learning how to motivate people. Essentially, **motivation** has to do with *energizing and directing our efforts toward a meaningful goal*. Our motivation is affected by many influences, some of them rather obvious but others less so. We'll begin by discussing a popular theory of motivation, Abraham Maslow's theory. Then we'll briefly explore some of our basic needs, like hunger. In a later section, we'll consider several basic motives that are shaped mostly by learning and the environment, like achievement motivation. **Needs** are *tension states that arouse us to seek gratification*; **motives** are *goal-directed activities that energize and direct behavior*. Later we'll look at the issue of personal motivation.

Many psychologists agree that emotions (the second topic in this chapter) and motivation are closely linked (e.g., Arkin, 2005; Efklides, 2005; Reeve, 2004; Rorty, 2004). When we feel happy, we are eager to continue to feel happy. When we are sad, we are motivated to end the pain as quickly as possible. In the last few parts of the chapter, we will turn our attention to emotions—what they are and how they are expressed verbally and nonverbally. Here is an interesting example, regarding the September 11, 2001, terror attacks on New York and Washington, of the grip emotions have and their relationship to motivation. Dr. Tedd Mitchell (2003) said:

> Conflicting emotions set in: the fear of travel—the defiant need to travel; resignation that another attack was inevitable—and a resolve to prevent an attack no matter what: emotional exhaustion from reliving the event over and over in the media—and an inability to turn off the TV. . . . fortunately the negative emotions brought on by the tragedy were counter-balanced by a flood of positive energy [p. 4].

At the end of this chapter, we will concentrate on specific emotions, such as anxiety, anger, and jealousy, that are problematic to adjustment. To end the chapter on an upbeat note, we will finish with information on happiness.

Understanding Your Needs

Your understanding of motivation may be enhanced by study of Maslow's growth model of motivation, the **hierarchy of needs**. Maslow's (1970) growth model is related to the humanistic perspective described in Chapter 2. Maslow suggests that our *needs and motives function in a hierarchical manner from the bottom up according to how crucial the need is for survival*. The higher needs are experienced only to the degree that the more basic ones have been relatively satisfied. He describes five levels of needs, from most basic to higher level needs, as follows:

(1) *Physiological needs* include the need for food, sleep, and sex.
(2) *Safety needs* include the need for protection from bodily harm and security from threat, as well as the need for order and stability.
(3) *Love and belongingness needs* include the need for acceptance, affection, and approval.
(4) *Esteem needs* are the need for self-respect and the sense of achievement.
(5) *Self-actualizing needs* include a variety of needs, such as the need for autonomy, uniqueness, aliveness, beauty, and justice in our lives.

Maslow suggested that fewer individuals have the top needs (e.g., esteem and self-actualizing needs) satisfied compared to basic physiological needs (e.g., fresh water and food). Du's parents, for example, worried about his meeting basic needs: "Du, become a doctor, earn lots of money, then you can feed yourself and care for us in our old age," they pleaded. Du, on the other hand, was more concerned with self-esteem needs; his primary goal was to improve and improve his golf game until he felt satisfied that he was the best player he could be.

Maslow theorized that the lowest level of unmet needs remains the most urgent, thus commanding our attention and efforts. Once a given level of need is satisfied, we become more motivated by the unmet needs at the next-higher level. To that end, as we satisfy our needs for food and shelter we become more concerned about things like job security. Maslow also pointed out that our needs typically remain only relatively satisfied. He once estimated that the average person is only 85 percent satisfied in terms of physiological needs, 70 percent in safety needs, 50 percent in love needs, 40 percent in esteem needs, and only 10 percent in self-growth needs. Therefore, he stated there is constant motivation to meet needs, and recent research has borne him out. The need for self-determination, competence, and autonomy (e.g., self-actualizing needs) may well be universal (Deci & Moller, 2005; Grouzet et al., 2005) as is the opposing need for survival (Grouzet et al.). Such striving is part and parcel of personal growth.

An important implication of Maslow's growth model of motivation is that we aren't content to achieve a stable, harmonious state. Instead, once we've reached a relative level of satisfaction, biologically and psychologically, we're increasingly motivated by growth needs. This theory helps to explain why successful people are rarely satisfied to rest on their previous accomplishments. They're constantly striving to attain something better. For example, Du won a junior golf championship at a public course when he was just 14 years old. While happy with the win, he was not completely satisfied; he wanted to play in the "big leagues" as he said. Similarly, people who are happily retired seldom sit around doing nothing; they're forever developing new interests and deepening their relationships with others. It seems we're happiest when we're growing and actualizing ourselves.

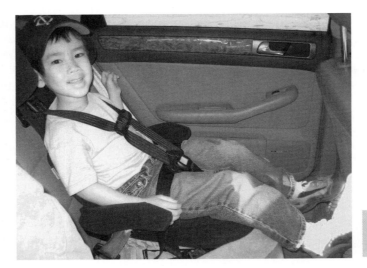

According to Maslow, safety needs are the most basic of needs.

Differences Between You and Others

Although each of us desires the creature comforts of food and sleep, as well as higher goals such as success in education or sports, the relative strengths of such motives differ from one person to another (Hinsz & Jundt, 2005). Accordingly, we need to think in terms of the individual's personal hierarchy of motives as well as Maslow's generalized pattern. Which motives have top priority for a given person will depend on factors such as inborn dispositions, culture, personal values, gender roles, and past experiences. For example, firstborn individuals tend to have a more intensive achievement motivation than their brothers and sisters, mostly because of the greater attention they received from their parents while growing up. In contrast, individuals who have been deprived of love and affection as children may be more motivated by the desire for approval than achievement. Our motives also change over time depending on the **motive targets** around us—*the people toward whom our attention or motives are directed*. At work you may have a strong motive to compete with your associates. In your leisure hours you may be more concerned about being accepted by your friends. Then again, at home you may feel inclined toward intimacy and involvement with your lover or spouse.

People searching for success favor positive role models who highlight strategies for success. Du's role model was Tiger Woods and his uncanny ability to concentrate on his game despite intense stress. People focusing on failure avoidance are inspired by negative role models who avoid negative outcomes (Lockwood, Jordan, & Kunda, 2002). As a result, our motives are constantly changing throughout the day, as we move from one situation to another and as we encounter various people. Furthermore, an individual's motives tend to vary across the entire life span and by culture, mostly because of one's experiences and personal growth. As a result, we often invest more or less of ourselves in the same career or same relationship (i.e., marriage) as we grow older.

Everyone's Basic Needs

Like all other beings, you and Du must eat, drink, and avoid extreme pain and injury if you are to survive. Although sex is not essential to our personal survival, it is necessary for the *survival* of the species. Such needs, though shaped by learning in varying degrees, have a clearer *physiological basis*. As a result, they are variously labeled **basic needs**, primary drives, or survival motives.

For the sake of example, let us discuss here only two basic needs, hunger and thirst. When you go without food or water for half a day, you feel hungry and thirsty—right? If you were deprived of food even longer, the effect would be more marked. People who are deprived of food or water for a long period of time become less efficient in their thinking and behavior. They become apathetic, irritable, and depressed. The desire for food and water dominates their daytime activities as well as their daydreams. In their home country, for example, Du's distant relatives were very poor and their daily life was centered on earning what little money they could and on growing their own food for their family. Fortunately, most of us never experience this extreme state, although we realize how important food is. Water is even more crucial to our survival. Although we can survive for weeks on minimal food, we can live only a few days without water.

Our eating and drinking behaviors are affected by a part of the brain known as the **hypothalamus**, *a small but important structure at the core of the brain that governs many aspects of behavior, such as eating and hormonal activity*. Eating is also affected by a variety of learned influences (Azar, 1998). In fact, some individuals learn to like food all too well and cannot control their eating or at the least find dieting difficult. Finally, some people may be supertasters who perceive taste intensely and thus avoid nutritious vegetables, which may be somewhat bitter (Duffy, Peterson, & Bartoshuk, 2004; Hunter, 1998).

Some of the more common cues about which we learn are the smell, sight, and taste of food; emotional stress; and self-control (over our eating habits). Culture also plays a large role in learning various eating habits. Most Americans, for example, prefer white eggs to brown ones; the brown ones appear dirty. On the other hand, Russians do not mind eating brown eggs; in fact, most of the eggs they eat have brown shells. There are other basic needs, such as the need for sleep, clean air to breathe, and—several people might add—sex. Let us move on to other types of motives closer to the top of Maslow's hierarchy.

Psychosocial Motives

The psychosocial motives have less to do with physical survival and more to do with our sense of well-being and psychological competence in dealing with our environment. The notion of *competence* brings us to two important distinctions related to human goals, especially pursuits of a psychosocial nature: intrinsic and extrinsic motivation. **Intrinsic motivation** concerns *active engagement with tasks that people find interesting and that, in turn, promote growth and are freely engaged in out of interest* (Deci & Ryan, 2000). In other words, the aim of intrinsically motivated behavior is not to succeed or to reach some other outcome but rather to engage in an activity naturally and spontaneously. Such behaviors are inherently satisfying to pursue in and of themselves (Grouzet et al., 2005). Alternatively, **extrinsic motivation** is *the desire to engage in an activity because it is a means to an end and not because an individual is following his or her inner interests* (Deci & Ryan). Extrinsically motivated behaviors are not based on an individual's need to feel competent and autonomous but on some external reward or outcome.

Du's life situation offers a good example of each type of motivation. Du loved golf. He liked the game's demands for concentration, the challenge of bettering his game each time, and communing with nature in a beautiful setting. Du was less concerned about earning "big bucks" as a professional golfer than he was with enjoying and improving his game. Du's desire to play golf was intrinsically motivated. On the other hand, Du's attending college was mostly his parents' idea. They deeply desired him to be a successful and rich doctor so that they could all become more "American." Thus, Du's college career was rather extrinsically motivated, although he, himself, did recognize the value of a good education.

Years of research have demonstrated that external rewards, surveillance, deadlines, and threats undermine intrinsic motivation (Deci & Ryan, 2000). These results are reminiscent of the concept of *locus of control* as reviewed in the previous chapter (Chapter 6). Persons with an external locus of control see their fates controlled by forces outside of themselves. Individuals with an internal locus of control feel they control their own fates. Not only do such external influences or controls undermine autonomy and thus intrinsic motivation, they also weaken creativity and problem solving. Then again, internal control or intrinsic motivation has generally been demonstrated to result in increased satisfaction and enhanced well-being (Deci & Ryan). This need for self-determination and need for autonomy is so strong that Grouzet et al. (2005) recently demonstrated its robustness and universality in 15 other cultures.

Some psychosocial motives—such as the motives for stimulation, curiosity, and exploration—seem to be largely inborn and are sometimes labeled *stimulus* needs. Others,

Achievement motivation—a social motive—often manifests itself at school first.

like *achievement motive*, are shaped more extensively by psychological, cultural, and social influences. Because of the complexity of human behavior, there is no one authoritative list of our psychological and social motives. Some of these motives are addressed in other chapters, such as our sexual motives, friendship needs, and the need for personal freedom and control. Here, we'll focus on two of the psychosocial motives not covered elsewhere, namely, the need for stimulation and for achievement.

Stimulation.   We need both sensory and social stimulation. People deprived of both, for instance, prisoners in solitary confinement and subjects in sensory deprivation experiments, display symptoms of stress, including distorted perceptions. They see and hear strange things; they hallucinate, have delusions, and fear losing their sanity. Military personnel in lonely outposts have shown similar reactions, though to a lesser degree. Most of us are rarely placed in a situation in which we suffer from extreme sensory or social isolation. But even after several hours of studying alone, you may feel a need to listen to the radio, call someone on the phone, or talk to a friend, mostly for variation in stimulation.

Perhaps you've noticed how some people have a greater need for trying novel experiences and meeting new people. Others prefer more peaceful activities, such as reading or stamp collecting. Marvin Zuckerman (1990a; 2005; Zuckerman & Kuhlman, 2000) attributes such differences in human behavior to the relative strength of the **sensation-seeking motive**. This motive is *our tendency to seek out stimulating and novel experiences.*

Zuckerman (2005) and others (e.g., Hansenne et al., 2002) believe our sensation-seeking motive may be partly dependent on biological factors, like brain stimulation and bio-chemical secretions (especially dopamine), so that each of us has an optimal arousal level. Whenever we find ourselves in situations that arouse us to a significantly lesser or greater extent than our optimal arousal, we become uncomfortable. If not sufficiently aroused, we seek greater stimulation; if we're overly aroused, we try to reduce the stimulation. Partly because of its biological basis, sensation seeking is at a peak during the college years and tends to diminish with age.

Research on sensation seeking in traditional college-age students might interest you. One study (Hansen & Breivik, 2001) found that those high in sensation seeking take more risks—both positive (e.g., kayaking) and negative (e.g., shoplifting). Another study demonstrated that college men who report high condom use had lower sensation-seeking scores than men who report less condom use (Arnold, Fletcher, & Farrow, 2002). In college students, the higher the sensation-seeking score, the more drugs consumed (Simons, Gaher, Correia, & Bush, 2005; Roberti, 2004). As you can see, sensation seeking influences many aspects of our lives, not all of them positive. In mainstream American culture, risk taking, bravado, and sensation seeking predominate. There are, however, individual differences in sensation-seeking and risk-taking behavior. Although both men and women can be sensation seekers, studies have demonstrated that men often score higher than women on sensation seeking (Arnold et al.; Wills, Vacaro, & McNamara, 1994) and that men are more prone to boredom (or lack of novelty, which is part of sensation seeking) than women (Vodanovich & Kass, 1990).

Differences in sensation seeking may also influence the way we relate to one another. Low-sensation seekers may feel that high-sensation seekers are foolhardy and hungry for attention. In contrast, high-sensation seekers may feel that low-sensation seekers are timid and boring. A scale for you to assess your level of sensation seeking is provided in Activity 7–1.

ACTIVITY 7–1

HOW MUCH STIMULATION DO YOU NEED?

The need for stimulation is related to sensation seeking. Circle which of the two choices for each statement best describes you.

1.	I prefer to	A. read a book.	B. do something physically exciting.
2.	When driving a car, I generally drive	A. at about the speed limit.	B. over the speed limit.
3.	I would like to	A. return to a place I have already visited.	B. visit a foreign country.
4.	I would describe myself as	A. an introvert.	B. an extrovert.

5.	I like to listen to	A. the same music over and over again.	B. recently released or new music.
6.	As a general theme in my life, I favor	A. risk taking.	B. security.
7.	I would describe my best friends as	A. quirky.	B. conventional.
8.	I often watch	A. adventure movies.	B. romantic movies.
9.	When I know water is cold, I	A. jump right in.	B. submerge myself slowly.
10.	I think I would	A like hang-gliding.	B. stay anchored on the ground.

SCORING: First, realize that this scale was specially designed for this book. A high score does not necessarily indicate that you are a sensation seeker or an avid escapee from boredom. Similarly, a low score does not necessarily mean that you don't take risks or seek adventure. This scale should be used to help you think about yourself and as a stimulus to class discussion.

For Items 1–5: Answer "A" indicates low need for stimulation or sensation seeking. Answer "B" indicates a high need for thrill seeking and/or avoidance of boredom. Total number of "Bs" _____

For items 6–10: Answer "A" indicates a need for thrill seeking or avoidance of boredom. Answer "B" indicates low need for stimulation or for sensation seeking. Total number of "As" _____

Now add your scores from both lines here. _____

A total composite score of 1–3 indicates a low need for sensation; a score of 4–7 indicates a moderate need for sensation seeking, and a score of 8–10 indicates a high need for sensation seeking. Using your score, think about whether you are prone to taking unnecessary risks, whether your life needs a little more spark, or have you found just the right balance between serenity and thrill seeking?

Achievement.   Perhaps you've noticed how your friends differ in achievement motivation. Some relish taking on a challenge. No matter what the task, they strive to do their best. Others seem to be happy just getting the job over and done with. In our opening case, Du had a strong motive to succeed, but his desire to succeed at golf eclipsed his need to achieve in his class work.

Achievement motivation is *the desire to accomplish or master something difficult or challenging as independently and successfully as possible.* Actually, achievement motivation is a complex combination of several factors (Senko & Harackiewicz, 2005). Two such elements are the **desire for success** or *the urge to succeed* and the counteracting **fear of failure**, fear *that we will be humiliated by shortcoming.* Each of us has a different mixture of these tendencies, mostly because of our personal makeup and past experiences (Komarraju & Karau, 2005). As a result, the difficulties of the tasks people choose differ. For example, someone who has a strong desire for success and a low fear of failure is more apt to choose moderately difficult but realistic tasks, thus maximizing the chances of success. Another person with an intense desire for success yet coupled with a high fear of failure will set a much lower goal and perhaps be more anxious about achieving these goals.

Although our achievement motivation remains fairly stable over time (Senko & Harackiewicz, 2005), it may vary according to several factors, an important one of which is self-efficacy (also discussed in other places in this book). Albert Bandura (1997, 2000) defines **self-efficacy** as *beliefs in one's capabilities to organize and execute the courses of action required to produce given attainments.* Self-efficacy affects our cognitions, our health, athletic and career functioning, and other activities and behaviors. For example, athletes like Du must learn the required skills, survive a highly competitive selection process, and then execute their skills perfectly in each game. Any and all of these processes can be affected by a sense of self-agency or self-efficacy. "I can do it" is what the efficacious person says. Belief in the power to make things happen is essential to self-efficacy (Bandura, 2000). But where does this come from? Bandura says families can provide experiences that build self-agency. First, young children try to get adults to produce desired outcomes that the children themselves cannot produce. Second, parents need to be responsive to their children's behavior and create opportunities for efficacious actions by providing an enriched physical environment, freedom for exploration, and varied mastery experiences. In this manner, children learn healthy self-appraisal skills. When they then move out into the school environment, self-efficacy continues to unfold if the same type of environment is created. We will return to the concept of self-efficacy in several other places in this book.

The information on self-efficacy probably holds true for most White Americans. In other cultures, self-promotion, achieving one's own goals, and competition with others is not viewed positively. Indeed, another factor that affects achievement is the prevailing environment and the social values revered in that environment. For example, Steele (1992) claims that over half of African American college students fail to obtain their diplomas due to racial stigmatism on campuses; very few fail to obtain degrees because of lack of ability. Blacks and their achievements are devalued in schools and American society. As if stigmatization is not bad enough, Steele continues with the point that African American children disidentify with school; that is, to salvage their self-esteem because their achievements have been ignored, the children decide they do not like school and drop out.

In collective (as compared to individualistic) societies where individual gain is shunned in favor of the collective good, achievement motivation occurs in a different form. Achievement motivation and satisfaction are not derived from personal accomplishment. Instead, positive feelings about the self come from fulfilling tasks associated with being *inter* dependent with others (Markus & Kitayama, 1991; Matsumoto, 2000). For example, a study of Japanese youngsters demonstrated that self-promotion in the collective society of Japan is viewed quite negatively even by young children. One peer was presented as modest whereas another was presented as a self-promoter. The more modest peer was actually perceived as more athletically competent than the self-promoter was.

Personal Motivation

A secret of being an active, motivated person is setting personal goals and then striving hard to reach them. In one sense, goal setting comes naturally in that we tend to be future-oriented. Most of us are more concerned about today and tomorrow than yesterday. However, it takes some thought and soul-searching to set personal goals or objectives, which is why a lot of people don't bother to do it. Nevertheless, the risk of not doing it can be costly in terms of wasted time and energy.

There are several types of personal goals:

- *Long-range goals* are concerned with the kind of life you want to live with regard to your career, marriage, and lifestyle. It's wise to keep these goals broad and flexible, especially during your college years.

- *Medium-range goals* cover the next 5 years or so and include the type of education you're seeking or the next step in your career or family life. You have more control over these goals, so you can tell how well you're progressing toward them and modify them accordingly.

- *Short-range goals* apply from the next month or so up to 1 year from now. You can set these goals quite realistically and should try hard to achieve them.

- *Mini-goals* cover anything from 1 day to a month. You have a lot of control over these goals and should make them specific.

- *Micro-goals* cover the next 15 minutes to a few hours. Realistically, these are the only goals over which you have direct control.

As you can guess, the shorter the time span covered, the more control you have over your goals. It is only through achieving the modest, short-range goals that you'll ever attain your medium- and long-range goals. Du, for example, wanted to succeed in college so that he could please his parents. He knew that no matter how often his fantasies turned to his golfing dreams, he needed to concentrate on each exam and each semester as short-term goals. Then and only then, he reasoned, would he be able to graduate and please his parents. Maybe then, he reasoned, his parents would let him pursue his golf career (a long-range goal) if only for a few years.

Too often, people make the mistake of setting grandiose or idealized goals (Kayes, 2005) and then quickly become disillusioned because they're making so little progress toward achieving them. It's far better to set *realistic* but desirable goals and then concentrate on achieving your day-to-day goals, which will make it possible to reach your "dream" goals. Remember also that once you've achieved a goal, it's important to set new ones. Keep in mind also that some individuals set large goals even though they would experience less distress day by day if they set smaller goals.

UNDERSTANDING EMOTIONS

We can only imagine the disappointment Du felt when one of his final exams was scheduled at the same time as an important amateur golf tournament in which he hoped to play. Compounding Du's conundrum was his anxiety about approaching the professor to see if the exam could be rescheduled to accommodate Du. Once again, Du was torn between following his golf dreams and obtaining the education his parents so fervently desired for him. With this example, we turn next to the study of emotions, which, as mentioned earlier, are motivating in and of themselves.

What Are Emotions?

Experts vigorously differ concerning how much each emotion is inborn or learned. In fact, understanding emotions continues to be a challenge for both researchers and laypeople. Today, we still lack a single, unifying theory of emotions, although the work of Robert Plutchik is closing in on such a theory (Plutchik, 2001). Nevertheless, many experts would agree that an **emotion** is *a complex pattern of changes that includes physiological arousal, subjective feelings, cognitive processes, and behavioral reactions*—all in response to a situation we perceive to be personally significant. Accordingly, an emotion has four components:

1. **Physiological arousal.**   Emotions involve the brain, nervous system, and hormones, so that when you're emotionally aroused your body is aroused. Intense or constant emotional arousal uses up valuable energy and may lower our resistance to illness.

2. **Subjective feelings.**   Emotions also include subjective awareness, or "feeling," that involves elements of pleasure or displeasure, liking or disliking. Thus, in studying emotions or knowing another person's feelings, we must rely heavily on that person's own self-reports.

3. **Cognitive processes.**   Emotions also involve cognitive processes such as memories, perceptions, expectations, and interpretations. Our appraisal of an event plays an especially significant role in the meaning it has for us.

4. **Behavioral reactions.**   Emotions also involve behavioral reactions, both expressive and instrumental. Facial expressions, as well as gestures and tones of voice, serve to communicate our feelings to others (expressive reactions). Cries of distress and running for our lives are also adaptive responses that may enhance our chances for survival (instrumental reactions). In sum, an individual may experience a threat (*arousal*), which triggers the *subjective feeling* of fear and therefore the *cognition* of risk or danger. The *behavioral reaction* will probably be to escape the threatening stimulus or event (Plutchik, 2001).

Here is a more specific example. Because he was already doing poorly in his organic chemistry class (cognition of risk or failure) and consequently feeling anxious (fear), Du was especially anxious (arousal) about the exam he might miss. While he would like never to take the exam (escape), he would at least like to delay taking the exam (behavioral reaction) not solely because of the tournament but to have more time to study.

Although some theories of emotion emphasize physiological factors such as the central nervous system and the endocrine system (Howlett, 1999), many contemporary theories of emotion now emphasize the role of cognitive factors (Beitel, Ferrer, & Cecero, 2005; Bonanno, Papa, Lalande, Westphal, & Coifman, 2004; Plutchik, 2001). An experience arouses our emotions mostly when the individual *appraises the stimuli as having personal significance*. In this view, an emotional experience cannot be understood as something that happens solely in the person or in the brain but more in our relationship to the environment. The particular emotion that is felt depends largely on how we label a given situation, that is, on how we interpret the personal meaning it has for us. Here is another example. While Du viewed the conflict between his exam schedule and the golf tournament schedule as anxiety producing, another student might view prepping for both as a challenge and approaching the professor as a welcome opportunity to interact one-on-one with the well-liked professor.

A major implication of the cognitive view of emotions is that each of us has more potential control over our feelings than what was once popularly believed. Whenever we feel angry, jealous, or depressed, we are not simply at the mercy of our momentary feelings (Richards, 2004). Nor should we take our "gut" reactions as infallible, as important as these may be. Instead, it's better to realize that our momentary feelings are partly the result of the way we perceive and respond to an event. Particularly for negative events, it is also important to know that most people fail to understand just how well and how quickly they can cope with them (Wilson & Gilber, 2005).

Another implication of the cognitive perspective is that interpretation of personal emotions may well underpin psychological adjustment (Bonanno, Papa et al., 2004). Perhaps anxiety over emotional expression creates problems for us, or perhaps we consistently misinterpret our own and others' emotional reactions. As Plutchik states, "Most of us often censor our own thoughts and feelings, and we have learned to be cautious about accepting other people's comments about their feelings" (2001, p. 344). Alternatively, perhaps some other mechanism accounts for emotions and adjustment. The following research illustrates another possibility. Bonanno, Papa et al., after the terrorist attacks on New York City, examined emotional expressiveness and adjustment in college students from New York. As expected, they found a link between emotionality and adjustment; the link was complex, though. Participants were asked to either suppress their emotions or enhance them. What the researchers found was that those participants who were most *flexible* in their emotional responses, that is, were best able to use both enhancement and suppression where *appropriate*, were best adjusted. Thus, a larger repertoire of emotions and ability to call on each where appropriate may be the key to healthy adjustment.

Experiencing Emotions

Emotions are a kind of barometer of our inner world, giving us an intuitive knowledge about ourselves and our involvement with others at the moment. On the one hand, intense emotions tell us our lives are strongly affected by some person or event and prompt us to act accordingly. On the other hand, when we feel little or no emotion in a given situation, chances are our needs, goals, or values are not affected; that is, we're not "emotionally involved." Perhaps that's why we're constantly asking each other, "How do you feel about this?" or "What's your reaction to that?" Unfortunately, it's not always easy to say, is it? A major reason is that we often have trouble identifying our feelings at the moment, and even more finding the right words to express them (Solomon, 2005). Then, too, our emotions are in a state of constant flux or change so that we may feel pleased one moment and annoyed the next. Also, our feelings may represent a mixture of various primary emotions and thus defy easy labels. Primary emotions, or basic emotions, probably combine to produce more complex or secondary emotions. Du, for example, was anxious about both his golf and his exams, but he found the golf anxiety mostly to be exhilarating and the exam anxiety to be stressful.

Although psychologists do not yet agree on how many primary emotions exist, Plutchik's model (2001) is often cited as a good starting point. He identifies eight primary emotions: joy, acceptance, fear, surprise, sadness, disgust, anger, and anticipation. These emotions can be experienced more or less intensely to create other emotions. Think about disgust and its complexities (Marzillier & Davey, 2004). For example, when you are intensely disgusted with someone, you may experience loathing; when you are moderately disgusted, you may feel dislike; and when only mildly disgusted, you may experience mild disapproval.

Besides Plutchik's theory, other models of emotions also exist (Trierweiler, Eld, & Lischetzke, 2002). For example, when people from various cultures are asked to report their experience of different emotions, they seem to place emotions along two

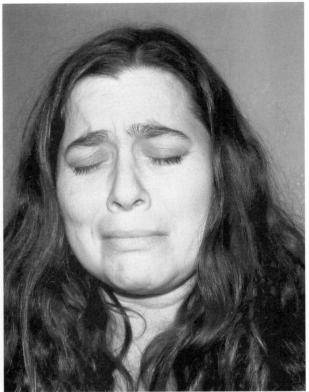

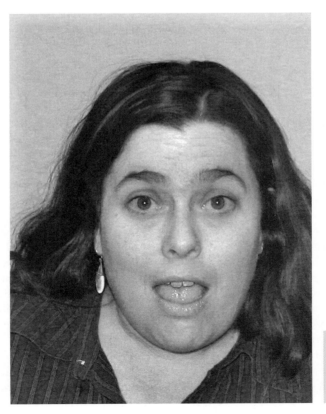

Some psychologists believe that certain emotions are universally expressed and understood. Which emotions are expressed here?

dimensions—*pleasant versus unpleasant* and *intensely versus weakly aroused* (e.g., Tsai, Knutson, & Fung, 2006). Thus, the emotions of contentment, joy, and love would fall into the category of pleasant or positive emotions, whereas anger, disgust, and sadness fall into the category of unpleasant emotions. On the intensity (arousal) scale, rage is more intense than anger, which in turn is more intense than annoyance. On the other hand, love is more intense than liking.

Also with regard to universality, facial expressions accompanying many emotions are interpreted the same way across cultures. In fact, six different primary emotions are expressed commonly on the human face from a very early age: anger, fear, happiness, sadness, surprise, and disgust (Ekman, 1993; Matsumoto, 2004). Based on cross-cultural research, Matsumoto (2000) claims that there exists a seventh universal emotion—contempt; others (Sabini & Silver, 2005) claim that jealousy and (primarily parental) love should also be considered universal emotions.

Expressing Emotions

Emotions not only motivate us to do certain things and to approach or avoid particular situations, they offer a primary means of communicating with others. However, we often assume it is not always safe to share our intimate feelings, even when casually greeting a good friend. How often has someone asked, "Hey, how ya doin'?" and you answered "Great" when you really were feeling glum or overwhelmed by too much to do? Sharing our feelings is risky and makes us vulnerable to the judgments of others. Some people are so afraid of their inner feelings that they're unable to experience, much less express, their deeper emotions, such as in times of great joy or profound sorrow. Others more in touch with their emotions disclose their feelings freely, whether the emotion be anger or love. Whichever way you're inclined, the most important thing is to find that balance of expression and control of feelings with which you and those around you are most comfortable.

Emotional balance is all the more difficult because of some of the individual differences in emotional expressiveness. Women, for example, report sadder responses to negative personal events than do men (Hess et al., 2000). And Fischer, Rodriguez Mosquera, van Vianen, and Manstead (2004) found that in a wide variety of cultures men more frequently report power*ful* emotions (e.g., anger) while women are more likely to report power*less* feelings (e.g., fear). Scientists have yet to tease out whether such differences are learned or biological.

Individual differences also exist in our ability to recognize and interpret others' emotions. For instance, researchers have consistently found that women are better decoders than are men of others' emotions, especially of body postures (Brody & Hall, 1993). Likewise, everyone is a better decoder of emotions expressed by members of their own culture rather than of another culture (Beaupré & Hess, 2005). In terms of understanding and recognizing our *own* emotional states, researchers have found that men more than women ruminate about upsetting events and report more inhibition of hostile feelings (McConatha, Lightner, & Deaner, 1994). Similarly, older persons rehearse more about upsetting events and express emotions less frequently than younger individuals, whereas other researchers have found that the elderly—contrary to stereotypes—are still highly capable of experiencing profoundly positive emotions (Carstensen & Charles, 1998).

As you might guess, culture also plays a major role in our emotional affairs (Spielberger, 2000). Matsumoto (1993) found that there are differences in how African American, Asian,

White, and Hispanic Americans display emotions. Japanese Americans, for example, report the lowest expressiveness in romantic relationships (Aune & Aune, 1996). Furthermore, several studies consistently reveal that Asians report the lowest intensity of positive emotions (e.g., Scollon, Diener, Oishi, & Biswas-Diener, 2004).

For years, psychologists and laypersons have regarded faces as the key to emotional expression (Bower, 2001; Coulson, 2004). There is little doubt that the face is important, but body postures, vocal changes (e.g., pitch modulation and speed of speech), and hand gestures also signal us as to what others are actually feeling (Azar, 2000; Pell, 2005). Research results illustrate that deciphering these and other nonverbal information is complicated. Coulson (2004), for instance, found that body posture greatly helps us decode anger and sadness but helps little in gauging others' level of disgust.

Another factor that makes recognition and interpretation of expressed emotions slippery is that some individuals purposely try to deceive us by manipulatively using many of these same nonverbal devices (e.g., posture). For example, if Du mustered the courage to approach his professor to change the exam date thus enabling Du to play in the tournament, Du might appear deferentially apologetic and remorseful in front of the professor but privately feel elation about the prospect of delaying the exam to play his much-loved game. Du, like anyone else, will probably monitor his self-presentation so that the elation does not show.

If others do attempt to deceive us, how can we detect their dishonesty? Put another way, how could the professor tell whether Du's deferential apology is sincere and whether the professor should honor Du's request for an exam delay? One helpful aid is **microexpressions**, or *fleeting facial expressions that last only a fraction of a second* (Ekman, 1985b). Microexpressions can be ephemeral, but they are still detectable by the astute observer (Dimberg, Thunberg, & Elmehed, 2000). Many people try hard to control their outward facial expressions because they believe we think the face is the primary clue to their secrets. Deceivers, however, may blink more or smile more broadly in an effort to deceive (Baron & Byrne, 1997) and thus can be exposed. In addition, yet another individual hoping to deceive you may express one emotion followed quickly by another, which can indicate that the person is lying. Some individuals are so good at monitoring and controlling their faces that their true feelings are difficult to detect. Watching for **body leakage**, *where body postures rather than the face leak the truth*, can be just as revealing of emotional deceit. While individuals are concentrating on monitoring their words and their facial expressions, they attend less to their bodies, which consequently betray their true feelings. Du would be well served by minding his facial *and* postural expressions when he visits his professor!

Managing Emotions

Because emotions are related to psychological adjustment (Bonanno, Papa et al., 2004; Eisenberg, Fabes, Guthrie, & Reiser, 2000; Izard et al., 2001), it is desirable to manage our feelings well. Learning to express feelings effectively involves a suitable balance between spontaneous expression and deliberate, rational self-regulation. Areas of emotional management needing improvement vary somewhat from one person to another. Some people who are overly emotional and impulsive may blurt out their feelings without much thought; they need to develop better self-control. On the other hand, those who keep their emotions under tight control may need to loosen up, to become more aware of their feelings and more comfortable expressing them appropriately to others.

We can become more adept and practiced at expressing our emotions by sharing our everyday feelings more readily with family and friends we trust, who can provide productive feedback. There often are times when we feel pleased about something a person has spontaneously done for us. Why not share your feelings of happiness and gratitude? At other times, someone may make you angry, for example, because they are very, very late and cannot provide you with a reasonable excuse. It is OK to express your sense of disappointment and frustration with that person in appropriate ways. As you become accustomed to sharing your emotions, you'll get in better touch with your feeling life. Then, when you experience an intense emotion, like rage or extreme disgust, you should find it easier to recognize your feelings and be more willing to express them *but in appropriate and modulated ways.* More often than not, it's a risk worth taking. When you express your feelings openly *and* in a constructive manner, it helps to clear the air and facilitate communication. Sharing your feelings with a willing person may also help you clarify your emotions, especially when several come flooding forward at the same time.

A technique that is particularly useful for expressing intense emotions, especially negative ones, is the use of an **"I" message**, as explained by Tom Gordon (Gordon & Sands, 1984). Essentially, this message *consists of saying what you honestly feel in a way that encourages others to listen and cooperate. "I" messages are especially helpful in expressing your feelings about someone whose behavior has become a problem for you.* We would hope that when someone takes issue with one of your behaviors, that person will also use an "I" message. An "I" message consists of four components.

- First, *describe the other person's objectionable behavior* in specific but nonjudgmental terms. For instance, you might use the phrase "when you fail to return my book on time" instead of "you're irresponsible." Avoid using fuzzy and accusatory responses or guessing the person's motives. Such communication only intensifies the person's resistance to changing the behavior.

- Second, *point out the specific ways in which that person's behavior affects you.* In most instances, people are not deliberately trying to make life miserable for you; they simply aren't aware of the consequences of their actions. Once a person becomes more aware of how the behavior has become a problem for you, the person is usually willing to modify it.

- Third, *tell the person how you feel about the behavior in a way that "owns" your emotions.* To do this, you should generally start your sentences with the pronoun *I*. Say "I feel hurt" instead of "you hurt me." Avoid projecting your emotions onto the other person.

- Finally, *tell the person what you want done to correct the situation.* For example, if you object to the casual way telephone messages are left for you, you might say something like this: "I don't have the information I need and I feel frustrated when you don't write down my telephone messages. I'd appreciate your writing down my telephone messages."

Initially, "I" messages may seem a bit contrived or stiff. But as you become more experienced in using them you'll feel more comfortable expressing your feelings in this way. Table 7–1 provides more tips on "I" messages.

Let's next look at specific emotions in more detail. Although we will concentrate on troubling emotions such as anxiety and anger, we will end on an upbeat note—happiness.

TABLE 7–1

EXAMPLES OF "I" MESSAGES

Nonjudgmental Description of Person's Behavior	Concrete Effects on Me	My Feelings About It	What I'd Prefer the Person to Do
1. If you don't complete what you promised to do	then I have to do it in addition to my other tasks	and I feel annoyed	I wish you would do what you've promised
2. Each time you criticize my work without telling me what I'm doing wrong	I don't know how to improve it	and I feel frustrated and resentful	Tell me what I'm doing wrong so I can correct it
3. When you change your mind at the last minute	it's too late to make other plans	and I feel angry and disappointed	Give me more advance notice when you think things may not work out

Special Emotions

Anxiety.   Du probably felt as much anxiety about his examinations as he did his somewhat unrealistic prospects as a golf professional. **Anxiety** is *a vague, unpleasant feeling that serves as an emotional alarm signal, warning us of an impending threat or danger* (Gorman, 2002). Anxiety is a complicated emotion and therefore a complex topic. In ancient times, anxiety may have been evoked by natural disasters, predators, or interclan hostilities (Zeidner & Matthews, 2005); its arousing nature may have been adaptive in that it helped humans survive. Today, our worries tend to be related less to survival and more to everyday frustrations, bureaucracies, personal achievements, and other non–life-threatening issues (Zeidner & Matthews). Unfortunately, we sometimes feel quite anxious when there is little actual danger, for example, when making a speech or going to the dentist. As a professor once said, "There is little point to test anxiety; I have yet to see a midterm leap off a desk and viciously attack someone."

When a threat is real (not imagined) and can be pinpointed, such as the fear of failing an examination or visiting a prominent professor's office to request a favor, moderate levels of anxiety may motivate us to take the necessary steps to avoid a gaffe. On the other hand, people who are prone to unusually high, chronic, "free-floating" anxiety tend to overreact to stressful situations, frequently making the situations worse. Furthermore, high levels of anxiety can distort our perception and thinking so much that our performance is impaired. Finally, anxiety siphons off energy by keeping us mobilized for action when none is needed. It makes us tense and tired, thereby robbing us of much of the enjoyment of life. Anxiety in modern life does not seem to serve to protect us and improve our survival; it is the bane of modern existence for many.

You are not alone if you suffer from anxiety; Zeidner and Matthews (2005) report that all types of anxiety are quite common. Somewhere between 20 and 50 percent of adults have math and computer anxiety. Many more adults, 60 percent, suffer from social anxiety or general timidity about social situations. And evaluation apprehension (the fear of others' appraisals of us) is nearly universal across people of different ages, genders, and cultures. One specific form of evaluation apprehension is test anxiety, which also appears to be widespread. Test anxiety is a familiar problem for most students like you and Du. Does test anxiety help you to learn better or does it interfere with your performance? A lot depends on you *and* on your situation. Read on.

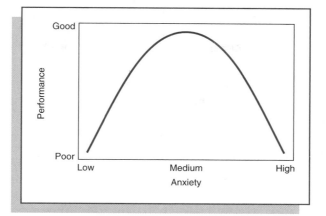

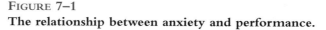

FIGURE 7–1
The relationship between anxiety and performance.

Generally, the relationship between anxiety and test performance takes the form of an inverted-U curve, as depicted in Figure 7–1. That is, at low levels of anxiety, we remain unmotivated and perform well only on easy, not difficult, tasks. Moderate levels of worry tend to enhance performance (Perkins & Corr, 2005), at least up to a point. But at high levels of anxiety, many people become distracted and overwhelmed, thereby performing more poorly on tests. Recognize, too, that people differ widely on their optimal level of anxiety—the degree of anxiety at which they do their best (Zeidner & Matthews, 2005). People with relatively low levels of anxiety often do their best only when challenged, as in a highly competitive situation. Those with characteristically high levels of anxiety tend to do better, at least on difficult tasks, under conditions of less pressure. Which of these two patterns do you most resemble? Do you find it depends somewhat on the situation as well as on your own mastery of required skills and motivation?

In a review on how to cope with anxiety, Zeidner (1995) found at least two important generalizations about test anxiety. First, adaptive coping in exam situations involves a flexible and combined use of several coping strategies. When one strategy does not work, the individual needs to be able to turn to another. Second, effective coping strategies should match both the context and the individual. This means that the individual needs to be comfortable with the strategy and also that the strategy should be appropriate to the level of challenge of the examination. Happily, Zeidner also reports that most students cope effectively because they utilize active coping, in which they plan study time and techniques, suppress competing activities (such as socializing with friends), and reframe the stressful event positively (e.g., "A good grade means a higher GPA and perhaps a better job when I graduate").

If your academic performance is hindered by test anxiety, you may benefit from a number of anxiety-reducing strategies. For instance, when you find yourself getting anxious during a test, you can employ anxiety-reducing statements such as "I know I can do it" and "I'll take one question at a time and do my best on each question." Much research has documented that students who take the *opposite* route (e.g., "I'm going to fail this test" or "All of these questions are too hard") become mentally distracted from the primary task of exam taking and therefore perform poorly (e.g., Hopko, Crittendon, Grant, & Wilson, 2005; Keogh, Bond, French, Richards, & Davis, 2004). Another effective method for coping with test anxiety is to study hard and learn well (Beilock, Kulp, Holt, & Carr, 2004), a strategy that increases confidence and thus decreases test anxiety. Good study techniques were reviewed in the "How to Study" section (PQ4R) at the beginning of this book. You might want to look them over again.

Anger.   Du's roommate often teases him that he is as bad a golfer as he is a student and that he is going "nowhere fast". Du loses his temper because he feels humiliated and is tired of the teasing, no matter how good-natured. Du is not alone in his angry moments. A basketball coach yells profanities at the referee after a controversial call. A teenage girl screams "I hate you" at her mother who won't let her stay out as late as her friends' parents allow. A red-faced worker slams his fist on the table to make his point during a dispute with his boss. All these people are venting **anger**—*feelings of displeasure or resentment over (perceived) mistreatment.*

Psychologists have been investigating whether venting anger or holding it in is more productive. Many of you have grown up with the idea that when you're angry, it's healthy to "get it off your chest" or "let it all hang out." Holding anger in, goes the popular notion, leads to all kinds of problems—high blood pressure, increased risk of heart attacks, depression, and suicide. On the other hand, we have all seen people blowing off steam and who afterward seemed pleased or relieved. What exactly is the truth?

The scientific truth is rather mixed. Many studies (e.g., Bushman, 2002) find that **catharsis** or *venting anger* only results in more anger and aggression. On the other hand, in a recent study, McGuire, Greenberg & Gevirtz (2005) found that expressive writing (designed to express emotions, especially negative ones like anger) actually helped lower blood pressure in participants in the research. Sometimes doing nothing or displacing anger onto a more productive project (chopping wood) may be an effective way to manage anger. There is some truth to the notion that people who unduly suppress or hold in their high levels of anger are more prone to high blood pressure and heart attacks. Psychologists have discovered a syndrome known as the Type A personality. **Type A individuals** *tend to be competitive, argumentative, time-urgent, ambitious, impatient, and sometimes hostile* (Friedman & Rosenman, 1974). Other research has added yet a different dimension to Type A syndrome—*distrustfulness* (Catipovic-Veselica, 2003). In any event, Type As are far more likely than others to suffer from coronary heart disease (Gallacher, Sweetnam, Yarnell, Elwood, & Stansfeld, 2003; Olson et al., 2005). **Type Bs,** on the other hand, are *relaxed, easygoing individuals.* Type As and Type Bs are such opposites that they are happiest when they do not have to work with each other (Keinan & Koran, 2002). Research has now found that hostility (loosely, anger) is the primary dimension responsible for the coronary troubles of the Type As (Contrada, Leventhal, & O'Leary, 1990; Olson et al.). Whether held in or exploded, hostility and anger are not beneficial to us. We therefore need to learn to address them better.

There is lots of evidence that we can learn to effectively manage our anger (Deffenbacher, Oetting, & DiGiuseppe, 2002; Potter-Efron, 2005). First, certain child-rearing practices can go a long way toward preventing inappropriate forms of anger expression (Meesters & Muris, 2002). Developmentally appropriate strategies for encouraging children to responsibly manage anger include modeling by parents of appropriate anger management, avoiding shaming a child's anger, and increasing the child's understanding of anger as well as the sense of control over anger-arousing events (Marion, 1994). Likewise, parents who encourage secure attachment to them inspire better anger management techniques and less aggression in their children (Meesters & Muris). Securely attached children have parents whom they love and trust and want to emulate.

Eliminating exposure to aggressive models also helps (Kirsh, 2006). Parents might want to monitor their child's television watching. There is much evidence that watching televised violence desensitizes us to its effects. Parents also need to be cautious about physically punishing their children, especially when the child has a temper tantrum or has acted aggressively toward another. Such parents are modeling the very behavior they are trying to eliminate in their children. Children and adults who are isolated also have difficulty managing anger. Perhaps it is the individual's failure to properly manage anger or some other negative traits that has turned friends away. Box 7–1 further suggests that school bullies are often depressed and angry and, thus, turn their anger on their victims. On the other hand, increasing social supports so that the angry person can discuss anger with others often improves anger management (Dahlen & Martin, 2005).

Training in social skills that teach us to get along with others is another option. If we don't know how to respond appropriately to others, we sometimes lose our tempers or they lose theirs. Social skills training helps individuals find alternative solutions to provocations. Such training is effective, often after only a few hours (Martsch, 2005; Renshaw, 2002). For other individuals, therapy might be the only answer. Therapy should convey the sense that anger is destructive and that better communication and problem-solving skills and increased empathy for the target of the anger all reduce anger. Such therapy has been shown to be effective for adolescents and adults who show strong levels of anger and little control (Acton & During, 1992; Wilcox & Dowrick, 1992).

Jealousy.   Essentially, **jealousy** is *a complex emotion that occurs when we fear losing a close relationship with another person or have lost it already* (Marazziti et al., 2003). Jealousy can be contrasted with **envy** (Parrott & Smith, 1993), *which is distinguished by feelings of inferiority, longing, resentment, and disapproval.* Jealousy is characterized by fear of loss, distrust, anxiety, and anger (Parrott & Smith). Jealousy is especially apt to occur in romantic and sexual relationships, so that it is popularly known as romantic jealousy. Romantic jealousy can be normal or pathological (obsessional); today, many Americans view jealousy as an embarrassing emotion at best (Marazziti et al.).

It is commonly thought that jealousy is a measure of devotion and that the lack of jealousy means the absence of love. Admittedly, jealousy may contribute positively, however indirectly, to close relationships like marriage. Laypeople may believe that high jealousy is linked to "strong love," "establishing ground rules," and an "increased commitment" in the marriage. However, some Americans as well as some psychologists regard jealousy as an unnecessary and destructive emotion in close relationships (Bringle, 1991). In fact, recently Tallis (2005) has raised the issue that passionate love with its dark side of jealousy, dependence on another, and consequential anxiety is related to mental illness. What do you think about the possibility that love and/or jealousy may be forms of psychopathology?

The occurrence of jealousy depends largely on the interaction between jealousy-evoking situations and the personalities of the people involved as well as their relationship. Some situations are especially apt to trigger jealousy, such as the following:

- The person you like goes out with someone else.
- Someone gets closer to a person to whom you are attracted.
- Your lover or spouse tells you how sexy a former boyfriend/girlfriend was.
- Your lover or spouse visits a person he or she used to go out with.

Box 7–1

BULLYING—A NATIONAL EPIDEMIC

Just what is bullying? A good definition comes to us from the childhood education literature. **Bullying** is *repeated, unprovoked, harmful actions by one child or children against another.* The bullying acts can be physical (e.g., punching or kicking) or psychological (e.g., name-calling or taunting) (Bullock, 2002).

Bullying may be rampant in U.S. schools (Nansel et al., 2001; Flynt & Morton, 2004). One out of every five children reports being a bully while 25 to 50 percent of the children report being the victim of bullying (Bullock, 2002; Flynt & Morton). Interestingly, boys are stereotyped as bullies because aggression, which is linked to anger, is one of the only acceptable emotions for males (Elias, 1999b; Flynt & Morton). Girls tend to bully as much as boys (Bullock; Hoffman, 2002), but the type of bullying may vary. Girls are more likely to use gossiping, taunting, glaring, and bad-mouthing (James & Owens, 2005; Underwood, 2004), whereas boys are more likely to use physical forms of aggression (Bullock; Hoffman). Girls essentially use *relational* bullying (manipulating peer relations by spreading nasty gossip or bad-mouthing the victim); boys use *direct bullying, which is more physical* in nature (Woods & White, 2005).

Bullies have different motives for picking on other children. Some children may bully because they have too high or too low self-esteem (Bullock, 2002). Other children have learned from their parents to hit back or become more aggressive when their self-esteem is threatened. Other bullies taunt and bully because they, themselves, have been bullied (Elias, 1999b). And some studies show that bullies may be depressed. For these children, especially for boys, the most acceptable way to express their misery is to act macho rather than sad (Elias).

Victims of bullying may go largely unnoticed by teachers and parents, in part because teasing in childhood is sometimes considered "normal" (Bullock, 2002). Teasing and bullying are not normal or acceptable, because bullying has serious psychological and social consequences for those who bully and are bullied (Nishina, Juvoven, & Witkow, 2005; Woods & White, 2005). Depression, low self-esteem, social isolation, and behavior problems are some of the effects (Bullock; Pace, 2001).

Victims of bullies tend to be children who are different from the typical student in the school (e.g., Flynt & Morton, 2004). Because schools, themselves, may inspire a "culture of sameness," children who are different and do not fit in are bullied (Anonymous, 2002). Such children are ethnically or racially different, dress differently, are weaker or smaller, disabled, or more passive (Bullock, 2002; Elias, 1999).

There are steps that parents and teachers can take to help victims of bullying (Smith, Pepler, & Rigby, 2004). The first is to recognize signs of victimization. If a child is experiencing the following, suspect bullying:

- Behavioral changes (e.g., more aggressive or more withdrawn)
- Frequent crying or depression
- Lower self-esteem
- Unexplained injuries
- Academic difficulties not manifested earlier
- Unexplained health problems such as stomach pains or fatigue
- Fear of school or desire to avoid school

After both teachers and parents observe the symptoms, they should talk in private to the children whom they suspect are bullies or victims. Second, many schools have instituted bullying prevention programs, although many programs have not been assessed at present. Some of these programs include using a peer mediator (someone empowered to intervene in the bullying) or a mentor who can help protect the victim (such as an adult or an older student). Finally, children can be taught not to tolerate bullying but rather to report it to parents, teachers, or other adults.

- You find that your partner is having an affair.
- You are the second spouse of your mate and he or she has to pay support to the first spouse.

The response to jealousy also depends on the exact situation and the personalities of the individuals involved. How would you respond if you found yourself in these situations? How do you think your partner would respond? Some people are especially prone to jealousy; such individuals are characterized by low self-esteem, high levels of anxiety, a negative view toward the world, low levels of life satisfaction, little control over their lives, low threshold of emotional arousal, and a greater sensitivity to threatening stimuli in social environments (Bringle, 1991; Guerrero & Andersen, 1998).

Beyond these characteristics, those with pathological (obsessional) jealousy possess unfounded suspicion of a partner's fidelity. These suspicions modify thoughts, feelings, and behaviors. For example, a pathologically jealous person obsessively checks the whereabouts of the object of affection and argues often with that person about jealousy or makes groundless accusations against that person (Marazziti et al., 2005).

Although the potential for jealousy may be inherent in our biological makeup (DeSteno, Bartlett, Braverman, & Salovey 2002), cultural influences carry as much or more weight in determining which situations provoke jealousy and how it is manifested. For instance, when jealous, the French get mad, whereas the Dutch become sad. The Germans prefer not to fight about it but rather to talk it out, while the Italians don't even want to talk about it. It appears that Americans are mostly concerned about what their friends will think (Bryson, 1991; Zummuner & Fischer, 1995).

How people *appraise* and then *cope* with jealousy-evoking situations is especially important. Heterosexual men and women as well as gays and lesbians often show the same levels of jealousy (Harris, 2002; Sheets & Wolfe, 2001), but there are some individual differences. For instance, men and women have jealousy mechanisms that are activated by different types of infidelity. Men appear more upset over sexual infidelity while women seem more upset over emotional infidelity (Murphy, Vallacher, Shackelford, Bjorklund, & Yunger, 2006; Schützwohl, 2006).

Yoshimura (2004) conducted an extensive study of coping with jealousy and communication between romantic partners. To list but a few strategies, coping and communication methods can vary from

- face-to-face interactions with the partner to avoidance of the partner or the rival;
- jealous violence to more positive solutions such as initiating an open discussion;
- problem-focused coping such as repairing the relationship to emotion-focused coping such as soothing the other person.

Some methods of coping are productive, such as using apologies, increasing affection, and using reassurances; others are less productive, such as making up excuses, being manipulative or vengeful, and arguing. What perhaps is most important about Yoshimura's research is that the *initial* expression of jealousy strongly influenced the trajectory of the rest of the cycle. In other words, positive communications at the onset, such as "I'm sorry I made you feel jealous; I want to reassure you that I love you very much" resulted in the most positive response from the partner. As expected, initial negative communications such as "You're just insecure" disintegrated into further negative interactions.

Along the same line of research, Shackelford, Goetz, Buss, Euler, and Hoier (2005) investigated romantic jealousy and how it devolves into violence. They investigated this issue using men's jealousy because of their support of evolutionary psychology (i.e., prevention of paternity uncertainty) and because men are more likely than women to commit partner violence. They identified several different strategies for men to deal with jealousy. One is *direct guarding*, where, for example a man drops in unexpectedly to see what his girlfriend is doing. Another is what the researchers call *negative inducement*, as in threatening a romantic partner who has shown attention to another man. A third method men use to guard against rivals is through *public signals of possession*, such as holding a wife's hand when other men are around. Yet another approach is *positive inducement*, where the man helps a woman when she really needs help or brings flowers to cheer her up. Not surprisingly, the first three tactics are much better predictors of the use of violence toward romantic partners to keep them in line than was the last, more positive approach. The strongest predictor of all for violence was emotional manipulation that included pleading that the man cannot live without his female partner or that he would die if she ever left. High vigilance as in direct guarding and monopolization of time also predicted violence toward the female partner as well.

Happiness.   Imagine Du's happiness and surprise when his professor readily agreed to delay Du's exam. In fact, Du was amazed at the professor's warmth and approachability. Du's only other experience with the professor was attending his lectures in a large auditorium. The professor revealed to Du that he, too, loved golf and had hoped to pursue golf professionally only to have his efforts thwarted by his parents who wanted him to obtain an advanced, prestigious degree. The professor continued that a Ph.D. in chemistry with weekend golf outings and well-timed golfing vacations was the compromise that met both his personal needs and his parents' lofty wishes.

Psychologists, as noted elsewhere in this book, have traditionally concerned themselves with psychopathology rather than wellness and happiness. In 2005, Kim-Prieto, Diener, Tamir, Scollon, and Diener reported that in the leading search engine for psychologists there are only 4,000 studies listed for happiness but 30,000–40,000 studies of stress and depression. However, in 1995 David Myers and Ed Diener reviewed all of the available literature on happiness. At the time, the good news was that many studies reveal that happiness is more abundant than believed. **Happiness**, or what Myers and Diener called **Subjective Well-Being (SWB)**, *includes a preponderance of positive thoughts and feelings about one's life*. People high in SWB have a global sense that work, marriage, and other life domains are satisfactory. They experience and report pleasant rather than anxious, angry, or depressive emotions. Happy people are less self-focused, less hostile, and less vulnerable to disease. They are more loving, forgiving, trusting, energetic, decisive, creative, helpful, and sociable than unhappy people (Myers, 1993; Lyubomirsky, Sheldon, & Schkade, 2005). Study after study shows that happy people have high self-esteem, a sense of personal control, optimism, and extroversion (e.g., DeNeve, 1999; Diener & Seligman, 2002); happy people often lose a sense of time and self because they find a task challenging and absorbing (Myers & Diener, 1995).

Myers and Diener dismiss many myths about happiness. For example, happiness does not discriminate between genders; in cross-cultural research both men and women have equal opportunities to find happiness (Michalos, 1991). The sources of men's and women's happiness, however, may differ. Cross-cultural studies suggest that men's well-being is better predicted by self-esteem, whereas women's well-being or happiness was predicted somewhat by self-esteem but also by relationship harmony (Reid, 2004). Aging does not necessarily involve a decline in happiness either (Shmotkin, 2005; Westerhof & Barrett, 2005). There is also only a modest correlation between wealth and happiness

(Diener & Biswas–Diener, 2002; Diener, Sandvik, Seidlitz, & Diener, 1993; Shmotkin). As Myers and Diener (1995) persuasively state, "[wealth's] absence can breed misery, yet its presence is no guarantee of happiness" (p. 13). Race, culture, and ethnicity are also not predictors of happiness.

Several studies point out that happy people outnumber unhappy people in many cultures (Rice & Steele, 2004; Shmotkin, 2005; Suhail & Chaudhry, 2004), perhaps because one of the overarching principles of happiness is a sense of "owning" one's goals, that is, pursuing one's life goals because of an authentic desire to do so (Sheldon et al., 2004). Research has demonstrated that members of both individualistic and collective cultures experience well-being when they pursue self-chosen goals. True, in an individualistic culture a self-selected goal may be "a better life for myself" while in a collective society a self-selected goal may be "to fit in better". Nonetheless, when individuals' goals are self-concordant, the individual reports higher levels of happiness and well-being than when goals are not self-selected (Sheldon et al.). Everyone, then, has the possibility for happiness. Motivation and emotion indeed are related. If by now you have not set life goals for yourself, isn't it time to think about doing so in order to promote your own subjective well-being?

SUMMARY

UNDERSTANDING MOTIVATION

Maslow's hierarchy of needs is a popular theory of motivation. At the bottom of the hierarchy are basic needs such as the need for food and the need for safety or security. The middle but narrower level involves the need for belonging or the need to fit in and be accepted. At the top levels are self-esteem needs and self-actualizing tendencies, respectively. Self-esteem needs involve the need to feel a sense of self-worth and achievement, whereas self-actualization includes a sense of autonomy and uniqueness. These higher-level needs cannot be met if the lower-level needs are unfulfilled.

Hunger is an example of a basic need. Most basic needs are biological but can be shaped by learning. Psychosocial needs are related to our sense of competence, include the need for stimulation and novelty, of which one form is sensation seeking, and achievement or the need for success. Such motives vary by individual. Culture, gender, and other factors that influence learning shape our individual methods for responding to and meeting these needs.

EXPERIENCING EMOTIONS

Emotions are complex changes that include physical arousal and cognitive interpretations of a situation. Emotions are very important to psychological adjustment. The cognitive view of emotions is that our interpretation of them is actually more important in influencing our reaction than the actual arousal or the provoking stimulus. Although psychologists have not yet agreed on the primary emotions, there is general agreement that several emotions are universally expressed: anger, fear, happiness, sadness, and surprise. Culture can greatly influence the intensity of emotional expression, though. Another tricky part of emotions is that people attempt to deceive us about their emotions by altering their nonverbal communications (the face and the body). We can learn healthy methods for managing our emotions so that we express them at socially appropriate times and in acceptable intensities and ways.

Anxiety is a common unpleasant emotion, but it can serve as a useful alarm that warns us of threat. Most causes for anxiety in modern life are less related to survival and more related to dealing with everyday frustrations. One example is test anxiety, which is especially detrimental to unprepared students, as it can diminish performance. Being well prepared for an examination helps overcome test anxiety.

Anger is yet another problematic emotion. Research with perpetually hostile individuals, Type As, has shown that hostility can lead to coronary disease. Learning to respond in nonhostile ways is therefore important to mental and physical health. One good method for avoiding anger and aggression is to raise children to recognize their anger and to manage it when they are young. Angry, depressed children often bully their peers. Parents can and should act as positive role models for their children.

Jealousy is a third negative emotion with which individuals have to cope. Jealousy often occurs in a romantic context. Many individuals need to learn to cope with jealousy in active and constructive ways where they express their intention of improving the relationships. Extreme forms of jealousy and manipulative strategies can sometimes result in violence against romantic partners.

Happiness is a positive emotion associated with subjective well-being. According to research, happiness is available to everyone regardless of sex, race, or income level. Happy people are less hostile, less vulnerable to disease, and more forgiving, trusting, and energetic than unhappy people.

SCORING KEY

ANSWERS AND EXPLANATIONS TO THE QUIZ ON WEIGHT CONTROL

1. True. A daily 10-minute walk raises energy levels and reduces tension for 2 hours.

2. False. Only about half of the obese people who lose weight regain it within 3 years, though almost all of them do so by 10 years.

3. True. Excess weight in the stomach area poses a greater risk of heart disease, diabetes, and gallstones than excess weight in the hips and thighs.

4. True. Compared to other body tissues, fat tissue can be maintained with fewer calories.

5. False. This eating pattern, which is common among obese people, actually slows down metabolism.

6. True. One reason is that the calories from a recent meal are consumed before the food has an opportunity to leave the stomach and become absorbed into the body tissues.

7. True. This is a major finding from research on starvation.

8. False. Regular exercise not only burns up calories but increases your resting metabolism as well.

9. False. Most authorities now discount willpower as an explanation for obesity, giving greater weight to individual differences in body chemistry and genetics.

10. True. This remains the basic strategy for losing weight.

SELF-TEST

1. In Maslow's concept of the hierarchy of needs, the most urgent need commanding our attention is
   a. self-actualization.
   b. security.
   c. belongingness.
   d. the lowest unmet need.

2. The part of the brain that is especially responsive to the changes in blood chemistry associated with hunger is the
   a. hypothalamus.
   b. medulla.
   c. cerebellum.
   d. frontal lobe.

3. Research demonstrates that differences in our sensation-seeking motives are thought to be partly dependent on
   a. biological factors.
   b. educational levels.
   c. intelligence.
   d. age.

4. Individuals with a strong need for achievement tend to choose tasks with
   a. low risks.
   b. minimum rewards.
   c. maximum rewards.
   d. medium risks.

5. Which of the following best expresses self-efficacy?
   a. "I can do it."
   b. "Maybe tomorrow."
   c. "Some things are better left unsaid."
   d. "I hope I get a better grade than my classmate."

6. The cognitive appraisal view of emotions holds that our emotions depend primarily on
   a. how people treat us.
   b. hormonal arousal.
   c. how we interpret situations.
   d. activity on the left side of the brain.

7. Fleeting facial changes that last only a second that tip us off to a person's true emotions are known as
   a. body leakage.
   b. microexpressions.
   c. unconscious denial.
   d. "I" messages.

8. Responding to someone's objectionable behavior with an "I" message normally includes our
   a. perception of the other person's feelings.
   b. positive rather than negative emotions.
   c. opinion of the person's behavior.
   d. nonjudgmental description of the person's behavior.

9. People who are the most successful in interpreting nonverbal messages are
   a. likely female, not male.
   b. live in individualistic societies.
   c. low in expressiveness themselves.
   d. high in creativity.

10. Jealousy is a blend of emotions, predominated by
    a. anticipation.
    b. disgust.
    c. love.
    d. fear of loss.

1. *Examine your eating habits.* Describe your eating habits in a page or so, including your responses to the following questions: How healthy are your eating habits? Do you know how many calories a day you consume? How does this figure compare with others of your age and lifestyle? Good nutrition requires eating food from the basic food groups—bread and cereal, fruits and vegetables, dairy products, and meat. Are your meals well balanced? Do you have any bad eating habits, such as overeating at mealtimes, snacking between meals, or frequently dining in fast-food restaurants?

2. *Seeking new experiences.* Sometimes the stimulation from new experiences helps to revitalize your motivation and zest for life. You might try several of the following suggestions: Taste a food you've never tried. Take up a new sport or hobby. Invite someone out socially you would like to know better. Attend a workshop or a special course you're interested in. Perhaps you can add other ideas. Try several of these suggestions, and write about your reactions in a page or so. Would you agree that variety is the spice of life?

3. *Assess your achievement motivation.* Look at your achievement motivation in a specific area of your life—a class you're taking, your motivation in school as a whole, your job, or progress toward your career goals. Then answer the following questions:

   - How strongly do you want to succeed?

   - Do you believe your ability is crucial, or is success mostly a matter of luck?

   - How much do you enjoy what you're doing?

   - Do you have the skills needed to succeed? If not, what are you doing about this problem?

   Honest responses to such questions may help you to understand the strength of your achievement motivation and what's needed to increase it.

4. *Personal goals.* Do you set goals for yourself? If so, describe in a page or more some of your long-range, medium-range, and short-range goals. Even if you don't usually formulate personal goals, try writing out some of your important goals as explained in this chapter. You might find goal setting especially helpful in the areas of career, marriage, and family life. After you develop your list, ask yourself whether these goals are self-concordant or not.

5. *What are your primary emotions?* What emotions do you think you express most freely? Which emotions do you tend to disguise or conceal from others? If you are somewhat deceptive in sharing emotions with others, do you think this affects your interactions with them? Are others likely to hide some of their emotions from you? Which ones?

6. *Share your everyday feelings.* Do you share your feelings as readily as you'd like? If not, you might try this exercise. A good way to begin sharing your feelings is to share some of the safe, everyday feelings. For example, whenever you're especially pleased by something another person has done for you, tell this person how you feel about it. The practice of sharing these safe feelings may help you to become more aware of and comfortable in sharing your deeper feelings.

7. *Practice sending "I" messages.* Think of several situations in which someone else's behavior has become a problem for you. Then write out the appropriate "I" messages under

the respective four headings, as explained and illustrated in this chapter. If you feel comfortable doing so, you might try expressing some of these "I" messages in person.

8. *Explore the effects of anxiety in your life.* As you may recall, anxiety can have positive and negative effects in our lives. Think of at least two situations in your life, one in which anxiety stimulated you to do your best and one in which anxiety interfered with your performance. How do you account for the difference?

9. *Anger.* Recall a situation in which you became very angry. Did you tend to lose control, saying and doing things you later regretted? Or did you respond to the situation in a way that made known your grievance and helped to restore your sense of control? Looking back, what would you have done differently?

10. *Happiness.* Are you generally a happy person? Why did you come to the answer you did? If yes, what can you do to maintain your current level of well-being? If not, can you think of ways you can improve your general level of happiness?

QUESTIONS FOR SELF-REFLECTION

1. What are some of the dominant motives in your life?

2. How important to you are incentives like money and success?

3. Have overeating or snacking between meals become a problem for you?

4. How strong is your sensation-seeking motive?

5. How strong is your achievement motive in school? In your career?

6. Are you a self-starter? Or do you work better "under pressure"?

7. What are your personal goals for the next year? What about the next 5 years?

8. When asked, can you readily say "how you feel"?

9. Would you characterize yourself as an emotionally expressive person?

10. Did you grow up in a home in which people expressed their feelings freely?

11. Which emotions are the hardest for you to express?

12. How do you usually cope with anxiety?

13. When it comes to anger, do you think before you speak?

14. When you feel jealous, what do you say and do?

15. What makes you happy?

FOR FURTHER INFORMATION

RECOMMENDED READINGS

BLAIR, G. R. (2005). *The ten commandments of goal-setting.* Syracuse, NY: The GoalsGuy. This book provides a blueprint for achieving goals you set.

EKMAN, P. (2004). *Emotions revealed: Recognizing faces and feelings to improve communication and emotional life*. New York: Owl Books. This book discloses how to read faces; the information is based on scientific research.

HIRSCH, G. (2001). *Helping college students succeed: A model for effective intervention*. New York: Brunner-Routledge. If you are having trouble making your way through college, this is the book for you.

MCKAY, G., & DINKMEYER, D. (2002). *How you feel is up to you: The power of emotional choice* (2nd ed.). Atascadero, CA: Impact Publishers. A book that discusses the power of emotions and emotional regulation.

POTTER-EFRON, R. (2001). *Stop the anger now: A workbook for the prevention, containment, and resolution of anger*. Oakland, CA: New Harbinger Publications. A book about anger management.

WEB SITES AND THE INTERNET

http://www.helpself.com/iq-test.htm   Test your emotional IQ at this site. A self-help site with other useful information besides emotional intelligence.

http://www.mtn.org/EA/   The site of Emotions Anonymous. The site offers to use social support to assist individuals over the Internet to deal with a variety of troubling emotions.

http://elvers.stjoe.udayton.edu/history/history.asp   A site to research Abraham Maslow and his motivational theory. In fact, link to the psychology part of the site and you can find biographical information on many well-known psychologists.

http://www.mindtools.com/page6.html   A site designed to help you improve your goal-setting strategies. The site also contains information on time management, decision making, interpersonal communication, and other necessary life skills.

http://www.authentichappiness.sas.upenn.edu/   Dr. Martin Seligman's web site for positive psychology. The site contains questionnaires, newsletter articles, and more.

Making and Keeping Friends

MEETING PEOPLE
Are First Impressions Most
    Important?
Mistaken Impressions
Shyness

KEEPING FRIENDS
Friendships Are Precious
When Friends Get Together
Self-Disclosure—Those Little
    Secrets
Same-Sex, Opposite-Sex Friends
Staying Friends
Loneliness

SUMMARY
SELF-TEST
EXERCISES
QUESTIONS FOR SELF-REFLECTION
FOR FURTHER INFORMATION

Anita and Gale were best friends. They probably never would have met were it not for their positions at Ramona Community College. Both had obtained their master's degrees in psychology, Anita in California and Gale in Minnesota. Gale's husband's job created a career move for him so she and her husband moved away from the Midwest as soon as she finished her degree. Gale grew up in a middle-class family in Minnesota, where her father was a journalist and her mother an engineer. Anita grew up in Texas. Her life trajectory was not as easy as Gale's. Anita's father left her mother when Anita was very young. Anita's mother worked at various low-paying jobs, such as housekeeper at a motel. Her mother always said that she wanted her daughter to have a better life. Her daughter did. Anita's mother ensured that Anita had the opportunity to attend first a community college and then a good 4-year college. Anita was encouraged by her professors to continue her education. She pursued a master's degree and soon found herself in the position of being a new professor at Ramona. When Anita arrived, Gale was already a professor there. Gale was in her 40s, Anita in her late 20s. Gale was White and middle class; Anita was Latina and, before acquiring her education, decidedly lower class.

The two women seemingly had nothing in common, but Gale was immediately taken by this intelligent and personable young woman. Because they were the only two women in the department, Gale decided to informally mentor Anita through her early years as a fledgling professor. That is how their friendship began. Both women soon learned that they really did have common interests. Each enjoyed rhythm and blues, foreign films, and Tex-Mex cuisine. Their attitudes about politics and religion were very different, though. Gale was strongly Republican, rather conservative, and hardly religious. Anita was devoutly religious and a solid Democrat. Is the story of their friendship typical? How do people form friendships? Why do friendships dissolve? These and other issues are the focus of this chapter.

In our fast-paced, mobile society we come in contact with more people than did our parents and grandparents. Sadly, however, we have fewer close relationships. Today, there's a tendency to form many short-term acquaintances on the basis of shared interests and satisfactions rather than fewer, long-term friendships. This is especially true for well-educated individuals like Gale and Anita, who are some of the most mobile in our society. If you were to keep track of all the different people you come into contact with, say, during a 3-month period, you might be surprised to learn that you have met as many as several hundred people. Yet most of these contacts are fleeting and superficial.

Meeting a great variety of people enables us to develop a wide range of interests and relationships, but today there is also a greater risk of loneliness. As a result, more people are now engaged in the search for closer, more satisfying social ties, that is, lasting friendships and romantic attachments. The portrayal of close relationships on television—in which people move from shouting matches to lovemaking in a matter of minutes—tends to oversimplify the realities involved. Consequently, people's expectations of friendship, indeed their sense of entitlement to it, often exceed their understanding of what is involved, much less their ability to attain and maintain it.

MEETING PEOPLE

Like Anita and Gale, do you have at least one good friend with whom to share secrets, troubles, and joy? Each of us needs intimate as well as more superficial social relationships. On the one hand, we need a network of people to fulfill a variety of needs, such as the exchange of services and the alleviation of stress through friendly activities. On the other hand, each of us also needs a deep, caring relationship with one or more special persons, such as a close friend, lover, or spouse. Sharing our deepest thoughts and feelings with an understanding companion who accepts us—despite our faults—is one of life's most satisfying experiences (Steiner, 2002). It makes us feel at home in the world despite the usual ups and downs in everyday life. Those who lack close relationships often experience emotional isolation and loneliness, regardless of their network of other acquaintances.

At the same time, people differ in their respective needs for social relationships. Some people prefer a variety of relationships that satisfy different needs, often with little emotional depth. Others value the closeness that comes with the more intense emotional involvement of fewer people, such as a circle of close friends. Then, too, the same person's need for companionship fluctuates according to the mood of the moment. Most of us like to share happy occasions such as a birthday or a promotion at work, but we like to be alone when physically tired or embarrassed about something.

Are First Impressions Most Important?

When Gale first met Anita, Anita seemed very bright and engaging. Anita, on the other hand, wondered if a woman so senior to her would ever be friendly. From the beginning, they were busy forming **first impressions** of each other. *These are the initial impressions we form of others in which we tend to judge them on the basis of very little information.* Forming such impressions seems to be a very natural and inescapable process (Ybarra, 2001). Research, where strangers meet one another and then decide whether to interact, suggests that impressions are formed after very brief first encounters but endure for weeks later (Sunnafrank, Ramirez, & Metts, 2004).

In impression formation, we do not treat all information equally. Upon meeting a new person, incoming negative and positive information is used differently (Denrell, 2005). Negative information is given more weight (Ybarra, 2001) and remains more stable (Denrell). But why? Because positive behavior is the expected social norm. When someone does something nice for us, we *expect* it. We simply anticipate positive behavior from all people, including those who are secretly heartless. When someone behaves badly, though, there is little doubt in our minds what the behavior means and why it was done. We assume the behavior was done intentionally; thus, the person is evaluated as being bad. Similarly, we are unlikely to interact further with that person, thus allowing our initial negative impression to maintain itself (Denrell).

All of us do this—form indelible first impressions of other people. Again, why? One reason has to do with the need for understanding people around us, especially if we think we may have to interact with them in the future. We think forming impressions of others helps us better predict their behavior. Another reason may be **social comparison,** *which involves using others as a source of comparison to understand who we are relative to them* (e.g., comparing ourselves to classmates on intelligence). We often prefer friends (Gabriel, Carvallo, Dean, Tippin, & Renaud, 2005; Rüter & Mussweiler, 2005) or others engaged in the same task (Gaines, Duvall, Webster, & Smith, 2005; Seta, Seta, & McElroy, 2006) with whom to compare ourselves. Whatever the reasons, the basic principle of person perception remains the same: We frequently tend to form extensive impressions of others on the basis of very little information.

One other generalization has also been demonstrated, that first impressions probably are *most* important (Ybarra, 2001). That is, subsequent impressions or interactions little alter our first impressions. But how are these first impressions formed? At first, when people such as Anita and Gale meet, they have *surface contact* or *zero acquaintanceship.* They see each other and perhaps only exchange greetings at most. After this stage, though, people need to decide whether to continue the interaction. Psychologists have explored the factors that determine whether we indeed will continue the interaction. While luck plays a role, there are other factors that predictably attract us to others (Foster, 2005). Let's explore these factors.

Physical Attractiveness.   Another person's physical appearance is important in determining our impressions of them, whether they be potential friends or prospective romantic partners. Being pretty or handsome makes a strong first impression on others. Height, weight, sex, facial features, and dress all affect our senses and feelings. In fact, much research has concluded that physical appearance may be one of the most powerful determinants of our impressions of others even though we won't often admit this (Sangrador & Yela, 2000; Smith & Weber, 2005). The more physically attractive someone is, the more positively we judge that person (Byrne, Ervin, & Lamberth,

2004; Katz, 2003; Jackson, Hunter, & Hodge, 1995). When people have been asked to give their impressions of others, they attribute all sorts of positive qualities to attractive people. Many of these qualities actually have little or nothing to do with a person's physical appearance (Johnstone, Frame, & Bouman, 1992). Attractive people are judged to be more interesting, intelligent, compassionate, sociable, and better adjusted than less attractive people (e.g., Diener, Wolsic, & Fujita, 1995; Eagly & Makhijani, 1991; Langlois et al., 2000). They are regarded as more successful in their careers and happier in their personal lives. Physical attractiveness is also associated with such diverse accomplishments as earning higher grades, landing better jobs, and obtaining faster promotions, as well as having less serious psychological disorders than others (e.g., Jackson et al.).

People in our society are considered attractive if they have an appropriate waist-to-hip ratio with the waist circumference about 70 percent or 80 percent of the hip circumference (Furnham, Lavanchy, & McClelland, 2006; Singh, 1995; Streeter & McBurney, 2003), have symmetrical faces (Rhodes ,Yoshikawa, Clark, Leen, McKay, & Akamatsu, 2001), and are fairly thin (Henss, 1995). Some of these same effects are often found in other cultures (Rhodes et al.). In fact, there are so many cultural similarities in the parameters of attractiveness that some researchers believe they are biologically determined (Furnham et al., Langlois et al., 2000). D. Jones (1995) found that Americans, Brazilians, and Russians preferred large eyes, small noses, and full lips. And Hatfield and Sprecher (1995) gathered data from college students in the United States, Russia, and Japan on preferences for marital partners. In all three countries, men cared very much about physical attractiveness, and men cared more than women about appearance. The most likely explanation is that because of cultural conditioning, women in these cultures are less likely than men to initiate opposite-sex relationships.

These generalities are true up to a point. Individuals within various ethnic and racial groups tend to show some degree of ethnocentrism when judging the attractiveness of others. They find members of their own group more attractive than members of other groups (Freedman, Carter, Sbrocco, & Gray, 2004; Liu, Campbell, & Condie, 1995; Schooler, Ward, Merriwether, & Caruthers, 2004). Another caveat is this: Most of these standards are the typical "White" standards in our society (Poran, 2002). When standards of this group are used as ideal reference points by other groups, such as African Americans, for judging their *own* attractiveness, a slow but definite erosion of self-esteem can occur (Hall, 1995).

As you look around, it is obvious that few people of either sex have an ideal face or figure. Most of us have some attractive features as well as others we'd like to change. At the same time, each of us manages to modify the cultural expectations regarding physical attractiveness to fit our partners and ourselves (Fudge, Knapp, & Theune, 2002). For example, the better we like someone, the more we modify our subjective evaluation of that person's physical attractiveness. Beauty undeniably is in the eye of the beholder. Hence, there are any number of people in the world who would consider each one of us attractive—a good thing for you to keep in mind.

Each of us may fantasize about having a highly attractive romantic partner. In reality, when it comes to choosing a date or romantic partner, *we usually settle for someone like ourselves, at least in regard to physical attractiveness.* This tendency has been labeled the **matching hypothesis.** For example, Little, Burt, and Perrett (2006) asked independent raters to rate faces on attractiveness and other factors; the rated individuals were married (unbeknownst to the raters). Results showed that raters perceived similar levels of attractiveness for pairs of married partners.

Box 8–1

MEETING PEOPLE THROUGH PERSONAL ADS

Today, there is a booming business related to meeting people in our mobile, technocratic world. In 2004, Internet dating alone made $500 million in North America and over $250 million in Europe (Johnson, 2005). In recent years, the number of such ads and revenue have tripled, with the leading web site, Match.com, experiencing 154 percent growth (Donaldson-Evans, 2003). Online personals are especially interesting because they allow users to market themselves to a very broad audience, to present themselves via a number of different media (e.g., prose, video), and to interact with potential dates fairly anonymously (Gibbs, Ellison, & Heino, 2006). Gibbs et al., explain that the Internet is different from other media, first in that it has a broader user base than other media and that there are substantively different capabilities available to users. For example, not only can users take advantage of text-based descriptions, they can post photographs and video records as well as interact with potential dates using both asynchronous communication like e-mail and real-time communication such as instant messaging and chat rooms.

Perusing the personal ads provides a good window on interpersonal relationships in different cultures. For example, personal ads in China emphasize family and society whereas ads in America emphasize individualism (Parekh & Beresin, 2001). Here are some other findings. Lance (1998) found that men tend to emphasize their personality, good looks, slimness, and professional careers. Women also emphasized personality, good looks, slimness, and professional careers. In other words, advertisements heterosexual men and women fashion about themselves do not differ very much. While heterosexual men rarely mention gender roles in their ads, Phua (2002) found that gay men often reveal their gender or sex-role preference in their ads. Smith and Stillman (2002), however, discovered that lesbians rarely express a role preference as to "butch" or "femme," and when they do, it is for the more feminine role.

Several other studies have analyzed ads placed by gay men. Bartholome, Tewksbury, and Bruzzone's (2000) research demonstrated that in gay personal ads, there is a strong emphasis on physical appearance and sexual relations. The AIDS epidemic, however, has somewhat tempered partner seeking of gay men. Phua, Hopper, and Vazquez (2002) found that gay men more than any other individuals were more likely to mention health issues. In particular, Hatala, Baack, and Parmenter (1998) found that HIV-positive men tend to discuss health issues in their ads, whereas HIV-negative men are more likely to specify their seriousness of purpose and the desired characteristics of their future partners.

Some had predicted that race would play a large role in personal ads. Yancey and Yancey (1998) predicted that Whites would offer their higher-status race in exchange for attractiveness or financial security with regard to a partner of another race. Minorities, they assumed, would offer financial security or attractiveness to find a White partner. Yancey and Yancey were unable to support their hypothesis. Interestingly, race was *not* a significant factor in most personal ads.

Perhaps the most significant aspects of personal ads are whether they are honest and effective. Gibbs et al., (2006) research offers some insights. They found that not all individuals using the Internet for personal ads seek long-term relationships. Those who are seeking such relationships, however, are cognizant that an eventual face-to-face meeting is possible. Such individuals tend to be more honest, disclose more, and make their disclosures more consciously and intentionally than those not interested. Their disclosures, though, are not necessarily more positive than those placing less importance on face-to-face meetings or dates. The researchers also found the norm of reciprocity evidenced in the fact that when one participant disclosed more, the recipient felt obligated to disclose more. (The **norm of reciprocity** is *an unwritten rule that guides reciprocal behavior related to the granting of favors.*) Similarly and surprisingly, the researchers also found that greater honesty actually had a *detrimental* effect on success as measured by establishing a long-term relationship; being honest about a personal flaw made one less likely to find a long-term relationship. Additionally, while the vast majority of research participants (94 percent) said that they had been honest about their own disclosures, they felt that others misrepresented themselves (87 percent).

In terms of effectiveness (e.g., did the ad result in an acquaintanceship?), positive self-disclosures appeared most effective. Similarly, those who disclosed a lot were more likely not only to find success but to learn more about the recipient of the advertisement, perhaps due to reciprocity. On the other hand, honesty had a negative effect on success, perhaps because honesty involves revealing one's foibles as well as one's talents.

Taken as a whole, all of this research on Internet personal ads suggests that ". . . the Internet [is] a medium for identity manipulation . . . or at least selective self-presentation (Gibbs et al., p. 169). Buyer beware.

People are turning more to dating services or to personal ads to find romantic partners (although, interestingly, not necessarily to find friends). In these ads, they often describe their appearance. Box 8–1, "Meeting People Through Personal Ads," reveals research about this fascinating trend.

If you're in a stable romantic relationship, to what degree does the matching hypothesis apply to your relationship? Can you think of couples that are exceptions to this rule? All things considered, how important do you think physical attractiveness is in love and marriage? How important is it to friendships, whether same-sex or opposite-sex?

People we regard as physically unattractive are typically judged unfavorably. Like beauty, ugliness is mostly in the eye of the beholder. For some, obesity or homely facial features appear to be ugly, as are irregular features such as large noses, discolored skin, or physical handicaps (Crandall, 1994). Whatever the case, unattractive people may be discriminated against for no good reason. One young student in Gale's class who was confined to a wheelchair since an automobile accident observed, "Even when people hold the door open for me, they avoid touching me or looking me in the eye." Other students who had gotten to know this young man were able to look past his handicap at the person himself and liked him very much. Individuals such as this young man need friends and lovers as much as we all do.

Reputations.   Someone's reputation also affects our first impressions and whether we respect a person (Sleebos, Ellemers, & deGilder, 2006). Suppose Gale is your friend and says, "I can't wait for you to meet Anita." Even before you meet Anita, you'll probably find yourself forming a positive image of her based on what Gale tells you. Should you later discover Anita has some unfavorable qualities Gale didn't tell you about, chances are you'll give her the benefit of the doubt. Of course, it works the other way, too. If someone says, "I hear that professor named Gale is a terrible teacher," you may find yourself forming a negative impression of her, rightly or wrongly (Graziano, Jensen-Campbell, Shebilske, & Lundgren, 1993). Such is the power of reputation.

Similarity.   One other reason that we initially notice and decide to like others is that they seem similar to us; some scientists have even posited genetic and evolutionary reasons for this notion (Rushton & Bons, 2005). Anita and Gale quickly came to realize that they both liked Tex-Mex food and rhythm and blues. Even if people are not really similar to us, we often assume that they are. Research has shown there is a strong correlation between liking and similarity (Byrne et al., 2004; Morry & Gaines, 2005). In particular, people with the same attitudes are attracted to one another. "Birds of a feather [really] do flock together." How does this happen? When people interact, they cannot help noticing each other's age, sex, height, and other physical features. Shortly after, they begin to disclose attitudes and values to each other. Research has shown that the *proportion* of similar attitudes, not the raw number of similar attitudes, is most important. Figure 8–1 depicts how attitude similarity and liking are related.

There is less agreement about the importance of similarity based on needs and personal traits. According to one view, people with similar needs and personalities are attracted to each other; the other view is that people who are complementary (opposite but compatible) in their needs and traits are attracted. Actually, the theory of complementarity tends to apply mostly to *specific* traits rather than to the meshing of two personalities as a whole. A talkative person may therefore become attracted to someone who is quiet; a dominant individual might seek out a more dependent partner. Also, complementarity probably isn't important in the early stages of attraction, though it may become more important in a long-term relationship like marriage. Nevertheless, even

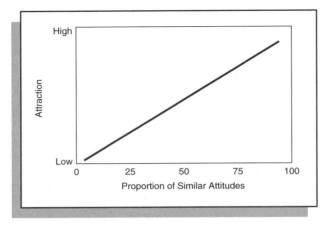

FIGURE 8–1
Attitude similarity and friendship.
The higher the proportion of similar attitudes between two people, the more they like each other.

among married couples, the weight of evidence seems to favor similarity as most influencing liking (Myers, 1998).

Propinquity.   Chances are that at some point in time your friends lived nearby, attended the same school, or worked at the same place, just as Gale and Anita did. Geographic nearness is especially important in the early stages of attraction, although the Internet is quickly changing this (Jacobson, 1999). First, the more you come into contact with people, the more opportunities you have for getting to know them better (Denrell, 2005). This factor is called proximity or propinquity. **Propinquity** means *physical closeness.* Many studies (e.g., Sias & Cahill, 1998; Smith & Weber, 2005) have demonstrated that the farther away a person lives or sits (in class, for example), the less likely that person is to become a friend. Being in close proximity also exposes us more to that individual so that we apparently come to know him of her better. Again, ample research has demonstrated this effect (e.g., Moreland & Beach, 1992). It is also true that "the better I know you, the better I know you." In other words, as we become more familiar with someone, we become better judges of that person's facial expressions and other nonverbal cues (Ansfield, DePaulo, & Bell, 1995; Sternglanz & DePaulo, 2004).

There's also a strong association between interaction and liking. That is, "the more I see you, the more I like you." And it works the other way, too: The more you like someone, the more you *want* to socialize with him or her (Vittengl & Holt, 2000). We also tend to emphasize the positive qualities and minimize the negative qualities of people we like to associate with (Denrell, 2005). Otherwise, we would feel we're stuck with an unpleasant friend, coworker, or roommate and may feel a lot of resentment. Then, too, our mainstream American social norms imply *cooperative* relationships with others. We, therefore, make a special effort to get along with people we live or work with, or else life might just be too miserable.

If it's true that the more you associate with someone, the more you like that person, then the longer couples are married the happier they should be—right? Because this is obviously not the case for many couples, other factors, such as compatibility, are involved. As a result, when there are serious differences or basic incompatibilities between two individuals, close contact may lead to overt conflict, resentment, and alienation. In such cases, "familiarity breeds contempt." It is well known among those who work in the justice system that in assault and murder cases, the leading suspects are likely to be lovers, spouses, or ex-spouses.

Nonverbal Signals.   Our impressions of others are also shaped by a variety of nonverbal signals (Ambady, Hallahan, & Rosenthal, 1995; Aronoff, 2006). In general, if a new acquaintance's face or gestures remind us of someone else that we know and like, we transfer our positive feelings about the old acquaintance to the new one. On the other hand, we also tend to transfer our negative feelings about a disliked person onto a new acquaintance who reminds us of the disliked person (Anderson & Berk, 1998). Additionally, a person's posture and gestures affect our impressions in other ways. Those who stand erect or walk youthfully make a more favorable impression than those who slouch. Also, people who point, glare, and interrupt a lot make a more negative impression than those who are attentive to what we say.

As you might guess, the face plays an especially vital role in our perception of others (Gladwell, 2002). Gaze, or looking into someone else's eyes, is very important (MacCrae, Hood, Milne, Rowe, & Mason, 2002). We are favorably impressed with people who smile and look us in the eye. People who make eye contact with us are apt to be seen as more trustworthy and likeable unless they gaze into our eyes for an uncomfortably long time. Those who avoid our gaze, whether from shyness or deceit, may strike us less favorably. In addition, those whose faces appear angular seem to us to be threatening or angry while those whose faces appear rounded are perceived as happy and likeable (Aronoff, 2006; Bar & Neta, 2006). Look at the faces in Figure 8–2 to see how they affect you.

There is a long-running theme in psychology that some facial expressions are universal (Matsumoto, 2002). (See also Chapter 7, which includes information on emotions.) In other words, a smiling face in Nigeria communicates joy in much the same way a smiling face communicates joy in Germany. A caveat is that Marsh, Elfenbein, and Ambady (2003) and Beaupré and Hess (2005) have been able to demonstrate that facial expressions of emotion can contain nonverbal "accents" that identify the expresser's nationality or culture. Their research suggests that just as languages and voices contain accents, so, too, may nonverbal cues.

Verbal Signals.   There are also dimensions of other people's verbal communication patterns that shape our perceptions of them—not the words and their meanings, but other features of verbal communication such as the rate of speech, pauses, and pitch.

FIGURE 8–2
We perceive rounded faces as happier and more likeable than angular faces.

These unspoken but important features of spoken communications are called **paralinguistics** (Epley & Kruger, 2005). Use of e-mail and the Internet to communicate greatly decreases the use of paralinguistic cues and perhaps decreases our accuracy and comprehension of others (Epley & Kruger; Kruger, Epley, Parker, & Ng, 2005) as well as decreases the possibility that a long-standing relationship will form (Bertacco & Deponte, 2005). On the other hand, certain paralinguistic cues—such as gestures—when used without speech, can actually take on the full burden of communication to another person (Goldin-Meadow, 2006). The message is that when you communicate electronically, it is important to communicate clearly.

Recently, paralinguistic cues have been used to detect deception and lying. Davis, Markus, Walters, Vorus, and Connors (2005) videotaped criminal suspects and found that cues discriminating true versus false statements included such things as word repeats, speech speed, and nonverbal animation level. Surprisingly, most people are not very good at detecting deception and lying even though it is important to business dealings, law enforcement, political life, and interpersonal relations (O'Sullivan, 2005). There also are nonverbal as well as verbal communication differences between men and women. You can read more about the relationships of gender to paralinguistics and spoken communications in Box 8–2, "When Men and Women Communicate."

Mistaken Impressions

Anita initially assumed that Gale would not be interested in being friends with her because of their age difference. Anita was mistaken. The biggest single reason we misjudge others is the lack of sufficient information about them, as first happened when Anita

---

Box 8–2

WHEN MEN AND WOMEN COMMUNICATE

When a man and a woman converse with each other . . .

- Men interpret "backchannels" (e.g., "uh-huh") differently from women as if they were raised in two different cultures (Mulac et al., 1998).

- Women and men respond similarly to comforting messages that are person-centered (Jones & Burleson, 2003).

- Men have more difficulty interpreting what women are saying than women have interpreting what men are saying (Edwards, 1998).

- In terms of nonverbal communication, women more directly orient their bodies to the speaker and use gaze, while men lean forward and show more postural congruence with the speaker (Guerrero, 1997).

- Women underestimate men's commitment, and men overperceive women's sexual intent (Haselton, 2003; Haselton & Buss, 2000).

- Men increase their responsiveness when women use a facilitative style; on the other hand, women maintain a similar rate of response regardless of the gender of the facilitative speaker (Hannah & Murachver, 1999).

- Men do most of the talking, more of the interrupting, and raise fewer topics than women (Atwater, 1992).

Some of these differences may be meaningless, because Basow and Rubenfield (2003) suggest that it is not "men" versus "women" per se, but rather masculinity and femininity that are traits available to both men and women that create the differences.

met Gale. Nor should this be surprising, given our tendency to "size up" people so hastily. When we quickly assess someone, we generally use **heuristics** or *mental short-cuts* for making complex decisions. One such shortcut or heuristic is the **false consensus effect,** *in which we assume others feel as we do* (Alicke & Largo, 1995; Lapinski & Rimal, 2005; Pinel, Long, Landau, Alexander, & Pyszczynski, 2006). We might guess, then, that if Gale initially liked Anita, she also falsely assumed that Anita liked her in return. Additionally, we also form mistaken impressions of others because of false cues, such as stereotypes and underestimating the importance of the situation the other people are in. **Mistaken impressions** are *false or erroneous perceptions of others, often based on insufficient evidence.*

False cues consist of various signals and indirect suggestions that unconsciously trigger certain associations in our minds. Signs of money and status often lead to mistaken impressions, especially to the unsuspecting. Because people who are successful and financially well off frequently live in large, impressive houses and drive expensive cars, we assume mistakenly that anyone who indulges in expensive cars and clothes is rich. Unscrupulous individuals deliberately take prestigious addresses and entertain at lavish parties to impress others. One man and his wife who lived in Ramona where Gale and Anita worked and were living on Social Security transformed themselves into jet-setters by displaying the signs of wealth even though they were poor. They let it be known that they were soon to inherit millions from a rich uncle. Then they ran up huge charge account bills against their anticipated fortune. In due time, however, their unpaid creditors became suspicious and the couple was brought to justice. Because this couple acted rich, most people merely assumed they were.

We also misjudge people because of **stereotypes**—*widespread generalizations that have little, if any, basis in fact and typically are held about groups of people.* Whenever people begin statements with phrases such as "*all* teachers" or "*women* drivers" or "*those people* are all the same,*" they're slipping into stereotypical thinking. Stereotypes are learned in one of two ways—by actual contact with an individual from the stereotyped group or

We often form impressions of another person based on little actual information, such as whether the individual wears glasses.

by discussing the stereotyped group with others (Ruscher, Cralley, & O'Farrell, 2005; Thompson, Judd, & Park, 2000). Research shows that the tendency to stereotype is, unfortunately, quite natural or automatic in humans (Lepore & Brown, 2002; Paul, 1998). Moreover, stereotyping might be our *dominant* response, not just in private but in public settings as well (Lambert et al., 2003). Unfortunately, if the stereotype is negative, the biased holder of the stereotype is unlikely to associate further with the target of the bias, thus maintaining the stereotype (Sherman, Stroessner, Conrey, & Azam, 2005).

A stereotype held by many of us is that people who wear glasses are smarter than those who don't (Huguet, Croizet, & Richetin, 2004). The unspoken assumption is that such people need glasses because they've strained their eyes from so much reading. The truth of the matter is that the need for glasses depends more on heredity than on one's study habits. Here are some other stereotypes: Men with beards, mustaches, and an abundance of body hair are more masculine and virile than those with less hair. Brunette women are seen as more intelligent and responsible than blondes—the latter as funnier and sexier than brunettes. Redheads of both sexes are seen as more "hot-tempered" than people with other hair colors. Do you use stereotypes? Why? Do you, yourself, sometimes feel misunderstood because of stereotypes? If so, which ones? How do you respond to others when they aim a stereotype or prejudice against you? Is your response productive?

We also *tend to label people good or bad because we know they possess (at least) a few good or a few bad characteristics.* This is called the halo effect or devil effect (Godoy et al., 2005). In the former case, it's as if the people we like wear a halo (ring of light) over their heads, like an angel, and can do no wrong. In other words, the **halo effect** *is inferring uniformly positive traits from the appearance of a few positive traits.* We're especially apt to like these people if we perceive them to be warm and sociable. When we regard people as warm and outgoing, we're apt to attribute all sorts of other positive qualities to them, such as intelligence and industriousness. Conversely, if we see others as cold and with-drawn, we tend to attribute additional negative qualities to them. Hence, the **devil (or horns) effect** means *inferring uniformly negative traits from an appearance of a few negative traits.* In reality, of course, few individuals are all good or all bad. Instead, you should bear in mind that each of us is a complex mixture of traits, some desirable and others not so desirable.

Another source of error is that we frequently misjudge people by not taking suffi-cient account of *situational* influences on their behavior. We assume that people are *always* acting in character (i.e., the behavior is trait induced). For example, if Anita dropped her coffee, Gale might think of her as clumsy rather than attribute the spill to the fact that the coffee was hot. The truth is that people are often constrained by their immediate situations. *The tendency to **over**attribute people's behavior to their personalities rather than to their circumstances* is so pervasive and of such importance to social perception that it has been called the **fundamental attribution error** (e.g., O'Sullivan, 2003; Truchot, Maure, & Patte, 2003). Here is another example: One day Gale and Anita had a verbal skirmish. Anita was angry with Gale because Gale had criticized Anita's grading strate-gies. "Too many high grades," growled Gale, "You'll make the rest of us unpopular with the students." Little did Anita know that Gale simply was exhausted from staying up late the night before to grade her own students' papers. To avoid misjudging people, we must take account of the powerful and changing influences of their situation. Thus, it is wise to observe someone in a *variety* of different situations *across time* in order to know what that person is really like.

Shyness

"Everyone but me was having such a good time laughing and talking," said Anita after the fall opening-day faculty reception. "Gale was moving around the room greeting friends. There I was trying to think of something to say to this woman I hardly knew. She must have felt sorry for me. I couldn't wait until the party was over."

Does this sound familiar? **Shyness**—*the tendency to avoid contact or familiarity with others*—afflicts people of all ages, but especially the young. A large number of Americans identify themselves as shy (Schrof & Schultz, 1999b), and almost half of all Americans report a chronic problem with shyness (Carducci, 1999; Carducci & Zimbardo, 1995; Marano, 2005). Similarly, about 80 percent of American college students report they have been shy at some point in their lives (Carducci; Carducci & Zimbardo). It is now thought that more women suffer from shyness than men (Schrof & Schultz, 1999b; Walsh, 2002). Shyness is typically consistent across situations and over time; in other words, shyness seems to be an enduring personality trait (Crozier, 2005). Shyness means different things for different people and covers a wide range of feelings and behaviors, but overall the experience of shyness (e.g., fear of social rejection and of social incompetence) is essentially the same in most cultures (Jackson, Flaherty, & Kosuth, 2000).

At one end of the shyness spectrum are those people who are not especially apprehensive about meeting people. When they are alone, it is because they prefer being in nature or working with ideas or things rather than with people. In the middle range are those who are sometimes embarrassed or occasionally lack self-confidence and prefer their own company (Crozier, 2005). Such individuals hesitate to ask for a date or a favor from others.

At the other extreme are individuals whose shyness has become a sad form of self-imprisonment. *In its extreme form, shyness is called* **social anxiety** *or* **social phobia** *and may severely interfere with a person's life* (Albano & Hayward, 2004; Schrof & Schultz, 1999b). For example, some individuals with social phobia turn to alcohol to lubricate their social interactions; they drink to inhibit their shyness and to enhance their sociability (Santesso, Schmidt, & Fox, 2004; Walsh, 2002). Social phobia is a problem of living but is also considered a psychological disorder with lifetime prevalence of between 10 and 15 percent of the population (Walsh). For this extreme form of shyness, antidepressants or antianxiety medication can be used for treatment (Capista, 1999). Other psychological interventions, such as social skills training, may work equally well (Albano & Hayward; Walsh).

Almost all of us tend to be shy in some situations, such as meeting strangers, dealing with people of the opposite sex, and being in large groups. To learn more about your own shyness level, answer the quiz on shyness found in Activity 8–1, "How Shy Are You?"

People who are habitually shy are different: They see shyness as something within themselves, that is, as a personal trait (Bruch & Belkin, 2001). They dislike being shy, though. Shyness also creates many problems for them: feeling lonely (Jackson, Fritch, Nagasaka, & Gunderson, 2002), being overly self-conscious and unassertive, having difficulty making friends (Bruch, Hamer, & Heimberg, 1995), being unable to think clearly in the presence of others, or freezing up in the middle of a conversation (Carducci, 1999; Carducci & Zimbardo, 1995). Shy people are often depressed, too (Jackson et al.), and misunderstood by others. They are apt to be regarded as aloof, condescending, emotionally "cold," and egocentric rather than shy.

In American culture, we value freedom, cherish our independence, and celebrate bravado, so shy people do not fit our mainstream culture. This is not true in all cultures.

ACTIVITY 8–1

HOW SHY ARE YOU?

INSTRUCTIONS: *For each of the following statements, indicate your level of agreement on a scale of one (1) = "strongly disagree" to seven (7) "strongly agree."*

1. I like to go on blind dates or to go out with someone I hardly know.

   Strongly disagree   1   2   3   4   5   6   7   Strongly agree

2. When I have to give a speech or participate in a debate, I approach the task with confidence.

   Strongly disagree   1   2   3   4   5   6   7   Strongly agree

3. I am assertive enough to stop a stranger on the street and ask what time it is.

   Strongly disagree   1   2   3   4   5   6   7   Strongly agree

4. When there are lots of strangers at a social gathering, I enjoy meeting them.

   Strongly disagree   1   2   3   4   5   6   7   Strongly agree

5. I am not bashful about meeting other people I do not already know.

   Strongly disagree   1   2   3   4   5   6   7   Strongly agree

6. When a small group of people is talking, I am one of the individuals who participates most.

   Strongly disagree   1   2   3   4   5   6   7   Strongly agree

7. I do not mind riding in crowded elevators even if all of us strangers should become trapped together.

   Strongly disagree   1   2   3   4   5   6   7   Strongly agree

8. If I think that my grade is incorrect, I am not timid about approaching the professor.

   Strongly disagree   1   2   3   4   5   6   7   Strongly agree

9. I feel I can readily ask my neighbors or friends for favors.

   Strongly disagree   1   2   3   4   5   6   7   Strongly agree

10. I generally feel comfortable the first day of class whether or not I know anyone else in the room.

    Strongly disagree   1   2   3   4   5   6   7   Strongly agree

SCORING: Add up your scores and record the total here:_____

The highest possible score is 70. If you scored at the high end of this scale (i.e., 50–70), you likely have confidence in your social skills and enjoy the company of other people, whether they are friends or strangers. If you scored at the low end of the scale (0–20), you might want to think about how shy you really are and what you can do to overcome shyness if it is a detriment to you. Remember, though, that the scale was developed for this book and is not scientific. The scale is intended to start you thinking about your own level of comfort around other people.

In many Asian cultures, the Chinese and Japanese cultures, for example, reticent individuals might be construed as more socially sensitive than extroverted individuals and therefore be more accepted by their peers (Carducci & Zimbardo, 1995; Chen, Rubin, & Sun, 1992; Sakuragi, 2004). Cross-cultural research shows that Israelis tend to be the least shy (Carducci & Zimbardo).

Where does shyness originate? Although some shyness can be traced to biology (Aron, Aron, & Davies, 2005), most psychologists assume it is learned in childhood (Walsh, 2002) or at least might be the result of *both* nature and nurture (Aron et al.). On the other hand, the cause may be related to the process of **attribution** (Bruch & Belkin, 2001), *in which we search for the causes for our own or someone else's behavior.* In Japan, for example, when children succeed, parents get the credit, so the child may be construed as shy. In Israel, a child who *tries* gets rewarded regardless of the child's success. Israeli, then, but not Japanese children take chances and do things that make them stand out and seem less shy (Carducci & Zimbardo, 1995).

If you or someone you know suffers from shyness, rest assured that shyness can be reduced by learning to modify shyness when it creates problems (Albano & Hayward, 2004; Scholing & Emmelkamp, 1990). Here's how:

- First and foremost, strive to reduce the inner monitoring of your own thoughts, feelings, and actions, especially the concern for how people see you and whether they will reject you. Instead, focus on your participation in the activity.
- Second, identify those aspects of situations that elicit shyness, such as meeting new people, as well as the social skills you may be lacking.
- Third, develop your social skills, such as how to initiate and carry on a conversation and how to assert yourself. In other words, allow yourself some successes on the interpersonal front.
- Fourth, keep in mind that shyness subsides when you step out of your usual identity, as in when you become totally absorbed in something or when you are helping others.
- Fifth, try to stop being so self-critical and perfectionistic. If shyness has become too disabling, seek counseling or therapy.

Interestingly, shyness is on the rise in America. The advent of technology in the form of e-mail and voice mail has reduced the need for us to meet face-to-face (Schrof & Schultz, 1999b; Yuen & Lavin, 2004). Some experts claim that these electronic means of communication have the potential to isolate us from others (Scealy, Phillips, & Stevenson, 2002) or can be addicting (Campbell, Cumming, & Hughes, 2006). Research has indeed borne out that the Internet can reduce our social well-being and increase our isolation (Kraut et al., 1998; Moody, 2001). By using the Internet and other less personal means of communication, the opportunities for shy people to practice their face-to-face interpersonal skills is decreased. On the other hand, if face-to-face interaction is so feared that individuals are lonely and isolated from others, technology may afford some opportunities for meeting others (Campbell, Cumming, et al.). Probably a balance of electronic and interpersonal communication is best.

KEEPING FRIENDS

While we treasure our solitude, most of us cherish time with our friends and family. The desire for human connectedness and attachment is a fundamental human motive (Asher & Paquette, 2003; Baumeister & Leary, 1995). Perhaps it was Gale and Anita's desire to have a good friend inside the psychology department that brought them together in the first place. Think about how you've met your good friends. Can you recall what attracted you to one another? Did you become friends instantly or did the relationship grow slowly? Did you actively have to cultivate the friendship?

Frequently, we're attracted to people with whom we have a lot in common, as mentioned earlier. We may be interested in the same career goals or taking the same classes. In some instances, we're attracted to people who are different from us; they complement us in some way. Then, too, a lot depends on the "chemistry," or subjective factors, when people meet. And, surely, you have noticed how we seem to get along with some people better than others almost from the start.

Friendships Are Precious

After we have formed our first impressions and decided whether we want to continue the interaction, the more we get to know someone the more likely our relationship will ripen into friendship as did Gale and Anita's. **Friendship** can be defined as *the affectionate attachment between two or more people.* We usually think of a friend as someone we've known a long time, which is often true. Yet friendship has more to do with *the quality of the relationship* rather than with the frequency of association (Berndt, 2002). A high-quality friendship is characterized by helping one another, intimacy or the disclosing of secrets, mutual praise for successes, loyalty, and other positive features (Berndt). Friendships provide warmth and closeness that are often missing in other daily transactions. As society becomes more complex and mobile and thus more impersonal, we cherish close friendships even more. Close friendships can save us from depression and loneliness and thus enhance our mental and social well-being (Knickmeyer, Sexton, & Nishimura, 2002; Oswald & Clark, 2003; Zea, Reisen, Poppen, Bianchi, & Echeverry, 2005). Friendships in childhood are especially crucial and have been demonstrated to be related to whether a child is victimized or accepted by peers (Asher & Paquette, 2003).

When Friends Get Together

Not surprisingly, one of the most common activities among friends is having an intimate talk. This is one of the activities most frequently mentioned by men, women, and children (Berndt, 2002). Just as Anita and Gale might, you may call a friend to tell her about an embarrassing incident that happened to you in class. Or your friend may want to talk about the trouble he's having with his girlfriend. In both instances, sharing your feelings and getting someone else's reaction on the subject may be extremely helpful. Another frequently mentioned activity, especially for men, is doing a favor for a friend. Perhaps you ask to borrow a friend's car. Or your friend may want you to pick her up after work. Asking or doing a favor for someone else presupposes a great deal of trust as well as give-and-take in a relationship, both important qualities of friendship.

As mentioned in the chapter on stress, one of the greatest favors friends can do for each other is to lend a listening ear. This form of social assistance is called **social support** (Duffy & Wong, 2003) and is defined elsewhere in the book as *a process whereby one individual or group offers comfort and advice to others who can use it as a means of coping.* Although people who report good general well-being have only a few close friends, they often report high levels of sharing of intimate and personal information with those friends (McDonough & Munz, 1994; Reynolds & Repetti, 2006). Sometimes a casual friend becomes a close friend *because* that person listens sympathetically to some personal problem. Faced with crises, many people will turn to a friend before talking about it with their families, because a friend may serve as a sounding board and provide needed support without the conflict of kinship loyalties. Do you have friends you could turn to in a personal crisis? If so, who are they? Remember, though, that people who frequently ask their friends to share serious problems that are more properly discussed with a professional may be asking too much. In these instances, it's often best to refer a friend to the appropriate help, while you remain supportive. Box 8–3 further elaborates upon this theme.

Self-Disclosure—Those Little Secrets

As the relationship between two people progresses from strangers to acquaintances to close friends, individuals disclose a greater breadth and depth of information about themselves. Disclosure is a way to bring us closer to others (Gibbs et al., 2006). **Self-disclosure** is *the sharing of intimate or personal information with others.* For example, Anita and Gale shared an apartment for a month when Anita's new apartment was being refurnished, so Anita met Gale's husband, Rick. At first Rick and Anita talked about common, benign topics such as their favorite movies, baseball teams, and foods. By the end of Anita's stay, all three felt more comfortable talking about a greater variety of subjects, such as their career goals, leisure activities, and more intimate matters like health concerns, families, religious beliefs, and political preferences. As Rick and Anita became good friends, they developed greater trust in each other and shared matters that might have threatened a weaker relationship.

Much research demonstrates that self-disclosure, especially of personal secrets, has health benefits. For instance, research shows that gay men who keep their sexual orientation to themselves are at greater risk for cancer and infectious diseases than those who do not conceal their sexual orientation (Kelly, 1999; Zea et al., 2005). What is it about disclosure that promotes well-being? One notion is that the teller of the secret gains new insights into the secret so no longer has to expend effort hiding it.

Increasingly higher levels of self-disclosure do not always lead to greater intimacy between two people and can sometimes backfire (Kelly, 1999). Ordinarily, the more you disclose about yourself, the more your friend will reciprocate (Levesque, Steciuk, & Ledley, 2002; Morry, 2005). If your friend does not feel sufficiently comfortable or trustful in the

Box 8–3

To Whom Can You Turn?

There's an old saying—"A friend in need is a friend indeed." With this in mind, think of all the people you call your friends. Now list the names of those

> who would really listen to you when you need to talk;
>
> with whom you can share your innermost feelings;
>
> to whom can you turn when you're very upset;
>
> with whom you can be totally yourself;
>
> whom you can count on to help during a personal crisis.

If you can name only two or three people, your personal support system may be too narrow. Perhaps your name isn't on enough other people's lists, too. After all, friendship is a two-way affair.

Young adults are more apt to turn to their peers than their families when in need. People who are middle-aged or older are more inclined to seek out members of their families (Steiner, 2001), perhaps because the current generation of older people has been socialized this way. With a growing population of elderly and the development of adult communities, perhaps future generations of older people will be more peer-oriented (Buys, 2001).

relationship, however, he or she may not reciprocate such intimate self-disclosure. Knowing intimate details about you would help your friend hold a power advantage over you. Eventually, you'd back off and restrict your communication to more superficial matters to balance the power. In other instances, someone may share information that presents a conflict in the relationship, so that both partners may retreat to more superficial levels of sharing.

For example, a young man in his late 30s disclosed to his wife a brief sexual affair he'd had while out of town on business a few months earlier. He reassured his wife that he felt no affection for this other woman and promised never to see her again. The young man also said he felt better for having told her and hoped it would bring them

Self-disclosure occurs when we share personal or intimate information with others. Individuals with high self-esteem are more likely to feel comfortable disclosing information to others.

closer together. He was wrong. His wife became extremely angry, resentful, and suspicious. Ever since then, she has doubted that he loves her and is worried about what he's doing while he's out of town. Both partners have become more guarded, a reversal of their former intimacy.

Gale and Anita were fortunate in that they each shared intimate information with the other, trusted the other to maintain confidentiality, and forgave one another for angry outbursts. Other individuals, however, differ in their willingness to share personal information for several reasons. Those who enjoy high self-esteem feel not only more comfortable sharing personal information about themselves but also greater security that comes with close relationships. Those with low self-esteem are more apt to withhold personal information and thereby fail to learn about themselves through closeness with others.

Men and women also differ in their willingness to share personal matters face-to-face or even electronically (Colley & Todd, 2002; Fehr, 2004; Oxley, Dzindolet, & Miller, 2002). Pairs of women characteristically engage in more intimate disclosure than do pairs of men (Dolgin, Meyer, & Schwartz, 1991). In fact, female–female friendship pairs seem particularly close (Dolgin & Kim, 1994). Disclosure by men is less reciprocal. That means men disclose less than is disclosed to them (Parker & deVries, 1993), and their disclosures are apt to cover less personal topics such as politics or school (Colley & Todd; Oxley et al.). Some psychologists suspect that women use disclosure to enhance interpersonal connectedness, whereas men use disclosure to strive for mastery and power (Suh, Moskowitz, Fournier, & Zuroff, 2004). However, with the diminishment of gender-role stereotypes, we can expect men to engage in more self-disclosure than has been the case in the past.

There are also significant cultural differences in how acceptable self-disclosure is. Several studies (Asai & Barnlund, 1998) have found that the Japanese are less likely to explore their inner reactions as frequently and thoroughly as do Americans. The result is less self-disclosure in Japan than in the United States (Kito, 2005). Another study replicated this finding (Chen, 1995) in yet another group of Asians (Taiwanese college students). On the other hand, Americans disclosed more information, especially on superficial topics, such as interests, work, and finances, than did the Taiwanese. Thus, there are general cultural differences between Eastern and Western societies in self-disclosure. Finally, Goodwin Nizharadze, Luu, Kosa, & Emelyanova (1999) found differences in self-disclosure in two seemingly similar cultures, the former Soviet-bloc countries of Hungary and Russia. Self-disclosure was far more common in Hungary than in Russia. We might conclude that even among apparently similar cultures there exist differences in self-disclosure.

Same-Sex, Opposite-Sex Friends

Friendship is not necessarily more important to one sex than to the other, but it does tend to have different meanings for men and women. More specifically, intimacy plays a more central role among women friends (Fehr, 2004), so the case of Anita and Gale in this chapter fits our subject well. Women generally are more physically and emotionally expressive in their friendships than men. Also, as we've already seen, women are more apt to share intimate details about their lives, such as their worries, joys, and secrets (Oxley et al., 2002). At the same time, women experience greater anxiety over close relationships. Tensions, jealousies, and rejections are more common in friendships between women, whereas men are apt to engage in outright disputes over money, property, and dominance. Usually, men are not as emotionally close in their friendships with other men (Oxley et al.). Instead, they are more likely than women to seek out a male friend to share in a particular activity, like tennis or hunting, or to ask a favor. Yet, when in the throes of a serious personal problem, men are just as inclined to seek out a close friend.

In addition, with changing gender roles, neither the "activity friend" nor the "all-purpose friend" friendship style is distinctively male or female. Women, whose active lives now include everything from working lunches to health-club workouts, are discovering the pleasure of activity friends. And men, realizing the importance of a personal support system, are discovering the value of an all-purpose friend with whom they share their deeper feelings and concerns. Neither friendship style gives an advantage in mental health, achievement, or the enjoyment of life. Most of us are better off with a mixture of both types of friends of both sexes. Each type of friend brings out and sharpens different aspects of ourselves.

Can you be a close friend with someone of the opposite sex without being romantically or sexually involved with this person (Bleske & Buss, 2000)? Some people remain skeptical; but now that men and women are working side by side just about everywhere, more people of both sexes are choosing friends of the opposite sex. Most people feel that opposite-sex friendships are different, in that they may easily turn into erotic (Chatterjee, 2001) or romantic relationships that are clearly more intense and dynamic than friendships (Collins & van Dulmen, 2006). There is new research emerging on this type of friendship, although the literature remains rather sparse (Messman, Canary, & Hause, 2000).

Evolutionary psychologists say that opposite-sex and same-sex friendships are different from each other. In Buss's research (Benenson & Alavi, 2004; Bleske & Buss, 2000), men perceived sex with their women friends as more beneficial than did women friends with their men friends. On the other hand, women reported more benefit from receiving protection from their men friends than men reported about their women friends. There was one similarity, however, between the two sexes. Each reported turning more to opposite-sex than same-sex friends to learn how to best attract a mate.

Because an opposite-sex friend is a potential mate, do men and women friends have to work to keep their friendships platonic? The answer seems to be yes. Messman et al., (2000) studied motives for remaining in a platonic state with someone of the opposite sex. In their study, the reported motives for maintaining the relationship as friends only were, in order from most to least important,

- wanting to safeguard the friendship as a friendship;
- not being physically attracted to the other person;
- fearing disapproval from a network of mutual friends;
- already being committed to a third party;
- avoiding risk (i.e., experiencing hurt) related to the relationship;
- not being ready to be in a romantic relationship with the friend.

The researchers also found that the main maintenance strategy was to play a supportive role to the opposite-sex friend. In fact, this supportive role (giving comfort, advice, and encouragement) as well as taking part in shared activities was related to positive friendships where no one in the pair benefited from the relationship more than the other person. When there was imbalance (or inequity), negative maintenance strategies (to avoid a romantic involvement) were likely to be employed, such as fearing disapproval of mutual friends. Opposite-sex friendships indeed are different from same-sex friendships.

Staying Friends

"There's no friend like an old friend," goes the time-honored saying. With old friends we can relax and be ourselves without much fear of rejection. We're familiar with each other's mannerisms and make allowances for each other's weaknesses. Staying friends depends more on the special qualities of the relationship (Bagwell et al., 2005) and less on the frequency of contact between two people. Most of us have some friends we don't see very often, but we still consider them friends. We may keep in touch by calling occasionally or exchanging cards, letters, or e-mails. Class reunions and vacations also afford opportunities for renewing old ties. At the same time, physical separation often exacts a toll on friendship, as when high school best friends attending separate colleges (Oswald & Clark, 2003). When people are asked why friendships cool off, the most frequently cited reason is that one person has moved away. In fact, the most common reason people cite for the breakup of friendships is simply life transitions; 77 percent of American adults said that their friendships ended because of life changes (Davis, 1996). One person's life situation changes and the other person's does not. Specific life changes that affect friendships include marriage, childbirth, new jobs, and different schedules.

Apart from life transitions, the most common reason friendships end is feeling betrayed by a friend; in other words, trust is broken. **Trust** can be defined as *people's abstract, positive expectations that they can count on friends and partners to care for them and be responsive to their needs, now and in the future* (Berscheid, 1994). The importance of trust and the ability to keep a confidence in friendship cannot be overestimated. In Russia, it is the leading cause for friendships to break up (Sheets & Lugar, 2005). In one American study, about one-third of the people said that their basic expectations in friendship had been violated by a best or close friend. In some instances, there were minor infringements, such as using a personal item without asking permission. Other cases involved more serious offenses, such as "repeating things I said in confidence" or "trying to seduce my wife." Sadly, trust in others has declined steadily in the United States. In fact, if trust continues to decline at its present rate, our society may well become pervaded by mistrust rather than trust (Robinson & Jackson, 2001).

There are yet other reasons friendships cool. Friendships may also break off because the individuals discover they have very different views on matters that are important to them. Not surprisingly, this is the third most frequently cited reason for ending a friendship. Curiously, in some cases, increasing intimacy between friends, such as may be occasioned by taking a vacation together, may make them more aware of their differences than their similarities, or they find they have less in common than originally believed. But friendship is such a deeply satisfying experience that each of us will continue making new friends throughout life, while cherishing the special closeness that comes with a long-lasting friendship.

Loneliness

Anita was fortunate to have someone like Gale meet her, mentor her, and befriend her. On the other hand, some people have trouble forming or keeping close friendships, and they experience loneliness. Essentially, **loneliness** is *a subjective state reflecting* *the fact that the quality and quantity of relationships wanted is lower than the quality and quantity of relationships available* (Archibald, Bartholomew, & Marx, 1995). Do not confuse loneliness with solitude, which is a more objective and, often, a desired state denoting the absence of people. You can feel lonely despite being surrounded by others if you don't feel close to those people. On the other hand, in terms of solitude, you have many friends but deliberately seek brief periods away from them without feeling lonely. It thus appears that loneliness is largely a state of mind that results from the gap between our desire for closeness and the failure to find it (Rokach & Neto, 2005). Loneliness can be associated with depression, anxiety, unhappiness, and shyness (Asher & Paquette, 2003; Neto, 1992). It is also associated with other health factors (Pressman et al., 2005). Lonely people, for instance, tend to smoke more, have a more sedentary lifestyle, and be more obese than those who are socially connected (Cacioppo, Hawkley, & Berntson, 2003). Interestingly, the *duration* of loneliness rather than the intensity of it may be related to reported psychological and somatic stress symptoms (DeBerard & Kleinknecht, 1995).

Ironically, traditional college students who are surrounded by hundreds, even thousands, of peers suffer more loneliness than any other age group (Wiseman, Mayseless, & Sharabany, 2006). Having loosened ties with their parents, people this age are actively seeking intimacy with their peers, especially those of the opposite sex. The idealism of youth, plus the desire for intimacy and a happy marriage, makes them especially sensitive to the discrepancy between their expectations of intimacy and their actual relationships. Moreover, transition to college may be the first time some adolescents are detached from their parents. Securely attached individuals, however, experience less loneliness at college than less securely attached students (Wiseman et al.). Loneliness tends to decline over the years, leveling off throughout middle age, though less so among women than men. Although older adults spend much of their time alone, most of them are less prone to loneliness than popularly depicted, probably because they have learned to put their need for companionship in better perspective. However, loneliness appears to increase again among those in their 80s, reflecting, in part, the greater sense of disengagement from life among those at an advanced age (Perlman, 1991). General loneliness in our society may increase in the future due to changes in our population. In the past decade, the number of people living alone has increased by 20 percent and the number of single-parent households has increased by 21 percent (Cacioppo et al., 2003).

Think about how often you feel lonely—rarely, sometimes, or often? Which areas of your life are most affected—your social life or your love life? Then read the next few paragraphs and see if any of the information describes you.

Many factors contribute to loneliness. People who have grown up with warm and helpful parents (i.e., securely attached to their parents) are less likely to report loneliness in adulthood than those who describe their parents as disagreeable and unhelpful. Some of the loneliest people are those whose parents divorced when they were younger than 6 years old, partly because young children misperceive parental divorce as abandonment. In contrast, people who have lost a parent through death experience no corresponding increase in loneliness, probably because they realize that the loss was not intentional or their fault. People with low self-esteem tend to experience loneliness more than people who have high esteem. Individuals with low esteem are often lonely because their beliefs in their own unworthiness limit their recognition of positive feedback from others. This keeps them from taking steps to reduce their loneliness.

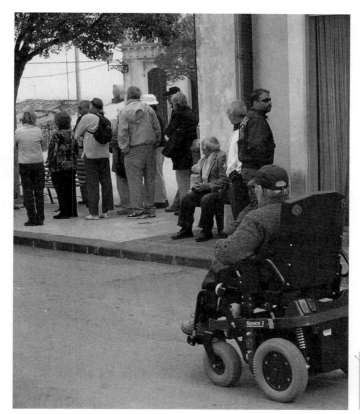

When both the quality and quantity of relationships with others is low, a person can experience loneliness.

Another reason for loneliness is that some individuals are rejected by others because they have poor social skills (Braza, Braza, Careras, & Muñoz, 1993). Children who lack appropriate social skills are sometimes rejected by their friends because they are aggressive, withdrawn, or fail to show appropriate responses to others' needs. These people are low in **emotional intelligence or EI**. *Emotional intelligence is the ability to regulate one's own emotions and to be empathic for others' emotions* (Lyons & Schneider, 2005). Specifically, emotional intelligence is comprised of four abilities (Salovey & Grewal, 2005), the ability

- to detect and decipher emotions in the self or others;
- to harness emotions to facilitate various cognitive activities such as problem solving;
- to comprehend emotion language such as slight variations between emotions (e.g., happy versus ecstatic);
- to regulate one's own and others' emotions.

Studies show that people with high EI engage in better-quality interactions with their friends and possess better impression management skills (Lopes et al., 2004). Other research indicates that those high in EI advance their careers even faster than people with high levels of general intelligence (Cremona, 2004; Schutte, Malouff et al., 2001), and they show better levels of performance under stress than those low in EI (Lyons & Schneider).

Culture affects loneliness, too (Ditommaso, Brannen, & Burgess, 2005; Rokach & Neto, 2005). The emphasis on personal fulfillment, often at the expense of stable relationships and commitment to others, is thought to make Americans especially prone to loneliness. Immigrants and long-term visitors to the United States are likely to report feeling very lonely, too, but for other reasons (Ditommaso et al.; Nah, 1993). In one study of international students, cultural distance predicted mood disturbance or maladjustment (Ward & Searle, 1991). In other words, the further the student's culture was sociologically from American culture, the more lonely and depressed was the student. Canadian students are less apt to be lonely than students from Nigeria. Befriending international students and helping them adjust by assisting them with understanding our culture would be a very kind and considerate thing to do. At the same time, you would have the interesting opportunity to learn more about their culture.

How well we cope with loneliness depends largely on how we interpret its causes. People who suffer the most from loneliness tend to exaggerate its internal aspects and minimize its external ones. Thus, people who blame their loneliness on their personal inadequacies ("I'm lonely because I'm unlovable" or "My lover and I have split up because I gained too much weight and have no will power") make themselves even more lonely and depressed. Cognitive therapy to change this schema may prove useful in this instance (Hope, Holt, & Heimberg, 1995). In contrast, people are more likely to overcome their loneliness when they focus on the *external, situational* factors that contribute to it: "It's hard to meet people in large classes" or "I'll stop working so much and get out and meet more people." Similarly, people who react to loneliness in passive ways—watching television, crying, and sleeping—feel even lonelier. Those who adopt more active or behavioral strategies—writing a letter or calling up an acquaintance—are more likely to alleviate their loneliness. Social skills training can help change behaviors, too (Hope et al.). The best course is to continue developing your interpersonal skills so that you always have access to a broad network of social ties as well as a circle of close friends.

SUMMARY

MEETING PEOPLE

We began the chapter by pointing out that each of us tends to have both a network of social ties with which to fulfill a variety of needs *and* a smaller circle of close friends with whom we can be more intimate. We begin acquaintances with surface contacts; then, based upon first impressions, we decide whether to continue the interaction.

We're attracted to people for a variety of reasons, including such factors as familiarity, physical attractiveness, and similarity to us, especially similarity to our attitudes. The more we interact with someone, the more we tend to like that person, unless we discover serious differences or basic incompatibilities. Also, we tend to judge physically attractive people more favorably than others, even on matters that have little or nothing to do with physical appearance. In long-term relationships, however, we're often attracted to someone on the basis of a mixture of similar and complementary needs.

When meeting people, we tend to form erroneous impressions of others on the basis of limited information, usually judging by such factors as a person's physical appearance (especially attractiveness), stereotypes, and nonverbal cues such as gaze. Not surprisingly, the most common reason for misjudging people is the lack of sufficient information, causing reliance instead on false cues and stereotypes, and the failure to account for the situational influences on people's behavior. Shy people, in particular, tend to be misperceived as aloof and disinterested, largely because of their silence and lack of eye contact. Shyness can be overcome.

KEEPING FRIENDS

As society becomes more complex and impersonal, we value close friends even more. At the same time, we're choosing friends from a wider diversity of people than in the past, including more opposite-sex friends. Close friends frequently get together for good talk and companionship, in addition to sharing a variety of other activities. There's a close link between friendship and mutual self-disclosure, so that emotional sharing often strengthens the bond of friendship. Generally, opposite-sex friends tend to supplement rather than displace our same-sex friends and may or may not be part of a sexual relationship; certain reasons are cited by same-sex friends for not turning the friendship into a romantic alliance. Staying friends with someone depends more on the special quality of the relationship than on the frequency of contact. The two most common reasons friendships break up are that one person moves away or one feels betrayed by the other.

Essentially, loneliness is a state of mind that results from the gap between our desire for closeness and the failure to find it. People who suffer the most from loneliness tend to blame themselves for their plight or resort to passive strategies, such as watching television or sleeping. In contrast, those who cope best with loneliness tend to recognize the situational factors involved and take more active steps to alleviate them, such as calling up a friend. Immigrants or international visitors often have problems adjusting to their new culture and therefore feel lonely.

SELF-TEST

1. Our initial impressions of people are generally based on
  a. their family backgrounds.   c. very little information.
  b. negative stereotypes.   d. their body language.

2. We often misjudge people when we fail to consider how their behavior is affected by
  a. situational influences.   c. moral principles.
  b. social status.   d. unconscious motives.

3. Shy people are especially apt to be misjudged by others as
  a. intelligent.   c. aggressive.
  b. cold.   d. undersexed.

4. The more familiar we become with a person, the more we tend to
  a. envy that person.   c. criticize that person.
  b. dislike that person.   d. like that person.

5. Research suggests we're attracted to people according to the proportion of shared
   a. attitudes.
   b. interests.
   c. motives.
   d. traits.

6. According to the fundamental attribution error, we often blame _____ rather than _____ for others' behaviors.
   a. traits/situations.
   b. friends/family.
   c. strangers/friends.
   d. situations/traits.

7. One of the most important activities among same-sex and opposite-sex friends is
   a. taking a vacation together.
   b. having an intimate talk.
   c. sharing a beer.
   d. All of these are equally important.

8. The process of revealing intimate information about ourselves is called
   a. self-disclosure.
   b. bragging.
   c. attribution.
   d. all of these.

9. Almost half of Americans report that they feel
   a. renewed nationalism and pride.
   b. chronic shyness.
   c. in love with another person.
   d. closer to opposite- than same-sex friends.

10. The most frequently cited reason for friendships breaking up is that one person has
    a. moved away.
    b. borrowed money.
    c. been promoted at work.
    d. inherited lots of money.

EXERCISES

1. *First impressions.* Look around in your classes and select someone you haven't met. Jot down your impressions of this person. Then make it a point to introduce yourself and become better acquainted. To what extent was your initial impression accurate or inaccurate? What steps can you take to improve your accuracy next time you meet a stranger?

2. *Shyness.* Do you ever suffer from shyness? If so, in which situations? How has shyness affected your life? What steps have you taken to overcome it?

3. *Write a personal ad about yourself.* Suppose you were writing a personal ad for the classified section devoted to introducing singles. How would you describe yourself? How would you describe the type of person you're looking for? Write a paragraph about why you gave those particular descriptions.

4. *Self-disclosure.* Write a paragraph or two including your thoughts on the following matters: How comfortable do you feel sharing personal information with friends? With whom do you share the most? Which topics do you share? If married, do you share more with your spouse or with your friends? Are the friends to whom you disclose same-sex or opposite-sex? Would you agree that the rewards of mutual self-disclosure outweigh the risks?

5. *Social support.* To whom can you turn? If you were experiencing a personal crisis, to whom would you turn for help—your family or friends? Which person would you seek out first? Explain the reasons for your answers. If you do not have good social support, how can you cultivate some friends to whom to disclose?

6. *Intimacy and growth.* Think of a close friendship or love relationship. Then describe your relationship in a page or so, including your thoughts on the following points: Do you both maintain other friendships? If lovers, are you also friends? Can each of you experience closeness without giving up your individuality? To what extent does this relationship encourage each of you to grow as a person?

QUESTIONS FOR SELF-REFLECTION

1. How much do you judge by first impressions? Are they accurate?

2. Do you make a good first impression on others? If not, how can you correct this?

3. Are you ever bothered by shyness? Loneliness? How can you overcome each?

4. Do you usually find that the more you know someone, the better you like the person?

5. How important are good looks to you in being attracted to someone of the opposite sex?

6. Do some of your friends have interests and personalities quite different from yours?

7. Who is your best friend? With which people do you feel most comfortable sharing secrets?

8. Do you have a close friend of the opposite sex? Do you have a close friend of the same sex? If you have both, how are these two friends similar? How are they different?

9. Have you ever been betrayed by a close friend? How did you react?

10. Have you ever befriended another person from a different country? How was that person's culture similar to yours? How was it different?

FOR FURTHER INFORMATION

RECOMMENDED READINGS

HILLIARD, E. B. (2005). *Living fully with shyness and social anxiety: A comprehensive guide to gaining social confidence.* New York: Marlowe & Company. A therapist-written book that provides practical but small incremental steps toward overcoming shyness and social anxiety.

GOLEMAN, D. (2005). *Emotional intelligence: 10th anniversary edition.* New York: Bantam Books. Learn all about EQ and why it is just as or more important than IQ. An updated version of Goleman's incisive book on emotional intelligence.

COPELAND, M. E. (2002). *The loneliness workbook: A guide to developing and maintaining lasting connections.* Oakland, CA: New Harbinger Press. A practical handbook for those who are lonely.

PAUL, M. (2005). *The friendship crisis: Finding, making, and keeping friends when you're not a kid anymore.* Emmaus, PA: Rodale. Emphasizing women's close relationships, Paul reveals how friendships can make or break our lives. There is something to be learned for men in this book also.

YAGER, J. (2002). *When friendship hurts: How to cope with friends who betray, abandon, or wound you.* New York: Simon & Schuster. Our friends can hurt us in a number of ways such as betrayal. This book helps heal the pain of a betrayed friendship.

WEB SITES AND THE INTERNET

http://www.cyberparent.com/friendship/   A site with click-on links to information about friendship, for example, how to make friends, maintain friends, and why friendships end.

http://www.adaa.org/   Anxiety Disorders Association of America. A site where you can find much information about social phobias.

http://www.shyness.com/   If you are shy or want to research shyness and social anxiety, this is the page for you. There are resources and links to other sites, a shyness questionnaire, and social support for shy people offered on the site.

http://www.bbbsa.org/   This is the web site of a truly amazing organization—Big Brothers/ Big Sisters. This organization provides older mentors or friends, usually college students, for children who need good role models. Research demonstrates that this program is highly successful in that the "bigs" steer the "littles" toward better lives.

http://www.WeboOfLoneliness.com/   A site that explains what loneliness is, what causes it, and how others have coped. Essays and poems about loneliness are also available.

Leader or Follower?

KINDS OF GROUPS
Favored Groups—Primary Groups
Bigger Than Both of
    Us—Secondary Groups
What Goes Wrong at Rock
    Concerts?—Collectives
"Us" Versus "Them"— In-Groups
    and Out-Groups

HOW DO GROUPS FORM?

WHY JOIN A GROUP?

WHAT GOES ON IN GROUPS?
What Did You Say?—
    Communication Patterns
You Want Me to Do What?—Social
    Influence
Let the Other Guy Do It—Social
    Loafing
All in Favor Say "Aye"—Group
    Polarization

ARE LEADERS MADE OR BORN?
The Great Man Theory
Situational Explanations of
    Leadership
Contingency Theory
Contemporary Theories
Gender and Leadership
Culture and Leadership

WHEN GROUPS GO WRONG
The Fiasco of Groupthink
A Little Shove Goes a Long
    Way—Group Conflict

SUMMARY
SELF-TEST
EXERCISES
QUESTIONS FOR SELF-REFLECTION
FOR FURTHER INFORMATION

Roy grew up in the cornfields of Iowa. His father, Harry, inherited the family farm and soon married Sara, Roy's mother. Sara and Harry were excited and proud the day their baby boy, Roy, was born. Sara and Harry developed great plans for their child from the moment of his arrival. Sara and Harry hoped that Roy would attend college and become an engineer or a lawyer so that he would not have to lead the hard farming life they had.

Sara and Harry pushed hard for Roy to achieve in school. High grades, they thought, were Roy's ticket out of the cornfields. Although Roy was resistant at first, much like any child who enjoyed playing rather than studying, he soon settled into his studies and was near the top of his class. Upon graduation, Roy was accepted to a large university in the East and even landed a good scholarship, thus relieving his parents of a huge financial burden.

September 5, 2003, was a day his parents were never to forget. Roy left for college and rarely returned to the cornfields. What happened to Roy? While at college, Roy became fascinated with a local group called the Akaries, a group that worshiped the sun, moon, and stars and believed that soon the world would end. Once Roy became fully initiated into this group, a well-known cult in the same city as the university, Sara and Harry never heard from him again.

How do groups such as the Akaries form? Why do some individuals such as Roy become followers, whereas others become revered leaders? Do all groups function the same? Do all groups have leaders? Is there such a thing as a dysfunctional group? These and other questions are the focus of this chapter on being part of a group.

KINDS OF GROUPS

Groups are all around us. Everywhere we look we see people in groups. People congregate in their places of worship, families can be seen in restaurants around America, and college classrooms are filled to the brim with eager students. Football fans collectively cheer for their favorite teams, and sororities and fraternities hold their deliberations on new members in the privacy of their houses. Everywhere—groups.

What kinds of groups are there and how do they differ? There are many different kinds of groups, each with its own characteristics, but we have space to review only a few of them here.

Favored Groups—Primary Groups

Perhaps the most immediately important group in your life is your **primary group**. *This group is important because it is small, intimate, and interacts face-to-face.* For these and other reasons primary groups have much influence on us. Of course, in turn, we can have great impact on them. Primary groups typically function through face-to-face interaction, as do families or suitemates in residence halls. A nuclear family, for example,

Primary groups are small, close-knit groups. Secondary groups are larger and come together for a specified purpose. Which group is represented here?

has immense impact on its members. The parents instill in their children the same values, dreams, and culture as the parents. Children often adopt their parents' religion, political views, and other likes and dislikes. College roommates sometimes become more like each other the more they live together. Happy husbands and wives often influence each other; they share the same friends, the same preferences for politicians, music, and television programs. Sometimes wives and husbands even laugh, walk, and talk the same way. The Akaries, although somewhat large with 22 members, could be classified as a primary group because the members were so close-knit and interdependent on one another.

Bigger Than Both of Us—Secondary Groups

Another type of group is a **secondary group**. *These groups are usually larger than primary groups, have a formal or contractual reason for coming together, often disband when the reason for their existence evaporates, and are less likely to engage in regular face-to-face interaction.* An example of this type of group would be the class for which you are reading this book. The class has a formal reason for coming together (to learn about adjustment and personal growth) and may not engage in much face-to-face (student-to-student) interaction. Other examples would be a church congregation or a social club such as the psychology club. Secondary groups, then, often configure in an audience rather than in a face-to-face, interaction pattern.

What Goes Wrong at Rock Concerts?—Collectives

You may have read about stampedes of people and riots in the streets. The cheering football spectators mentioned earlier can number in the tens of thousands if the stadium is large enough. Fans at a rock concert offer another example. The crowd that gathered to watch the twin towers of the World Trade Center burn after the terror attacks offers a third example. These groups, called **collectives**, *tend to be very large and are less likely to have a true leader or clear rules* compared with primary and secondary groups. Collectives often form and disband for no readily apparent reasons.

Because collectives are large and without clear-cut rules, they can often be disorderly. Americans have witnessed the tragedy of this disorderliness, especially at rock concerts where crowds distressed over the long wait spread rumors that there were too few seats. Pushing and shoving began and fans were trampled to death in the ensuing stampede. Other instances come to us from the sports world where crowds have rioted when their favorite teams have lost; fights start in the stands and spread throughout the stadium or tumble into the streets.

"Us" Versus "Them"—In-Groups and Out-Groups

There are two other very important groups that influence you (Hewstone, Rubin, & Willis, 2002). One is *the group with which you identify*—the **in-group**. The in-group can be contrasted with the **out-group**, *the group that we perceive as being different from (outside of) your own group*. In-group/out-group perceptions can develop based on ethnicity, gender, age, religion, occupation, attitudes, athletic prowess, academic ability, and income level, among other factors. To the locals around Roy's campus, the Akaries in their strange wardrobes and weird haircuts were clearly the out-group; to the Akaries, the rest of the world was the out-group. Their own respective group was the in-group.

> [o]ne of the most pervasive forms of categorization among humans is the distinction between *us* and *them*. People generally view ingroup members, i.e., "us," more positively than outgroup members, i.e., "them," and also allocate more rewards to the ingroup, compared to the outgroup. . . . This occurs when participants are divided into groups arbitrarily in the laboratory . . . as well as when group membership is based on longstanding cultural or social relations (Brown, Bradley, & Lang, 2006, p. 303).

What is most important about the distinctions we make between our own group and the out-group is that these differentiations often result in prejudiced attitudes and negative behavior against the out-group (Brown et al., 2006; Fiske, 2002; Mackie, Devos, & Smith, 2000). The distinction can be based on barely visible differences such as skin tone shades, with individuals having darker skin experiencing more prejudice than individuals of the same race with lighter skin (Brown, 2004). **Prejudice** is *an unfair, often negative attitude toward another person or group based solely on group membership* (Dovidio & Gaertner, 1999; Dovidio, Glick, & Rudman, 2005). Prejudice is sometimes accompanied by behaviors whereby the group against which the prejudice is held is discriminated against or treated worse than our own group. *When we apply unfair or negative treatment to groups on the basis of such features as age, sex, or race*, this is called **discrimination**. Although the two usually occur together, prejudice can occur without discrimination and discrimination can occur without prejudice. For example, a restaurant owner could harbor negative attitudes toward Native Americans but still serve them in his restaurant because of the laws against discrimination. Prejudice can also prompt **stereotypes**, or *widespread generalizations about people (based solely on their group membership) that have little if any basis in fact*.

Psychologists are concerned about prejudice, discrimination, and stereotypes because they invariably lead to negative and unfair evaluations of individuals in the out-group (Bodenhausen, 1990; Ensari & Miller, 2005). Prejudice and its correlates produce stress in the out-group (Contrada et al., 2000) and may cause damage to the self-esteem of the targets of prejudice (e.g., Platow, Byrne, & Ryan, 2005). Interestingly, one reason causing biased individuals to hold prejudices is that they seek to enhance their own self-esteem by viewing their group as superior to the out-group (Major & Eccleston 2005). Similarly, in-groups can be hard on their own members when a member deviates from or disagrees with the group (Conway & Schaller, 2005; Marques, Abrams, & Serodio, 2001). The overarching message you should take away from this information is that group dynamics can be harsh and unpleasant, but they need not be. For example, while *intergroup* contact is not always successful at breaking down stereotypes, prejudice, and in-group—out-group barriers (Antonio, 2004), some research shows that it does work (Quillian & Campbell, 2003).

Another significant point about in-groups and out-groups is that their importance varies by culture (Matsumoto, 2000; Hornsey & Jetten, 2005). We have already made the distinction elsewhere in this book between collectivistic and individualistic cultures. To review, **individualistic cultures** *value the individual's gains (needs, wants, and autonomy) over those of the group*. In an individualistic culture, people have more in-groups; that is, they belong to more organizations such as music clubs, Girl Scouts, and so forth (Matsumoto). Therefore, people in individualistic cultures are not as attached to any particular in-group as are people in **collectivistic cultures**, in which *collective or societal gain is cherished over individual advancement*. Perhaps because of their multiple memberships, individuals in individualistic cultures make fewer distinctions between in-groups and out-groups (Matsumoto). In collective societies, people have fewer in-groups, so they are more attached to the groups of which they are members (Matsumoto). Survival of the group is more dependent on the effective functioning of the group as a whole rather than that of individuals. Similarly, members of individualistic cultures self-enhance on independence (from the group) dimensions, whereas members of collective societies self-enhance based on loyalty to the group (Hornsey & Jetten). Finally, Johnson, Kulesa, Cho, and Shavitt (2005) believe that in individualistic cultures, people are far more expressive of their own independent views, whereas in collectivistic cultures, individuals, seeking harmony, are more likely to take a middling approach to volatile issues.

HOW DO GROUPS FORM?

Think about a fairly new group that you recently joined. How and why did the group form? Why did you join? Did the group evolve or change from its original form or purpose? The group may have been one from your campus and perhaps was a secondary group. Suppose that the group was initiated by a group of disgruntled commuter students who felt there was an insufficient number of parking spaces and too few evening classes to accommodate their busy schedules.

The initial stage in group development is **forming** (Tuckman, 1965; McGrew, Bilotta, & Deeney, 1999), *where individuals come together to form the group*. When Roy became entranced by the Akaries, the group was already well formed. In other groups, in the forming stage, members sometimes do not know each other as well as they will later in the developmental process; they are simply coming together as a group. In the commuter group, one concerned individual may call the meeting, which is initially attended by many strangers. Even in a new marriage, where the couple has dated for months, the new wife may not know that her new husband squeezes the toothpaste in the middle when she prefers to squeeze neatly from the bottom. Neither does she know that her new husband prefers to watch game shows rather than the political debates she favors. If enough of these differences exist, friction can build and squabbles might begin in any group. Initially, though, most group members step forward with their best and most cooperative foot as the group forms and people (sometimes secretly) jockey for positions.

When group members learn more about each other's attitudes and predilections, differences among individuals lead to *the second stage*, **storming** (Tuckman, 1965). In this stage, which can follow quickly on the heels of the first, *individuals disagree or often openly conflict when they learn each other's opinions*. In the commuter group, some individuals may prefer a university-sponsored bus service, whereas others argue for more parking spaces.

This stage is a troublesome one. Members may decide too much friction exists and so leave the group. For example, some individuals initially attracted to the Akaries did not remain long when they realized how extreme the Akaries were. Other members may decide that it is best to remain passive rather than be pulled into the fray, and others are so vociferous and aggressive about promoting their agendas that the remaining members intensely dislike them. At this point it may seem that the group will never start functioning. If group members recognize that this is a normal group stage, however, they

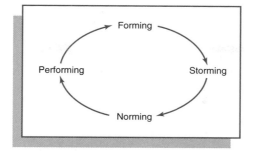

FIGURE 9–1
The cycle of group formation.

can move beyond their differences to the next, more productive stage. As with personal growth, group growth can happen in stages and develop via adversity.

When roles become more sharply defined, when groups finally come to terms with how they will function, when rules by which they will function become clearer, the group is said to be **norming** (Tuckman, 1965). That is, through discourse and debate *the group eventually comes to consensus about the rules under which it will operate.* As just mentioned, roles start to emerge in groups in the storming and norming stages. A **role** is *a set of rules that defines how an individual in a particular post in a group will behave.* Also as mentioned previously, each group develops its own idiosyncratic **norms**, *standards or unwritten rules by which it will function and by which it will exert pressure on nonconforming members.* For example, the married couple with one television may agree that the husband will squeeze the toothpaste from the end because it creates less waste. The wife may agree that every other night they will watch what her husband prefers and on off nights the couple will watch what she likes. Suitemates in residence halls may ultimately decide that the one who stays up late watching television has to go to the downstairs lounge to do so; otherwise, she disturbs those enrolled in early-morning classes. The Akari group had very strange norms to outsiders. In his posh bedroom, the leader, Otu, was allowed to have sex with any woman in the group, except married women and young girls. Other single men had to remain celibate and live in their collective bunkroom.

Once a group has formed, has worked through its initial disagreements, and has developed norms, the group is ready to function well. **Performing** (Tuckman, 1965) *is the final stage of group development. It is during this stage that the group functions better and actually performs its business,* whether it is the rearing of children in a marriage or developing a strategic plan for a work team. Once this developmental pattern has been played out by a group, new issues can arise or new members can be added. The group then cycles through these stages again (see Figure 9–1). Be aware, though, that some theorists have suggested that other processes exist, such as de-norming, de-storming, and de-forming (McGrew et al., 1999).

WHY JOIN A GROUP?

Why would individuals follow a cult leader such as Otu? What would draw intelligent men and women to the Akaries? What would attract any individual to a cult? What makes you join some clubs, teams, or committees but resist pressure to join others?

Social psychologists have identified a multitude of reasons for people's joining groups. People sometimes connect with groups because groups offer possibilities not available to us as individuals. One possibility that groups offer is the chance to **affiliate**, *to be with others who are similar to us or whom we like.* Sororities and fraternities fill this need by attracting new members who generally are very similar to existing members. Synagogues, churches, and mosques offer more than religious support; they also offer the chance to socialize with members of the same faith. The Akaries afforded the opportunity to individuals with the same spiritual and political attitudes to be with similar others and test out their novel, but bizarre, ideas.

Groups also offer us information we might not otherwise possess. Although most people in America have access to the media, some do not avail themselves of television and newspapers because they do not have the time, do not speak English, or eschew or cannot afford electronic media. Groups to which we belong can keep us informed about important as well as mundane issues. Groups, however, offer us more than mere facts. Groups help us *understand* whether we harbor attitudes that represent a minority or majority position in a group. Groups also help us understand our position in the social order. For example, you do not know whether you are brilliant until you debate with several opposing individuals who eventually attack and erode your viewpoint. Another example is this: When you receive examinations back in a college class, you may think that a score of 37 is terrible until you see that the classmates around you received 25, 19, and 32. Now the 37 feels better, doesn't it? *Groups, then, allow us to compare ourselves to others and understand who we are relative to them.* This is the process of **social comparison**. We generally select another person with whom to compare ourselves based on that person's expertise, similarity to us, and previous level of agreement (Schwinghammer, Stapel, & Blanton, 2006; Suls, Martin, & Wheeler, 2002).

The concept of social support (Duffy & Wong, 2003), introduced elsewhere in the book, is important to groups. You may recall that **social support** is *a process whereby one individual or group offers psychological and sometimes physical aid to another individual or group.* Primary groups, especially of friends and family, can offer us much-needed social support. When something goes wrong in our lives, when we have difficult decisions to make, and even when something wonderful has happened (for instance, receiving a promotion), groups can give us a needed boost. Coworkers can help us ponder the advantages and disadvantages of various alternatives that confront us when we have to make an important decision. Friends can give us affection and sympathy when we suffer the loss of a loved one. Our families can enhance our joy when we have succeeded. Groups, then, offer social support that research has repeatedly demonstrated is important to our mental health (e.g., Helgeson & Cohen, 1996; Duffy & Wong).

Groups also give us more collective power. There may be needs we have that we simply cannot meet alone. For example, the Akaries may have been composed of individuals who for one reason or another were failures elsewhere. By joining, members realized their collective power and ability to influence others. One individual who was influenced by the Akaries was John, Roy's roommate, who was educated in journalism but who joined the Akaries shortly after applying to and being rejected by journalism graduate schools.

Labor unions offer another example. Unions can collectively and typically negotiate better raises and working conditions than any individual member can. Alliances and coalitions can better lobby governments for needed legislation. And student groups, such as your student government, possess consolidated power compared to each individual student. The student government with the force of hundreds or thousands of students behind it can better approach the administration to advance student causes, such as assistance for commuting students, on your campus.

WHAT GOES ON IN GROUPS?

You have already been introduced to two group processes, development of roles and development of norms. There are other processes that are unique to groups and would rarely be discussed with regard to an individual. These processes include communication, social influence, social loafing, and group polarization, which are all important to decision making and performance in groups.

What Did You Say?—Communication Patterns

One of the most important group processes is communication. Intragroup communication is important to all the other processes discussed next. *Intragroup* means *within* a group; communication within a group allows group members to coordinate their actions, share information, and express emotions and ideas—all of which are important to decision making and performance.

Networks. Some of the earliest research on group communication concerned communication networks within groups (Davis & Newstrom, 1985). There are **centralized communication networks** *in which one or two individuals control the flow of information.* One such network is the wheel, in which a centralized individual or node with spokes or channels extends outward to other individuals or nodes. The wheel is similar to a university, where all department chairs go to a dean or vice president who makes final funding, personnel, and other decisions. Certainly, Otu was the important focal point or the center of the group known as the Akaries. The wheel and other networks are depicted in Figure 9–2.

Centralized networks can be contrasted to *decentralized communication networks.* In **decentralized communication networks**, *individuals can communicate relatively freely with one another.* An example of a decentralized network is the circle, also shown in Figure 9–2. Rumors that pass from one person to another, then to yet another, and back

Compared to face-to-face communication, electronic communication may result in more miscommunication because it lacks subtle cues such as facial expressions.

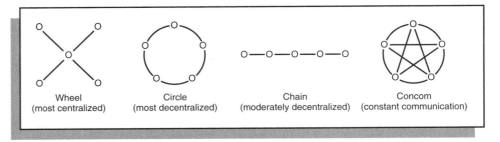

FIGURE 9–2
Examples of various communication networks.
"O" represents an individual, and the lines represent the communication links between individuals.

to the original source offer an example of the circle. Of course, there are other centralized and decentralized systems. Can you think of other concrete examples for all of the networks represented in Figure 9–2?

Centralized and decentralized networks result in different types of performance in groups. In research on groups, performance (how many widgets were made, how long the group met, how good was the group's decision, for example) is usually measured. Centralized networks are much more efficient and thus work capably and effectively, but mostly on simple tasks or simple decisions. When tasks are complicated or decisions require complex input and deliberation, decentralized networks are generally best. You certainly already know that there are other dimensions that count as much or more than performance. Satisfaction of the members with their group experience, direction of communication, power inequities of the members, and other factors are also important measures of group dynamics.

Group Size. As you might well imagine, one other group factor that affects quality of communication and therefore quality of the group's work and members' satisfaction is the *size* of the group. Groups vary in their size depending on the situation. Juries are usually composed of 12 individuals, university academic departments can be as small as 2 people or as large as 60, and families typically average between 3 and 5 members in the United States. A group with many members has more resources available, so may be able to generate more ideas. However, the number of ideas generated is not directly proportionate to group size. Curiously, as the size of the group increases, the number of ideas increases at a slower rate. Interactions and communications are also more likely to be formalized in a larger group. For instance, large groups, such as the United States Congress, are more likely to set agendas and to follow Roberts' Rules of Order to control discussions.

Other factors related to group size are how the communications are perceived. In small groups, group discussions actually appear to be interactive dialogues or conversations. In larger groups, the discourse resembles a monologue in which a few individuals dominate or speak sequentially (Fay, Garrod, & Carletta, 2000). Note also that some individuals may be shy about participating in large groups but not in small groups, so participation is usually pretty uneven.

Electronic Communication. As our society turns more and more to electronic forms of communication, it will be interesting to determine whether the principles just described will still hold true. For example, in electronic communication such as e-mail, the impact of nonverbal cues is lessened, so there may be more opportunity for miscommunication. However, Finholt and Sproull (1990) analyzed incoming and outgoing electronic messages of 96 employees and found that most of the employee groups behaved like real social groups. This was true despite the fact that the groups did not share physical space and that their members were essentially invisible. Other research has established that status inequalities are reduced with electronic participation (Dubrovsky, Kiesler, & Sethna, 1991). This is important because in face-to-face groups, often the highest-status members do the most communicating. Dubrovsky et al.'s research shows that with electronic communication each group member has a greater likelihood of participating. Given this, the group has a better chance of maximizing the potential of all its members.

There are some downsides to electronic communication, especially e-mail (Whitty & Carr, 2006). Morris, Nadler, Kurtzberg, and Thompson (2002) recognized the importance of "schmoozing," as they called it; by schmoozing, they meant establishing rapport by sharing personal information before formal interactions begin. Electronic communication compared to face-to-face communication cuts down on schmoozing, and, thus, in their research Morris et al. found that there was less trust and less rapport in electronic communications. They suggested face-to-face meetings first when possible; then if electronic communication is required, people will feel they know one another better. Wilson, Straus, & McEvily (2006) also found that trust is greater in face-to-face rather than electronic meetings. Likewise, electronic communication lacks subtle communicative cues (e.g., facial expressions and vocal intonations) for communicating, for example, the differences between sarcasm versus genuine humor. Because of this, miscommunication can frequently occur. Moreoever, research shows that e-mail users are largely unaware of this limitation; they know what they intended to communicate, so they assume that their audience does as well (Kruger, Epley, Parker, & Ng, 2005). Other researchers have found that electronic communication, especially at workplaces, is more task-oriented and more efficient than face-to-face meetings (e.g., Lantz, 2001). This effect may be alright, but only if group members do not miss the socializing aspects of work.

Electronic communication also enables its users to expand their group's size and influence and to heighten social contact. Drentea and Moren-Cross (2005) found that cyberspace does foster social capital and social support. More specifically, they found that the use of the Internet helps build community spirit as well as provides both emotional and instrumental support to its users. On the other hand, the Internet can also be used to promote racism, terrorism, and other harmful movements (Adams & Roscigno, 2005). Finally, several studies (e.g., Adrianson, 2001; Lind, 2001; Sánchez-Franco, 2006) have found gender differences in the way men and women use and respond to technology. Sánchez-Franco noted that males tend to be more focused and intentional in their Internet use (e.g., newsrooms) whereas females utilize the Internet for social engagement (e.g., chat rooms). Additionally, females report lower computer self-efficacy than do males.

You Want Me to Do What?—Social Influence

Certainly, many other people have tried to use social influence on you. What is social influence? **Social influence** involves *efforts on the part of one person to alter the behavior or attitudes of one or more others.* Otu and other cult leaders have immense social influence over their followers. Other groups and leaders have such influence, too, although often not to

Conformity consists of a change in behavior in response to the influence of others. Compliance entails a direct request for a behavior, while obedience involves a direct command. Which method of social influence is depicted here?

the extremes of cults. Social influence can occur at three different levels. We can publicly go along with others but refuse to change our private beliefs. An example of this would be that you are seated in the snack bar between classes and three friends all declare that they are voting for a political candidate whom you detest. In a hurry to make your next class, you do not want to debate with them so nod your head in agreement. Another level of social influence is when you behave like others or are influenced by others because you are attracted to them. Very often when you begin to steadily date someone, you adopt the new date's tastes for food and music. If you and your date then part company, you return to your own tastes in cuisine and melody. The third level is one where someone has truly influenced you so much that you change forever. At this level, an individual or group convinces you that you should adopt their ideas, behaviors, and tastes. This third and most important type of influence is the kind Otu exerted over his followers, Roy, and the rest of the Akaries.

How and why do people gain influence over others? Three processes—conformity, compliance, and obedience—shed light on the mechanisms.

Conformity.   You may already have a nodding acquaintance with conformity, but let's define it anyway. **Conformity** is a *change in behavior due to the real or imagined influence (pressure) of other people.* When American youths started wearing baseball caps backwards, they were conforming to age-mate pressure to conform, to be like others their age. No one issued official orders or laws proclaiming that youths needed to wear their caps backward. There was subtle peer pressure to conform.

Conformity has been well examined since the seminal research of Solomon Asch. Asch (1951) requested subjects to come to an experimental room one at a time. When the subject entered the room, the subject was confronted by what appeared to be other subjects. These other subjects actually were **confederates** or *friends of the experimenter who were told by the experimenter how to behave.* The subject and confederates were asked to judge lines similar to those in Figure 9–3. One at a time, each was to say aloud which line of the three, B, C, or D, was closest in length to the standard line A.

At first, confederates gave correct answers; for example, in Figure 9–3 the confederates would answer that line B was closest in length to line A. Then confederates gave wrong answers, for example, that line C was closest in length to line A. Asch reasoned that the real subjects would stand their ground and give the correct answer, thus refusing

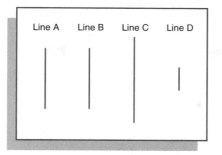

FIGURE 9–3

The Asch conformity experiment.
Subjects sat with confederates and looked at the lines. The subject and confederates were to compare line A with lines B, C, and D and state which of the three was closest in length to line A. Confederates often gave the wrong answer; results indicated that many subjects simply conformed to the confederates' wrong answers.

to conform. Asch, to his surprise, found that many subjects conformed to the apparently wrong answer. Specifically, Asch found that of 123 subjects, 94 subjects, or 76 percent, gave the wrong answer at least once. Asch concluded that the tendency to conform in our society is strong, even on obviously easy tasks and even when no one forces conformity.

Since Asch's initial research, scientists have discovered factors that enhance or reduce conformity. We are most likely to conform to the wrong answer when our responses are public and face-to-face (Bond, 2005) and when the proportion of other conformists is high (Coultas, 2004). Not all groups function exactly according to these findings on conformity. The Akaries group was fairly large, so exerted much influence over its members.

It is also important to comment on individual and cultural differences in conformity. Despite Asch's results, many Americans espouse independence and autonomy, so shun conformity. Cultures that emphasize **interdependence** (*mutual dependence among individuals in a given group or society*) also exist. Many of these are collectivist societies. Conformity and harmony is an integral part of the social fabric of these cultures (Johnson et al., 2005). Some examples of more interdependent cultures (where conformity to group norms is *expected*) are the Japanese, Zimbabwean, and Lebanese cultures (Smith & Bond, 1993). Schwartz and Rubel (2005), however, found no sex differences in the value of conformity across 70 different cultures; in each culture, men and women conformed equally frequently.

Compliance.   Another process of social influence is compliance. **Compliance** may be defined as a *change in behavior in response to a direct request from another person to do so*. Compliance, like conformity, is an everyday phenomenon. When your professor requests that you take your seats so that she can begin lecturing, you sit down, thus complying with her entreaty. When your sister calls you to the dinner table, you usually come in response to her request. And when you ask to borrow your roommate's extra umbrella, she usually lends it in a demonstration of friendship. Each offers an example of compliance. Note that we sometimes comply publicly but disagree with the request privately, just as is true for conformity.

There are conditions under which we are more or less likely to comply. In mainstream American society, a **norm of reciprocity** is common. *This unwritten rule guides* *reciprocal behavior related to the granting of favors.* If someone does you a favor, you feel compelled to return (reciprocate) the favor. For example, when you borrow your roommate's umbrella, you are obligated (tit for tat) to let her borrow something of yours. When food companies give away free samples, there is some feeling of obligation on the consumer's part to buy the product. Charities often send free address labels or calendars in hopes that you will reciprocate with a donation.

Another method to induce compliance is **ingratiation**, which involves *managing the impressions you leave on others so that they will like you more and comply with your requests.* Flattery is a form of ingratiation by which the flatterer hopes that the flattered individual will give in to a certain request. Another form of ingratiation is *opinion conformity,* in which one individual publicly agrees with another so that the other person will like the ingratiator. The ingratiator who uses opinion conformity can later ask the other individual for a favor.

Sometimes a two-step approach to compliance increases its likelihood. There are several two-step processes, one of which will suffice as an example here. In the **door-in-the-face effect**, *the requester first issues a large, unreasonable request. When the respondent answers "no," the requester makes the truly desired but smaller and more reasonable demand.* Not wanting to appear difficult or stubborn, the respondent often answers "yes" to the second, smaller request. For example, a rather calculating friend may ask to borrow your new, expensive car to impress his new date. Not having driven the car much yourself, you quickly answer "no." The friend then asks to borrow $15 for the same date, to which you more readily agree.

As you can see, both ingratiation and the door-in-the-face technique are manipulative ways to bring about compliance. These methods are not presented here so that you can hone your skills using them. Rather, it is good for you to recognize when others are manipulating you with these techniques.

Obedience.   **Obedience** involves *following a direct order or command.* The command typically comes from someone who has the capacity to enforce the order if it is not followed. You probably think of an army officer issuing an order that soldiers follow. Otu's followers were surely obedient to him, but are other individuals so servile? Surprisingly, many Americans are obedient to different authority figures. A classic series of studies on obedience demonstrates our propensity to obey.

In 1974, Stanley Milgram published his dramatic *Obedience to Authority.* In this book he detailed a series of studies on obedience to authority figures that rattled the psychological world. Imagine that you are in the following prototype of Milgram's experiment. You are led to a room and introduced to Mr. Wallace, a kindly older man who is to be the learner in the study. You are going to be the teacher. Mr. Wallace is to learn a list of words. Each time he errs, you are to give him an electric shock that you are both told will be painful but will cause no permanent tissue damage. For each error, you are to proceed up the shock generator one step. The first step is 15 volts and labeled "slight shock." The other end is 450 volts and labeled only with "XXX"—to designate its dangerous nature. As the teacher you are not aware that the experiment is fixed such that you are not really administering shocks and that Mr. Wallace is really a confederate (the experimenter's assistant) and has been told how to act.

As you proceed up the shock generator, you hear Mr. Wallace's groans. Eventually, Mr. Wallace refuses to continue and states that he has a heart problem. Finally, Mr. Wallace becomes silent. Each time you query the experimenter (the authority figure) about Mr. Wallace's condition, the experimenter urges you to continue. The experimenter reminds you that although the shocks may be painful, they cause no permanent damage. The experimenter requests that you continue.

The most dramatic and disconcerting part of these studies was that 65 percent of the American subjects went all the way up the shock generator at the urging of the experimenter. It would be easy to explain away these results by suggesting that the subjects were disturbed or that they were all aggressive men. Milgram assured us that all subjects were mentally healthy and that even women shocked the learner at about the same rate. If for some reason obedience is not desirable, there are techniques for reducing it. Placing the "victim" closer to the obedient person or putting the authority figure farther away are two such methods.

Let the Other Guy Do It—Social Loafing

Have you ever "goofed off" in a group? If you haven't, have you observed others "not holding up their end of the deal"? Another process that occurs in groups is loafing. **Social loafing** *means that individuals contribute less to a group effort than they would contribute to an individual effort* (Smith, Kerr, Markus, & Stasson, 2001). For example, if individuals are asked one at a time to paint a mural or to clap for an athlete, they put more effort into the performance than they would if asked to perform as a their performance (i.e., the more the social loafing). Relatively new research also indicates that social loafing may be a particular problem of on-line communities (Chidambaram & Tung, 2005; Ling et al., 2005), perhaps because they are so large and so anonymous.

Groups can reduce social loafing in a number of ways (Karau & Williams, 1993). When people believe their performance will be evaluated, when the task is important or meaningful, when failure is possible if loafing occurs, or when individual members value the group, loafing is minimized. People who enjoy the challenge of cognitive tasks are also less likely to loaf whether alone or in a large group (Smith et al., 2001). The **nominal group technique**, which is *a systematic (round-robin polling) approach to soliciting individual input into a group project*, also reduces social loafing (Asmus & James, 2005).

There are also cultural differences in amounts of social loafing. As mentioned elsewhere, many Western societies are individualistic; individuals are expected to be independent and autonomous, so they contribute less to group efforts. In more collective societies in which group effort is valued, social loafing is less likely to occur (Triandis, 2004).

All in Favor Say "Aye"—Group Polarization

Surely you have worked in groups that make decisions requiring consensus or unanimity. This is how most committees function. Indeed, consensus is the foundation for democracy.

In 1964, Kogan and Wallach compared how individuals versus groups make decisions. In their study, participants were given a series of social dilemmas and asked to select a solution for the dilemma. For example, participants were asked to decide whether a risky experimental drug should be administered to a dying patient. The solutions varied on amount of risk. Kogan and Wallach determined that *groups coming to consensus make riskier decisions than individuals*. They labeled this phenomenon **risky shift**. The researchers explained that *individuals in groups feel less responsible for the risk so are willing to make riskier decisions in groups*, in a process known as **responsibility diffusion**.

Subsequent research (Myers & Arenson, 1972), however, demonstrated that some groups tend to make more conservative decisions than individuals. That is, if individuals in the group made fairly conservative decisions before joining the group, they tend to make

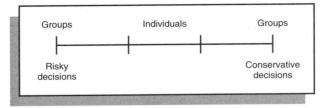

FIGURE 9–4
The group polarization effect.
Groups often make more extreme decisions (conservative or risky) than individuals.

even more conservative decisions in a group. In other words, *groups are likely to shift to either a more conservative or a riskier decision than individuals alone make.* This newer phenomenon is the **group polarization effect** (Prislin & Wood, 2005), as depicted in Figure 9–4. One factor that predicts whether individuals in a group will press for caution or for risk is—you guessed it—culture. In African cultures, for example, caution is valued over risk. In American culture, risk and bravado are valued over caution (Gologor, 1977). Given that you, too, spend so much time in groups, you need to be aware of these effects so that you can override their consequences and make the best possible decisions.

ARE LEADERS MADE OR BORN?

Have you ever led a group? Do you think you have leadership qualities? Or would you rather sit back silently and let someone else have the limelight? By reading the next passages, you should understand yourself better as well as the challenges facing all leaders of groups.

In almost all groups, someone rises as leader. Committees elect their leaders; corporations retain presidents appointed by the board of directors; some countries are governed by a self-appointed dictator while others have hereditary rulers. Leaders are vitally important because research has confirmed that groups with leaders outperform groups without leaders (De-Souza & Klein, 1995). How do leaders emerge and what qualities make for good leadership? The answers to these questions are difficult because each situation is so different from the next. A summary of some of the literature is all that space allows here. For more information on groups and leaders, see the recommended readings at the end of the chapter. Let us first examine theories about the origins of leaders.

The Great Man Theory

Did Otu possess certain traits at birth that set him on the path to leadership? The earliest theory of leadership was the **great man theory**. The theory predated feminism so the term "man" was used. This theory suggests that *great leaders are born with a certain common set of traits.* If an individual possesses these traits, such as good public speaking skills, then that person will become a leader. If not, the individual is out of luck. Researchers assumed that they ought to be able to assess great leaders and find common characteristics. Simonton (1987) did just that. Simonton gathered information from a variety of sources about the presidents of the United States. Information collected included personality attributes as well as demographic and educational factors. Out of 100 characteristics, only

3 correlated with how effective each president was in office. One factor was family size, another was height, and the third was number of books published. Presidents are more likely to have been born into small families and to be tall. There were no personality factors that consistently correlated with performance in office. The great man theory has essentially been abandoned in favor of other notions of leadership.

Situational Explanations of Leadership

Other explanations for the emergence of leaders involve the situation people find themselves in. In other words, perhaps being in the right place at the right time means that you are likely to become a leader. For example, if you sit at the head of the table with everyone else seated at the sides, you might be appointed leader of the group (Jackson, Engstrom, & Hassenzahl, 2005). If someone else sat in the same seat, that person instead might emerge as leader. Another example is this: A tour group is visiting France. Only one person in the group speaks French. This person interprets and translates for everyone else in the group, so becomes the leader. It would be a different story if the same person were in Tibet and could speak only French. The French speaker would probably not be the leader. In other words, according to this notion of leadership, the situation creates the leader. Perhaps Otu found some dejected social outcasts who needed a leader or a spiritual "center" (as Otu called it) at that moment in their lives, and he deftly slipped in as leader of these needy people.

Contingency Theory

Some of the most popular theories of leadership are those that combine personal factors with situational factors (Somech, 2006). In other words, the theory suggests that you have to have the right leadership qualities for that particular situation. Then and only then will you be an effective leader. One such theory is Fiedler's (1978) **contingency theory of leadership**. *The theory identifies two attributes or styles of leaders known as people-oriented or task-oriented, which are effective at leading in different situations.* **People- or relationship-oriented leaders** *concern themselves with members' feelings and relationships.* **Task-oriented leaders** *are primarily concerned with getting the job done well and in a timely fashion.* Fiedler measures these two styles by asking leaders to rate their least-preferred coworker. Interestingly and not unpredictably, the people-oriented leader sees the good in this coworker even though the worker is not well liked. The task leader, interested more in performance than people, has stronger negative feelings toward those coworkers who do not do their jobs well (Kaplan & Kaiser, 2003). Activity 9–1 presents a scale similar to that of Fiedler.

The situations differ under which each of these leaders is effective (DeYoung, 2005; Judge, Piccolo, & Ilies, 2004; Morris, Brotheridege, & Urbanski, 2005). Without a doubt, you know social situations in which the task to be done is clear and members of the group have good relationships. This is what Fiedler calls a *high control situation* as compared to *low or medium control situations*. Results of research demonstrate that task-oriented leaders are most effective in high or low control situations. On the other hand, people-oriented leaders are most effective in medium control situations. Fiedler strongly suggests that leader style should match the situation, as depicted in Figure 9–5. One style alone does not produce an effective leader across the board. Stated another way, a balance between task- and people-oriented when matched to appropriate situations results in maximal effectiveness of leaders in their groups (Kaplan & Kaiser, 2003).

ACTIVITY 9–1

WHAT TYPE OF LEADER ARE YOU?

INSTRUCTIONS: *Rate your* least favorite classmate *on the following dimensions by placing an "X" in the appropriate space. First impressions are best.*

Friendly	_ _ _ _ _ _ _	Unfriendly
Cold	_ _ _ _ _ _ _	Warm
Strong	_ _ _ _ _ _ _	Weak
Honest	_ _ _ _ _ _ _	Dishonest
Active	_ _ _ _ _ _ _	Passive
Bad	_ _ _ _ _ _ _	Good
Intelligent	_ _ _ _ _ _ _	Unintelligent
Closed-minded	_ _ _ _ _ _ _	Open-minded

Now rate your most favorite classmate *on the following scale by placing an X in the appropriate space. First impressions are best. Try not to let your ratings of the least favorite classmate influence these ratings (i.e., don't use comparisons).*

Friendly	_ _ _ _ _ _ _	Unfriendly
Cold	_ _ _ _ _ _ _	Warm
Strong	_ _ _ _ _ _ _	Weak
Honest	_ _ _ _ _ _ _	Dishonest
Active	_ _ _ _ _ _ _	Passive
Bad	_ _ _ _ _ _ _	Good
Intelligent	_ _ _ _ _ _ _	Unintelligent
Closed-minded	_ _ _ _ _ _ _	Open-minded

Look at how close the Xs are for each designated classmate. Were your ratings for least favorite classmate similar to the ratings for your most favorite classmate? In other words, were the Xs located in about the same position on the scales? If yes, then you possess a person-oriented leadership style. If they are farther apart (at opposite ends of each scale), then you may possess a task-oriented leadership style. This scale is designed to assist you in thinking about your own personal style of leadership. Remember that both styles have their advantages. Good leaders learn to adopt each style when the situation dictates.

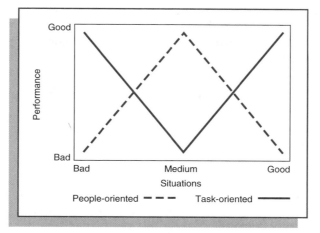

FIGURE 9–5
Graph of the effects of people-oriented versus task-oriented leaders on group performance.

Contemporary Theories

Emotional intelligence, or EI, is explained in more detail elsewhere in the book (see Chapter 8). Briefly, **emotional intelligence** is *the ability to regulate one's own emotions and to be empathic for others' emotions.* Leaders high in EI are self-aware, have exceptionally good interpersonal skills, evince self-control and social awareness, and know how to manage interpersonal relationships (e.g., possess good conflict management skills) (Dearborn, 2002). Leaders with EI are also confident without being arrogant. These traits make the person with EI very popular with others. Daniel Goleman (2005), who has written much about this concept, empirically examined whether people with EI are also good leaders. The answer is yes. Goleman found that EI is twice as important as any other personal characteristic (e.g., possession of technical skills) for predicting who will achieve the highest roles in organizations. Moreover, EI accounted for 90 percent of the difference in the profiles of high- versus low-ranking individuals in organizations, with high-ranking individuals having much EI. Goleman also found that high EI distinguishes outstanding leaders from mediocre leaders as well as predicts which leader will have high organizational performance; of course, high-EI leaders performed better than their low-EI counterparts (Goleman, 1998; 2005).

Emotionally intelligent leaders may share some traits with another type of leader—**the charismatic leader**—(Brown & Moshavi, 2005), especially in the realm of self-awareness (Sosik, 2001). *This type of leader inspires social change, is visionary, and appeals to followers' self-concepts and values.* The charismatic leader often guides followers to solutions that alleviate the problems they face. Some experts on leadership have also linked charismatic leaders to transformational leaders (Jacobsen & House, 2001). Leaders high in emotional intelligence may also resemble **transformational leaders** (Barbuto & Burbach, 2006; Bass & Riggio, 2006; Mandell & Pherwani, 2003). Transformational leaders *stimulate interest among colleagues and followers to view their work from a new perspective. The leader does this by generating awareness of the mission or vision of the organization and helps members to look beyond their own interests* (Mandell & Pherwani). Such leaders raise their followers to a higher level of morality and motivation by moving followers to work toward the greater good or shared goals (Alimo-Metcalfe & Alban-Metcalfe, 2001; Bass & Riggio). No matter what label we apply to these types of leaders, they usually have a positive impact on their followers (e.g., Stewart, 2006; Xirasagar, Samuels, & Stoskopf, 2005). On the other hand, these same leaders can be detrimental to their followers, for example, when they foster dependency on the leader, as Otu did (Kark, Shamir, & Chen, 2003). As much as they may appeal to you, such leaders are also unpopular in times of threat when task-oriented leaders are most preferred (Cohen, Solomon, Maxfield, Pyszczynski, & Greenberg, 2004).

Gender and Leadership

As you can tell from the dated name of the "Great Man Theory," interest in women as leaders has developed only recently, in part because of the feminist movement and in part because there are now more women involved in leadership roles, such as Coretta Scott King and Hillary Clinton. In 1976, 21 percent of all managers were women; by 1999 the percentage had increased to 46 (Powell, Butterfield, & Parent, 2002). Researchers examining acceptance of women as leaders have found that while people today place less emphasis on masculine traits for leaders, a good leader is still perceived as more masculine than feminine (Powell et al.; Sczesny, Bosnak, Neff, & Schyns, 2004). Perhaps because of this, women are not as likely as men to become leaders (Ritter & Yoder, 2004), and when they do lead, they are still not as well received as men (Koch, 2005).

Several studies examine the styles with which men and women lead. Sczesny et al. (2004) found that the scientific literature supports that women are more people-oriented and men more task-oriented. Regarding the characteristic of transformational leadership, some studies have found no sex differences (e.g., van Engen, van der Leeden, & Willemsen, 2001) while others have found that women are more likely to be transformational leaders than men (van Engen & Willemsen, 2004), perhaps because women have higher emotional intelligence (Mandell & Pherwani, 2003).

Women also tend to consult more with subordinates, that is be more democratic, utilize larger social networks, and share more information and power with colleagues than do men (Helgeson, 1990). Eagly and Johnson (1990) as well as Wheelan and Verdi (1992) contend that women are every bit as task-oriented as men, especially because this is a criterion by which organizations select and train leaders. In a later study, Eagly, Karau, and Makhijani (1995) found that men and women are equally effective as leaders, but women are more effective when their roles are defined in feminine terms; men are more effective when their roles are defined in masculine terms.

If women are equally as effective as men (but perhaps retain different styles) (Eagly & Johannesen-Schmidt, 2001), why are there so few women leaders? At least two factors help explain this societal phenomenon. As you read this passage, see if you can think of other reasons. Eagly, Makhijani, and Klonsky (1992) in another literature review found that women leaders tend to be slightly less positively evaluated than men while Koch (2005) found that women leaders have more negative affect directed at them than do men. Butler and Geis (1990) found that this is especially true when men are doing the evaluating. Another reason fewer women achieve top leadership positions may be that because of societal pressure they are more conflicted about mixing career and family (Crosby, 1991). For example, although most women work outside the home, it is still relatively common to see television portray women as homemakers (Jewell, 1993) and not in leadership roles (Lauzen & Dozier, 2005). Additionally, women's magazines are still more likely to carry articles about cooking and home products than careers or managerial skills (French, 1992). As you can see, the *stereotyped* sex differences between men and women leaders are probably overstated (Vecchio, 2002).

Culture and Leadership

The literature on culture and leadership is ever increasing, first, because the American workforce is diversifying, and second, because different leadership expectations and styles are firmly ensconced in other cultures. Just as important is the fact that many American, Canadian, and other companies have "gone global" with offices or factories scattered around the world.

One extremely important dimension of leader or managerial style that differs across cultures is **power distance** , which is *the idea that people in groups accept the concept that people in an organization rightfully have different levels of power and authority* (Hofstede, 2001; Johnson et al., 2005). In a high-power-distance culture, the leader makes decisions because he or she has the authority to do so. That is, the subordinates accept large distances in the distribution of power and expect leaders to behave autocratically, be somewhat paternalistic, be subject to different rules than subordinates, and enjoy privileges not available to subordinates. In other words, the managers or leaders are not psychologically close to their subordinates. Examples of high-power-distance cultures are Mexico and India.

In medium-power-distance cultures such as the United States, Canada, and Italy, subordinates expect to be consulted but will sometimes accept autocratic behavior. Subordinates also expect rules and policies to apply to all; however, they will accept some status differences between superiors and subordinates. In low-power-distance cultures, subordinates expect to be consulted on most issues, prefer a participatory and democratic style of leadership, and often rebel if superiors appear to be stepping outside their authority or possess status symbols. Rules are seen as applicable to all. Examples of such cultures are those of Denmark and Israel.

Research has begun on the effects of various levels of power differences on groups and performance (Johnson et al., 2005). Erez, Kleinbeck, and Thierry (2001) report that, in high-power-distance societies, motivational strategies designed to get groups to work harder are more effective if they are initiated and implemented by superiors with high status. Furthermore, negative supervisory reactions toward subordinates— such as criticism—are more demoralizing and trigger stronger defensive reactions in high-power-distance societies. Cho and Cheon (2005) found that in terms of Internet communications, members of high-power-distance societies (e.g., Japan and Korea) are more likely to interact with one another rather than superiors as compared to members of low-power-distance societies (e.g., the United States and Britain), who are likely to interact with (and have greater access to) authority figures.

WHEN GROUPS GO WRONG

On May 24, 2005, Sara and Harry received the sad news that their son Roy was dead. The Akaries had committed mass suicide the day after their predicted doomsday when the world did not end. You will likely agree that the Akaries functioned in a peculiar and dysfunctional manner, as can any group. In this last section, we will look at dysfunction in groups.

The Fiasco of Groupthink

There are several important concepts related to dysfunction in groups. One such concept is groupthink, introduced extensively to the psychological literature by Irving Janis (1982). **Groupthink** is *the tendency for groups to reach a consensus prematurely because the desire for harmony overrides the process of critical thinking and the search for the best decision.* Groupthink occurs when a group becomes more concerned with maintaining consensus and cohesion than with developing good ideas. Let us look at how groupthink develops and how it can be prevented. When groupthink is not present, well-functioning groups make sound decisions.

Antecedents of Groupthink.   Groupthink begins when a group is close-knit and the members view the group as attractive. In other words, people strive to be members of the group, just as Roy strived to become a member of the Akaries. In fact, cohesiveness or how close group members are to one another is posited to underlie much of the groupthink phenomenon (Henningsen, Henningsen, & Eden, 2006). The group becomes somewhat isolated. The leader usually is directive, that is, controls the discussion or promotes his or her own preference (Ahlfinger & Esser, 2001). As with many cults, the Akaries kept outside influences to a minimum; Otu himself was also very directive, especially about the planned suicide the day after the failed doomsday prediction.

Symptoms of Groupthink.   Janis as well as Henningsen et al. (2006) have detailed symptoms of groupthink for us. Knowing these symptoms, you should be able to sense groupthink commencing and stop it before poor decisions are made.

One symptom of this phenomenon is the illusion of invulnerability. The group is so close-knit and in agreement that *the members believe they are invincible; they can do no wrong.* This occurs because no one in the group wants to dissent and break the cohesiveness. In fact, dissenters are quickly dismissed or pressured to conform to the group's sentiments. In the Akaries, individuals were physically punished with spanking or were dumped in a pit of raw sewage when they disagreed with Otu. *The individuals who take it upon themselves to censor dissenters* Janis labeled **mindguards.** When Sara and Harry investigated this strange cult to which their son had belonged, the authorities told them that the Akaries had had special lieutenants who saw to the punishment of errant group members. In groupthink, members eventually censor their own behavior; thus, it *appears* that there is little to no disagreement. Because dissension then ceases, the group comes to think that it is unanimous and morally correct. What makes the process of unanimity and self-righteousness likely is that the group also stereotypes the out-group (the opposition). Members may denigrate the out-group as lazy, stupid, or incapable. Do you recall the information on in-groups and out-groups in an earlier section of this chapter? If not, go back and review it.

Consequences of Groupthink.   You are aware by now that groupthink results in defective decision making and in most cases disastrous decisions. These decisions are a consequence of several other processes. The group

- generally discusses only one or two ideas;
- fails to survey all possible alternative solutions;
- commits the blunder of not looking at all possible risks;
- avoids discussing the downside of its chosen alternative;
- and never develops any contingency plans in case something goes wrong.

Groupthink is a sinister and destructive process that is best avoided by groups.

Preventing Groupthink.   Fortunately, groupthink can be averted. One means to prevent it is to promote open inquiry and skepticism, something Otu did not allow. Perhaps the group can appoint an official devil's advocate, or the group leader can invite criticism and open debate about each alternative. To ensure that a number of alternatives are generated, subgroups can be formed. Each group should produce its own solutions; consequently, several alternatives result. Once an alternative has been selected, a second-chance meeting should occur. In this way the group has the opportunity to rethink its position and to express any remaining doubts. The leader also should refrain from expressing his or her opinion at the outset so as to foster the generation of options. One last recommendation is to call on outside experts so that the group does not remain isolated and decisions can be made by better-informed group members. You should fill out the information requested in Activity 9–2, to see whether you recently have been subjected to groupthink.

A Little Shove Goes a Long Way—Group Conflict

When you enthusiastically join a group, you hope that the group is free of conflict; however, all of us probably can recall instances of intragroup (within–group) and intergroup (between–group) conflict. When Roy called his parents to tell them that he had joined the Akaries, his parents were shocked. They threatened to cut off any financial support to him and to disinherit him so that he would not inherit the family farm. This open conflict between Roy and his parents offers a poignant example of the first type of conflict—intragroup (or intrafamilial) conflict. As for intergroup conflict, the taunting of the Akaries that some of the university students carried out offers another moving example.

The Good Side of Conflict.   Conflict need not always be deleterious (Bippus, 2005; De Dreu, 2005). In fact, some experts in the field of conflict resolution think conflict can be pleasurable (Harper, 2004). Conflict can be useful in terms of testing and assessing ourselves, others, and the issues facing us. Conflict challenges us to develop creative responses and solutions. Conflict can also result in much positive social change. Witness, for example, how the civil unrest of the 1950s resulted in advances for African Americans and other people of color. Conflict with a second group can sometimes increase cohesiveness within a group. Conflict, then, is not always bad.

The Downside of Conflict.   Conflicts typically are the result of complex mixed motives. In other words, a number of divergent motives fuel the conflict. Individuals and groups generally want more than just to win the conflict. Sometimes they also hope to inflict revenge, humiliation, or punishment on the other side or to make the other side suffer a greater loss than they themselves. One other major problem with conflict is that it sometimes seems to escalate out of control. In other words, a little shove goes a long way (De Dreu, 2005). Besides being unpleasant, conflicts are complex and often difficult.

Many factors contribute to conflict escalation (Heifetz & Segev, 2005; Rubin, Pruitt, & Kim, 1994). Threats are one such factor. When one group or party threatens another, the other side often responds with a like threat. For example, in international conflict, if one country threatens invasion, the threatened country often responds with a counterattack or at least a threat of retaliation (Huntington, 1999). You will recall that this was President George W. Bush's response to the terrorist attacks of 2001. The United States entered a war in Afghanistan against Al Qaeda and Osama bin Laden in retaliation for their attacks.

Activity 9–2

Groupthink—Has It Happened to You?

INSTRUCTIONS: *Think about a group situation you were in where the group made an important decision. Using the following true (T) or false (F) scale, indicate whether the following statements describe the situation.*

1. Early in our deliberations, the group leader announced his   T   F
   or her preferences.

2. Our group was particularly friendly and close-knit.   T   F

3. The group was not very tolerant of dissent or disagreement.   T   F

4. Once we understood the issue, we developed our ideas quickly.   T   F

5. I don't think the group ever recognized the ramifications of its   T   F
   final decision.

6. The group did not generate ideas in case things went   T   F
   wrong after our decision was implemented.

7. Our group was a bit self-righteous during our deliberations.   T   F

8. People outside the group were ignored or even made fun of.   T   F

9. Once we decided what we wanted to do, we quickly went   T   F
   off topic and chatted about personal issues.

10. The group looked unanimous, but I think some   T   F
    people privately disagreed.

   • Count up the number of Ts. _____ The higher the number, the more
     likely your group suffered from groupthink.
   • Now examine how good your decision was. Did it work?
   • Were others outside of the group pleased with the decision?
   • Did anything go wrong during implementation or afterward?

If your group was fraught with groupthink as indicated by your score (a high number of "trues"), then your answers should indicate the final decision was rather poor. Was it? If yes, what will you do differently next time?

Are threat and retaliation advantageous reactions to conflict? In classic research, Morton Deutsch and Robert Krauss (1960) found that many people use coercive means and threats *even if* they also result in damage to their *own* outcomes. This may be true because threats at first appear to offer quick resolution to the conflict and are easy to use. You may recall how events in Afghanistan and, later, Iraq dragged on for years. As another example, in his junior year of college, when Roy informed his parents that he had joined the Akaries, Sara and Harry threatened him with financial withdrawal, as mentioned earlier. Roy threatened back that he would break all contact with his parents. As threats from each side increased and promises were broken, trust decreased. It is no wonder that the conflict finally spiraled out of control, and Sara and Harry never heard from their son until they were notified of his death.

Our biases toward others, such as stereotypes and prejudice, also fuel conflict escalation (Bargal, 2004). Such perceptions divide conflicting groups into "us" versus "them," or in-group and out-group, quite easily. The **fundamental attribution error** in part also accounts for this division. When you fall prey to the fundamental attribution error, you *overattribute other people's behaviors to personality (traits) rather than to situations*. If a divorcing spouse does something negative such as threaten the other spouse with stopping child support, the threatened spouse asserts that the threatener is inherently bad. It does not occur to the threatened partner that something in the situation (such as a bad day at work or fatigue) accounts for the threat. Once this negative image is established, the self-fulfilling prophecy sustains it. The **self-fulfilling prophecy** *occurs when people's expectations become a reality by virtue of their own behavior*. Once the spouse threatens to stop payments, the other spouse becomes embittered and counterthreatens. The counterthreat induces further threats and negative behaviors from the first spouse and so on. The conflict spirals out of control.

One other reason conflict escalates is that once we are committed to a position, we tend to devote time and energy to that position (Cardona-Coll, 2003) rather than to investigate a second position. Interestingly, people do not seem to cut their losses when they begin to lose. *This process of throwing more time, energy, or money into a bad situation* is called **entrapment**. Entrapment occurs when commitments to a failing course of action are increased to justify investments already made. Entrapment contributes to conflict escalation by motivating the losers to keep trying to win. Have you ever been involved in entrapment? If not, watch for it in your future.

Culture and Conflict.   International conflict was mentioned earlier. However, much conflict also occurs within a culture. Psychologists, sociologists, and anthropologists have noted that different cultures manage conflict differently (e.g., Cushner, 2005). Specifically, the distinction between collectivistic cultures and individualistic cultures again becomes important (Hofstede, 2001; Johnson et al., 2005; Oetzel & Ting-Toomey, 2003). Recall that collectivist societies value group efforts over individual efforts, but the converse is true for *individualistic cultures*. Many Asian cultures are far more collectivistic than American, Canadian, and Western European cultures (Johnson et al.; Matsumoto, 2000). In collectivistic cultures, face-saving is important so that the self-respect and image of the disputants is maintained (Ulijn, Rutkowski, Kumar, & Zhu, 2005). In many collectivistic cultures, opponents would purposely try to avoid humiliating or conflicting with others. In individualistic societies, individuals are more concerned with saving their *own* images, so might well debase or denigrate their opponent.

Oetzel and Ting-Toomey (2003) examined face-saving in conflict situations between these two types of cultures. **Face-saving** *relates to saving one's own or someone else's image*. The researchers thought that the strategies individuals in these two cultures adopted for managing conflict might differ due to face-saving strategies. In collective or interdependent cultures, results revealed that negotiators in conflicts appear to help the *other* party save face, while in individualistic cultures, *self*-face-saving was more predominant. Furthermore, participants from individualistic cultures used dominance as a style of negotiating, whereas individuals from collective cultures were more likely to utilize avoidant or integrative solutions. You will read about integrative solutions just soon.

Conflict Management.   Luckily, experts in conflictology have developed several strategies for dealing with conflict. When conflict is completely settled, the experts say that conflict *resolution* has occurred. At other times, conflict can at best be *managed*; that is, conflict cannot be settled but only contained or kept from escalating. Groups are more likely to be fiercely competitive with each other than are two individuals in conflict (Insko, Schopler, Hoyle, Dardis, & Graetz, 1990).

Because most conflicts are mixed-motive conflicts (e.g., "Even if I lose, I want to keep my opponent from gaining much"), it is not always true that when one side loses, the other must win. Groups and individuals in conflict can look for integrative solutions. **Integrative solutions** are *those that take into account the needs of both sides such that both sides can win something.* At first, it may sound as if integrative solutions involve compromise. In compromise, though, each side must also lose a little to win a little. Integrative solutions go *beyond* compromise. Thompson (1991) examined compromise versus integrative solutions in a study in which she asked students to play the role of buyer or seller of a car. As you know, selling or buying a car involves trust, financial arrangements, warranties, delivery dates, and so forth. The parties—buyer and seller—could negotiate almost anything they wanted. To the buyer, warranty was most important. To the seller, finance rate was most important. What Thompson found was that the students simply compromised or split everything down the middle (between highest and lowest bid). It was not until participants were specifically told to ask the other party exactly what was wanted that integrative solutions were found where the buyer was pleased with the warranty period and the seller was pleased with the finance rate. The lesson here is that when in conflict, it is important to *know exactly what the other party seeks.* If you do not ask, you may make mistaken assumptions.

Charles Osgood (1962) introduced another negotiating technique designed to end or lower the level of conflict. The technique is known as **GRIT, or graduated and reciprocated initiatives in tension reduction**. With this technique *each side gradually concedes something to the other side.* For example, in international conflict, one side might concede a small piece of disputed territory. Because of the norm of reciprocity (mentioned earlier), pressure exists on the other side to concede something as well, perhaps a partial troop retreat in international war. Often these concessions are made *public* so as to keep pressure to reciprocate on both sides. The key here, then, is *communication with the public* as well as with the other side. There is always a danger with GRIT that one side will not reciprocate and in fact take advantage of the other, conceding side. Should this happen, the side that made the concession needs to respond with a like competitive action so that the other side knows the first will not be taken advantage of.

There are other possibilities for conflict management and resolution. One final method to be addressed here is the intervention of a third party (Wilburn, 2006). Third parties are usually mediators or arbitrators. **Mediators** are *neutral third parties who intervene in conflict and who help the two disputing parties come to common agreements via communication, creative problem solving, and other techniques.* **Arbitrators** are similar to mediators in that they are *neutral third parties who, using the same techniques, assist the parties with the conflict, hope that the parties can resolve their differences, but if they cannot, render a binding decision upon the parties* (Duffy, Grosch, & Olczak, 1991; Duffy & Wong, 2003).

Every state in the United States houses mediation or neighborhood justice centers as alternatives to the courts (McGillis, 1997). The typical case is a two-party dispute over property, but some centers handle felonies such as rape where the rapist and victim meet face-to-face. Mediators and arbitrators are used in many different arenas to facilitate the resolution of conflict. Mediators, in particular, have been assigned to international, environmental, business, family, neighborhood, and other conflicts with a high degree of success (Beardsley, Quinn, Biswas, & Wilkenfeld, 2006; Duffy et al., 1991; Duffy & Wong, 2003). Empirical research has also demonstrated that mediation involves a humanistic growth process. Individuals who successfully mediate their conflicts function at a higher level on Maslow's needs hierarchy (see Chapter 7) after mediation (Duffy & Thomson, 1992).

As you can ascertain, we rarely operate in isolation. Most humans are social beings; for that reason, groups affect us daily in a myriad of ways. Understanding how groups form and function, comprehending why people join groups, recognizing detrimental group processes when they first develop, and knowing how to correct dysfunctional group behaviors are valuable skills.

SUMMARY

KINDS OF GROUPS

There are several different types of groups to which we can belong. The most important group is our primary group, the small, close-knit, face-to-face groups formed by family or friends. Secondary groups are larger and less intimate, whereas collectives are very large. We usually also distinguish our own group, or in-group, from other outside groups, or out-groups. In-groups are our reference points for our feelings about ourselves.

HOW DO GROUPS FORM?

Groups go through a developmental process just as do humans. Groups come together in the forming stage and then usually move quickly to the storming stage when friction exists. Once the storming is over, the group agrees on norms or rules by which it functions and then moves to the performing or productive stage. Groups sometimes slide back to one of these stages and the process recycles.

WHY JOIN A GROUP?

Individuals join groups for a variety of reasons. One reason is that groups furnish us with the opportunity to affiliate or to be with similar others; groups also provide us with social support or psychological aid. Groups, too, often possess more information and more collective power than a single individual would.

WHAT GOES ON IN GROUPS?

Several processes operate no matter what the type of group. Various centralized or decentralized communication systems typically develop. Individuals in groups also try to influence one another through pressures to conform, comply, or obey. Some individuals feel they do not have to work as hard in a group, in which their individual efforts are less likely to be noticed, a phenomenon known as social loafing. Groups often become polarized in their decision making, whereby groups make more extreme decisions than individuals. This is known as the group polarization effect.

ARE LEADERS MADE OR BORN?

Psychologists are unsure exactly why someone in a group emerges as leader. Traits, the situation (i.e., someone being in the right place at the right time), or some combination of the two may account for leader evolution. Several theories have attempted to explain why people emerge or are effective as leaders, but no one theory to date has successfully explained this phenomenon. Contingency theory appears to be one of the better theories. The theory posits that there are two leadership styles—person-centered, in which the leader attends to group members' feelings and relationships, and task-centered, in which the leader is concerned about success and about meeting goals. The effectiveness of the group is dependent or contingent on leader style and the quality of the situation in which the group finds itself. There are several styles of leadership, including the self-aware (high emotional intelligence), charismatic, and transformational.

Research has also examined gender issues related to leadership. Women are just as effective as men in leadership positions, although the stereotype of the typical effective leader is masculine. Women, however, often are not found in such positions for reasons including the perception that they should not act in task-oriented or assertive (masculine) ways.

WHEN GROUPS GO WRONG

There are several negative group processes. One is groupthink, where groups value cohesiveness or "sticking together" over sound decision making. Groupthink often ends in disastrous decisions. Another is conflict. Although conflict is not always bad, conflict can sometimes keep a group from performing well. There are known techniques for overcoming both of these phenomena. For example, appointing a devil's advocate who criticizes the group's decisions is helpful in preventing groupthink. For conflict, integrative solutions provide the opportunity for the parties in conflict to come to some mutual understanding.

SELF-TEST

1. A family represents which type of group?
   a. primary.
   b. secondary.
   c. a collective.
   d. out-group.

2. The group with which we identify most is known as our
   a. in-group.
   b. aggregate group.
   c. norming group.
   d. secondary group.

3. The second stage of group formation is the _____ stage.
   a. forming.
   b. storming.
   c. norming.
   d. performing.

4. For what reasons do members usually join groups?
   a. affiliation.
   b. collective power.
   c. social comparison.
   d. all of these.

5. An example of a centralized group communication network is
   a. circle.
   b. chain.
   c. wheel.
   d. hierarchy.

6. When people issue a request for us to do something, they are actually requesting that we
   a. obey.
   b. conform.
   c. comply.
   d. collectivize.

7. Tony realizes that his psychology class is large, so he need not contribute often. This is an example of
   a. social loafing.
   b. authoritarianism.
   c. norm of reciprocity.
   d. group polarization.

8. People-oriented leaders are most effective in
   a. all situations.
   b. poor situations.
   c. moderately good situations.
   d. good situations.

9. The phenomenon in which groups value cohesiveness over sound decision making is known as
   a. groupthink.
   b. conformity.
   c. norming.
   d. responsibility diffusion.

10. An outside, neutral person who has the power to make *binding* decisions in a conflict is a
    a. mediator.
    b. arbitrator.
    c. expediter.
    d. GRIT.

EXERCISES

1. *Kinds of groups.* Think about the primary and secondary groups to which you belong. Do the characteristics of your groups fit the descriptions in the book? If not, why not?

2. *New groups.* Watch a newly forming committee or some other group. Did the group go through the stages of group development as outlined in this chapter?

3. *Why join groups?* Ask a number of people why they join the groups they choose. Do the reasons conform to those cited in the book? Are they different from your reasons?

4. *Social support.* Make a list of occasions on which someone offered you social support in the last 2 months. Do the occasions have anything in common? What kinds of support were offered?

5. *Electronic communication.* Have you ever used electronic communication in a group of which you are a member? Write a few paragraphs about how these communications differed from face-to-face communications.

6. *Group consensus.* Observe a group coming to consensus about some issue. Do you see any signs of groupthink? How could the group have avoided this phenomenon?

7. *Leadership.* For the groups of which you are a member, think about how the leader was selected. Can you add anything to the literature on leader emergence based on your experience? How well does your experience fit any of the theories presented?

QUESTIONS FOR SELF-REFLECTION

1. Why did you join the groups you did? Why did you leave any of the groups?

2. Who are the members of your in-group? Do you think that your in-group will remain the same over a lifetime? Why not?

3. Be honest—are there out-groups in your life? Who are the members? Would it be better for you and for them if they weren't in your out-group? How can you overcome stereotyping this group or conflicting with them?

4. When groups are storming, have you contributed to the storming or tried to move the group toward norming and performing? What were your motives for doing what you did? Did others resist you? Why?

5. Are you as likely to offer social support to someone in need as others are to offer you support?

6. What do you enjoy more—face-to-face communication with others or electronic (phone, e-mail, etc.) communication? Why?

7. Are you a conformist or a nonconformist? Is one better than the other for you given your life circumstances? Could you change strategy if you wanted to?

8. Do you do your fair share of work in the groups of which you are a member? Why or why not? Do you think you need to change your contribution level?

9. Are you a leader of any groups? If you are a leader, why? If you do not lead any groups, why not? Are you more comfortable being a leader or a follower? Why?

10. Reflect on your life; have you experienced groupthink? What were the results of the groupthink process? Can you reverse any poor decisions?

FOR FURTHER INFORMATION

RECOMMENDED READINGS

BOYATZIS, R. E., & MCKEE, A. (2005). *Resonant leadership: Renewing yourself and connecting with others through mindfulness, hope, and compassion.* Cambridge, MA: Harvard Business School Press. The authors propose that leaders with emotional intelligence need to move beyond using solely this quality to lead; otherwise, they burn out. Boyatzis and McKee provide useful suggestions for executives who want to motivate their employees and improve the bottom line.

HARPER, G. (2004). *The joy of conflict: Transforming victims, villains, and heroes in the workplace and at home.* British Columbia, CA: New Society Publishers. Written by a real mediator and conflict management expert, the book provides practical, humorous, and well-received methods for managing conflict.

KOUZES, J. M., & POZNER, B. C. (2002). *The leadership challenge.* Boston, MA: Wiley. Leadership is critical to our modern, shrinking world. Leaders need to experiment, take risks, and learn from their mistakes.

PERLOW, L. A. (2003). *When you say yes, but mean no: How silencing conflict wrecks relationships and companies ... and what you can do about it.* New York: Random House. We are fond of silencing conflict and taking an easier way out. Sometimes ignoring conflict can be as destructive as surfacing it. Why this is so and what to do about it are the topic of this practical book.

WHEELEN, S. (2004). *Group processes: A developmental perspective*. Boston, MA: Allyn & Bacon. This book provides a standard social psychological viewpoint of group processes. The author provides both theory and research to address issues specific to group dynamics.

WEB SITES AND THE INTERNET

http://www.managementhelp.org/grp_skll/theory/theory.htm A web site on group dynamics which includes information on how groups form, how to conduct team building, etc. There are also links to library and other resources.

http://www.alleydog.com/links-sp/social.asp This site offers links to other sites that are concerned with social psychology, including topics on group behavior.

http://www.richmond.edu/~dforsyth/gd/ A site that contains much information on the history of study of groups, how research on groups is performed, how groups structure themselves, the nature of group influence, and more. It reinforces many of the concepts in the chapter.

http://www.factnet.org/ Interested in knowing more about those special groups we call cults? This information page discusses a multitude of important questions about cults.

http://www.uiowa.edu/~grpproc/index.html A site sponsored by the Center for the Study of Group Processes. It includes free access to the electronic journal *Current Research in Social Psychology*.

CHAPTER 10

At Work and Play

CHOOSING YOUR CAREER
Taking Stock of Yourself
Identifying Compatible Careers
Arriving at Your Career Decision
Preparing for Your Career

YOUR CAREER OUTLOOK
Forecasting Your Career's Growth
Changing Jobs or Careers

CONTEMPORARY ISSUES IN THE WORLD OF WORK
Job Satisfaction
Technology and Work
Diversity in the Workplace

LEISURE TIME
What Is Leisure?
Work and Leisure
Using Leisure Positively

SUMMARY
SELF-TEST
EXERCISES
QUESTIONS FOR SELF-REFLECTION
FOR FURTHER INFORMATION

Kristin was thrilled. She had just marched down the aisle of the stadium at her university to celebrate her graduation. Her parents and her grandmother were there with flashbulbs popping. Of course, Kristin was saddened to be leaving her good friends. "There is always e-mail or my cell phone," she thought to herself.

The next day was Sunday, so Kristin lounged around the house. In fact, she continued this routine in the days that followed. She lazed her time away watching TV, talking on the phone, and helping her parents around the house. In the third week after her graduation, her father asked, "Krissy, do you have a résumé?" "Sure, Dad," she answered. "The university career center helped me assemble it." "Krissy, tomorrow we are getting in the car and we are going to drop off your résumé in downtown Manhattan." Kristin was startled by her father's abruptness, but she agreed to accompany him. She took her résumé and cover letter to over 45 different businesses during the next week. Nothing happened. The phone never rang; no one asked for interviews. Kristin was disheartened. Her parents kept insisting that she get out of the house and find a job. She finally landed a job waiting on tables at the local country club. "Sure, I am earning money," she thought. "But I had hoped for a job that would better utilize my skills and training." Kristin was a psychology major with a business minor and had hoped to work in the human resources department of a big company. Specifically, Kristin hoped to be a recruiter for new employees or a trainer for new hires. None of this was coming true. Kristin kept sending her résumé and cover letters. She was determined that waitressing was only a means to pay off her student loans until something better came along.

One day her dream really did come true. A large department store in New York City requested an interview. The store was interested in Kristin because she had completed an internship in a human resources department for a smaller store near her university. Kristin landed the job of her dreams. She was indeed to be a recruiter—but not just any recruiter. Her job was to hire celebrities for big publicity functions at the flagship store.

CHOOSING YOUR CAREER

Kristin's experience illustrates some of the perils and promises of finding your own niche in the **workplace**, or *place of paid employment outside the home*. On the minus side, you can see that no matter how well educated you are, you can still end up without a **job**, *a position of employment or set of work activities and responsibilities associated with a given position*. A major reason for unemployment is often the lack of a good system for matching people with careers and jobs. As a result, in addition to millions of unemployed people, it has been estimated that many people in the United States are **underemployed**—*working in a job beneath their abilities or education*.

On the plus side, Kristin's success story shows what you can do when you take the initiative and make the most of your opportunities. Notice that in reassessing her **career**—*one's purposeful life pattern of work, as seen in the sequence of jobs held throughout one's life*—Kristin needed to take stock of what she had to offer and what she really wanted. One of the keys to Kristin's success was her eventual emphasis on a positive, take-charge attitude, as opposed to the conventional image of the job applicant as a prospective employee cowering before employers. All of these points are relevant for our own lives because we, too, face the challenges of choosing a compatible career and finding a job that uses our talents.

Taking Stock of Yourself

When choosing a career goal, it's best to begin by taking stock of yourself. Such self-assessment should include a consideration of your interests, abilities, personality, and personal values. What are your interests? Which school subjects do you like the most? The least? Which hobbies do you enjoy? Which recreational and sports activities do you play or follow? In each case, try to determine what it is that most interests you, whether it's the activity itself or the people you're doing it with. Generally, the intrinsic or internal enjoyment of the activity is one of your best guides to the choice of a career.

What are you good at? People often balk at this question. They say, "I haven't done anything but go to school" or "I've been busy raising three kids." The implication of such remarks is that these people don't have any marketable skills. But when they are confronted with a checklist of things they can do, the picture brightens. For example, a woman who has organized a mothers' cooperative day care, planned field trips for children, and managed the family budget has had considerable experience with management skills, a very important ability for a variety of jobs. *A* **skill** *is the ability to perform a task well. It is usually developed over time through training or experience.* A skill can be used to do work in many jobs or it can be used in learning. To start you on appraising the skills you have, read Box 10–1.

Another way to find out what you're good at is to reflect upon your achievements, including those in school or elsewhere. Perhaps you won a spelling bee or were the all-around athlete-scholar. You may have been elected to an office of a large student

Box 10–1

What Skills Do You Possess?

Occupations are classified based on how frequently skills are used and by what level of skill is usually needed. Most occupations offer some exceptions. For example, a high level of math skills is not required for some computer programmers, such as those who work on user interfaces, but high-level math skills are required for most computer programmers—including some who prepare physics simulations that require calculus. Based on the level of skills that most of these workers need, mathematics ability is rated as essential for computer programmers. In another example, managerial skills are rated as being of basic importance for construction and building inspectors, who are primarily independent but sometimes must advise other workers. The skills—artistic, communication, interpersonal, managerial, mathematical, mechanical, and scientific skills—are described here.

Artistic skills. Occupations that require artistic skills tap workers' sense of what is beautiful or well designed. The level of creativity needed may depend on how structured an occupation is. Workers in occupations that identify art as being somewhat important use artistic creativity occasionally or use artistic originality within precise guidelines. Highly artistic occupations are most likely to require a great deal of independent composition, production, or performance.

Communication skills. As mentioned previously, nearly all workers need communication skills. Occupations in which basic communication skills are needed involve speaking and writing clearly, reading, and giving descriptions or instructions. Occupations in which communication skills are somewhat important require persuasive communication, the use of technical jargon, or writing reports or other documents. Occupations that require the highest level of communication skills use vocabulary appropriate for complicated subjects, explain complicated subjects orally and in writing, and include communication as a primary component of the work.

Interpersonal skills. Interpersonal skills refer to workers' ability to interact effectively with other people and to be persuasive. The level of interpersonal skills required in each occupation is based on workers' frequency of contact with the public, other employees, or clients. Beyond dealing with people courteously, workers in occupations that place some importance on interpersonal skills need an ability to sell products, ideas, or services in a convincing manner. Occupations in which interpersonal skills are of high importance might draw on the ability to analyze and solve workplace conflicts.

Managerial skills. Managerial skills include the ability to organize, direct, and instruct other workers. Many occupations do not require managing others. But in occupations in which these skills are of some importance, workers should be able to motivate and inspire individuals or teams. When managerial skills are essential in an occupation, workers must be able to guide others and to accept responsibility for others' work and actions.

Mathematics skills. Mathematics skills refer to more advanced ability than the core math skills required in nearly all jobs. Occupations in which basic math is needed require that workers be comfortable using numbers and performing arithmetic; some workers in the occupation might use a higher level of skills—for example, to draft a budget—but these skills are not essential across the occupation. In occupations in which math skills are somewhat important, quick calculations and number analysis are often required; these occupations might also involve a working knowledge of complex mathematical theorems, such as algebra, geometry, or statistics. High-level importance is indicated when many workers use algebra, geometry, or statistics frequently or when mathematical decision making is a primary responsibility of most workers; these occupations might also require study of both linear algebra or calculus and advanced statistics.

Mechanical skills. Mechanical skills include a broad range of abilities, such as installation, maintenance, troubleshooting, and quality control analysis. Occupations in which these skills are somewhat important might require basic mechanical ability, such as an understanding of the relationship between moving parts. Higher-level mechanical skills may require knowledge of operations as well as an ability to diagnose and repair failures of equipment, machines, or systems.

(continued)

Box 10–1 *(continued)*

Science skills. When basic science skills are often needed in an occupation, workers must have an ability to apply some scientific theories and to communicate about science at a basic level. When science skills are deemed somewhat important in an occupation, workers need a theoretical knowledge of the principles of life, physical, or computer sciences, including biology, ecology, chemistry, and physics; or, they might need to communicate with science experts. In-depth practical knowledge often is required in highly scientific occupations, particularly in those related to scientific research and development; workers in these occupations almost always study science in college.

SOURCE: Adapted from the Bureau of Labor Statistics (2004). http://www.bls.gov/opub/ooq/2004/fall/art01.pdf

organization. Select several achievements in each of the 5-year periods of your life. What do these achievements have in common? What characteristics do they *not* share? What can you learn about yourself and your goals and skills from your achievements?

Your personality also offers valuable clues for choosing a compatible career. Each of us possesses a unique combination of traits, needs, and motives that make some work environments more compatible for us than others. For example, a meticulous homemaker may be good at working on computers, a field that requires the ability to manage details with precision. A young man who has never cared much for school may like working with his hands, such as rebuilding car engines. Many times our experience in part-time and summer jobs helps us see which type of work environments we like the most as well as which we don't like. For example, after spending a summer working with a tree service, one friend of Kristin's realized how much she enjoyed working outside, so she became a national park ranger. Kristin loved her position in the human resources department at the store, in part because it matched her training, including her business skills and her desire as a psychology major to work with others.

Your values are also an important consideration, especially your **work values—** *what brings you the most enjoyment or satisfaction in a career or job.* All too often, we take our work values for granted, becoming aware of them only when faced with job dissatisfaction, job changes, or decisions about jobs. An example is the choice between a job we enjoy that doesn't pay well and one that we don't especially like that does. However, the sooner we clarify our work values, the easier it will be to make a satisfying decision regarding a career or job.

Identifying Compatible Careers

Once you have a better understanding of your interests and abilities, you're ready to match yourself with a compatible career. With more than 20,000 different careers to choose from, this can be a formidable task. Fortunately, there are many helpful resources such as the *Occupational Outlook Handbook* (OOH) published by the Bureau of Labor Statistics. This handbook contains more than 20 basic career groups, each with dozens of related occupations. An **occupation** is *the activities and responsibilities necessary to perform given work tasks in a particular line of work,* such as nursing or marketing. For example, health-related careers include physicians, physician's assistants, registered nurses, practical nurses, medical technicians, and the like. For each career, the handbook provides information on the type of work involved, places of employment, entrance requirements, working conditions, and employment outlook. The OOH also has an introductory section with helpful information on such topics as how to find a job and employment opportunities. The OOH, revised every 2 years, is available in most libraries and job counseling centers or

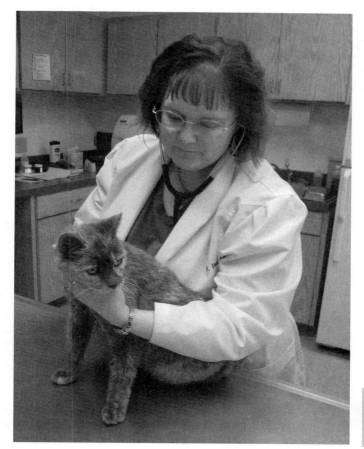

With more than 20,000 types of jobs available, choosing a career can be a formidable task.

can also be found online at http://www.bls.gov. In addition, the book provides job search tips and links to information about the job market in each state. Another book that you may find helpful is *The Guide to Job Opportunities* from the College Board in Princeton, New Jersey.

In identifying compatible careers, it's often advisable to talk over your plans with an interested teacher, school counselor, mentor, or someone in your field of interest. Professionals in university counseling centers and career development centers spend a good part of their time assisting people with their career planning. They also have access to a wide assortment of psychological inventories for this purpose. These inventories may furnish valuable leads to compatible careers for someone with your interests, especially when discussed with a counselor. Don't wait until you are looking for a job to assess your strengths and values; working with these centers while you are a freshman or sophomore can be an invaluable guide to planning your education before you graduate or hit the job market.

The *Strong Interest Inventory* probably dominates the field of career assessment as the most popular instrument (Watkins, 1993) and has been demonstrated to be very effective in dealing with the complexities of career interests (Donnay & Borgen, 1996; Hansen & Dik, 2005). This same inventory has also been used in research with college freshmen. Freshmen with "flat" profiles (i.e., students with less differentiated interests) have more difficulty selecting a major, have less career certainty during college, and are more likely to change jobs than those freshmen with well-developed interests (Sackett & Hansen, 1995).

The *Strong Interest Inventory* is usually administered by a professional counselor and is widely used for career guidance. Using this inventory, you indicate your preferences (like, dislike, or indifferent) for various careers, school subjects, activities, amusements, and types of people as well as indicate something about your own personal characteristics. Computer-scored printouts organize the results around six basic categories, which are briefly described here:

- *Realistic*—practical, stable, persistent (example: engineer)
- *Investigative*—task-oriented, introspective, and independent (example: biologist)
- *Artistic*—creative, impulsive, and expressive (example: musician)
- *Social*—sociable, responsible, and humanistic (example: social worker)
- *Enterprising*—aggressive, confident, and energetic (example: stockbroker)
- *Conventional*—predictable, conforming, conscientious, and obedient (example: accountant)

The results of the *Strong Interest Inventory* include information on general career themes, basic interests, and specific careers with which you are most compatible. Discussion of the results with a counselor usually provides valuable leads to the most compatible careers for you. To help you prepare to see a career counselor, think about which of these descriptors best fits you. Which others come close to describing you, and which do not describe you at all?

Several other inventories exist (Betz & Rottinghaus, 2006), so an important question is "How helpful are these inventories?" A lot depends on how they are used. If you take them in hopes that they'll tell you which career you should choose—a common misunderstanding—you'll probably be disappointed. Nor will the results predict how successful or happy you'll be in a given career, inasmuch as these factors depend on your abilities, personal motivation, and so on. Instead, these inventories are best used as an aid in making an *informed career choice*. For instance, the results of the *Strong Interest Inventory* have proven quite useful in predicting which people will remain in a given field (Hansen & Dik, 2005; Sackett & Hansen, 1995). Those who choose careers very similar to their career profiles tend to remain in their careers, whereas those who enter careers highly dissimilar to their profiles eventually tend to drop out of them. When you consider all the time and money invested in preparing for a career, this information can be extremely helpful to you.

Arriving at Your Career Decision

If you're like most people, you'll end up with not just one but a number of potentially compatible careers. Ultimately, you must make a decision about which is the best career for you. The process is so important that there is a special chapter (Chapter 6) devoted to it; the chapter is called "Taking Charge" and is about personal control and decision making. You might pay close attention to the steps in decision making—especially the balance-sheet procedure in that chapter. This step consists of listing all the pluses and minuses involved in a given course of action, like the choice of a career goal. Such an approach helps you make a comprehensive appraisal of what is involved. It also promotes contingency planning, that is, figuring out what to do if one or more of the unfavorable consequences in the minus column should materialize.

In the process of deciding on a career, you should guard against certain pitfalls. One is the accidental choice, which consists of choosing a career mostly because of attraction to one's first job. People who fall into this trap may discover later, to their regret, that they would have been happier or more successful in another line of work. Another pitfall is the choice of a career or job because of its external trappings, like money, prestige, power, or security. In the long run, it's better to choose a work activity that is enjoyable in itself, as long as the financial rewards are adequate. A major mistake is not exploring your career options sufficiently. Kristin, for example, knew she did not want to be a waitress all of her life. On the other hand, she was not sure about what she did want to do. Just as with Kristin, you must take the initiative and engage in an *active* process of finding a compatible career, as already discussed. Still another pitfall has to do with the timing of your decision, with the risk of making a premature decision or of waiting too long to decide. People who make strong career commitments in their 20s, before they are fully informed about careers, often regret their choices later. On the other hand, those who delay making a career commitment until their 30s (e.g., stay-at-home mothers) usually deprive themselves of the necessary work experience to make a wise choice. Thus, you need to choose a career goal but be willing to modify that choice in light of your subsequent experiences and personal growth.

Preparing for Your Career

Once you've determined your career goal, you'll need to know how to prepare for it. Kristin was only partly prepared in that she had held a single internship and at the last minute developed her résumé. She had no further strategies for finding her first professional-level job until her father told her to drop off her résumé at various businesses. As you might expect, there are many ways to prepare for a career. Some careers are entered through an apprenticeship, vocational-technical school, internships, or on-the-job training programs. Others require a 2-year or 4-year college degree. In addition, careers such as teaching, accounting, and nursing also require a state license or some type of certification. Professions such as clinical psychology, medicine, and law also require an advanced degree, supervised training, and a state license. Because you are already enrolled in some sort of post–high school education, you may have begun the appropriate education for your career. On the other hand, others of you, especially those in a liberal arts program, may not have arrived at a firm career goal. But in either case, an integral part of career planning is finding out the appropriate educational requirements for your chosen career.

As you know, more people are choosing to attend college today than in the past. Whereas only one-third of high school graduates went on to college in the 1960s, more than half of them do so today. In turn, this ratio raises the educational attainment of people in the workplace, as well as the value of a college education.

College is supposed to make you a better-informed person and provide access to higher status and better-paying careers. Naturally, college graduates continue to have higher lifetime earnings and lower unemployment rates than high school graduates, as shown in Table 10–1. For instance, people with a 4-year college degree earn substantially more than high school graduates the same age. Those with graduate or professional degrees enjoy an even greater advantage. Of course, people's salaries vary considerably depending on many factors, such as the field of study, actual position held, and geographic location. Given the rapid changes in the job market, and the fact that one in nine persons changes careers every year, some of the most valuable but often overlooked advantages of a college

TABLE 10–1

EDUCATION AND PAY: THE BETTER THE EDUCATION, THE BETTER THE PAY

Average earnings in 2004, based on education level, for people 18 or older

Education Level	Average Salary
No high school diploma	$22,232
High school diploma	30,640
Some college, no degree	35,970
Associate degree	37,480
Bachelor's degree	53,581
Master's degree	67,361
Doctoral degree	93,096
Professional degree	115,292

SOURCE: U.S. Census Bureau (2005). http://pubdb3.census.gov/macros/032005/perinc/new04-001.htm.

education are the abilities for critical thinking, appreciation of lifelong learning, and enhanced adaptation to continuing change.

There are several important aspects pertaining to landing your first full-time professional position. One important aspect, as Kristin found out, is the résumé. Another important step is the job interview. It is never too early to start preparing yourself for both. Activity 10–1 introduces you to some of the complexities of the job interview and preparing for it.

Perhaps you believe as Kristin did that she merely had to look at the newspaper classified advertisements to find a position. She did this dutifully each day shortly after she graduated. Her parents, however, knew that 80 percent of available jobs are never advertised and that over half of all employees obtain their jobs through people they know (U. S. Department of Labor, 2004). Although not exhaustive, here is a list of possible places to search for a position:

• Apply in person or walk in the door with your résumé as did Kristin.
• Search Internet job sites such as Monster.com.
• Use an employment agency or recruiter that hires individuals for companies.
• Find a position through the university or college career service center.
• Use your and your parents' networks of personal contacts to find job openings.
• Look in professional journals and newsletters or attend professional conferences.
• Visit job fairs or other venues where jobs are posted.

Do you know which of these is most fruitful and, on the other hand, which search strategy results in few good matches, if any, between job seekers and employers? With the proliferation of job search engines on the World Wide Web, you might think that this is the most productive method. Wrong! Knowing now what Kristen's parents know about the value of personal contacts in job searches, you should be cultivating contacts with knowledgeable others—perhaps alumni from your campus, neighbors, volunteer or internship supervisors, or other mentors you know—who can point you to job openings upon your graduation. This strategy is called **networking** or *using personal contacts to establish career opportunities*. You might think that this provides you with an unfair advantage over any other candidates—which it might. This is, however, a perfectly acceptable and ethical technique, especially given that up to half of all position openings are unadvertised.

ACTIVITY 10–1

THE JOB INTERVIEW

Securing a job usually involves one or more formal interviews. Your major goal is to convince the employer that you are the person for the job, that is, that you have the necessary qualifications and personal qualities and would fit into the organization. It's best to create a favorable impression. Be confident and ambitious, emphasizing your strengths. If asked about your weaknesses, admit a minor one such as "At times I'm too conscientious." Also, it's generally best not to furnish more information than requested by the employer. Finally, a crucial part of a successful job interview is preparing for the interview. Consider the following job interview tips.

Preparation:
- Learn about the organization.
- Have a specific job or jobs in mind.
- Review your qualifications for the job.
- Prepare answers to broad questions about yourself.
- Review your résumé.
- Practice an interview with a friend or relative.
- Arrive before the scheduled time of your interview.

Personal appearance:
- Be well groomed.
- Dress appropriately.
- Do not chew gum or smoke.

The interview:
- Relax and answer each question concisely.
- Respond promptly.
- Use good manners.
- Learn the name of your interviewer and greet him or her with a firm handshake.
- Use proper English—avoid slang.
- Be cooperative and enthusiastic.
- Use body language to show interest.
- Ask questions about the position and the organization, but avoid questions whose answers can easily be found on the company web site. Also avoid asking questions about salary and benefits unless a job offer is made.
- Thank the interviewer when you leave and, as a follow-up, in writing.

Test (if employer gives one):
- Listen closely to instructions.
- Read each question carefully.
- Write legibly and clearly.
- Budget your time wisely and don't dwell on one question.

Information to bring to an interview:

- Social Security card.
- Government-issued identification (driver's license).
- Résumé. Although not all employers require applicants to bring a résumé, you should be able to furnish the interviewer information about your education, training, and previous employment.
- References. Employers typically require three references. Get permission before using anyone as a reference. Make sure that they will give you a good reference. Try to avoid using relatives as references.
- Transcripts. Employers may require an official copy of transcripts to verify grades, coursework, dates of attendance, and highest grade completed or degree awarded.

SOURCE: Adapted from U.S. Department of Labor, Bureau of Labor Statistics (2005). *Occupational Outlook Handbook.* http://www.bls.gov/oco/oco20045.htm.

YOUR CAREER OUTLOOK

How promising your job is often depends on the outlook for your field. Do you know the outlook for your chosen career? Are the job openings in your field expected to remain stable? Or is rapid growth of jobs projected? Kristin based her career choice of wanting to work in human resource management on her love of psychology and the results of the *Strong Interest Inventory*, which indicated she was also attracted to business environments. Although it's difficult to answer all possible questions about specific jobs, the Bureau of Labor Statistics (BLS) periodically makes informed projections of jobs in the various careers. Because employment projections, by their nature, are somewhat imprecise, you should not use them as the sole basis for a career decision. But such projections can help you assess future opportunities in the careers that interest you.

Forecasting Your Career's Growth

The number and types of jobs available in the years ahead depend on the interaction of many factors, especially economic, demographic, and technological factors. By analyzing changes in the economy and the factors involved, the Bureau of Labor Statistics develops projections of future demands for many careers. To make these projections, authorities must make some assumptions about the growth of the labor force, economic inflation, and unemployment. You can find the BLS web site and other federal sites at www.firstgov.gov. (By the way, this is an excellent site for assembling up-to-date statistics for term papers.)

As projected through 2010 by the U.S. Department of Labor (2000), total employment is expected to increase by 15 percent. The service sector (finance, real estate, health care, communication, data processing, etc.) is expected to dominate employment growth, adding up to 20.5 million jobs. Many of the fastest-growing occupations are computer-related. Manufacturing, goods-producing services, and administrative support positions are expected to grow at a much slower rate, if at all. Examples of such positions include construction, farming, office assistant, and mining. Table 10-2 provides you more detail on which employment sectors are most expected to grow.

TABLE 10–2

INDUSTRIES WITH THE LARGEST WAGE AND SALARY EMPLOYMENT GROWTH (NUMBERS IN THOUSANDS)

Industry	Employment 2004	Employment 2014	% Change
Employment services	3,470.3	5,050.2	45.5
Local government—educational services	7,762.5	8,545.5	10.1
Local government	5,485.6	6,249.3	13.9
Physicians	2,053.9	2,813.4	37.0
Full-service restaurants	4,226.4	4,927.8	16.6
Hospital services	4,050.9	4,699	16.0
Limited-service restaurants	3,726.7	4,318.6	15.9
Home health care services	7,73.2	1,310.3	69.5
Colleges, universities and professional schools	1,377.5	1,849.8	34.3
Management, scientific, and technical consulting	779	1,250.2	60.5

SOURCE: Bureau of Labor Statistics. stats.bls.gov/news.release/ecopro.to3.htm.

Changing Jobs or Careers

Looking over the job projections and alternative career patterns may start you thinking about your own career goal. Perhaps you already have a firm career direction and are busily preparing for it. Someone else may have doubts or reservations. Either way, remember that it's perfectly natural to modify your career goal with experience and with greater knowledge of career opportunities. People are often reluctant to change their career goals for many reasons. Sometimes they would rather keep to their original goal than risk disappointing their parents, spouses, or peers. They forget they are choosing for *themselves*—not for anyone else. People also fear that switching career goals may be regarded as an admission of failure, but to continue in a direction you have misgivings about will only make matters worse. Then, too, individuals may overestimate the price of changing career goals. After gathering all the facts, you may find that the penalties are not as great as expected. The longer you delay changing career goals or careers, the more difficult it is. More often than not, the positive gains outweigh the costs.

People are changing jobs more frequently than in the past. The time a worker keeps a job has steadily declined, and the typical American worker has more jobs (or employers) in his or her lifetime than workers during the 1950s. The typical pattern is that an individual tends to hold several brief jobs in the first few years after graduation, then settles into a position that lasts several years. Workers in their 30s who stay with the same employer for 5 years or more are likely to remain in that job for a long time. As men and women get older, they make fewer job changes. By the age of 40, workers will make about two more job changes; at 50, only one more. Few people change jobs in their 60s, and most of them are probably moving into second careers because of retirement. At the same time, there are exceptions to this pattern. A small number of workers exhibit extremely stable job patterns throughout their careers. Others change jobs every few years until they reach retirement.

There are many reasons individuals change careers, jobs, or employers. One important and oft-overlooked reason is burnout. Burnout in our fast-paced work-a-day life is a problem more and more psychologists are researching and trying to understand. Box 10–2 explicates some of the issues surrounding burnout. Some of the other reasons for changing jobs or careers, such as low job satisfaction, are reviewed next.

Box 10–2

JOB BURNOUT—DON'T LET IT HAPPEN TO YOU

There are many factors that can make a job unsatisfying. Some work is dangerous—for example, working on a construction crew. Other jobs are boring and monotonous, like assembly-line work. In other instances, employees may not be well matched to or well trained for their jobs. Some positions provide solitary work, where employees cannot socialize or talk to one another during the course of the day. Other occupations allow little room for advancement or new skills acquisition. Some posts provide for little responsibility or underutilize the individual's education or capabilities. Other jobs might require individuals to work too hard and, thus, to experience overload. One other very important aspect of job satisfaction and performance is job burnout.

Burnout is *a psychological syndrome of emotional exhaustion, depersonalization, and reduced personal accomplishment that occurs among individuals, especially those who do "people work"* (Schutte, Toppinene, Kalimo, & Schaufeli, 2000). Let's look in greater detail at this definition. Emotional exhaustion is the primary symptom or characteristic of burnout. Emotional exhaustion typically means that the person feels exhausted or drained from the stress of the job. Stress can come from a steady stream of problematic clients, long work hours, too much responsibility, and a myriad of other factors. Depersonalization means that clients, customers, or others with whom the burned-out individual comes in contact are not seen as particularly human anymore; they are numbers or faceless souls. The burned-out employee interacts with them in a detached, impersonal, and cynical manner. Finally, the sufferer's performance may decline or the individual may feel that he or she no longer makes a difference—no matter how well or how many hours the individual works. Human service workers are probably most affected by burnout (Adams, Boscarino, & Figley, 2006), although those in other occupations certainly are eligible as well. Teachers, nurses, police, and social workers are good examples of people prone to burnout.

Men and women are equally likely to burn out, although women's health may suffer more from job stress (Toker, Shirom, Shapira, Berliner, & Melamed, 2005), and those who are unmarried are more prone to it. Some researchers suggest that low levels of hardiness, poor self esteem, an external locus of control (e.g., being controlled by forces beyond the individual), and an avoidant coping style typically constitute the profile of a stress-prone or burned-out individual (American Psychological Association, 2006; Maslach, Schaufeli, & Leiter, 2001). Other researchers suggest that yet different personality dimensions result in burnout, for example, neuroticism, conscientiousness, and even high self-efficacy (Burke, Matthiesen, & Pallesen, 2006). We should not forget, however, that certain job characteristics can also contribute to burnout and job fatigue, namely time pressures, role ambiguity, long working hours, low control over the work, and so forth (Sonnentag & Zijlstra, 2006).

The best way to avoid burnout is to prevent it in the first place. Before you take a job, consider whether you and the job are a good fit. If the job requires you to report early to work, are you an early riser? If you like being creative on the job, is there room for creativity in the day-to-day routine of the job? If you are a social butterfly, does the position provide you possibilities for interacting with customers and coworkers? Does the job require public speaking; are you frightened to get up in front of a large audience? Consider all aspects of the position as well as your personality and preferred work environment. Don't take the job if it isn't a good match.

If you find yourself victimized by burnout, you can still escape some of its consequences. One of the most important ways to reduce the effects of burnout is to have a good social support system. Perhaps coworkers feel the same way you do but cope better; talk to them and see what helps them. Family members who know about your work may also offer a sympathetic ear and some good advice for how to deal with burnout. A good sense of humor and the ability to have fun can also help you better manage this type of job stress. Perhaps you can put up some funny pictures or cartoons in the break room or ask coworkers to bring in the joke of the day. Be sure that you allow for leisure time, covered elsewhere in this chapter, off the job, too. Try not to come home from work so exhausted that you can't do a few fun things after work.

You might also think about how you do your job. Are there positive aspects you could focus on more? Why did you take the position in the first place? Perhaps

(continued)

Box 10–2 (*continued*)

you can realign your work values with the initial aspects of the job that interested or excited you. Perhaps you or your supervisor can think of ways to expand your job to include elements that make the job less boring, more exciting, or more rewarding. Maybe there are new skills you can learn or utilize, too. If you are a good employee, your boss will want to keep you and keep you happy.

Finally, as can any other type of stress, burnout can cause physical and mental health problems, so it is best to confront it when it happens. If burnout becomes too intense and too much for you to handle, perhaps it is time to do another self-assessment and find a new job in a different company or even a new occupation. Don't let burnout get the best of you.

CONTEMPORARY ISSUES IN THE WORLD OF WORK

During our teens and 20s, most of us gain considerable work experience through a variety of part-time and summer jobs and, in many cases, full-time jobs. Although these jobs may not have been especially interesting or related to our career goals, they do provide practical knowledge. Experience in the workplace teaches us how to budget our time; take responsibility for a job; and, most important, get along with other people. Finding and holding our first satisfying full-time job in our chosen career is much more involved and important, however. Following are some issues important to any job.

Job Satisfaction

Job satisfaction is *people's feelings about different aspects of their jobs; how well one likes a given job, depending on such factors as pay and coworkers.* People who are satisfied with their jobs not only are less susceptible to stress-related illnesses but also visit the doctor less frequently and live longer than those who are dissatisfied in their jobs—all important considerations.

Despite all the griping you hear (and perhaps your own choice comments) on the job, a substantial majority of Americans are satisfied with their jobs (Souza-Poza & Souza-Poza, 2000; U.S. Merit Systems Protections Board, 2005). Many of these same individuals say they would continue to work even if they didn't need the money (AARP, 2002). This does not mean, though, that these same individuals are happy with all aspects of their jobs. College-educated workers, especially those in the professions and executive positions, are generally more satisfied with their jobs than those with less education. Workers in unskilled and service jobs tend to be less satisfied. Sales personnel tend to fall below the norm in job satisfaction, despite being fairly well compensated.

Satisfaction on the job depends heavily on the work activity itself. People generally prefer work that involves contact with others, is interesting, offers the opportunity to learn new skills, and allows them some independence (Hugick & Leonard, 1991; Mohr & Zoghi, 2006; Sousa-Poza & Sousa-Poza, 2000). Interestingly, how well you feel you perform on the job is only somewhat related to your level of job satisfaction. That is, only a moderately positive relationship exists between performance and job satisfaction (Joner, 2005; Schleicher, Watt, & Greguras, 2004). Some people who love their jobs perform well while others who love their jobs do not. Some people who do not acquire satisfaction from their jobs perform well anyway; others who do not like their jobs do not perform well at all. Thus, there are other reasons that explain our job performance outside of job satisfaction.

Job satisfaction also depends to a great extent on the working conditions of the job. In addition to a rewarding job, workers generally prefer having a job that provides opportunities for advancement, job security, and good working hours. They also want friendly, cooperative coworkers and considerate supervisors. Workers also experience less stress at work when they are allowed some control or can make decisions on their own (Spector, 2002). Pay for work is not only a means of recognizing job performance or success; it also may be used to purchase other items we want. One study demonstrated, however, that going after the highest-paying job does not necessarily result in high job satisfaction (Iyengar, Wells, & Schwarz, 2006). For the majority of people in the middle and working classes who are caught between materialistic aspirations and economic pressures, pay has become an increasingly important part of job satisfaction.

Many other variables affect satisfaction on the job. Age and years on the job continue to be important considerations. Recent graduates initially enjoy high job satisfaction, as did Kristin. As soon as the novelty of the work wears off and reality sets in, job satisfaction can drop sharply. The drop occurred for Kristin when she realized that another employee doing much the same job but with a little less experience was earning almost 15 percent more than she was. After 5 years on the job, satisfaction tends to rise steadily with age and years on the job. Major reasons include greater job security and better pay as well as more realistic expectations. The rising level of education among younger workers helps account for the relative dissatisfaction among younger, better-educated workers. The major exception is for workers with professional and graduate degrees, such as doctors and lawyers, who generally are happy in their work. However, unlike blue-collar workers, who reach a plateau in earnings relatively early, college-educated workers generally reap the rewards of greater education in the later years of their careers.

Workers who are not promoted often complain of favoritism, suggesting that getting ahead on the job depends more on "whom you know" rather than on what you know. Surveys of larger samples of workers provide a more balanced view; when asked about ways to get ahead in the job, most workers emphasize the importance of performing the job well, working extra hours, and being willing to accept responsibility. At the same time, almost half of them realize the importance of knowing the "right people" and having highly visible work assignments.

These issues suggest the importance of knowing how promotions are made in the organization you work for. Many companies make their policies on promotion clear in the employment interview or at the time of hiring. If not, you should inquire about them. You should know to what extent promotions are based on such factors as education, work experience, job performance, and seniority. For example, Kristin was hired by the department store to bolster sagging sales, which she did in record time. She initiated an innovative advertising campaign based on celebrity appearances and never hesitated to take work home during evening hours or over weekends. As a result, Kristin believed she was responsible for the increase in sales. When her supervisor was promoted, Kristin hoped to be considered for the job, but someone from the outside was brought in to become the new manager. When Kristin asked why, she was told that coworkers and a few celebrities had complained of her aggressive, high-handed style. Kristin had expected to be promoted primarily because of the sales results, but her superiors had judged her by a broader standard, including how well she related to people. Such misunderstanding could have been avoided if either Kristin or her boss had clarified the standards for promotion at the outset.

Technology and Work

The addition of technology into American work sites is affecting how people work and whether they are satisfied with their jobs. Computers, palm pilots, voice mail, and teleconferencing are but a few of the innovations. Estimates are that by 2010 there will be

20 million full- and part-time telecommuters working in the United States (Kirk & Belovics, 2006). Many Americans seem to have a love–hate relationship with electronic communication, especially with computers. In a series of studies, Nass and Moon (2000) found that we mindlessly apply social rules and expectations to computers. For example, some individuals employ gender stereotypes toward computers ("*She* is giving me trouble again") or think that their computers have minds or personalities of their own ("Oh, so you're going to be difficult today"). How often do you find yourself talking to a computer or a television set? How do you think this will go over at your work site? Do you think others chat with their electronic appliances or perceive human qualities in them, too? Probably!

In one study of the impact of technology on work behavior, Akkirman and Harris (2005) found that virtual office workers were more satisfied with their work than were traditional office workers. In yet another study, Cameron and Webster (2004) found that instant messaging as a means to enhance collaboration among employees spread out geographically resulted in increased informality and an enhanced perception of privacy. On the other hand, results also indicated that employees missed the richness of face-to-face communication and found instant messaging to be distracting.

Interestingly, some employees are being fired because they spend *too much* time playing with technology, such as the World Wide Web. **Cyberslacking** is *the overuse of the Internet in the workplace for purposes other than work* (Whitty & Carr, 2006). Because of cyberslacking, some employers monitor their employees' on-line behavior; this raises interesting and difficult ethical issues (Armour, 1999a). Cyber harassment, chain e-mails, joke e-mails, and other objectionable forms of communication are proliferating in the workplace, too, with women more likely to be the recipients of these than men (Whitty & Carr).

Employment situations are constantly shifting due to changes in technology, increased diversity in the workplace, and other factors. For example, employment opportunities in the manufacturing sector are expected to decline, whereas employment opportunities in the technology sector are expected to increase.

Another way technology is changing our working life is by **e-recruiting**, in which *job candidates are screened by phone, video, or computer* (Armour, 1999b) rather than in a face-to-face interview. If this happens to you, you might want to practice with a friend who can give you feedback before the actual interview, because there is much less nonverbal feedback from an interviewer using an electronic method of interviewing.

Diversity in the Workplace

One of the major shifts in the workplace between now and 2050 will be the changing demographic picture of the labor force. Although Whites will continue to account for the vast majority of workers, as they did in 1990, their share will decline from 73 percent to 52.8 percent (see Figure 10–1). In contrast, both the number and the proportion of minority workers will increase. Hispanics, non-Hispanic Blacks, and Asian and other ethnic groups are projected to account for an increasing share of the labor force. By 2050, Hispanics will constitute a greater share of the labor force than will Blacks. Asians and others continue to have the fastest growth rates but still are expected to remain the smallest of the four labor force groups (U.S. Department of Labor, 2006a, b).

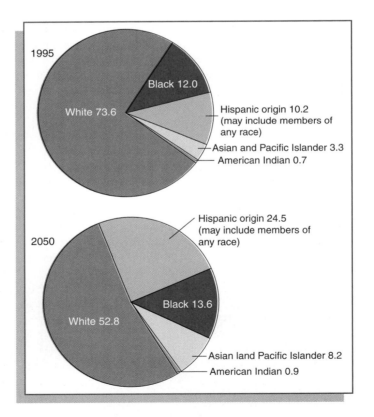

FIGURE 10–1
The U.S. workforce is more diverse.
SOURCE: Bureau of Labor Statistics. http://www.dol.gov/asp/programs/history/human/reports/
futurework/report/chapter1/chart1. . . .

A majority of new jobs will require some form of postsecondary or college education. For example, employment in occupations requiring at least a bachelor's degree is expected to grow 21.6 percent by 2010, and jobs requiring an associate's degree are projected to grow 32 percent (U.S. Department of Labor, 2000). The gap between the limited educational level of some immigrants and minorities coupled with the rising demand for educated workers will make it difficult for some to find a job or, once hired, to find job satisfaction and advancement.

A key factor will be improving the educational level of minority students. Although high school graduation rates have improved among minority groups in the past 20 years, especially among African Americans, they still lag compared to that of Whites. Minority groups earn an even smaller proportion of master's and doctoral degrees. Consequently, unless colleges attract more minority students, minority group members will lack the necessary skills to succeed in the workplace. In turn, this lack will not only add to the existing frustration and poverty of minorities but also create labor shortages and jeopardize the overall economy.

Research on job satisfaction in multicultural organizations has just begun and is admittedly rather scant (Rodriguez-Calcagno & Brewer, 2005; Tangri, Thomas, Mednick, & Lee, 2003). In some studies, African Americans report lower job satisfaction than Whites (Mau & Kopischke, 2001). One study also revealed that Hispanic Americans are particularly likely to experience more job stress than non-Hispanics (Rodriguez-Calcagno & Brewer). Other studies show few to no race or ethnic differences (Greenhaus, Parasuraman, & Wormley, 1990) or even demonstrate high job satisfaction for minorities (e.g., Tangri et al.). One reason for these findings may be differences in the kinds of jobs and organizations analyzed in the various studies. Another factor might be whether the researched organizations were fairly diverse (heterogeneous) or not (Wharton, Rotolo, & Bird, 2000). In any event, White Americans (and Canadians) will face the same problems as minorities because North American corporations are internationalizing and sending their employees to other countries or bringing people from other countries to work in the home organization (Matsumoto, 2000).

Internationalization of American business means that we will need to understand cultural similarities and differences better if we are to work together. This means it will be wise for you to understand others' work habits and work values. Throughout this book, we have made the distinction between two general types of cultures—*collectivistic* and *individualistic*—so we will use this distinction again to elucidate differences in work behaviors. In individualized cultures like the mainstream American one, people have an easier time distinguishing between work time and personal time and also between work activities and social activities. In such cultures, initiative, challenge, and freedom on the job are valued and encouraged. On the other hand, in collectivistic societies, people view their work groups and work organizations as fundamental parts of themselves (like families), so the bonds between individuals and organizations are stronger. Work is also seen as the fulfillment of an obligation to a larger group (e.g., to family or to society) rather than as a means to accumulate money. Organizations in collectivistic societies are considered morally responsible for the welfare of their employees and are expected to care for them across their life spans (Matsumoto, 1996).

Women are making the workplace more diverse, too. In 1988, women comprised 45 percent of the workforce and men 55 percent. By 2008, women are expected to make up about 48 percent of the labor force and men 52 percent. Women usually work to support themselves or to help with the family income. Although Kristin was not married and was without children, she wanted to work to support herself and to be able to buy some of the niceties that she had deprived herself of when she was in college. The excitement of living on her own, without her parents, also attracted her to the job market. Jobs, then, provide women (and men) with a sense of competence and a chance to apply talents not used in other roles.

The most notable inequity between men and women in the workplace is the earnings gap. In 2005, women's pay was 81 percent of men's (U.S. Department of Labor, 2006c). A major reason for the earnings gap is that many women enter lower-paying service jobs such as secretarial positions. Until recently, most women have been crowded into less than 10 percent of the Labor Department's job categories. Women are overrepresented in careers such as secretaries, nurses, and librarians; they are underrepresented in careers such as engineers, dentists, and physicians. Another reason for the discrepancy in pay between the sexes is that women workers have had less education and work experience, but this factor, too, is changing. Entering college classes now contain slightly more women than men—a relatively recent phenomenon. Although the proportion of women in the traditional male careers remains small, the rate of increase has been dramatic. For instance, in the past 40 years the percentage of college professors who are women has increased. Compared to the past, there are now more women physicians, more women in the life and physical sciences, and more women engineers, lawyers, and judges.

Among the other issues that concern women in the workplace are role conflicts between home and work, opportunities for advancement, sexual harassment, and child care. For example, working women report spending more time on various chores at home than do men (Erickson, 2005). And although few studies report sex differences in job satisfaction, women are less happy about opportunities for advancement. Admittedly, some companies offer better opportunities for women than others.

Additionally, ambitious women often feel that their careers are hindered by a glass ceiling (Ryan & Haslam, 2005). They can't see and can't pass beyond this ceiling, mostly because of stereotyped attitudes and expectations in the workplace. For example, a smaller percentage of the top management jobs are held by women than men. Similarly, women who are promoted into better managerial positions are likely to have salaries that lag behind those of their male colleagues.

Sexual harassment is a problem faced more often by women than by men. **Sexual harassment**—*any unwanted attention of a sexual nature occurring in the workplace that interferes with a person's ability to work*—is now illegal. Sexual harassment includes but is not limited to unwelcome sexual advances, physical contact, offensive language, and threats of punishment for rejection of these acts. Instances of sexual harassment still abound in many places and create double jeopardy (prejudice and harassment) for minority women (Berdahl & Moore, 2006). A woman might have been having an affair with the head of her division. She notifies him that she wants to break it off, and he retaliates by saying she will not get the promotion she has been expecting. In order to reduce such instances, the Equal Employment Opportunity Commission (EEOC) has issued guidelines for preventing sexual harassment. These guidelines suggest that employers should raise the consciousness of employees about the subject of sexual harassment, express strong disapproval of such behavior, inform all workers of their right to raise the specter of sexual harassment, explain the appropriate procedures for making a complaint, and sensitize everyone concerned. Box 10–3 further discusses how you can better cope with sexual harassment.

Still another issue for women and also men is balancing family and work responsibilities (Day & Chamberlain, 2006). A good example is finding adequate child care such that both the mother and father can work. Today, most married women—the traditional child care providers—in the workplace have children; over half have preschool-age children. High-quality day care is hard to find, difficult to afford, and still not fully tax deductible in most cases. Presently, only a small proportion of employers provide child care facilities for their workers. As an increasing proportion of women

Box 10–3
COPING WITH SEXUAL HARASSMENT ON THE JOB

At a workshop on this topic, when women were asked to share their experiences, a recently hired college graduate said, "My boss hinted I'd get a raise faster if I went out with him." A young married woman complained, "One man makes these suggestive remarks like 'You look happy today—it was that kind of night, eh?' " A middle-aged woman said, "A male colleague can't keep his hands off me."

Sexual harassment in the workplace takes many forms. A familiar practice is directing catcalls, whistles, and demeaning words like "doll" at women. Another one is recurring, offensive flirtation. Although most sexual harassment is verbal, physical patting, pawing, or sexual advances are not uncommon. Soliciting sexual favors for promotion at work is often cited in lawsuits against large companies.

Although each situation is different, some suggested strategies are usually helpful in dealing with sexual harassment on the job.

1. Make it clear when you disapprove. Say directly but tactfully something such as, "I find that remark offensive."

2. Jot down the time, place, and manner of such incidents. Who are the biggest offenders? Under what circumstances?

3. Talk about the incident to other workers. Find out how many other women (or in some instances, men) have been harassed.

4. Take positive steps in raising the awareness of male workers. Report offensive incidents to supervisors. Discuss problems of sexual harassment at staff meetings. Encourage workshops on the subject.

If necessary, make an official complaint to your employer, either orally or in writing, depending on the situation. As a last resort, contact federal agencies, like the Equal Employment Opportunity Commission.

enter the workplace, issues such as maternity leaves and subsidized day care may become valued fringe benefits (Duffy & Wong, 2003). There are other issues where work matters spill over to home and vice versa. For example, studies (e.g., Matjasko & Feldman, 2006) indicate that emotional transmission, that is, carrying anger or anxiety from one place to another, occurs from work to home for both men and women. Today, many Americans are still searching for a good balance between home and work activities.

LEISURE TIME

No matter how much you like your job, it's important to have sufficient time off to do many of the other things you enjoy in life. In other words, **leisure** (*time free from work or duty that may be spent in recreational activities of one's choice*) is as important as work. Most Americans feel that they are working more and playing less—a perception now being confirmed. In 1987, Lou Harris pointed out that in little more than a decade, the number of hours Americans work would increase from about 40 hours per week to 48 hours. That time has passed, and Harris has been proven right; the amount of leisure time available to the average person has dropped (Lagerfeld, 1999). Interestingly, Americans, unlike their other Western counterparts, are likely *not* to use all the vacation time they have earned (Guinto, 2005).

This dramatic change can be accounted for in several ways. A major factor is the growing practice of businesses and other organizations to employ fewer workers, often assigning additional responsibilities rather than hiring more full-time workers. The stated aim is to increase productivity, but the average worker often feels overworked. As Kristin remarked after several years on the job, "I find that I'm working harder just to stay even." Working more than 60 hours a week, administrators and managers are most apt to put in the longest workweek (Brett & Stroh, 2003). Many baby boomers, perhaps your parents or grandparents, work over 50 hours a week. Small-business people also work over 50 hours a week. Although women in dual-income families work almost the same number of hours as men do, they have less leisure time, mostly because they do many more chores at home, as mentioned earlier. Ironically, the most affluent sectors of society—college graduates, professionals, and those with incomes of $50,000 or more—work the longest hours and have the least time for leisure.

This trend runs counter to predictions 25 years ago, when it was assumed that automation and technology would shorten the workweek and give us more leisure time (Hunter, 1999; Whitty & Carr, 2006). Actually, the opposite has occurred, perhaps because computer owners are determined to perfect and re-perfect their work. Another factor that accounts for less leisure time is that our work often *spills over* into our leisure time (Snir & Harpaz, 2002). For example, some people go on vacation but take work or at least their computer or Blackberry with them. Another factor that contributes to the seeming compression of leisure time is that more and more people are working from home; they use computers or other electronic methods for connecting to their workplace, so the distinction between work and home is blurring (DeBell, 2001; Kirk & Belovics, 2006).

The growing commitment to work has heightened the nation's productivity, helping the United States to compete in the global market. But by the same token, the precarious balance of work and play (Greaves, 2005) has become even more threatened. Many people are becoming so absorbed with work that they aren't giving the loving attention needed to make their marriages work or providing growing children with enough attention or taking part in community endeavors. Meanwhile, time is at a premium in our society such that leisure time is an even more precious commodity. People must now think carefully about the most desirable way to spend their leisure hours.

What Is Leisure?

There are many things we do outside of work that are anything but leisure, for example, cleaning up after meals, dusting our homes, studying, and visiting the dentist. Such activities are usually labeled **maintenance activities**, *nonleisure and nonwork time spent in activities necessary for the maintenance of life*. In contrast, leisure has to do with the way we use our free time, our motivation for doing it, the meaning it has for us, and how it affects our lives. The purpose of leisure, Aristotle believed, is the cultivation of the self and the pursuit of the higher things of life. Playing a musical instrument primarily for the enjoyment of it or bicycling for pleasure are examples of **unconditional leisure**; these are *activities freely chosen, excluding work and maintenance activities*. People who have a satisfying leisure life, such as Kristin, who played tennis with her friends in her spare time, often find they must acquire certain skills and play often enough to keep up their game. At the same time, individuals who are highly competitive or perfectionistic may become so concerned about their performance that the pleasure in their leisure activities is lost. True leisure, then, is considered something we do primarily for the enjoyment we get out of it.

Work and Leisure

Most Americans regard their work and leisure activities as separate—and perhaps unrelated—parts of their lives. When Kristin was disappointed that she did not receive her promotion after her supervisor was promoted, she nonetheless enjoyed her friends and recreational life, especially tennis. Another person may have a very satisfying career, with little or no time for play. In each instance, a person's involvement and satisfaction in work and leisure are related to personal characteristics, needs, and values.

Researchers have studied leisure activities based on sex, race, and age. For example, Talbot, Fleg, and Metter (2003) examined women's and men's leisure activity levels over several decades. Their results indicate that especially for men, national recommendations to become more physically active appear to have had a modest effect. Several studies have found that African Americans have lower levels of leisure-time activity than Whites (e.g., Stodolska, 2005) and that this difference might be accounted for by discriminatory behavior (Stodolska) or differences in preferences for leisure activities (Shinew, Floyd, & Parry, 2004).

Not everyone in these particular demographic classifications fits neatly into these patterns. What pattern describes your involvement and satisfaction in work and play? Are you more work-oriented or more leisure-oriented? In what ways would you like to change your pattern? The answers to these questions are just as important to your mental health as are notions about what career you think is best for you. Multiple studies have shown that leisure activities help us cope better with negative life events, assist us in our overall adjustment (Kleiber, Hutchinson, & Williams, 2002), and improve our physical well-being (Hébert, 2005).

Using Leisure Positively

By the time people have arrived home after a hard day's work and eaten dinner, they're often too tired to do anything else. When asked their favorite way to spend an evening, the majority, including Kristen, says watching television. Adults now watch television an

Some activities can be considered work or play, depending on the reason for performing them.

average of 4 to 6 hours a day, most of it in the evening. Although people watch television primarily for entertainment and to a lesser extent for the news, watching television is also a time to relax and unwind, or to recuperate, which is mostly a maintenance activity, as described earlier. The ease with which someone may push a button and be entertained for hours on end remains a great temptation. At the same time, individuals who have curtailed their TV habits are usually amazed at how many other interesting things there are to do in life.

In contrast, the *positive* use of leisure requires a certain degree of choice and planning (Hébert, 2005). Ideally, you should select activities that are compatible with your interests and lifestyle rather than simply doing whatever is convenient at the time or what your friends want to do. Kristin was fortunate to have friends who also enjoyed tennis. They typically played every other Saturday morning. Kristin knew, however, that there were Saturdays when she would be too tired to play and preferred instead to sleep late. She would call her friends on Friday night to inform them of her decision.

To enjoy an activity to the fullest, you usually have to acquire the necessary skills. You must also budget your time and money to keep up the activity. For example, people who take pride in their tennis game tend to play regularly and probably derive greater satisfaction than those, like Kristin, who play only occasionally. If learning the skills and budgeting time and money are too stressful for you, perhaps you should switch to another form of leisure activity. Leisure activities can become stressful (Hébert, 2005) but needn't be.

A favorite American form of leisure is taking a vacation. About half the population takes some type of vacation each year, typically a 1- or 2-week vacation. Most people feel little or no guilt taking time off for a vacation. When asked the main reasons for taking a vacation, their responses reflect a variety of motives. The most common motive is to relax. Other motives are intellectual stimulation, family togetherness, adventure, self-discovery, and escape. After the vacation, most people are glad to be back home and look forward to returning to work. Only a few feel depressed at facing the familiar routine. Many Americans feel that work is more important than leisure, and they seek not so much a leisure-filled life as a better balance of the two. Now that more women are working outside the home, leisure has become even more important for families. Furthermore, the advent of more flexible work schedules enables people to take long weekends, which promise to make short vacations a regular event rather than a once-a-year affair.

Leisure becomes increasingly important from midlife on because of all the changes in people's lives. By this time, people are reassessing their needs and values and what they want out of life. Also, people this age tend to have more job security, more discretionary income, more free time, and more paid vacation time than younger adults. For many, this may be the first time they've been able to follow their own inclinations without having to worry about the productivity of their efforts. Now they can take up interests and express abilities not previously used in career and family responsibilities. In short, leisure becomes a means of personal growth.

Constructive leisure activities are also an important way to prepare for retirement. People who have developed rewarding leisure activities as well as a network of social and family relationships are more able to make the crucial shift from full-time work to a satisfying retirement. A common and very constructive leisure activity is performing volunteer work. You can read more about volunteering in Box 10–4.

Box 10–4

VOLUNTEERING IN AMERICA

Volunteering is good for you! Or so says research. Harris and Thoreson (2005) found that frequent volunteers among the elderly had significantly reduced mortality, and Lum and Lightfoot's research (2005) established that volunteering reduces health problems and depression levels in older Americans.

You don't have to wait to retire or be elderly to jump on the volunteer wagon. You can join over 65 million American volunteers (almost one-third of our population) now. In fact, nonprofit organizations appear to be flourishing because of their volunteer base. In the 1970s, there were only 5,000 nonprofits registered with the federal government. Today, the number has soared to nearly 45,000 (Russo, 2005). Those individuals who do not volunteer report that they often lack time, have health or medical problems, or family responsibilities that interfere.

All types of people volunteer, although middle-aged persons and teens have the highest volunteer rates, as do married and employed persons. Both men and women spend an average of about 50 hours a year volunteering at various organizations, including educational, religious, and community service organizations (U.S. Department of Labor, 2005b). Volunteers complete a wide variety of tasks for their organizations, such

as fund-raising, food service, general labor, transportation, and teaching (from highest to lowest in frequency). These individuals either step forward of their own initiative or are asked by the organization to volunteer.

Volunteering not only gives back to your community or organization for everything it has done for you but also provides free on-the-job training, helps you explore possible careers, builds your résumé, and establishes networking connections (and perhaps letters of recommendation) for use after your graduation. And a recent survey of volunteers also found that volunteer work was directly linked to career advancement because volunteers learned leadership skills, developed confidence, practiced interpersonal cooperation, and enhanced communication skills while they volunteered (*Women's Way*, 2006). A wonderful web site exists to get you started searching for a volunteer opportunity if you have not already found one: www.volunteermatch.org. At this site, you can search by zip code and interest area (such as emergency services, animal care, arts and culture, religion, etc.). Your campus might also house a volunteer office or you can ask the local Chamber of Commerce for a list of nonprofits (or even for-profits) that take volunteers.

SUMMARY

CHOOSING YOUR CAREER

We began the chapter by discussing the process of choosing a career, one's overall or life pattern of work. In choosing a career goal, it's best to begin by taking stock of yourself, including your interests, abilities, personality, and work values. Then you're ready to explore the career options available to you, realizing that there are a variety of career inventories that may help to identify the most compatible careers for someone like yourself. A commonly utilized scale is the *Strong Interest Inventory*, but others exist. You should also be aware of certain pitfalls in decision making, such as arriving at a career goal prematurely or unduly delaying the choice of a career. It's best to keep your career goal somewhat flexible and to be willing to modify it in light of subsequent experience, especially while you are in college.

YOUR CAREER OUTLOOK

Career outlook depends on the interaction of many factors, especially the makeup of the labor force and the growth of the various careers as well as one's own career choice. Major changes in the labor force include the increase of minority and women workers. Because jobs for college-educated workers will grow faster than average, college graduates will continue to have higher rates of employment and lifetime earnings. In contrast, people with less than a high school education will find it difficult to get good jobs with good pay and chances for advancement. There is also more mobility in the workplace today, with the typical American worker now having more jobs in his or her lifetime.

CONTEMPORARY ISSUES IN THE WORLD OF WORK

Satisfaction on the job depends heavily on how interesting and meaningful the work activity itself is, as well as the conditions on the job itself. One major change in our working lives is the increase in technology. Technology on the job affects different employees in different ways—sometimes increasing or decreasing job satisfaction. Another major shift now taking place in the workplace is the increase in the number and proportion of minority and international workers. Our workplaces are indeed becoming multicultural. However, because of the gap between the limited educational level of many of these individuals, such as recent immigrants, and the rising demand for educated workers, it will be difficult for some individuals to find a suitable job, much less achieve job satisfaction and advancement. Also, more women now work outside the home; among the many issues that concern modern employees are the earnings gap between the sexes, opportunities for advancement, sexual harassment, role conflicts between home and work, and availability of child care.

LEISURE TIME

No matter how much you like your job, it's important to have time off for other things you enjoy. Most Americans are working more hours per week and having fewer hours for leisure than they did in the past. Consequently, leisure—time free from work that may be spent in meaningful activities—becomes more and more of an issue in our society. The value of leisure and whether we engage in leisure activities varies with gender and race. A favorite form of leisure is taking a vacation, and half the population takes some type of vacation each year. The positive use of leisure becomes increasingly important from midlife on as we reassess what we want out of life. Volunteer work is a valuable and common form of leisure activity.

SELF-TEST

1. In choosing a career goal, it's best to begin by
   a. taking a test.
   b. seeking counseling.
   c. taking stock of yourself.
   d. getting parental advice.

2. Inventories such as the *Strong Interest Inventory* help to predict which careers you
    a. are most compatible with.   c. you are best trained for.
    b. will succeed in.   d. will be happy in.

3. Which of the following is widely regarded as the major advantage of a college education?
    a. greater social skills.   c. advanced cognitive abilities.
    b. better job opportunities.   d. more factual knowledge.

4. Above all, most people are looking for a job that provides
    a. interesting work.   c. a feeling of accomplishment.
    b. contact with other people.   d. all of the above.

5. Which of the following groups will have a smaller proportion of people in the workplace by the year 2010?
    a. Whites.   c. Hispanics.
    b. Asian Americans.   d. African Americans.

6. The greatest inequity between men and women in the workplace is the gap between their
    a. earnings.   c. education.
    b. job productivity.   d. job qualifications.

7. In the future, which jobs are expected to have the biggest numerical increase in workers?
    a. health care.   c. manufacturing.
    b. mining.   d. agriculture.

8. Which statement is true about American workers changing their careers?
    a. Americans seek jobs and then keep them a long time.
    b. Job changes are more common in late career rather than early career.
    c. Americans are fairly prone to changing jobs.
    d. In the 1950s Americans changed jobs frequently.

9. Compared with people in the 1970s, the average American now
    a. works more hours a week.   c. works fewer days a week.
    b. has more leisure time.   d. takes longer vacations.

10. The most common reason for taking a vacation is
    a. self-discovery.   c. family togetherness.
    b. relaxation.   d. escape.

EXERCISES

1. *Explore your career interests.* Make an extensive list of all the activities you've enjoyed, including school courses, extracurricular activities, full- and part-time jobs, hobbies, and sports. Then select a dozen of the most satisfying activities and rank them from the most enjoyable down. Ask yourself what made each activity satisfying. Was it the activity itself? Or was it mostly the people you did it with or the recognition or money involved? Activities that are intrinsically enjoyable are usually the best indications of the types of careers you'll enjoy.

2. *Identify compatible careers.* Go to your campus career development center or career guidance center and take some type of career inventory like *Holland's Self-Directed Search* or one that requires professional supervision, like the *Strong Interest Inventory*. Then review the results with a trained counselor.

3. *Become better informed about your career goal.* How much do you know about your chosen career? You might find it helpful to look up some basic information about it in a resource like the *Occupational Outlook Handbook*. Look up your chosen career or one you're interested in. Then write down information on the following: (1) description of the work, (2) typical places of employment, (3) educational and entry requirements, and (4) employment outlook. This exercise should give you a more realistic view of your career goal and how to prepare for it.

4. *Write about your experience finding jobs.* If you've held part- or full-time jobs, how have you found out about them? Did a friend tell you about the job? Or did you use the want ads or see a notice posted? How much luck was involved? Would you agree that to find a job you need to use as many different resources as you can?

5. *Describe your experience as a woman or minority in the workplace.* If these categories don't fit you, interview someone who fits. Describe your or their experience in part-time and full-time jobs, paying special attention to the working conditions on the job, such as pay, supervision, and promotion. If you're married and have children, has your family been supportive? If you're a single parent, what special problems has this presented for you?

6. *Favorite leisure activities.* What do you like to do in your leisure time? Do you have enough time for play and leisure? Do you like solitary or social leisure activities? What can you learn about yourself given your analysis of leisure time?

7. *Think about your work and leisure cycles.* In what ways would you like to change your patterns of work and play? How would you keep your patterns the same? Why?

QUESTIONS FOR SELF-REFLECTION

1. Do you have a specific career goal?

2. If not, are you actively engaged in choosing a career—or are you "waiting for things to just happen"?

3. Do you believe that hard work eventually pays off?

4. What are the three most important things you look for in a job?

5. If you won a million dollars in the state lottery, would you continue to work? Why?

6. What is the projected outlook for your chosen career?

7. If you were to change careers, what would your alternate career choice be?

8. Have you ever been unemployed? What did it feel like? How did you overcome these feelings?

9. What is the most important thing you've learned from part-time jobs?

10. What is your favorite leisure activity?

FOR FURTHER INFORMATION

RECOMMENDED READINGS

BOLLES, R. N. (2003). *What color is your parachute? A practical manual for job hunters and career seekers.* Berkeley, CA: Ten Speed Press. A classic on matching your personal needs and desires to various jobs.

IBARRA, H. (2003). *Working identity: Unconventional strategies for reinventing your career.* Cambridge, MA: Harvard Business School Publishing. Many Americans change jobs; Ibarra examines this trend and how to successfully and creatively switch careers.

LEITER, M. P., & MASLACH, C. (2005). *Banishing burnout: six strategies for improving your relationship with work.* San Francisco, CA: Jossey-Bass. A very readable book on an important subject by some of the leading experts on the topic.

POLLAN, S. M., & LEVINE, M. (2002). *Creating the life you really want, building the career you truly desire.* Boston, MA: HarperCollins. The authors take the reader on a journey through self-assessment to help the individual find the most compatible career.

SCHEIN, E. H. (2006). *Career anchors: Self-assessment.* Hoboken, NJ: Pfeiffer. Besides providing a self-survey to discover your own strengths and talents, this book includes basic career descriptions so that readers can find the jobs with which they are most compatible.

WEB SITES AND THE INTERNET

http://www.monster.com A site for anyone who wants work, is working, or has retired from work. Something for everyone.

http://www.employmentguide.com/site/index.html Here you can search for a job by type of job, by specific employers, or by geographic location.

http://www.careers.org Another site that can help you find jobs and information about work, including information about working in other countries.

http://www.collegegrad.com A job site designed specially for recent college graduates.

http://www.dol.gov The web site of the U.S. Department of Labor with an abundance of information on job search strategies, data on career outlook, the *Occupational Outlook Handbook*, affirmative action, and other important issues.

CHAPTER 11

Sexuality

MEN AND WOMEN
Changing Views of Sexuality
Sexual Communication
Initiating and Refusing Sex

SEXUAL RESPONSIVENESS
The Sexual Response Cycle
Individual Differences
Love and Sex

PRACTICAL ISSUES
Sexual Dysfunctions
Contraception
Sexually Transmitted Diseases
Sexual Victimization

SUMMARY
SELF-TEST
EXERCISES
QUESTIONS FOR SELF-REFLECTION
FOR FURTHER INFORMATION

After taking a test during their evening class, Carol and Kim stood in the hallway discussing some of the questions. Both felt tense, and both agreed they needed some time to unwind. They decided to visit a café near the campus. Because the café was crowded, they had to share a table with two male students whom they didn't know. Striking up a conversation, they soon discovered several areas of mutual interest. Carol found that Steve was also a psychology major and shared her career aspirations with him. Kim soon discovered that she and Bob, Steve's friend, liked the same musical groups. Initially, the four of them enjoyed talking and interacting. However, as the evening wore on, the men began drinking too much beer and telling sordid jokes. The women felt very uncomfortable. Furthermore, Carol and Kim became aware that what the women intended as friendliness was being perceived by the men as a sexual invitation. Sensing that an awkward situation was imminent, the women excused themselves and left.

MEN AND WOMEN

Changing Views of Sexuality

As intimated in the opening vignette, a cogent question is: Do men and women misunderstand each other sexually? This question has intrigued poets, philosophers, songwriters, and psychologists for decades. The experience of Kim and Carol and Steve and Bob demonstrates how our understanding of sex continues to be hampered by **gender stereotypes**—*widespread generalities about the characteristics and behaviors of men and women that exaggerate the differences between the sexes*, thereby setting the stage for misunderstanding and frustration. In this section, we'll examine several gender and sexual stereotypes and their implications for men's and women's sexual behavior. We'll next look at a healthier view of sexuality that is emerging along with the extensive changes in gender roles in our society.

There's a long-standing belief that men have a stronger sex drive than women and that they enjoy sex more than women do. Although this stereotype is beginning to diminish as younger generations are socialized differently, there is ample evidence that men and women still subscribe to it in varying degrees (Impett & Peplau, 2003; McCabe, 2005; Regan & Atkins, 2006; Regan, Durvasula, Howell, Ureño & Rea, 2004). Similarly, women fantasize about having sex with familiar partners while men often fantasize about sex with strangers. Thus, men's attitudes are more permissive and promiscuous than women's when it comes to sex; these gender differences generally hold for homosexuals, too (Missildine, Parson, & Knight, 2006; Peplau, 2003). There are some scientists who believe that these sexual attitudes are programmed into men and women by nature because they are evolutionarily advantageous (Knight, 2002). Further research is needed to establish this latter point (Diamond, 2004).

There's also the notion that men are inherently sexually assertive, with some men downright aggressive (Chung, 2005; Peplau, 2003). Women, on the other hand, are perceived as less sexually aggressive. Thus, a man may tend to regard a woman as a challenge, in other words, to see "how far" he can go with her. Maybe that is what Steve and Bob were up to in the café. Some men might actually become aggressive, the extreme form of which is rape. Having been taught that men are lustful creatures with "sex on the brain," a woman might feel she must assume the role of "controller." Instead of enjoying cuddling and kissing, she may be thinking about how to keep his hands off her breasts. Several studies support the conclusion that men are more sexually aggressive (e.g., Peplau) or at least more powerful sexually (Missildine et al., 2006). For example, Anderson, Cyranowski, and Espindle (1999) found that men's sexual self-concepts are characterized by a dimension of aggression. This dimension includes power, experience, and domination. A similar dimension did not exist for women.

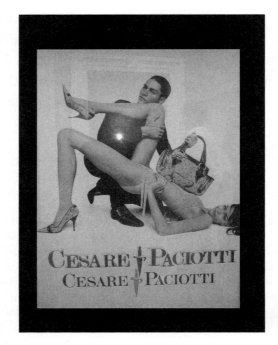

Gender stereotypes exert a direct effect on our dating behavior and sex lives.

Still another stereotype is that masculinity and femininity are polar opposites, inherent in the biological makeup of men and women, respectively. Thus, certain behaviors such as initiating sex or expressing affection are thought to be the natural prerogative of one sex or the other. For example, women (more than men) tend to "romanticize" or feel that love ought to play an important role in sexuality (Regan et al., 2004). Women are also more likely to endorse sexuality in a *committed* relationship, whereas men are more likely to engage in *casual* sex (McCabe, 2005; Peplau, 2003).

Behavioral scientists, armed with research findings in this area, find few people are 100 percent masculine or feminine. In fact, recent research has shown that gender roles are changing (American Academy of Pediatrics, 2006), especially with women becoming more masculine (Guastello & Guastello, 2003; Wilde & Diekman, 2005) and men becoming more androgynous (see below) (Guastello & Guastello). Gender characteristics are thought to coexist in varying degrees in individuals of both sexes, mostly because of important learned gender-role influences on behavior as well as individual differences. Considerable attention has been given to the concept of psychological **androgyny**—*the combination of desirable masculine and feminine characteristics in one person.* Based on the opening vignette, Carol and Kim and Steve and Bob are probably traditionally sex-typed, not androgynous. Just as traditional sex roles affect multiple behaviors, androgyny can also apply to many different behaviors, not just to sexual behavior. Our topic here, though, is sexuality. Because Steve and Bob are masculine and Carol and Kim are feminine, they played the typical roles, respectively, of "initiators" and "controllers." On the other hand, an androgynous woman might initiate sexual activity (traditionally a masculine role) but do so in a way that is both warm and sensitive to her partner (a traditionally feminine role).

Overall, however, social scientists disagree over the desirability of androgyny for men's and women's optimal adjustment (Woodhill & Samuels, 2003), because an individual who is androgynous in one situation might not behave androgynously in another context. There exists research, however, that indicates that androgynous individuals are more comfortable with same- and opposite-sex touching (Crawford, 1994) and that androgyny is the preferred sex-role orientation in various types of relationships (Green & Kenrick, 1994). Whatever your personal view in this matter, certain things seem clear: Traits labeled masculine and feminine are mostly learned, coexist to some extent within each of us, and can be a benefit or detriment depending on the situation.

The ongoing changes in gender roles taking place in our society are giving rise to a new, healthier view of sexuality. As Masters, Johnson, and Kolodny (1995) point out, many men and women are discovering that they cannot achieve the satisfaction they want until they realize sex is not something a man *does to* or *for* a woman, or vice versa. Instead, men and women are learning that sex is something a man and a woman *do together as equal participants.* The woman who affirms her sexuality learns that she can, when she so chooses, express the full range of her excitement and involvement without feeling guilty—and not primarily to please the man. Similarly, the man who appreciates his sex partner may not always feel compelled to take the initiative or assume total responsibility for satisfying her. Instead, each partner can appreciate the other's emotional needs and sexual urges—which vary with mood, time, and place—without labeling them as masculine or feminine (Greene & Faulkner, 2005). When sexual needs conflict, as sometimes happens with partners, they can negotiate a solution, less as adversaries than as two separate partners united by a common concern. The same advice holds true for homosexual partners.

The Masters and Johnson team also discovered that at least half the potential pleasure of sexual experience comes from the partner's response. If one partner is critical, unresponsive, or at best passive, the emotional vitality of the couple's sex life steadily weakens and eventually withers away. However, when both partners are actively involved and when each person spontaneously communicates feelings, the other person's excitement and responsiveness is heightened. What he gives her returns to him, and what she gives him comes back to her. All too often the relationship between the sexes is marred by a misleading image—two people on a seesaw, with power as the pivot. If one goes up, the other goes down; what one gains, the other must lose. The sexual relationship among couples with a satisfying sex life shows this image to be false. The quality of a couple's sex life, along with their overall relationship, is greatly enriched by a fully shared partnership (Greene & Faulkner, 2005).

Sexual Communication

The extent to which we share our desires and feelings about sex with a partner is an integral part of our communication pattern, especially in regard to intimate matters. Carol and Kim obviously were not interested in having a sexual relationship with Bob and Steve that night but were not assertive enough to openly express it. Even when we know someone better than Carol and Kim knew these two men, it is not always easy to express our sexual desires. How easily can you communicate with your partner your sexual needs and wants? To assess your own level of communication in intimate relationships, you and your partner could complete Activity 11–1 and then discuss the results.

One of the most astounding things about sexual behavior is the reluctance of most people to talk about sex with their lovers or spouses. It's as if talking about sex would spoil the spontaneity—which might be only partly true. A lot depends on how you talk about your sex life. Sex therapists discover over and over again that people don't have the foggiest notion of their partner's sexual likes or dislikes. Consequently, well-intentioned caresses are not fully appreciated because they're either too heavy-handed, too quick, or too far off the mark—all matters that could be easily corrected by a few words murmured at the right time. Better yet, couples might set aside some time to share their feelings about sex—what was most satisfying and what might be improved. However, it's best to avoid discussing sex in a calculating or clinical way. Likewise, it might be best if couples avoid talking about sex immediately before or after, lest it put their partner on the defensive.

Communication in sexual matters, as with almost all other aspects of life, is most successful when it is two-sided (Greene & Faulkner, 2005), with both partners expressing themselves clearly as well as actively listening to each other. It is unfortunate that the taboo against doing this is so strong that Carol and Kim could not express their reasons for their reluctance to continue talking to Steve and Bob. Perhaps sex wasn't really on the young men's minds. Maybe they were just trying to impress the young women as a prelude to a request for a date. The most important part of sexual communication is the attitude you and your partner have toward each other. Especially crucial is the sense of trust and mutual empathy—the sense that each cares for the other and knows this feeling is reciprocated (Vangelisti & Gerstenberger, 2004). A lot depends on the spirit and tone of voice in which you say something and your partner's willingness to discuss it in good faith. For instance, in making a request, you might say something like "I'd prefer doing something together before we have sex, such as taking a walk on the beach." Such

ACTIVITY 11–1

HOW WELL DO YOU AND YOUR PARTNER COMMUNICATE SEXUAL FEELINGS?

This exercise is designed to give you some indication of your level of communication in close relationships. This survey was designed specifically for your own self-understanding. It is not a scientifically derived survey.

With your partner or significant other in mind, respond to each of the following questions by answering true (T) or false (F) in the blank.

_____ **1.** I readily tell my partner my wishes and needs.

_____ **2.** My significant other knows my favorite foods, television shows, and hobbies.

_____ **3.** My partner and I calmly discuss financial problems.

_____ **4.** My partner and I are able to give each other criticism without becoming angry.

_____ **5.** My companion and I are able to understand each other even without speaking.

_____ **6.** We discuss with sensitivity and sympathy one another's problems at work.

_____ **7.** If my partner does something I do not like, I can straightforwardly tell him or her.

_____ **8.** When we fight, our fights are problem-focused and of short duration.

_____ **9.** My significant other enjoys my sense of humor, even if he or she is the target of it.

_____ **10.** My partner and I know each other's sexual desires and preferences.

_____ **11.** When my companion tells me a secret, it remains a secret with me.

_____ **12.** My partner and I rarely lie to each other about anything.

_____ **13.** If my partner makes me jealous, I express my jealousy in productive ways.

_____ **14.** My significant other and I pretty much agree on the types of people we both like.

_____ **15.** I provide feedback to my partner without hurting his or her self-esteem.

_____   **16.** We regularly and calmly disclose personal information to each other.

_____   **17.** I easily communicate with my partner when he or she has had a bad day.

_____   **18.** My partner and I frequently and effortlessly make joint decisions.

_____   **19.** I am just as happy to be a follower as a leader where my companion is concerned.

_____   **20.** My significant other and I don't have to "give in" to each other to keep the peace.

SCORING: Add up the number of "true" or Ts; chances are, the higher your score, the better your communication skills with your intimate companion, with 20 being the highest score. If you had a low score (for example, below 7), you don't necessarily have poor communication skills. You might, however, want to sit down with your partner and discuss whether there are better ways to communicate with each other.

personal sharing tends to elicit a similar disclosure from your partner. You may also want to use questions to discover your partner's preferences. You might ask a yes-or-no question, such as "Did you enjoy that?" Or you could ask an open-ended question, such as "What part of our sexuality would you most like to improve?" Some individuals prefer either-or questions such as "Do you want to talk about this now or at a later time?" Open-ended and either-or questions encourage more participation from your partner than simple yes-or-no questions. It's also important to use questions selectively and, most important, as a means to the end of *really* listening to what your partner is saying to you.

Giving and receiving criticism regarding sexuality is a touchy but important matter. In fact, some highly destructive patterns have been identified (Gottman, 1994; Gottman & Carrere, 2000). One pattern is **criticism** *that entails attacking the partner's character,* for example, calling the partner "selfish." Another pattern is **contempt,** *in which insults are used to denigrate the partner's sexuality.* A third damaging type of communication is **defensiveness,** *in which we make excuses or refuse to take responsibility for our sexuality or use some other self-protective defense.* Finally, withdrawal is lethal to sexual relationships. In **withdrawal** *we ignore our partners by watching TV or turning our backs on them.* There are much better means to communicate our sexual feelings. Perhaps the cliched "not tonight dear; I've got a headache" isn't such a shabby response.

When you feel the urge to criticize, ask yourself, "What's the reason for my saying this?" If there's no good reason, perhaps it's better *not* to say it. Also, waiting for the most appropriate time and place to offer criticism can go a long way toward sexual harmony. When you feel you must criticize, express your remarks in a nonjudgmental way—using "I" messages, as discussed in the chapter on emotions and motivation (Chapter 7). Whenever possible, demonstrate what you mean. If one person feels a partner has been too rough during foreplay, he or she might place one hand on the partner's and demonstrate a gentler method, saying, "This is what I prefer." When receiving criticism, try not to overreact. Remember that criticism is often how your partner shows that he or she cares for you. Look beyond the words to what your partner is trying to tell you. Ask what the person would prefer you to do; then try to take it to heart. Finally, remember that much of our communication is nonverbal, especially in sex.

Initiating and Refusing Sex

Nowhere is sexual communication put to the test more than in initiating and refusing sex, as Carol and Kim discovered. Some people don't communicate very well in this area and expect their partners to be mind readers. Others have developed nonverbal cues or elaborate rituals to signal their interest in sex. For example, one of Carol's friends once said to her, "When John gets out the champagne and suggests we watch a sexy movie on TV, I know what he's thinking."

Men have traditionally taken the initiative in sexual intercourse in heterosexual couples, but nowadays men and women are moving away from such restricted notions of what "men must do" or what "women must not do" (Greene & Faulkner, 2005; Wilde & Diekman, 2005). The more couples can initiate and refuse sex on an equal basis, however, the more satisfied they are with their sex lives. Not surprisingly, they also engage in sex more frequently than other couples. Among married, cohabiting, and committed couples alike, most couples who share the initiator and refuser roles equally are more satisfied with the quality of their sex life, compared to couples for whom sexual initiation is not equal.

Finally, it is not just our sexual desires that we need to communicate to our partners; we also need to discuss with our partners their and our sexual histories. Few people are comfortable asking partners, both romantic partners and relative strangers, if they have been exposed to sexually transmitted diseases or whether they use contraception (Goldmeier & Richardson, 2005). But these are *very important* aspects of human sexuality in this day and age, so broaching the subject with our partners is a must. If you consider that your partner is already receiving sexual communications from friends, family, peers (Hyde & Jaffee, 2000), and especially the media (e.g., Baker, 2005), why not take the steps to ask the questions of your partner that may protect you? In fact, research demonstrates that wise individuals almost always ask about their new sex partner's sexual history (Hyde & Jaffee). Such individuals tend to use contraception, be less likely to use drugs and alcohol, and believe in committed relationships (Moore & Davidson, 2000).

SEXUAL RESPONSIVENESS

Let's assume that a week later, Carol is in the Student Union with another girlfriend, and Steve is also there. They immediately recognize each other. He comes over to her, apologizes for his drunken behavior, and starts talking to Carol and her friend about college life. They soon find that they went to high schools in the same city and enjoy basketball and Thai food. Carol and Steve leave to go to a favorite Thai restaurant, spend the night talking, and eventually agree to begin dating one another. Their dating soon leads to a sexual relationship.

Much sexual behavior, especially intercourse, takes place in private, so it's difficult to know what occurs. Despite people's reluctance to discuss their sex lives, researchers have been able to better understand human sexuality due to the pioneering work of William Masters and Virginia Johnson.

The Sexual Response Cycle

Through an extensive series of interviews and controlled observations of volunteers masturbating and engaging in **sexual intercourse** (here defined as *penetration of the vagina by the penis*), Masters and Johnson identified *the basic sexual response patterns of men and women*. These patterns consist of certain common physiological changes that occur in a predictable sequence and are collectively labeled the **sexual response cycle**. What follows is a modified version of the cycle, incorporating some of the recent changes suggested by other authorities in the field. We'll describe five phases of the sexual response cycle: (1) transition, (2) excitement, (3) plateau, (4) orgasm, and (5) resolution. Before reading further, it is important for you to know that although Masters and Johnson's work is seminal work in the field of human sexuality, it is not without criticism. Tiefer (1991), for example, claims that their studies are replete with experimenter and methodological biases as well as participant-selection biases. For example, most Americans simply would not allow scientists to observe them having sex.

Transition (or Desire).   In the sexual response cycle, **transition** is *the gradual shift from a nonsexual to a sexual state of being and includes the awakening of sexual desire and a readiness for sexual arousal*. We're all familiar with the importance of "getting ready" for a special evening out. The same is true with sex. Although individuals vary widely in regard to what puts them in the mood for sex, some things commonly facilitate the transition. Anything that induces relaxation, with a shift from a goal-centered to a more process-centered awareness, almost always helps. Some people enjoy a relaxed, candle-lit meal; others may prefer dancing, listening to certain music, or watching a romantic or erotic movie. Touching, massage, and relaxing in hot water are favorite ways to get into the mood for sex. It is quite possible that the lack of sexual desire stems from one partner's unreadiness for sex. Men in particular tend to be more impatient and less in tune or interested in the need for transition than women. Many women prefer a more gradual transition, accompanied by emotional sharing and tender caressing and kissing. Some partners like to use erotic materials to stimulate each other. Interestingly, most of the erotica produced in the United States is designed to stimulate sexual interest in men, not women (Attwood, 2005; Hyde & DeLameter, 1997). This may be because men find visual images more sexually arousing than do women (Canli & Gabrieli, 2004).

Excitement.   *Sexual arousal*, or excitement, involves a combination of mental and sensory stimulation. **Excitement** means that *sexual arousal causes increased muscle tension, engorgement of the genitals with blood, and increased heart rate*. Each partner's anticipation of sex is an important part of getting in the mood. Sexual desire is also heightened through the stimulation of the senses. Although individual preferences vary widely, sights and sounds, the sense of smell, and even taste all combine to heighten the mood. Mutual caressing of various parts of the body, especially the erogenous zones, almost always intensifies sexual arousal, even when sexual desire is initially low in one partner. As Carol once said, "Sometimes in the beginning I'm not much in the mood for sex, but I rarely end up feeling that way." It is during this stage that the man's penis becomes erect and the woman also experiences arousal (or engorgement with blood) of her sex organs. The length of this stage varies greatly among individuals and couples.

Sexual arousal also depends greatly on psychological changes in the central nervous system, such as thoughts and feelings about a specific partner or the sexual act (Janssen, Carpenter, & Graham, 2003). As you might suspect, men and women are often aroused by different stimuli (Canli & Gabrieli, 2004; Janssen et al.), thereby setting the stage for

Media images serve at least three purposes with regard to human sexuality: they provide stimuli for sexual fantasies, shape gender role stereotypes, and influence ideal body.

misunderstanding between the sexes. At the same time, individual differences tend to outweigh gender differences, so that each person needs to be appreciated in terms of his or her own preferences.

Many people become aroused more readily through erotic fantasies covering a wide range of situations (Meana & Nunnink, 2006). For some, fantasy provides an initial boost to sexual arousal. Others use a treasured fantasy to move them from nonarousal to arousal. Some individuals can't experience orgasm without it. Erotic fantasy serves a variety of functions, ranging from the reduction of anxiety to the focusing of our thoughts and feelings, thereby avoiding distraction (Meana & Nunnink). Sexual fantasies are especially helpful in counteracting boredom, a common obstacle in long-term relationships like marriage. Common fantasies include reliving a past sexual experience with another attractive person or even having sex with a famous partner.

There are some gender differences in fantasies (Canli & Gabrieli, 2004; Leitenberg & Henning, 1995; Peplau, 2003). Men fantasize about women's bodies, physical appearance, and sexual activity, whereas women fantasize about their own attractiveness to men. Men are likely to fantasize about being dominant (Zurbriggen & Yost, 2004), and women fantasize about the emotional or romantic context of the sexual activity. Men and women, though, seem equally likely to fantasize. Interestingly, research on the fantasies of gay men and lesbians has found similar gender effects except that the fantasized partner is usually of the same sex (Chivers, Rieger, Latty, & Bailey, 2004; Leitenberg & Henning).

Plateau.   The **plateau** phase *occurs just before orgasm; in this phase, sexual arousal becomes more pronounced*. It is usually quite brief, lasting anywhere from a few seconds to several minutes. It's difficult to define the onset of this phase because there is no clear outward sign, such as erection of the man's penis or lubrication of the woman's vagina. Actually, the usual signs of sexual arousal become more pronounced as the individuals approach orgasm. The heart beats faster and breathing grows more rapid. Increasing muscle tension and blood pressure lead to engorgement of the sex organs, promoting the partner's readiness for orgasm. Men rarely lose their erection at this phase. Women also experience a marked increase in the swelling of the outer third of the vagina, making stimulation even more pleasurable. At this point, the partner who is moving faster toward orgasm, often the man, may need to slow down or vary the stimulation from time to time so that both partners can reach orgasm at the same time if they so desire.

Orgasm.   **Orgasm** is *the climax of sexual excitement that is pleasurable and releases tension.* As this climax of sexual excitement approaches, the partners may sense that orgasm is inevitable. Men usually realize orgasm accompanied by tingling muscle spasms throughout the body and perhaps uncontrollable cries and moans. However, women may arrive at the heightened sexual tension of the plateau phase without necessarily experiencing orgasm, as scientists have observed. This is sometimes the case during penile-vaginal intercourse when the man reaches orgasm first or when he replaces manual or oral stimulation with penetration as the female approaches orgasm.

Muscles in and around the man's penis contract rhythmically, causing the forcible ejaculation of semen. Similarly, the outer third of the woman's vagina contracts rhythmically along with the pulsation of her uterus. For both sexes, the first few contractions are the most intense and pleasurable, followed by weaker and slower contractions. Individuals of both sexes vary considerably in their subjective reports of orgasm.

Resolution.   When no further stimulation occurs, orgasm is immediately followed by the **resolution phase**, where *the body returns to its normal, nonexcited phase.* Heart rate, blood pressure, and breathing quickly subside. Muscle tension usually dissipates within 5 minutes after orgasm. Men lose about 50 percent of their erection within a minute or so after orgasm, and the remainder in the next several minutes. Men also enter into a **refractory period**—*a time when added stimulation will not result in orgasm.* The length of time varies widely, from a few minutes to several days, depending on such factors as the man's age, health, and frequency of previous sexual activity as well as his sexual desire for his partner. Women experience no equivalent refractory period. Most women are physically capable of another orgasm, though they may not desire it or experience it. Women who have not experienced orgasm after high levels of arousal usually experience a slow resolution. However, when both partners have attained orgasm, they generally find this a pleasant and relaxed time.

Individual Differences

We've stressed the similarity in men's and women's sexual response in accordance with the more recent knowledge of the sexual response cycle. This knowledge helps to dispel the old notion that men and women are worlds apart in their experience of sex, encouraging better communication between them. There are, however, some important differences between men's and women's experience of sex in addition to the refractory period in males.

First, there are marked differences in sexual arousal in men and women. Some of the differences have already been noted. One major difference is that brain imaging studies of men and women have revealed that even when men and women view identical sexually arousing material, the male amygdala and hypothalamus are more strongly activated *even when women report greater arousal* (Canli & Gabrieli, 2004). Women report higher levels of overall distraction as well as higher levels of appearance-based distractions than do men during sexual activity (Meana & Nunnik, 2006). When viewing sexual material, men respond to the sexual attractiveness of the female participants and to watching as an observer or imagining oneself as a participant. Women, on the other hand, tend to respond more exclusively to imaging themselves as a participant.

Much of the difference in sexual activity between the sexes may be due to cultural factors, especially those that restrict women's sexuality more than men's. One of the clearest examples is the double standard in sex, which implies that the same sexual behavior is evaluated differently, depending on whether a man or a woman engages in it. At the same time, there are other factors not easily classified as biological or cultural that may contribute to the differences in sexual arousal between men and women. For instance, when asked, "What has prevented you from freely expressing your sexuality?" women are more likely than men to report being affected by fear of pregnancy, guilt, lack of desire, and social disapproval. The fact that women can become pregnant and men do not remains a factor even in this era of more effective contraceptives. If you don't believe this, consider that nearly half of all pregnancies in the United States are unintended (Ross, 2002).

Also, the differences between male and female sexuality tend to change across the life span (Kaplan, 1983; Sex Information and Education Council of the United States [SIECUS], 2002). The teenage male's sexuality is very intense and almost exclusively genitally focused. But as he ages, his refractory period becomes longer, he becomes satisfied with fewer orgasms a week, and his focus of sexuality is not so completely genital. Sex becomes a more sensuously diffuse experience, including a greater emotional component in relation to his partner. In women, the process is often quite different. Their sexual awakening may occur much later. While they are in their teens and 20s, their arousal and orgasmic response may be slow and inconsistent. However, by the time they reach their 30s, women's sexual responsivity has become quicker and more intense, especially among sexually experienced women. In sum, men seem to begin with an intense, genitally focused sexuality and only later develop an appreciation for the sensuous and emotional aspects of sex. In contrast, women have an earlier awareness of the sensuous and emotional aspects of sex and tend to develop the capacity for intense genital response later. Put somewhat differently, adolescent male sexuality is body-centered, and the person-centered aspects are incorporated only later. Adolescent female sexuality is more person-centered, and the body-centered aspects of sex tend to be added later in women's development (Hyde & DeLameter, 1997). Thus, the differences in sexual arousal between men and women tend to diminish with greater maturity and sexual experience of individuals of both sexes, often aided by social and cultural changes that encourage equality between the sexes. For example, 80 percent of postmenopausal women and a similar 82 percent of men partnered with menopausal women report that sex is very to somewhat important to them (SIECUS).

Another major difference between the sexes is the greater orgasmic variation among women compared to men, both in the physiology of orgasm and in the individual's subjective awareness of sexual climax. Masters, Johnson, and Kolodny (1988b) identified three basic patterns of the sexual response cycle in women, though only one for men.

- One pattern resembles the male pattern and differs mainly in the woman's capacity for additional orgasms.
- A second shows a prolonged, fluctuating plateau phase, with small surges toward orgasm, followed by a gradual resolution. This is sometimes referred to as "skimming" because of the lack of a single, intense climax and is most often reported by young or sexually inexperienced women.
- Another pattern shows a rapid rise in sexual excitement leading to a single, intense orgasm and quick resolution.

Masters et al. suggest that after many experiences of intercourse, some women gradually change their sexual response from one to the other of the patterns.

Although men exhibit fewer variations, it would be a mistake to assume that all men experience the sexual response cycle in the same way. Some men have reported extended periods of intense sexual stimulation before reaching orgasm. Others have experienced several mild sexual climaxes, finally leading to an expulsion of semen. Still others have prolonged pelvic contractions after ejaculation. A marked difference between the sexes is **multiple orgasms**—*two or more sexual climaxes within a short period of time*—with women more likely to have multiple orgasms. Although it is not uncommon for women to have several orgasms in quick succession, multiple orgasms are the exception rather than the rule for men. Multiple orgasm, though, is best seen as a potential area to be explored by some rather than an ultimate goal for all.

Another individual difference relates to *preference* for sex partners. Some individuals have an *emotional and sexual preference for partners of the opposite sex* and are considered to be **heterosexual** or to practice heterosexuality. Others have an *emotional and sexual preference for partners of the same sex* and are referred to as **homosexual** or to practice homosexuality. Homosexual men often prefer to call themselves gay, whereas homosexual women may prefer to call themselves lesbian. Some lesbians also use the term *gay* to describe themselves. Most homosexuals, though, would be quick to point out that homosexuality does not pertain simply to sex but rather to a particular orientation that is but one part of an individual's multifaceted life (SIECUS, 2003). Researchers have also discovered that some people's sexual orientation is fluid; that is, they go from bisexuality to homosexuality or heterosexuality to homosexuality as they develop (Rosario, Schrimshaw, Hunter, & Braun, 2006). Sexual orientation is defined and further discussed in Box 11–1. In the early study of human sexuality, sexologist Alfred Kinsey (Kinsey, Pomeroy, & Martin, 1948) determined that men and women are not always exclusively heterosexual or homosexual. Rather, there are gradations of sexual preference, which include, for example, bisexuality. **Bisexuality** means that *the individual prefers sex with partners of either sex*. There are other preferred but less common patterns related to sexuality, as explored in Box 11–1.

No one knows how many heterosexuals, homosexuals, and bisexuals live in the United States (Diamond, 2003; Savin-Williams, 2006). These numbers are extremely difficult to ascertain. Homosexuality in particular carries a social stigma and thus is a difficult and complex developmental process for some individuals (Kurdek, 2005; Rosario et al., 2006) and keeps some homosexuals "closeted" or secretive about their sexual orientation (Kurdek; Rosario). In fact, homosexuality was so stigmatized in the past that the American Psychiatric Association in its *early* history considered homosexuality to be a mental disorder. *This is not true today.*

Furthermore, there are heterosexual individuals who are **homophobic** (Green, 2005) and, thus, stigmatize variations on sexual orientation; that is, they are *afraid of homosexuals or hold negative attitudes toward homosexuals* for various reasons, causing the targets of their negative attitudes to keep their orientation to themselves. Interestingly, one reason for homophobia might be that homophobic heterosexuals are uncomfortable with their own sexual impulses (Herek, 2000a). Homophobia, as a psychological construct, has been reviewed in the literature. Gregory Herek (2000b) suggests that better terminology might be **sexual prejudice**—*all the negative attitudes based on sexual orientation, whether the target is homosexual, bisexual, or heterosexual*. Some would argue that sexual prejudice can also occur when homosexuals are phobic about or afraid of heterosexuals (Haldeman, 2006). These attitudes, especially against homosexuals, have declined somewhat over the last two decades. In the 1970s and 1980s, two-thirds of surveyed Americans said that homosexuality was "always wrong." That figure dropped to 56 percent by the 1990s. Many Americans now also believe that a gay person should not be denied employment and that same-sex domestic partners should have some rights, such as employee health benefits (Herek, 2000b). When such prejudice does exist today, it is likely found in older, less educated, conservative Americans (Herek, 1994). Sexual

Box 11–1

What You Should Know About Sexual Orientation

Sexual orientation, as defined in this book, is *a component of sexuality and is characterized by enduring emotional, romantic, or sexual attraction to a particular gender.* The three main sexual orientations include **homosexuality**, *which involves attraction to someone of the same sex*; **heterosexuality**, *which involves attraction to someone of the opposite sex*; and **bisexuality**, *which involves attraction to members of either sex* (American Psychological Association, 2007).

There are, however, other orientations and issues, most of which are transgender. They include but are not limited to:

- **Crossdressers:** These are individuals who *occasionally wear clothing of the opposite gender.* Most crossdressers are heterosexual.

- **Transvestites:** Transvestites are people who *dress to look like the opposite gender.* Some transvestites wear other-gender clothing full-time and successfully pass as the opposite sex.

- **Transsexuals:** Transgendered people who *believe that they were born into the body of the wrong sex* are called transsexuals. They sometimes want to change this situation through hormone therapy and gender reassignment surgery.

- **Hermaphrodites:** These individuals *exhibit sexual characteristics of both genders.* Hermaphroditism often occurs at the embryonic stage of development.

- **Intersexed persons:** Some people *are born with chromosomal or hormonal birth defects so that they do not readily fit into "male" or "female" categories.*

Perhaps you wonder whether all of these individuals are happy with their orientation and, if not, whether they ever alter their orientation. Some studies indicate that lesbians and their heterosexual sisters differ little on mental health and happiness (Rothblum & Factor, 2001). If an individual so chooses, though, sex and gender reassignment techniques are available. To date, scientific data are lacking that show sexual-orientation modification techniques effectively change an individual's sexual orientation. The small number of attempts that have been adequately documented appear to have been unsuccessful. On the other hand, it is possible that some individuals who enter therapy (psychological or medical) eventually do make a successful change. Some people, too, may have changed their sexual orientation without intervention.

Because there is often sexual prejudice (Herek, 2000b) against individuals who differ from the majority, the federal government believes that sexual orientation merits special attention. It prohibits federal employees from discriminating against job applicants and fellow employees on the basis of sexual orientation as well as on the basis of race, color, sex, religion, national origin, age, disability, marital status, or political affiliation. The Sex Information and Education Council of the United States (SIECUS) also notes that many public schools are now trying to reduce sexual prejudice and discrimination by offering education to students about sexual orientation. Nearly half of a random sample of high school health teachers said they formally taught about homosexuality in their classes. Most teachers offering the information were health teachers. Apparently, there is a need for such information in the schools. Compared to heterosexual students, gay, lesbian, and bisexual youths are four times as likely to be threatened with a weapon on school property, and over 86 percent of them report hearing homophobic remarks from classmates or school staff (SIECUS, 2001).

prejudice is also more likely to be manifested in individuals who do not personally know or think they know any homosexuals (Herek, 2000a) and in very religious individuals or those who possess anxiety about gender roles (Green).

Pioneering sex researchers Masters and Johnson (1966, 1979) compared the actual sexual behaviors of male and female heterosexuals and homosexuals. The physiological responses of the genitals of heterosexuals and homosexuals were nearly identical. In other words, Masters and Johnson found the very same sexual response cycles in homosexual men and women as they did in heterosexual men and women. (These are the cycles described earlier.) Masters and Johnson (1979) also reported that for homosexual men and women, there was more communication about preferred sexual activities and these preferred activities were engaged in for longer periods of time than between heterosexual partners.

There is a question in the adjustment literature about whether homosexuals cope well in the face of the strong stigma against their sexual orientation (Safren & Pantalone, 2006). D'Augelli, Hershberger, and Pilkingston (1998) suggest that disclosure of homosexual orientation to friends and family is the second most significant life stressor for homosexuals, with the most significant being initial discovery of their own homoerotic attractions. One reason disclosure is difficult is because unlike other marginalized groups (e.g., African Americans), most young homosexuals are not raised in a community of similar others (Rosario et al., 2006). Edwards (1996a, 1996b), however, found in two different studies that homosexual youth cope as well as and are as well adjusted as heterosexual youths. This seems especially true when homosexual individuals accept their sexual orientation (Dupras, 1994). And, as mentioned elsewhere in this book, the same can be said for the gay individual whose family or friends are supportive when disclosure about homosexuality is made (Elizur & Ziv, 2001; Kurdek, 2005; Saltzburg, 1996; Safren & Pantalone). On the other hand, there exist studies that show homosexual individuals report more suicidal ideation, suicide attempt, self-injurious behavior, and use of therapeutic interventions than heterosexuals do (e.g., Balsam, Beauchaine, Mickey, & Rothblum, 2005). Although homosexuality is not considered a form of mental disorder, the stigma attached to it can contribute to depression and other mental disorders.

Love and Sex

So far we've been emphasizing the physical aspects of sex. What about the attitudes and relationships between the partners? For example, if Carol and Kim had become sexually involved with Steve and Bob on the first night, would they have experienced guilt and shame? Would they find themselves more attracted to the men? Must they have been in love to enjoy sex? Healthy, guilt-free people can function well sexually and derive pleasure from sex without being in love. Masters and Johnson observed that there is nothing inherently "bad" about sex without love, especially if both parties consent. Under certain circumstances, for some people, sex without love may be enjoyable in its own right (Masters et al., 1995). However, in reality a great deal depends on the individuals involved, especially their value systems. For example, Carol did not want to have sex with Steve the first few nights she dated him. Another woman might have reacted quite differently and have seen the opportunity for sex on the first date to be an exciting adventure or a way to feel closer to her date, but Carol wanted to get to know Steve better and feel that he acknowledged some commitment toward her before even thinking of having sex with him.

It is worth emphasizing that love can enrich sex, especially in a long-term relationship like marriage. The affection and commitment two people enjoy in their relationship can enhance their overall pleasure, compensating somewhat for the loss of sensual excitement that can occur after years in a committed relationship. In contrast, couples that have sex mechanically, especially when one or both partners have little or no affection for the other, soon discover that sex itself is no longer satisfying.

Romantic love, *which consists of intimacy or closeness and passion*, may lead to satisfying sex, at least for a while, though the satisfaction may soon diminish as romantic ardor cools. In contrast, for couples in a long-term relationship, romantic love often matures into **companionate love**, *a kind of loving but practical relationship based primarily on emotional closeness and commitment rather than physical, sexual intimacy*. Indeed, many sex therapists have worked with hundreds of couples with a loving, committed relationship (companionate love) whose sex life is disappointing. In America at least, the ideal type of love remains that of **consummate love**, *a complete and balanced love characterized by emotional closeness, sexual intimacy, and commitment between the partners*. It is worth noting that marital happiness and a satisfying sex life are positively correlated, though it is almost impossible to distinguish between cause and effect. Thus, for most couples, but not necessarily all, a good sex life and happy relationship go together. Love not only strengthens the closeness and commitment between a man and woman but also engenders better sex. It is no coincidence that most couples refer to sexual intercourse by the phrase "making love"; sex and love seem to go together in mainstream America. We will discuss love and commitment extensively in Chapter 12.

PRACTICAL ISSUES

The emphasis on sexual fulfillment in recent years has had some beneficial effects. Today, there appears to be more objective information about sex, increased sexual communication between partners, and less anxiety and guilt over harmless sexual practices like masturbation. At the same time, such changes have been accompanied by new anxieties. Many sexually normal men worry about their sexual performance. A woman who is not orgasmic may suffer the same loss of self-esteem as the man who has a fairly flaccid erection. Then, too, the increasing sexual activity outside of marriage today has accentuated the perennial problems of birth control, unwanted pregnancies, and sexually transmitted diseases such as AIDS. Most disturbing of all is the increasing occurrence of sexual victimization in our society, as seen in rape, for example.

Sexual Dysfunctions

Even sexually experienced couples discover that each time they engage in sex, it is different. Sometimes sex is highly pleasurable for both partners; at other times it is less satisfying for one or both of them. Such occasional problems are usually not serious; they often are caused by fatigue, or stress. Alcohol consumption, a particular inclination of college students, can be especially troublesome in terms of interfering with sexual activity (Johnson, Phelps, & Cottler, 2004). When sexual disorders persist or become distressful to individuals such that they cannot enjoy sex, the disorders typically are classified as sexual dysfunctions. Unfortunately, because sexual performance is sometimes associated with a loss of self-esteem and may result in stigmatization within certain cultures, individuals may resist seeking help. Fortunately, this situation is changing with the greater societal openness about sex and the general availability of sex therapists.

Sexual dysfunctions include *persistent problems that prevent an individual from engaging in or enjoying sexual intercourse*. Sexual dysfunctions may be grouped according to the phase of the sexual response cycle in which they occur. They include difficulties of desire, arousal, and orgasm. **Hypoactive sexual desire**, sometimes called **inhibited sexual desire**, refers to a *lack of interest in sex*. There is a higher incidence of this disorder in women than in men (Rosen & Leiblum, 1995). In some instances, the lack of desire may be a realistic response, such as with a partner who practices poor hygiene or is verbally abusive. In many cases, it reflects the individual's preoccupation with a life problem such as a death in the family or a problem at work. Emotional factors are often involved, and boredom is a frequent cause of inhibited sexual desire; so is anger, especially buried anger. Other factors are anxiety, guilt, low self-esteem, depression, and the fear of intimacy. Prolonged frustration from the lack of arousal or orgasm may result in low sexual desire. And a person who feels pressured into sex or feels guilty about saying no may become less and less interested in sex. Some people may be so fearful of sexual pleasure or closeness that they unconsciously prevent themselves from feeling sexual desire by developing a "turn-off" mechanism. By becoming angry, fearful, or distracted, they draw on the natural inhibiting mechanisms that suppress sexual desire, and the lack of desire appears to emerge automatically.

Emphasis should not necessarily be placed solely on the psychological causes of this disorder because the cause can also be physiological. For example, in women who have experienced menopause, low estrogen levels or lack of vaginal lubrication can reduce sexual feelings or make sex painful. In fact, the literature seems to be moving away from the emphasis mainly on psychological causes as promoted by Masters and Johnson toward biomedical and organic causes of sexual disorders (e.g., Dennerstein & Hayes, 2005; Rosen & Leiblum, 1995). Similarly, the issue of low sexual desire often stems from the fact that one partner simply has a higher level of desire so thus defines the partner with lower desire as having a disorder.

Aversion to sex refers to *anxiety, disgust, repulsion, and other negative emotions toward sex*. Although both men and women experience sexual aversion, it is more common among women. Individuals who are repelled by sex often have a history of childhood sexual abuse, such as incest, or have been victims of sexual assault. In some instances, such individuals have been subject to constant pressuring or bargaining for sex in a relationship. Repeated but unsuccessful attempts to please a sexual partner may eventually lead to the avoidance of sex. Finally, anxiety about conflicts in one's sexual identity or orientation may also create fear of sex (Masters et al., 1995).

Another type of sexual dysfunction is **inhibited sexual arousal**, which is *insufficient sexual arousal*. This disorder occurs most as **erectile inhibition** (*impotency*) and **inhibited vaginal lubrication** (*when insufficient vasocongestion and insufficient lubrication occur in women*). Men who suffer from inhibited sexual arousal usually have **secondary erectile inhibition**—that is, *they've previously experienced erections but are consistently unable to have an erection of sufficient firmness to penetrate the woman's vagina*. Most men have occasional difficulties with erections, usually because of fatigue or stress. It's only when this difficulty continues to occur or becomes distressing to the man or his partner that it should come to the attention of a professional. Many factors may contribute to erectile inhibition.

Physiological factors related to erectile inhibition include severe diabetes and the effect of certain drugs, especially alcohol, narcotics, amphetamines, and some prescribed medications. Worry and criticism from a partner may also lead to erectile inhibition. In most instances, erectile inhibition is only a passing problem, but sometimes these experiences may generate such concern and anxiety that they develop into a chronic pattern. The man's anxiety assumes the form of a "spectator's role." That is, instead of relaxing and letting his erection occur spontaneously, he watches and judges his own performance. Thus, his self-critical attitude and tenseness contribute to the erectile problem. Treatment consists of helping the man learn how to relax and let things happen. It's especially important not to overreact to the temporary loss of erection.

Inhibited vaginal lubrication in the woman is similar to the man's lack of erection because in both cases *insufficient vasocongestion and lubrication of the vagina occurs*. Normally, during sexual stimulation the congestion of blood vessels causes the vaginal walls to secrete droplets of fluid, which eventually form a shiny film on the walls of the vagina. Lack of lubrication doesn't always mean something is wrong. Frequently, the woman is not sufficiently stimulated. Also, during prolonged intercourse with lengthy plateau periods the woman may have a decrease in vaginal lubrication. In such instances, increased stimulation of the woman's clitoris or other parts of her body may help to increase vaginal lubrication. Older women who have passed the age of menopause sometimes supplement their vaginal lubrication by adding small amounts of vaginal jelly or use a cream containing estradiol (by prescription from a physician) to enhance the thickness of their thinning vaginal walls.

The most common difficulty of the orgasmic phase in the sexual response cycle is **premature** (*early orgasm in a man*) or **retarded ejaculation** (*the delay or absence of orgasm in a man*) and *delay or absence of orgasm for the woman* known as **female orgasmic disorder**. Premature ejaculation consists of experiencing orgasm so quickly that the man's enjoyment of sex is significantly lessened or his partner is not contented. It is a common problem for men. As many as half of the cases of erectile disorder may be due to organic factors (Richardson, 1991). Another common reason is that men have become accustomed to experiencing orgasm quickly so as to demonstrate their sexual prowess or avoid discovery of the couple having sex. Fortunately, this condition is readily treatable through such measures as the stop-start technique in which the man, usually with the aid of his partner, practices recognizing the sensations of impending orgasm and momentarily stops stimulation until he gradually learns to delay ejaculation.

The most common problems for women are slowness or inability to experience orgasm. Because orgasm is a reflex, an involuntary reaction, and differs considerably from one individual to another, it may help to see this problem in the context of women's overall sexual response. On one extreme are the women who have never climaxed at all. Next are the women who require intense clitoral stimulation for orgasm. Third are women who need direct clitoral stimulation but are able to climax with their partners. Also near the middle are women who can climax during sex but only after lengthy and vigorous stimulation. Near the upper range are women who require only brief penetration to climax, and at the very extreme are the women who can experience orgasm via fantasy or breast stimulation alone.

Women who have never experienced orgasm sometimes lack knowledge of their own sexual response cycle, something that is often learned by other women through masturbation. These women may become orgasmic by minimizing their inhibitions and by maximizing their sexual stimulation through masturbation. A more common issue is slowness or failure to climax through intercourse with a partner. This problem is not surprising, considering that orgasm is usually triggered through sensory stimulation of the clitoral area, which is accomplished only indirectly during intercourse. Consequently, only about one-half of women experience orgasm regularly through intercourse (Masters et al., 1995). Those who prefer vaginal orgasm and are unable to experience it may need more intense thrusting on the man's part.

There are many more women who need direct clitoral stimulation, either by manual or oral stimulation from the man or who prefer self-stimulation, in addition to the penile-vaginal thrusting during intercourse to reach climax. Women frequently complain that men don't know how to provide clitoral stimulation. Men tend to be impatient, rubbing the clitoris directly or too long, thereby irritating it. Women usually prefer a more indirect, playful approach, which may include caressing one side of the clitoral shaft or use of an indirect, circular motion of the whole clitoral area. Keep in mind that even healthy, sexually experienced women do not always reach orgasm, either because of fatigue or temporary, situational factors. Also bear in mind that this need not necessarily be a problem. You might want to (re)read the information presented in Chapter 3 on Viagra and other medications designed to help alleviate some of these sexual dysfunctions.

Contraception

The availability and use of reliable birth control and contraceptive methods has become increasingly important in recent years for several reasons, especially because half of all pregnancies are unplanned (Guttmacher Institute, 2004) and because of the deadly AIDS epidemic. Most couples want to avoid an unwanted pregnancy and sexually transmitted diseases. Although Carol liked Steve very much, she knew she was not ready to have his children or to marry him. Even among married couples, there's a tendency to have planned and wanted children.

American women are not particularly happy with the contraceptive choices available to them. They also are not happy that the burden of birth control typically falls on them, with fewer methods available to men. As their relationship progressed, Carol and Steve had several discussions about birth control. Steve wanted Carol to start using birth-control pills; she replied that she did not want to do so and that he should just buy condoms. Unlike Carol, most women have tried several contraceptive methods in the search for one that suits them best, but they feel that every method requires trade-offs among safety, convenience, and effectiveness. What most women and men want are birth-control methods that do not require them to make trade-offs.

The effectiveness of the various contraceptives, along with their general type and a brief description, are shown in Table 11–1. Typically, condoms and birth-control pills are most popular among people in their teens and 20s. It is important for couples to choose the method of protection that suits them best. The primary concern for heterosexual and gay partners is that the method be effective without jeopardizing either partner's health or the spontaneity of sex.

Shared responsibility for contraception can enhance a relationship. When one partner takes an active interest in contraception, the other is less likely to feel resentment over assuming all the responsibility. Men and women can share responsibility for contraception in several ways. An important step is discussing the matter of protection or prevention before first engaging in intercourse. Unfortunately, this initial step is rarely taken, mostly because of the fear of spoiling the spontaneity of sex. Figure 11–1 depicts the most popular methods of birth control that Americans have settled on for now. Note that nonusers included women hoping to become pregnant, women not currently engaging in intercourse, and women already sterile due to surgery. In the large "other methods" category, male sterilization was a common method. For more in-depth information on birth control, go to Guttmacher.org, which stays up-to-date on the newest methods being introduced to our society.

Sexually Transmitted Diseases

When Steve and Carol first started having sex, they did not discuss whether each of them was sexually healthy. Carol, in particular, did not know that Steve had had a variety of other sex partners, each of whom could have been a risk to Carol as well as Steve. As one sex educator was fond of stating, "You are having sex with everyone your sex partner has had sex with," the gist of which is that you need to know your sex partner's or partners' histories. Many **sexually transmitted diseases (STDs)**, a broader and less value-laden term than *venereal disease, may be transmitted primarily through sexual interaction.* Although many of these diseases can be treated successfully, many are on the rise, because of increased sexual activity and a tendency to have more than one sexual partner, especially during one's youth. The incidence of STDs is highest among those in the 20- to 24-year-old group, with the

TABLE 11–1

COMPARATIVE EFFECTIVENESS OF BIRTH-CONTROL METHODS

Contraceptive Type	Definition	Type	Failure Rate
Birth-Control Pill (Oral Contraceptive)	A hormonal pill taken daily to prevent ovulation or fertilization.	Hormonal	8%
Implants	Small capsules inserted into the arm that release hormones to prevent ovulation.	Hormonal	<1%
Injection	An injection of a hormone that prevents ovulation.	Hormonal	3%
Emergency Contraception	An emergency, high dose of birth-control pills taken within 72 hours (three days) of unprotected sex.	Hormonal	25%
IUD	A T-shaped, plastic device placed inside the uterus that contains copper or hormones.	Hormonal	<1%
IUD	A T-shaped, plastic device placed inside the uterus that contains copper or hormones.	Other	<1%
Male Condom	A thin, latex or polyurethane sheath that covers the penis.	Barrier	15%
Female Condom	A polyurethane sheath or pouch that lines the vagina.	Barrier	21%
Cervical Cap	A small rubber or plastic cup that fits over the cervix	Barrier	16–32%
Diaphragm	A round rubber dome inserted inside the vagina to cover the cervix.	Barrier	16%
Contraceptive Sponge	A foam sponge containing spermicide placed inside the vagina.	Barrier	16–32%
Spermicide	A cream, foam, jelly, or insert that kills sperm.	Barrier	29%
Natural Family Planning	Avoiding sexual intercourse near the time of ovulation, when pregnancy is most likely to occur.	Other	25%
Sterilization	A permanent, surgical procedure that blocks the pathways of egg or sperm.	Other	<2%

SOURCE: U.S. Department of Health and Human Services. *Sexual development and health: Issues.* http://www.4parents.gov/topics/contraception.htm.

next highest incidence among those in the 15- to 19-year-old group and then among the 25- to 29-year-olds. Those age groups represent many traditional college students or recent college graduates.

Chlamydia—*a bacterium that is spread by sexual contact and that affects both males and females*—has rapidly become one of the most common sexually transmitted diseases and continues to be widespread (Centers for Disease Control and Prevention [CDC], 2002a). In 2004, there were over 900,000 cases of chlamydia reported to the government, although this number is thought to be grossly underestimated. As many as 2.8 million Americans may be infected each year (CDC, 2006b). An estimated 10 percent of all college students are affected by this disease. A condom can help prevent the spread of chlamydia.

Men who contract the infection have symptoms similar to gonorrhea, such as a discharge from the penis and a mild burning sensation during urination. Women with

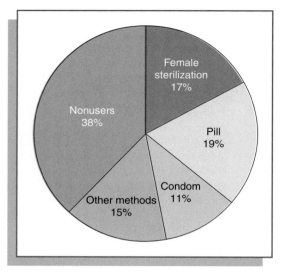

FIGURE 11–1
Current contraceptive status of Americans.
SOURCE: Mosher, W. D., Martinez, G. M., Chandra, A.,
Abma, J. C. and Willson, S. J. (2004). Use of contracep-
tion and use of family planning services in the United
States: 1982–2002. Advance Data: From Health and Vital
Statistics, 1–46.

chlamydia infections show little or no symptoms and are often unaware of the disease until they are informed by an infected partner. On the other hand, a woman may have the infection for a long time, during which period she may pass it on to her sexual partners. If left untreated in women, it may result in cervical inflammation or pelvic inflammatory disease and, if a woman is pregnant, may cause eye damage to infants at birth. In men, it may spread to the prostate. It is important that an infected person get a laboratory diagnosis before receiving treatment because the symptoms are often confused with those of gonorrhea, though the disease is usually treated with a different drug, tetracycline, rather than penicillin as is used in gonorrhea.

Gonorrhea continues to be *another common sexually transmitted bacterial infection that sometimes produces a cloudy, smelly discharge and a burning sensation upon urination*. Gonorrhea increased dramatically through the 1960s and 1970s, but the trend has slowed (Centers for Disease Control and Prevention, 2002a). Nonetheless, there were over 700,000 cases reported in 2002 (CDC, 2006a). A condom may help prevent the transmission of gonorrhea during intercourse, but it doesn't guarantee immunity. Early symptoms in men include a bad-smelling, cloudy discharge from the penis and a burning sensation during urination. Many women fail to seek treatment because they have so few early symptoms that they don't realize they are infected. Untreated gonorrhea is the single most common cause of sterility among men. Women with untreated gonorrhea may experience inflammation of the fallopian tubes, infertility, birth malformations, or menstrual disorders. Fortunately, in most cases when it is discovered, it is easily treated with penicillin.

Genital herpes is *one of several herpes viral infections (human papillomavirus) that are primarily transmitted through sexual contact*. It has increased dramatically in recent years, with 6.2 million new cases each year and over 20 million currently infected Americans

(CDC, 2006a). Symptoms usually appear within several days after sexual contact with an infected partner: one or more small, red, painful bumps (papules) in the genital area, such as on the man's penis and the woman's labia and inner vaginal walls. These bumps change into blisters, which eventually rupture into painful open sores. The person continues to be contagious throughout this time. In addition to the periodic discomfort, genital herpes can have serious complications. Pregnant women may require a cesarean section if active herpes is in the birth canal at the time of delivery. Furthermore, women infected with genital herpes are more likely to contract cervical cancer than others. So far there is no real cure for genital herpes, but medical researchers are pursuing effective treatments. Current treatment consists of the drug acyclovir, which reduces discomfort and assists healing during an outbreak.

Syphilis, though less common now than herpes and gonorrhea (CDC, 2002a), is a far more serious disease. *Syphilis is caused by a spiral-shaped bacterium, or spirochete.* Although fewer than 32,000 new cases of syphilis are recorded each year, the actual incidence is thought to be much higher. Syphilis is caused when the spiral-shaped bacteria are transmitted through sexual contact. It is not transmitted exclusively by vaginal sex; other organs of the body can be the sites of entry. The early signs of syphilis are painless sores at the place of sexual contact, usually the man's penis and the inner walls of the woman's vagina or cervix in heterosexual couples. Although the sores usually disappear within a month or two, in later stages, a skin rash and other sores may appear, along with sores on other parts of the body. These symptoms eventually disappear, but if the disease is left untreated it may progress to an advanced stage, causing brain damage, heart failure, blindness, or paralysis. Fortunately, syphilis is readily detected through a blood test, and there is a highly effective treatment when it is detected in its *early* stages.

Compared to other STDs, **AIDS** (*acquired immune deficiency syndrome, which is caused by a virus known as HIV and transmitted primarily through body fluids*) is a fairly new disease by historic standards that has achieved national and worldwide prominence in recent years because of its growing threat. Also in comparison to other STDs, AIDS is far more deadly. By 2003, more than 1 million persons in the United States had been diagnosed with the AIDS virus and more than 500,000 of them had died (CDC, 2006b). Public health officials believe that the numbers are even greater than this; a large number of people have AIDS but do not yet know it. Knowing about AIDS, then, might literally save your life. To test your knowledge, take the AIDS Quiz in Activity 11–2.

People who are initially infected generally show no symptoms and have no antibodies to the disease, so blood tests may come back negative. Individuals can carry this disease and be asymptomatic for long periods of time, years in fact. Because the AIDS virus destroys the T-helper cells in the body's immune system, infections that would ordinarily be less harmful to a person with a normal immune system can produce devastating, ultimately lethal diseases in the person with AIDS, for example, a common cold. This is often when it becomes apparent that the individual has AIDS. By this time it may be too late for the infected individual's sex partners; they may have already contracted the illness.

Although AIDS or HIV is classified as a sexually transmitted disease, it is communicated through blood or blood products containing the virus, so can be transmitted in ways other than sexual activity. Infection with other STDs increases the transmission probability for HIV. By all indications, HIV does not readily penetrate intact body surfaces, so there is little danger of getting it through a kiss, a sneeze, a handshake, or a toilet seat. Instead, HIV is acquired by direct exposure of one's bloodstream to the virus, which is carried by body fluids—notably blood and semen. The stereotype in the United States is that HIV or AIDS is a gay man's disease. Gay men represent the largest group living with AIDS (47 percent of all AIDS patients) followed by heterosexuals

ACTIVITY 11–2

AIDS QUIZ

Which of the following statements are true?

1. You can tell by looking that someone has the AIDS virus.

2. People cannot become infected with the HIV virus by donating blood.

3. The AIDS virus can enter the body through the vagina, penis, rectum, or mouth.

4. It's possible to get the AIDS virus from hugging, kissing, or a toilet seat.

5. Condoms are an effective but not a foolproof way to prevent the spread of the AIDS virus.

6. The AIDS virus may live in the human body for years before symptoms actually appear.

7. The AIDS virus may be spread through sneezing and coughing.

8. Any unprotected person can become infected with the AIDS virus through sexual intercourse.

9. If you think you've been exposed to the AIDS virus, you should get an AIDS test.

10. Presently, there is no cure for AIDS.

Answers: Numbers 1, 4, and 7 are false. The others are true.

SOURCE: *Understanding AIDS* (1988). (HHS Publication No. 88-8404). Washington, DC: U.S. Government Printing Office.

(27 percent), and intravenous drug users (22 percent). Of all adults in the United States, African Americans and Whites have been hardest hit by this epidemic (CDC, 2006a).

Among homosexually active men, the main source of transmission has been anal intercourse. The risk of HIV infection for intravenous drug users, who are likely to share needles, comes through direct exposure of the bloodstream to someone else's infected blood. The virus can also be transmitted through vaginal intercourse, from men to women or, less commonly, from women to men. Although heterosexual infection has accounted for only a small number of AIDS victims in the United States so far, this proportion is rising rapidly. The risk of catching AIDS through blood transfusions has diminished considerably because of more careful screening of blood donors and programs for intravenous drug users.

No single pattern of symptoms fits all cases of AIDS. Some common symptoms include a progressive, unexplained weight loss; persistent fever (often accompanied by night sweats); swollen lymph nodes in the neck, armpits, and groin; reddish purple spots on the skin; chronic fatigue; and unexplained diarrhea or bloody stools. Symptoms may remain unchanged for months or may be quickly followed by additional infections. There are psychological symptoms as well because HIV has a direct effect on the central nervous system (Matlin, 1999). These symptoms include altering the neurotransmitter dopamine, as well as cognitive problems such as difficulty remembering and paying attention. People afflicted with the AIDS syndrome tend to have one overwhelming infection after another until their immune system gives out. AIDS in the past was usually fatal, though with today's modern cocktails of medication some individuals are surviving much longer.

People can reduce their risk for AIDS by following some practical guidelines, such as those shown in Box 11–2. Using latex condoms is a good start. Research has demonstrated that although college students and others seem to possess knowledge about the transmission of AIDS, their behaviors, such as engaging in casual sex, leave them at risk (Roberts & Kennedy, 2006). As psychologists know, behaviors do not always follow from attitudes. Ultimately, of course, the surest way to prevent the infection will be the development of a vaccine. Although research efforts are being intensified, there are no guarantees, and a vaccine may very well take a long time. Meanwhile, the threat of AIDS will and should be a major influence on people's sexual habits and lifestyles for the foreseeable future.

Sexual Victimization

Another issue that attracts public concern is **sexual victimization**, which *occurs when a person is coerced to engage in sexual acts under duress or force.* To go back to our opening vignette, Carol was fortunate that she found Steve, who turned out to be a loving, sensitive man who had merely fallen prey to his buddy Bob's pressure the night she first met him. Other people are not so fortunate; they become victims of sexual exploitation when they are forced to comply with sexual acts under duress. Sexual victimization may take many forms, ranging from the sexual abuse of a child by a parent, relative, or family friend to an adult who feels coerced to engage in offensive sexual acts by his or her partner. In this section, we'll focus on two particularly exploitative forms of sexual victimization: sexual abuse of children and rape.

Sexual Abuse of Children.   Approximately 90,000 children are victims of sexual abuse every year (Finkelhor & Jones, 2004). Most often the abuser is a family member, close relative, or friend—usually a man. Women can also sexually abuse children, and their abuse can be just as severe (Orange & Brodwin, 2005; Rudin, Zalewski, & Bodmer-Turner, 1995). Not uncommonly, the abuser has been a victim of sexual abuse as a child (Prentky, Knight, & Lee, 2006). In many instances, sexual abuse is not limited to a single episode and may not involve physical force. Sexual interactions generally consist of touching and fondling the genitals of the child, though some child molesters may engage in intercourse. Sexual abuse is most likely to involve prepubescent children between 9 and 12 years of age.

The immediate effects of child sexual abuse include increased anxiety, anger, eating or sleep disturbances, guilt, withdrawal, and other psychological problems of adjustment (Jumper, 1995). Abused children are sometimes preoccupied with sex, as seen in an unusual interest in the sex organs, sex play, and nudity. They're also likely to exhibit a host of physical complaints, such as rashes, headaches, and vomiting, all

Box 11–2

HOW TO REDUCE YOUR RISK OF GETTING AIDS

You can reduce your risk of getting AIDS by following these guidelines:

- Avoid sexual contact with people known to have AIDS or suspected of having AIDS.

- Do not use intravenous or other illicit drugs. If you use intravenous drugs, do not share needles or syringes (boiling does not guarantee sterility).

- Do not have sex with people who use intravenous drugs.

- Avoid anal intercourse, with or without the use of condoms.

- Avoid oral contact with semen.

- Do not have sex with prostitutes.

- Have sex only with someone you know well, preferably a person who has not had multiple sex partners. *Always* ask your partners about their sex histories.

- Use *latex* condoms during sexual intercourse. Condoms are an effective, though by no means foolproof, way of preventing the spread of AIDS.

without medical explanation. The child's emotional trauma can be magnified when parents overreact to the discovery of sexual abuse. It is important, however, that parents show sufficient concern, such as making certain the child is not left alone with the suspected abuser as well as reporting incidents of sexual abuse to the police. Above all, the child needs to know that the parents will protect the child from other abuse and that the parents still love the child.

In adulthood, even when there are no serious psychological problems, victims of sexual abuse often have other problems, such as difficulty engaging in sex or compulsively engaging in sex. Also, abused women may feel isolated and distrustful of men. They're likely to feel anxious, depressed, and guilt-ridden. One of the most disturbing findings is the effect childhood sexual abuse has on the next generation. Boys who are abused are at increased risk of becoming child molesters themselves, and girls are more likely to produce children who are abused. Fortunately, most victims of childhood sexual abuse—and molesters—can benefit from psychotherapy.

Child Pornography.   Child pornography—in fact, all pornography—has been around for centuries. However, the Internet has greatly increased the possibility that more and more people have access to it despite the fact that *all* states have laws against it. **Child pornography** is *a visual depiction of a minor engaging in sexually explicit conduct, especially one lacking serious literary, artistic, political, or scientific value* (National Center for Missing and Exploited Children, 2006). Most children depicted in pornography are girls between the ages of 6 and 12. The main exploiters or consumers of child pornography are White, unmarried men older than 25 years of age, although individuals attracted to child pornography come from all economic and educational levels and all types of communities. Some, but not all, consumers have criminal histories and are socially isolated (National Center for Missing and Exploited Children).

Children engaged in these activities are altered forever, not just by the exploitation but by the fact that the pornographer, using modern technology, can keep reproducing the images of the child over and over again. The pornographer can also use these images to blackmail the child into silence. These children not only suffer physical trauma such as

Child sex trafficking remains an enormous problem, especially in some developing countries.

bruising and STDs but also experience depression, withdrawal, anger, and mental disorders (National Center for Missing and Exploited Children, 2006). These effects can linger into adulthood if left untreated.

Rape.   Rape—*sexual intercourse under conditions of actual or threatened force that overcome the victim's resistance*—has long been a problem in American society. Although the rape of males has increased in recent years, the overwhelming majority of rapes involve male rapists and female victims. One of the most disturbing findings is that almost half of all rape victims are younger than 18 at the time of the attack (Rape, Abuse, and Incest National Network, [RAINN] 2006b). Equally unsettling is the fact that only a few rapes are ever reported to the police. Contrary to popular myth that strangers hiding in bushes commit rape, most rapes are committed by *someone known to the victim* (RAINN).

Date rape—*coercive sexual activity that occurs during a date*—has become a widespread problem on many college campuses and elsewhere. However, victims (women) of date rape are often reluctant to label such assaults rape, mostly because of the common misconception that rape must be committed by a stranger under conditions of extreme force. "Force," however, means something different to each sex. Women tend to say they were physically coerced to have sex, whereas men are more apt to feel they were responding to psychological pressures. (Box 11–3 discusses other misconceptions or myths about rape.) Such gender differences are also reflected in the long-term effects of rape. The majority of women feel that the date rape had a long-term impact on them, whereas most men disbelieve such effects.

Studies of rape victims show that rape usually has a devastating effect on the victim's mental health (RAINN, 2006a). Almost one-third of all rape victims develop rape-related posttraumatic stress disorder (RR-PTSD) sometime during their lives. In turn, RR-PTSD dramatically increases the victim's risk for major alcohol and drug abuse problems. Rape survivors may experience a variety of emotional repercussions in two phases. The acute phase begins immediately after the assault and may continue for hours, days, or weeks. During the first few hours after being assaulted, the woman may react in an expressive manner—crying and being very upset. Or in some instances, a woman may maintain a controlled, subdued manner and only later become aware of her feelings. Victims commonly report anxiety, shame, anger, guilt,

Box 11–3

MYTHS ABOUT SEXUAL ASSAULT

Myth #1: *Victims provoke sexual assaults when they dress provocatively or act in a promiscuous manner.*

Fact: Rape and sexual assault are crimes of violence and control that stem from a person's determination to exercise power over another. Neither provocative dress nor promiscuous behavior is an invitation for unwanted sexual activity.

Myth #2: *If a person goes to someone's room or house or goes to a bar, she assumes the risk of sexual assault. If something happens later, she can't claim that she was raped or sexually assaulted because she should have known not to go to those places.*

Fact: This "assumption of risk" wrongfully places the responsibility of the offender's actions on the victim. Even if a person went voluntarily to someone's residence or room and consented to engage in some sexual activity, it does not serve as a blanket consent for *all* sexual activity. When someone says "No" or "Stop," that means STOP. Sexual activity forced upon another without consent is sexual assault.

Myth #3: *It's not sexual assault if it happens after drinking or taking drugs.*

Fact: Being under the influence of alcohol or drugs is not an invitation for nonconsensual sexual activity. A person under the influence of drugs or alcohol *does not cause* others to assault her; *others choose* to take advantage of the situation and sexually assault her because she is in a vulnerable position. Many state laws hold that a person who is cognitively impaired due to the influence of drugs or alcohol is *not able to consent* to sexual activity.

Myth #4: *Rape can be avoided if women avoid dark alleys or other "dangerous" places where strangers might be hiding or lurking.*

Fact: Rape and sexual assault can occur at any time, in many places, to anyone. According to a report based on FBI data, almost 70 percent of sexual assaults reported to law enforcement occurred in the residence of the victim, the offender, or another individual.

Myth #5: *A person who has really been sexually assaulted will be hysterical.*

Fact: Victims of sexual violence exhibit a spectrum of responses to the assault, which can include: calm, hysteria, withdrawal, anger, apathy, denial, and shock. Being sexually assaulted is a very traumatic experience. Reactions to the assault and the length of time needed to process through the experience vary with each person.

Myth #6: *All sexual assault victims will report the crime immediately to the police. If they do not report it or delay in reporting it, then they must have changed their minds after it happened, wanted revenge, or didn't want to look like they were sexually active.*

Fact: There are many reasons why a sexual assault victim may not report the assault to the police. It is not easy to talk about being sexually assaulted. The experience of retelling what happened may cause the person to relive the trauma. Other reasons for not immediately reporting the assault or not reporting it at all include fear of retaliation by the offender, fear of not being believed, fear of being blamed for the assault, fear of being "revictimized" if the case goes through the criminal justice system, belief that the offender will not be held accountable, wanting to forget the assault ever happened, not recognizing that what happened was sexual assault, shame, and/or shock. In fact, reporting a sexual assault incident to the police is the exception and not the norm. Victims can report a sexual assault to criminal justice authorities at any time so long as the incident is reported within the jurisdiction's statute of limitations.

Myth #7: *Only young, pretty women are assaulted.*

Fact: The belief that only young, pretty women are sexually assaulted stems from the myth that sexual assault is based on sex and physical attraction. Sexual assault is *a crime of power and control* and offenders often choose people whom they perceive as most vulnerable to attack or over whom they believe they can assert power. Sexual assault victims come from all walks of life.

Myth #8: *It's only rape if the victim puts up a fight and resists.*

Fact: Many states do not require a victim to resist in order to charge the offender with rape or sexual assault.

(continued)

Box 11–3 *(continued)*

In addition, there are many reasons why a victim of sexual assault would not fight or resist her attacker. She may feel that fighting or resisting will make her attacker angry, resulting in more severe injury. She may not fight or resist as a coping mechanism for dealing with the trauma of being sexually assaulted.

Myth #9: *Someone can only be sexually assaulted if a weapon was involved.*

Fact: In many cases of sexual assault, a weapon is not involved. The offender often uses physical strength, physical violence, intimidation, threats, or a combination of these tactics to overpower the victim. As pointed out above, most sexual assaults are perpetrated by someone known to the victim. An offender often uses the victim's

trust developed through their relationship to create an opportunity to commit the sexual assault.

Myth #10: *Rape is mostly an interracial crime.*

Fact: The vast majority of violent crimes, which include sexual assaults and rapes, are intraracial, meaning the victim and the offender are of the same race. This is not true, however, for rapes and sexual assaults committed against Native women. American Indian victims reported that approximately 8 in 10 rapes or sexual assaults were perpetrated by Whites. Native women also experience a higher rate of sexual assault victimization than any other race.

SOURCE: U.S. Department of Justice, Office of Violence Against Women (2006). *Myths and facts about sexual violence.* http://www.usdoj.gov/ovw/MythsFactSexualViolence.htm.

---

self-blame, and a sense of powerlessness. Physical symptoms include headaches, nausea, premenstrual disturbance, and pain syndromes.

Nervousness and fear may continue into the second, reorganization phase, which may last for years. Women often fear retaliation by the rapist. They might also harbor negative feelings about sex. Some date rape victims greatly reduce the frequency of their sexual activity or discover that they have sexual disorders. Rape, therefore, is usually a very traumatic experience, which interferes more with the psychological aspects of sexual activity than the physiological response. Fortunately, the passage of time, combined with gentle support from others and psychotherapy, can help to alleviate the effects of rape for many victims. Furthermore, improvements in the police and court system, which make them more sensitive to and supportive of rape victims, along with the establishment of rape victim advocate programs, not only increase the likelihood that victims will report the crime but also help them in making an effective recovery.

SUMMARY

MEN AND WOMEN

At the outset, the chapter helped you to understand that our attitudes about sex are often distorted by gender stereotypes. At the same time, the ongoing changes in gender roles in our society are giving rise to a healthier sexuality; for example, sexual intercourse is understood as something partners do together as equal participants. Personal communication about sexual matters tends to be more effective when partners express themselves clearly and listen to each other. Nowhere is sexual communication put to the test more than in initiating and refusing sex. Although the more emotionally expressive partner tends to initiate sex most of the time, couples whose partners share the initiator and refuser roles equally tend to have more satisfactory sex lives than other couples.

SEXUAL RESPONSIVENESS

There are five phases of the sexual response cycle: transition, excitement, plateau, orgasm, and resolution. A major difference between the sexes is the greater variation among women in the physiology and subjective awareness of orgasm, especially in the woman's ability to have several orgasms in quick succession. At the same time, individual differences tend to outweigh gender differences, so that each person needs to be understood and appreciated in terms of personal preferences. Some people now feel it is necessary to be in love to enjoy sex. Love, rather, can enrich sex, especially in long-term relationships.

PRACTICAL ISSUES

Common sexual dysfunctions include the lack of sexual desire, erectile inhibition and premature ejaculation in men, and inhibited vaginal lubrication and female orgasmic disorder in women. Each method of birth control has its advantages and disadvantages, with the final choice often involving a trade-off among safety, convenience, and effectiveness. Sexually transmitted diseases, such as chlamydia, gonorrhea, genital herpes, and syphilis, continue to present a health hazard, though they can be effectively treated. In contrast, AIDS is a deadly disease that poses a growing threat. Although the majority of AIDS victims in the United States have been homosexuals and intravenous drug users, the risk of AIDS from heterosexual intercourse is increasing. Another problem attracting public concern is sexual victimization, including sexual abuse of children and rape. One of the most disturbing findings is that most rape victims are younger than 18, and the rapist is known by the victim. Although coercive sex continues to be a problem, improvements in the justice system, along with the establishment of sex victim advocate programs, increase the likelihood that victims will report the crime and be helped in making an effective recovery.

SELF-TEST

1. Traits such as masculine and feminine are best understood as
   a. mere stereotypes.
   b. rare.
   c. largely learned.
   d. androgynyous.

2. The most important part of sexual communication is the partners'
   a. persuasive skills.
   b. use of questions.
   c. factual knowledge of sex.
   d. attitudes toward each other.

3. Married and unmarried couples alike tend to be more satisfied with their sex lives when the initiative for sexual intercourse is
   a. taken mostly by the man.
   b. shared equally by both partners.
   c. taken mostly by the woman.
   d. always taken by the man.

4. The sex fantasies of men and women
   a. are identical to one another.
   b. are different from one another.
   c. occur in the excitement phase.
   d. occur in the resolution phase.

5. Multiple orgasms are
   a. more common in women.
   b. experienced by most men.
   c. more common in men.
   d. equally common for men and women.

6. Is love necessary to a sexual relationship? Love
   a. is necessary to enjoy sex.
   b. must be experienced before orgasm is possible.
   c. enriches sex.
   d. interferes with the enjoyment of sex.

7. The most common sexual dysfunction among men during the orgasm phase of the sexual response cycle is
   a. premature or retarded ejaculation.   c. difficulty maintaining an erection.
   b. inhibited sexual desire.   d. inhibited sexual arousal.

8. Which of the following birth-control techniques has the best effectiveness rating?
   a. cervical cap.   c. birth-control pills.
   b. condom.   d. diaphragm.

9. The most common sexually transmitted disease in the United States is
   a. gonorrhea.   c. AIDS.
   b. genital herpes.   d. chlamydia.

10. Victims of childhood sexual abuse are most likely to be
    a. boys 13 to 15.   c. girls 3 to 7.
    b. girls 9 to 12.   d. children under 7.

EXERCISES

1. *Gender stereotypes.* Select a specific gender stereotype you disagree with, whether discussed in this chapter or not. Then write a page or more telling why you feel so strongly about it. Is there any truth to this stereotype? What is the evidence against it? Why do you think this stereotype persists? What can we do to eliminate this bias?

2. *Sexual communication.* What has been the most difficult part of sexual communication for you? Have you discovered your partner's sexual likes and dislikes? Do you have difficulty initiating sex? How well can you refuse an unwanted sexual invitation or accept rejection?

3. *How important is love for sex?* Do you feel two people can enjoy sex without being in love? Or do you feel people must be in love to have good sex? Write a short paragraph explaining your views about sex and love.

4. *Sharing sexual fantasies.* If you're married or sexually active in a secure relationship, share some of your sexual fantasies with your partner. Such sharing is usually more helpful when it is mutual. It may be wise to begin with mild fantasies that can help desensitize fears and embarrassment and enable you to judge the impact of such sharing on your partner as well as yourself. It's also best to avoid sharing fantasies that would shock your partner or threaten the relationship.

5. *Shared responsibility for contraception.* How do you feel about men sharing the responsibility for birth control? What are some of the pros and cons? Does it present any special problems for the woman?

6. *Sexual victimization.* Suppose you were asked to suggest ways to decrease the incidence of sexual victimization, for example, childhood sexual abuse and rape, in our society. Write a page or more describing the changes you would propose.

QUESTIONS FOR SELF-REFLECTION

1. When was the last time you read a book about sex by a recognized authority in the field?

2. How well do you and your partner communicate about sex? How can you improve your communications?

3. Do you and your partner share the initiative for sex? Or does one of you usually initiate sex?

4. Must physical hugging and touching always lead to sexual intercourse?

5. Are you aware of what is sexually arousing for your partner?

6. Do you and your partner agree about the relationship between sex and love?

7. Are you aware that an occasional sexual dysfunction may be due to emotional stress that particular day?

8. How safe is your method of contraception? Does your partner share your concerns about contraception?

9. Can you recognize the symptoms of prevalent STDs?

10. Are you familiar with the practical guidelines for avoiding AIDS?

FOR FURTHER INFORMATION

RECOMMENDED READINGS

COMFORT, A. (2002). *The joy of sex*. Victoria, BC, Canada: Crown Publishing. Fully revised and completely updated for the twenty-first century. This is a classic that swept in on the heels of the sexual revolution.

CROOKS, R. L., & BAUER, K. (2004). *Our sexuality*. Belmont, CA: Wadsworth. One of the leading books on all aspects of human sexuality.

DOMITRZ, M. (2005). *Voices of courage: Inspiration from survivors of sexual assault*. Greenfield, WI: Awareness Publications. You will read the stories of survivors of sexual assault. Their experiences and their recovery are made very real by means of their own essays, poems, and memoirs.

KAMINSKY, N. (2003). *Affirmative gay relationship*. Binghamton, NY: Haworth Press. The author takes gays and lesbians through the steps of finding a life partner.

WOODS, S. G. (2002). *Everything you need to know about STDs*. New York: Rosen. Important and timely information on sexually transmitted diseases.

WEB SITES AND THE INTERNET

http://www.ngltf.org   A good place to find information on gay and lesbian issues.

http://www.siecus.org   The site of the Sexuality Information and Education Council of the United States (SIECUS), a national, nonprofit organization that affirms sexuality as a natural and healthy part of living.

http://www.4parents.gov   A government web site that guides parents through helpful information on a variety of topics, especially teen sexuality. The site provides helpful tips for parents who find discussing such topics with their children difficult.

http://www.arhp.org   A site maintained by the Association of Reproductive Health Professionals with much information about reproductive health.

http://www.sexuality.org/safesex.html#C2   A place to find quality information about safe sex. There is some fairly explicit information here, but it is presented in a no-nonsense style.

CHAPTER 12

Love and Commitment

LOVE AND INTIMACY
The Ingredients of Love
Love and Close Relationships

COMMITMENT
Cohabitation
Marriage and Other Committed
    Relationships

**ADJUSTING TO INTIMATE
RELATIONSHIPS**
Sharing Responsibilities
Communication and Conflict
Making the Relationship Better
Sexuality
Changes Over Time

DIVORCE AND ITS CONSEQUENCES
The Divorce Experience
Single-Parent Families
Remarriage

SUMMARY
**SCORING KEY FOR THE MARITAL
    MYTHS QUIZ**
SELF-TEST
EXERCISES
QUESTIONS FOR SELF-REFLECTION
FOR FURTHER INFORMATION

David and Diane, both in their early 20s, have been going together for 3 years. They met at their community college in biology class. They're in love with each other and have discussed the possibility of living together as well as of marriage. Both left home and first took apartments with their high school friends who are attending the same college. Dave and Diane soon realized, however, that they could share an apartment, spend more time with each other, and save more money.

Having worked through many of the differences in their interests, they enjoy spending as much time together as their busy schedules permit. Because they attend some of the same classes, they also study together. Both want a close, rewarding relationship, in which they're best friends as well as lovers, but they're having some difficulty achieving it. Diane complains that David is preoccupied with his part-time automobile parts sales job. She also complains that when they are together, all he wants to do is watch sports on television. Although Diane likes basketball, she detests football. David argues that he is too tired to go to a movie or to dinner after attending classes, studying, and working. Even when they're together, Diane says David doesn't share his feelings with her. This trait has become especially troublesome when he's moody and won't explain why. In David's view, Diane doesn't understand that this is a critical stage in his plans to become a car dealership manager and that Diane is more concerned about getting married than about him and their careers. Also, David feels Diane is too possessive at times, for example, her recent jealousy over his casual friendship with a woman at the district sales office. David readily admits that talk of marriage at this point in his life makes him feel "trapped." Diane believes that David's feelings have been shaped, at least in part, by his parents' recent, messy divorce. Consequently, she worries about how committed David is to their relationship and about their future together.

LOVE AND INTIMACY

Like so many other couples in their young adulthood, David and Diane want a great deal of closeness in their relationship. At the same time, they're having difficulty developing it partly because they've both grown up in families lacking the very warmth and intimacy they seek. Consequently, David feels uneasy when people get too close to him, and Diane worries about loved ones leaving her, resulting in an anxious–ambivalent relationship. Some couples grow in love and understanding and eventually achieve a satisfying relationship despite their different backgrounds and shortcomings. Other couples are not so fortunate. Faced with frustration and disillusionment, many of them simply split up. Countless others continue in conflict-laden relationships or empty marriages. Let's see what happens to David and Diane.

We'll begin the chapter by exploring the essentials of love as well as the different ways people approach intimate relationships. We'll also look at the practice of couples living together and the process by which couples move toward marriage or some other form of commitment, such as a commitment ceremony between gays. We'll discuss some of the major areas of adjustment, including sharing responsibilities, communication and conflict, sex, and relationship changes over time. Finally, we'll describe what happens in divorce, single-parent families, and remarriage.

Please note that this chapter could well be about love, marriage, and divorce. However, with high levels of cohabitation as well as increasing awareness of various sexual orientations such as homosexuality and bisexuality, it is important to take such relationships into account. It is probably judicious to discuss *commitment* to a significant other, of which marriage is but one form, rather than to speak solely of marriage. If you aren't familiar with the terms *sexual orientation*, *homosexuality*, and *bisexuality*, Box 12–1 might prove helpful.

The Ingredients of Love

Psychologists recognize that **intimate relationships** (or *close relationships*) and friendships overlap to a considerable extent. Both lovers and friends initially seek out others who are similar to them (Lucas et al., 2004; Whitbeck & Hoyt, 1994). Both types of couples enjoy each other's company, despite occasional disappointments. Individuals in both types of relationships generally accept each other as they are, without trying to make their partner over into a different person. We apparently want friends and lovers who can validate our self-concept (Swann, De LaRonde, & Hixon, 1994). Both friends and lovers know they can count on each other in times of need. Also, they can confide in each other without fear of

Box 12–1

WHAT IS SEXUAL ORIENTATION AND WHY IS IT IMPORTANT?

Sexual orientation, *a component of sexuality, is characterized by enduring emotional, romantic, or sexual attraction to individuals of a particular gender.* The three major sexual orientations are **homosexuality,** *which involves emotional and sexual preference for partners of the same sex;* **heterosexuality,** *which involves emotional and sexual preference for opposite-sex partners;* and **bisexuality,** *which involves a preference for sexual activity with partners of either sex* (American Psychological Association, 2003). Psychologists are still trying to ascertain why a particular sexual orientation develops, but a combination of nature and nurture is believed to be involved.

The American Psychological Association (2004) states that it is important for society to be better educated about sexual orientation:

> Educating all people about sexual orientation and homosexuality is likely to diminish anti–gay prejudice. Accurate information about homosexuality is especially important to young people struggling with their own sexual identity. Fears that access to such information will affect one's [own] sexual orientation are not valid.

Discovering that one's sexual orientation is not heterosexual—the predominant orientation in our society—can be distressing because of societal stigmas and prejudices against homosexuality. *When an individual accepts his or her sexual orientation as homosexual (or bisexual) and then tells others,* this is called **coming out.** Research has found that coming out involves many processes for the homosexual individual (as well as for others who are told), including but not limited to challenging one's own beliefs and self-concept, developing new methods of communication, managing conflicts differently, changing established relationships with other people, and asking questions of the self and others (Oswald, 2000).

When the gay person's family and friends are supportive, the individual copes much better with this revelation (Elizur & Ziv, 2001; Willoughby, Malik, & Lindahl, 2006). Gay men, however, seem to be more estranged from their families, especially their fathers, than heterosexual men (Bobrow & Bailey, 2001) and lesbians. Surprisingly, gay men and lesbians report that their intimate relationships with their partners are not very affected by parental disapproval (LaSala, 2002). In fact, in relationships where the homosexual partner is fairly visible, families (siblings and parents) are more likely to include the partner in family rituals (e.g., birthday celebrations) (Oswald, 2002). When families do not accept or support their homosexual family member, involvement in the gay and lesbian community and support at school can help diminish psychological distress and even reduce suicidality (Lasser, Tharinger, & Cloth, 2006; Morris, Waldo, & Rothblum, 2001).

betrayal. Friends and lovers understand each other and make allowances when the other person occasionally acts in an unexpected or annoying manner. Finally, research demonstrates that we want the same personal characteristics in friends and lovers—warmth, kindness, openness, acceptance, respect, trust, and understanding—but we prefer *higher* levels of these attributes in our lovers than in our friends (Beste, Bergner, & Nauta, 2003; Sprecher & Regan, 2002).

At the same time, love relationships are distinctively different from friendships. Essentially, it appears that love heightens the potential for both positive and negative aspects of close relationships, making love relationships not only more rewarding but also more frustrating. **Love** can be defined as *deep and tender feelings of affection for or attachment to one or more persons.* Love relationships include characteristics such as fascination, sexual desire, and exclusiveness, such that lovers (but not friends) tend to be preoccupied with their partners in an exclusive sexual relationship (Lucas et al., 2004; Simpson & Gangestad, 1992). There is also more intense caring for each other in love relationships, even more so than in friendship, for example, being an advocate for a lover and giving more of one-self, with the result that lovers are willing to give their utmost to their partners. However, because of the greater exclusiveness and emotional involvement between them, lovers also experience greater conflict, distress, and mutual criticism in their relationships than do friends (Rogge, Bradbury, Hahlweg, Engl, & Thurmaier, 2006). In its extreme form, this can result in partner abuse (Feinberg, 2002), which is discussed in detail later in the chapter. In sum, love relationships are both more rewarding and more volatile than friendships.

The Internet has certainly changed the way some individuals search for romantic partners. Box 12–2 discusses this new "marketplace" through the eyes of psychologists. Read it and then ponder whether you think this is a good way to meet potential lovers.

The intensely satisfying but unstable nature of love relationships is often attributed to a special variety of love—**romantic love**—*the strong, emotional attachment to a person of the opposite sex and, on occasion, the same sex*. Faith in romantic love is widespread in Western culture (Kim & Hatfield, 2004; Reade, 2002). The interest in romantic love has prompted the development of several theories regarding love. One such theory has been advanced by psychologist Elaine Hatfield (1988; Kim & Hatfield). Passionate and companionate love are the two types of love identified. Passionate love best fits our notion of romantic love. **Passionate love** is *an intense emotional reaction to a potential romantic partner who may not even love you in return*. This is the "head-over-heels" reaction some of us experience when we first realize we are in love. This type of love is what David and Diane first experienced. One day, Diane invited Dave to join her and her friend for lunch. They walked to the class after lunch and became acquainted. Within days, David had a desperate crush on this gentle, pretty young woman. Diane soon "fell" for David, too. As is true of passionate love, they were initially blind to each other's foibles and faults (Aloni & Bernieri, 2004; Neff & Karney, 2005; Reade).

Hatfield claims that three conditions must be met in order for individuals to feel they have fallen madly in love.

- First, the individuals must be exposed to romantic images (as in the media) and role models that lead to the expectation that love is possible. (Love, therefore, is not always found in every culture.)

- Second, the individual must come into contact with an appropriate person to love. "Appropriate," of course, is culturally defined. We will consider cultural variations in notions of love soon.

- Finally, Hatfield states that an intense arousal must be present. For example, fear, sexual excitement, even drunkenness can all change our arousal level, and we can confuse them with perceptions that we are in love.

Another type of love identified by Hatfield is **companionate love**, defined as *a loving but practical relationship based primarily on emotional closeness and commitment rather than physical, sexual intimacy*. This is a practical kind of love that involves trust, caring, and tolerance for the partner's flaws. Companionate love is more moderate emotionally than passionate love; it also takes longer to develop than passionate love. Companionate love tends to be more characteristic of long-term relationships, including many happy marriages and some friendships. Perhaps this kind of love had not yet developed between Diane and David, for they were becoming more critical of each other as their relationship evolved over time.

A **triangular theory of love**, *a theory that suggests there are three components to love*, has also been proposed. After studying various types of relationships to figure out what

Box 12–2

ROMANCE ON THE INTERNET

On-line matchmaking has become a culturally legitimate approach to mate selection (Houran, Lange, Rentfrow, & Bruckner, 2004), whereas in the past online dating or the posting of personal ads in newspapers was stigmatized as a crutch used only by those desperate for a date (Gibbs, Ellison, & Heino, 2006). The Internet is a rapidly growing venue for meeting people and forming relationships (Hardey, 2004; Ben-Ze'ev, 2004), so social scientists have begun researching the pros and cons of this medium.

Three recent studies are important to this topic. First, some on-line dating services claim that their matches are based on scientific strategies. On the contrary, Houran et al. (2004) found that one on-line service's selected variables, research design, and sampling techniques were seriously flawed. Second, those individuals who spend a great deal of time on the Internet or who have an affinity for the Internet are more likely to hold favorable (but not necessarily more accurate) perceptions of Internet dating services (Anderson, 2005). Finally, and important to the main topic of this book—personal growth—Yurchisin, Watchravesringkan, and McCabe, (2005) found that the act of individuals' posting their own personal profiles on Internet dating services had an impact on the individuals beliefs about themselves. In other words, individuals sometimes learn and grow from such experiences.

If you choose to seek out partners on the Internet, here are some useful guidelines you can follow to keep yourself safe and to improve your chances of high-quality relationships and personal safety (Onguard.gov, 2006):

- Think about how different sites work before deciding to join a site. Some sites will allow only a defined community of users to access posted content; others allow anyone and everyone to view postings.

- Think about keeping some control over the information you post. Consider restricting access to your page to a select group of people.

- Keep your information to yourself. Don't post your full name, Social Security number, address,

phone number, or bank and credit card account numbers—and don't post other people's information, either. Be cautious about posting information that could be used to identify you or locate you offline. This would include the name of your school, where you work, or where you hang out.

- Make sure your screen name doesn't say too much about you. Don't use your name, your age, or your hometown. Even if you think your screen name makes you anonymous, it doesn't take a genius to combine clues to figure out who you are and where you can be found.

- Post only information that you are comfortable with others seeing—and knowing—about you. Many people can see your page, including your parents, teachers, the police, the college, or an employer.

- Remember that once you post information on-line, you can't take it back. Even if you delete the information from a site, older versions exist on some people's computers.

- Consider not posting your photo. It can be altered and broadcast in ways you may not be happy about. If you do post one, ask yourself whether it's one your mother would display in the living room.

- Flirting with strangers on-line could have serious consequences. Because some people lie about who they really are, you never really know who you're dealing with.

- Be wary if a new on-line friend wants to meet you in person. Before you decide to meet someone, do your research: Ask whether any of your friends know the person, and see what background you can dig up through on-line search engines. If you decide to meet, be smart about it: Meet in a public place, during the day, with friends you trust. Tell a responsible person where you're going and when you expect to be back.

- Trust your gut if you have suspicions. If you feel threatened by someone or uncomfortable because of something on-line, tell someone you trust and report it to the police and the social networking site. You could end up preventing someone else from becoming a victim.

differentiates romantic relationships from other types of love, Robert Sternberg and Susan Grajek (1984; Sternberg, 2004) developed their triangular theory built around the three components of love—intimacy, passion, and commitment. **Intimacy** is *the emotional aspect of love and includes closeness, sharing, communication, and support.* Intimacy tends to develop slowly in the beginning and then progress more steadily until it levels off and later declines. An apparent lack of intimacy may mean that the relationship is dying. Or intimacy may be present but taken for granted, requiring some disruption such as a family crisis or separation to make people more aware of how close they really are.

Passion, *the emotional or motivational aspect of love, involves physiological arousal and an intense desire to be united with the loved one.* Unlike intimacy, sexual motivation blossoms quickly. But after a while, you get used to it, or "habituated," so that increased exposure to the person no longer brings the arousal and satisfaction it once did. Worse still, when you break up with the person, you may experience withdrawal symptoms—depression, irritability, and loss of desire.

Commitment, *the cognitive aspect of love, includes both the short-term affirmation of your love for the person and the long-term commitment to maintain that love.* This may well be the aspect that was missing long-term from Diane and David's relationship. Commitment usually develops in a more straightforward manner than does intimacy or passion. In long-lasting relationships, commitment increases gradually at first and then more rapidly. As the relationship continues, the amount of commitment levels off. If the relationship begins to weaken, the level of commitment will decline. And if the relationship falls apart, commitment falls back to zero. In contrast to romantic love, the love of a parent for a child usually is marked by a high and unconditional level of commitment. The triangular theory of love is not the only theory of love (see Beste et al., 2003), but it is the best known in the psychological literature. Can you think of any other components of love that are missing from either of these theories? Does one of these theories better describe your current or past love relationship? Why? As mentioned earlier, the perception of love is influenced by culture (Kim & Hatfield, 2004; Matsumoto, 2000). Many social scientists are discovering that love is a rather universal phenomenon (Hatfield & Rapson, 1993). However, its importance in helping us select appropriate others to whom to commit or to marry varies by culture. Elsewhere in this book we have discussed two main types of cultures: individualistic and collectivistic societies. In **individualistic societies** *the goals of the individual are more important than the goals of the collective (or of society)*, and in **collective societies** *the goals of society or the collective are more important than the goals of the individual.* The United States embraces a decidedly individualistic culture, whereas India, Japan, and other Asian countries promulgate collectivism. Dion and Dion (1993; 2005) propose that romantic love is more likely to be an important basis for marriage in individualistic than in collectivistic societies. Similarly, psychological intimacy in marriage is more important for marital satisfaction in individualistic than in collectivistic societies.

Finally, although intimacy is important in individualistic marriages, intimacy can be more problematic because of individualism in such societies compared to collective societies. Research supports some of these contentions. Levine, Sato, Hashimoto, and Verma (1995) studied attitudes about love and marriage in college students from 11 different countries. They found that for college students from Western or individualistic cultures such as the United States as compared to collectivistic or Asian societies, there was more emphasis placed on love as a basis for establishing a marriage. Love was also a stronger reason for establishing a marriage in individualistic cultures than for dissolving a marriage. Those students who assigned greater importance to love came from countries with higher economic standards than those who did not do so. This means that the students from the United States assigned the highest worth to love, whereas students from India, a country whose economy is Third World, emphasized love the least in selecting marriage partners. In such cultures, rather than marrying the loved person or romantic partner, couples *learn* to love each other after they marry (Matsumoto, 2000). In Japan (a collectivistic society), the ratings of the value of love by college students fell somewhere between those of the other two. Interestingly, countries that do not emphasize romance in mate selection have lower divorce rates.

In the United States, Canada, and other Western societies, as repeatedly mentioned, there is a variety of subcultures. Contreras, Hendrick, and Hendrick (1996) conducted research on Hispanic Americans and Anglo Americans to determine whether each group differentially values love in marital relationships. They found that Hispanic respondents were more pragmatic about love and less idealistic about sex than Anglo Americans. In both subcultures, the researchers also found that passionate love was also correlated with marital satisfaction. That is, the higher the passion, the higher the marital satisfaction. We might conclude from all of these cross-cultural studies what others have concluded—that many groups in today's world believe in and value romantic love. In this regard, they are more similar than dissimilar in their views about love and intimacy (Hatfield & Rapson, 1993).

Love and Close Relationships

Diane sometimes accused David of being "just like his father," whom she judged to be lazy—a couch potato who would rather watch sports on TV than attend community events or help with housework. The way people approach close relationships as well as their view of love can be a reflection of their personal development. More specifically, their characteristic styles of attachment to their parents probably influence their attachment style to their romantic partners. **Attachment style** means *our typical style of becoming involved with others*. Early attachments (refer back to Chapter 2) often give children a working model of relationships that they later emulate (Hazan & Shaver, 1994).

A series of studies by Cindy Hazan and Phillip Shaver (1994) show an interesting similarity among people's romantic relationships, beliefs about love, and the kind of attachment they formed with their parents during childhood. The researchers polled 620 adults and 108 college students, asking them how they typically approach close relationships, their important romantic experiences, their beliefs about love, and their childhood relationships with their parents. Based on the responses, Hazan and Shaver classified each person into one of three groups.

Securely attached people *believe it's easy to get close to others, and they report happy and trusting love relationships*. Their romances last the longest and end in divorce least often. Many of them feel that romantic love never fades. People in this group saw their parents as especially loving, responsive, and warm. Neither David nor Diane apparently was securely attached to their parents in childhood, but neither was willing to discuss this with the other.

Those who form **avoidant attachments** *feel uneasy when people get too close to them*. Because they fear intimacy, they have trouble trusting and depending on others and are prone to jealousy. They hold a cynical picture of love, believing that the head-over-heels romantic love depicted in movies and novels does not exist in real life. Instead, they feel, it is rare to find someone to fall in love with, and even then romantic love seldom lasts. Avoidant adults generally rated their parents rather harshly, seeing their mothers as not very likeable, if not rejecting, and their fathers as uncaring. Although the college students

Individuals who, as children, were securely attached to their parents have longer-lasting romantic relationships and are less likely to divorce.

often rated their parents more positively than the older adults, the researchers speculated that the unduly rosy picture of their childhood is destined to become more realistic, and hence more negative, as they get older.

The third group, called **anxious–ambivalent**, *includes people who desire a high level of closeness* many partners don't seem willing to give. They also worry a lot about loved ones leaving them. Accordingly, these people experience emotional extremes as well as jealousy in their relationships. They find it easy to "fall in love" but difficult to find "true love." They generally gave more mixed reports about their parents than did those in the other two groups. Box 12–3 discusses another important but more troubling type of relationship, partner abuse.

There is some evidence that we *do* attach to our romantic partners as we did to our parents. Kanemasa and Daibo (2003), using a Japanese sample, found that as adults, securely attached individuals have relatively positive images of romantic love and value the

Box 12–3

PARTNER ABUSE

Despite better education and more laws, one in four American women is estimated to experience domestic violence in her lifetime. Although men can be victims of domestic violence, women comprise 85 percent of all victims (National Coalition Against Domestic Violence [NCADV], 2005). Intimate partner violence makes up about 20 percent of all nonfatal violent crimes experienced by women (Rennison, 2003). Over half of all women and one-third of all men murdered are killed by their significant others (Kessler, Molnar, Feurer, & Applebaum, 2001).

Just what is partner abuse or domestic violence? The National Coalition Against Domestic Violence (2005) provides this definition: **Battering** is *a pattern of behavior used to establish power and control over another person through fear and intimidation, often including the threat or use of violence. Battering happens when one person believes he or she is entitled to control another.*

Domestic violence against intimate partners can involve married or unmarried heterosexual women and men as well as lesbian and gay couples. The most common abusive situation involves a man and a woman, with the woman as the victim (Rennison & Welchans, 2000). This situation, in which a man is abusive toward a woman, results in the most negative consequences of all, such as serious physical injury (Holtzworth-Munroe, 2000). Trends in partner abuse and violence fortunately indicate that this type of violence may be declining (Rennison, 2003). Figure 12–1 depicts these trends in more detail.

According to the National Coalition Against Domestic Violence, many theories have been developed to explain why some men use violence against their partners. These theories include family dysfunction, inadequate communication skills, provocation by women, stress, chemical dependency, lack of spirituality, and economic hardship. While such issues may be associated with battering of women, they are not the true causes. Why? Removing these associated factors will not end men's violence against women. The batterer begins and continues his behavior because violence is an effective method for gaining and keeping control over another person, and he unfortunately does not usually suffer adverse consequences as a result of his behavior. Risk

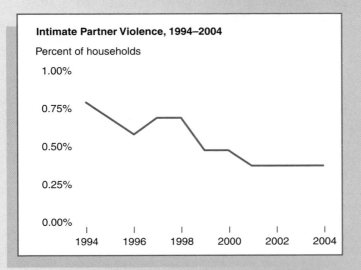

Intimate Partner Violence, 1994–2004

Percent of households

FIGURE 12–1

Intimate partner violence.

SOURCE: Bureau of Justice Statistics (April 2006). Crime and the Nation's Households, 2004. U.S. Department of Justice: Washington, DC.

(continued)

Box 12–3 *(continued)*

factors that predict violence against a partner include unemployment, drug use, having witnessed similar violence as a child, low income, and low educational levels, especially for male abusers. Very few of these men are truly antisocial, but most lack good communication skills and have a high need to control and overpower their partners (Ingrassia & Beck, 1994). Cohabiting men are most likely to kill their partners (Shackelford & Mouzos, 2005), with the risk for abusive murder going down with the women's age.

Batterers come from all groups and backgrounds and from all personality profiles. However, some characteristics fit a general profile of a batterer:

• A batterer objectifies women. Overall, he sees women as property or sexual objects.

• A batterer has low self-esteem and feels powerless and ineffective in the world. He may appear successful, but inside he feels inadequate.

• A batterer externalizes the causes of his behavior. He blames his violence on circumstances such as stress, his partner's behavior, a "bad day," alcohol, or other factors.

• A batterer may be pleasant and charming between periods of violence and is often seen as a "nice guy" to outsiders.

• A batter provides behavioral warning signs, including extreme jealousy, possessiveness, a bad temper, unpredictability, cruelty to animals, and verbal abusiveness (NCADV, 2005).

Abusive partners frequently minimize or deny what they have done and frequently blame the victim. Much of the violence occurs in a predictable cycle or pattern, too. First comes *the stage of escalation or tension building*, which many victims learn to recognize and thus try to avoid with such techniques as sidestepping certain topics or avoiding various conversations. The second stage in the cycle of violence is *the actual violence*, which is often explosive. The third stage, strangely enough, *involves the abuser begging for forgiveness*, offering love and promises never to batter again and even engaging in sex with the victim.

The victims of such abuse find extricating themselves from such relationships difficult. Besides the horror of the physical bruises, victims often suffer loss of self-esteem, repeated threats of violence, debilitating depression, and stalking if an escape to safety is attempted. Given these, many victims find leaving the abuser to be impossible. Historically, violence against women has not been treated as a "real" crime. Thankfully, today assault, battering, and domestic violence are generally considered crimes. In recognition of this cycle and that victims are unable to escape, some states have passed laws mandating the arrest of batterers. Police, however, sometimes have little training in such matters or find domestic disputes unglamorous or downright dangerous (Duffy & Wong, 2003). There is increasing evidence, though, that battering or domestic violence is being taken more seriously by the justice system, with increased rates of police notification, arrest, and judicial involvement (Cho & Wilke, 2005). Sadly, when the police do intervene, they often arrest both parties—even the victim—rather than the primary aggressor (Finn, Blackwell, Stalans, Studdard, & Dugan, 2004).

Psychologists have tried to intervene in this cycle and typically work with the batterer. Some counselors offer group therapy for abusers in which the abusers confront each other. Other therapists offer anger management classes for abusers. Other therapists suggest treatment with medication.

In the meantime, the cycle of violence continues. If you are a victim or know a victim of partner violence, you can receive referral and support information by calling the National Victim Center (800-FYI-Call); there is also a web site for more information: NVCV.org. Other resources include the National Coalition Against Domestic Violence at www.ncadv.org/ and The National Domestic Violence Hotline: 1-800-799-7233.

importance of relationships. Avoidant individuals had relatively negative images of romantic love and do not regard romantic relationships as important. Finally, ambivalently attached individuals view romantic relationships as ones that impose restraints on them from their partners. An additional study adds more information. In an American sample, Schachner and

Shaver (2004) found that attachment style influences motives for sex, with *anxiously* attached individuals reporting having sex to reduce insecurity and to enhance the intensity of closeness to the partner. On the other hand, anxiously attached individuals report having sex, especially casual, uncommitted sex, to impress their peer group. The latter study demonstrates that not only are attachment style and sexual behavior related, it also insinuates that the relationship between sex and love is very complicated (Hendrick & Hendrick, 2004).

Some researchers have questioned whether factors in intimate relationships that are important to women are as important to men. Emotional intimacy is of almost equal importance for the happiness of both sexes. However, men and women often differ in how they experience intimacy. For women, emotional intimacy generally leads to greater happiness in their relationships as wives and mothers. Women also value respect from, open communication with, and fidelity by, their partners more than men do (Hall & Mosemak, 1999).

COMMITMENT

Once a couple has formed, the individuals often indicate their commitment to each other by living together (cohabitation) or becoming engaged and later married. In both cases, they often are committed to each other exclusively; that is, they do not date or feel romantic attraction to others. Let's look at each of these states in more detail.

Cohabitation

Couples who begin living together, as did Diane and David, often experience greater intimacy than other dating couples their age, at least in the short run. Although people of varying ages and prior marital statuses engage in **cohabitation** or *the practice of unmarried persons living together, sharing bed and board*, the largest proportion is in their 20s to 40s (Smith, 2003). Some drift into this type of arrangement (Peterson, 2002), often keeping a place of their own. Others deliberately set up a joint household from the outset, as did Diane and David. The number of cohabitating couples in the United States has grown sixfold from the 1970s (Smith). The last national census found that 5.5 million couples were living together, up from 3.2 million in 1990, with economics driving this increase (i.e., it is cheaper for two people to live together than apart) (Smock, Manning, & Porter, 2005). While most of these couples were of the opposite sex, about one in nine couples (Kurdek, 2005) had same-sex partners. Some investigators state that cohabitation in the United States is now the modal (most common) path to marriage (Smock et al., 2005). Others note that cohabitation is far more common elsewhere, for example, Sweden (Kiernan, 2004).

Some people who cohabit have a different set of values, believing that relationships are breakable if they're not personally satisfying. In fact, early researchers identified the **cohabitation effect** (Cohan & Kleinbaum, 2002; Phillips & Sweeney, 2005), *where couples that cohabit first have greater marital instability than couples that do not cohabit*. Cohabitation often does not result in marriage, and, when it does, it is more likely to result in divorce (Manning & Smock, 2002; Centers for Disease Control and Prevention [CDC], 2002c). Subsequent research is proving that this finding is simplistic. Race, length of the cohabitation, reasons for cohabiting (e.g., a test of compatibility before marriage), and other factors all must be taken into account. Some cohabiting couples can and do go on to successful marriages (Phillips & Sweeney).

About one-half of cohabiting couples eventually marry. Some researchers claim that it is men, in particular, who are less committed to the institution of marriage (Peterson, 2002) or even to cohabitation. As a result, they are more likely to stay single and simply cohabit or divorce once married rather than stay in a less-than-satisfying relationship. Some of these individuals tend to be independent-minded and believe that their right to personal happiness takes precedence over a marital relationship, or they do not have strong respect for marriage as a social tradition. At the same time, much of this research evidence reflects the increasing economic status of women, who may have less financial need to marry than in the past. Also, today there is a greater acceptance of sex outside of marriage and a greater emphasis on personal satisfaction in close relationships. Perhaps this was David and Diane's problem, even after they married. (Yes, they did marry, one warm, June Saturday as friends and family looked on.)

Marriage and Other Committed Relationships

Although marriage as an institution is being challenged by alternative arrangements such as cohabitation, it is not going out of style. **Marriage** is *the state of being married, usually the legal union of two people.* Most people in the United States still want to marry, though they usually don't condemn someone who isn't married. There are other forms of commitment, too, such as common-law marriages (recognized in some states) and committed gay relationships. Some states as well as Canada allow marriage between same-sex couples. We may value marriage for heterosexual couples, but attitudes toward homosexual or gay marriages tend to vary immensely. While the issue of gay marriage is "emotionally charged and highly politicized" (Leiblum, 2004), the issue is advancing through American society faster than other, similar issues, such as interracial marriage, did (Wilkinson & Kitzinger, 2005).

Many Americans consistently report believing same-sex marriage undermines the traditional American family or their own religious beliefs, but a majority of Americans *do* support some sort of rights to civil unions, inheritance, access to the partner's health insurance, and so forth for gays (Brewer & Wilcox, 2005). About this societal division, Andrew Sullivan (2003) says, "Every day, if you're a gay person, you see amazing advances and terrifying setbacks. . . . Wal-Mart set rules . . . to protect its gay employees from discrimination [but] the Vatican comes out and announces that granting legal recognition to gay spouses will destroy the family and society" (p. 35). Most Americans also think children should be reared within a marriage. Marriage is seen as promoting the welfare of children and the stability of society (Naples, 2004). Ironically, this pits against each other the issues of the value of marriage to children and of gay parents raising children (Naples). The matters of gay marriage and gay parenting will likely continue to be debated in courtrooms, in legislative chambers, and at kitchen tables for years to come (Rosato, 2006).

Kurdek (2005) recently reviewed the psychological literature on gay and lesbian couples. He found that relative to heterosexual couples, gay partners tended to assign household labor more fairly, resolve conflicts more constructively, and experience a more equal level of satisfaction with the relationship. Overall, then, scientific research paints a more positive picture of gay and lesbian couples than popularly believed and indicates that they tend to be more similar to than different from heterosexual couples.

All couples today in nearly all regions of the world tend to wait a bit longer to marry, with the median age of first marriages rising slightly each year (Saardchom & Lemaire, 2005). Consequently, many people marry during their 20s and 30s. Perhaps this is a

Most Americans believe in voluntary marriages that are based on love rather than involuntary marriages that are based on some arrangement between families.

positive trend, because the older people are when they marry, the longer the marriage lasts (CDC, 2001). The reasons for this are varied, but a rise in education and economic modernization is thought to explain this trend (Saardchom & Lemaire).

For the most part, heterosexuals and gays tend to marry or commit to partners of similar age, education, ethnic or social background, race, and religion. Much of this tendency reflects the ways we have been socialized as well as the opportunities for meeting people, with physical proximity increasing the chances for attraction. As our society becomes more mobile and diverse, however, people are marrying or committing to others who cross many of these familiar boundaries, because factors such as similar values rather than similar demographics play a more important role in today's world. According to Matsumoto (2000), however, these diverse marriages (e.g., intercultural marriages) are especially prone to conflicts about love and intimacy, but surprisingly, such marriages are *not* more divorce prone.

Many people tend to marry or make commitments to significant others out of mixed (multiple negative and positive) motives, many of them unclear even to themselves. The tradition of marriage, along with the social, legal, and especially economic advantages of marriage, plays a larger role than is commonly realized (Smock et al., 2005). When asked, though, most Americans characteristically say they marry because they are in love. Now that marriage is no longer necessary for economic survival, the satisfaction of sexual desire, or, for that matter, the rearing of children, love has become the major rationale for getting and staying married. Even upper-class couples and royalty, who have traditionally married for social reasons, now prefer marriages based on love.

Most American couples believe in voluntary marriage. **Voluntary marriages** are *ones based on the assumption that two people will remain married only as long as they are in love.* When they are no longer in love, it's mutually understood they will separate. This seemed to be David and Diane's mode of operating as well. As they came to understand that they no longer loved each other, divorce became a stronger option. When people marry or commit to a significant other on the basis of romantic love—with its emphasis on emotional and physical intimacy—it's no surprise so many relationships and marriages fail; that is, if the love diminishes, the marriage fails. On the other hand, the longer a couple lives together, especially in a satisfying, committed relationship, the more both partners come to value companionate love, with a greater emphasis on personal intimacy and commitment than physical attraction.

The alarming marital divorce rate, hovering at about 50 percent for some groups (Maher, 2003), has prompted social scientists to turn their attention to successful marriages and what makes them work. Until recently, marital "success" meant longevity, that is, how long the marriage lasted. Divorce was universally regarded as a failure on the part of both partners. However, the changes in values in recent years have shifted the emphasis to the *quality* of the marital relationship rather than its duration. Success in marriage is interpreted more in terms of marital satisfaction, especially in the relationship aspects of marriage, such as mature love, intimacy, and companionship. **Marital satisfaction** is *the sense of gratification and contentment in a marriage.* David and Diane's marital satisfaction was often quite low because they argued a great deal. Divorce is often taken to be the price one pays to end a dead or destructive relationship, often to seek a more satisfying one. Such changes pose some nagging questions. Must marital happiness exact such a high price? Can't people live in long-lasting relationships without becoming bored or having a devitalized relationship? In other words, is it possible to have marriages that are both happy *and* enduring? To test your attitudes about marriage, take the Marital Myths Quiz provided in Activity 12–1.

Let's first look at *new* marriages. What are they like? How can we predict whether a new marriage will survive? John Gottman and Sybil Carrere (2000) have longitudinally studied marriages. When a newly married couple argues—and most do—Gottman claims he can tell within 3 minutes whether the marriage will flourish or fail. Newlyweds heading for divorce start an argument by sending out hostile vibes through their tone of voice, facial gestures, and what they say. The biggest problems occur when the woman brings up an issue "harshly" and critically, and the man responds with great negativity. Other research has shown that women initiate discussion about relationship problems about 80 percent of the time (Peterson, 1999a).

Happy couples argue, but when they do, they use five times more positive than negative behaviors (Fincham, 2003). For example, when the wife is angry, the husband might inject humor into one of his responses. Such playfulness helps to reduce emotional tension caused by the conflict. Happy couples also accept the fact that they will have differences with which they will always have to cope. For instance, one partner might not be very talkative while the other partner prefers to engage in extensive conversations. Tolerating these inevitable differences leads to happier marriages.

Other research exists on what keeps love alive. Becoming more attitudinally similar is one factor (Kalmijn, 2005). When a couple's attitudes are measured early in their relationships, the partners' attitudes may differ. However, with the passage of time there is attitude alignment, wherein their attitudes become more similar and, thus, less likely to cause arguments. An example of this is where the couple initially disagrees about methods of birth control (e.g., he wants her to use birth-control pills; she fears side effects and wants him to use condoms, which he hates). Later in the relationship, there may be more attitudinal similarity, with partners settling on a third type of birth control.

Because it is thought to serve as a maintenance strategy to keep the relationship alive, self-disclosure is also important. **Self-disclosure** is *the sharing of intimate or personal information with another.* Sprecher and Hendrick (2004) found that men and women

---

ACTIVITY 12–1

MARITAL MYTHS

Some truisms about marriage follow. Indicate which of them you think are true (T) and which are false (F). Then check your responses by consulting the correct answers at the end of the chapter.

1.	More than 9 out of 10 Americans eventually marry.	T	F
2.	Partners who live together before marriage are less apt to get divorced than those who did not do so.	T	F
3.	Marriage should be a 50–50 partnership.	T	F
4.	Husbands and wives should be best friends.	T	F
5.	Differences and incompatibilities between partners are the major causes of marital dissatisfaction.	T	F
6.	Married people are happier and healthier than those who remain single.	T	F
7.	Most divorces are initiated by women.	T	F
8.	Extramarital affairs will destroy a marriage.	T	F
9.	Children are damaged more by a legal divorce than by remaining in an intact but unhappy home.	T	F
10.	Married people tend to live longer than unmarried people.	T	F

---

indicate similar high levels of self-disclosure in close relationships. When high disclosure is present, the researchers established that there are high relationship esteem (i.e., confidence in the partner), good relationship quality, and high responsiveness between the partners. Couples who eventually marry typically maintain the same high levels of disclosure. Self-disclosure, then, is a good quality, so even though raising the issue about a partner's sexual history is sticky, it is often the safest route to safe sex and may bolster the relationship.

On the other hand, self-disclosure carries the risks of rejection due to a particular disclosure and of ensuing insecurity. In order to feel secure in a relationship, people need to believe that their partners see qualities in them that merit attention, nurturance, and care (Murray, 2005). When one partner of a couple feels threatened and rejected, his or her self-esteem may diminish, which subsequently diminishes closeness. Murray suggests that only when people are able to quell their concerns about self-protection are they free to think and behave in ways that create the kinds of bonds that will satisfy their need for connectedness.

Gottman (Gottman & Carrere, 2000) also claims there are certain emotions and styles that prove toxic for new marriages. Criticism, contempt, defensiveness, and withdrawal tend to be particularly destructive. Not being good friends is one other factor that destroys marriages—one partner does not give the other partner the benefit of the doubt in difficult times or remains emotionally disengaged in the relationship. Similarly, Rauer and Volling (2005) discovered that negative emotions also end relationships or cause discord, especially men's negative emotions.

The flip side of the question, then, is what characterizes long-term, satisfactory marriages. First, a major factor identified in almost every longitudinal study of marriage is "joint problem-solving ability." This factor is mentioned by over two-thirds of the highly satisfied couples but by one-third of the unsatisfied couples. Second, when asked specifically to cite the factors they believe contribute to the longevity of their relationship, almost half of the satisfied couples say they "have fun" together and cherish such experiences, yet fun, humor, and playfulness are not even mentioned by the mildly satisfied and unsatisfied couples.

Third, one of the best predictors of marital success is the quality of the couple's communication—even before marriage—presumably because it is more *how* differences and problems are handled than how frequently they occur. David and Diane thought they were good communicators before they were married, but perhaps they were not, because rather than discuss negative events they both suppressed their anger and withdrew from one another until the pent-up anger made them explode in rage. Fourth, one of the strongest predictors of marital success is "affective affirmation"—the communication of loving, accepting attitudes or the unconditional approval of one's mate. Diane's sometimes sharp criticism of David's couch potato behavior certainly was not approving or affirming of him. David's taunting of Diane when she went into one of her sulks was also not productive. We would predict that Diane and David need to improve their communications if they are to have a long and happy relationship.

Other factors found to contribute to long and happy relationships include empathic ability for understanding a partner's feelings, a good balance of time spent together and separately, a satisfying sexual relationship, and mutual willingness to make adjustments to each other (Schwartz, 2002). Finally, there are demographic factors that also correlate with successful marriages (Bramlett & Mosher, 2003). If the wife grew up in a two-parent home, is college-educated, is White, and has a religious affiliation of any kind, the marriage is more likely to last (Heaton, 2002). Marital stability is good in the sense that research finds that marriage provides a protective factor to partners; that is, marriage, but not necessarily cohabitation, enhances one's psychological well-being (Kim & McKenry, 2002).

Such findings support the importance of companionate love in long-term happy marriages and other committed relationships. That is, happy couples are more apt to place importance on interpersonal intimacy and commitment to a lasting relationship than on physical satisfaction. Couples who are fortunate enough to sustain a vital sex life, more often because of the quality of their sex life than the frequency of intercourse, may experience **consummate love**—*the balanced combination of intimacy, commitment, and passion.*

ADJUSTING TO INTIMATE RELATIONSHIPS

Whether or not couples achieve a lasting, happy relationship depends to a large extent on what happens after they marry or commit to one another in some other way—over and above how well matched they are in such matters as compatibility. Of great importance is each partner's flexibility and willingness to change, especially in our rapidly changing society. A major difference between today's couples and those of the past is the lack of clearly defined roles for each partner. The changing nature of gender roles creates problems for all types of couples as they settle down to live together. Even the most mundane tasks may become a problem, as with David and Diane. Who cooks? Who takes out the trash? Who writes the checks? Getting along in a committed relationship, though, involves the larger questions of authority, fairness, power sharing, and fulfillment of needs. In this section, we'll discuss several important areas of adjustment, including the sharing of responsibilities, communication and conflict, sex, and the changes in the relationship over time. Here, **couple adjustment** means *the changes and adjustments in a couple's relationship during the course of their committed or married life.*

Sharing Responsibilities

Partners, especially marriage partners, are sharing responsibilities to a greater degree today than in the past. As a result, the respective role expectations between partners, especially married couples, are becoming more flexible and functional. More women, for example, are sharing the provider role by working outside the home. Interestingly, women are better than men at preventing stress spillover between work and home (Martin, 1999). Men are expected to provide greater emotional support in the relationship, including help with child rearing. Decision making has also become more democratic, especially among dual-income couples.

A major area of adjustment for many couples concerns employment outside the home. Today, most women like the option of working outside the home and feel it helps their relationship and family. Realize, however, that household tasks and the amount of time needed to complete them are constant whether both individuals in a relationship work outside the home or not. In American families, women overall perform 65 to 75 percent of the household chores. Diane often complained to David that after they started living together, she did 150 percent of the daily chores! David retorted that this was fair. He was going to school *and* working; she, on the other hand, was only attending school.

If women do work outside of the home, does this mean that they will do fewer chores or that their mates will assist with housework? Several studies demonstrate that women still do more housework than men even when the women work outside of the home (Sayer, 2005). Consequently, when the woman serves in other multiple roles such as child or parent care provider and is also employed, she might well feel exhausted. Besides her anger with David, this feeling will likely be one Diane experiences if and when she obtains a job.

Although egalitarian relationships seem to be the ideal, one difficulty that comes with the increased sharing of responsibilities is the issue of fairness. More specifically, there is a tendency for each partner to want greater rewards at no additional costs. Indeed, perceived inequity is one of the great instigators to conflict (Fincham, 2003). One person may want the partner to work to help pay the bills but still expect the partner to continue doing all the same chores as before. In turn, the other partner may want to keep most of his or her earnings but expect the other partner to help out more around the house. Research has shown that when husbands increase their share of the housework, marital quality improves for women but not for men (Amato, Johnson, Booth, & Rogers, 2003). Interestingly, gay couples are more likely to have a fair distribution of domestic duties as well as incomes that are more similar (Dunne, 2000; Kurdek, 2005). More couples need to learn means to resolve these issues so that domestic work is equitably distributed. Three interactive factors that boost men's housework performance are: whether in their childhoods their mother worked, a father was present in the home, and the man currently is married (Gupta, 2006). Married men who live in divorce-friendly societies are also more likely to help with housework (Yodanis, 2005).

Communication and Conflict

These ongoing historic and marital changes in responsibilities make communication and conflict management even more important in committed relationships. Few committed couples never argue. Although many couples argue, the priorities of particular problems vary from couple to couple. For instance, some couples feel conflicts over money are one of their leading problems. Some regard sexual incompatibilities as the major problem. Other couples complain of unrealistic expectations, lack of affection, and power struggles. Other problems include problems related to child rearing; with the birth of a child comes a decline in passionate love (Puterbaugh, 2005; Ceballo, Lansford, Abbey, & Stewart, 2004) and an increase in dissatisfaction (Kantrowitz & Wingert, 1999). Other issues that create conflict are in-laws and romantic or sexual affairs (Yarab & Allgeier, 1997). Drugs, problematic drinking or money spending, and jealousy also predict conflict (Fincham, 2003). However, the most common problem, appearing at the top or next to the top of almost every list, is difficulty in communication. Again and again, husbands and wives like David and Diane complain, "We just can't talk to each other." For example, adult children often find themselves sandwiched between caring for their aging parents and their own children as well as holding jobs (Lawrence, Goodnow, Woods, & Karantzas, 2002). Such multiple roles are often, but not always, stressful (Stephens & Franks, 1999). The stress might be miscommunicated or not communicated at all until it explodes in a fight. If members of a couple would discuss what is bothering them at the onset rather than waiting for the issue to escalate, there likely would be fewer fights in intimate relationships.

Why can't couples communicate? They usually communicate very well with their friends and siblings. Partners do talk to each other all the time. They say such things as "What are we having for dinner?" and "I'll be home later than usual tonight." This type of communication is easy enough. The failure in communication tends to occur at a deeper level of sharing feelings, expectations, intentions, and personal needs. It's in these areas that partners have trouble getting through to each other. In most instances both partners long for intimacy and tenderness. The price of being open, however, may be vulnerability. Settling into a kind of guarded communication, each partner may tend to hold back. These difficulties in communication are further compounded as couples try to mesh their lives more closely. As they become involved with each other, some areas of disagreement are inevitable, much as was true for Diane and David. As couples struggle to resolve their disagreements, the sparks can fly. Interestingly, anger is not always the most destructive emotion in marriage, since both happy and unhappy couples fight.

Making the Relationship Better

Some marital conflict prevention programs are available that couples can utilize *before* they marry (Halford, O'Donnell, Lizzio, & Wilson, 2006). Research has demonstrated that premarital education results in higher levels of satisfaction, better commitment to marriage, lower levels of conflict, and also reduced chances of divorce (Stanley, Amato, Johnson, & Markman, 2006). For those couples that marry and cannot alter their own relationship, after-the-fact couples therapy might be a viable solution (Wood, Crane,

Schaalje, & Law, 2005). The assumption here is that conflict is not all bad. Indeed, conflict is an inevitable part of vital, close relationships; it may help individuals learn more about themselves and each other and may deepen their relationship. Stated a different way, marital discord can be a growth experience.

One approach advocated by couples counselors is emotion-focused therapy, which has been demonstrated in a statistical literature review (meta-analysis) to be the most effective of all therapies for relationship problems (Wood et al., 2005). **Emotion Focused Therapy or EFT** is *a cognitive therapy that provides a technique for changing basic thought and emotional patterns* (Underwood, 2002a). Specifically, the goal of EFT is to help partners feel securely connected by fostering feelings of safety, accessibility, and responsiveness. Couples are usually taught active listening, where one partner can paraphrase what the other has said, in order to encourage a better relational environment between them. Once the feelings of security and receptiveness develop, couples can better process and send clear messages to each other, see each other's perspective, and do collaborative problem solving (Johnson & Patz, 2003). The success rate for this form of couples therapy is claimed to be high, purportedly as high as 70 to 75 percent (Underwood).

Couples therapy, however, cannot redeem all marriages. A review of the therapy literature demonstrates that couples of younger ages, lower levels of depression, flexibility regarding gender roles (Bray & Jouriles, 1995), and egalitarian attitudes (Gray-Little, Baucom, & Hamby, 1996) leave therapy the most satisfied. Likewise, couples in therapy who are similar in their coping strategies are more satisfied with their marriages than those whose strategies differ (Ptacek & Dodge, 1995). Similarly, couples that use "repair attempts" (such as humor in midfight) have happier marriages in the end (Fincham, 2003; Kantrowitz & Wingert, 1999).

David and Diane, rather than engage a family therapist, used another option—a family mediation service. **Mediation** is *intervention in a conflict by a neutral third party who assists the conflicting parties in managing or resolving their disputes* (Duffy, 1991). Mediators, the neutral individuals, can manage more than family disputes, whether the conflicts are between married individuals or couples seeking to dissolve their marriages. For example, mediators are often used to intercede in neighborhood, school, consumer, and other disputes. Here the focus is on committed relationships, such as marriage. In family mediation, the mediator listens as both sides tell their stories and then tries to help them find concrete and mutually agreed-upon solutions to their problems. For example, Diane complained that David did little housework, and David defended himself by saying that he was tired from work. The mediator worked out an agreement that Diane would cook dinner and David would do the dishes each night. On evenings when they were too tired to prepare dinner and do the dishes, they would go out to an inexpensive restaurant and split the bill. Unfortunately, the process did not work well for David and Diane, but for other couples, family mediation has a remarkable success rate, varying from 80 percent to 90 percent agreement, satisfaction with the process, and compliance with the mediated agreements (Duffy). There are family mediators and mediation centers in every state in the United States; most large cities have their own centers. Mediation as an alternative to courts, especially when children are involved, has grown enormously in the last few years (McGillis, 1997; Underwood, 2002b).

Sexuality

Partners such as newlyweds bring greater sexual knowledge and experience to their marriages today than in the past, but they're also more likely to judge their sex lives by higher standards. Couples today are engaging in sexual intercourse more frequently than couples did in the past (Smith, 2003), with an average of two to three times a week for couples in their 20s and 30s. They're also open to a wider array of sexual practices, use a greater variety of sexual positions, and engage in sex for a longer time.

The longer couples—unmarried and married alike—live together, the less frequently they have sexual intercourse (Brewis & Meyer, 2005; Smith, 2003). Reasons usually cited include the lack of time or physical energy. Perhaps a more important factor is the decline of sexual ardor because the partners have become "accustomed to each other." The decrease in physical vigor associated with aging is also a related factor, especially among couples in middle and late adulthood. Couples with children also complain about the lack of privacy. Actually, the longer couples are married, the more attention they pay to the *quality* of sex rather than to its frequency, though these two are related. Do couples have sex more frequently because they are happy in their marriage? Or does the frequency of sex serve to strengthen a couple's love? It's hard to tell. One point is clear: For most couples, though not necessarily all, a good sex life and a happy relationship go together.

Most couples aspire to the ideal of sexual monogamy, whether they adhere to it or not. But when asked if they've ever had sex outside of marriage, it's a different story. Traditionally, the double standard in heterosexual sex has permitted men (e.g., husbands) to engage in extrarelational sex more than women (Masters, Johnson, & Kolodny, 1995), but this too is changing. Today, researchers estimate that between 20 to 50 percent of American women and 30 to 60 percent of American men have engaged in extramarital sex (Vangelistic & Gerstenberger, 2004). Note that the estimates vary wildly depending on the study methodology and samples polled. Infidelity is both a cause and consequence of poor marital quality (Previti & Amato, 2004). Having had a high number of prior sex partners, being male or African American, and thinking about sex several times a day are also predictors of marital affairs (Treas & Giesen, 2000).

Changes Over Time

Around the same time that David and Diane married, two of their friends from the same college, Reshia and Erwin, also married each other. After only 2 years of marital bliss, Diane and David's marriage goes steadily downhill. One squabble leads to another; within a few years they are headed to divorce court. On the other hand, their friends who married one another the same summer report that their marriage has become happier with each passing year. They are saddened to learn that their friends David and Diane are on the brink of divorce.

How do these patterns develop? What makes them persist? Is there any hope that unhappy marriages can be saved? Let's look at the communication and thought patterns in which happy and unhappy couples find themselves. Couples who are happy tend to make relationship-enhancing attributions for the partner's behaviors. Couples who are unhappy tend to make distress-enhancing attributions (Gordon, Friedman, Miller, & Gaertner, 2005). To make an **attribution** *means to search for the cause of our own or another person's behavior.* We can attribute the cause to the person, such as blaming traits, or to something external, such as to fate or to the situation. If a husband, for example, does something negative such as forget his wife's birthday, the wife can attribute the forgetfulness to the fact that her husband is unreliable and uncaring *or* so busy at work that he simply and unintentionally forgot. In happy couples, the wife makes the attribution that the husband is just plain busy and unintentionally forgot. In unhappy couples, the wife makes the attribution that the husband is unreliable and uncaring.

TABLE 12–1

AN EXAMPLE OF ATTRIBUTIONS OF HAPPY AND UNHAPPY COUPLES

	In *Happy* Couples the Wife Says:	In *Unhappy* Couples the Wife Says:
Positive event: The husband remembers his wife's birthday with a present.	"He's so sweet; he never forgets my birthday."	"Hah, he's up to something; he never gives me gifts unless he wants something from me, like forgiveness."
Negative event: The husband forgets his wife's birthday.	"He hardly ever forgets: he must be having a hard week at work."	"That's just like him to forget; he never remembers events important to me."

On the other hand, if a wife does something positive for her husband, such as surprise him at work with a birthday party, the attributions are the reverse. In the happy couple, the husband attributes the surprise to his wife's kind heart. In the unhappy couple, the husband assumes his wife merely wants to impress his coworkers or check up on him because she doesn't trust him. Research has shown that intentional negative trait attributions distance partners and hurt feelings (Vangelisti & Young, 2000). Attributions play a large role in causing and maintaining relationship distress (Gordon et al., 2005). They can also play a role in relationship happiness.

The lesson here is that couples need to monitor the attributions they make toward each other early in their relationships. If they find themselves in the distress-maintaining attributional mode, they should talk about why they are making these attributions, decide what they can do to reverse the types of attributions they are making, and take other appropriate measures. Table 12–1 provides another example of these attributional styles. Early in their marriage, Diane and David had unfortunately developed this negative attributional style. Let's see what happens to them next.

DIVORCE AND ITS CONSEQUENCES

Diane and David eventually concluded that their marriage could not be salvaged. Unfortunately, like Diane and David's marriage, many marriages now end in **divorce**, *the legal dissolution of marriage*. The divorce rate among Americans has more than doubled in the past 40 years, with approximately one out of every two marriages now ending in divorce. Each year over 1 million couples get divorced, most of them within the first 7 years of marriage (CDC, 2002b; Kantrowitz & Wingert, 1999; Maher, 2003). Twenty percent of first marriages end within 5 years and 33 percent of first marriages end within 10 years (Maher). These data mean that by age 18, 40 percent of American children will have experienced parental divorce (Greene, Anderson, Doyle, & Riedelbach, 2006).

Why the dramatic rise in the divorce rate in America? Many different reasons, ranging from the lack of preparation for marriage to fading religious values, have been put forth. A major factor has been the gradual shift away from the traditional notion that marriage is forever to the idea that the primary goal of marriage is happiness and fulfillment. This shift in values has also been accompanied by changes in the laws that make it easier for couples to get divorced.

The Divorce Experience

The decision to divorce usually comes after a long period of mutual alienation, often accompanied by a separation, in which both partners suffer from damaged self-esteem, hurt, and loneliness. This sounds like Diane and David, doesn't it? In some instances, the estranged couple may have sought help from professionals such as couples counselors, family therapists, or family mediators. Studies by psychologists and sociologists indicate that the wife is the key player in divorce and adjusting to it (Amatoa & Previti, 2003; Crane, Soderquist, & Gardner, 1995). As is true for dating relationships, in heterosexual relationships women are more likely to initiate the breakup than men (Helgeson, 1994). In fact, women make more specific plans and are more likely to implement their plans for divorce. Women also think more about divorce and talk to their friends during the decision making (Crane et al.).

No matter how good or bad the relationship has been, the process of getting divorced is almost always painful (Hendrick, 2006), but it needn't be (Barber, 2006; Rutherford, 2001). Recognize also that for gay couples, the breakup of a long-term, committed relationship can be equally traumatic and distressing. Divorce and the end of a committed relationship, as in cohabitation, is a complex experience because so many things are happening at once. The partners tend to withdraw emotionally from each other or coexist with a great deal of mutual antagonism. The legal aspects of the breakup are not only expensive but emotionally draining as well, including the settlement of property, money, and child custody/visitation issues. Disapproval and rejection by friends, family members, and coworkers can also be distressing. Separating oneself from the influence of a former partner and becoming an autonomous social being again can be difficult. By way of example, David and Diane divorced after 7 years of marriage. They both found it hard to reenter the world of dating and to set up and support independent households. These changes may be quite intimidating and draining at first, but some are potentially the most constructive aspects of divorce in that the individual may experience considerable personal growth (Barber). Nevertheless, it takes most people 2 or 3 years to recover fully from the distress of a divorce, and many do not recover completely (Lucas, 2005). Men typically come out of a breakup with only moderate financial declines while for women the consequences frequently prove more precipitous (Avellar & Smock, 2005). The increasing number of support groups available for divorced people helps to alleviate much of the loneliness and emotional pain that inevitably accompany divorce.

A divorce involving parents can be particularly painful for the parents *and* for the children (Kantrowitz & Wingert, 1999; Maher, 2003; Pedro-Carroll, 2005; Wallerstein & Lewis, 2004, 2005). The courts tend to follow the principle of "the best interests of the child," which traditionally meant that custody was given to the primary nurturer, the wife. Today, there is a tendency to award **joint or shared custody** (*which usually means joint decision making about the child's care*) and in some cases to award custody solely to the father. The partner who is not granted residential custody of the children (i.e., the parent with whom the child does not reside) is usually granted certain visitation rights.

Single-Parent Families

How children are affected by their parents' breakup varies considerably, depending on such factors as the intensity of the parental conflict, the child's personality, the age and sex of the child, whether the child is uprooted from familiar friends in the process, and the custodial parent–child relationship. Some psychologists argue that divorce makes children vulnerable to depression and other psychological disorders (Maher, 2003;

Wallerstein & Lewis, 2004, 2005). On the other hand, studies show that parental discord before and after a divorce influences children's adjustment more powerfully than does the actual divorce (Derdeyn, 1994). Grandparents also suffer when their adult children divorce, because they may not be able to see their grandchildren as frequently as before or at all (Gray & Geron, 1995).

Divorce typically provides children with a double dose of stress. Immediately after their parents' divorce, many children feel resentful and depressed (Maher, 2003). Older children and adolescents are especially apt to exhibit heightened aggression. However, within a few years, most children do adjust to the new living arrangements. Then, about 3 to 5 years after the divorce, there may be a second dose of stress associated with either parent's remarriage (Dunn, O'Connor, & Cheng, 2005). Because most divorced mothers and fathers remarry (CDC, 2002b), many children of divorce gain a stepparent. The stepparent's intrusion into the home may initially be an unwelcome event, disrupting the single parent's relationship with his or her children. All of this turmoil necessitates another period of readjustment.

Children and adolescents today are more likely to grow up in single-parent families, in part due to higher divorce rates and to fewer marriages by pregnant women (Rubin, 1999). The high rate of out-of-wedlock births combined with the greater proportion of women who never marry and those who remain single after divorce all contribute to the increase in female-headed homes and subsequent problems, such as poverty. Children living with a single mother are *six times* more likely to live in poverty than are children with married parents (Maher, 2003). However, this problem is an integral part of a larger, more complex pattern attributable to a combination of social, economic, and cultural factors. Other major factors include the high rates of unemployment, poverty, and housing instability of such single mothers (Sleek, 1998). Many single mothers either hold dead-end jobs or require public assistance or do not receive their child support. This means a large number of children and teenagers are growing up in father-absent, economically deprived homes, thereby setting the stage for problem behaviors such as dropping out of school, delinquency, alcohol and drug abuse, and unwed pregnancy (Maher, 2003). Given these discouraging statistics about the effects of divorce on children, couples need to think carefully about developing a committed relationship that may

More children today are living in single-parent homes due to high divorce rates or to fewer women marrying their babies' fathers.

result in children, especially if the relationship is not a solid one at the onset. There are successful programs designed to assist children of divorce cope better with the myriad stressors associated with family dissolution. One such program is Pedro-Carroll's (2005) *Children of Divorce Intervention Program.*

Remarriage

Despite the painful experience of divorce, most divorced people remarry—one-fourth within 1 year of their divorce (CDC, 2002c; Maher, 2003). Diane did eventually remarry, but David never did. In most instances, a divorced person marries another divorced person, probably because they share similar experiences or are the same age. Then, too, participation in various support groups that have been recently formed, such as Parents Without Partners, increases the likelihood of meeting and marrying someone like themselves.

You might ask, "How successful are these second marriages?" To be frank, it's difficult to answer because the record is mixed. Statistically, second marriages are even more likely to end in divorce (CDC, 2002c). You should be aware, however, that there are a small number of "repeaters," who marry and divorce several times, thus inflating the overall divorce figures for remarriages. Many second marriages are successful both in terms of marital happiness and longevity. When the divorce repeaters are removed from consideration, the outlook for second marriages may be better than previously thought. At least 6 out of 10 remarriages last, which is higher than first marriages. Partners in a second marriage often benefit from their mistakes in an earlier marriage. They know full well the value of give-and-take in a close relationship like marriage. Age and maturity also help. Most of all, remarried people usually realize the value of commitment and thus work harder at their second marriage.

An increasing number of remarriages now involve stepchildren (Pacey, 2005), as mentioned. About half of these children have stepparents, mostly stepfathers because of the tendency for children to live with their mothers. Other children are born after the remarriage of the partners. The majority of remarried couples, however, have children only from the previous marriage, with no children from the remarriage. Only a very small number of *remarried couples have children of their own in addition to children from previous marriages of both partners. Such families are called* **blended families**.

Remarriages involving children pose special demands on the adults as well as the children. The man Diane married after her divorce had two preteen daughters. Diane found coping with the new marriage and her ready-made family trying, especially because she and her husband had little child-free time to build mutual understanding and acceptance of each other (Pacey, 2005). As with Diane, when partners perceive that stepchildren cause family problems, they report more marital unhappiness and more thoughts about divorce in their remarriages (Knox & Zusman, 2001). When the children are young, the stepparent has more opportunity to develop rapport and trust with the children, but when adolescents are involved, it's more difficult for everyone. If the new partner too quickly assumes parental authority, especially in matters of discipline, the children may be resentful. Both parents must make allowances for the children's initial suspicion and resistance.

Part of the problem is that the role of stepparent is not well defined. This problem is often compounded by the child's continued interaction with the remaining biological parent. When both parents in the home develop a good working relationship, talking things out and cooperating on parental issues, stepparent families can do at least as well as intact families, if not better, in many cases.

SUMMARY

LOVE AND INTIMACY

We began the chapter by discussing the intensely satisfying but often unstable nature of love relationships. Although most people retain a stubborn faith in romantic love, they regard it as only the first stage of love, from which a more mature love should grow. Individuals from most Western (individualistic) societies have been exposed to romantic images in the media, have come in contact with someone to love, and have experienced the strong emotional arousal they label as love. Thus, they report the experience of passionate or romantic love. A second type of love, companionate love, in which the company and friendship of the lover is enjoyed, can develop later. Sternberg's view is that ideal love includes equal and generous amounts of the three essential components of love—intimacy, passion, and commitment.

COMMITMENT

Couples who live together before marriage may enjoy greater intimacy than other dating couples; this type of union is known as cohabitation. Cohabitation, however, does not always result in marriage, and marriages after cohabitation are not as likely to last. Most Americans will eventually marry, most of them in their 20s and 30s. People who marry, especially those from individualistic societies, believe in voluntary marriage—the assumption that they will remain married only as long as they are in love. When they are no longer in love, it's mutually understood they will divorce. In contrast, one of the keys to lasting, happy marriages is the couple's commitment to marriage as a long-term relationship and their willingness to communicate and work through their conflicts.

ADJUSTING TO INTIMATE RELATIONSHIPS

A major change in marriage is today's lack of fixed roles for husbands and wives and other committed couples, with a greater sharing of responsibilities between partners than in the past. Difficulty in personal communication continues to be a major problem for many couples. In contrast, good communication is necessary for resolving the inevitable differences and conflicts that surface in any close relationship.

A satisfying sex life is also an important part of a committed relationship like marriage, with a strong association between a satisfying sex life and satisfaction with the relationship itself. Although the average committed relationship tends to devitalize over time, partners who remain open to each other and continue growing in their relationship report increasing happiness.

DIVORCE AND ITS CONSEQUENCES

The divorce rate has more than doubled in the past few decades, with about one out of every two marriages now ending in divorce. Getting a divorce or breaking up a long-term committed relationship involves overlapping and painful experiences, including the emotional, legal, economic, parental, and community aspects. How children are affected by divorce depends on a variety of factors, such as the age and sex of the child and custody arrangements.

Most divorced people eventually remarry, some of them achieving happy marriages. Remarriages involving children from a previous marriage pose special demands on the adults as well as the children. Such families are called blended families. For families troubled by conflict, family mediation and Emotion Focused Therapy offer effective solutions.

SCORING KEY FOR THE MARITAL MYTHS QUIZ

1. True. More than 9 out of 10 Americans eventually marry, most of them in their 20s and 30s.

2. False. As discussed in the text, couples that live together before marriage may be more apt to divorce than other couples, mostly because of the attitudes and values they bring to the marriage. Newer studies, however, are indicating that these findings may be changing.

3. False. Changing circumstances often trigger differing ratios of input between partners. For instance, a 30–70 ratio of husband to wife might be characteristic of a newly married couple in which the man is busy starting a new business, though the ratio might well be reversed (70–30) later in the marriage if the wife works and assumes more responsibilities at home because her husband has a life-threatening illness.

4. True. This factor is mostly true in that love and friendship are overlapping relationships. Sexuality adds a special dimension to marriage and love relationships that is not found in friendships.

5. False. It is the lack of high-quality communication in discussing their differences rather than the differences themselves that is a major cause of marital dissatisfaction.

6. True. Studies show that married individuals report being healthier and happier than single individuals.

7. True. In contrast to the past, most divorces are now initiated by women. One reason may be women's greater concern with the quality of the marriage relationship, with divorcing women reporting more dissatisfaction with their marriages than divorcing men.

8. False. This factor varies. Extramarital affairs may rejuvenate some marriages, make no difference to others, and prove downright destructive to still others. A lot depends on how both partners deal with an extramarital affair.

9. False. Although studies vary, there is mounting evidence that children are damaged more by the conflict-ridden atmosphere of an intact home, especially when it is long-standing, than by the legal divorce itself.

10. True. On the average, married people, not simply happily married couples, live longer than unmarried people. One reason may be the need to look after someone else; another may be the emotional support people receive from their partners.

SELF-TEST

1. Compared to close friendships, romantic relationships are characterized by greater
   a. stability.
   b. trust.
   c. volatility.
   d. acceptance.

2. Couples in long-term relationships characterized by intimacy and commitment but little or no passion exhibit
   a. romantic love.
   b. companionate love.
   c. consummate love.
   d. empty love.

3. A common and destructive emotion in an unhappy marriage is
   a. all of the following.
   b. rejection.
   c. anger.
   d. contempt.

4. Couples with happy and enduring marriages attribute their success to _____ attachments in childhood.
   a. secure.
   b. avoidant.
   c. ambivalent.
   d. intense.

5. Sexual orientation is generally distinguished by
   a. mental illness and extreme emotionality.
   b. attraction to individuals of a particular gender.
   c. transsexuality and bisexuality but not heterosexuality.
   d. confused gender role and hermaphroditism.

6. The most common conflict among married couples is
   a. sharing household chores.
   b. sexual incompatibility.
   c. problems with in-laws.
   d. who earns the most money.

7. Partners in unhappy marriages make _____ attributions about each other.
   a. positive and negative.
   b. distress-enhancing.
   c. neutral but emphatic.
   d. humorous and playful.

8. A blended family is
   a. racially mixed.
   b. like a business partnership.
   c. involves stepparents and their children.
   d. all of the above.

9. Most divorced people tend to
   a. never marry again.
   b. remarry the same partner.
   c. remarry someone who has never been married.
   d. remarry within 1 year of their divorce.

10. What process attempts to bring together divorcing couples with a neutral person to come to agreements about how they will reduce conflict?
    a. family mediation.
    b. cohabitation.
    c. blending.
    d. family therapy.

EXERCISES

1. *Qualities desired in a significant other.* Make a list of some personal qualities you would like in a significant other. You might list a dozen such qualities; then go back and check the three most important ones. Write a short paragraph telling why these three qualities are the most important. You might do the same for personal qualities you would *not* like in a partner. Again, list a dozen such qualities and check the three most important ones. Why do you think these qualities are undesirable?

2. *Qualities you offer to a prospective significant other.* Make a list of the major personal strengths and weaknesses you would bring to a committed relationship. What are the three most desirable qualities you have to offer? What are some of your less desirable qualities that might affect the marriage? If you are already committed to someone or if you are married, you might ask your partner to add to your list. Try to list more desirable qualities than undesirable ones.

3. *Cohabitation.* If you are currently living with a significant other or have had such an experience, write a page or so telling what you learned from this experience. To what extent is your experience similar to that of cohabiting couples described in this chapter? Did cohabitation include serious plans for marriage? What are some of the values of cohabitation? The hazards? Would you recommend this experience to others?

4. *The marriage relationship.* If you are going steady, engaged, living with someone, or married, describe the type of relationship you have with your partner. Are you also friends? Do you and your partner return each other's love? Or is one of you more emotionally involved in the relationship than the other? To what extent are both of you relationship-oriented?

5. *Adjustment.* If you're living with someone or married, what has been your major adjustment in learning to live together? Has it involved learning how to communicate and handle conflict? Or has it had to do with specific problems involving money, house chores, or sex? Select one or two of the most difficult adjustments you've had in your current relationship, and write a page or so about it. Is there anything you learned in this chapter that can help you better adjust?

6. *Your attitudes toward homosexuality.* Have you closely examined your attitudes toward homosexuality? Think about your past reactions when you have found out that someone is gay or have been introduced to a gay person. Have you been open-minded? Have you behaved the same way you did toward other people? If you answer "no" to these questions, why do you think you hold the attitudes you do? Do you think you can or should change your attitudes with regard to the issue of homosexuality?

7. *The divorce experience.* If you have gone through a separation or divorce, write about your experience in a page or so. How has the divorce experience influenced your desire to remarry or recommit to another? If you came from a home with divorced parents, you might write about your experience, telling how you have been affected by your parents' divorce. How has your experience influenced your outlook on marriage? On divorce?

QUESTIONS FOR SELF-REFLECTION

1. Can you be in love with more than one person at a time?

2. How can you tell whether your partner loves you?

3. Are you and your partner equally emotionally involved in your relationship?

4. Do you believe that living together before marriage ensures a happier marriage?

5. If you are living with someone or are married, to what extent are the household chores shared? Is your arrangement fair? Would your partner agree?

6. Do you and your partner "fight fair" so that you can disagree without undermining your relationship?

7. To what extent do you feel that sexual satisfaction and relationship satisfaction go together?

8. If you or your parents have gone through a divorce, what was the hardest part for you?

9. As a single person or single parent, which characteristics do you most desire in a mate?

10. If your current situation—married, cohabiting, single, or otherwise—involves children, how does the presence of children influence your prospects for love and commitment in the future?

11. If you're happily remarried or with another life partner, what makes this relationship better than your earlier ones?

FOR FURTHER INFORMATION

RECOMMENDED READINGS

FRIEL, J. C., & FRIEL, L. D. (2002). *The seven happy things couples do . . . plus one.* Deerfield Beach, FL: Health Communications. Drawing on private practice and research, psychologists reveal what makes couples happy.

GOTTMAN, J., GOTTMAN, J. S., & DECLAIRE, J. (2006). *Ten lessons to transform your marriage.* New York: Crown. Leading relationship experts, cited in the text, present their views and research on making marriage work.

LOVE, P. (2001). *The truth about love: The highs, the lows, and how you can make it last forever.* New York: Simon & Schuster. A therapist discusses the psychological and physiological components of love and the predictable patterns of highs and lows related to it.

MERCER, D., & PRUETT, M. (2001). *Your divorce advisor: A lawyer and a psychologist guide you through the legal and emotional landscape of divorce.* New York: Simon & Schuster. This book shows divorcing persons how to negotiate, keep a healthy perspective, and protect assets.

ROSENBLUM, K. E. & TRAVIS, T. C. (2005). *The meaning of difference: American constructions of race, sex and gender, social class, and sexual orientation.* New York: McGraw-Hill. The authors examine the concept of "difference" in America, with sexual orientation being one difference. They acknowledge that the same social processes may underlie how all differences are construed.

WEB SITES AND THE INTERNET

http://www.smartmarriages.com   The site for the Coalition for Marriage, Families, and Couples Education.

http://www.aamft.org   This site is supported by the American Association of Marriage and Family Therapists. It is a general information source on families; also contains referral information for family therapy.

http://www.qrd.org   This site presents the "Queer Resources Directory." It contains lots of information on homosexuality concerning families, religion, health, gay culture, and so forth.

http://www.divorcecentral.com   This site is for individuals contemplating or experiencing divorce. Laws are available by state as well as chat lines and other supports.

http://www.gettingremarried.com   A web site for those considering remarriage with helpful advice on blended families, second weddings, prenuptial agreements, financial planning, etc.

CHAPTER 13

Stress!

OH NO!—UNDERSTANDING STRESS
Conceptualizing Stress
Stress and You

YIKES!—REACTIONS TO STRESS
Physiological Stress Reactions
Psychological Stress Reactions
How Do You React to Stress?

PHEW!—MANAGING STRESS
Modifying Your Environment
Altering Your Lifestyle
Using Stress for Personal Growth

SUMMARY
SELF-TEST
EXERCISES
QUESTIONS FOR SELF-REFLECTION
FOR FURTHER INFORMATION

Steve arrives at the office late, after a harrowing 30-minute delay on the expressway. He is told the boss wants to see him right away. "I wonder what that's about?" Steve muses to himself, as he takes off his coat and heads upstairs. He's ushered inside the boss's office, only to find the boss pacing back and forth. The boss is furious. The big deal they were counting on with a major corporation has just fallen through. The boss makes it clear that if Steve values his job he'd better have a good explanation. Steve gropes for words. "Frankly, I'm stunned. I can't imagine what happened," he says. "Let me call and talk to the people over there and find out the story." Steve's boss continues making accusations about Steve's incompetence and his uncertain future with the company. Eventually, Steve feels enraged at being treated this way. He is tempted to yell back at his boss but knows this is neither a mature nor productive response. Instead, he returns to his office to cool off. His stomach churning, his neck muscles tense, and his blood pressure rising, he sits down at his desk. He reaches for a Maalox and an aspirin.

OH NO!—UNDERSTANDING STRESS

Steve is discovering that the modern world is no less perilous than the jungle. He feels that extra burst of adrenaline that primes his muscles and steadies his nerves for a fight. Steve knows that the primitive "fight or flight" response used by his Stone Age ancestors is no longer appropriate; in fact, it's dangerous. When people like Steve lash out aggressively with their fists or weapons, they jeopardize the very welfare of society itself. Should they try to escape through alcohol or drugs, they only succeed in making their problems worse (American Psychological Association [APA], 2006a, b). Instead, they must learn how better to manage stress and the intense emotions it arouses in a manner more appropriate for our times.

TABLE 13–1

STATISTICS ON STRESS

- Over half of Americans view job stress as a major problem in their lives.
- One-fourth of American workers say that their stress is so severe that they feel a "nervous breakdown" is imminent.
- More than three out of every five doctor's office visits are for stress-related problems.
- Up to 90% of reported illnesses and disease is stress-related.
- More women than men report feeling superstressed, including 23% of female (as opposed to 19% of male) executives and professionals. In college, about 38% of women as compared to 20% of men report high stress levels.
- Young people are more affected by stress; 75% of 18- to 24-year-olds have suffered from stress at work.

Stress takes a heavy toll on our nation's well-being (Stambor, 2006). Leaders of industry are alarmed about stress causing absenteeism, decreasing productivity, and increasing medical expenses, all of which are estimated to cost businesses over $300 billion a year in the United States (Daniels, 2002). Stress has also become a major contributor, either directly or indirectly, to coronary heart disease, cancer, lung ailments, accidental injuries, cirrhosis of the liver, and suicide—six of the leading causes of death in the United States. Many of the deleterious effects of stress are due to its effect on the immune system (Segerstrom & Miller, 2004). In short, it seems as if our modern way of life has become a major source of stress. Table 13–1 presents other important statistics on stress so that you can judge for yourself how large a problem stress is for modern life.

Just like Steve, a majority of adult Americans experience "high stress" at one time or another. Many report that they feel "great stress" at least once or twice a week or live with high stress every day. Stress has become the price paid for being affluent and successful. Twice as many high-income as low-income people suffer from the tension of stress. Also, the more educated people are, the more likely they are to suffer extreme stress. Executives, managers, and professionals suffer more heavily from stress than those in other occupations. Interestingly, most executives do not use all the vacation time they are entitled to (Daniels, 2002; Guinto, 2005).

Conceptualizing Stress

Stress is difficult to define, partly because it means different things to different people. The overall experience of stress can include instigating causes or stimuli followed by various stress responses, as well as our perception of what is stressful to us as individuals. Most definitions tend to emphasize one of these aspects of stress more than the other. Those that emphasize the *stimuli or instigating factors* describe stress in terms of **stressors**—*the variety of external and internal stimuli that evoke stress*, such as a highly competitive work environment or college roommate conflicts. Not surprisingly, it is often a combination of events or of stimuli that causes stress—such as not being able to start the car on the morning you want to arrive early for an important test. In this case, stress includes the specific efforts needed to start the car (or get a ride) *and* to take the test.

Other specialists believe **stress** can be defined as *the pattern of responses individuals make to events that disturb their equilibrium or exceed coping abilities.* When events disrupt our usual level of functioning and require us to make an *extra effort* to reestablish our equilibrium, we

Daily hassles, such as waiting in long lines, sometimes exert a greater effect on our moods and health than do the major misfortunes of life.

experience stress. Accordingly, besides *behavioral reactions*, stress also involves *physiological reactions* that occur in response to stressful events, such as the increased flow of adrenaline that mobilizes us for an extra effort.

Other experts emphasize the importance of our *perception* of such events. One person, for example, may perceive the car's not starting and being late for the test as a normal part of life. Another person, who responds quite differently, might feel extremely distressed at being late for the exam and that the stress will affect the exam outcome.

We should be careful not to equate stress solely with distress. Instead, stress is a multi-faceted phenomenon that also may even have beneficial effects in some cases, such as when an athlete needs a little stress to become motivated for a big game. Hans Selye (1991; McEwen, 2005), a noted stress researcher, has described four basic variations of stress, each with its own label. *When events have a harmful effect*, stress is correctly labeled **distress**. Unfortunately, much of the stress in modern society is distressing. As noted, stress may also have a beneficial effect (Almeida, 2005; Daniels, 2002; Linley & Joseph, 2004; Oxington, 2005). Beginning a new job, getting married, or taking up an exciting sport like skydiving may have a stimulating effect that results in personal growth. Selye suggests we call this **eustress**, or *good stress*. He has also described two more variations of stress. **Hyperstress**, or *excessive stress*, usually occurs when events, including positive ones, pile up and stretch the limits of our adaptability. For example, individuals who are already under stress at work and home may experience hyperstress when a terrorist attack occurs. **Hypostress**, or *insufficient stress*, is apt to occur when we lack stimulation. Monotonous jobs typically inspire hypostress. Bored people may resort to sensation-seeking behaviors mentioned elsewhere in the book, such as experimenting with drugs or taking up a risky sport such as hang gliding.

There are other ways of categorizing or conceptualizing stress. The study of major life events as obvious stressors comes to mind. Holmes and Rahe (1967; Cassidy, O'Connor, Howe, & Warden, 2004; Almeida, 2005) realized that negative life events, such as the loss of a job or the death of a loved one, are usually quite stressful. At the same time, they acknowledged that positive events such as beginning college or getting married can be stressful, too. Consequently, the most important factor in this approach is *the total impact of various life changes*, both positive and negative, in combination with *the amount of readjustment* these events require. Many studies have found that changes in life intensity as measured by Holmes and Rahe's scale is closely linked with the onset of various illnesses. Accordingly, the combined stress of life events has been related to sudden cardiac death, stroke, diabetes and other chronic illnesses, depression, complications of pregnancy and birth, everyday colds, flare-up of multiple sclerosis, and many other physical problems (Cropley & Steptoe, 2005; Tosevski, & Milovancevic, 2006).

Despite its usefulness, the life-events approach to stress has several limitations (e.g., Bennett & Miller, 2006). First, the particular events selected may not be equally relevant for all groups of people, such as blue- versus white-collar workers or *young adults versus the elderly*. Second, the life-events approach does not take into account how individuals perceive a given change, much less how well they adapt to it. Third, because the life-events approach is built around change, it fails to include a great deal of stress that comes with chronic or repeated conditions, such as a boring job or a long-lasting unsatisfying marriage. Finally, it leaves out the "little things" in everyday life that often get to us, such as losing your car keys or snapping a shoelace when you're in a rush in the morning.

More recently, attention has turned to stress associated with everyday difficulties, such as concerns about owing money or about being stuck in traffic (Bennett & Miller, 2006). Steve, the individual in our opening case, was facing several hassles the day his boss confronted him. He was not only dismayed that his boss was angry and accusatory but he was also confused about why the big deal did not go through. In addition, Steve was having renewed difficulties with his former wife about his visitation with their children. His ex-wife also wanted to increase the amount of child support he paid her, which would financially strap him. Finally, Steve thought he had better buy a new car soon, because his old car had broken down three times in the previous 2 weeks.

Lazarus (1993; Almeida, 2005) has found that daily hassles sometimes have a greater effect on our moods and health than do the major misfortunes of life. However, people vary considerably in terms of what bothers them (Almeida). Among traditional college students, the most commonly reported hassles are anxiety over tests and grades (Kieffer, Cronin, & Gawet, 2006; MacGeorge, Samter, & Gillihan, 2005). Box 13–1 presents supplementary information on college students and stress. Middle-aged people are bothered more by worries over health and money. Professional people feel they have too much to do and not enough time to do it and have difficulty relaxing. Daily hassles common to all groups are misplacing or losing things, worrying over physical appearance, and having too many things to do. Lazarus has found a strong link between daily hassles and psychological and physical health, with people who suffer frequent, intense hassles having the poorest health.

A final approach to conceptualizing stress is *the self-perception of "global"* (or *generalized and pervasive*) *stress* in our lives. Some psychologists call this **chronic stress** as opposed to **acute stress**, which is *stress that is a momentary response to imminent danger and is relieved when the danger is over* (Dinan, 2005; Sagy, 2005). Most medical professionals consider *chronic* stress the most harmful. Steve's boss's surprisingly angry outburst at Steve might be considered an acute stressor, while Steve's long-running feud with his ex-wife is more typical of chronic stress.

Box 13–1

College Students and Stress

College students experience lots of stress, and the causes of stress are often different from those for other groups in our general population. College students, especially in their first year, are exposed to new social norms and customs, different peer groups, work overload, a change in lifestyle, as well as more demands on their time and their self-control than in high school. While in secondary school, an individual may have had guidance from parents on curfews, bedtimes, study routines, and so forth. A college freshman, on the other hand, might attend a college or university where peer pressure to stay up all night and study is the norm.

The transition to college is particularly difficult, with a large number of freshmen reporting overwhelming stress (Pritchard & Wilson, 2006; Reisberg, 2000), but college alone, no matter what year a student is in, stimulates additional stress. For example, one in four students expects to have to work full-time while attending college (*Techniques*, 2000). Curiously, the data on college students also mimic the data on the population at large in that college women report more stress than college men (Hudd et al., 2000; Reisberg) and rely more on emotion-focused coping than do men (MacGeorge et al., 2005).

Stress in college students has been associated with a variety of negative outcomes. Increases in smoking, drinking (especially beer), consuming junk food, and committing suicide among distressed college students have all been documented by researchers (Hudd et al., 2000; Kieffer et al., 2006). A concomitant decline in healthy eating habits, fitness, and other positive health behaviors, such as vitamin taking, are also well documented. Additionally, stressed students are significantly less pleased with their grade-point averages and their health (Hudd et al.). It is unclear whether high levels of stress produce lower grades and poor health or whether poor levels of academic performance and fitness result in added stress (Hudd et al.).

Faculty who are often requested to mentor students have a difficult time gauging how much stress the students are under (Misra, McKean, West, & Russo, 2000). Faculty might not be the best first line of defense for recognizing and reducing college student stress. On the other hand, many campuses offer counseling services for their students as well as workshops on stress reduction, study habits, and career counseling. Many campuses house support groups for common disorders that accompany stress, such as eating disorders or depression.

Do you know what services your campus has available? Perhaps you need to explore them for yourself or someone close to you?

Stress and You

How you perceive a given stressor may make it more or less stressful. Some people take criticism of their work as a personal attack, become highly distressed as Steve did, and waste a lot of energy defending themselves. Other people may take similar criticism as a challenge to improve their work, thereby experiencing less stress. A lot depends on our personal makeup. People plagued by inner doubt, low self-esteem, and suspiciousness may misconstrue even the most routine demands of everyday life as stressful. Age and gender were mentioned earlier as individualized factors that contribute to the perception of stress, with women and young individuals more likely to report higher stress. Other factors, such as personality traits like neuroticism (Zautra, Affleck, Tennen, Reich, & Davis, 2005), can be a factor in the experience of stress. One well-known personality syndrome is the Type A personality, described elsewhere in the book (Chapter 7). Type As are more likely to develop stress-related illnesses because of personal traits. (**Stress-related illnesses** are *those illnesses affected by our emotions, lifestyles, or environment*, such as a stress-related heart attack). People with **Type A personality** syndrome tend to be *competitive, argumentative, time-urgent, ambitious, and impatient as well as hostile* (Jamal, 2005). They judge themselves and others by rigorous standards. When others fail to maintain the high standards set by the Type A individual, the Type A person can be nasty. As a result, Type As keep themselves (and others) under constant stress and are more likely to develop heart disease (Mohan, 2006) than other, more *relaxed* individuals known as **Type Bs**.

Another factor that can add to distress is other people's reactions to us. Prejudice against us because of the groups to which we belong is but one example (Harrell, 2000; Thompson, 2002). Cassidy, O'Connor, Howe, and Warden (2004) sampled young, ethnic minority people (Chinese, Pakistani, and Indian) to examine the relationship between perceived ethnic discrimination and psychological distress. The researchers found that anxiety (distress) significantly predicted levels of perceived discrimination; that is, higher anxiety was related to higher perceived discrimination. The authors caution that cause and effect are not yet known, but this and other research clearly demonstrate a link between stress and discrimination.

Many other *situational factors* (factors outside of the individual) can contribute to our experience of stress. Here are some additional situational factors that contribute alone or in combination to add to our experience of distress:

- *Physical stressors* such as too much to do or too many demands on our time and attention
- *Lack of control* over decisions and demands in our personal life or our work life
- *Unpredictability* of events that therefore find us unprepared to cope with them
- *Lack of social support* from friends and family
- *Poor interpersonal relations* with family members, friends, or coworkers
- *Role conflict* in which one role (for example, a job) conflicts with another role (for example, being a readily available parent)
- *Career concerns* including finding a job, receiving a promotion, and being unemployed
- *Unpleasant or dangerous physical conditions* such as a noisy work environment

With the possibility of affecting thousands of people at a time, terrorism is now a major threat and stimulant for stress in the United States. Terrorism's unpredictability and uncontrollability render it a topic for special treatment and is pursued further in Box 13–2. The list of situational factors certainly is not exhaustive. This unit is long enough, however, to convince you that there are multiple factors, both personal and situational, that contribute to the rising level of stress in the United States.

YIKES!—REACTIONS TO STRESS

Stress manifests itself in a variety of ways. The most common sign of stress is increased nervousness, anxiety, and tension. Many people experience tension headaches, and others say their stress shows up as anger and irritability with others. Some Americans report that stress also takes its toll in fatigue or depression. Other symptoms of stress include muscle aches, stomachaches, an overall feeling of being upset, insomnia, loss of sleep,

Box 13–2

TERRORISM, MASS TRAGEDIES, AND THEIR EFFECTS

Americans need ways to cope with the anxiety produced by senseless tragedies such as the terrorist attacks in New York and Washington, not to mention the continued threat of future attacks. Recent natural disasters such as hurricanes also distress many. No one who sees or hears about a tragedy of this kind is untouched by it—and in an era of instant mass communications, the number of people exposed to such violence in one way or another is significant. Most of us will experience some anxiety and stress that usually fades over time. For some, however, such feelings may not go away on their own.

WHAT ARE COMMON REACTIONS?

Mass tragedies can affect us in many ways: physically, emotionally, and mentally. They can make people feel angry, enraged, confused, sad, or even guilty. When those feelings don't go away over a few weeks, or when they seem to get worse, it may be appropriate to seek help for yourself or the person in your life who is experiencing these difficulties. Among the signs to look for over time are:

- Feeling tense and nervous
- Being tired all the time
- Having sleep problems
- Crying often or easily
- Wanting to be alone most of the time
- Drinking alcohol or taking drugs more often or excessively
- Feeling numb
- Being angry or irritable
- Having problems concentrating and remembering things

THINGS TO REMEMBER WHEN TRYING TO UNDERSTAND DISASTROUS EVENTS

- No one who sees a disaster is untouched by it.
- It is normal to feel anxious about your and your family's safety.

- Profound sadness, grief, and anger are normal reactions to an abnormal event.
- Acknowledging your feelings helps you recover.
- Focusing on your strengths and abilities will help you to heal.
- Accepting help from community programs and resources is healthy.
- We each have different needs and different ways of coping.
- It is common to want to strike back at people who have caused great pain. However, nothing good is accomplished by hateful language or actions.

WAYS TO EASE THE STRESS

- Talk with someone about your feelings—anger, sorrow, and other emotions—even though it may be difficult.
- Don't hold yourself responsible for the disastrous event or be frustrated because you feel that you cannot help directly in the rescue work.
- Take steps to promote your own physical and emotional healing by staying active in your daily life patterns or by adjusting them. This healthy outlook (healthy eating, rest, exercise, relaxation, meditation) will help yourself and your family.
- Maintain a normal household and daily routine, limiting demanding responsibilities on yourself and your family.
- Spend time with family and friends.
- Participate in memorials, rituals, and use of symbols as a way to express feelings.
- Use existing support groups of family, friends, and church.
- Establish a family emergency plan. Feeling that there is something that you can do can be very comforting.

As the anniversary of a disaster or traumatic event approaches, many survivors report a return of restlessness and fear. The psychological literature calls it the **anniversary reaction** and defines it as *an individual's response to unresolved grief resulting from significant losses.* The anniversary reaction can involve several

(continued)

Box 13–2 (*continued*)

days or even weeks of anxiety, anger, nightmares, flashbacks, depression, or fear. Not all survivors of a disaster or traumatic events experience an anniversary reaction.

On a more positive note, the anniversary of a disaster or traumatic event also can provide an opportunity for emotional healing. Individuals can make significant progress in working through the natural grieving process by acknowledging the feelings and issues that surface during their anniversary reaction. These feelings and issues can help individuals develop perspective on the event and figure out where it fits in their hearts, minds, and lives.

SOURCE: Adapted from the web site of the U.S. Department of Health and Human Services—Substance Abuse and Mental Health Services Administration, Mentalhealth.org (February 2003).

compulsive eating or loss of appetite, a feeling of frustration, crying, yelling, and screaming. Research demonstrates that people under stress have more heart attacks and strokes, catch more colds, and respond less well to flu vaccines (Adler, 1999).

Many of these symptoms are part of the body's physiological stress response—automatic, built-in reactions over which we have little control. As previously mentioned, the familiar symptoms of stress can result from our psychological reactions to events that are more dependent on the way we *perceive* the world and our capacity for dealing with it rather than to the actual stressor. In this section, we'll examine both physiological and psychological reactions. We'll also look at how individuals differ in their characteristic responses to stress.

Physiological Stress Reactions

Hans Selye (1991), a pioneer in the study of how stress affects the body, maintains that in addition to the body's specific responses to a particular stressor (e.g., sweating in response to heat), there also is a characteristic pattern of nonspecific physiological mechanisms that are activated in response to almost any stressor. Selye called this pattern the **general adaptation syndrome**. It *consists of three progressive stages: the alarm reaction, the stage of resistance, and the stage of exhaustion.*

Alarm Reaction. In *the initial emergency response to stress-provoking agents, the body attempts to restore its normal functioning.* The **alarm reaction** consists of complicated body and biochemical changes that produce similar symptoms regardless of the type of stressor. For this reason people in the beginning stages of different illnesses often complain of common symptoms such as fever, headache, aching muscles and joints, loss of appetite, and a generally tired feeling.

Stage of Resistance. If our exposure to stressful situations continues, the alarm reaction is followed by the **stage of resistance**, in which *the human organism develops an increased resistance to the stressor.* The symptoms of the alarm stage disappear, and body resistance rises above its normal level to cope with the continued stress. The price of this resistance includes increased secretions from various glands, lowered resistance to infections, and the "diseases of adaptation." Stress-induced peptic ulcers and high blood pressure are common examples, though not all cases of these disorders are induced by stress.

In an important literature review, Segerstrom and Miller (2004) examined the relationship between stress and immune system functioning. They found that many studies emphasize the causal link between exposure to chronic stressors and suppression of the immune system. Furthermore, Glaser (2005) in another review of studies on stress and health confirms that stress makes us more susceptible to viruses —not just colds but HIV, which causes AIDS—and diminishes wound healing as well as induces lower immunity at the cellular level.

Stage of Exhaustion.   If chronic stress continues too long, the **stage of exhaustion** is reached. *The body is unable to continue secreting its hormones at the increased rate, so the organism can no longer adapt to chronic stress. Body defenses break down, adaptation energy runs out, and the physical symptoms of the alarm reaction reappear.* The symptoms of this stage are similar to aging in many respects, except that the symptoms of exhaustion, depending on the severity of one's condition, are more or less reversible.

Selye (1980) originally held that the stress response occurs in reaction to various stressors, including illness. However, his theory also relates how a chronic stress reaction can itself lead to illness and accentuate aging. Continued stress responses use up the body's store of adaptive energy. Although the person who is successfully coping with specific stressors may lead an active, healthy life, each experience of stress uses up some adaptive energy. It might be better to use our energy more wisely rather than wasting it on so many false alarms, which are better ignored. Continual stress can eventually damage the various organs of the body, but different parts of our bodies do not suffer stress at an even rate. Instead, illness or death usually occurs when the weakest parts of our bodies give out. Each person's "weakest link" is determined partly by genetic vulnerability and partly by the type and severity of the stress experienced. In any event, reducing our level of stress may help us lead longer and healthier lives.

There exist today explanations other than Selye's to explain the effects of stress on us. Psychologists often speak of the **fight or flight response** with regard to stress (Korte, Koolhaas, Wingfield, & McEwen, 2005). **Fight**, of course, means *confronting the stressor*, and **flight** means *fleeing from the stressor*. When the stressor is insurmountable, we flee; when it is capable of being vanquished, we often fight it. Specifically, a stress response starts in the brain when the brain detects or perceives a stressor. Certain parts of the brain, such as the **amygdala** (*which directs signal traffic in the brain and triggers an all-systems alarm*) and the **pituitary gland** (*the master gland of the endocrine or hormonal system*), signal the rest of the body to prepare to fight or to flee. The body responds by increasing the flow of various hormones such as adrenaline and cortisol (*Harvard Women's Health Watch*, 2003). Similarly, nerve cells release and respond to various neurotransmitters. These changes cause the rest of the body to change. For example, nonessential processes slow down while the heart races, the senses sharpen, the lungs work harder, and the muscles tense (Johnson, 2003; Lemonick, 2003a; National Institute of Mental Health [NIMH], 2001).

When the stressor disappears or subsides, so, too, do many of the physiological responses, and the body relaxes. Fight or flight is no longer necessary. On the other hand, if the stress response is activated too often or turned on for too long, these emergency responses to stress can actually turn against the body, causing damage. One of the reasons that protracted stress is so detrimental is that certain hormones can stay elevated. Most hormones return to their base rate or to normal after the stressor is gone, but glucocorticoids (e.g., epinephrine) can stay elevated indefinitely, especially if the stress is chronic. Chronic elevation can actually reduce the effectiveness of the immune system some studies show (Lemonick, 2003b). Prolonged physiological response to stress consequently can cause or worsen many of the health problems described earlier (*Harvard Women's Health Watch*, 2003; Shafirkin, 2003).

Other scientists have found the fight or flight explanation of stress responses too simplistic and at the same time have criticized Selye's model for not being more inclusive regarding the physiological mechanisms involved in stress responses. McEwen

(2005) suggests the concepts of allostasis and allostatic load. **Allostasis** means *achieving stability through changes via a process that maintains balance among the physiological factors essential for life,* such as body temperature, blood pressure, heart rate, and oxygen level. **Allostatic load** refers to *cumulative changes that reflect the cost to the body of adapting repeatedly to demands (i.e., stresses) placed upon it.* This view takes into account a time frame. Over the short run, bodily functions associated with allostasis provide *protective* effects *against* stress, but over the long run, stressors can have *damaging effects* and adversely affect our life by resulting in poorer health (McEwen; Almeida, 2005). Put another way, allostasis helps us physiologically manage stress but chronic allostatic overload means we eventually become too distressed. It is, as McEwen suggests, the difference between "stressed" and "stressed out."

Psychological Stress Reactions

Unlike the body's stress reactions, our psychological reactions typically are shaped by learning and are heavily dependent on the way we perceive our world. Included here are a wide variety of cognitive, emotional, and behavioral responses to stress.

Because most stressors evoke **anxiety**—*the vague, unpleasant feeling that something bad is about to happen*—the most familiar psychological reactions to stress are defense mechanisms. They are called **defense mechanisms**, or sometimes "ego defense" mechanisms, because they are used to protect oneself from perceived threat (Cramer, 2003; Thobaben, 2005). Although defense mechanisms are influenced to some extent by learning, many psychologists believe they are *automatic unconscious mechanisms that protect us from the awareness of anxiety, thereby helping us to maintain a sense of self-worth in the face of threat* (see Table 13–2 for examples). The notion of defense mechanisms was dismissed by academic psychology years ago. More recently, social and cognitive psychologists have found evidence for such processes (Baumeister, Dale, & Sommer, 1998; Thobaben).

TABLE 13–2	
DEFENSE MECHANISMS	
Defense Mechanism	**Definition**
Repression	Excluding unacceptable ideas or feelings from consciousness
Denial	Misperceiving threatening objects or events as harmless
Fixation	Continuing a kind of gratification after one has passed through the stage at which it was appropriate
Regression	Reverting to a form of behavior that was more appropriate at an earlier stage of development
Rationalization	Justifying our unacceptable behavior with "good" reasons
Intellectualization	Reducing anxiety by analyzing threatening issues in an emotionally detached way
Projection	Attributing our unacceptable ideas or feelings to others
Displacement	Redirecting threatening ideas or impulses onto less threatening objects
Sublimation	Channeling socially unacceptable urges into acceptable behaviors
Acting out	Relieving anxiety or unpleasant tensions by expressing them in overt behavior
Reaction formation	Developing conscious feelings and behaviors opposite to the unconscious, anxiety-arousing ones

Each of us relies on such mechanisms at one time or another, especially when we feel threatened, and whether the objective situation warrants it or not. As emergency reactions, they diminish our awareness of anxiety and help to maintain our sense of adequacy and self-worth in the face of threat. Because defense mechanisms also involve self-deception and a distortion of social reality, habitual reliance on defense mechanisms can prove maladaptive and can stifle personal growth.

Once a stressor has been interpreted as threatening, a variety of other cognitive functions may be affected. We may become so preoccupied with the stressor that our attention and perceptions are greatly restricted. Memory can also be influenced because of the reduced attention given to the overall situation. Stress can also interfere with our judgment, problem solving, and decision making. Whenever we're under intense stress, we tend to revert to rigid and stereotyped thinking rather than engaging in creative problem solving.

How people behave under stress depends partly on the level of stress experienced. Mild stress can energize us to become more alert, active, and resourceful. Medium stress tends to have a disruptive effect on our lives, especially on complex behaviors such as writing a term paper. Very high levels of stress can be extremely troublesome. Under such stress, people become less sensitive to their surroundings, easily irritated, and more apt to resort to unhealthy coping devices such as consuming too much alcohol or not getting enough sleep. Stress also evokes a wide range of emotions, ranging from a sense of exhilaration in the face of minor, challenging stressors to the more familiar negative emotions of anxiety, anger, fear, jealousy, and discouragement. Stressful life experiences involving separation or loss of friends and loved ones are frequently associated with depression, which is discussed elsewhere in the book.

Fortunately, Steve, the man in the opening vignette, did not suffer from severe stress. Steve was lucky, because at its highest level, stress can be debilitating. Severe stress tends to inhibit behavior and may lead to apathy and immobility, as in clinically depressed individuals who feel helpless in the face of overwhelming frustration or deprivation. In addition, survivors of traumatic events, such as rape victims, terrorists' hostages, and veterans of combat, may cope well at the time of the trauma but months later experience a delayed emotional reaction known as posttraumatic stress disorder (PTSD). **Posttraumatic stress disorder** is *a severe anxiety disorder characterized by symptoms of anxiety and avoidance behavior, resulting from an unusually distressing event such as being assaulted.* Box 13–3 discusses posttraumatic stress disorder in more detail.

How Do You React to Stress?

Each of us reacts to stress, even a repetitious stressor such as college examinations, somewhat differently. Some anxious individuals are more apt to react with bodily symptoms. They may feel jittery, have stomach acid, develop a splitting headache, or experience diarrhea. Others react to stress mentally. Preoccupied by worries, they find themselves unable to concentrate. In many instances, people experience a mixture of physical and psychological symptoms, depending on the particular stress.

There are recognized individual differences in the experience of stress and in coping. Gender, for example, may serve as a valuable "window" that influences not only how individuals appraise stress but also how they cope with stress (Gianakos, 2002). Peter, Hammarström, Hallqvist, Siegrist, and Theorell (2006) suggest that occupational gender segregation and unequal power and control issues exist that may affect how men and women perceive and cope with stress. Vegg, Spielberger, and Wassala (2002) add that

Box 13–3

Posttraumatic Stress Disorder (PTSD)

Posttraumatic stress disorder (PTSD) is an anxiety disorder that can develop after exposure to a terrifying event or ordeal in which grave physical harm occurred or was threatened (NIMH, 2001). The types of events that trigger PTSD usually lie outside the realm of ordinary human loss and grief. Examples are plane crashes, earthquakes, floods, assaults, rapes, hostage taking, torture, murders, and military combat. The most frequent cause for Americans is automobile accidents (Blanchard & Hickling, 2003). Nearly half of the American adult population is exposed to at least one traumatic event during their lifetimes, yet only 10 percent of women and 5 percent of men develop posttraumatic stress disorder (Ozer & Weiss, 2004).

As many as a million Vietnam veterans who took part in heavy combat show signs of serious PTSD—sometimes known as the Vietnam syndrome. The severity of their symptoms is partly due to two factors not present in previous wars. For one thing, civilian casualties were higher in Vietnam than in earlier wars, leading to feelings of guilt. Then, too, the controversial nature of the Vietnam war left many returning veterans feeling unwelcome, giving rise to resentment and rage against society. As a result, Vietnam veterans have experienced above-average rates of divorce, suicide, and hospitalization for alcohol and drug abuse. Many veterans continue to have difficulties readjusting to civilian life. The war in Iraq is predicted to produce an even higher rate of mental casualties than other wars (Baum, 2004; Zabriskie, 2004).

The symptoms of this disorder can begin immediately after the traumatic event or 3 to 6 months afterward (McFarland, 2005). However, it is not unusual for the symptoms to emerge only after a much longer period, which is characteristic of the chronic or delayed forms of the disorder (NIMH, 2001a). Victims involuntarily re-experience the past traumatic event in dreams, which include "flashbacks" of the event accompanied by the original emotions of fear, shock, and horror, especially when they experience reminders of the trauma. They also experience an emotional numbness toward their everyday world. Frequently, they have trouble concentrating at work during the day and difficulty sleeping at night. Feeling alienated from others, they may also lose interest in people. Angry outbursts and irritability are also signs of PTSD. The possibility of PTSD is greatest for those who have suffered past traumas (Ai, Evans-Campbell, Santangelo, & Cascio, 2006). Interestingly, scientists using brain imaging and other sophisticated techniques have found neural changes in victims of PTSD; these physiological changes may account for some of the more chronic symptoms, such as flashbacks and blunted emotions (NIMH).

Scientists today are trying to discover what treatments work best for individuals with PTSD. Possibilities include various medications, group therapy, cognitive-behavioral therapy (discussed elsewhere in the book), and exposure therapy, where the individual repeatedly and gradually relives the trauma under controlled conditions (National Institute of Mental Health, 2001a). Early research also showed that giving individuals the chance to talk about the trauma very soon after the event might reduce the symptoms of PTSD. However, a recent literature review indicates that crisis intervention or debriefing actually may *not* work and, in fact, might impede natural recovery (McNally, Bryant, & Ehlers, 2003). It may also be that various treatments work best for different types of trauma (NIMH) or victims.

women experience multiple and overlapping roles (e.g., occupation versus family) that can create more stress than men experience. Women also react to a wider range of stressors and say they feel stress more often than men (Matud, 2004). Research has also shown that women are more likely to cope with stress through social support (sharing emotions and stressful experiences with their friends) than are men (APA, 2004b).

Finally, Matud (2004) reported more emotion-focused coping on the part of women and more problem-focused coping on the part of men. In **emotion-focused**

Some individuals manage stress with solitude or relaxation while others manage stress by means of social interaction or exercise.

coping *the individual tries to alter the emotional reaction to stress*, for example, by expressing rather than suppressing feelings. In **problem-focused coping** *the individual tries to change the environment or find a solution*, for example, by applying lessons learned from earlier experiences. In the past, psychologists have considered emotion-focused coping less adaptive than problem-focused coping (Austenfeld & Stanton, 2004). However, newer studies are demonstrating that emotion-focused coping is just as adaptive (Austenfeld & Stanton). In fact, positive emotions such as gratitude and love buffer stress during crises such as the terror attacks of September 11, 2001 (Fredrickson, Tugade, Waugh, & Larkin, 2003).

Once you get a personal grip on stress, you can deal with it more effectively. For instance, if you are the physical type, you might choose one of the following relaxers: aerobics, biking, swimming, walking, progressive relaxation, or soaking in a hot bath or sauna. However, if you're more of a cerebral type, you might try one of these relaxers: meditation, reading, crossword puzzles, television, chess or card games, or any absorbing hobby. In most cases, you can choose a combination of ways to unwind. The important thing is to find what works best to reduce stress for you.

Another individual difference is that some individuals seem better able to take stress in stride. Studies of top executives in *Fortune* 500 companies have shown that those who cope with stress most successfully have what the researchers call **psychological hardiness**—*the attitude that allows them to make the most of the situation.* The three trademarks of hardy individuals are feelings of *challenge* (instead of threat), *commitment* (rather than alienation), and *control* (as opposed to powerlessness) (Bonanno, 2004; Maddi, 2005). The executives who do well with stress feel stimulated by change and stress (challenge). They are also intensely involved in what they are doing (commitment), and they are not usually overcome by feelings of powerlessness even in very difficult situations (control). The last issue, control, is especially noteworthy. In probing the relationship among stress, physical illness, and psychological disorders, the importance of personal control recurs again and again. Being able to acknowledge heightened stress, as well as its effects on you, while maintaining reasonable control of yourself and, if possible, the situation at hand is vital to managing stress successfully.

A related concept is **resilience** (Almedom, 2005), or *positive growth or positive adaptation following brief periods of stress after some stressful disruption or extreme adversity* (Campbell-Sills, Cohan, & Stein, 2006). Resilience was once thought to be rare or even pathological; today, however, psychologists understand that it is more common than previously believed (Bonanno, 2004; 2005). Interestingly, it now appears to be the most common trajectory of all after distress and trauma (Bonanno, 2005).

Resilience after trauma is quite different from recovery after trauma. Resilience is characterized by relatively *mild and short-lived disruption* and a *stable trajectory* of healthy functioning across time. Mere recovery after trauma is typified by *significant* disruption to normal functioning that *declines only gradually* (Bonanno, 2005). In other words, resilient individuals bounce back from stressful experiences quickly and effectively (Tugade & Fredrickson, 2004). Such people use humor, positive emotions, cognitive flexibility, cognitive reappraisal, social support, and optimism to cope with adversity (Southwick, Vythilingam, & Charney, 2005), Stress and trauma, therefore, need not be negative or stressful. The important message here is that individuals can and do experience personal growth during adverse times.

By taking the self-assessment in Activity 13–1, you can begin to identify your own stress-coping style.

ACTIVITY 13–1

WHAT'S YOUR STRESS STYLE?

INSTRUCTIONS: *For each of the following statements, indicate your level of agreement by circling the appropriate number below the statement.*

1. When I am under stress, I become angry more quickly than usual.

   Strongly disagree   1   2   3   4   5   6   7   Strongly agree

2. During stressful times, my health habits (such as maintaining a good diet) decline.

   Strongly disagree   1   2   3   4   5   6   7   Strongly agree

3. When I am under stress, I have difficulty concentrating.

   Strongly disagree   1   2   3   4   5   6   7   Strongly agree

4. Despite being in sticky situations, I find I can resort to humor or positive thinking to help myself get through it.

   Strongly disagree   1   2   3   4   5   6   7   Strongly agree

5. When I am under stress, I react with more anxiety than do other people.

   Strongly disagree   1   2   3   4   5   6   7   Strongly agree

6. At times of stress, my nervous habits (such as nail biting or hair twisting) become more prevalent.

   Strongly disagree   1   2   3   4   5   6   7   Strongly agree

7. Stress makes my memory worse.

Strongly disagree   1   2   3   4   5   6   7   Strongly agree

8. When I am under stress, I become easily frustrated and tense.

Strongly disagree   1   2   3   4   5   6   7   Strongly agree

9. Stress makes me cry more easily than at other times.

Strongly disagree   1   2   3   4   5   6   7   Strongly agree

10. I have a harder time learning as well as studying for exams when under stress.

Strongly disagree   1   2   3   4   5   6   7   Strongly agree

11. I find stress challenging at times and sometimes even exhilarating.

Strongly disagree   1   2   3   4   5   6   7   Strongly agree

12. After a distressing event, I take a few quiet moments to learn about myself and my reaction.

Strongly disagree   1   2   3   4   5   6   7   Strongly agree

SCORING: This self-assessor was designed specially for this book. Your findings, therefore, should be used only as a tool to stimulate critical thinking about how you cope with stress.

Emotional reactions to stress are measured in questions 1, 5, and 8.

Behavioral reactions to stress are measured in questions 2, 6, and 9.

Cognitive reactions to stress are measured in questions 3, 7, and 10.

Resilient reactions to stress are measured in questions 4, 11, 12.

Add up your points for each reaction cluster and write your total for that cluster in the space provided below:

Emotional reactions _____

Behavioral reactions _____

Cognitive reactions _____

Resilient reactions _____

Total for all reactions _____

Now decide if the scale did an accurate job measuring your typical reaction. For example, would your family or best friend concur with your scores? If you scored highest for emotional reactions, would they agree that you are emotional in stressful situations? Also, consider your total score. In some ways it indicates whether your reactions to stress are too strong or perhaps whether you are under high levels of stress. Now think about ways that you can better react or cope with stress and how you can reduce the total amount of stress that you have.

PHEW!—MANAGING STRESS

Managing stress successfully involves more than relying on the automatic, symptom-reducing reactions to stress, as helpful as these may be. Managing stress means taking charge, directing and controlling our responses to stressors, thereby modifying the overall stress. Steve, for example, realized that punching his boss was not a productive response to the distress and, in fact, could cause him much trouble. Instead, he returned to his office to process thoughtfully what had happened. While there are many other ways to cope with stress, most of them fall under two major headings: modifying your environment and altering yourself or your response.

Modifying Your Environment

Soon after his boss berated Steve, a camera he had on special order finally arrived. He quickly discovered it was not exactly what he wanted. What should he do? What would you do? You could return to the store and tell the clerk a mistake had been made and then proceed to order the correct model of camera. Or you could simply accept the camera on hand and leave, making sure never to buy anything in that store again. There's yet another option: You could refuse to accept the order and, instead, choose another camera more to your liking from among those already in stock.

These responses illustrate some of the basic ways to modify your environment: assertiveness, withdrawal, or compromise. They are considered *environmental* rather than personal responses to stress because they either change your environment or change the responses of others who are creating stress for you. Let's look at each of these strategies.

1. Assertiveness is the preferred way to manage stress whenever there is a reasonable possibility of success. Assertiveness is *the expression of one's rights and feelings in a direct way without violating the rights of others*. Such an approach consists of direct attempts at modifying the stressful situation itself. Common examples are returning a defective product to a store or speaking up in response to an unreasonable request (see Box 13–4).

For example, if Steve were an unassertive person, he could have let his boss take advantage of him on various occasions, which would only build up Steve's resentment. Then in the moment of anger when his boss confronted him about the deal falling through, he might have lashed out aggressively, making the situation even more stressful. In contrast, assertiveness has to do with expressing rights and desires without infringing on those of others. Assertiveness is a rational and constructive way of handling stress, which in turn tends to alleviate the stress involved. Steve could have assertively told his boss how frustrated he became when he was given conflicting orders, as when the boss wanted him to close two important deals at the same time. As often happens, his boss might be unaware of the inconsistencies in his requests and change his ways, alleviating much of Steve's stress.

2. Withdrawal means *removing oneself physically or emotionally from an activity, organization, or person*. Withdrawal may be an appropriate response to stress, especially when a stressful situation cannot be successfully modified through assertiveness or compromise (discussed next). By returning to his office the day his boss yelled at him, Steve practiced withdrawal. Another example of withdrawal would be the consumer

Box 13–4

HOW ASSERTIVE ARE YOU?

Assertiveness has to do with expressing your rights, thoughts, and feelings in a direct way without violating the rights of others. Imagine yourself in each of the following situations. What would you say?

- When your parents are giving unwanted advice
- When a friend asks you for a loan
- When you're being pressured to buy something
- When refusing an unreasonable request
- When interrupted while you're speaking

In the last situation, to keep quiet would simply be nonassertive, but to blurt out "Shut up!" would be aggressive or hurtful. Instead, an assertive response might be, "Excuse me, I'd like to finish what I was saying."

Ironically, the lack of assertiveness in everyday relationships produces more resentment and alienation in the long run than assertiveness. In contrast, assertive responses not only preserve your self-respect but also facilitate good communication, which is essential for mutually satisfying relationships.

who actively shops at a different store after getting no satisfaction from the first store's customer service center. Withdrawal is neither good nor bad in itself. Much depends on how it is used. On the one hand, if someone habitually withdraws from stressful situations, that person may drift into a constricted lifestyle that prevents adequate adjustment or personal growth. On the other hand, the use of withdrawal as a temporary strategy may be a valuable means of coping with stress that has become overwhelming or detrimental to one's health. Some examples of temporary withdrawal are destitute students dropping out of school until they can earn more money, or marital partners agreeing to a separation while they seek counseling. When no suitable solution is forthcoming, despite the best efforts of the people involved, a permanent withdrawal may be more appropriate.

3. **Compromise** is still another adaptive response to stress and *occurs when an adjustment is made by modifying opposing ideas or behaviors.* In contrast to withdrawal, compromise allows us to remain in the stressful situation but in a less active way than does the assertive approach. Compromise is most likely to be used when someone holds a higher rank or authority than another or when both participants are at a standstill. The three most common types of compromise are conformity, negotiation, and substitution.

Conformity *as a response to stressful situations involves a change in our behavior due to another's direct influence.* Let's say you work as a buyer for a large corporation that has just established a more elaborate procedure for purchasing, including much more paperwork and more signatures for approval. At the outset, you detest the change. You may comply outwardly by adopting the new procedure even though you dislike it. Or you can conform to the new demands because you like your superiors and coworkers enough to accommodate the added stress. In as much as jobs are not easy to get or hold, you may take the new procedures in stride and decide that changing your attitude is the most realistic approach, because endless strife and resentment may be more stressful than accommodation or outright assertion. The key question in any type of conformity response, however, is whether the price of the compromise is worth it.

Negotiation is a more active and promising way to achieve compromise in many stressful situations. Negotiation means that *we make mutual concessions with another person.*

Steve, for example, might have calmly negotiated more time to explore what went wrong with the big deal, with his boss agreeing that he would give Steve only 3 days to explore the deal and navigate it again before their next meeting. Often used in the public area of labor management and political disputes, negotiation has now become more widely used at the interpersonal level among coworkers, marriage partners, and friends. Negotiation is preferable to conformity wherever possible because it involves mutual accommodation among the participants.

Substitution means that *we seek alternative goals with another person*. Substitution is another way to achieve compromise with another person when negotiation or conformity is not appropriate. If a woman desires to resume her college education but has small children and cannot enroll full-time, she may decide that the best alternative is to attend part-time. In this case, a substitute means was found to achieve the same goal. At other times, it may become necessary to choose a completely different substitute goal. For example, if Steve explores why the deal fell through, finds that indeed it was his fault, and does not want to be on the receiving end of his boss's ire, he might seek a position with a different company.

Compromise itself is neither good nor bad. Much depends on the relation between the satisfaction achieved and the price paid for the reduction of stress. Habitual compromise may bring more frustration and conflict than a more assertive approach. Too many people suffer in stale jobs or conflict-ridden marriages longer than necessary because compromise has become the easy way out. A life of passive accommodation to undue stress may be more stressful than an assertive or avoidant approach.

Altering Your Lifestyle

We ultimately have more control over ourselves than over our environment. As a result, we may choose to modify something about ourselves or about our behaviors as a way of better managing stress. There are many possibilities, including developing greater tolerance for stress, altering our everyday habits, learning to control distressing thoughts, acquiring problem-solving skills, and seeking social support.

First, *build up a greater tolerance for stress*. **Stress tolerance** can be defined as *the degree of stress you can handle or how long you can put up with a demanding task without acting in an irrational or disorganized way*. Many of the competent, successful people we admire are probably under a great deal more stress than we realize; they've simply acquired a high tolerance for it. Greater tolerance for pressure—deadlines, competition, criticism from others—usually comes with greater experience and skill. People in high-pressure jobs such as police, surgeons, and firefighters have learned how to stay calm in the face of stress through months and years of experience on the job. Our tolerance for frustration can also be improved by selecting reasonable goals and adjusting our expectations to match the realities of the immediate situation. Likewise, expecting too much of ourselves is a frequent source of frustration. Each of us is disappointed with ourselves from time to time. Rather than wallow in self-pity, it's more helpful to ask what we can do to remedy the situation and then learn from our experience for future reference.

Another important aspect of stress tolerance is the ability to function well despite anxiety. There are many instances when it is normal to feel anxious in the face of uncertainty, such as going for our first job interview or flying in a plane during times of imminent terrorist attacks. Competence in these situations may mean carrying out our responsibilities despite feelings of anxiety. Remember, mild to moderate doses of anxiety can stimulate us to do our best, though too much anxiety can interfere with our

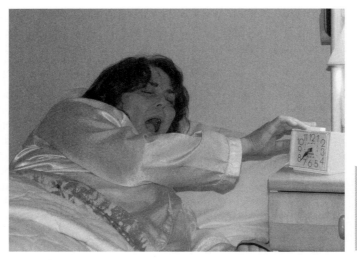

What strategies for managing stress outlined in the text do you practice? For example, do you get enough sleep? Do you get up early enough so as not to be late?

performance. In this case, you may need to control your distressing, anxiety-arousing thoughts, as explained later in this section.

Second, *change your pace of life.* Steve had probably experienced traffic delays before; had he only left earlier on that fateful morning, he would have experienced less stress when his boss was furious over the deal that fell through. You might be bringing a lot of stress on yourself by rushing around and trying to accomplish too much in too little time. A fast pace of life makes you walk, talk, conduct business, and do almost everything faster. Kircaldy, Furnham and Levine (2001) has shown that the pace of life in the United States is already much faster than in other countries. Only Japan seems to have a faster pace. Individuals as young as 18 who feel time pressure have blood pressure that is much higher than individuals who don't put themselves under such pressure (Gupta, 2002). Slowing down, then, serves us well. Frequently, we could lighten the stress by better time management.

In other cases, we need to pace ourselves better. The particular adjustments needed vary with each of us, but consider the following suggestions:

- Get up early enough to avoid rushing.
- Set a radio–alarm clock to your favorite station.
- Take time for breakfast.
- Make a list of things to do; put the most important things first.
- Allow enough time to drive to school or work without rushing.
- Avoid scheduling all your classes back-to-back or on only a few days a week.
- Walk at an unhurried pace.
- Share at least one meal each day with other people.
- Avoid the excessive use of caffeine, alcohol, or drugs.
- Take some time to relax each day. Go for a walk, ride your bike, or take a hot bath.
- Try to exercise regularly. Because the biochemicals related to fight or flight may not dissipate immediately, exercise may help dissipate stress.

- Avoid procrastination; the sooner you begin a task, the less you'll worry about it.
- Concentrate on the task at hand. Unplug the phone if necessary.
- Have a contingency plan in case things go wrong.
- Take time to talk with your friends, especially nonworriers.
- Set aside regular times for study.
- Schedule some relaxation for the weekends to break the cycle of stress.
- Jot down things you don't get done that you'd like to do the next day.
- Unwind before going to bed. Read, listen to music, meditate, or watch comedy on television.

Perhaps there are other changes needed in your lifestyle. What are they? Add them to your list of suggestions for managing stress.

Third, *learn to control distressful thoughts*. Perhaps you've had the experience of glancing at the first question on a test and muttering to yourself, "If the rest of this test is this hard, I'm going to flunk it." Ironically, such negative self-monitoring interferes with your performance, making you do worse on the test. You can control distressful thoughts by using the following strategy. First, become aware of your negative, catastrophic manner of thinking. You'll probably notice how such thoughts lead you to assume the worst, such as "I'll never make it," "How did I get into this mess?" or "What the heck am I going to do now?" Second, formulate positive thoughts that are incompatible with your distressful thoughts. Some examples are "I can do it; just take it one step at a time," and "I'll keep doing my best and see how things turn out." It also helps to relax and give yourself a mental pat on the back when you've successfully managed distressing thoughts. Take a few minutes to acknowledge to yourself, "I did it; it worked. I'm pleased with the progress I'm making."

Another way to manage distressing thoughts is to replace them with humorous thoughts; humor really works to reduce stress (Garrick, 2006; Godfrey, 2004). Do not minimize your stress by making fun of distressing events; rather, take some time to enjoy humor. Read some cartoons, go to lunch with a friend and tell jokes, recall funny events from your life. Humor is a valuable form of coping and can have physiological as well as psychological benefits for distressed individuals. When people laugh, there is a reduction in at least three chemicals associated with stress, and the activity of the immune system frequently is enhanced (Martin, 2001). Humor can also mitigate trauma reactions (Garrick) and reduce anxiety (Szabo, Ainsworth, & Danks, 2005).

Fourth, if needed, *seek help with problem-solving skills*. Most colleges and many community agencies offer a variety of workshops on topics such as assertiveness training, job-hunting skills, and stress management. Some people are wise enough to take such training as a way of bolstering their repertoire of social skills. Others seek it only after encountering problems. Another means for finding help is simply to turn to friends. Numerous studies have shown that we manage stress and trauma more successfully when we have the support of a spouse, close friend, or support group (e.g., Scarpa, Haden, & Hurley, 2006).

Having access to friends and support groups may help to alleviate stress in several ways. Perhaps if Steve had had a trusted office mate with whom he could share his stressful ordeal with the boss, he could have coped better. Why? First, close relationships provide the opportunity to share painful feelings, which if kept to ourselves become more burdensome. Second, friends provide emotional support through their expressions of concern and affection. Third, the understanding and reassurance of our friends may bolster our self-esteem throughout the low periods of our lives. Fourth, concerned friends and support groups may provide information and advice that may help us to reach more effective solutions to our problems, especially support groups that are oriented to a particular problem, such as the death of a spouse. Fifth, friends can enhance positive experiences in our lives (Duffy & Wong, 2003). Remember, though, we don't have to turn to friends only in times of trouble; friends can enhance the experience of joy, too.

Be mindful of the fact that at times other people in our lives may cause more distress than support. Some would call such individuals "toxic people," who drop stress on others without much thought. Here, you are probably thinking of the judgmental spouse, a friend who constantly asks for favors, or a perpetually difficult boss—like Steve's—who puts people under even greater pressure during times of stress. On balance, people under stress who have access to close and supportive relationships enjoy greater emotional and physical health than those without close social ties.

Using Stress for Personal Growth

How we choose to alter our lifestyle or modify our environment is up to us. Stress management, like stress itself, is a personal matter. Each of us faces a different combination of stressful events at work and at home. Also, each of us has our own characteristic level of stress tolerance, such that we experience stress differently. The important thing to remember is that we can do something to manage stress more effectively. We don't have to be passive victims to whom things happen. Instead, we can look at ourselves as active agents who take charge of our lives. No matter how stressful the situation, there's always something we can do to reduce the stress.

Keep in mind that stress can be a valuable means of self-understanding. We don't fully know what we can do until we have to do it. Each time we successfully get through a stressful situation, like a difficult course at school or a trying problem in our love life, we gain in self-confidence. Even experiences of disappointment and failure are sometimes blessings in disguise. Perhaps we weren't ready for the task at hand, or we were pursuing the wrong goals. Sometimes a minor failure today can save us from a bigger letdown later on.

Finally, we can make stress work for us. Remember that stress is not synonymous with distress or stressed out. Too little stress and we become bored and lazy. Too much and we become tense, make mistakes, and get sick more easily. To get the most out of life, each of us needs to find our optimal level of stress and the types of stress we handle best. Properly managed, stress gives zest to life. A stressful situation can challenge us to try harder, evoking our best and bringing personal growth. Managing stress well is a lot like making music with a stringed instrument. Too little pressure and the strings moan and groan. Too much and they snap. But apply just the right pressure and we get beautiful music.

SUMMARY

OH NO!—UNDERSTANDING STRESS

The great majority of adult Americans experience a high level of stress at one time or another. One in four people lives with high stress daily. Stress is defined as the pattern of specific and nonspecific responses an organism makes to stimulus events that disturb its equilibrium and tax its ability to cope. However, stress may have beneficial as well as harmful effects, depending on the person and the situation. A major source of stress is the combination of various life changes, both positive and negative, including major life events as well as daily hassles. At the same time, our overall experience of stress is affected by a variety of personal and situational factors, such as how we perceive events and the degree of control we believe we have over them.

YIKES!—REACTIONS TO STRESS

Some reactions to stress occur more or less spontaneously, including physiological reactions as well as certain emotional, behavioral reactions. Many of our body's reactions to stress can be understood in relation to Selye's general adaptation syndrome, either in the initial alarm reaction or the successive stages of resistance or exhaustion. Another explanation for the effects of stress on our bodies relates to the notion of fight or flight, which also produces physiological responses to stressors. A third conceptualization is that of allostasis and allostatic overload. Psychological reactions to stress include the familiar defense mechanisms, or emergency responses, such as rationalization as well as other emotional reactions that vary somewhat with the level of stress. At the same time, each of us experiences the same stressful situations somewhat differently, depending on our particular personality and coping strategies.

PHEW!—MANAGING STRESS

Managing stress successfully involves more than automatic, symptom-reducing reactions to stress. Stress management means taking charge, directing and controlling our responses to stress so that we modify the overall stress. The two major ways of doing so are modifying our environment and altering our lifestyle. The three main ways of modifying the situational sources of stress are assertiveness, the preferred response; withdrawal, when appropriate; and compromise, especially negotiation, because it involves mutual accommodation among participants.

   Alleviating stress by altering our lifestyle includes building greater stress tolerance, changing our pace of life, controlling distressful thoughts, and acquiring problem-solving skills. Finally, remember that stress is not synonymous with distress. Instead, to get the most out of life, each of us needs to find our optimal level of stress and use it as a method of growth.

SELF-TEST

1. Stress that has a beneficial effect on us is called
   a. eustress.   c. distress.
   b. hypostress.   d. hyperstress.

2. When under stress, how do people react? With
   a. cognitive changes.   c. behavioral changes.
   b. emotional changes.   d. any of the above.

3. An alternative explanation to Selye's general adaptation syndrome to explain the body's reaction to stress is
   a. the fight or flight response. c. the alarm reaction.
   b. eustress vs. distress. d. social isolation response.

4. The first stage in the general adaptation syndrome is
   a. any of the following can be first. c. alarm.
   b. exhaustion. d. resistance.

5. Symptoms of stress-related illnesses such as a peptic ulcer are most likely to develop in which stage of the general adaptation syndrome?
   a. exhaustion. c. alarm reaction.
   b. resistance. d. flight.

6. The exclusion of unacceptable ideas or feelings from consciousness is called
   a. suppression. c. repression.
   b. rationalization. d. denial.

7. One *environmental* means for managing stress is
   a. using compromise. c. building stress tolerance.
   b. self-deprecation. d. using problem-focused coping.

8. You're returning a recently purchased, defective coat. An assertive response would be to
   a. apologize, then ask to have the coat repaired.
   b. threaten to sue the store and a specific employee.
   c. complain about the poor quality of the merchandise.
   d. ask for another coat without the defect.

9. A desirable way of handling stress that involves mutual accommodation among all the participants is
   a. denial. c. negotiation.
   b. conformity. d. withdrawal.

10. New research indicates that most people manage distress and even trauma
   a. with resilience or hardiness. c. via anxiety and depression.
   b. very poorly at best. d. by withdrawal or compromise.

EXERCISES

1. *Take an inventory of your stress.* List the most common ways you manage stress. When you think back over the past 6 months, did you handle stress well? If not, why not? Do you think that if you changed how you react to stress, you would manage stress better?

2. *Daily hassles.* Jot down some of the little things in everyday life that annoy or distress you, for example, a friend who is perpetually late or being stuck in traffic. How does your list compare with the survey of daily hassles described in the text? Which hassles bother you the most? Select two or three of them and suggest specific ways you could make them less troublesome.

3. *Defense mechanisms.* Think of a particular situation in which you reacted defensively. Which defense mechanism(s) did you rely on? How well did you cope with this

situation? If you face a similar situation in the future, would you handle it differently? How so?

4. *Describe your most stressful experience.* In a page or so, tell what made the incident or experience so stressful and how you coped with it. How well did your coping mechanisms work in this situation?

5. *Managing stress assertively.* Recall a stressful situation that you handled in an assertive manner. Describe the situation, how you handled it, and how it turned out. An alternate exercise is to relate a similar situation that you wished you had handled in a more assertive manner. How did you react in this situation? What happened as a result? If you're faced with a similar situation in the future, how could you handle it more assertively?

6. *Altering your lifestyle.* Review the suggestions for reducing stress by changing your pace of life. If there are other changes especially needed in your daily habits, what are they? Select two or three of your suggested changes and apply them to your daily life for a week. If you find these changes helpful, why not continue altering your lifestyle to reduce your everyday stress?

QUESTIONS FOR SELF-REFLECTION

1. Can you recall several instances when stress had a beneficial effect?

2. Which situations do you find most distressing?

3. What are some of the "little things" that get you down?

4. Would you agree that having some control over your work activities makes them less stressful?

5. How can you tell when you're under a lot of stress?

6. When you become defensive, how do you behave?

7. Are you inclined to abuse alcohol or drugs when under stress?

8. What are some ways you've modified your environment to decrease stress?

9. Have you tried altering your lifestyle as a way of alleviating stress?

10. Do you believe that you have the traits of hardiness and resilience?

11. All things considered, how well do you manage stress?

FOR FURTHER INFORMATION

RECOMMENDED READINGS

CHARLESWORTH, E. A., & NATHAN, R.G. (2004). *Stress management: A comprehensive guide to wellness.* New York: Ballantine Books. The authors not only discuss stress and how to manage it, they highlight how to move beyond recovery to wellness.

EPSTEIN, R. (2000). *The big book of stress-relief games.* New York: McGraw-Hill. A fun book filled with ways to help relieve stress.

McEwen, B. S., & Lasley, E. N. (2002). *The end of stress as we know it.* Washington, DC: Joseph Henry Press. A scientific book that examines how the brain and stress respond to each other with an eye toward understanding how to prevent the physiological damage stress creates.

Preston, J. (2002). *Survivors: Stories and strategies to heal the hurt.* Atascadero, CA: Impact Publishers. Using the stories of four different people, the book shows how people cope with difficult experiences.

Scaer, R. C. (2005). *The trauma spectrum: Hidden wounds and human resilience.* New York: W.W. Norton. An exceptionally good book on trauma with new information on resiliency.

WEB SITES AND THE INTERNET

http://www.stressrelease.com   Contains lots of information on stress, such as the reasons for it and tips on stress management. Check out their on-line resources section.

http://www.stress.org   The site for the American Institute of Stress, which is committed to developing a better understanding of how to tap into the vast innate potential that resides in each of us for preventing disease and promoting health.

http://www.humorproject.com   A site with many humor resources and products and information.

http://www.mentalhealth.org   The site of the U.S. Department of Health and Human Services—Division on Substance Abuse and Mental Health Services Administration. Excellent information on trauma and terrorism, especially for parents and teachers.

http://www.psychologymatters.org/trauma.html   Part of the American Psychological Association's on-line public information site. Includes material on trauma, stress, and hardiness.

CHAPTER 14

Understanding Mental Disorders

PSYCHOLOGICAL DISORDERS
What Are Psychological
    Disorders?
How Common Are Psychological
    Disorders?
How Are Disorders Classified?

**ANXIETY DISORDERS: THE MOST
COMMON DISORDER**
Generalized Anxiety Disorder
Phobias: Fear of Something That
    Won't Really Hurt
Obsessive-Compulsive Disorder:
    The Doubting Disease
Trauma and Disaster

MOOD DISORDERS
What Is Depression?
Suicide: Who and Why?
What Is Bipolar Disorder?

OTHER COMMON DISORDERS
Do You Have an Eating Disorder?
What Are Personality Disorders?
Schizophrenia—The Enigmatic
    Disorder

SUMMARY
SELF-TEST
EXERCISES
QUESTIONS FOR SELF-REFLECTION
FOR FURTHER INFORMATION

Learning Objectives

After completing this chapter, you should be able to

1. Describe the distinguishing features of a psychological disorder.
2. Be able to discuss the prevalence and incidence of various disorders.
3. Know what the DSM is and how disorders are diagnosed.
4. Differentiate the various anxiety disorders from one another.
5. Distinguish between major depression and other mood disorders.
6. List the warning signs of suicide and predict who is likely to commit suicide.
7. Describe the characteristics of eating disorders such as anorexia and bulimia.
8. Explain the diathesis-stress hypothesis as well as the symptoms of schizophrenia.

With a good job in the loan department of a bank, Lisa, age 23, was a happy young adult, or so it seemed. She began working for the bank immediately upon her graduation from college and slowly worked her way up through the ranks such that she held a good mid-level management job. She was engaged to Hans, a modest young man who worked in a different department of the bank. Lisa had recently moved back home in the same city to live with her widowed mother, who was having some heart problems, one of which was a deep depression due to the recent loss of her husband. Although Lisa was not very happy about this arrangement, as it restricted her freedom after work and the time she could spend with Hans, she nonetheless felt it was her duty as a good daughter—as an only child—to care for her ailing mother. Just when Lisa thought her mother was improving, her mother suddenly died. The surprise of this event deepened Lisa's angst. At the same time, her mother's health care and funeral left Lisa and the estate with some large unpaid bills. Lisa became more depressed as she tried to manage the aftermath of her mother's death, including paying the bills and estate taxes, negotiating with the funeral home, and settling other matters related to her mother's estate. Three months after her mother's death, Lisa was greeted by another unpleasant surprise. Hans announced that he had been given a promotion, was seeing someone else, and wanted to break their engagement. In the time that Lisa had been caring for her mother, Hans had met another woman. Again, Lisa was stunned and dismayed. As if this weren't enough to worry her, there were rumors at the bank that her department would shortly be downsized. With all this bad news,

Lisa soon found that she had difficulty getting out of bed each morning. She would then stand in her closet for a long time trying to decide what to wear to work. In fact, Lisa began missing work; she would call in sick even though she really felt she was "just tired." Eventually, Lisa's coworkers began noticing that she appeared somewhat disheveled, not the old meticulous, orderly Lisa. Lisa's formerly short hair went uncut and unkempt. Sometimes she wore the same sweater and wrinkled skirt all week only to have the same garments reappear the following week. Lisa's coworkers also noticed she was losing weight. One day Lisa did not materialize for work and neither did she call in sick. After this happened 3 more days in a row, one of her closest coworkers went to Lisa's house to find her in bed alternately staring at the ceiling and sobbing. Lisa appeared normal, at least she was able to carry on a rather normal conversation, albeit groggily, but she did not want to get out of bed or to eat anything. The coworker also found that the house was a mess. There was garbage overflowing the cans, newspapers piled in front of the door, and clothing strewn everywhere; the mail was unopened, and old cat food containers littered the kitchen. "What was wrong with Lisa?" wondered her friend.

PSYCHOLOGICAL DISORDERS

Among themselves, Lisa's coworkers and friends might call her "neurotic" or "nuts." Others might refer to her as a "flake" or a "weirdo." Upon hearing of her admission to the local hospital, they might say Lisa was having a "nervous breakdown." Psychologists and other mental health professionals generally avoid such terms because not only are they negative, they are stigmatizing. Instead, specialists tend to focus on more relevant matters, such as Lisa's intense personal distress and the degree of impairment in her everyday behavior. In short, mental health professionals would be concerned about the type and severity of Lisa's disorder and, thus, how best to help her. As it turned out, Lisa was suffering from a major depressive episode, one of the more common and disabling disorders, as you will see later in this chapter.

The study of psychological disorders is often associated with abnormal behavior because many disorders involve thoughts, feelings, or actions that are not considered "normal." Abnormal behavior and psychological disorders, however, are not synonymous. For instance, some forms of depression are too common to be labeled abnormal or statistically "out of the normal" but are nevertheless classified as psychological disorders. Other behaviors may be considered socially deviant or unusual, such as running nude across the field at a soccer game, without being considered a psychological disorder. Consequently, we'll begin by looking at some of the common standards used in defining psychological disorders and the incidence of such disorders. We will then turn to how disorders are classified, so as to provide you with some general background on this topic.

What Are Psychological Disorders?

Throughout this book, you are learning about mental health, adjustment, and personal growth. In this chapter, we turn to the challenge of mental disorders. You may be surprised to know that there is no precise and universally agreed-on standard that distinguishes between abnormal and normal behavior or, for that matter, between the presence of a psychological disorder and no disorder. Probably the most widely accepted guide in these matters is the *Diagnostic and Statistical Manual of Mental Disorders*, Fourth Edition (text revision), or DSM-IV-TR, published by the American Psychiatric Association. This manual is popularly referred to in shorthand as the DSM (American Psychiatric Association, 2000). The DSM is a controversial manual and may soon undergo yet another revision (*Clinical Psychiatry News*, 2001; *Harvard Mental Health Letter*, 2002a; Genova, 2003). At the outset, the authors acknowledge the difficulties in defining a psychological disorder, much less specifying precise boundaries for particular disorders. For now, let us define **psychological disorder** as *a clinically significant behavioral or psychological pattern that is associated with* (1) *present personal distress;* (2) *disability or impairment in one or more important areas of functioning, e.g., maladaptive behaviors;* (3) *significantly increased risk of suffering disability, pain, or death; and* (4) *an important loss of freedom or personal control* (American Psychiatric Association).

As noted in the definition, a major factor in diagnosing a disorder is the individual's level of **personal distress**, which is *intense or chronic negative self-awareness that interferes with one's sense of well-being or functioning.* Someone with a chronic fear of heights or a marked change in mood such as Lisa's severe depression might be diagnosed as having a psychological disorder. When Lisa would not get out of bed or take out the trash because it seemed too onerous, we begin to suspect that Lisa had a mental disorder. On the other hand, people who behave in an unusual or eccentric way but are otherwise happy would probably not be so diagnosed. If Lisa were artistic and saved empty cat food cans and other pieces of metal to produce sculptures, we would not assume that she was "ill." As useful as this standard of personal distress is, it isn't sufficiently comprehensive to help us define or diagnose a mental disorder.

Another important feature in defining a disorder is **maladaptive behavior**, *significant impairment in one or more areas of psychological functioning, especially the ability to work and to get along with others.* As implied in the definition, people with psychological disorders usually suffer from a significant impairment in their inability to work, to care for themselves, or to get along with family and friends. This is a *practical* approach because it focuses on behavior that is relevant to daily living. Accordingly, when Lisa manifested intense grief in response to her mother's death, she was not considered to have a disorder because she was able to plan and attend her mother's funeral in appropriate ways. It was her eventual inability to care for herself and her apartment as well as her inability to get out of bed and go to work that led others to believe she was experiencing problems.

A third issue of relevance is the individual's *increased risk for suffering disability, pain, or death.* Individuals who exhibit maladaptive behaviors and impairments in daily living put themselves at risk for harm. People who are addicted to certain substances or too anxious to pay attention to their driving are more prone to car accidents. Lisa, too, had stopped taking care of herself; she did not take showers, comb her hair, or brush her teeth. Neither did she maintain a healthy diet; in fact, some days she would eat nothing—thus, the weight loss. The inactivity and weight loss were placing Lisa at risk for health problems. In fact, her friends wondered if she were suicidal or had an eating disorder. Lisa did not keep her apartment clean but allowed the trash to pile up as she sank deeper and deeper into depression. Her coworker was concerned that the unclean apartment might also fill with flies and other disease-carrying pests.

Another dimension of mental disorder is *the violation of social norms*. **Social norms** are *generalized expectations regarding appropriate behavior in a given situation or society*. People in every studied society live by certain rules of what is acceptable and unacceptable. When an individual repeatedly violates commonly accepted social norms, that person may be considered to have a psychological disorder if other conditions also prevail. Such rule violations can result in *the loss of freedom and control* for the individual because others fear the individual will hurt them or hurt him- or herself. For example, the standard dress code for women at Lisa's bank consisted of skirted suits of various dark colors such as navy blue, black, and gray. In addition, there was an expectation that no one would

---

Box 14–1

ANTISTIGMA: DO YOU KNOW THE FACTS?

Stigma is not just a matter of using the wrong word or action. Stigma is about disrespect. **Stigma** is *the use of negative labels to identify a person living with a mental disorder or with another distinguishing feature and who you believe differs from you*. Stigma is a barrier, because it causes exclusion, rejection, and devaluation of the stigmatized individual (Weiss & Ramakrishna, 2006). Fear of stigma, and the resulting discrimination, discourages individuals and their families from getting the help they need (Gary, 2005; Vaccaro, 2004). An estimated 22 to 23 percent of the U.S. population experiences a mental disorder in any given year, but almost half of these individuals do not seek treatment.

The following information encourages the use of positive images to refer to people with mental disorders and underscores the reality that mental disorders can be successfully treated:

- Do you know that an estimated 44 million Americans experience a mental disorder in any given year?

- Do you know that stigma is not a matter of using the wrong word or action?

- Do you know that stigma is about disrespect and using negative labels to identify a person living with a mental disorder?

- Do you know that stigma is a barrier that discourages individuals and their families from seeking help?

- Do you know that many people would rather tell employers they committed a petty crime and served time in jail than admit to having been in a psychiatric hospital?

- Do you know that stigma can result in inadequate insurance coverage for mental health services?

- Do you know that stigma leads to fear, mistrust, and violence against people living with mental disorder and their families?

- Do you know that stigma can cause families and friends to turn their backs on people with mental disorders?

- Do you know that stigma can prevent people from getting access to needed mental health services?

DO'S

- Do use respectful language.

- Do emphasize abilities, not limitations.

- Do tell someone if they express a stigmatizing attitude.

DONT'S

- Don't portray successful persons with disabilities as superhuman.

- Don't use generic labels such as *retarded* or *the mentally ill*.

- Don't use terms like *crazy, lunatic, manic-depressive*, or *slow-functioning*.

SOURCE: SAMHSA's National Mental Health Information Center (2003). The Center for Mental Health Services. http://www.mentalhealth.org/publications/allpubs/OEL99–0004/default.asp.

wear the same suit day after day after day. At the beginning of her depression, when Lisa started showing up to work in the same sweater and wrinkled skirt many days in a row, she violated the social norm or unwritten dress code. In addition to her other symptoms, her coworkers were probably correct in noticing this marked change in Lisa. In fact, Lisa's supervisor was thinking of talking to her about her recent and too casual mode of dress as well as her unkempt hair. It may well be the violation of social norms that intimidates others when they witness the socially inappropriate behavior of someone with a mental disorder. This fear factor can lead to stigmatization of those with mental disorders. The U.S. government is so concerned about the effects of stigmas on individuals with disorders that it has provided us with some helpful information, as detailed in Box 14–1.

You already know that social norms not only vary from culture to culture but sometimes vary within a culture. In most societies, people commonly eat in public but do not urinate in front of others. Each society has social norms about what is appropriate to eat (yogurt or pig's intestines) and how to eat (for example, with chopsticks or a spoon). In America, it is often acceptable to eat food at a rock concert or sporting event but not at a church or funeral service. It would be unusual, though, to see an American consuming blini (Russian pancakes) and borsch (beet soup) at a basketball game.

If you understand the significance of these cultural differences, you should not be surprised to know that the frequency of mental disorders varies from culture to culture, too (Osborne, 2001; Xiao-Ping, 2004). For instance, the prevalence of depression is low in China and many parts of Africa—just the opposite of its occurrence in the United States. One explanation is that in Western societies, individuals are more likely to be held personally responsible for their failures and misfortunes and thus may be more susceptible to depression as they turn their focus inward to their own perceived deficits. Box 14–2 discusses the issue of diversity and mental disorder in more detail.

As you can see, there is no simple way of determining when someone has a psychological disorder. In practice, mental health professionals rely on a combination of standards to determine whether a given behavior is normal or not. To review, the four factors most likely taken into account when arriving at a diagnosis are (1) personal distress, (2) significant impairment in one or more areas of functioning, (3) the social acceptability (norms) of the individual's behavior, and (4) an important loss of personal control.

How Common Are Psychological Disorders?

Mental disorders are a burden worldwide. Surprisingly, mental disorders rank second after cardiovascular diseases in the **global burden of diseases**, which is *a measure of years of life lost to disability throughout the world*. Donna Shalala, former U.S. Secretary of Health and Human Services, in a major report on the subject said that the burden of mental disorders has long been profoundly underestimated. Shalala said that major depression is equivalent in terms of hardship to blindness or paraplegia (Shalala, 1999). Approximately 14.8 million American adults alone have a depressive disorder in any given year (National Institute of Mental Health [NIMH], 2006a). And worldwide, schizophrenia is listed as the eighth leading cause of disability-adjusted (reduced) life years, not to mention the burden it places on the caregivers (Rössler, Salize, van Os, & Riecher-Rössler, 2005). Thus, it is important for us to understand and to study mental disorders.

Much information about the extent of psychological disorders comes from in-depth surveys of representative samples of the population, along with admission figures

Box 14–2

Diversity and Mental Disorder

America is home to a boundless array of cultures, races, and ethnicities. Diversity has enriched our nation by bringing global ideas, perspectives, and productive contributions to all areas of contemporary life. The enduring contributions of minorities, like those of all Americans, rest on a foundation of mental health. Mental health is fundamental to overall health and productivity. It is the basis for successful contributions to family, community, and society. Throughout the life span, mental health is the wellspring of thinking and communication skills, learning, resilience, and self-esteem. It is all too easy to dismiss the value of mental health until problems appear.

Major mental disorders like schizophrenia, bipolar disorder, and depression are found worldwide, across all racial and ethnic groups, wherever researchers have surveyed. In the United States, based on the available evidence, the prevalence of mental disorders for racial and ethnic minorities is similar to that for Whites. There are, however, several documented and important disparities affecting mental health care of racial and ethnic minorities compared with that of Whites (Gary, 2005; Nelson, 2006; Schraufhagel, Wagner, Miranda, & Roy-Byrne, 2006):

- Minorities have less access to and availability of mental health services.

- Minorities are less likely to receive needed mental health services.

- Minorities in treatment often receive a poorer quality of mental health care.

- Minorities are underrepresented in mental health research.

A constellation of barriers deters minorities from reaching treatment. Many of these barriers operate for all Americans: cost, fragmentation of services, lack of availability of services, and societal stigma of mental disorders. But additional barriers deter racial and ethnic minorities: mistrust and fear of treatment, racism and discrimination, and differences in language and communication (Nelson, 2006). The ability of clients and health care providers to communicate with one another is

essential for all aspects of health care, yet it carries special significance in the area of mental health because mental disorders affect thoughts, moods, and the highest integrative aspects of behavior. The diagnosis and treatment of mental disorders greatly depend on verbal communication and trust between patient and clinician. More broadly, mental health care disparities may also stem from minorities' historical and present-day struggles with racism and discrimination (Nelson), which affect their mental health and contribute to their lower economic, social, and political status. The cumulative weight and interplay of all barriers to care, not any single one alone, is likely responsible for mental health disparities between Whites and other groups.

Ethnic and racial minorities collectively experience a greater disability burden from mental disorders than do Whites. This higher level of burden stems from minorities' receiving less care and poorer quality of care, rather than from their disorders being inherently more severe or prevalent in the community. From not receiving effective treatment, they have greater burdens of disability in terms of lost workdays and limitations in daily activities. Most troubling of all, the burden for minorities is growing. Racial and ethnic groups are becoming more populous, all the while experiencing continuing inequality of income and economic opportunity.

Culture also plays a pivotal role in mental health, mental disorder, and mental health services. Understanding the wide-ranging roles of culture enables the mental health field to design and deliver services that are more responsive to the needs of racial and ethnic minorities. **Culture** is broadly defined as *the ideas, customs, arts, and skills that characterize a group of people during a given period of history*. The term *culture* is as applicable to Whites as it is to racial and ethnic minorities. History has focused on the beliefs, norms, and values of European Americans, the dominant culture for much of United States. Today's America, though, is unmistakably multicultural, and because there are a variety of ways to define a cultural group (e.g., by ethnicity, religion, geographic region, age group, sexual orientation, or profession), many people consider themselves as having multiple cultural identities.

(continued)

Box 14–2 (*continued*)

With a seemingly endless range of cultural sub-groups and individual variations, culture is important because it bears upon what *all* people bring to the clinical setting. It can account for variations in how consumers communicate their symptoms and which ones they report. Some aspects of culture may also underlie **culture-bound syndromes**—*sets of symptoms much more common in some societies than in others*. More often, culture bears upon whether people even seek help in the first place, what types of help they seek, what coping styles and social supports they have, and how much stigma they attach to mental disorder. All cultures also feature strengths, such as resilience and adaptive ways of coping, which buffer some people from developing certain disorders. Clients of mental health services naturally carry this cultural diversity directly into the treatment setting.

Culture is a concept not limited to individuals with mental disorders and their families. It also applies to the professionals who treat them. Every group of

professionals embodies a "culture" in the sense that they, too, have a shared set of beliefs, norms, and values. This is as true for health professionals as it is for other professional groups such as engineers and teachers. A professional's culture can be gleaned from the jargon used, the orientation and emphasis in their textbooks, and the mindset or way of looking at the world. It also means that clinicians view symptoms, diagnoses, and treatments in ways that sometimes diverge from their clients' views, especially when the cultural backgrounds of the consumer and provider are dissimilar. This divergence of viewpoints can create barriers to effective care.

The main message, then, is that culture, race, and ethnicity count. Cultural and social influences are not the only influences on mental health and service delivery, but they have been historically underestimated—and they do count.

SOURCE: Adapted from *Mental health: A report of the Surgeon General* (1999). http://www.mentalhealth.org/cre/execsummary.

to various mental health facilities such as psychiatric hospitals and community mental health clinics. Two frequently used terms are *incidence* and *prevalence*. **Incidence** refers to *the number of new cases of disorders reported during a given period*. This term is usually distinguished from **prevalence**, which refers to *the total number of active cases that can be identified in a given population at a particular time* (Duffy & Wong, 2003).

During any 1-year period, mental health professionals estimate that one in four adults will suffer from some type of psychological disorder (NIMH, 2006d). Overall, about one out of every three persons will experience at least one significant psychological problem in his or her lifetime. Fortunately for you, college graduates generally report fewer such ailments than non-college graduates. This, then, makes Lisa's case a bit unusual.

People who have a psychological disorder usually experience their first symptoms by early adulthood (NIMH, 2006d); three-fourths of those surveyed reported their first symptoms by age 24. In this case, Lisa is typical. However, symptoms of alcohol abuse, obsessive-compulsive behavior, bipolar disorder, and schizophrenia appear somewhat earlier, at a median age near 20. Table 14–1 shows the numbers of Americans with selected disorders.

There is a popular notion that more women than men are "emotionally disturbed." Is there any truth to this view? Apparently not. When all disorders are taken into account, men and women are equally likely to suffer from psychological disorders. However, the patterns of disorders differ somewhat between the sexes (World Health Organization [WHO], 2006). Women suffer more from phobias (intense and irrational fear) and depression (a sense of hopelessness and lack of pleasure in life much like that experienced by Lisa), and men are more apt to abuse alcohol and drugs and exhibit long-term antisocial behavior

TABLE 14–1

PREVALENCE OF SELECTED DISORDERS IN ANY GIVEN YEAR IN THE UNITED STATES

Disorder	Prevalence
All disorders (including individuals with dual diagnoses)	57.5 million
Anxiety disorder	40 million
Mood disorders	20.9 million
Schizophrenia	2.4 million

SOURCE: National Institute of Mental Health (2006d). http://www.nimh.nih.gov/publicat/numbers.cfm#Intro.

(WHO). At the same time, women are twice as likely as men to seek help, which may have given the mistaken impression in the past that women were more troubled by mental disorder than men.

How Are Disorders Classified?

Because there are no sharp boundaries between the various psychological disorders (Office of the Surgeon General, 1999), or between a psychological disorder and no disorder, you can readily appreciate the difficulty of classifying disorders. The coworker who went to Lisa's home was fairly sure there was something amiss with Lisa but was not certain what it was. A psychologist or psychiatrist might also need some time to diagnose the type and extent of Lisa's disorder. However, within the limitations mentioned earlier, the DSM classifies, defines, and describes over 200 psychological disorders, using practical criteria as the basis of classification. To arrive at a **diagnosis**—*in which the problem is classified within a set of recognized categories of abnormal behavior*—the clinician compares the behavior of the "patient" with the description in the manual and then selects the label of the description that best fits the problem. The purpose is to provide an accurate description of the person's overall problem and functioning, along with a prediction for the course of the disorder, which helps during treatment. The diagnosis also helps professionals communicate with and understand one another.

Throughout the DSM, the emphasis is on classifying behavior patterns, *not* people, as is often thought. Thus, the manual refers to "people who exhibit the symptoms of schizophrenia" rather than to "schizophrenics." Also, the terminology refers to "mental health professionals" and "clinicians" instead of "psychiatrists," thereby acknowledging the broader range of professionals who deal with people with psychological disorders. Finally, the emphasis is on describing rather than interpreting psychological disorders, especially when the causal factors are unknown. Thus, the DSM gives clinicians a practical, behavioral approach to dealing with people exhibiting symptoms of psychological disorders.

In the rest of this chapter, we'll describe two different sets of disorders: (1) the more common disorders, such as the anxiety disorders, affective or mood disorders, and personality disorders, as well as (2) the more serious but less common disorders such as schizophrenia. In addition, some of the other disorders as well as some thought-provoking issues will be highlighted in separate boxed items.

ANXIETY DISORDERS: THE MOST COMMON DISORDER

Most of us experience anxiety or fear some of the time; it is a natural emotional response to stress and is often a normal part of life (*Harvard Women's Health Watch*, 2002). Being anxious before a big job interview is to be expected. In fact, when Lisa first interviewed for her bank job, which she really wanted when she was fresh out of college, she felt jittery but was able to compose herself.

Sometimes anxiety can be energizing; extremely high levels of anxiety, though, can be immobilizing. High anxiety can prevent people from leaving their homes. It can also make them block out daily news events, avoid other people, refuse to answer the phone, and in general not enjoy everyday life. In individuals with **anxiety disorders**, *a group of disorders characterized by symptoms of excessive or inappropriate anxiety or attempts to escape from such anxiety*, the anxiety is out of all proportion to the stressful situation. In fact, anxiety may occur in the absence of any specific danger. In brief, anxiety disorders may be experienced in several ways:

- **Generalized anxiety disorder** identified as *a chronic state of diffuse or free-floating anxiety*. In this disorder, the anxiety itself becomes the predominant disturbance.
- **Phobic disorder** is *intense anxiety evoked by some specific and irrational object or activity*, such as flying in a plane.
- **Obsessive-compulsive disorder** is marked by *the involuntary dwelling on an unwelcome thought or the involuntary repetition of an unnecessary action*.

Let's review these in detail.

Generalized Anxiety Disorder

The main characteristic of generalized anxiety disorder is a persistent sense of "free-floating" anxiety. The person is anxious most of the time or suffers from periodic panic attacks, as occurs in the closely related panic disorder. People who are chronically anxious can't say what they are afraid of. All they know is that they feel on edge all the time. They generally worry a lot and anticipate the occurrence of something bad. Lisa, for example, felt this way when her mother was ill, but the anxiety did not yet incapacitate her. She did not feel all of the symptoms associated with anxiety, such as cold sweat, pounding heart, and dry mouth, as do people with generalized anxiety disorder. Lisa also knew the cause of her anxiety, her beloved mother's illness. Anxiety may disrupt the everyday functioning of individuals with generalized anxiety disorder such that they may find it hard to concentrate and make decisions. At the time of her mother's illness, Lisa was still able to function adequately. People with this disorder may also develop headaches, muscular tension, indigestion, a strained face, and fidgeting. Frequently, they become apprehensive about their anxiety and fear their condition will give them ulcers or a heart attack or make them go crazy.

Chronically anxious people can also suffer from **panic attacks**, *characterized by the occurrence of severe panic*. These intense attacks occur in the absence of a feared situation and usually last 15 to 30 minutes (Mentalhelp.net, 2000a). In some instances, the attack occurs in response to a specific phobic situation, such as driving in city traffic or speaking publicly. At other times, the panic does not seem to be produced by a specific instigator. In a panic attack, anxiety increases to an almost intolerable level. The individual breaks out in a cold sweat, feels dizzy, and may have difficulty breathing. Victims almost always have a feeling of inescapable doom, as if they won't make it to safety or will die. Panic attacks usually last only a few minutes but may continue for hours. Afterward, the victims feel exhausted. Because panic attacks are unpredictable, they often create additional anxiety, and the victims avoid certain situations in which they fear losing control, being helpless, or experiencing panic.

By way of example, Cynthia, a young woman who graduated from the same university as Lisa, suffered from periodic panic attacks while at college. At times, she couldn't concentrate on her studies, had difficulty sleeping, and complained of stomach pains. As the end of the semester approached, she became more susceptible to panic attacks. In her discussions with the counselor, Cynthia discovered that her anxiety was precipitated by problems at home. She felt caught in a conflict between her parents, who were divorcing. Because she was unable to cope with the pressure to side with her mother or father, the prospect of going home for the holidays evoked intense anxiety. To determine your own general level of anxiety, try the scale in Activity 14–1.

ACTIVITY 14–1

How Anxious Are You?

The following scale was developed for this book. It is designed for you to think about your characteristic anxiety level or your trait anxiety. This is not a scientific scale. If you have a high score, you might think about whether anxiety interferes with your academic performance or other important behaviors and then consider ways you can lower your anxiety level.

Place a check mark next to each statement that is typical or characteristic of you:

_____ I often have a sense of dread or impending doom but cannot always identify what it is I fear.

_____ I find that I am afraid of things others do not seem to be afraid of.

_____ My friends think I worry more than they do about examinations, meeting deadlines, and so forth.

_____ I seem to have more stomachaches, headaches, and other signs of anxiety than others do.

_____ I frequently feel restless and tense and do not sleep as well as I should.

_____ Many times, I try to avoid situations that cause me anxiety, such as public speaking or meeting strangers.

_____ I probably perspire and have rapid heartbeats when it is inappropriate (e.g., when I have not been exercising).

_____ Decisions are usually difficult for me to make, especially important decisions.

_____ Compared to others, I feel that I have difficulty concentrating on even the simplest of tasks.

_____ My friends are not as afraid as I am of everyday situations, such as becoming lost in a new part of a city.

SCORING: Add up the number of check marks. The highest score you can receive is 10. If you scored 7 or higher, you might want to consider whether you have high anxiety levels and whether these high levels interfere with your life. If you decide "yes," you should explore ways to reduce your anxiety. Professional help or some of the techniques in the following chapter on psychotherapy may prove useful.

Phobias: Fear of Something That Won't Really Hurt

Phobic disorders are *characterized by a persistent and irrational fear of a specific object or activity, accompanied by a compelling desire to avoid it.* The object or activity typically does not merit such intense fear. Most of us experience an irrational avoidance of selected objects, like spiders or snakes, but it usually has no major impact on our lives. In contrast, when the avoidance becomes a *significant* source of distress to the individual and interferes with everyday behavior, the diagnosis of a phobic disorder is warranted. There are several major types of phobic disorders: simple phobias, social phobias, and agoraphobia.

Simple phobias are *the most common type of phobia in the general population. Commonly feared objects include animals, particularly dogs, snakes, and insects.* Other simple phobias are **acrophobia**, *the fear of heights*, and **claustrophobia**, *the fear of closed places*. Most simple phobias originate in childhood and disappear without treatment. However, the more intense fears that persist into adulthood generally don't disappear without treatment.

A phobia is a persistent and irrational fear of a specific object or activity, accompanied by a compelling desire to avoid it.

Social phobia is *an extreme form of shyness that can interfere with an individual's daily life and involves a chronic, irrational fear of and a compelling desire to avoid situations where others may scrutinize the individual.* If confronted with the necessity of entering such a situation, the person experiences marked anxiety and attempts to avoid it. Examples are an intense fear of speaking or performing in public, eating in public, using public lavatories, and writing in the presence of others. Although this type of disorder itself is rarely incapacitating, it does result in considerable inconvenience, such as avoiding a trip that involves the use of a public lavatory. Also, in an effort to relieve their anxiety, individuals with this disorder often abuse alcohol, barbiturates, and other anti-anxiety medications. A unit in the chapter on meeting friends (Chapter 8) differentiates shyness from social phobia, so you might want to examine that section.

Agoraphobia, classically known as *"fear of open spaces,"* is typically the most severe phobic reaction and the one for which people most often seek treatment. Agoraphobia is *a cluster of different fears, all of which evoke intense anxiety about crowds or open spaces*, such as crowded stores, elevators or tunnels, or public transportation. This type of phobia tends to occur in the late teens or early 20s, though it can occur later in life. During outbreaks of this phobia, refusing to go outside, the victims are often housebound. If they go out, they take great care to avoid certain situations, such as being in an elevator. Box 14–3 presents the names and descriptions of other types of phobias. Some "medicate" themselves with alcohol or other substances so as to curb their fear.

Obsessive-Compulsive Disorder: The Doubting Disease

The essential feature of **obsessive-compulsive disorder** (OCD) involves the *involuntary dwelling on an unwelcome thought or the involuntary repetition of an unnecessary act.* It has sometimes been called the "doubting disease" (Groopman, 2000) because many individuals

---

Box 14–3

Do You Recognize Any of These Phobias?

Acrophobia—fear of heights

Androphobia—fear of men

Arachitbutyrophobia—fear of peanut butter sticking to the roof of your mouth

Autophobia—fear of oneself

Decidophobia—fear of making decisions

Ergophobia—fear of work

Gamophobia—fear of marriage

Gynephobia—fear of women

Hypergiaphobia—fear of responsibility

Monophobia—fear of being alone

Mysophobia—fear of dirt

Nyctophobia—fear of darkness

Ophidiophobia—fear of snakes

Topophobia—fear of performing (stage fright)

Triskaidekaphobia—fear of the number 13

Tropophobia—fear of moving or making changes

Zoophobia—fear of animals

with OCD develop habitual behaviors to help them avoid anxiety. Anxiety occurs when the individual does not engage in a particular thought or avoidance behavior, for example, repeatedly checking a door previously locked or compulsively washing one's hands.

Research suggests that a critical feature of OCD is an *overinflated sense of responsibility* (Mentalhelp.net, 2000a). Specifically, an **obsession** is *a thought or image that keeps recurring in the mind, despite the individual's attempts to ignore or resist it.* Similarly, a **compulsion** is *an act that the individual feels compelled to repeat again and again, usually in a ritualistic fashion or according to certain rules.* The act is performed with a sense of compulsion, coupled with a desire to resist such action, at least initially. The individual usually realizes that the behavior is senseless and does not derive pleasure from carrying it out, though doing so provides a release of tension. OCD is thought to be caused by disruption of the basal ganglia of the brain. The basal ganglia is a region in the brain that filters messages (*Harvard Mental Health Letter*, 1998).

Most of us experience mild obsessions from time to time. Lisa sometimes found herself repeatedly humming a tune she didn't even like. Others might find their thoughts going back to an article they read in the daily newspaper about a tragic accident. These minor obsessions are temporary and do not interfere with everyday activities. In contrast, pathological obsessions reoccur day after day. They sometimes involve thoughts of lust and violence, partly because of their association with the individual's anxiety and guilt, which makes the thoughts even more disruptive. Examples are the fear of being contaminated by germs, the fear that one will kill one's child or spouse, or the temptation to have sex with a forbidden partner. Such compulsions tend to fall into several categories (Mentalhelp.net, 2000a), such as *hoarders*, who collect almost anything and cannot get rid of it; or *repeaters*, who feel they must repeat a behavior a set number of times; or *orderers*, who want their possessions in certain places and arranged in certain ways.

By this point in the chapter, you may be thinking that some of the symptoms of the disorders described thus far sound familiar to you, in fact that they *do* describe you. You probably are perfectly healthy or else you would not be attending college, working at a job, or enjoying your marriage. It is quite normal to introspect about your mental health; in fact, it is healthy. However, if you think you are prone to one of the disorders discussed so far, you might want to visit your campus health clinic or counseling center for a discussion with a professional.

Trauma and Disaster

Let's return to our discussion of anxiety disorders. Because terrorist activity has haunted Americans since before September 11, 2001, psychologists have turned concerted attention to victims of trauma and disaster. Psychologists have always been interested in trauma, but recent historic events have heightened our attention and our need for more information.

In the chapter on stress, **posttraumatic stress disorder** (or PTSD) is briefly reviewed. In short, *PTSD is a severe anxiety disorder characterized by symptoms of anxiety and avoidance behavior; this disorder results from an unusually stressful event such as being assaulted.* Of course, other events can be traumatic and include but are not limited to the devastation of wars, natural disasters, sniper attacks, rapes, plane crashes, terrorism, horrific car accidents, and murders. As you can see, most of the causes of PTSD involve life-threatening events (*Harvard Women's Health Watch*, 2005). PTSD is commonly typified by intense fear, flashbacks (reliving the event over and over again), and nightmares (Nemeroff et al., 2006). Other signs that a person is suffering from PTSD include:

- Mood swings, irritability, depression, and sadness; crying often
- Limited attention span, difficulty concentrating, and confusion
- Poor work or school performance
- Physical symptoms such as headaches, sleep disturbance, or stomach problems
- Guilt and self-doubt
- Fear of crowds, strangers, or being alone
- Self-medication with drugs or alcohol
- Difficulty communicating thoughts

Certain individuals are more prone to PTSD than others (McNally, Bryant, & Ehlers, 2003; Nemeroff et al., 2006). These persons include those directly exposed to the trauma, such as witnesses, fire or police personnel, victims who narrowly escape death, emergency rescue workers and medical workers, and those who have already lost a loved one, especially in a traumatic fashion. Women are more likely than men to be vulnerable to PTSD (NIMH, 2006e); children are also more vulnerable than adults, especially if they have been abused or are suffering from chronic stress such as living in a war zone. People who lack social support or have a preexisting mental disorder are also more susceptible to PTSD (*Harvard Mental Health Letter*, 2002; McNally et al.).

There is much you can do to help yourself (or someone else) cope better with trauma. Here are some ways to ease the stress (Center for Mental Health Services [CMHS], 2003).

- Be sure to talk to someone about your feelings, no matter how difficult this may be.
- Spend time with family and friends, particularly in enjoyable activities.
- Do not hold yourself responsible for the event or for not responding sooner or better.
- Promote healing by staying active in daily patterns. Continue to work, rest, relax, and exercise.
- Maintain normal routines but limit demanding responsibilities.
- Participate in memorials, rituals, and other symbolic events related to the trauma.
- If self-help strategies are not working, seek professional help.

MOOD DISORDERS

What Is Depression?

Most of us go through periods of time when nothing seems to go right. For example, when Lisa's mother became ill and Lisa decided to move in with her, Lisa's car died. Her old landlord informed her that she would not receive back the security deposit for her apartment. Then Lisa lost her purse and was so worried about identity theft that she spent hour upon hour on the phone to cancel her credit cards and change her bank accounts. Like Lisa, you and other individuals lose their wallets, experience car trouble, and may have problems in their close relationships all at the same time. We may say we're "depressed," but we're usually not suffering from a diagnosable psychological disorder. Our mood is one of mild dejection or dysphoria that generally passes within a matter of days. In contrast, when the disturbance of one's mood is more severe and persistent just as Lisa's eventually became, it may be classified as depression, one of the various mood disorders. **Depression** is *an emotional state characterized by intense and unrealistic sadness that may assume a variety of forms, some more severe and chronic than others.* Depression is one of the most common disorders in our society. It is sometimes referred to as "the common cold of mental illness." Whereas the common cold rarely kills anyone, clinical depression often does. Many suicides in the United States are committed by people suffering from depression (Rochford.org, 2000; Schindehette, Calandra, Podesta, & Williams, 2004; Williams, Crane, Barnhofer, Van der Does, & Segal, 2006).

Depression can assume a variety of forms. In many instances, people experience the symptoms of depression only to a mild or moderate degree, so they may continue their everyday activities. Others may suffer from any number of the common symptoms of depression, including decreased energy, loss of interest in everyday activities such as eating, feelings of inadequacy, periods of crying, and a pessimistic attitude. You may have recognized some of these symptoms in the case of Lisa.

It is estimated that three-quarters of all college students suffer some symptoms of depression during college, one-quarter of them at any one time. In almost half of these students, the depression is serious enough to require professional help. Depression may be triggered by the stress of student life, academic pressures, and the felt need to make a career decision. Depression is often brought on by cognitive distortions, such as exaggerating the importance of getting good grades or the loss of a love relationship. When students confront their actual problems instead of dwelling on their distorted self-perceptions, they tend to have more success in breaking out of their depression. People who suffer from major depression experience many of the same symptoms, but in a more severe and chronic way. In some cases, major and severe depression may include psychotic features such as delusions and hallucinations. This condition almost always interferes with everyday functioning, and in some instances, periods of hospitalization and medication may be necessary (Hanson et al., 2005). Contrary to popular belief, a major depression can occur at any age. The age of onset is fairly evenly distributed throughout adult life. It is estimated that depression affects over 18 million Americans at any given time, with women *possibly* affected more than men (Schrof & Schultz, 1999a; NIMH, 2006a). Box 14–4 discusses in some detail these sex differences. More than half of those who experience one episode of major depression will eventually have another within 2 years.

Some people are more vulnerable to *depression at certain times of the year, especially the winter months.* They suffer from a peculiar mood disorder commonly labeled **SAD— seasonal affective disorder.** The causes of this recently recognized disorder remain unclear. Because more than two-thirds of those with this syndrome have a close relative with a mood disorder, genetic factors are suspected. Another theory is that gloomy winter weather disturbs the body's natural clock, affecting the production of serotonin and melatonin. The presence or absence of light is thought to be a major factor. During darkness, the pineal gland in the brain secretes larger amounts of the hormone melatonin, associated with drowsiness and lethargy. Light suppresses the secretion of this chemical. Although the extra melatonin secreted in winter doesn't disturb the body's chemical balance in most people, those with SAD may suffer from an overdose of this

Box 14–4

MEN, WOMEN, AND DEPRESSION

Depression has been called the common cold of mental disorders. In other words, depression is very widespread. Women are more prone to depression than men; at least that is what is believed by American psychologists and psychiatrists. Women, therefore, are twice as likely as men to be diagnosed with depression (Mentalhelp.net, 2005). Let's look a little closer at this issue.

Why are women more depressed? Or are they? One might readily assume that there are biochemical differences, for example, hormonal differences, between men and women that leave women more vulnerable to depression. In support of this view, the differences in depression between men and women do not emerge until after puberty (Mayo Clinic, 2002; Mentalhelp.net, 2005; NIMH, 2006g). It was also once believed that women were simply more likely to seek professional help for depression compared with men, inflating the figures for women. Studies have demonstrated that this is not true; women really do suffer more from depression (NIMH).

There are other plausible explanations for the higher rates of depression in women than in men. Many of the other explanations pertain to societal and cultural causes (Mayo Clinic, 2002; NIMH, 2006a). Women have unequal power and status compared to men. For example, there is generally more discrimination against women in the workplace. Minority women face the double whammy of race *and* sex discrimination. Discrimination is a difficult burden to bear. Furthermore, women are more likely to live in poverty than men; many are single mothers.

Women also do more housework than men; few people report liking such chores. In fact, one study demonstrated that there is a relationship between amount of household strain, housework performed, and depressive symptoms (NIMH, 2006g). Working and married women, then, juggle multiple tasks and suffer from work overload (Mayo Clinic, 2002; Mentalhelp.net, 2003).

Newer brain imaging research has also shown that the brain region affected by depression is eight times larger in women than in men (Foote & Seibert, 1999). Women and men also learn to manage stress and emotions in different ways. Women may be less inclined to act on their problems and more inclined to dwell (ruminate) on them (Mayo Clinic, 2002; Mentalhelp.net, 2003). These and other factors, then, are likely to contribute to higher rates of depression in women than in men (Mayo Clinic).

hormone. Interestingly, new research reveals that not everyone living in winter darkness suffers from SAD. Icelanders, for example, have lower levels of SAD than Americans, perhaps because of some unique adaptive mechanism (Raymond, 2000). So far, people with SAD are finding relief with light therapy (Mallikarjun, 2005; Sher, 2004). During the winter months, they spend time each day in front of a sun-box, a device fitted with powerful fluorescent lights that emit the full spectrum of natural daylight. One young man, who suffered from near-suicidal depression and weight gain of up to 30 pounds, found light therapy liberating. "It's given me more energy and a sense of well-being—something I haven't had during winter until now."

Depression has been attributed to a variety of causes, ranging from biological factors such as genes and biochemical processes to social and cultural influences (*Harvard Mental Health Letter*, 2005; Kelsey, 1999). Cognitive theorists point out that people can make themselves depressed by negative thinking or pessimistic cognitive styles (Alloy, Abramson, & Frances, 1999; NIMH, 2002). In contrast, some types of depression run in families, suggesting that biological vulnerability can be inherited. In some families, major depression also seems to occur generation after generation. However, it can also occur in people who have no family history of depression. Whether inherited or not, major depressive disorder is often associated with changes in brain structures or brain function (NIMH).

Depression is one of the most treatable of all disorders, but only about half of the sufferers will be adequately diagnosed. Perhaps only 15 percent of those diagnosed will get adequate treatment, because some family physicians see depression as a character weakness rather than as a health issue (Kelsey, 1999; Schrof & Schultz, 1999a).

Suicide: Who and Why?

Astonishingly, suicide is more common than homicide (murder) in American society (NIMH, 2003). In fact, suicides outnumber homicides five to three. Suicide also outranks AIDS/HIV deaths by two to one (NIMH). As mentioned, people who take their own lives, or attempt to do so are very often depressed (Rochford.org, 2000; Schindehette et al., 2004; Williams, Crane, et al., 2006); thus, our discussion of suicide is subsumed under the topic of mood disorders. Accurate figures on suicide are even more difficult to obtain than statistics on depression. One reason is that many people who commit suicide prefer to make their deaths look accidental, enabling their survivors to be spared the stigma associated with suicide. If the truth were known, as many as one out of six single-car accidents might actually be a suicide. Despite incomplete statistics, official figures indicate that about 30,000 people commit suicide each year in the United States (Rochford.org). However, most authorities estimate the actual cases of suicide to be two or three times that number. Thus, about every 5 minutes someone takes his or her life. If suicide *attempts* are included, someone somewhere is contemplating self-destruction every minute.

Adolescents and the aged are the most likely to commit suicide. White elderly men have the highest suicide rate of any group (NIMH, 2003). Especially alarming is the fact that the suicide rate for young people in the 15- to 24-year-old group has tripled in the last 30 years; suicide is now the third leading cause of death for them. Suicide rates generally increase with age before decreasing, except for male Caucasians. Men are more likely than women to commit suicide, and Whites are more likely than African Americans. Men are more successful than women, partly because men tend to use swifter and more violent means, such as a gun. In contrast, women are more likely to take pills or turn on the gas, which often allows time for intervention.

Why do people commit suicide? Surprisingly, suicide is more prevalent in affluent societies, so much so that it has been described as a disease of civilization. At the level of individual behavior, many possible motives have been suggested: escaping from pain or stress, trying to eliminate unacceptable feelings, turning aggression inward, punishing others by making them feel guilty, and acting impulsively on momentary feelings of desperation. Suicidal people often suffer from "tunnel vision"—the misperception that suicide is the *only* alternative to seemingly unsolvable problems in living. The tragedy is that such problems are often transitory, whereas the solution of suicide is permanent.

As mentioned previously, suicide is related to psychological disorders, especially depression, so it should be no surprise that Lisa's coworkers began to worry that Lisa might be suicidal. A study of adolescents attempting suicide found that compared to nonattempters, attempters were more likely to report a past suicide attempt, to report suicidal ideas in the past, and to be depressed (Rotheram-Borus, Walker, & Ferns, 1996). Curiously, severely depressed people are more likely to take their lives *as their situations improve*. When they are most depressed, they may not have sufficient energy to take their own lives, as was true for Lisa. Usually, it's when depressed individuals start to feel better and get their energy back that they commit suicide. In addition, autopsies of suicide victims have found abnormally low levels of **serotonin**—*a neurotransmitter that has been linked to depression*—suggesting that biochemical deficiencies may play a role in suicide. Box 14–5 alerts you to some of the other warning signs of an impending suicide.

The prevention of suicide has received great attention in recent years. Environmental approaches include tightening control over prescription sedatives, controlling gun purchases through legislation, and increasing protective measures (e.g., putting fencing around the observation platform of the Empire State Building in New York City). Another approach is to increase community awareness and resources for dealing with suicide. Many communities now have suicide and crisis intervention hotlines available 24 hours a day. Do you know whether your community or campus has a crisis line and how to reach it? Volunteers at these crisis services usually have specific goals, such as determining the seriousness of the suicide threat, establishing and conveying empathy, understanding of the caller's problems, describing available resources, and getting some sort of agreement that the caller will seek help.

Contrary to the myth that people who threaten to kill themselves seldom do so, most people who commit suicide express some suicidal intent, directly or indirectly, within several months before their deaths. It helps to recognize the warning signs, as noted in Box 14–5. Perhaps you've heard that questioning depressed people about their suicidal ideas will give such thoughts greater force. *This isn't true.* Providing an opportunity to talk about suicidal thoughts often helps these people overcome such wishes and know where to turn for help. If you notice the warning signals of suicide in a family member or friend, do your best to see that he or she gets professional help.

What Is Bipolar Disorder?

Unlike Lisa, some people experience *an alternation of elated and depressive moods, popularly known as manic depression* but now termed **bipolar disorder** (Perry, 2005). Usually, this disorder first appears as **mania**, in which *the individual exhibits such symptoms as an expansive*

Box 14–5
Warning Signs of Suicide

Some warning signs of suicide:

- Expression of suicidal thoughts or a preoccupation with death

- Prior suicide attempts

- Death of a close friend or family member

- Giving away prized possessions

- Depression or hopelessness

- Despair over a chronic illness

- Social isolation

- Change in sleeping and eating habits

- Marked personality changes

- Abuse of alcohol or drugs

- Sense of hopelessness

- Neglect of personal welfare

- Self-inflicted injury or other reckless behavior

- Divorce or stress in the family

- Job loss or loss of esteem or sense of security

mood, increased social activity, talkativeness, sleeplessness, and reckless behavior. For example, a college classmate of Lisa's had his first manic episode at the age of 19 when he was still living in a residence hall. His speech and behavior became frenetic and fast-paced. At first his close friends thought he was taking drugs or "uppers." The young man stayed up all night and moved all of the lounge furniture from every lounge in the dormitory into the main lounge. There were many lounges because the residence hall and the university were large. The next morning he woke all of his friends and invited them to his new "breakfast club," designed just for them so that they could eat breakfast in their pajamas rather than dress to go to the dining hall.

The subsequent episodes can occur in any one of several patterns. The initial manic episode may be followed by periods of normal activity, followed by a depressed episode and then another normal period. Or one mood may be followed immediately by its opposite, with normal intervals occurring between the manic-depressive pairs. In rare forms, the person's mood may alternate between manic and depressive episodes, with no intervals of normal functioning. In another rare form, the mixed type, the individual may experience symptoms of both moods simultaneously, that is, being expansive and yet weeping and threatening suicide at the same time.

In addition to the manic episodes, there are other characteristics that distinguish bipolar disorder from major depression. First, bipolar disorder is much less common than major depression, affecting between 0.4 and 1.2 percent of the population. Second, bipolar disorder is equally prevalent among men and women. Third, unlike major depression, which occurs more frequently among the lower socioeconomic classes, bipolar disorder is more prevalent among the upper classes. Fourth, although married people are less susceptible to major depression, they enjoy no such advantage in regard to bipolar disorder. Fifth, although major depression can occur at any time in life, bipolar disorder usually appears before the age of 30. Sixth, bipolar episodes tend to be briefer and more frequent than those in major depression. Finally, bipolar disorder is more likely to run in families. In fact, scientists are hot on the trail of the unique metabolic activity of the brains of bipolar individuals (Perry, 2005).

OTHER COMMON DISORDERS

Many other psychological disorders are described in the DSM, covering almost every conceivable complaint, from compulsive gambling to delusional (paranoid) disorder. We cannot possibly cover all disorders in this chapter; your college may offer an abnormal psychology course that you can take if you wish to learn about other diagnoses. Here, we'll describe three types of disorders that are of special interest because they are commonly misunderstood or are found with some frequency among college students: eating disorders; personality disorders; and schizophrenia, one of the most disabling of all disorders.

Do You Have an Eating Disorder?

Pam is Lisa's second cousin. She was a 17-year-old who was somewhat overweight for her age. She blamed much of her weight-gain troubles on her mother, who constantly urged her as a child to eat more. "Think about all the starving kids in _____ who'd love this food," admonished her mother. Pam also blames her current boyfriend, who threatens to break off their relationship "if you get any fatter." Pam suffers from an intense fear of getting even fatter. Her fears, coupled with a desire to become socially attractive, have led her to experiment with strict diets. As a result, Pam's weight recently plunged from 153 pounds to 99 pounds in less than a year.

Pam was recently diagnosed as having **anorexia nervosa**, *an eating disorder characterized by a severe loss of appetite and weight. The essential features of this eating disorder are a fear of becoming fat along with a disturbance in body image and a refusal to maintain normal weight.* In other words, the individual relentlessly pursues thinness. Eating disorders are not due to a failure of will or behavior; rather, they are real, treatable medical illnesses in which certain maladaptive patterns of eating take on a life of their own (NIMH, 2006b). Being 85 percent of normal body weight, along with other physical signs such as the suspension of menstrual periods, is usually sufficient for this diagnosis. When Pam stopped menstruating, she feared she was pregnant; how wrong she was! The weight loss is usually accomplished by a reduction in total food intake, especially foods high in carbohydrates and fats, use of laxatives or diuretics, and sometimes strenuous and excessive exercise.

Anorexic disturbance is *the way in which one's body weight or shape is experienced and includes undue influence of body weight or shape on self-evaluation or denial of the seriousness of the current low body weight* (NIMH, 2006b). Those who suffer from this disorder do not realize they are getting dangerously thin, even when they examine themselves in the mirror. "Dangerously thin" is not a misstatement; up to 20 percent of people who have an eating disorder die from it (Anred.com, 2000; NIMH, 2006b). It is also conjectured that the eating habits of these girls may have been so regulated by their parents that they have not learned to interpret the inner signals that they are hungry. Instead, they have an obsessional need to control their lives primarily through their eating habits, often engaging in elaborate rituals to ensure they will not eat too much. For example, Pam was observed to push her food around her plate a number of times before nibbling a tiny bit of it and then licking her empty fork several times. It appeared that she was eating because of all the commotion. In actual fact, she was eating very little.

Cheryl lives in the same large city as Lisa and Pam. Cheryl is 5 feet, 10 inches tall, is 20 years old, and had always been somewhat chubby for her age. For the past several years, however, she has begun to indulge in binge eating followed by purges of the consumed food. For instance, Cheryl will eat a quart of ice cream and a plate of brownies, gobbling the food down quite rapidly, with little chewing. Once she has started to eat, she feels a loss of control. She feels as though she cannot stop eating. Later, in secret, she induces vomiting by sticking her finger down her throat. The vomiting decreases the physical pain of overeating, thereby allowing either continued eating or termination of the bingeing. The entire cycle is followed by self-criticism ("Why do I eat so much?") and depression ("I'll never be able to stop myself; I am a failure").

Cheryl's condition is **bulimia nervosa**, *an eating disorder characterized by excessive overeating or uncontrolled binge eating followed by self-induced vomiting.* This disorder is closely related to but different from anorexia, which is more common (NIMH, 2006b). Whereas the aim of the anorexic is to lose weight, the bulimic attempts to eat without gaining weight. The essential features of this disorder are episodic eating sprees, or binges, accompanied by an awareness that this eating pattern is abnormal—a fear of not being able to stop eating voluntarily and a depressed mood and self-disparaging thoughts. "You have no self-control—shame on you!" criticizes the little voice in the bulimic's head. The bulimic is also unhappy with her body image, as is the anorexic (Joiner, Wonderlich, Metalsky, & Schmidt, 1995; NIMH). Individuals who suffer from bulimia sometimes diet excessively between binges.

Like anorexia, bulimia is more common among girls, especially those in the middle and upper socioeconomic groups. Although the estimated frequency of the disorder varies considerably, about one in four college-age women are involved in bulimic behavior (Anred.com, 2000). Research also indicates that gay men are prone to eating disorders because they, too, hope to please male partners. On the other hand, lesbians and heterosexual men are less prone to eating disorders (Siever, 1994). Similarly, African American women are less critical of their bodies and therefore less likely to develop an eating disorder than White women (Powell & Kahn, 1995).

Certain types of obesity can also be considered eating disorders. Compulsive or binge eaters constitute a distinct subgroup. **Binge eating** is *characterized by eating an excessive amount of food within a discrete period of time and by a sense of lack of control over eating during the episode* (NIMH, 2006b). Whereas most overweight people generally consume more calories than they expend over the course of each day, compulsive overeaters or binge eaters consume large amounts of food in a very short time without the subsequent use of purgatives or exercise. Often the binge eater eats alone due to embarrassment about the loss of control. It is estimated that about one-third or more of all individuals in weight-control programs report frequent episodes of compulsive overeating. Compulsive overeaters exhibit a higher-than-average incidence of psychological problems, especially depression. Eating more often in response to positive or negative emotional states (NIMH), compulsive overeaters also tend to experience greater mood fluctuations during the course of the day. Binge eating is commonly triggered by tension, hunger, consumption of any food, boredom, craving for specific foods, and solitude or loneliness. Think here about your pattern of eating. Do you overeat? Undereat? Get enough exercise? Are you prone to changing your eating habits at particularly stressful times? Do you have the potential to develop an eating disorder?

One of the most useful approaches to compulsive overeating is to set a weight goal that is more consistent with one's weight history than that obtainable from a normative chart or from images in the mass media. Thus, a 5-foot, 5-inch woman whose weight

Do you have an eating disorder?

was 165 pounds because of binge eating might be better off striving for the 135-to 145-pound range than trying to get down to a model-thin 100 pounds. Such an approach reduces the need for stricter diets, which in turn can sometimes contribute to additional binges. The chapter on the body and health discusses planning a healthy diet. If you are overweight, a binge eater, or are experiencing another eating disorder, you may want to access that information.

What Are Personality Disorders?

Personality traits are *enduring patterns of thinking, feeling, acting, and relating to others that we exhibit in a wide range of situations.* However, *when personality traits are so inflexible and maladaptive that they cause marked impairment in individuals' social and occupational life*, they may have one of the **personality disorders**. These disorders are generally longstanding and result in a pattern of deviation from accepted social norms. They are unique in that they tend to cause less distress to the individuals themselves than to others who live and work with them. As a result, these individuals resist getting professional help. Scientists now believe that many of the personality disorders described here are caused by childhood abuse and neglect (Battle et al., 2004). Several personality disorders that rank among the most common will be discussed here.

The **narcissistic personality** is *a disorder characterized by an undue sense of self-importance, often accompanied by a sense of inferiority.* This disorder is thought to be the characteristic personality disorder of our time, mainly because so many otherwise normal individuals in our society exhibit undue self-interest. Whereas a certain degree of self-interest may shield us from the effects of criticism or failure, excessive self-interest can be maladaptive, especially when the cravings for affection and reassurance become insatiable. People with this disorder generally exhibit a grandiose sense of self-importance in behavior or fantasy, often accompanied by a sense of inferiority. They exaggerate their talents and accomplishments and expect to be treated as special without the appropriate achievements. They are, however, hypersensitive to others' evaluation and react to criticism with arrogance and contempt. They believe they are unique and can be understood only by special people.

Psychologists differ about the causes of narcissistic personality disorder. Psychodynamic (Freudian) theorists believe narcissistic personalities compensate for the inadequate affection and approval they received in childhood. In contrast, cognitive and social learning theorists see narcissistic people as the products of exaggerated expectations during childhood of what they will achieve in adulthood. Whatever the primary cause, narcissism may be fostered by many forces in today's society, such as our preoccupation with self-fulfillment, the "overvaluing" of children, heightened expectations and sense of entitlement among youths, the prominence of television, and our pervasive consumer orientation.

One of the most unsettling personality disorders is the **antisocial personality**, *another personality disorder characterized by long-standing habits of maladaptive thought and behavior that violate the rights of others*—formerly called the psychopathic or sociopathic personality. These people have a history of chronic antisocial behavior, in which they disregard others' rights, usually starting before midadolescence. They tend to get in trouble with the law because of their predatory attitude toward people and their disregard for others' rights. They may act in an impulsive manner, such as stealing a pack of cigarettes or a car—whichever seems easier at the moment. Also, they are irresponsible, often walking out on their jobs or spouses. Antisocial personalities lack a normal conscience and, with little or no guilt, are manipulative toward others. One real example of antisocial personality is a man who courted and married 105 women, all without benefit of a divorce!

You well might ask, "How can people get away with such outrageous behavior?" One explanation may be their superficial charm, poise, and intelligence, all of which disarm their victims. Also, lacking a sense of responsibility, these individuals can engage in spontaneous behavior, giving the appearance of being free-spirited. In many cases, they have grown up in a family in which they have been undersocialized, with one or more of their parents exhibiting antisocial behavior. Western society may encourage antisocial tendencies by glamorizing fame and success, so that superficial charm and lack of concern for others may help antisocial people get ahead.

Another common personality disorder is **borderline personality disorder**. *The individual who suffers from this disorder shows impulsive behaviors and unstable social relationships as well as unstable self-image.* The impulsiveness is often self-damaging, such as substance abuse or reckless driving. This individual may also make suicidal threats or may self-mutilate in a desperate move to capture the attention of those who might abandon him or her. The individual's mood is also unstable, with intense or inappropriate episodes of irritability, anxiety, combativeness, and even euphoria. The individual manifests these symptoms in a variety of settings such as work or home. This personality disorder, in particular, is very disturbing to those close to the borderline individual; it strains interpersonal relationships to the breaking point. Psychotherapists often do not like to work with such individuals because of their manipulativeness and their tendency to want help at all times (Perry, 1997). Box 14–6 discusses other prevalent personality disorders.

Schizophrenia—The Enigmatic Disorder

Most of us can understand what it's like to be panic-stricken or depressed, but the bizarre behavior of a person with schizophrenia remains a mystery to us. Schizophrenia is a chronic and very disabling disorder (NIMH, 2006f); it baffles and frustrates

---

Box 14–6

OTHER PERSONALITY DISORDERS

Paranoid personality: Characterized by a basic distrust of others. Usually such distrust and suspiciousness is without basis.

Schizoid personality: Evidenced by social isolation and shallow emotions. Lacks close friends or confidants.

Schizotypal personality: Typified by social unease and eccentric behavior. Also manifests odd beliefs or magical thinking that is inconsistent with cultural norms.

Histrionic personality: Characterized by attention seeking and excessive emotionality. Uses dramatic behaviors and physical appearance to draw attention to self.

Avoidant personality: Demonstrated by social constriction, low self-esteem, and extreme avoidance of negative self-appraisals.

Obsessive-compulsive personality: Not to be confused with OCD. Marked by need to maintain control and order. Has a preoccupation with perfection, details, rules, and so forth that interferes with task completion.

psychologists. Schizophrenia erroneously has been called "split personality" by the public. Here are some facts about schizophrenia (NIMH):

- In the United States, approximately 2.4 million adults, or about 1.1 percent of the population age 18 and older in a given year, have schizophrenia.
- Rates of schizophrenia are very similar from country to country—about 1 percent of the population.
- Schizophrenia ranks among the top 10 causes of disability in developed countries worldwide.
- The risk of suicide is serious in people with schizophrenia.

Because *schizophrenia* is a label given to a group of related disorders, it's impossible to describe the "typical" person with schizophrenia. We might define **schizophrenia** as *a group of related psychotic disorders characterized by severe disorganization of thoughts, perceptions, and emotions; bizarre behavior; and social withdrawal.* The essential features of these disorders include **psychotic symptoms,** *symptoms that are signs of psychosis and that include hallucinations such as hearing voices, marked impairment in self-care and social relationships, and other signs of severe disturbance.* To diagnose schizophrenia or other disorders where psychotic symptoms are apparent, there must be continuous signs of the disturbance for at least 6 months, including an active phase of at least 1 week or less if the symptoms have been successfully treated (American Psychiatric Association, 1994). Here are other symptoms:

1. Disorders of speech. One of the most striking features of individuals suffering from schizophrenia is their peculiar use of language—in both the form and the content of thought and speech. There is a loosening of associations of thought and rambling, disjointed speech. Words that have no association beyond the fact that they sound alike, such as *clang* and *fang*, may be juxtaposed with each other.

2. Distorted beliefs. This major disturbance in the content of thought involves **delusions**—*beliefs that have no basis in reality.* For example, individuals may feel they are being spied on or plotted against by their families.

3. Distorted perceptions. Individuals suffering from schizophrenia seem to perceive the world differently from other people. They have difficulty focusing on certain aspects of their environment while screening out other information. Instead, their inner world is flooded with an undifferentiated mass of sensory data, resulting in odd associations, inner confusion, and bizarre speech. In addition, many schizophrenics experience **hallucinations**—*sensory perceptions that occur in the absence of any appropriate external stimulus.* The most common hallucination is hearing voices that characteristically order these people to commit some forbidden act or that accuse them of having done some terrible misdeed.

4. Blunted or inappropriate emotions. Schizophrenia is characterized by a blunted affect (emotions), or in more severe cases, a lack of emotions. Schizophrenic individuals may stare with a blank expression or speak in a flat, monotonous voice. Or they may display inappropriate emotions, such as giggling when talking about some painful experience.

5. Social withdrawal. People who eventually have a schizophrenic episode tend to be loners, preferring animals, nature, or inanimate objects to human company.

Perhaps they are preoccupied with their inner world, or having learned that they are often misunderstood, they prefer to keep to themselves. When in the presence of others, they avoid eye contact and tend to stand or sit at a greater distance from people than others do. They are also emotionally distant, making it difficult to establish satisfying close relationships with them.

Despite extensive research, the causes of schizophrenia are not fully understood. For a long while, a dysfunctional family environment was regarded as a major cause of this disorder, but in recent years there has been increasing evidence that genetic, neurological, and biochemical factors may play an even greater role (NIMH, 2006f). Nevertheless, about half of the identical twins that share the same genes with a schizophrenic twin do not develop this disorder (NIMH). Thus, a predisposition by itself does not appear sufficient for the development of schizophrenia. The **diathesis-stress hypothesis** views *schizophrenia as the interaction of a genetic vulnerability (the diathesis or predisposition) with environmental stressors.* That is, schizophrenic individuals tend to inherit a lower threshold to certain types of stress, which, if exceeded, may precipitate an acute episode of the disorder. If an individual manages to keep the level of environmental stress well below a particular threshold and despite a genetic predisposition, that person may never experience an acute episode of schizophrenia. The initial onset of schizophrenia usually occurs in adolescence or early adulthood. You might think that Lisa, a young adult under stress,

Schizophrenia is distinguished by a wide array of seemingly disparate symptoms; no one individual, however, manifests all of the symptoms all of the time.

would be a candidate for schizophrenia, but without the genetic propensity for schizophrenia, she instead developed depression.

Schizophrenia may appear abruptly, with marked changes in behavior in a matter of days or weeks, or there may be a gradual deterioration in functioning over many years. During this initial phase, individuals are socially withdrawn. They display blunted or shallow emotions and have trouble communicating with others. They may neglect personal hygiene, schoolwork, or jobs. By this time, such individuals may have begun to exhibit the bizarre behavior and psychotic symptoms signaling the onset of the active phase. The *active phase* of the disorder is often precipitated by intense psychological stress, such as the loss of a job, rejection in love, or the death of a parent. During this period, the psychotic symptoms become prominent. Schizophrenic individuals begin to hallucinate, hold delusions, and exhibit incoherent and illogical thought and bizarre behavior. However, no one person manifests all these symptoms; each individual exhibits a somewhat different pattern.

In the *residual phase*, individuals with schizophrenia may recover from the acute episode in a matter of weeks or months. Some of the psychotic symptoms, such as hallucinations or delusions, may persist, although they are no longer accompanied by intense emotion. These individuals may continue to exhibit eccentric behavior and odd thoughts, for example, believing they are able to control events through magical thinking. As a result, many of them are not ready to fully resume everyday responsibilities, such as holding a job or running a household.

Box 14–7

OUTLOOK FOR RECOVERY

How well an individual recovers from the active phase of schizophrenia depends on a variety of factors, especially the following:

1. *Premorbid adjustment.* The more adequately the person functioned before the disorder, the better the outcome.

2. *Triggering event.* If the disorder is triggered by a specific event, such as the death of a loved one, the possibility of recovery is more favorable.

3. *Sudden onset.* The more quickly the disorder develops, the more favorable the outcome.

4. *Age of onset.* The later in life the initial episode of schizophrenia appears, the better. Men are more at risk before the age of 25; women are more at risk after 25.

5. *Affective behavior.* Symptoms of anxiety and other emotions, including depression, are favorable signs. A state of hopelessness not accompanied by depression is a poor sign.

6. *Content of delusions and hallucinations.* The more delusions involve feelings of guilt and responsibility, the better the outlook. Conversely, the more the delusions and hallucinations blame others and exonerate the individual, the more severe the disorder.

7. *Type of schizophrenia.* Paranoid schizophrenia, the most common type, has a better outlook, mostly because the individual's cognitive functioning remains relatively intact compared with other types of schizophrenia.

8. *Response to the disorder and the treatment.* The more insight individuals have concerning what makes them ill, the more responsive they are to the medication; and the more cooperative they are with their therapists, the better their chances of recovery.

9. *Family support.* The more understanding and supportive these individuals' families are, the better their chances of a good recovery.

There is a considerable difference of opinion about the outlook for individuals who have suffered an acute schizophrenic episode. Traditionally, clinicians adhered to the principle of thirds; that is, about one-third of the people who have experienced a schizophrenic episode make a good recovery, another one-third make a partial recovery with occasional relapses, and still another one-third remain chronically impaired. However, with improved methods of treatment, powerful antipsychotic drugs, more favorable attitudes toward those afflicted with this disorder, and more sophisticated research strategies, a larger proportion of schizophrenic individuals are making at least a partial recovery (NIMH, 2006f). How well an individual recovers from an acute schizophrenic episode depends on many factors. Box 14–7 details some of the other factors that predict who possibly will recover from schizophrenia.

Once again, if you or someone you know appears to have one of these disorders, the best thing to do might be to get professional help. If you are going to an educational program in a community unfamiliar to you, your campus counseling center, the dean of students, a dormitory adviser, or a psychology professor could help you find appropriate assistance.

SUMMARY

PSYCHOLOGICAL DISORDERS

We began the chapter by noting that there is no simple way to determine whether someone has a psychological disorder. In practice, professionals rely on a combination of standards, such as the presence of personal distress, significant impairment in behavior, the social acceptability of the behavior, and an important loss of personal control. Overall, about one out of every three persons will experience at least one significant psychological problem in his or her lifetime, ranging from the mildly disabling anxiety disorders to severe ones like schizophrenia. In the DSM, an authoritative guide to the various disorders, the emphasis is on describing the characteristic behavior patterns of the various disorders rather than interpreting the possible causes, which are often unknown.

ANXIETY DISORDERS: THE MOST COMMON DISORDER

In an anxiety disorder, the level of anxiety is out of proportion to the stressful situation or may occur in the absence of any actual danger. Anxiety may be experienced in different ways in the various disorders. In the general anxiety disorder, a chronic sense of diffuse or free-floating anxiety becomes the predominant disturbance, and the person is anxious most of the time. In contrast, the phobic disorders are characterized by a chronic, irrational fear of a specific object or activity, together with a compelling desire to avoid it, that is, avoidance behaviors. The essential features of obsessive-compulsive disorder are recurrent obsessions or compulsions or both, as seen in people preoccupied with various checking and cleaning rituals.

MOOD DISORDERS

The mood disorders involve different types of mood disturbances, including extreme elation and depression. Depression may range from mild despondency to a major depressive disorder that is so disabling it requires hospitalization. Seasonal affective disorder is a form of depression that seems to be caused by the short and dark winter days in some parts of the world. Suicide now ranks as one of the leading causes of death among young men and women. Suicide is also more common among the elderly. In contrast, bipolar disorder, popularly known as manic depression, involves depression alternating with extreme elation and usually appears in young adults.

OTHER COMMON DISORDERS

Anorexia is an eating disorder primarily of adolescent girls that is characterized by a disturbance in body image and eating habits and results in a loss of normal body weight. Bulimia, a related eating disorder, involves episodic eating binges accompanied by a fear of not being able to stop eating voluntarily, eventually followed by a depressive mood. Recently, attention has been given to compulsive or binge eaters, those who consume large amounts of food in a very short time without the subsequent use of purgatives or exercise.

People with personality disorders are characterized by maladaptive behavior patterns that impair their social and occupational lives. The disorder may be more noticeable to those around the individual rather than to the individual. Those with a narcissistic personality disorder have an exaggerated sense of self-importance and need constant reassurance to maintain their inflated esteem. In contrast, those with an antisocial personality disorder get into trouble because of their predatory attitude toward people and their disregard for others' rights. The borderline personality is impulsive, has disturbed interpersonal relationships, is manipulative, and can be self-damaging. Other personality disorders exist.

Schizophrenia, one of the most severely disabling of all the psychological disorders, affects about 1 percent of the American population sometime during their lives. Symptoms include disordered thought, imaginary voices, blunted emotions, and social withdrawal. Although the causes of schizophrenia are not fully understood, it is thought that it results from an interaction of a genetic predisposition and environmental stress.

SELF-TEST

1. A major factor in determining whether someone has a psychological disorder is the presence of
   a. interpersonal conflicts.
   b. personal distress.
   c. lack of behavior.
   d. anxiety.

2. The most common group of psychological disorders in the United States are the
   a. anxiety disorders.
   b. personality disorders.
   c. schizophrenic disorders.
   d. mood disorders.

3. A chronic state of free-floating anxiety is often the main symptom in which one of the following disorders?
   a. phobic disorder.
   b. generalized anxiety disorder.
   c. bipolar disorder.
   d. personality disorder.

4. An example of a social phobia is someone with an intense fear of
   a. closed places.
   b. crowded stores.
   c. public speaking.
   d. being in elevators, even if alone.

5. The person who reenters the house several times to make certain the stove has been turned off before leaving for work probably has
   a. a mood disorder.
   b. a simple phobia.
   c. a personality disorder.
   d. obsessive-compulsive disorder.

6. In contrast to major depression, bipolar disorder
   a. commonly appears before age 30.
   b. affects more women than men.
   c. results in suicidal tendencies.
   d. is less likely to run in families.

7. Which statement regarding suicide is correct?
   a. More women succeed in committing suicide than men.
   b. Suicide is more common in the old than in middle-aged adults.
   c. Suicide is less prevalent in affluent than impoverished societies.
   d. Suicide goes hand in hand with phobias.

8. The eating disorder characterized by episodic eating binges and purges is called
   a. anorexia nervosa.
   b. fasting disorder.
   c. bulimia nervosa.
   d. compulsive overeating.

9. People who have a history of chronic "deviant" behavior with little or no regard for the rights of others probably have
   a. a schizophrenic disorder.
   b. antisocial personality disorder.
   c. bipolar disorder.
   d. multiple personality disorder.

10. Which of the following factors generally indicates a *favorable* sign of recovery for someone experiencing an acute schizophrenic episode?
    a. sudden onset.
    b. resignation to being sick.
    c. lack of emotions.
    d. onset in adolescence.

EXERCISES

1. *Have you ever experienced a panic attack?* Even if you've only experienced intense anxiety, write a page or so describing what it was like. Be sure to include what occasioned the anxiety and how it affected you. Also, write about how well you cope with similar situations today.

2. *Are you bothered by an intense fear or phobia?* If you were to list your worst fears, which ones would you include? Do you share some of the more common fears, such as the fear of snakes or spiders? Or are you bothered by other fears? What are you doing to overcome your fears?

3. *Managing the "blues."* Most of us have times when we feel down. The important thing is knowing how to handle ourselves so that we can snap out of such low moments. Write a page or so describing how you cope with discouragement and depression. How effective is your approach?

4. *Feeling better.* When you feel down, do you try to think of happier moments? What makes you happy? What makes you sad? Do the two "triggers" have anything in common, or does each moment have its own trigger?

5. *Have you known someone who committed suicide?* To what extent did this person exhibit the characteristics discussed in the chapter? Also, in retrospect, did the person display any of the warning signs of suicide? At this point, do you think you're better able to recognize individuals with a high risk for suicide? If you suspected someone was suicidal, what would you do?

6. *Psychological disorders in the family.* Do you have relatives who have suffered from a psychological disorder? If so, which ones? Are any of these disorders those that tend to run in families, for example, schizophrenia or major depression? What steps, if any, are you taking to avoid such problems?

7. *Distinguish schizophrenia from the commonly used term "split personality."* People tend to confuse these two. Do you know the difference between them? Can someone have a split personality? To test yourself, you might write a paragraph or so explaining how the two terms differ. Ask your instructor to check your answer to make certain you really understand the differences.

QUESTIONS FOR SELF-REFLECTION

1. Do you believe society tolerates greater deviance than in the past? What are the advantages and disadvantages of greater toleration?

2. When you become anxious about something, how does this affect you? Does anxiety energize you? When you are relaxed, how do you feel? How is your behavior different in these two situations?

3. How do you cope with occasional feelings of despondency or depression? Do you live in a climate that might induce seasonal affective disorder? Do you suffer from it? What can you do about this disorder?

4. Do you think women are more apt to seek professional help for their mental disorders than men? Why?

5. Would you agree that depression among men is often masked by drinking or drug problems?

6. Do you know someone who has attempted suicide or who succeeded? How did the suicide affect you?

7. How would you account for the high suicide rate among older White men? Do you think the reasons adolescents and the elderly commit suicide are different from White men's reasons?

8. What are some of the chronic self-destructive behaviors people engage in? Why do you think people engage in these behaviors? Can people change voluntarily, or do most people need therapy?

9. Are you aware that some individuals who have experienced acute schizophrenic episodes resume normal lives? What do you think brings on remission from schizophrenia? Can you imagine what it is like to live as an individual with schizophrenia?

FOR FURTHER INFORMATION

RECOMMENDED READINGS

AMEN, D. G., & ROUTH, L. C. (2004). *Healing anxiety and depression*. New York: Penguin. Two well-trained scientists highlight the similarities between anxiety and depression by demonstrating that both appear to be brain disorders. They use neuroimaging and case studies to elucidate their main points.

BOURNE, E. J. (2005). *The anxiety and phobia workbook*. Oakland, CA: New Harbinger Publications. This workbook discusses the causes of fears and anxieties, treatments for anxiety, the relationship of self-esteem to anxiety, and lifestyle changes designed to help you overcome anxiety and phobias.

FAIRBURN, C. G., & BROWNELL, K. D. (2005). *Eating disorders and obesity: A comprehensive handbook*. New York: Guilford Press. The second edition of this well-reviewed book offers a compendium of the latest information on all types of eating disorders, including obesity.

SOLOMON, A. (2002). *Noonday demon: An atlas of depression*. New York: Simon & Schuster. This book examines depression from personal, social, and scientific perspectives.

TORREY, E. F. (2001). *Surviving schizophrenia: A manual for families, consumers, and providers*. New York: Harper Perennial. A handbook for families of schizophrenics and others touched by this baffling disorder.

WEB SITES AND THE INTERNET

http://www.psycom.net/depression.central.html   A site provided by a psychiatrist about depression in all ages and groups of people with information on genetics and other causes of depression. The site also contains information on other mood disorders and links to other sites.

http://www.save.org/   A valuable site on suicide, its warning signs, misconceptions about suicide, and how a forgotten group, survivors, can better cope with their loss.

http://www.mentalhealth.com/   Contains information about all types of mental disorders with good information on a large variety of personality disorders and phobias. The information includes symptoms, treatments, and relevant research on each.

http://mentalhelp.net/   A good general resource for information on a variety of disorders. Has chat rooms, book lists, possibilities for participating in research projects, and so forth.

http://www.nimh.nih.gov/publicat/schizoph.cfm   A government web site with a wealth of information about schizophrenia for individuals with schizophrenia, their family members, and their friends.

CHAPTER 15

If You Go for Help

INSIGHT THERAPIES—THE
TALKING CURE
Psychoanalysis
The Person-Centered Approach
A Variety of Approaches

COGNITIVE-BEHAVIORAL THERAPIES
Behavioral Therapies
Cognitive Therapies
Status of Psychotherapy Today

OTHER APPROACHES TO TREATMENT
Family, Couples, and Relationship
    Therapy
Biomedical Therapies
Community-Based Services

HOW WELL DOES THERAPY WORK?

FINDING HELP

SUMMARY
SELF-TEST
EXERCISES
QUESTIONS FOR SELF-REFLECTION
FOR FURTHER INFORMATION

Since moving back home 3 months ago, Sergei has been at odds with his parents, who emigrated with him from Russia when Sergei was 10. Sergei admits he's going through a difficult time in his life. He recently lost his job—again—and is having trouble making the payments for his car. To make matters worse, he has just asked his father for another small loan to help him through his present financial crisis. Sergei's parents see things differently. They feel that Sergei is floundering and has no sense of direction in his life. His friends think he is depressed, as seen in his constant but vague complaints, fatigue, and boredom. Since the recent breakup with his girlfriend, Sergei has been staying out late and drinking heavily several evenings each week and then refusing to get up in the morning. Sergei's friends are concerned and insist he get therapy. Sergei agrees very reluctantly after they apply much pressure to him. "But I'll see the shrink just once," he says, "mostly to satisfy you I'm not crazy." His parents, however, are Russian immigrants and do not want Sergei sharing their family problems with a stranger. They remember all too well when secrets shared with strangers in Soviet Russia resulted in the informant's disappearance. Sergei's friends insist that he should give the therapist a chance. "Okay, okay, I'll give it a try. But I'm not making any promises."

Why are people like Sergei so reluctant to seek professional help? The answers probably vary from one person to another. Some individuals, especially those with little education, resist getting help because of the stigma associated with mental disorders. In the popular mind, psychotherapy is for people who are "crazy." Unfortunately, seeking assistance for a mental disorder remains stigmatized (Gary, 2005; Shalala, 1999; Vaccaro, 2004; Weiss & Ramakrishna, 2006).

Psychotherapy is *the helping process in which a trained, socially sanctioned therapist performs certain activities that will facilitate a change in the client's attitudes and behaviors.* In practice, psychotherapy is more likely to be used by people with the milder disturbances, who seek it as a means of personal growth as well as for the relief of symptoms. However, in our society, which places a high value on self-sufficiency, getting help may be seen as an admission of weakness. This is probably the major reason men are less likely than women to seek professional help for psychological problems. It's more acceptable for women to express their emotions and admit weakness. Men are expected to cope on their own and, as a result, often mask their problems with alcohol and drugs, as Sergei is doing. In many instances, people don't know how to go about getting help, or they may feel that therapy is too costly. In any event, only about one in five adults with a serious psychological problem will seek help from a mental health professional such as a psychiatrist or psychologist. Family physicians, clergy, and other types of counselors such as social workers will see many other individuals.

Would you recognize when to seek help? If you have been in counseling, have you reassessed yourself lately to see if you could use a mental health tune-up? Do you have friends like Sergei does who would encourage you to seek assistance if they thought you were depressed or were drinking too much? Or would you do what thousands of Americans do, avoid therapy because of the stigma, cost, or inconvenience? To assess whether you might be a candidate for psychotherapy or some other form of assistance for a mental disorder, complete the assessment found in Activity 15–1.

A major problem in choosing a **therapist**—*a person trained to help people with psychological problems*—is sorting through the various approaches to therapy. There are now close to 270 different forms of therapy, including various insight therapies as well as many types of behavioral and group therapies. Despite their differences, most therapies share certain common goals. All of them afford clients relief from their symptoms, such as intolerable anxiety or depression. Many of them offer clients better understanding of their thoughts, feelings, motives, and relationships. They also help clients modify their problem behaviors, such as excessive fear (e.g., phobias) or compulsive gambling. In addition, many therapies help clients to improve their interpersonal relationships at home and work. Different schools of therapy emphasize some of these goals more than others; some may put more emphasis on adjustment, whereas others may concentrate on growth or address emotional

---

ACTIVITY 15–1

Taking a Look at Yourself

INSTRUCTIONS: *The following self-assessor was developed by the federal government to help consumers understand if and when they might need assistance with mental health issues. Do any of the following feelings or experiences make you feel miserable or get in the way of doing the things you want to do most or all of the time? Place a check mark in front of those statements that do.*

_____ **1.** Feeling as though your life is hopeless and you are worthless

_____ **2.** Wanting to end your life

_____ 3. Thinking you are so great that you are world famous, or that you can do supernatural things

_____ 4. Feeling anxious

_____ 5. Being afraid of common things like going outdoors or indoors, or of being seen in certain places

_____ 6. Feeling as though something bad is going to happen and being afraid of everything

_____ 7. Being very "shaky," nervous, continually upset and irritable

_____ 8. Having a hard time controlling your behavior

_____ 9. Being unable to sit still

_____ 10. Doing things over and over again—finding it very hard to stop doing things like washing your hands, counting everything, or collecting things you don't need

_____ 11. Doing strange or risky things—like wearing winter clothes in the summer and summer clothes in the winter, or driving too fast

_____ 12. Believing unusual things—such as that the television or radio is talking to you, or that the smoke alarms or digital clocks in public buildings are taking pictures of you

_____ 13. Saying things over and over that don't make any sense

_____ 14. Hearing voices in your head

_____ 15. Seeing things you know aren't really there

_____ 16. Feeling as if everyone is against you or out to get you

_____ 17. Feeling out of touch with the world

_____ 18. Having periods of time go by when you don't know what has happened or how the time has passed—you don't remember being there but others say you were

_____ 19. Feeling unconnected to your body

_____ 20. Having an unusually hard time keeping your mind on what you are doing

_____ 21. A sudden or gradual decrease or increase in your ability to think, focus, make decisions, and understand things

_____ 22. Feeling as though you want to cut yourself or hurt yourself in another physical way

If you answered "yes" to any of these experiences, you might want to discuss your feelings or behaviors with your family physician or a mental health professional.

SOURCE: SAMHSA. http://www.mentalhealth.org/publications/allpubs/SMA-3504/taking.asp (accessed July 14, 2003).

responses. There are three main schools of psychotherapy: insight therapies (e.g., psycho-analysis), person-centered therapies, and cognitive-behavioral therapies (Demorest, 2005). Because they appeared first on the psychotherapy landscape, we'll begin with the **insight therapies**—*those that bring change by increasing self-understanding.* A controversy exists in the current therapy literature as to whether **insight** or *self-understanding* is necessary for therapeutic change. Some experts claim that self-understanding leads to symptom reduction and improvement in mental health (e.g., Kivlighan, Multon, & Patton, 2000), whereas others claim insight is not necessary for meaningful change to occur (Norum, 2000).

INSIGHT THERAPIES—THE TALKING CURE

Psychoanalysis

According to Sigmund Freud (1965), the founder of psychoanalysis, psychological disturbances are due to anxiety about hidden conflicts among the different parts of our unconscious personality. (See Chapter 2 for a review of Freud's theory and a description of the parts of personality.) Thus, **psychoanalysis** involves *psychotherapy aimed at helping the person gain insight and mastery over unconscious conflicts.* If not expressed directly, these unconscious impulses and conflicts seek *indirect* release in all kinds of symptoms. The therapist's or analyst's purpose is to help the individual gain insight and conscious awareness of these unconscious desires or conflicts, thereby gaining emotional release and eventual mastery of them (Stern, 2006).

The core of the psychoanalytic approach is the analysis of **transference**—*the unconscious tendency of clients to project onto the therapist their feelings and fantasies, both positive and negative, about significant others in their childhood.* Therapists deliberately foster the development of the transference relationship through their own neutrality and relative passivity. Then, as the therapy proceeds, the therapist analyzes or explains the transference process to help clients achieve insight into the influence of the past on their present behavior (Stern, 2006).

"Working through" the transference relationship involves an exploration of unconscious material and defenses and includes a variety of techniques. One of the historically

Sigmund Freud, founder of psychoanalysis.

earliest of these was **free association**. In classic psychoanalysis, the individual is asked to lie down on a couch, relax, clear the mind of everyday thoughts, and then *say whatever comes to mind regardless of how trivial it sounds*. Sometimes clients are encouraged to talk about their dreams. Though these recollections might appear irrelevant, the well-trained analyst may use dream interpretation to shed light on the clients' problems. *When an individual hesitates or is reluctant to talk about some painful experience*, this is seen as a sign of **resistance**. For example, if Sergei had elected to see a psychoanalyst, he might have been reluctant to discuss his immigrant background. The therapist would have viewed this as important simply because Sergei would not talk about it. The therapist may wait or may use another approach to the area of resistance, so that eventually this problem can be overcome. By analyzing resistances, the therapist helps the clients see how they handle anxiety-provoking material. Today, some of these psychoanalytic concepts, such as resistance, have been accepted by other practitioners and therapists, although the assumed causes and methods for dealing with it may differ (Beutler, Moleiro, & Talebi, 2002; Grabhorn, Kaufhold, Michal, & Overbeck, 2005). Other Freudian concepts have also stood the test of time and, in fact, may be making a comeback because of recent scientific support (Gedo, 2002).

Traditionally, psychoanalysis involved hour-long sessions 3 to 5 times a week, often lasting several years. At the level of current fees, this schedule would make psychoanalysis prohibitively expensive for all but a privileged few. As a result, there have been many changes in this approach. Now psychoanalytic therapy may involve only 1 or 2 sessions a week and often lasts only 20 or 30 sessions. The therapist sits facing the client and takes a more active role in therapy compared to the impenetrable "mirror" role advocated by Freud. Psychoanalytic therapists are also likely to be more eclectic than in the past, using techniques from other approaches when appropriate. At the same time, the emphasis remains on gaining insight and self-mastery of the unconscious forces affecting one's behavior. There are few definitive studies showing analysis to be effective compared to no treatment or to be better than other therapies, but the results of the bulk of studies are encouraging (American Psychoanalytic Association, 1999). Recently, Blatt and Shahar (2004) demonstrated that psychoanalysis is more effective with clients who are ruminative, self-reflective, and introspective than is therapy such as the person-centered approach, described next.

The Person-Centered Approach

One of the major alternatives to psychoanalysis is Carl Rogers's humanistic approach to therapy. Toward the end of his career, Rogers (1980; Cornelius-White & Cornelius-White, 2005) changed the name of his approach from *client-centered therapy* to **person-centered therapy**, as a way of indicating that the same principles apply to a variety of fields of human interaction as well as to psychotherapy. According to this view, *the helper's genuineness, acceptance, and empathic understanding of the client are necessary and sufficient conditions for producing therapeutic change.*

Rogers developed his view of therapy out of his own experience as a therapist. Early in his career he was counseling a mother about her son, who was having problems. No matter what strategy he tried, he got nowhere. Finally, he admitted his failure. As the mother walked toward the door, she turned and asked Rogers if he ever saw adult clients. Then the woman returned to her seat and began pouring out her own problems. She spoke of her own sense of confusion and failure and her despair about her marriage, all of which were more pertinent to her son's problems than the sterile case-history approach they had followed before. After many more interviews, the woman felt better about her marriage, and her son's problem behavior melted away as well. Rogers felt the improvement had come because he had followed her lead, because he had listened and understood rather than imposed his diagnostic understanding on her. This was the first of many experiences that gradually led Rogers to the view that therapeutic progress comes mostly from respecting and responding to the client's own frame of reference and inherent potential for growth.

Therapists using the Rogerian approach believe that all of us have within ourselves vast resources for self-understanding and for altering our behavior and that these resources can be tapped if the proper climate for change can be provided. According to Rogers (1980), *three* conditions must be present for a growth-producing therapeutic climate. All of them pertain to the client-therapist relationship.

- *First, the therapist must be genuine, or "congruent,"* in the relationship, rather than maintaining a detached professional facade. That is, there is a congruence, or close matching, between what the therapist experiences at the gut level and what is expressed to the clients.
- *The second essential is an attitude of acceptance and caring.* When the therapist is accepting of and caring toward the clients at the moment, therapeutic change is more likely to occur. The therapist accepts the clients unconditionally, so that they are free to feel what is going on at the moment—whether confusion, resentment, fear, or love. This *positive, unconditional acceptance* (and caring for) clients is called **unconditional positive regard** (Gibson, 2005; Greenberg & Watson, 2006).
- *The third aspect of the therapeutic relationship is empathic understanding.* That is, the therapist accurately senses the feelings and personal meanings that the clients are experiencing and communicates this understanding to them.

Recent research has borne out that Rogers's brand of therapy promotes client and therapist co-thinking and co-experiencing (Bohart & Byock, 2005) as well as supported Rogers's emphasis on the therapeutic relationship as a means to change (Kirschenbaum & Jourdan, 2005). Other studies of Rogers's therapeutic techniques have demonstrated that support for Rogers's concepts of empathy and unconditional positive regard as critical elements of effective therapy (Kirschenbaum & Jourdan). Rogers maintains that as clients are understood and accepted, they accept themselves more fully and listen more accurately to the flow of their inner experience. They also become increasingly self-directed and experience greater freedom to become the true, whole person they would like to be.

During the early stages of therapy, one young woman said that whenever she looked within herself she felt nothing but emptiness: "There was just a cavern." Later, speaking about the change in her life, the same woman said:

It's real: I am in a very dynamic process of becoming. I'm not on top of the world yet (maybe, as Joe suggests, I'm somewhere around five on the process scale), but now I know I will be. The cavern is filling with experiencing, and feeling—and I'm in there—ME—A PERSON [Rogers, 1980, p. 218].

A Variety of Approaches

New forms of insight therapy continue to appear and take their place alongside the more established ones just described. Many of these newer approaches are attempts to add or emphasize aspects of therapy thought to be missing in existing therapies. For instance, in contrast to the so-called value-neutral approach to therapy, other therapies have been developed. As practiced by Rollo May, **existential therapy** is *an approach that emphasizes the clients' capacity for growth through affirmation of their free choice and personal values.* Another approach to insight therapy is logotherapy, developed by Viktor Frankl. **Logotherapy** *stresses the importance of clarifying those values that give personal meaning and purpose to one's life.* Thus, individuals must have the courage to make choices, break away from restrictive lifestyles, and take responsibility for their lives. **Gestalt therapy**, founded by Fritz Perls, also *puts great value on the individual's responsibility in therapy but makes more use of here-and-now nonverbal behavior in the therapy session as a way of helping clients to unify their feelings and actions.* **Actualization therapy**, developed by Everett Shostrom, *combines elements of the person-centered approach, gestalt therapy, and rational-emotive therapy (discussed under cognitive therapies) as a way of maximizing the individual's growth or self-actualization.*

There are new approaches to therapy, not just insight therapy, developing every decade. For a glimpse at what else is available, turn to Box 15–1.

Box 15–1

WHAT ARE ALTERNATIVE FORMS OF THERAPY?

An alternative approach to mental health care is one that emphasizes the interrelationship between mind, body, and spirit. Although some alternative approaches have a long history, many remain controversial. The National Center for Complementary and Alternative Medicine at the National Institutes of Health was created in 1992 to help evaluate alternative methods of treatment and to integrate those that are effective into mainstream health care. It is crucial, however, to consult with your health care providers about the approaches you are using to achieve mental wellness. Also, before receiving alternative services, check to be sure the provider is properly certified by an appropriate accrediting agency. The following are examples and do not represent all possible alternative forms of therapy.

GENERAL THERAPIES

- Diet and Nutrition
- Pastoral Counseling
- Animal-Assisted Therapies

EXPRESSIVE THERAPIES

- Art Therapy
- Dance/Movement Therapy
- Music/Sound Therapy
- Acupuncture
- Yoga/Meditation

RELAXATION AND STRESS-REDUCTION TECHNIQUES

- Biofeedback
- Guided Imagery or Visualization
- Massage Therapy

SOURCE: SAMSHA. http://www.mentalhealth.org/publications/allpubs/ken98-0044/default.asp (retrieved July 14, 2003).

COGNITIVE-BEHAVIORAL THERAPIES

Just when you thought there couldn't possibly be other ways to address psychological problems, there are! Today, a large and diverse group of therapists characterize their orientation as *either behavioral or cognitive, which, respectively, attempts to modify maladaptive behavior or faulty thinking.* These psychologists practice **cognitive therapy**, **behavioral therapy**, or **cognitive-behavioral therapy**, depending on whether they combine the two approaches. Having developed from research psychology more than clinical practice, both approaches focus on the problems themselves and how to modify them rather than on what caused them or on the client's emotions. Although you will read the descriptions of the behavioral and cognitive approaches separately, keep in mind that the trend is toward combining elements of each into a more inclusive alliance labeled *cognitive-behavioral therapies.* Research now strongly supports that this combined approach results in both short- and long-term effectiveness for a variety of disorders (Butler, Chapman, Forman, & Beck, 2006), for example, depression, generalized anxiety disorder, panic disorder, posttraumatic stress disorder, chronic pain, bulimia nervosa, obsessive-compulsive disorder, and even schizophrenia.

Behavioral Therapies

Instead of searching for the underlying causes of the client's difficulties, as in many insight therapies, behavioral therapists focus directly on the problem behaviors involved. For example, instead of focusing on Sergei's Russian childhood and his reticence about disclosing personal information to strangers, behavioral therapists would focus on his present problems of drinking too much, being unemployed, and being adversarial toward his well-intentioned parents. Their aim would be to help Sergei replace these maladaptive behaviors with more appropriate and satisfying ones. Typically, **behavioral therapy** involves *discovering the factors that trigger and reinforce the problem behavior; specifying a target behavior to replace it; and then, by manipulating these factors, bringing out the desired behavior.* In the process, behavioral therapists help clients to develop the necessary skills or behaviors to cope more effectively with their life situations.

Behavioral therapists draw on a repertoire of behavioral methods of proven effectiveness, for example, desensitization, aversive counterconditioning, token economies, modeling, and social skills training such as assertiveness training. For instance, many of our fears are acquired through the process of conditioned responses, based on the principles of classical conditioning. One form of therapy for countering such fears is desensitization. **Desensitization**, developed by Joseph Wolpe, is a *method of controlling anxiety by learning to associate an incompatible response, like relaxation, with the fear-provoking stimulus.* By linking the feared object or situation to something pleasant, like relaxation, the client becomes "desensitized" to the fearful situation (see Activity 15–2).

Desensitization is especially effective with fears and phobias. Wolpe (1973) tells of a 24-year-old art student who came for treatment because of her fear of taking examinations, which had resulted in repeated failures. Wolpe began by making up a hierarchy of imagined situations that made her anxious, culminating with the day of the examination. Then he taught her how to relax her body muscles and gradually associate the relaxed state with each of the feared situations. After 10 sessions, the art student felt free from anxiety at the highest level of the hierarchy. Four months later, she took and successfully passed her examinations without any disruptive anxiety.

ACTIVITY 15–2

OVERCOMING YOUR FEARS

Although desensitization is ordinarily done under professional supervision, it also can be used on a do-it-yourself basis with mild fears. There are four steps in desensitizing yourself.

First, on separate 3 × 5-inch cards, write down each situation you associate with a given fear or apprehension. Include at least 10 but no more than 25 items in your stack of cards.

Next, arrange these cards in a hierarchy from the least to the most threatening situation, preferably with small steps of anxiety arousal between each. For example, suppose you are afraid of riding in a crowded elevator. You might construct a hierarchy that includes imagined situations such as the following:

1. You're entering a building that has an elevator.

2. You're walking down the hall toward the elevator.

3. You're standing alone in front of the elevator and so on.

The next step is to train yourself in relaxation techniques. Sit in a comfortable chair or lie on a couch or bed. Then, beginning with your forehead and scalp, practice relaxing and letting your muscles go limp. Then progress to your jaw muscles, your neck, and so on. You can vary this technique by alternately tensing and relaxing each set of muscles. Or you can combine it with deep breathing, as described in the chapter on stress. Whichever method you use, spend two or three sessions practicing your relaxation techniques until you can become reasonably relaxed.

Now you're ready for the fourth step. Take the top card from the pile and look at it. Then close your eyes and visualize the situation as vividly as you can. As soon as you experience any anxiety, stop imagining the scene and go back to your relaxation techniques. When you are completely relaxed, look at the card again. Repeat this process until you can look at the card without feeling anxious. Then progress to the next card. You can heighten the realism of the imagined scenes by using such aids as pictures, recordings, slides, and videotapes.

It is important not to rush. Don't be upset if you can visualize only a few scenes in the hierarchy in each session. Each person has his or her own rate of progress. It's also a good idea to begin each new session with the last hierarchy scene that didn't arouse anxiety in the previous session.

In addition to confronting the client with imagined scenes, as in systematic desensitization, therapists may also use variations of this technique. In **behavior rehearsal**, for example, *the client role-plays the feared situation.* In real-life or **in vivo desensitization**, *the individual gradually approaches the feared situation directly*; it is *a method of controlling anxiety by learning to associate an incompatible response, like relaxation, with the fear-provoking stimulus.*

In vivo desensitization is an approach often used in treating **agoraphobia,** or *a cluster of irrational fears of open spaces.*

Cognitive Therapies

Cognitive therapists, drawing on a different set of principles, *focus on faulty cognitive processes as the crucial element in maladaptive behavior.* A major reason for this focus is their belief that cognitive processes—such as attention, perception, thoughts, and beliefs—may affect behavior independently of the stimuli traditionally emphasized by behaviorists. Indeed, cognitive therapists claim that people's actions are often shaped more by their own *interpretation* and *reactions* to external events than to the events themselves. Albert Ellis's **rational-emotive therapy** (Dozois, Frewen, & Covin, 2006; Ellis & MacLaren, 1998) and Aaron Beck's **cognitive therapy** (1979; Dozois et al.) are both well-known cognitive therapies. Although these therapies differ in emphasis and tone, they share a common approach. *The central assumption is that the emotional and behavioral problems result from the individual's distorted thoughts and reactions to external events rather than from the events themselves. These approaches encourage people to think more rationally about themselves and their problems.* Stated another way, these therapies share the view that individuals' beliefs affect their interpretation and response to various life circumstances, thereby contributing to emotional adjustment or maladjustment (Dozois et al.).

For example, Melissa, a friend of Sergei's, discovered that she had earned a low grade on her first test in psychology. She felt discouraged and soon engaged in some self-defeating thinking: "How stupid can I be! I'll never make a good grade in this course. I might as well drop it." A therapist trained in rational-emotive therapy might point out that Melissa is "awfulizing," that is, overreacting to her poor performance. The therapist would point out the irrationality of Melissa's thinking and model a more realistic evaluation of her situation, for example: "This was just the first test, not the final exam; your grades in other classes are quite good." The therapist would then help Melissa take positive steps to improve her performance, such as talking to the professor to discover the particular reasons she did poorly on the test, getting suggestions for improving her performance on the next test, and finding out what her chances are for eventually earning a good grade in the course. The therapist might instruct Melissa in monitoring her self-defeating thoughts, correcting her thinking, and preparing more effectively for the next test now. All of us can awfulize or catastrophize. Do any of the statements in Activity 15–3 frequently pop into your head?

Cognitive therapists differ from insight therapists in that they do not probe for deep-seated causes of the client's problems. For example, they would not be as likely as a psychoanalyst to explore Sergei's Russian childhood. Instead, their goal is to identify faulty assumptions and thought patterns and then rely on established behavioral procedures such as behavior rehearsal or desensitization to alter the behavior.

Status of Psychotherapy Today

There are, as always, many therapists who continue to practice the type of therapy for which they have been trained, modifying their orientation somewhat with experience. An increasing number of therapists, however, would characterize themselves as eclectic, in the sense of having been exposed to more than one theoretical orientation in their

Activity 15–3

Are You an Awfulizer?

INSTRUCTIONS: *Place a check mark next to each statement that describes your worrisome thought processes.*

_____   1. When I am driving in a strange place, I am sure I will get lost.

_____   2. On the very day I don't do the reading assignment, the professor will call on me.

_____   3. I just know when I meet someone new that person will not like me.

_____   4. My alarm clock is least likely to work when I have an early morning commitment.

_____   5. When I get sick, I know I'll feel worse before I feel better.

_____   6. I am certain that if I buy something, I'll soon find it elsewhere at a better price.

_____   7. When I most have to perform well, I perform the worst.

_____   8. At work, when a piece of technological equipment starts to act up, it spells doom for me.

_____   9. Unlike others, I find I have a cloud hanging over my head much of the time.

_____   10. When my car makes a strange noise, I just know it will be something expensive.

How many check marks did you end up with? Even one check mark might indicate that you catastrophize or "awfulize," which can lead to self-defeating behaviors. For example, if you become extremely anxious about having a car accident, you just might!

For each statement where a check mark appears, recast the statement in such a way that it represents a more rational, reasonable, or positive view of life, which can lead to more competent, gratifying behavior and less anxiety on your part.

training and continuing to add new techniques to their repertoires. They seem more intent on being able to use the most appropriate treatment strategy for a given client's problems than remaining within a particular school of therapy. As a result, in practice, many therapists incorporate aspects of more than one insight therapy as well as different behavioral techniques. This eclectic approach indeed may be more effective than any single approach by itself (Kensit, 2000). One other pattern that has been documented is that all forms of psychotherapy take place over shorter periods of time; those with severe mental disorders are the only ones who are treated long-term (Olfson, Marcus, Druss, & Pincus, 2002). The probable cause of the decrease in time spent by clients is the limitation set by health insurance companies.

OTHER APPROACHES TO TREATMENT

In addition to the individual therapies discussed so far, there are a wide variety of other types of interventions. For instance, group therapies have mushroomed in number and type in the past several decades. Groups not only offer opportunities for people to interact with others with similar problems but also are more cost-efficient, saving time and money—an important consideration today. We'll especially examine family therapy because the disruption of marriages and families has become a major source of stress in our society. Also, the gains in medicine and technology have produced more powerful drugs and sophisticated biomedical therapies, which have become an integral part of many treatment programs. Finally, one of the most dramatic changes in regard to treating individuals with mental disorders is the shift away from prolonged stays in large institutions to the use of community-based services, as you will see shortly. Before you read further about professionally led groups, read Box 15–2 about mutual-help or self-help

Box 15–2
MUTUAL-HELP GROUPS

Today, more than 12 million people participate in an estimated 500,000 self-help or mutual-help groups—groups whose members share a common problem and meet regularly to discuss their concerns without the guidance of professionals.

Although these groups frequently have multiple functions, such as fostering self-help and lobbying for reform, most have the same underlying purpose—to provide social support as well as practical help in dealing with a problem common to all members. A major assumption is that no one understands you or can help you better than someone who has the same problem, whether it's obesity, depression, or alcoholism. New members may approach their first meeting with apprehension, wondering what the group can do for them or what it will ask in return. Experienced members, well aware of these mixed emotions, encourage new members to feel relaxed and welcome. In an atmosphere that is friendly and compassionate, new members soon realize that their participation is voluntary, with no strings attached.

There is usually an unwritten code of confidentiality within the group. Even when there is a series of steps to recovery, as in the various "Anonymous" groups, members can proceed at their own pace. Some groups, especially those that deal with addictive behavior or emotional disorders, may use a "buddy" system so that a new member can count on a familiar person for encouragement and support. All in all, mutual-help groups provide an atmosphere of acceptance and support that encourages their members to communicate more openly, view their problems more objectively, and find more effective coping strategies. Research demonstrates that most mutual-help groups are effective in producing member change (Duffy & Wong, 2003).

Numerous agencies and clearinghouses provide information on mutual-help groups. If you fail to find the mutual-help groups of interest in your phone book, visit the American Self-Help Clearing House web site at http://selfhelpgroups.org, which houses a directory of self-help groups.

groups in which laypersons assist one another. Sometimes the help of a professional is not necessary; a good friend can be just as healing.

Family, Couples, and Relationship Therapy

Relationship Therapy.   Married and unmarried couples alike usually come to relationship therapy because of some crisis, such as infidelity on the part of one partner or a breakdown in communication. A common problem encountered by therapists is the case in which one partner, usually the more dominant person in the relationship, threatens to leave, and the other partner wants to keep the marriage or relationship intact. Although each person tends to blame the partner for the predicament, therapists tend to focus more on the partners' interaction and relationship. For instance, if one person has engaged in an extramarital affair, instead of joining in the blame, the therapist may ask each partner what he or she thinks caused this situation. Perhaps the offending partner has a personality problem or wanted to get back at the other partner. Either way, the therapist helps both of them become more aware of how they treat each other; how they may unwittingly hurt each other; and most important, how they may nurture each other. The therapist often has to help the couple clarify the extent to which they really want to work at the marriage and, if so, how to proceed. Therapy that goes beyond individual intervention is more complex because of the various relationships and alliances involved (Rait, 2000). Despite the complexity, research reveals strong evidence of its effectiveness (Johnson & Lebow, 2000).

When couples chronically experience anger, defensive, or miscommunication, a good relationship therapist would ask to see both members.

Family Therapy.   **Family therapy**, as the name implies, *involves the larger family unit, including children and adolescents, on the assumption that the disturbance of one family member reflects problems in the overall family patterns*. There are now dozens of different types of family therapy, which vary in their theoretical approaches, range of techniques, and procedures. Some therapists prefer to see the entire family from beginning to end. Others may see the parents for a couple of sessions, then the children for a couple of sessions, and finally bring them all together. Still others, such as contextual therapists, who adhere to an intergenerational approach, may even involve members of the extended family in therapy. In Sergei's case, perhaps his grandparents would participate if they were available, particularly because in Russian culture extended families are considered very important. Implicit in all such therapies is the assumption that families function as systems, so the individual's problems are best understood and treated as an integral part of the family milieu. In Sergei's case, his parents might also be involved in Sergei's therapy so that they could learn to interact more effectively with their "Americanized" son.

Suppose a teenager is having trouble in school or is doing something that indicates a problem. The usual course of events is to make the teenager the client, leaving untouched the larger background of problems at home. However, professionals oriented to family therapy may discover upon further investigation that the identified client is simply the most sensitive and vulnerable person in the family and has become the scapegoat of a troubled family. When this is the case, it may be necessary to see other members of the family to get a better understanding of the family's dynamics to help the identified client. For example, Brad, another friend of Sergei's, reluctantly consulted a therapist because of parental pressure to do so. His parents complained that he was running around with a group that was into drugs and petty larceny. The therapist soon discovered that Brad's problems were fueled in part by his parents' serious marital problem and Brad was suffering from "split loyalty." His mother was resentful of the long hours her husband spent at work, along with numerous alleged extramarital affairs, and went to great lengths to make certain Brad knew about his father's disloyalty to the family. As a result, Brad felt pressured, mostly subconsciously, to take his mother's side in the family feuds. In doing so, however, he felt cut off from his father's influence and support. Brad responded by withdrawing from both parents, pretending he didn't care about his parents' marital problems and spending all his time with his friends, including the heavy-drinking Sergei. The therapist asked both parents to come in and gradually helped them to see how their marital problems were contributing to their son's troubles. Once the parents became aware of what they were doing to Brad, both of them made greater efforts to cooperate, at least as far as their son's welfare was concerned. Brad, in turn, felt less divided in his loyalty to his parents and spent his energy resolving his own problems. In fact, Brad's therapy was so successful that he was one of the friends who encouraged Sergei to see a mental health professional.

Biomedical Therapies

In contrast to the various forms of verbal therapy, **biomedical therapies** are *strategies that rely on direct physiological intervention to treat the symptoms of psychological disorders*. In recent years, there has been a rapid accumulation of evidence that many disorders are related to biochemical abnormalities, especially **neurotransmitters**—*chemical substances (or messengers) involved in the transmission of neural impulses between neurons*. As a result, psychoactive drugs have especially become an indispensable part of treatment. Many of

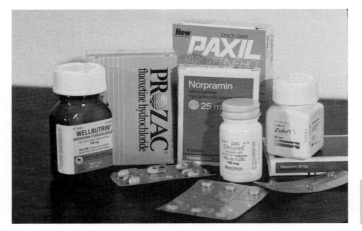

Drug therapies continue to be the most widely used biomedical therapies.

those with severe disorders like schizophrenia may be treated primarily with drugs. Those with less severe disorders may be treated with medication, but often in conjunction with the other therapies discussed so far. In fact, research demonstrates that this is a good strategy. Thase et al. (1997) analyzed the literature on psychotherapy compared to psychotherapy *combined with* biomedical therapies and found that for severe cases of mental disorder, combined approaches are most effective. For less severe cases, psychotherapy alone is as effective as the more expensive combination of psychotherapy with drugs.

Drug therapies continue to be the most widely used biomedical therapies. In fact, there have been significant increases in the use of psychotropic medications (Rubin, 2004). Whereas about one-third of psychotherapy users received a medication in 1987, almost two-thirds receive psychotropic medication today (Olfson et al., 2002). The three major medication categories are antianxiety, antidepressant, and antipsychotic drugs (National Institute of Mental Health [NIMH], 2006c). Sergei would be an unlikely candidate for such therapies. These medications do not mix well with alcohol.

Antianxiety drugs are the most commonly prescribed psychoactive drugs in the United States. These are *drugs that are used primarily for alleviating anxiety, including minor tranquilizers.* In most cases, family physicians prescribe a tranquilizer for people going through a difficult time, but these drugs are also used in the treatment of anxiety disorders, stress-related disorders, and withdrawal from alcohol or other drugs (NIMH, 2006c). As useful as these medications are, they are not without side effects. The most common are fatigue, drowsiness, and impaired motor coordination. Also, when used in combination with alcohol or other central nervous system depressants, these drugs can be dangerous or even fatal. Finally, the most common criticism of antianxiety medications is that they may provide such prompt alleviation of symptoms that people avoid solving their problems in behavioral or social ways. Consequently, these drugs may be most useful on a short-term basis.

Antidepressants *are used to treat depression and elevate mood, usually by increasing the level of certain neurotransmitters,* especially norepinephrine and serotonin. These drugs help to relieve many of the typical symptoms of depression, such as sleeplessness or excessive sleepiness, chronic fatigue, loss of appetite, loss of sex drive, sadness, and feelings of worthlessness. A significant disadvantage of these drugs is that they do not begin to take effect for about 2 to 4 weeks—which can be a long time for seriously depressed people waiting for relief. Newer, quicker-acting antidepressants have been introduced, but it remains to be seen whether they will be as effective. Antidepressants are the medication class whose use has most dramatically increased in recent years (Olfson et al., 2002).

Lithium—*a natural mineral salt and mood stabilizer—is used to treat people with bipolar disorder.* Lithium is capable of terminating three-fourths of all manic episodes (unduly elevated moods) and some cases of depression. When taken regularly, in maintenance doses, lithium eliminates or at least diminishes mood swings in bipolar disorder (NIMH, 2006c). However, because the effective dosage is close to a toxic one, it is difficult to prescribe the proper maintenance dosage of lithium. Furthermore, many patients stop taking their medication because lithium takes away the sense of well-being they feel in their manic or excited state. The interruption of lithium treatment usually leaves patients just as vulnerable to the disabling manic episodes as they were before treatment began.

Antipsychotic drugs, as the name suggests, are used to treat the symptoms of severe disorders such as schizophrenia (NIMH, 2006c). *These medications primarily relieve the symptoms of psychoses, such as extreme agitation, hyperactivity, hallucinations, and delusions.* As mentioned earlier, the use of antipsychotic drugs is often the primary treatment for patients with schizophrenia, especially those chronically impaired. These drugs are thought to work by blocking the activity of dopamine and other neurotransmitters, thereby reducing hallucinations, delusions, and bizarre behavior. However, they do not cure the apathy, social withdrawal, or interpersonal difficulties found in people with schizophrenia, for which psychotherapy is usually helpful. Antipsychotic drugs also have several side effects. In producing calm, they may produce apathy as well, reducing the patient to a zombielike state. Also, a small proportion of patients develop **tardive dyskinesia**, *characterized by jerking movements around the neck and face and involuntary protrusions of the tongue.* Today, newer medications with fewer side effects are available. These are called atypical antipsychotics and appear to be more effective than older medications (NIMH). Despite the disadvantages and the criticisms surrounding the use of such drugs, antipsychotic drugs have been the single biggest factor in reducing the institutionalized patient population in the United States from over half a million in the 1950s to about one-third that number today (Duffy & Wong, 2003). Over two-thirds of individuals with schizophrenia who regularly take their medication can remain out of the hospital. Consequently, most professionals who work with them believe the value of the drugs outweighs their potential for adverse side effects.

Electroconvulsive therapy (ECT), for reasons that are not completely understood, helps to relieve severe depression in some patients. ECT *involves the administration of an electric current to the patient's brain to produce a convulsion.* Although people often react negatively when it is mentioned, ECT has been refined and is done in a more humane manner than in the past (NIMH, 2006c). For severely depressed individuals for whom medication is ineffective, ECT usually involves 6 to 10 treatments, spaced over a period of several weeks. The patient typically is given general anesthesia and a muscle relaxant. Then an electric current of approximately 70 to 130 volts is administered to the temple area for a fraction of a second, causing convulsions for a minute or so. Within half an hour, the patient awakens and remembers nothing of the treatment. The most common side effect is memory loss, especially the recall of events before the treatment. Despite the controversy over ECT, its effectiveness in treating severe illness is recognized as useful by the American Psychiatric Association and similar organizations in other countries.

Box 15–3

ALLEVIATING DEPRESSION THROUGH EXERCISE

Dozens of studies link regular physical exercise with lower levels of depression and anxiety (e.g., Tkachuk & Martin, 1999; Barbour & Blumental, 2005). Most studies point to the fact that regular exercise is a cost-effective treatment for mild to moderate depression. Some studies also indicate that exercise may also be a viable treatment in conjunction with other treatments for schizophrenia and anxiety disorders (Tkachuk & Martin). In other words, people who exercise regularly are less depressed. Some researchers, however, realize it might work the other way around, namely, that people who are more depressed simply exercise less.

To demonstrate the link between exercise and depression, DiLoreno et al. (1999) had one group of individuals complete a 12-week fitness program and compared them to nonexercising participants. Results showed that the exercising participants experienced positive fitness changes as well as positive psychological benefits, including less depression.

It is not clear how or why exercise affects depression. Some explanations focus on the changes in body and brain chemistry (e.g., Zheng et al., 2006), resulting in rising levels of endorphins in the blood during exercise. Other explanations suggest that the sense of mastery over one's body gained through exercise may contribute to a greater sense of personal control over other aspects of one's life as well, thereby alleviating the passivity and helplessness often found in depressed people. Because the more severe types of depression typically result from a complex interaction of genetic, physiological, and psychological factors, exercise is best seen as only one factor in the overall treatment of depression—but one that should not be overlooked.

Psychosurgery is an even more drastic procedure (Egan, 2005), so much so that Sergei certainly would not be a candidate for it. This is *surgery designed to destroy or disconnect brain tissue in an attempt to regulate abnormal behavior.* Psychosurgery is aimed at reducing abnormal behavior. In the earlier prefrontal lobotomies, the surgeon severed the nerves connecting the frontal lobes of the brain with the emotion-controlling centers. Although many severely disturbed patients became calm, others emerged from surgery in a vegetative state. As a result, professionals welcomed the introduction of antipsychotic drugs, which produce similar results in a safer, reversible manner. Since then, the surgical procedure has been refined. However, lobotomies are still the treatment of *last resort* and are used only rarely, mostly for severely depressed, suicidal patients who have not responded to other treatments.

After reading these passages on biopsychological approaches to treatment of mental disorders, you may be wondering whether we can use less intrusive physiological methods for improving our mental status. After all, each of the techniques just described can have serious side effects. The answer is yes, as you will see in Box 15–3.

Community-Based Services

Is your stereotype of the mentally disordered that of a homeless person, sleeping on the streets, carting around possessions in a stolen grocery cart? Does your stereotype include the person begging, urinating on the street, and curling up on apartment house stoops during cold snaps? This is the image we often hold of the mentally ill. This description need not be the case but sometimes is.

The introduction of antipsychotic drugs, along with convincing evidence that custodial care in large mental hospitals is detrimental, led to the release of large numbers of ex-patients into the community over the past 40 years. Because most of these individuals require some type of treatment, as do others in the community who wish to avoid hospitalization, mental health professionals have responded by providing more **community-based services**. This is a general term meaning that *mental health services are located in the individual's own community or nearby*. The passage of the Community Mental Health Centers Act in 1963 aimed to create a **community mental health center** for every 50,000 people in the United States. These include *a variety of mental health services located in the patient's own community*. Everyone in the catchment area (an area of geographical coverage) for the center would have access to the needed psychological services at the center at affordable fees, without having to leave the community. Although the actual services provided by these centers have fallen far short of the initial vision, they have been a major factor in the nationwide shift away from hospitalization to community-based care (Duffy & Wong, 2003).

As you might expect, outpatient services are the most heavily used services of local mental health centers. The goal of outpatient services is to provide help for individuals without disrupting their normal routine. Most mental health centers offer short-term therapy for individuals in the community with a variety of problems, ranging from domestic disputes to severe emotional disturbances.

The more comprehensive centers also provide alternatives to hospital care, such as day hospitals, halfway houses, and emergency or crisis services. **Day hospitals** that *provide part-time care in a hospital setting for those with mental disorders* have been established throughout the United States. These treatment centers provide the needed therapeutic care to patients from morning until late afternoon and then allow them to return to their families in the evening. Another agency that has proliferated in recent years is the **halfway house**—*a residence in which newly released patients and ex-addicts can live under supervision for a short period of time while they make the crucial transition in their lives from a setting with close supervision and other restrictions*. Halfway houses are also called *group homes* and *board-and-care homes*. The best halfway houses are small residences that are staffed by paraprofessionals who help the residents learn to live together and acquire the appropriate skills for returning to community life (Duffy & Wong, 2003). **Crisis intervention** has also emerged in response to a widespread need for *immediate treatment for those who are in a state of acute crisis but do not need treatment for many sessions*. Most people who come for short-term crisis counseling do not continue in treatment for more than a few sessions. In addition, a variety of telephone hotlines is now available in many communities. Even police in some cities, who are often the first to come in contact with a mentally disordered person in crisis, receive some crisis intervention training (Duffy & Wong).

Community-based services often fall short of what is needed, mostly because of insufficient funding and the resultant inadequacies in facilities, staffing, and carefully thought-out and coordinated programs that address the needs of the community (Duffy & Wong, 2003). Because of these inadequacies, the return of former patients to the community has slowed significantly. Even when individuals return to the community, they lack the necessary supervision and support to stay there. In large cities, many of them become "street people" before returning to the hospital—hence, our stereotype. As a result, in many regions, *the number of admissions to mental hospitals has increased rather than decreased, leading to a "revolving-door" syndrome* or **transinstitutionalization** (Duffy & Wong).

The revolving-door syndrome and the presence of so many former mental patients in jails, on the streets, and in nursing homes remind us that although comprehensive community-based care is an excellent idea, it is far from achieving its original goals (Duffy & Wong).

HOW WELL DOES THERAPY WORK?

Have you ever wondered what therapy is like? Have you ever wondered if therapy would work for you? Better yet, have you ever questioned whether psychotherapy works at all? For many years, hardly anyone bothered to ask such a question. Therapists and clients alike held a kind of blind faith that therapy does work. Then after reviewing various studies on the subject, Hans Eysenck (1966) shocked the world of therapy by concluding that over time, clients *not in therapy* improved as much as did clients *in therapy*. Eysenck's claims were hotly contested and challenged by other researchers. Since that time, scientists have typically asked three major questions about the effectiveness of therapy:

(1) Is therapy better than no therapy?

(2) Is one particular type of therapy more effective than others?

(3) Are certain disorders more amenable to certain therapies?

Let's address these questions in order of presentation.

Is psychotherapy effective? Extensive studies have confirmed that therapy tends to have positive effects. For example, the American Psychiatric Association, which developed a commission on psychotherapy, says that based on research, at the end of therapy, the average treated patient is better off than 80 percent of untreated patients (Gabbard & Lazar, March 10, 2004). Another organization, the American Psychological Association, whose members are psychologists rather than psychiatrists, says:

> There is convincing evidence that most people who have at least several sessions of psychotherapy are far better off than untreated individuals with emotional difficulties. One major study showed that 50 percent of patients noticeably improved after eight sessions while 75 percent of the individuals in psychotherapy improved by the end of six months [American Psychological Association, 1998].

A *Consumer Reports* (2004) study of 3,079 readers who saw mental health professionals found that most individuals felt much better after therapy. These results are encouraging because a recent study found that the use of psychotherapy continues at the same or higher level for most people in the United States (Kessler et al., 2005) and has actually increased for some socioeconomically disadvantaged groups (Olfson et al., 2002).

Research subsequent to Eysenck's has also provided some idea about what elements make therapy effective, no matter what the theoretical underpinning (O'Donohue, Buchanan, & Fisher, 2000; Kolden et al., 2006). One important aspect found over and over again is *the match between the client and the therapist* (Kolden et al.). Recall Blatt and Shahar's study (2004) that demonstrated that psychoanalysis is most effective with clients who are ruminative, self-reflective, and introspective. Another way to provide a good match is for *the client to become an active consumer of information*, that is, to ask questions about the therapist's qualifications, for explanations about the diagnosis, and so forth. Another important ingredient is *length of treatment*, with longer treatments yielding better results (Seligman, 1995). In research on the number of sessions required for treatment, 20 or fewer sessions seem to be the norm today for effective treatment. Assigning "homework," focusing on skills building and problem solving, and repeating assessments also contribute to effective intervention (O'Donohue et al., 2000).

This leads us to our second question: *Is one type of psychotherapy more effective than another?* The answer the scientific literature provides is that *there is little difference among types of interpersonal psychotherapy* (Wampold, Minami, Tierney, Baskin, & Bhati, 2005). However, for a variety of reasons, various forms of interpersonal therapy increasingly are approximating cognitive-behavioral therapy (Ablon & Jones, 2002). Regardless of the type of psychotherapy, research on *early* stages of therapy suggests that a robust therapeutic relationship early on promotes therapeutic benefits, more productive sessions, as well as better mental health status. Such early gains lead to more expressive and receptive involvement in subsequent sessions. This openness, in turn, fosters further role investment in the therapeutic interaction (Kolden et al., 2006). As reviewed by Ackerman and Hilsenroth (2003), research on therapist characteristics that enhance the effectiveness of therapy shows that therapist flexibility, honesty, respect for the client, trustworthiness, warmth, and openness are very important to success. Similarly, the therapeutic techniques of reflection, accurate interpretation, facilitation of expression of affect, and free exploration of ideas and emotions are also important ingredients. In fact, many behavior therapists who traditionally have slighted the curative power of the therapeutic relationship are now emphasizing it to a far greater extent than in the past. According to all of this research, Sergei would be well served by psychotherapy. If his primary disorder is depression, what type of therapy do you think would work best in his case? Or do you believe medication would be better?

We now arrive at our last question: *Is one type of therapy better or worse for any particular disorder?* Although more research is merited on all of these issues, the answer to this third question at this point seems to be "yes." To date, cognitive-behavior therapies appear to be effective for anxiety disorders and depression (Butler et al., 2006). Psychoactive drugs are most effective for treating schizophrenic disorders (Hollon, Thase, & Markowitz, 2002). As more answers become available through research, psychotherapists may increasingly offer specific treatments for particular problems or integrate different approaches that may be more effective than a single approach with certain individuals.

Remember, too, that therapy is not exclusively dependent on the therapist's skills, the disorder, and the type of therapy. The client's traits and motives are also important (Vogel, Wester, Wei, & Boysen, 2005). The type of person likely to benefit most from psychotherapy is someone who is articulate, motivated, anxious to change, capable of becoming personally involved in therapy, and believes in psychological processes as explanations for behavior (Nietzel, Bernstein, & Milich, 1991). Another client (and therapist) characteristic that affects efficacy of therapy is cultural background (Kress, Eriksen, Rayle, & Ford, 2005). Recall that Sergei's Russian parents wanted to keep their family problems to themselves and not share them with a stranger, in this case his therapist. Some research has suggested that Asian and Hispanic Americans tend to underutilize mental health care services (Bui & Takeuchi, 1992; Sue, Fujino, Hu, Takeuchi, & Zane, 1991). Sue et al. argue that even when ethnic minorities seek mental health care, they tend to have higher dropout rates than Whites. What Sue et al. suggest is that the mental health care professional share the same ethnic background as the client.

FINDING HELP

Being knowledgeable about psychotherapy is one thing. Knowing how to get professional help for yourself and others is another matter. Should you or someone like Sergei have the occasion to seek professional help, you might consider the following questions:

1. When should you seek professional help? As you might expect, there is no simple answer to this question, as so much depends on the particular person and the situation. However, a simple rule is this: Whenever your problems begin to interfere with your work and personal life, it's time to seek professional help. Also, when your present methods of coping with your problems no longer work, that's another sign that you may need help, especially when your family or friends are tired of being used as therapists and become openly concerned about you. Most importantly, whenever you feel overwhelmed and desperate and don't know what to do, it's best to seek help.

You don't have to have a serious problem, much less a psychological disorder, to benefit from therapy. As mentioned earlier, more and more people are seeking therapy to find personal growth, improve their coping skills, and get more out of life.

2. Where do you find help? Help is available in a wide variety of settings. A large proportion of therapists work in comprehensive mental health centers that are now available in many communities. Staffed by a combination of psychiatrists, psychologists, social workers, and counselors, these centers offer a variety of services, including emergency help, all at a nominal fee that depends on income and ability to pay. See Box 15–4 for a description of the various types of mental health professionals available.

Many therapists work in private practice, either in a group or individual setting. They are usually listed in the yellow pages by their respective professions, for example, psychiatrists, psychologists, social workers, or family therapists. Although some are expensive, you may be reimbursed for part of the fee, depending on the type of insurance you have. Investigate with your health insurance company first. If you don't have insurance, some clinics provide low-cost or free services.

Many private social service or human service agencies provide short-term counseling and support for such matters as family problems, addiction problems, and career counseling. Also, many private and mental hospitals offer emergency help for psychological problems. Then, too, most high schools and colleges have counseling centers, which provide psychological help as well as academic guidance and career counseling. If all else fails, the American Psychological Association Practice Directorate at 800 374-2723 can aim you toward an appropriate state organization that can make a local referral.

3. What should you look for in a therapist? Among the major considerations for choosing a therapist should be (1) whether the therapist is professionally trained and certified and (2) how comfortable you feel with this person. Ordinarily, people must be properly qualified to list themselves as psychiatrists, psychologists, or social workers in the telephone directory. Also, professionals are encouraged to display

Box 15–4

WHO ARE THE THERAPISTS?

Unlike law or medicine, in which there is a single path to professional practice, there are many routes to becoming a psychotherapist. Because few states regulate the practice of psychotherapy as such, the question of who may legitimately conduct psychotherapy is governed by state law or professional boards within the respective professions.

- **Psychiatrists** *are medical doctors who specialize in the treatment of mental illness.* They usually spend 3 to 4 years training in a clinical setting following their medical degree and can treat the psychological disorders requiring drugs and hospitalization.

- **Psychoanalysts** *are psychiatrists or other mental health professionals who have received several years of additional training in personality theory and the therapeutic methods of one of the founding analysts,* such as Freud, Jung, Adler, or Sullivan.

- **Psychologists** *receive clinical training in the methods of psychological assessment and treatment as part of a program*

in clinical, counseling, or school psychology. They may have a Ph.D., Ed.D., or Psy.D. degree.

- **Psychiatric social workers** *receive supervised clinical training as part of their master's degree program in the field of social work, and some earn a doctorate as well.* They tend to be community-oriented and usually work as part of a clinical team, though many now enter private practice.

- **Counselors** *receive training in personality theory and counseling skills, usually at the master's-degree level. Their counseling emphasis tends to reflect their respective professional affiliations, depending on whether they are doing marriage counseling, career counseling, pastoral counseling (clergy), or some other type.*

- **Paraprofessionals** (*para* meaning "akin to") *have 2- or 4-year degrees (or sometimes no degree at all) and work in the mental health field.* Sometimes as many as half the staff members of a community mental health center work at the paraprofessional level, assisting in the helping process in a variety of ways.

their state license and other certificates in a prominent place in their office. But you will also want to feel comfortable talking to the therapist. Does this person really listen to you? Is the person warm and empathic without being condescending? Does this person understand and appreciate your particular point of view? Box 15–5 discusses a rapidly growing trend that will make therapy seemingly available to everyone, no matter how remote a region they live in. This trend involves therapy via computers and the Internet.

Once you've selected a therapist, it's appropriate to inquire in the initial session about such matters as the therapist's approach to therapy. Recall that the therapist's theoretical orientation may be less important than personal characteristics, professional experience, and skills. The relative influence of other matters, such as the therapist's age, gender, and ethnic background, depend largely on their importance to you. You will also want to discuss fees. Fees vary widely among private practitioners, with clinical psychologists and psychiatrists being the most expensive. Some practitioners do not accept insurance, and others are not recognized by various insurance companies, so check carefully.

4. What can you expect from therapy?   Most therapies provide certain common benefits, such as an empathic, caring, and trusting relationship; hope for the demoralized; and a new way of understanding yourself and the world. Beyond this, a lot depends on the goals and progress made in your particular therapy. People seeking relatively short-term therapy usually acquire a better understanding of their problems as well as the necessary skills to cope with a personal or family crisis. Those undergoing

Box 15–5

Computers and Therapy: Wave of the Future?

An increasing number of psychotherapists are offering on-line help; in fact, technology may become an important part of psychotherapy delivery in the next decade (Newman, 2004). There are now so many on-line therapists that no one quite knows what to name this new form of therapy: etherapy, ecounseling, cybertherapy, or telecounseling (Elleven & Allen, 2004).

Many therapists are setting up World Wide Web pages accessible to millions of Americans with credit cards and computers. Some therapists, however, provide the caveat that cybertherapy does not allow for as detailed probing as does face-to-face intervention. On the other hand, some clients may feel better about sharing their most intimate secrets with a computer rather than with a therapist in a face-to-face setting. Newman (2004) suggests that research now shows that contrary to many criticisms, technology need not necessarily compromise the all-important therapeutic alliance between client and therapist.

Critics of cybertherapy (Haveren, Habben, & Kuther, 2005) argue that ethical issues are beginning to emerge; for example, confidentiality may be betrayed if the wrong person receives an electronic message either to or from the therapist or client. Critics also argue that the client may know little about the on-line therapist's qualifications because of the geographic distance between client and therapist and that clients who are not computer savvy may feel uncomfortable with cybertherapy.

Other means for finding help on-line are rapidly developing. For example, social support is offered in the form of chat lines, bulletin boards, and news groups for individuals with specific disorders. Similarly, some psychological journals have gone on-line so that mental health consumers can do their own literature searches. One rich web site is the one offered by the American Psychological Association; see especially information on the link to "Monitor on Psychology".

Another new use for computers in therapy is virtual therapy. **Virtual therapy** *employs the high-tech tools of virtual reality, which essentially is often a computer-generated fantasy world that can be controlled by the client.* Virtual therapy has been used to distract burn victims from their pain as well as to engulf phobics with harmless but feared virtual stimuli such as spiders and snakes. Research on this type of therapy is just beginning, but one disadvantage is already well known—the expense of the hardware and software.

---

relatively long-term therapy, such as psychoanalytic therapy, aspire to more fundamental changes in their personality and may remain in therapy longer.

5. How long must you go?   In the past, the lack of objective guidelines made it difficult for therapists and clients alike to know how long therapy should last. However, the recent trend toward short-term therapies and the increased concern for containing health care costs have made the length of therapy a major issue. At the same time, the rate of improvement varies considerably among different types of clients. Consequently, the appropriate length of treatment often becomes an empirical issue to be decided by clients and their therapists with some interference from insurance carriers.

As a practical guide for deciding when to terminate therapy, consider two key questions: First, is the crisis or problem that brought you to therapy under control? You need not have resolved all of your difficulties, but you should have more understanding and control over your life so that your difficulties do not interfere with your work and personal activities. Second, can you maintain the gains acquired in therapy on your own? It's best to discuss these two issues with your therapist before deciding to terminate therapy. At the same time, bear in mind that in therapy, as in all close relationships, there will be unsettling as well as gratifying occasions. Therapy can become so uncomfortable that you may want to quit. If you put yourself into it and keep going, however, you'll eventually find it's a very rewarding experience.

SUMMARY

INSIGHT THERAPIES—THE TALKING CURE

At the outset, it was stated that many people suffering from a psychological disorder will not get help from a mental health professional, such as a psychologist. Many will be seen by their family physician or a counselor. Traditionally, clients have sought out insight-oriented therapies, which aim at bringing about change by increasing self-understanding.

Modern psychoanalytic therapists use a modified version of Freud's ideas and techniques to help clients achieve insight into and self-mastery of the unconscious forces in their lives. In contrast, Rogers's person-centered approach assumes that individuals have within themselves vast resources for self-understanding and growth, which may be actualized within a caring and empathic relationship conducive to change. In addition, a variety of other insight therapies, such as existential therapy, gestalt therapy, and actualization therapy, emphasize aspects of therapy thought to be missing in more mainstream therapies.

COGNITIVE-BEHAVIORAL THERAPIES

Cognitive-behavioral approaches developed out of research and experimental psychology and tend to focus on the maladaptive thoughts and behaviors themselves rather than on their causes or on emotions. Behavioral therapists focus directly on the client's problem behaviors, with the aim of replacing maladaptive behaviors with more appropriate and satisfying ones. For instance, in desensitization, the client learns to substitute a new response, such as relaxation, for an old, maladaptive response, such as anxiety or fear. Cognitive therapies tend to focus on the irrational thoughts and beliefs that contribute to problem behaviors.

Today, there is an increasing alliance between behavioral and cognitive therapies. As a result, more therapists characterize their orientation as cognitive-behavioral, with the goal of modifying faulty assumptions and thought patterns and then relying on established behavioral procedures like relaxation training to help modify the problem behavior. In many ways, this trend is incorporated in multimodal therapy, a comprehensive approach that uses a wide variety of cognitive and behavioral techniques with the aim of finding the most appropriate treatment for each client's problems.

OTHER APPROACHES TO TREATMENT

The various group therapies, including family and couples therapy, deal with the individual as a function of group dynamics or family structure and utilize the group process to help members achieve mutually satisfying solutions. Biomedical therapies treat the symptoms of psychological problems with direct physical intervention, including drugs—antianxiety, antidepressant, and antipsychotic drugs; electroconvulsive therapy; and psychosurgery.

One of the most dramatic changes in mental health care has been the marked shift from prolonged stays in large institutions to the use of community-based services. Although the latter have expanded to include a variety of services, such as day hospitals and halfway houses, outpatient services continue to be the most widely used.

HOW WELL DOES THERAPY WORK?

Studies show that psychotherapy generally works better than no therapy, and clients who have had therapy are better off than untreated clients. Much of the current research focuses on specific, measurable factors that make therapy effective, such as client characteristics. Also, some approaches appear to be especially well suited to certain problems, such as the cognitive-behavioral approach for people suffering from anxiety or mild to moderate depression.

FINDING HELP

Individuals who are considering professional help might benefit from asking the following questions: (1) When should I seek professional help? (2) Where can I find it? (3) What should I look for in a therapist? (4) What can I expect from therapy? and (5) How long must I stay in therapy?

SELF-TEST

1. The process of helping clients gain insight into their unconscious conflicts through such techniques as the analysis of transference is called
   a. behavior therapy.
   b. logotherapy.
   c. psychoanalysis.
   d. multimodal therapy.

2. To establish the proper climate for change, a person-centered therapist strives to be accepting, empathic, and
   a. genuine.
   b. interpretive.
   c. objective.
   d. judgmental.

3. Which one of the following therapies places central importance on the client's finding meaning and purpose in life?
   a. gestalt therapy.
   b. psychoanalysis.
   c. behavior therapy.
   d. logotherapy.

4. Which of the following techniques is especially effective in treating fears and phobias?
   a. transference.
   b. desensitization.
   c. logotherapy.
   d. gestalt therapy.

5. The therapeutic approach of modifying clients' behavior by changing their irrational thoughts is called
   a. cognitive therapy.
   b. existential therapy.
   c. psychoanalysis.
   d. actualization therapy.

6. Which of the following approaches assumes that people's problems are best understood and treated as an integral part of the groups to which they belong?
    a. existential therapy.   c. family therapy.
    b. logotherapy.   d. psychoanalysis.

7. Which of the following groups of psychoactive drugs are the most widely prescribed in the United States?
    a. antianxiety drugs.   c. lithium derivatives.
    b. antidepressants.   d. antipsychotic drugs.

8. The setting in which people with mental disorders receive part-time treatment in a hospital is
    a. day hospitals.   c. state hospitals.
    b. halfway houses.   d. inpatient services.

9. Comparative studies have shown that by eight sessions of therapy, improvement is seen in what proportion of clients?
    a. one-fourth.   c. one-half.
    b. one-third.   d. two-thirds.

10. Professionals who are medical doctors but who specialize in treating mental disorders are
     a. psychiatrists.   c. social workers.
     b. psychologists.   d. counselors.

EXERCISES

1. *How do you feel about getting help?* Write a paragraph describing your attitude toward getting help for a psychological problem. To what extent do you feel that psychological help is a sign of personal weakness? How severe would the problem have to be before you sought help? Be honest.

2. *To whom would you turn for help?* Suppose you needed psychological help immediately. To whom would you turn? Write down the name, address, and telephone number of the person or agency. If you're unable to do so, you might ask for appropriate referrals from your state psychological association or a local employee assistance program at work. You might also think about why you selected this person or agency.

3. *Distinguishing between psychiatrists and psychologists.* People often confuse these two professionals. Reread Box 15–4. Then write a paragraph or so describing the differences between these two types of professionals. What services are usually reserved for psychiatrists? What types of problems or psychological disorders are most appropriate for psychologists?

4. *First-person account of therapy.* If you've participated in counseling or therapy, write a page or two describing your experience. In what ways was it beneficial? Do you have any misgivings about it? On the basis of your experience, what suggestions would you make to those considering therapy? If you have never been in therapy, imagine that you have been for counseling and write about why you think it might be beneficial or not.

5. *Desensitization.* Reread Activity 15–2. Then apply the material to one of your mild to moderate fears, such as test anxiety or the fear of flying. If you're unsure of how to proceed, check with your instructor or an experienced counselor.

6. *Mutual-help groups.* Perhaps you've participated in a group like Parents Without Partners, Alcoholics Anonymous, or Toughlove. If yes, write a page or so describing your experience. If not, which type of mutual-help group would you be most interested in joining and why? You might visit the web site for the American Self-Help Clearing House to obtain a list of such groups (http://selfhelpgroups.org).

QUESTIONS FOR SELF-REFLECTION

1. Do you believe that friends can be good medicine?

2. If you were looking for a therapist, either for yourself or someone else, whose recommendation would you seek?

3. What are some personal qualities you would look for in a therapist? Professional qualities?

4. Have you ever considered using desensitization to reduce your own anxieties or fears?

5. Can you recall aggravating a problem by awfulizing?

6. Do you think some of your limitations or problems might be related to family patterns, present or past?

7. Have you ever belonged to a mutual-help or self-help group?

8. Would you agree that people have to want to change in order to benefit fully from therapy?

9. Do you think that asking for help when you need it is itself a mark of maturity? Weakness?

10. Are you aware that many people experience personal growth as well as the relief of symptoms in psychotherapy? How can therapy help people grow?

11. If you went for help, what kind of therapy (e.g., existential or behavioral) would you seek?

FOR FURTHER INFORMATION

RECOMMENDED READINGS

COREY, G. (2005). *Theory and practice of counseling and psychotherapy*. Belmont, CA: Brooks/Cole. A leading textbook on counseling and psychotherapy that covers the principles of counseling as well as explains the orientation and techniques of various theories of therapy.

HEALY, D. (2002). *Creation of psychopharmacology*. Cambridge, MA: Harvard University Press. This book discusses the history of the development of antipsychotic medication. The author takes the stance that politics and money rather than a desire to help the mentally disordered drive such discoveries.

MILLON, T. (2004). *Masters of the mind: Exploring the story of mental illness from ancient times to the new millenium.* Hoboken, NJ: Wiley. Millon is one of the leading authorities on mental disorders and interventions. Here he reviews the history of mental illness and its treatment.

NORCROSS, J. C. (2002). *Psychotherapy relationships that work.* New York: Oxford University Press. This is a book a psychotherapist would read. It reexamines therapy. Instead of the type or style of therapy, Norcross promotes the importance of the therapeutic alliance or relationship between client and therapist.

YALOM, I. D. (2003). *The gift of therapy: An open letter to a new generation of therapists and their patients.* New York: HarperCollins. Through cases and stories, Yalom examines therapy through the eyes of the therapist and the client.

WEB SITES AND THE INTERNET

http://www.compwellness.com   A web site devoted to less traditional forms of treatment for mental disorders.

http://www.apa.org   The American Psychological Association's web site that offers scientific and practical information on a variety of topics related to psychology, therapy, and other issues.

http://www.nami.org   The web site for the National Alliance for the Mentally Ill, an advocacy group for the mentally ill and their families.

http://nypsychotherapy.com   The site of the New York Psychotherapy Group; the site provides information on whether therapy helps, various forms of therapy, what to expect from therapy, the use of medications, and more. Click on "Articles and FAQs."

http://www.mentalhelp.net   A web site with a wealth of information for the lay consumer of mental health information, including information on all types of treatments for mental disorders.

CHAPTER 16

Good Grief and Death

DEATH AND DYING
Risks of Dying
Awareness of Death
Near-Death Experiences
The Experience of Dying

BEREAVEMENT AND GRIEF
Grief Work
Unresolved Grief
Good Grief

LIFE AND DEATH IN PERSPECTIVE
The Right to Die
A Natural Death
Funerals and Other Services
Death and Growth

SUMMARY
SELF-TEST
EXERCISES
QUESTIONS FOR SELF-REFLECTION
FOR FURTHER INFORMATION

Two people hold sharply contrasting attitudes toward death. Mark, who is in his late 40s, bristles at the mention of the word *death*. Those who know him well say this reaction may have something to do with the tragic loss of his older brother in a car accident when Mark was a young adult. In any event, Mark refuses to attend funerals, even for his closest friends. One can only speculate how Mark would react if his wife or children should die before he does. For years, Mark has boasted that the only way he'll ever go to a cemetery is "feet first" when he's carried there for his own burial.

Joanna, a widow in her early 80s, maintains a very different attitude toward death. She is grieving over the recent loss of her husband, to whom she was happily married for 52 years. She talks openly with her friends about how much she misses him. She regularly tends to the plants at the family plot. Knowing that her husband never liked being alone, she sometimes pauses by his grave to talk to him. "Don't worry," she says, "I'll be with you one day." Then she glances at the unused gravesite adjacent to her husband's, together with the stone containing her name: "Joanna C. Hunzinger, 1924-." How does she feel about seeing her own tombstone? "Well, you see," she replies, "we saved a little money by getting both at the same time." With which of these people's attitudes toward death do you most identify?

DEATH AND DYING

Death is a difficult concept to define, much less to think about and understand. A common definition of **death** is *the cessation of life as measured by the absence of breathing, heartbeat, and electrical activity of the brain.* Some of us would prefer to think we're like Joanna, with her open and matter-of-fact attitude toward death. At other times, we realize that we may be more like Mark, with his characteristic denial of death. Perhaps most of us fall somewhere in between these two extremes.

Actually, some denial of death such as Mark holds is probably necessary *and* normal to function effectively. Death, especially the possibility of our own death, is such a harsh reality that few people can face it directly. Denial helps to keep our anxiety level over the threat of our own demise at a low, manageable level. Denial also helps us to avoid thoughts of being separated from loved ones, whose relationship to us is essential to our self-esteem and well-being. Then, too, there's another reason for not thinking about death—the idea that it's futile to think about the inevitable. Because we aren't certain what comes after death—though some of us suspect it is nothingness—death typically is a most unpleasant thought. As Ben Franklin said, "In this world nothing can be said to be certain, except death and taxes." Interestingly, both Joanna and Mark, via their individual styles of coping with the prospect of death, agree with Franklin.

An excessive or inappropriate denial of death such as Mark's, however, tends to be counterproductive. For instance, people who constantly reassure themselves that "It can't happen to me" or who insist "I don't want to think about it" may continue to smoke, drink alcohol, eat junk food, and drive too fast, all of which increase their vulnerability. Similarly, the denial of death makes us avoid the aged or the seriously ill, who may remind us of our own mortality. Joanna, being more comfortable with death than Mark, was able to stay at her dying husband's side and support him through this passage. Then, too, as long as we mistakenly assume we are going to live forever, we tend to postpone doing the things that really matter to us, which can result in a superficial life. John, Mark's now deceased brother, regrettably spent most of his waking hours trying to increase his income and buy a bigger house rather than forming meaningful bonds with his children.

We'll begin this chapter by considering some of the realities of death, such as the everyday risks of dying, death anxiety, and the experience of dying. In the middle section, we'll describe the process of grief and the importance of working through emotions associated with personal loss. Then in the final section, we'll examine some of the ethical and practical issues associated with dying, such as the right to die, funerals, and how the awareness of our mortality and experiences of loss can enrich the meaning of life itself.

Risks of Dying

Every day each of us risks dying as a consequence of engaging or not engaging in certain activities. Risk-taking may increase death anxiety; in some people, however, it may not. To become more aware of your level of death anxiety, you can complete the Death Anxiety Scale in Activity 16–1 before reading further. After you know your score, contemplate how your level of anxiety affects your life, if at all. Do you take risks? Are you scared to death of death? Is your death anxiety keeping you from attending funerals of close friends and family or sitting with a loved one who is terminally ill?

People tend to overestimate the risk of death from sensational causes such as accidents and homicides and underestimate the risk of death from nonspectacular causes such as heart attacks, strokes, and diabetes. Such misjudgments arise from our tendency to believe an event is likely to occur if we can easily imagine or recall it, which is further compounded by the media's practice of overreporting dramatic, negative events such as accidents and homicides. Newspapers carry three times as many articles about death from homicide as about death from disease, although disease takes 100 lives to every 1 homicide. Because most of these deaths are noted in the obituary columns rather than the headlines, we underestimate the risk of death from familiar hazards such as

ACTIVITY 16–1

What's Your Level of Death Anxiety?

INSTRUCTIONS: *For each of the following statements, indicate your degree of agreement by circling the appropriate number below the statement.*

1. As I read this chapter on death and grief, I feel uncomfortable.

    Strongly disagree   1   2   3   4   5   6   7   Strongly agree

2. I am not distressed by the thought of planning my own funeral.

    Strongly disagree   1   2   3   4   5   6   7   Strongly agree

3. When I know someone is terminally ill, I find it difficult to visit.

    Strongly disagree   1   2   3   4   5   6   7   Strongly agree

4. If I knew it would save me money, I would buy a burial plot in advance.

    Strongly disagree   1   2   3   4   5   6   7   Strongly agree

5. I prefer not to attend funerals or other death-related events.

    Strongly disagree   1   2   3   4   5   6   7   Strongly agree

6. Thoughts of my own death do not significantly trouble me.

    Strongly disagree   1   2   3   4   5   6   7   Strongly agree

7. I am careful not to take physical risks other, more adventurous people might take.

    Strongly disagree   1   2   3   4   5   6   7   Strongly agree

8. The sight of cemeteries and funeral homes does not bother me.

    Strongly disagree   1   2   3   4   5   6   7   Strongly agree

9. I worry greatly that after death, there is nothingness.

    Strongly disagree   1   2   3   4   5   6   7   Strongly agree

10. I try to attend the calling hours for friends and family who have recently died.

    Strongly disagree   1   2   3   4   5   6   7   Strongly agree

SCORING: The even-numbered items need to be reverse scored so that disagreement signals higher death anxiety; that means for even-numbered items, a 1 becomes a 7, a 2 becomes a 6 and so on.

Total for odd-numbered items: _____

Total for even-numbered items (after reverse scoring) _____

Grand total _____

INTERPRETATION: This scale was developed for your own personal information and awareness. It has no scientific validity or reliability. A high score does not necessarily mean there is something wrong with you or that you suffer tremendous death anxiety. A low score does not necessarily mean that you manage the idea of death well. Instead, this scale is designed to stimulate you to think about the concept of death as well as about your level of death-related anxiety.

70–55 = You may have high levels of death anxiety.

54–40 = You may have moderately high levels of death anxiety.

39–25 = You are neither comfortable nor uncomfortable with the topic of death.

24–10 = You are only somehwat distressed by the topic of death.

9 and below = You may be at peace with the idea of death, or, on the other hand, uncaring.

smoking, surgery, and diseases. These are, however, the very things over which each of us has a great deal of control.

As you might suspect, the risk of dying varies greatly from one person to another, depending on such factors as lifestyle, heredity, and gender. Health habits and lifestyles, as mentioned elsewhere in this book, are especially important. People who smoke a pack or more of cigarettes a day can expect to die 5 or 6 years sooner than those who don't smoke. Similarly, those who are overweight by 50 pounds or more die many years sooner than those closer to their ideal weights.

People who have healthy eating and exercise habits not only keep themselves more fit but also tend to live longer than those with less healthy habits. Personality and stress management are also important. Whereas individuals who are intense, hostile, and easily angered tend to die sooner than average, those who are relaxed and easygoing live longer than average (Cohen & Pressman, 2006). Table 16–1 lists some of the leading causes of

TABLE 16–1

LEADING CAUSES OF DEATH IN THE UNITED STATES, 2004

Cause	Number of Deaths
Heart disease	685,089
Cancer	556,902
Stroke	157,689
Chronic lower respiratory disease	126,382
Accidents	109,277
Diabetes	69,301
Pneumonia/influenza	65,163
Alzheimer's disease	63,457
Kidney disease	42,453

SOURCE: Centers for Disease Control and Prevention, National Center for Health Statistics. http://www.cdc.gov/nchs/deaths.htm (accessed August 10, 2005).

death in the United States. Notice that the first few reasons are related to or caused by unhealthy lifestyles such as smoking.

Heredity also affects our life expectancy. It is well known that people with long-lived parents and grandparents tend to live longer than those whose close relatives die before 50. However, if your relatives are not noted for their longevity, you need not become fatalistic. Instead, you might make even greater efforts to adopt healthier eating and exercise habits. For instance, because most of the men in Mark's family died before the age of 50, he continued his "eat, drink, and be merry" outlook, believing he would be dead by middle age anyway. At the insistence of his doctor and wife, he underwent a coronary bypass operation and began eating healthier foods. He refused to exercise, though.

Awareness of Death

Despite attempts at denial, each of us, like Mark, has some awareness of our own mortality (Fawcett, 2004). For instance, suppose you were asked, "How often do you think about your own death?" If your reply is "once in a while," you've got a lot of company. About half the people asked this question answer "occasionally." Another fourth say "frequently" or "very frequently," whereas another fourth claim they rarely have thoughts about their own death.

Certain situations are likely to pique our death awareness, such as seeing a roadside memorial.

Actually, our personal awareness of death fluctuates somewhat every day. Most of the time, we have very little awareness of death. We avoid thinking about the possibility of our death and deny that someday our lives must end. The more intense the denial, the lower is our awareness of death. Other days, we're more aware that our life span is limited. Perhaps we've just seen a gory automobile accident, or we've learned that someone we know has a serious illness. When individuals are questioned directly about death, they rarely admit being fearful of it. When questioned with more indirect methods, such as fantasy and imagery, people express greater fears of death.

The personal awareness of death also varies somewhat by age. Interestingly, people in their late 20s are the most fearful of all, perhaps partly because they have most of their lives ahead of them. The terrorist attacks of September 11, 2001, however, served to make them and teens even more sensitive to awareness of death (Halpern-Felshner & Millstein, 2002). Then, too, the leading causes of death for youths—accidents, homicide, and suicide—imply that death often comes cruelly and tragically to them. Then, as individuals reach late adulthood, they generally *think* about death more often and talk about it more openly. The increase in chronic illnesses and the death of close friends at this age are all reminders that death is the natural end of life. Older people, however, are usually *less fearful* of death than other age groups. After all, they've already lived a reasonably long life and may feel they have less to look forward to. Also, those with a deep religious faith, including a belief in some kind of afterlife, are thought to be generally less fearful of death (Krause, 2005). Such a belief may provide an important mechanism for dealing with the anxieties of aging and death. When Joanna, a regular churchgoer, was asked if she feared death, she replied, "I'm more worried about ending up in a nursing home, being in pain, or becoming a burden to my children than I am of dying. I've made my peace with death." In fact, many Americans feel the same way; they are more afraid of *the process* of dying than death itself (Matousek, 2000).

Near-Death Experiences

Suppose you're knocked unconscious in an automobile accident and taken to the hospital. Critically injured, you're put on a life-support system that keeps you alive. After a couple of days, you regain consciousness, only to discover that you almost died. There's a chance you would have had a **near-death experience**—*the distinctive state of recall associated with being brought back to life from the verge of death.*

Accounts of these experiences show striking similarities. Initially, individuals experience a detachment from their bodies and are pulled through a dark tunnel. Then they find themselves in another kind of "spiritual body," in which physical objects present no barrier and movement from one place to another is almost instantaneous. While in this state they may have a reunion with long-lost friends and loved ones. One of the most incredible elements is the appearance of a brilliant light, perceived as a warm, loving "being of light," which fosters a kind of life review in a nonjudgmental way. Finally, people report being drawn back through the dark tunnel and undergoing a rapid reentry into their bodies (van Lommel, van Wees, Meyers, & Elfferich, 2001; *Harvard Health Letter*, 2002). For most people, the near-death experience brings a profound change in attitudes. They not only become less fearful of death but are also more concerned with loving and valuing the life they have (Koerner, 1997). There is also an increase in spirituality (Musgrave, 1997) as well as more concern for others and less concern for material possessions (Groth-Marnat & Summers, 1998).

Of the nearly 18 percent of Americans who claim to have been on the verge of dying, perhaps as many as a third may have had a near-death experience. No matter what their age, race, sex, or education level, the experience seems transforming. Alcoholics find themselves unable to imbibe beer; hardened criminals opt for a life of helping others. Atheists embrace religion or report feeling welcome in any church, temple, or synagogue. Although many who have had near-death experiences prefer to view them as spiritual encounters, researchers are taking the mysticism out of such occurrences by claiming that they are physiological events, hallucinations, or other changes in cognition created by the nervous system or anesthesia (Buzzi, Couper, Bardy, & Evans, 2002; Koerner, 1997). Others, such as Elisabeth Kübler-Ross (1997b), believe that near-death phenomena are an integral part of the more inclusive experience of dying, including the physical level (loss of consciousness), psychic level (out-of-body awareness), and spiritual level (glimpse of nonjudgmental light or the realm of God).

The Experience of Dying

By **experience of dying,** we mean *the sequence of physiological and psychological changes experienced by individuals who are dying.* Now that people are likely to die in a hospital, often sedated and isolated from all but their immediate family and hospital personnel, the experience of dying has become something of a mystery for the average person. Many people have never been in the presence of someone who is dying. Even people who have sat with a loved one or friend who is dying have only a limited awareness of the dying person's inner world or how to communicate with that person. For those who are heavily sedated, as was Joanna's husband when he died of cancer, perhaps the final moments are meaningless. Alternatively, some people with a terminal illness remain alert up to the end and have expressed their thoughts and feelings about dying, giving us a more accurate understanding of it.

One of the best-known pioneers in this field is Elisabeth Kübler-Ross. She and her colleagues interviewed more than 500 terminally ill people at the University of Chicago hospital. Kübler-Ross (1975) found that even when patients were not told of the seriousness of their illnesses, they usually sensed that fact as well as the approximate time of their deaths. Compared to the 1970s, doctors today are more likely to reveal to patients their terminal prognosis (Barnett, 2006; Field & Copp, 1999), because Kübler-Ross's efforts have made medical schools more likely to incorporate such information into their curricula (Block & Billings, 2005). Hence, there is a growing realization that when persons indicate a willingness to know the truth about their impending death, it may be wiser to give the relevant information than to protect them with a conspiracy of concealment (Barnett). This also provides them with some time to get their affairs in order, for example, write a will if they do not have one or say a special goodbye to loved ones. How the knowledge of impending death is conveyed is more important than the particular facts communicated. Furthermore, dying people have benefited from the opportunity to face death openly and to talk about it, removing much of the fear, sense of isolation, and mystery.

Kübler-Ross (1993, 1997b) noted that individuals tend to go through several stages in dying, although there is considerable overlap between these stages. The first stage consists of a **denial of death,** *with people characteristically feeling, "No, not me; this cannot happen to me."* Such denial protects them from the deep emotions associated with death and provides time to cope with the disturbing facts (Zimmermann, 2004). Later, individuals tend to show small signs that they are now willing to talk about death, but at this stage friends or professionals should talk about it only for a few minutes at a time, allowing the dying time to make the needed adjustment. In the second stage, denial eventually gives way to the emotions of anger and **resentment**, *especially toward individuals who are healthy*. "Why me?" people ask. The sight of others enjoying their health evokes envy, jealousy, and anger. The dying often take their feelings out on those closest to them, mostly because of what these people represent—life and health. Consequently, it is important for those nearby not to take these remarks personally, but to help dying individuals express their feelings.

The third stage characteristically consists of attempts to **bargain for time** in *which the dying individual attempts to negotiate with others (e.g., God) who might help them live longer*. Individuals at this stage often say, "I know I'm dying but. . . ." Then they indulge in a bit of magical thinking or negotiation: "If I cooperate with the doctor or my family, maybe God will let me live till my daughter graduates or my son gets married." When individuals tend to drop the "but" and admit, "Yes, I'm dying," they enter the fourth stage, **depression**, *characterized by intense and sometimes unrealistic sadness*. In a sense this is a natural response to the threat of losing their life, and it is very important to allow dying people to grieve and express their sadness. One of the worst things a friend can do is deny these feelings and say, "Cheer up." Thus, it is important for family and friends as well as professionals to learn to accept their own feelings about death so that they can help dying people accept their own impending death without dwelling on it unduly.

The final stage is the **acceptance** of death, though not all dying persons reach this stage. By this time, most *people who are dying have pretty much accepted death and have disengaged themselves from others*. They ask only for fewer visitors, but often they don't want to die alone. Although most people prefer to die at home (Administration on Aging, 2005), they are more likely to die in a hospital. In fact, much of the pain of dying comes from mental anguish, especially the fear of being separated from loved ones.

Elisabeth Kübler-Ross (1975, 1993) was the first to point out that the experience of dying is not a fixed, inevitable process and that many people do not follow these stages (Wright, 2003). For some, anger remains the dominant mood throughout, whereas others are depressed until the end, as was Joanna's husband, although he died quickly. Many experts go even further and hold that individual differences are more pronounced in the experience of dying than are differences in stages (e.g., Corr, 1993; Quigley & Schatz, 1999; Wright). Consequently, each person experiences the dying process in a unique way because of such factors as age, sex, and personality differences, as well as cultural backgrounds and the nature of various types of illnesses.

BEREAVEMENT AND GRIEF

To lose a loved one or friend through death is to lose part of ourselves. It's a very painful experience that is labeled variously as bereavement, grief, or mourning. **Bereavement** ("to be deprived of") is *the process of adjusting to the experience of loss, especially to the death of friends or loved ones*. It involves the overall experience of loss. **Grief** refers to *the intense emotional suffering that accompanies our experience of loss*, and **mourning** refers to *the outward expressions of bereavement and grief*.

Because death is one of the universal rites of passage, most societies have mourning customs to facilitate the expression of grief. In the past, in American culture, widows

Each of us grieves in our own healthy or unhealthy way. Unresolved or complicated grief occurs when a person's emotional reaction to loss remains repressed or is manifested in unexplained physical or psychological symptoms.

dressed in black and widowers wore black armbands. Such dress explained the show of grief on the part of the bereaved and afforded them an opportunity to talk about their loss and to receive the needed sympathy. However, many of these customs have been modified or given up. Wakes and visiting hours have been replaced by brief funerals and memorial services. Ordinarily, the bereaved today are expected to resume their usual dress and activities as soon as possible.

Grief Work

Our modern customs sometimes get in the way of grief work—the healthy process of working through the emotions associated with loss. **Grief work** consists of *freeing ourselves emotionally from the deceased, readjusting to life without that person, resuming ordinary activities, and forming new relationships*. The grief process parallels the experience of dying and involves many of the same emotions. Simply disclosing our grief to others, however, may not alleviate the grief (Stroebe, Schut, & Stroebe, 2005). Grief work takes time and is not always completed. Why? For one, there exist individual differences (Boerner, Wortman, & Bonanno, 2005) in how people grieve, but we will describe the typical experience.

Initially, we react to a person's death with a sense of shock and disbelief, especially when death occurs unexpectedly. When we've been anticipating a person's death, as in the case of a terminally ill friend, our initial response may be subdued and accompanied by a sense of relief. Joanna experienced a sense of relief after caring for her failing husband for several months. Her sense of relief, though, only served to make her feel guilty later. Guilt may be as normal to grief as is sadness.

After the initial shock wears off, we're likely to be bothered by memories of the deceased. This was the stage most bothersome for Mark when his brother died. He was very emotionally close to his brother. As may be the case, Mark did not feel like socializing with his friends, especially in activities that reminded him of his deceased brother. He missed a whole season of football games, sold a car they enjoyed riding in, and cut off his otherwise friendly relationship with his brother's girlfriend. Negative emotions such as anger and guilt are likely to surface at this stage. We may blame God, fate, or those who've been taking care of the deceased. It's not uncommon to blame the deceased person for having abandoned us, especially if that person committed suicide. Mark's brother did not commit suicide; he died in a car accident. Nonetheless, it is apparent that Mark had and still has a difficult time coping with his brother's death. We also may have feelings of guilt because of something we said or did or feel we should have done while the person was still alive. Some of our guilt may be "survivor's guilt," that is, feeling guilty simply because we're still alive and the other person is not.

The emotional intensity of grief in these early stages often appears in the disguise of physical symptoms, especially among older adults. In the early months of bereavement, the most common symptoms of grief are crying, depressed feelings, lack of appetite, and difficulties concentrating at work or at home. Another common symptom is lack of interaction with others (Monk, Houck, & Shear, 2006). Fortunately for Joanna, these symptoms did not last long, because she was a particularly resilient person. Many people rely on sleeping pills and tranquilizers at some point during their bereavement.

In the final stage of grief, we usually come to terms with our loss and resume our everyday activities. This stage may occur anytime from a few months to a year or more after the initial loss, depending on how close we were to the person and the circumstances surrounding the death. Research has shown that about 1 year is the norm for normal grief work (Lindstrom, 1995), but some professionals in the field of grief and bereavement find that normal grief can extend way beyond the first year (Davis, 2001). Depression and other emotional reactions to the death of a loved one generally decline over the first year (Grad & Zavasnik, 1999). From that time on, we're likely to recall the deceased person with pleasant memories. In some ways, we never fully get over the death of a loved one, such as a parent, child, or spouse. The more fully we work through our grief, however, the more likely we'll be able to get on with our normal lives.

Unresolved Grief

Psychological Reactions.   **Unresolved grief** *is a psychological state in which a person's emotional reaction to loss remains repressed, often being manifested in unexplained physical or psychological symptoms.* Also called **complicated grief,** this prolonged and impairing type of grief may assume a variety of forms, from unexplained physical complaints to psychological symptoms (Bonanno & Kaltman, 2001; Shear, Frank, Houck, & Reynolds, 2005; Warren, 1997). In some instances, the psychological reactions are obviously related to the loss. For example, some people avoid their grief (Bonanno, Papa, Lalande, Zhang, & Noll, 2005); they can't bring themselves to return to the house, hospital, or room where a person has died because of unresolved grief. In other cases, unresolved grief may be more disguised. A friend of Mark's complained that when she was a young child, her father died but she did not really experience any grief. She recalled that she never cried or experienced the usual grief reactions. It was later found that she was left out of the family bereavement process; that is, no one in the family had talked to her about her father's death, and she had not been allowed to accompany them when they attended the funeral or burial. Years later, this woman discovered that much of her resentment toward her mother and her apprehensiveness over her husband's traveling were related to unresolved grief over her father's death. As she expressed her pent-up tears and anger to her counselor, she gradually worked out her grief, which resulted in more satisfying relationships with her mother and husband.

On the other hand, some individuals do just the opposite. Instead of thinking too little about their loved one or the death, they think too much about their grief and the loss of their loved one. Studies have also shown that rumination about the death, that is, preoccupation with the death, can be detrimental (Michael & Snyder, 2005). Individuals who ruminate or constantly rehash details of the death, especially when they have few social supports and other stressors, experience more depression and are more pessimistic than those who don't ruminate (Nolen-Hoeksema, Parker, & Larson, 1994). Some bereavement experts suggest that this type of prolonged or complex grieving is abnormal or requires special attention by professionals (e.g., Shear et al., 2005). Others claim that there are really very few cases of delayed grief or abnormal bereavement (Bonanno & Kaltman, 2001).

Physical Reactions.   People who live alone, especially those without close friends, are perhaps the most likely to have difficulty working through their grief. They may be prone to a variety of illnesses like heart disease, strokes, cirrhosis of the liver, hypertension, and cancer, as well as premature death. For example, depending on the age of the individual, heart disease is anywhere from two to five times higher among the divorced, single, and widowed than among the married. Men are likely to die a few years after the death of their wives, although women's chances of dying are less affected by their husband's death. Similarly, there is little difference in the death rates between people who have lost a spouse in the past year and married people the same age. In the ensuing years, however, widowed men suffer a much greater mortality rate than their married counterparts. Widowed men between the ages of 55 and 65 die at a 60 percent higher rate than married men the same age. The most likely explanation is that the quality of life changes more drastically for men than for women, possibly because of their greater reliance on wives for their emotional and daily needs. Women tend to have a better support system for coping with their grief. However, when widowers remarry, they have an even lower mortality rate than their married counterparts who have never lost a spouse.

Good Grief

So far, we've seen that it is sometimes better to go through the full experience of bereavement, however painful it may be, than to get over it too quickly or to ruminate too intently. In this regard, Joanna was coping better with her loss than was Mark, even years later. There are, however, some positive aspects of grief. Grief may be a learning experience that helps us grow (Bonanno, Moskowitz, Papa, & Folkman, 2005; Gamino & Sewell, 2004). It is sometimes said that we don't fully appreciate something until we have lost it, which is especially applicable to human relationships. While people are still with us, we often have ambivalent feelings toward them. One moment we love them, another we're angry with them, and later we are indifferent to them. In retrospect, however, grief helps us appreciate loved ones and friends more fully despite their shortcomings. Grief also helps us value our relationships with those still living. In short, **good grief** means *that we have learned and grown in our bereavement.* In fact, there now exists some research that documents how bereavement indeed contributes to growth (Cadell, Regehr, & Hemsworth, 2003).

There are several ways to make the experience of bereavement more effective: talking it out, feeling it out, and acting it out. Even though it may be very difficult to talk about the death of a loved one for the first several weeks, this may be exactly when talking it out can be most helpful. The main thing to remember is that the focus is on *the feelings of the bereaved.* Whatever it takes, a friend should attempt to listen and help the bereaved person to talk out feelings rather than cut the mourner off. Although you may be uncomfortable discussing death, the bereaved person may well need someone to talk to.

Encouraging and empowering a bereaved friend to express feelings may also be cathartic. People tend to feel less embarrassed when they can do so in the company of a few close friends. Men usually have more difficulty expressing bereavement, largely because our society still considers a show of emotions by men to be a sign of weakness. It is also important to realize that the characteristic way of expressing emotions differs somewhat from one person to another. For some, moistened eyes and a warm handclasp are about as close as they ever come to expressing grief. Others may cry openly or weep unashamedly. Still others seem to be inclined toward more dramatic and at times hysterical expressions of grief, such as screaming and pounding the walls with their fists.

Another way of resolving grief is to express it in other relevant ways. Sometimes just sheer physical activity, such as a brisk walk, helps to alleviate the tension and sadness of bereavement, at least temporarily. Funeral rituals also can afford an outlet for grief. Taking care of the affairs of the deceased may be therapeutic as well as helpful. As the executor of her husband's estate, Joanna found herself faced with a great deal of correspondence and many legal transactions. She initially regarded it as a burden but soon realized it was one of the few tangible things she could do for her deceased husband and their grown children. It became her way of showing her love and respect for him as well as helping her express her grief. Individuals who are resilient or hardy are more likely to utilize problem-focused rather than emotion-focused coping (see Chapter 13) during bereavement. Those with adequate social support are less likely to be depressed (Stroebe, Zech, Stroebe, & Abakoumkin, 2005) and may recover from their grief faster, too (Caserta & Lund, 1992; Nolen-Hoeksema et al., 1994). Finally, many studies indicate that **grief therapy**, which *assists the bereaved to cope with the death of a loved one*, is effective in helping the survivor cope with intense grief (e.g., Allumbaught & Hoyt, 1999; Shear et al., 2005).

LIFE AND DEATH IN PERSPECTIVE

In 1900, more than half of all deaths were of children (Fulton, 1987). The children died early from disease and hunger. By 1955, life expectancy was 48 years of age, and by 1995, it was 65 years of age (Kleespies, 2004). Now that the average life expectancy is

TABLE 16–2	
LIFE EXPECTANCY IN THE UNITED STATES	
Variable	**Life Expectancy in Years**
Year	
2004	77.9
1900	47.3
Race & sex	
Whites	78.3
Males	75.7
Females	80.8
Blacks	73.3
Males	69.8
Females	76.5

SOURCE: Centers for Disease Control and Prevention, National Center for Health Statistics. www.cdc.gov (accessed August 10, 2006).

over 75 years, more people are apt to suffer from chronic diseases, such as many forms of cancer, heart disease, and kidney failure. Table 16–2 provides you with life expectancies in the United States by race and sex. Also included is information on historic life expectancy. As you read this table, try to figure out *why* there exist differences in life expectancy over time and by group. As you ponder these differences, attend also to the fact that some groups are more likely to have health insurance or higher incomes, which may allow them to die with better care.

Because Americans are living longer and are dying from chronic rather than acute illnesses, death comes more slowly and often occurs in a hospital. As you know, hospitals tend to be large and impersonal institutions, geared more to the treatment of acute illnesses and the prolonging of life. Consequently, this change in the context of death presents new ethical issues (Haddad, 2003; Kleespies, 2004; Anonymous, 2005), such as the use of lifesaving machines and the right to die in a dignified way. Examining such issues may help us put life and death in better perspective.

The Right to Die

Joanna remembers what her husband was like in the early years of their marriage. He was a fun-loving, hard-working, out-of-doors kind of person. Then, 8 months ago, Joanna's husband was diagnosed with melanoma (a skin cancer), which left him very incapacitated and eventually in a coma. His health disintegrated so quickly that he was unable to tell Joanna what his last wishes were. He was sustained in the end by a feeding tube and intravenous painkillers at the hospital, as there was no hospice or alternative care nearby. At that point, Joanna, together with her grown children, wanted to have the feeding tube removed. All of them believed that her husband would not want to continue existing in this way.

Patients like Joanna's husband pose an ethical dilemma for their families and doctors regarding the right to die. The **right to die** is *the legal and ethical view that competent individuals who are able to understand treatment choices and their consequences have the*

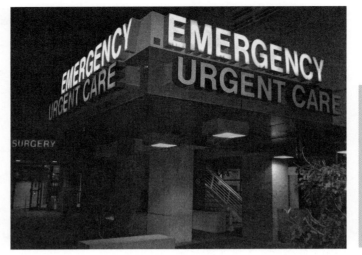

Today, hospitals and physicians are more likely to distribute health care proxies to patients. Because health care proxies and living wills are relatively new to our society, only time, experience, and more research will help us sort out all of the advantages and disadvantages of this new system of dying.

right to decide their own fate, such as the withholding of treatment that would delay death. Family members are torn between their desire to be loyal to their loved one and the emotional and financial realities of supporting someone in a permanent vegetative state (Doka, 2005; Kleespies, 2004). Doctors also face the conflict between their duty to sustain life and their obligation to relieve suffering. Doctors often continue treatment because of their moral commitments or the fear of the legal consequences of doing otherwise (Davidson, 2000; Jauhar, 2003). In recent years, the American Medical Association's Council on Ethical and Judicial Affairs has provided some guidelines for doctors in such situations. After struggling with the issue for 2 years, the seven-member panel affirmed that it is not unethical for doctors to discontinue all life-support systems for patients who are in an irreversible coma, as was Joanna's husband, even if death is not imminent. A more controversial provision includes food and water on the list of treatments that might be withheld. In each case, the patient's wishes—as far as can be determined—should be respected and the patient's dignity maintained. In fact, research has found that one of a dying person's main concerns is loss of dignity, such as becoming dependent on someone else for care (Chochinov et al., 2002). The council's decision reflects growing public support on such issues. Many Americans support the idea that terminally ill patients or patients in great pain should be allowed to die. Others support physician-assisted suicide; these supporters are likely to be less religious than those who oppose physician-assisted suicide (Westman, Hunt, Cicillini, & Lewandowski, 1999).

A president's commission on this subject, including doctors, lawyers, theologians, and others, has concluded that competent patients who are able to understand treatment choices and their consequences has an all but absolute right to decide their fate. When a person is incompetent, a surrogate, usually a family member, should be given the authority to make these decisions. Such thinking has led to the growing use of instruments like the so-called **living will**, in which *a person instructs doctors and family members to stop using life-sustaining procedures in the event of a terminal condition.* To date, only a small percentage of Americans have made out living wills. To encourage more people to do so, a new law requires all federally funded hospitals, nursing homes, and hospices to tell incoming patients of their right to write a living will. Living wills are

---

My Living Will to My Family, My Physician, My Lawyer, and All Others Whom It May Concern

Death is as much a reality as birth, growth, maturity, and old age—it is the one certainty of life. If the time comes when I can no longer take part in decisions for my own future, let this statement stand as an expression of my wishes and directions, while I am still of sound mind.

If at such time the situation should arise in which there is no reasonable expectation of my recovery from extreme physical or mental disability, I direct that I be allowed to die and not be kept alive by medications, artificial means, or "heroic measures." I do, however, ask that medication be mercifully administered to me to alleviate suffering even though this may shorten my remaining life.

This statement is made after careful consideration and is in accordance with my strong convictions and beliefs. I want the wishes and directions here expressed carried out to the extent permitted by law. Insofar as they are legally enforceable, I hope that those to whom this Will is addressed will regard themselves as morally bound by these provisions.

(Optional specific provisions to be made in this space)

Durable Power of Attorney (optional)

I hereby designate _____ to serve as my attorney-in-fact for the purpose of making medical treatment decisions. This power of attorney shall remain effective in the event that I become incompetent or otherwise unable to make such decisions for myself.

Optional Notarization:
"Sworn and subscribed to before me this _____ day of _____, 20_____."

Notary Public (seal)

Signed_____

Date_____

Witness_____

Address_____

Witness_____

Address_____

Copies of this request have been given to _____

FIGURE 16–1
A living will.

sometimes known as advance directives or health care proxies. Figure 16–1 gives an example of a living will.

Some right-to-die laws attempt to make these directives binding on doctors, who can transfer medical responsibility for the patient to another doctor if they disagree with the patient's wishes. A study of health care professionals found that many of them support the use of living wills because they encourage peace of mind in the will makers, allow caregivers to honor patient wishes, and stimulate better communication among all concerned (Thompson, Barbour, & Schwartz, 2003).

Living wills are not without controversy. While it is important for health care providers to honor patients' choices (Kleespies, 2004), doctors may be somewhat unwilling to care for dying patients (Jauhar, 2003). In fact, research suggests that living wills not only do not guarantee patients' wishes but suggests that the patient self-determination movement is a failure (Medical Ethics Advisor, 2005). Family members often experience ambivalence and even conflict as they struggle to meet the dying person's wishes. For example, one family member may hold the health care proxy, but other family members disagree with that individual's decisions. Family members may find it difficult to witness the slow deterioration of a loved one and even be repulsed by that person's appearance (Doka, 2005). Because living wills and health care proxies are relatively new to our society, time, experience, and more research are needed to sort out all of the advantages and disadvantages of this new system of dying.

Another legal document you might consider is an organ donation card. Many individuals die suddenly, as Mark's brother did in a traumatic accident. Their brains become incapacitated, but other organs such as their hearts, livers, and eyes remain unharmed. These individuals perhaps are candidates for organ donations, which involve the immediate transplantation of a vital organ from someone who has essentially died to a living person in need of the organ. Most states have means by which you can ensure that your healthy organs are donated. In instances of traumatic death, where doctors want to harvest organs quickly for transplant, families of the deceased can be put under immense pressure in a short amount of time, especially if the deceased has not signed an organ donation card or indicated his or her desires in advance.

A Natural Death

One of the dangers of the right-to-die movement is that it may unwittingly program people to die quickly. Which is better? A sudden death such as the one experienced by Mark's brother? Or one anticipated because of a terminal illness as in Joanna's husband's case? In sudden death, the dying are supposed to have been spared the suffering of a terminal illness. Also, in the case of sudden death, the survivors have been saved from the burden of taking care of an "invalid" or having to watch someone die slowly. A fast death helps us to avoid our social responsibilities, such as caring for the lingering convalescent and the aged. On the other hand, in the case of a prolonged death, everyone has more time to say goodbye, to put affairs in order, and to plan end-of-life care preferences, but watching a loved one's prolonged death distresses most families. Neither death is really "better" than the other. Interestingly, though, the revolt against needless prolongation of life may incline us toward an equally "unnatural" hastening of death. A quick, induced death, however, does not answer the key questions: How old is too old? How ill is too ill? At what point should a person on the heart-lung machine be allowed to die? When does life cease to have meaning? Death may be more of a problem for the survivors than for the dying.

Perhaps the nearest we come to a "natural" death is helping people die at their own pace and style. For example, if a young person has been an active, outdoor type, as was Mark's brother, and doesn't have the desire to adjust to a disabled state, perhaps that person should be allowed to die a dignified death. Others who may suffer from equally disabling handicaps but who prefer making the adjustment to their diminished capacities should be encouraged and supported in their efforts to go on living. Have you thought about these issues? Perhaps now is a good time to ponder them.

The hospice movement for the terminally ill represents a giant step toward the kind of humane and supportive community needed for a dignified death. In the Middle Ages, a hospice was a shelter for travelers who had nowhere else to go. Today, the hospice is a place or method for taking care of those approaching the end of their lives. Specifically, **hospice** is *a system of care that integrates a physical facility for the terminally ill with the patient's family and home to enable the patient to die with dignity.* As mentioned earlier, much of the suffering of the terminally ill consists of the treatments, the impersonal atmosphere, and the sense of isolation experienced in hospitals. In contrast, the hospice is a community that helps people to live, not merely exist, while they are dying (Hospice Foundation of America, 2003). Table 16–3 provides you with some interesting statistics about hospice care in the United States.

In some cases, patients may spend their final days at home being taken care of by loved ones and by trained volunteers. In addition to helping with such practical matters as pain control and preparing meals, hospice personnel also give emotional support and guidance to family members. The aim throughout is to provide a humane and supportive community in which the patient may die with dignity (Hospice Foundation of America, 2003). Begun in England, the hospice movement has since spread to other countries, including the United States and Canada. The increasing population of elderly people and rising costs of hospitalization are such that the hospice movement is likely to expand during the years ahead.

Research is just now revealing whether the hospice movement is successful. There are many reasons for the dying and their loved ones to be dissatisfied with hospice or palliative care (Shiozaki, Morita, Hirai, Sakaguchi, Tsuneto, & Shima, 2005). Some hospice professionals suggest that hospice stays are too short (Plonk & Arnold, 2005). The recommended hospice stay is 3 months to allow time to provide patients and their families adequate physical and psychological support (Shockett, Teno, Miller, & Stuart, 2005). As you read in Table 16–3, the typical stay is much shorter. One reason is that exact time of death is never clearly predictable in terminal illnesses. Also, physicians may be reluctant to make timely referrals to hospice because the patient and the family have not fully accepted that the illness is terminal. The reality today appears to be that physicians refer patients too late to hospice programs, which causes families to be less satisfied with the experience (Shockett et al.).

There are many individuals who prefer to die at home (with or without hospice services). One study, for example, found that 63 percent of terminally ill patients prefer to be at home when death occurs (Brazil, Howell, Bedard, Krueger, & Heidebrecht,

TABLE 16–3	
HOSPICE CARE (INCLUDING IN-HOME CARE) IN THE UNITED STATES, 2004	
• Number of hospice agencies	3,650
• Number of hospice patients	1,060,000
• Percent of in-home hospice patients	95.8
• Leading need for hospice care	Terminal cancer
• Median stay in hospice care	22 days

SOURCE: National Hospice and Palliative Care Organization (2004). *NHPCO 2004 Facts and Figures.* NHPCO.org (accessed August 10, 2006).

2005). Besides health care professionals, the families, friends, and other volunteers in the community provide much care to the dying. Box 16–1 discusses who these caregivers are, the immense stress they experience, and the need for caregivers to care for themselves. The self-control afforded the dying must be balanced with consideration for the well-being of these informal caregivers in the community (Brazil et al.).

Box 16–1

GUARDIAN ANGELS: CAREGIVERS

Older Americans, those dying from AIDS and cancer, the disabled, and others often need assistance from professional and lay caregivers. Some recipients require permanent care; others need assistance during convalescence. Friends and families often become the primary caregivers. They are not professional caregivers like home health aides, yet they are often expected to perform some of the very same duties. Dependent individuals typically cannot do their own shopping, bathing, or cooking, so depend on caregivers. Caregivers also act as chauffeurs, fill out insurance forms, give medications, take care of financial arrangements, and act as physical or emotional therapists, among other duties. One reason the number of caregivers has skyrocketed is that more Americans are living longer and more want to die in their own homes, which would not be possible without the assistance of voluntary caregivers. We seem, however, to be reaching a caregiver crisis (Gavzer, 2000), in that so many are expected to do so much.

Who are these guardian angels stepping in to help? Over 50 million American households report that their homes include someone who cannot care for him- or herself (National Family Caregivers Association, 2005); the care provided by these "angels" would cost $257 billion a year if provided by nonvolunteers (National Family Caregivers Association). Caregivers are frequently family members, typically women or grown daughters (Gavzer, 2000; Lawrence, Goodnow, Woods, & Karantzas, 2002). Many of these caregivers work part- or full-time in a highly mobile society, which means they may not live close by to the care recipient. Caregivers might also be neighbors, friends, church members, Kiwanis members, or anyone else. In fact, there are more nonpaid caregivers in the United States than paid or professional caregivers. The primary recipients of care are often families, but some

caregivers assist neighbors, friends, and, in some cases, individuals who are almost strangers, such as homeless or runaway children.

Some informal caregivers are full-time or nearly full-time caregivers. The stress of full-time caregiving can be enormous (Li, 2005; Pinquart & Sörensen, 2005). Individuals who have been caregivers for extended periods of time report depression and frustration (*Harvard Women's Health Watch*, 2003; Li; *Mental Health Weekly*, 2002; Pinquart & Sörensen). One study even found that heart disease is more prevalent in caregivers than noncaregivers (*Health & Medicine Week*, 2003).

Caregivers often need help themselves. They may need some medical training as well as emotional and social support. Caregivers also need respite from their many duties. Caregiving is both emotionally and physically exhausting. To assist caregivers, local support groups are springing up all around the country (Gavzer, 2000; Savard, Leduc, Lebei, Beland, & Bergman, 2006). These groups offer advice, emotional support, and often respite care in which another member fills in for a few hours a week. There are also nationwide organizations that publish newsletters, sell useful products, and provide other insightful information. If you are a caregiver or expect to be, you can join the National Family Caregivers Association (www.thefamilycaregiver.org). There are also specialized national groups for individuals caring for those with AIDS, Alzheimer's, physical disabilities, the elderly, and others requiring specialized assistance in living. Most of these organizations maintain easily accessible web sites. Other programs include community nursing and respite programs for the caregivers (*Hospice Management Advisor*, 2003). In any event, if you become a caregiver, don't forget to take care of yourself.

Funerals and Other Services

When death finally comes, it is typically recognized by the family and the community as a rite of passage. In most societies, parting with the dead is recognized by some kind of **funeral**—*the ceremonies and rituals associated with the burial or cremation of the dead*. Such rites may enable people to maintain order and experience a form of closure.

In earlier eras, when belief in an afterlife was a more dominant influence on human affairs, funerals were held primarily for the benefit of the dead. Death was seen as a passage to heaven or eternal life. Hence, some ancients not only buried the corpse but also included personal items of the deceased to be used on the "journey" to eternal life. Perhaps you have heard about the pyramids of Egypt, in which items were buried with the deceased to make their journey to and life in the afterworld easier. In today's more secularized American society, however, the emphasis on death and funerals tends to be humanistic and sometimes materialistic. Funerals have become the occasion for according the dead the recognition and honor they may not have achieved in life. Although it is the dead who are remembered at funerals, the ceremony often is more for the benefit of the survivors. Families sometimes get caught in a status game, selecting expensive bronze caskets, ornate headstones, and choice burial sites to maintain their position in society. Consequently, funerals have become increasingly lavish and expensive. The funeral industry has been criticized for exploiting people in their time of bereavement, but defenders point out that bereaved family members themselves are partly to blame because they choose on the basis of their emotions rather than common sense. Thus, whether out of respect, guilt, or vanity, many expensive funeral practices continue. Funerals are typically the fourth-largest consumer purchase, following a house, car, and wedding. We need to realize that the decisions made at such an emotional time are *our* decisions, and we must be sure that we are not being pressured into anything against our will.

Death and Growth

It may seem strange linking death to growth. Ordinarily, death is seen as the end of growth and existence. In the larger scheme of things, death is an integral part of life that gives meaning to human existence and, in fact, can foster further growth (Bonanno, Moskowitz et al., 2005; Gamino & Sewell, 2004; Kübler-Ross, 1997a). It sets a limit on our lives, reminding us to spend our days on the things that matter most. Individuals who have recovered from intense mourning also learn to hope that other adverse events can be overcome (Gamino & Sewell, 2004). Similarly, grieving over the loss of a loved one may help us relate more deeply to those who remain. Whether you are young or old, if you can begin to see death as an inevitable companion of life, it may help you to live your life fully rather than passively—not that you should rush out and begin doing all those things people fantasize about. Instead, the awareness that you have only so much time to live may help you make the most of your life—the disappointments and pains as well as the joy. As Joanna said, "I've begun to take time to smell the roses." Usually, it is those who have not lived their lives fully who are the most reluctant to die. Haunted by broken relationships and unfulfilled dreams, they grow ever more anxious and fearful in the face of death.

Far from being morbid, thinking about your own death may give you a new perspective on life. For instance, if you were told you had only a limited time to live, how would you spend the time? What unfinished business would you be most concerned about? Which people would you most want to be with? Pondering the answers to such questions may help you to clarify what is really important to you. You should plan to do these things before it's too late. Elisabeth Kübler-Ross (1975) stated that the greatest lesson we may learn from dying is simply "LIVE, so you do not have to look back and say, 'God, how I wasted my life'" (p. xix).

SUMMARY

DEATH AND DYING

The prospect of our own death is sometimes so frightening that a little denial of death is necessary for us to function effectively. However, people tend to underestimate the risk of death from nonspectacular causes, such as heart attacks, stress, and diabetes, and overestimate the risk of death from sensational causes, such as accidents and homicides. Although most people think about their own deaths occasionally, older people think about death more often but appear less fearful of it. Also, near-death experiences, often associated with the use of lifesaving machines, tend to make people less fearful of death and more appreciative of life. Terminally ill people tend to go through several stages of dying—denial, anger, bargaining, depression, and acceptance—with considerable overlapping between the stages and with the stages sometimes out of this order. Each person experiences the dying process somewhat differently, however, depending on such factors as personality and type of illness.

BEREAVEMENT AND GRIEF

It is important for the bereaved to engage actively in grief work, a process that parallels the experience of dying and involves many of the same emotions. People who have not been able to resolve their grief exhibit various symptoms, ranging from physical complaints to more persistent psychological symptoms. Those who live alone are especially likely to have difficulty working through their grief. Healthy grief consists of talking about our grief, sharing our feelings, and taking part in the rituals and activities that may eventually alleviate grief. Resilient individuals who use problem-focused coping and have social support are most likely to resolve their grief work in positive ways.

LIFE AND DEATH IN PERSPECTIVE

Now that people live longer, they are more apt to suffer from chronic and life-threatening illnesses and often die in a hospital. The increased use of lifesaving technology poses critical questions about prolonging life or letting someone die rather than suffer unduly. As a result, patients are being encouraged to express their own wishes through such instruments as the living will or health care proxy. The importance of providing terminally ill people with a humane and supportive community has led to the hospice movement, which is likely to expand in the coming years. It appears that a more realistic awareness of death as an inevitable companion of life, far from being morbid, may help each of us put our lives in better perspective and to live more fully.

SELF-TEST

1. Compared to young adults, older adults tend to
   a. become more fearful of death.
   b. think of death more often.
   c. become less religious.
   d. think of others' death, not their own.

2. Those who have experienced near-death generally
   a. become more spiritual.
   b. fear death more.
   c. become more self-centered.
   d. develop psychological problems.

3. According to Elisabeth Kübler-Ross, the second stage of dying consists of
   a. depression.   c. anger.
   b. bargaining for time.   d. denial.

4. The typical amount of time it may take a survivor of grief to overcome intense grief and depression is
   a. 6 months.   c. 5 years.
   b. 1 year.   d. never.

5. The group with a higher-than-average rate of death compared with others their age is
   a. widows over 55.   c. college graduates.
   b. married people.   d. widowed men over 55.

6. The constructive use of grief, involves
   a. repressing one's grief.   c. talking out one's grief.
   b. avoiding thoughts of death. d. trying to forget one's loss.

7. A living will almost always
   a. provides for organ donations.
   b. confers decision-making power on another individual.
   c. instructs doctors and families to stop life-sustaining procedures in cases of terminal illness.
   d. legally requests physician-assisted suicide.

8. A hospice is a supportive community that helps patients to
   a. live as long as possible.
   b. live and die with dignity.
   c. remain in the hospital to the end.
   d. die as quickly as possible.

9. Today's American funeral ceremony is primarily for the benefit of the
   a. survivors.   c. larger community.
   b. undertaker.   d. deceased.

10. In terms of personal growth, the realization that death is an inevitable companion of life
    a. usually hastens one's death.   c. may give life new meaning.
    b. is a morbid idea.   d. generally leads to depression.

EXERCISES

1. *Subjective life expectancy.* Simply knowing a person's age does not tell you how that person feels about his or her future. To discover this information, try the following exercise in subjective life expectancy. You may want your friends or other individuals to try it as well.

    1. I expect to live to age (circle your answer)

       30   35   40   45   50   55   60   65   70   75   80   85   90   95   100

    2. I want to live to age (circle your answer)

       25   30   35   40   45   50   55   60   65   70   75   80   85   90   95   100

    Are there discrepancies between your expressed desire and expectation? If so, what are the possible reasons? Are there differences in desires with increasing age? Usually, findings have shown that those past middle age expect and wish to live to a later age than younger people do. Did you find this to be true? When people expect to live less than the average life expectancy for their age, do they have a good reason? Did you find that some people were afraid to specify an age for fear it would somehow make death occur at that time?

2. *Your attitudes toward death.* Analyze your attitudes toward death. First, write down your actual experiences with death, such as the loss of a friend or loved one, the age at which it occurred, and so forth. Then describe some of your feelings and attitudes toward death. Include your own responses to the subjective life expectancy exercise as well.

3. *Death as an altered state of consciousness.* Some people have observed a similarity between dying and the marginal state of awareness experienced just before sleep. Try to catch yourself in this state some night and make a mental note of your reactions. Was it a peaceful state? Did you find yourself naturally giving in to it? How did you feel after the loss of control or power?

4. *Reflections on the experience of bereavement.* Recall a personal experience of bereavement, whether the loss of a loved one or that of a friend. Then describe your experience in a page or so. To what extent did your experience include the grief work process described in the chapter? In what ways was your experience unique? Finally, how has your experience of grief affected your life? Has it made you more cautious and, perhaps, bitter toward life? Or has it eventually become "good grief," leading you to make the most of life and to reach out to others in a more meaningful way?

5. *Disposing of your body.* If you had a choice, how would you want your body disposed of? Do you want to be embalmed and buried? Or would you rather be cremated? If so, what do you want done with your ashes? Some people want their ashes to be scattered over water or a favorite spot on land; others prefer their ashes to be left in a mausoleum or buried in a cemetery. People sometimes write down such preferences and leave them with their families or a memorial society.

6. *Organ donation.* Have you thought about donating organs from your body before you die? After you die? If so, which ones? Are you interested in leaving your body for medical science? Why or why not?

7. *Write your own obituary.* This isn't as strange as it may seem. Major newspapers have a file of obituaries written while celebrities and national figures are still alive, and then they update these accounts at the time of death. Try writing your own obituary in two or three paragraphs. In addition to giving the standard information, such as your name, age, and position at work, point out some of your major accomplishments. Which community activities would you mention? Who are your survivors? In addition, list your funeral and burial plans. What day and time do you prefer to be buried? Where is your service being held? Do you have any preferences regarding financial contributions to charities in lieu of flowers? Where do you want to be buried or have your ashes deposited?

QUESTIONS FOR SELF-REFLECTION

1. Do you occasionally think about the possibility of your own death?

2. Have you ever had a close brush with death?

3. Are you afraid of dying? Why? How do you cope with the thought?

4. How often do you think of someone who is dead?

5. Is there something you would especially like to do before you die? Why have you not done this thing?

6. Can you recall your first experience of grief? Whose death was it?

7. Have you experienced good grief?

8. Have you made a will? Do you have a health care proxy? Have you signed an organ donor card?

9. What kind of after-death service would you like, if any?

10. What do you believe happens to us after death?

FOR FURTHER INFORMATION

RECOMMENDED READINGS

KÜBLER-ROSS, E. (1997). *Death: The final stage of growth.* New York: Simon & Schuster. This famous author and researcher shares her views on why death can be a growth experience.

KÜBLER-ROSS, E., & KESSLER, D. (2005). *On grief and grieving: Finding the meaning of grief through the five stages of loss.* New York: Scribner. Kübler-Ross's last "gift" to us before her own death, the book is an interdisciplinary approach to understanding grief.

MITFORD, J. (2000). *The American way of death revisited.* New York: Vintage Books. Discusses the way Americans celebrate or grieve the death of a loved one.

UFEMA, J. (2006). *Insights on death and dying.* Philadelphia, PA: Lippincott, Williams, and Wilkins. This book is comprised of excerpts from columns written by a leading thanatologist.

WOODWARD, J. (2005). *At Issue series—The right to die.* Chicago, IL: Greenhaven. A legal and ethical examination of both sides of the right to die issue.

WEB SITES AND THE INTERNET

http://www.hospice-america.org   A site that includes a consumer guide to hospice care.

http://nfcacares.org   A site dedicated to assisting family caregivers.

http://www.near-death.com   A site with much information on near-death experiences and the afterlife.

http://www.griefnet.org   A site started by a clinical psychologist offering information on grief and coping in the form of support groups, literature, etc.

http://www.mindspring.com/~scottr/will.html   A site with links to lots of information on living wills and related issues.

Answers to the Self-Tests

Chapter	Questions									
	1	**2**	**3**	**4**	**5**	**6**	**7**	**8**	**9**	**10**
1	b	d	c	a	a	a	b	a	a	c
2	a	b	a	b	b	c	c	a	c	b
3	d	d	a	b	d	a	a	c	d	c
4	b	c	a	d	b	b	c	b	d	a
5	c	a	b	d	a	d	a	c	c	d
6	a	b	d	c	c	c	a	d	c	b
7	d	a	a	d	a	c	b	d	a	d
8	c	a	b	d	a	a	b	a	b	a
9	a	a	b	d	c	c	a	c	a	b
10	c	a	b	d	a	a	a	c	a	b
11	c	d	b	b	a	c	a	c	d	b
12	c	b	a	a	b	a	b	c	d	a
13	a	d	a	c	a	c	a	d	c	a
14	b	a	b	c	d	a	b	c	b	a
15	c	a	d	b	a	c	a	a	c	a
16	b	a	c	b	d	c	c	b	a	c

Glossary

acceptance. The final stage of death and dying, in which dying people have somewhat accepted death and have disengaged themselves from others.

achievement motivation. The desire to accomplish or master something difficult or challenging as independently and successfully as possible.

acrophobia. An irrational fear of heights.

actualization therapy. An approach that combines elements of the person-centered approach, gestalt therapy, and rational-emotive therapy (discussed under cognitive therapies) as a way of maximizing the individual's growth or self-actualization.

acute stress. Stress that is a momentary response to imminent danger and is relieved when the danger is over.

adherence to treatment regimens. The degree to which a person's behavior (e.g., taking medications, attending treatment sessions, etc.) coincides with medical or health advice.

adulthood. The period of life from physical maturity on, consisting of a sequence of physical and psychosocial changes throughout early, middle, and late adulthood.

affiliate. To be with others who are often similar to us or whom we like.

age-related changes. Changes that tend to occur at a given age, such as puberty.

ageism. Negative attitudes toward and treatment of older Americans.

aging. A decline in the biological processes that comes with advancing years, increasing the risk of illness and death and usually accompanied by appropriate psychosocial changes.

agoraphobia. A cluster of different fears all of which evoke intense anxiety about crowds or open spaces.

AIDS. Acquired immune deficiency syndrome, which is caused by a virus known as HIV and transmitted primarily through body fluids.

alarm reaction. Part of Selye's notion of the general adaptation syndrome of stress; the initial emergency response to stress-provoking agents when the body attempts to restore its normal functioning.

alcohol and drug abuse. Misuse or dependence on a psychoactive substance like alcohol.

allostasis. Achieving stability through changes via a process that maintains balance among the physiological factors essential for life.

allostatic load. Cumulative changes that reflect the cost to the body of adapting repeatedly to demands placed upon it.

altruism. A desire to help others at a cost to the helper.

Alzheimer's disease. A debilitating cognitive disorder that may, in fact, begin to develop in midlife but is often associated with old age.

amygdala. A part of the brain that directs signal traffic in the brain and triggers an all-systems alarm.

anal stage. According to Freud, the stage that occurs during the second year of life when the child's major source of physical pleasure becomes the releasing or retenting of feces.

androgyny (psychological). The combination of desirable masculine and feminine characteristics in one person.

anger. The feeling of extreme displeasure or resentment over (perceived) mistreatment.

anniversary reaction. An individual's response to unresolved grief resulting from significant losses.

anorexia nervosa. An eating disorder characterized by a severe loss of appetite and weight. The essential features of this eating disorder are a fear of becoming fat along with a disturbance in body image and a refusal to maintain normal weight.

anorexic disturbance. The way in which one's body weight or shape is experienced and includes undue influence of body weight or shape on self-evaluation or denial of the seriousness of the current low body weight.

antianxiety drugs. Drugs that are used primarily for alleviating anxiety; including minor tranquilizers.

antidepressant drugs. Drugs that are used to treat depression and elevate mood, usually by increasing the level of certain neurotransmitters.

antipsychotic drugs. Drugs that are used primarily to relieve symptoms of psychoses, such as extreme agitation, hyperactivity, hallucinations, and delusions.

antisocial personality. A personality disorder characterized by long-standing habits of maladaptive thought and behavior that violates the rights of others.

anxiety. A vague, unpleasant feeling that serves as an emotional alarm signal, warning us of an impending threat or danger.

anxiety disorder. A group of disorders characterized by symptoms of excessive or inappropriate anxiety or attempts to escape from such anxiety.

anxious-ambivalent (attachment style). An attachment style in which the individual experiences emotional extremes such as jealousy but in which the individual also desires extreme closeness.

arbitrators. Neutral third parties who, using the same techniques as mediation, assist the parties with the conflict, hope that the parties can resolve their differences, but if they cannot, render a binding decision upon the parties.

archival method. Method in which scientists examine existing data such as historical documents that were fashioned before anyone knew they would be the subject of study.

assertiveness. The expression of one's rights and feelings in a direct way without violating the rights of others.

attachment. A close, emotional tie with another person.

attachment style. Our typical style of becoming involved with others. This includes the *secure attachment style,* in which individuals find it easy to trust and love others; the *avoidant style,* in which individuals feel uneasy about getting close to others; and the *anxious-ambivalent style,* which involves individuals who want to be attached but find it difficult to commit to others.

attribution. Searching for the causes of our own or someone else's behavior.

aversion to sex. Anxiety, disgust, repulsion, and other negative emotions toward sex.

avoidance (as related to illness). A pattern an individual utilizes to minimize or deny that there are symptoms of illness to notice.

avoidant (attachment style). An attachment style that results in the individual's feeling uneasy when other people get too close.

bargain for time. The third stage of death and dying in which individuals attempt to negotiate with others who might help them live longer.

basic needs. Needs that have a clear physiological basis and are related to survival.

battering. A pattern of behavior used to establish power and control over another person through fear and intimidation, often including the threat or use of violence. Battering happens when one person believes he or she is entitled to control another.

behavior rehearsal. Therapy in which the client role-plays the feared situation.

behavioral therapy. Therapy that involves discovering the factors that trigger and reinforce the problem behavior; specifying a target behavior to replace it; and then, by manipulating these factors, bringing out the desired behavior.

behaviorism. The view that psychology is an objective science that studies overt or external behavior.

bereavement. The process of adjusting to the experience of loss, especially the death of friends or loved ones.

binge eating. Eating an excessive amount of food within a discrete period of time and with a sense of lack of control over eating during the episode.

biological perspective. Many of our personal attributes and much of our personal development may be attributable to genetic and other biological influences.

biomedical therapies. Therapeutic strategies that rely on direct physiological intervention to treat the symptoms of psychological disorders.

bipolar disorder. An emotional disorder characterized by alternation of elated and depressive moods, popularly known as manic depression.

bisexual, bisexuality. Preference for sexual activity with partners of either sex.

blended families. Families created when remarried couples have children of their own in addition to children from previous marriages of both partners.

body ideal. One's image of the ideal body.

body image. Refers to the mental image we form of our own bodies.

body leakage. The leaking of the true emotion through body postures rather than the face.

body mass index. A measure of total body fat calculated from an individual's height and weight.

borderline personality disorder. A personality disorder in which the individual shows impulsive behavior and unstable social relationships as well as an unstable self-image.

bulimia nervosa. An eating disorder characterized by excessive overeating or uncontrolled binge eating followed by self-induced vomiting.

bullying. Repeated, unprovoked, harmful actions by one child or children against another.

burnout. A psychological syndrome of emotional exhaustion, depersonalization, and reduced personal accomplishment that occurs among individuals, especially those who do "people work."

calories. A measurement of energy produced by food when oxidized, or "burned," in the body.

career. The purposeful life pattern of work, as seen in the sequence of jobs and occupations held throughout life.

catharsis. Venting (releasing) anger.

centralized communication networks. Communication in groups in which one or two individuals control the flow of information.

charismatic leader. This type of leader inspires social change, is visionary, and appeals to followers' self-concepts and values.

child pornography. A visual depiction of a minor engaging in sexually explicit conduct, especially one lacking serious literary, artistic, political, or scientific value.

chlamydia. A bacterium that is spread by sexual contact and that affects both males and females.

chronic stress. The self-perception of "global" (or generalized and pervasive) stress in our lives.

claustrophobia. An irrational fear of closed places.

climacteric. The loss of reproductive capacity.

cognition. A general term for information processing, including a variety of processes such as attention, perception, and memory.

cognitive-behavioral therapies. A large and diverse group of therapies that characterize their orientation as either behavioral or cognitive or both and that attempt to modify faulty thinking or maladaptive behavior.

cognitive dissonance. An uncomfortable feeling caused when one's actions do not match one's attitudes or when one has made the wrong decision.

cognitive psychology. A theoretical perspective that assumes learning and behavior involve higher-level cognitive functions or thinking.

cognitive therapies. Therapies in which the central assumption is that the emotional and behavioral problems result from the individual's distorted thoughts and reactions to external events rather than from the events themselves. This approach encourages people to think more rationally about themselves and their problem.

cognitive therapists. Focus on faulty cognitive processes as the crucial element in maladaptive behavior.

cohabitation. The practice of unmarried persons living together, sharing bed and board.

cohabitation effect. An effect whereby couples that cohabit first have greater marital instability than couples that do not cohabit.

collectives. A large group that is unlikely to have a true leader or clear rules.

collective societies (or cultures). Societies in which collective or societal gain is cherished over individual advancement.

coming out. When an individual accepts his or her sexual orientation as homosexual (or bisexual) and then tells others.

commitment. The pledge or promise to make something work, as in committing ourselves to a career or relationship. In love relationships, commitment is the cognitive aspect of love, which includes both a short-term affirmation of love and a long-term commitment to maintain love.

community-based service. The general term meaning that mental health services are located in the individual's own community or nearby.

community mental health center. A center designed to provide a variety of mental health services located in the patient's own community.

companionate love. A kind of loving but practical relationship based primarily on emotional closeness and commitment rather than physical, sexual intimacy.

compliance. A change in behavior in response to a direct request from another person to do so.

complicated grief. A psychological state in which a person's emotional reaction to loss remains repressed, often being manifested in unexplained physical or psychological symptoms.

compromise. When an adjustment is made by modifying opposing ideas or behaviors.

compulsion. An act that the individual feels compelled to repeat again and again, usually in ritualistic fashion or according to certain rules.

conditions of worth. The feeling most of us have that, instead of growing up in an atmosphere of unconditional acceptance, most of us feel we are loved and accepted only if we meet certain expectations and approvals.

confederates. Friends of the experimenter who have been told by the experimenter how to behave.

conformity. A change in behavior due to the real or imagined influence (pressure) of other people.

confrontation (as related to illness). A pattern an individual utilizes to directly note that there are symptoms of illness present.

consummate love. A complete and balanced love characterized by emotional closeness, sexual intimacy, and commitment between the partners.

contempt (in sexual relationships). A tactic in which insults are used to denigrate a partner's sexuality.

contingency theory of leadership. The theory identifies two attributes or styles of leaders known as people-oriented or task-oriented, which are effective at leading in different situations.

counselors. Professionals who receive training in personality theory and counseling skills, usually at the master's-degree level. Their counseling emphasis tends to reflect their respective professional affiliations, depending on whether they are doing marriage counseling, career counseling, pastoral counseling (clergy), or some other type.

couple adjustment. The changes and adjustments in a couple's relationship during the course of their committed or married life.

crisis intervention. A treatment for those who are in a state of acute crisis but do not need treatment for many sessions. Many cities possess these services in the form of telephone hotlines.

criticism (in sexual relationships). A response pattern related to human sexuality in which one partner attacks or criticizes the other partner's character.

crossdressers. Individuals who occasionally wear clothing of the opposite gender.

crystallized intelligence. The ability to use accumulated knowledge to make judgments and solve problems.

cultural diversity. The cultural pattern by which people from different cultural and ethnic backgrounds maintain in varying degrees both their national and their ethnic identities.

culture. The ideas, customs, arts, and skills that characterize a group of people during a given period of history.

culture-bound syndromes. Sets of symptoms much more common in some societies than in others.

cyberslacking. The overuse of the Internet in the workplace for purposes other than work.

date rape. Coercive sexual activity that occurs during a date.

day hospitals. Hospitals that provide part-time care for those with mental disorders during regular working hours and then allow them to return to their families in the evening.

death. The cessation of life as measured by the absence of breathing, heartbeat, and electrical activity of the brain.

decentralized communication networks. Communication in groups in which individuals can communicate relatively freely with one another.

decision making. The process of gathering information and relevant alternatives and making an appropriate choice.

defense mechanisms. Automatic unconscious mechanisms that protect us from the awareness of anxiety, thereby helping us to maintain a sense of self-worth in the face of threat.

defensiveness (in sexual relationships). A tactic in which we make excuses or refuse to take responsibility for our sexuality or use some other self-protective defense.

delusions. Beliefs that have no basis in reality.

denial of death. The first stage of death and dying, in which people characteristically feel that death cannot happen to them.

depersonalization. The sense of not being intimately attached to one's body.

depression. An emotional state characterized by intense and unrealistic sadness that may assume a variety of forms, some more severe and chronic than others.

desensitization. The method of controlling anxiety by learning to associate an incompatible response, like relaxation, with the fear-provoking stimulus.

desire for success. The urge to succeed. A social motive in which the individual hopes for achievement and success; in some individuals this motive competes with another social motive, the fear of failure. Both of these motives contribute to overall need for achievement.

development. The relatively enduring changes in people's capacities and behavior as they grow older because of biological growth processes and people's interaction with their environment, including their social environment.

devil effect. Inferring uniformly negative traits from an appearance of a few negative traits.

diagnosis. The classification of a disorder within a set of recognized categories of abnormal behavior.

diathesis-stress hypothesis. A proposal that views schizophrenia as the interaction of a genetic vulnerability (the diathesis or predisposition) with environmental stressors.

discrimination. When we apply unfair or negative treatment to groups on the basis of such features as age, sex, or race.

distress. Stress that has a harmful effect.

divorce. The legal dissolution of a marriage.

door-in-the-face effect. The requester first issues a large, unreasonable request. When the respondent answers "no," the requester makes the truly desired but smaller and more reasonable demand.

downward comparison (as related to health issues). A pattern of behavior individuals utilize to compare their own situation to others who are worse off.

early adulthood. The initial stage of adult development, from the late teens or early 20s through the 30s, characterized by the establishment of personal and economic independence.

ego. A direct outgrowth of the id and functions as a manager of personality, enabling the individual to cope with the conflicting demands of the id, the superego, and society.

Electra complex. The sexual attraction of girls to their fathers and envy of their mothers.

electroconvulsive therapy (ECT). The administration of an electric current to the patient's brain to produce a convulsion; sometimes used in the treatment of severe depression.

emotion. A complex pattern of changes that include physiological changes, subjective feelings, cognitive processes, and behavioral reactions.

emotion-focused coping. The attempt by the distressed individual to alter the emotional reaction to stress.

emotion-focused therapy (EFT). A cognitive therapy that provides a technique for changing basic thought and emotional patterns.

emotional intelligence (EI). The ability to regulate one's own emotions and to be empathic for others' emotions.

entrapment. The process of throwing more time, energy, or money into a bad situation.

envy. Feelings of inferiority, longing, resentment, and disapproval.

e-recruiting. A process in which job candidates are screened by phone, video, or computer.

erectile inhibition disorder. In sexuality, this is known as impotence or the inability of the man to experience erection.

eustress. Stress that has a beneficial effect.

excitement (stage in the sexual response cycle). A stage of sexual arousal that causes increased muscle tension, engorgement of the genitals with blood, and increased heart rate.

existential therapy. An approach that emphasizes the client's capacity for growth through affirmation of their free choice and personal values.

experience of dying. The sequence of physiological and psychological changes experienced by individuals who are dying, such as those with a terminal illness.

external locus of control. The belief by an individual that something outside of him- or herself, such as other individuals, fate, or various external situations, controls life events.

extrinsic motivation. The desire to engage in an activity because it is a means to an end and not because an individual is following his or her inner interests.

extroverts. Individuals who tend to be warm, outgoing, and involved in life.

face saving. Saving one's own or someone else's image

false consensus effect. An assumption that others feel or believe as we do.

family therapy. An approach that includes the larger family unit, including children and adolescents, on the assumption that the disturbance of one family member reflects problems in the overall family patterns.

fear of failure. Fear that we will be humiliated by shortcoming.

female orgasmic disorder. Delay or absence of orgasm in a woman.

fight response (to stress). Confronting the stressor. (See also **flight response.**)

first impression. The initial perception we form of others, in which we tend to judge them on the basis of very little information.

fixation. The emotional fixation of the personality at a particular anxiety-ridden stage that influences the individual to continue to act out symbolically any wishes that were overly inhibited or indulged.

flight response (to stress). Fleeing from the stressor. (See also **fight response.**)

fluid intelligence. The ability to process new information based on perceptual skills and memory.

forming (stage). The initial stage of group development, in which the members come together to form the group.

free association. Saying whatever comes to mind regardless of how trivial it sounds.

friendship. The affectionate attachment between two or more people.

fundamental attribution error. The tendency to overattribute people's behavior to their personality (traits) rather than to their circumstances or situations.

funerals. The ceremonies and rituals associated with the burial or cremation of the dead.

gender. Social and cultural distinctions between masculinity and femininity.

gender roles. Social and cultural expectations about what is appropriate for males and females.

gender stereotypes. Widely held generalizations about the characteristics and behavior of men and women that exaggerate the differences between the sexes.

general adaptation syndrome. According to Selye, the body's reaction to stress, which includes three progressive stages—alarm reaction, stage of resistance, and stage of exhaustion.

generalized anxiety disorder. A chronic state of diffuse or free-floating anxiety.

genes. The biochemical units by which characteristics are inherited.

genital herpes. One of several herpes viral infections (human papillomavirus) that are primarily transmitted through sexual contact.

genital stage. The stage that begins with the onset of puberty and sexual maturation, from about 12 years of age on. In this period the individual's sexual interests are reawakened and focus on gratification through genital or sexual activity.

gestalt therapy. An approach that puts great value on the individual's responsibility in therapy but makes more use of here-and-now nonverbal behavior in the therapy session as a way of helping clients to unify their feelings and actions.

global burden of disease. A measure of years of life lost to disability throughout the world.

gonorrhea. A common sexually transmitted bacterial infection that sometimes produces a cloudy, smelly discharge and a burning sensation upon urination.

good grief. Grief that leads to learning and growth in our bereavement.

great man theory (of leadership). A theory suggesting that great leaders are born with a certain common set of traits.

grief. The intense emotional suffering that accompanies our experience of loss.

grief therapy. A form of therapy that assists the bereaved to cope with the death of a loved one.

grief work. The healthy process of working through emotions associated with loss and death; freeing ourselves emotionally from the deceased, readjusting to life without that person, and resuming ordinary activities.

GRIT (graduated and reciprocated initiatives in tension reduction). A conflict resolution technique in which each side gradually concedes something to the other side.

group polarization effect. Groups are likely to shift to either a more conservative or a riskier decision than individuals alone make.

groupthink. The tendency for groups to reach a consensus prematurely because the desire for harmony overrides the process of critical thinking and the search for the best decision.

guided imagery. A procedure that helps a person shut off the outside world and bypass the censor we call the brain, enabling the person to see, experience, and learn from an intuitive, feeling, unconscious nature. (See also **visualization**.)

halfway house. A residence in which newly released patients and ex-addicts can live under supervision for a short period of time while they make a crucial transition in their lives from a setting with close supervision and other restrictions. Also called group homes and board-and-care homes.

hallucinations. Sensory perceptions that occur in the absence of any appropriate external stimulus.

halo effect. Inferring uniformly positive traits from the appearance of a few positive traits.

happiness. A state with a preponderance of positive thoughts and feelings about one's life.

health psychology. A subfield of psychology that is concerned with how psychological and social factors affect health, wellness, and illness.

heredity. The transmission of traits from parents to offspring.

hermaphrodites. Individuals who exhibit sexual characteristics of both genders. Hermaphroditism often occurs at the embryonic stage of development.

heterosexual, heterosexuality. Emotional and sexual preference for partners of the opposite sex.

heuristics. Mental shortcuts or rules of thumb for making complex decisions.

hierarchy of needs. According to Maslow, the hierarchical manner in which needs and motives function in relation to each other, so that the lowest level of unmet needs remains the most urgent.

homophobic. Term describing individuals who are afraid of homosexuals or hold negative attitudes toward homosexuals.

homosexual, homosexuality. Emotional and sexual preference for partners of the same sex.

hospice. A system of care that integrates a physical facility for the terminally ill with the patient's family and home to enable the patient to die with dignity.

hyperstress. An excessive amount of stress.

humanistic psychology. A group of related theories and therapies that emphasize the values of human freedom and the uniqueness of the individual.

hypoactive sexual desire or inhibited sexual desire. Lack of interest in sex.

hypochondriacs. People who habitually complain of unfounded ailments or exhibit an undue fear of illness.

hypostress. Insufficient stress.

hypothalamus. A small but important structure at the core of the brain that governs many aspects of behavior, such as eating and hormonal activity.

id. The unconscious reservoir of psychic energy for the overall personality and the source of later development when the ego and superego appear.

ideal body. The body we would like to have.

ideal self. The self we'd like to be including our aspirations, moral ideals, and values.

illusion of control. The mistaken belief that we can exercise control over chance-determined events.

"I" messages. Honest but nonjudgmental expressions of emotions about someone whose behavior has become a problem.

immune system. A complex surveillance system, including the brain and various blood cells, that defends our bodies by identifying and destroying various foreign invaders.

incidence (of disorders). The number of new cases of disorders reported during a given period.

individualistic societies (or cultures). Societies in which individual gain (needs, wants, and autonomy) is appreciated more than general societal gain.

infantilized. Treated like infants, as, for example, when other adults speak to them in baby talk..

ingratiation. Managing the impressions we leave on others so that they will like us and comply with our requests. An example is flattery.

in-group. The group with which we identify.

inhibited sexual arousal. Insufficient sexual arousal, such as the male's difficulty in sustaining an erection of his penis or the female's difficulty in generating sufficient vaginal lubrication.

inhibited sexual desire. Lack of interest in sex.

inhibited vaginal lubrication. When insufficient vasocongestion and insufficient lubrication occur in women.

insight. Self-understanding.

insight therapies. Any therapy that aims to bring change by increasing self-understanding.

integrative solutions (for conflicts). Solutions that take into account the needs of both sides in a conflict such that both sides can win something.

interdependence. Mutual dependence among individuals in a given group or society.

internal locus of control. An individual's belief that something within him- or herself controls life events.

intersexed persons. People who are born with chromosomal or hormonal birth defects that cause them not to readily fit into "male" or "female" categories.

intimacy. The emotional aspect of love that includes closeness, sharing, communication, and support.

intimate relationships. Emotionally close relationships between two or more persons, such as friends or lovers, that may or may not include physical, sexual intimacy.

intrinsic motivation. Active engagement with tasks that people find interesting and that, in turn, promote growth and are freely engaged in out of interest.

in vivo desensitization. A technique in which the individual gradually approaches the feared situation directly; it is a method of controlling anxiety by learning to associate an incompatible response, like relaxation, with the fear-provoking stimulus.

jealousy. A complex emotion that occurs when we fear losing a close relationship with another person or have lost it already.

job. A position of employment; the set of work activities and responsibilities associated with a given position.

job satisfaction. People's feelings about different aspects of their jobs; how well one likes a given job, depending on such factors as pay and coworkers.

joint or shared custody. Joint decision making by divorced parents about the child's care.

late adulthood. The final stage of adult development, from the mid-60s to death, characterized by adjustment to changing health, income, and social roles.

latency period. According to Freud, the period that takes place between 5 and 12 years of age. During this time the child's interests turn away from sexual satisfactions. Early sexual feelings are forgotten and sexual urges lie relatively dormant.

learned helplessness. Maladaptive passivity that frequently follows an individual's experience with uncontrollable events.

learned optimism. A learned way of explaining both good and bad life events that in turn enhances our perceived control and adaptive responses to them.

learning. A relatively permanent change in behavior.

learning theory. The systematic statement of principles that explains learning, defined as relatively permanent changes in behavior because of practice or experience.

leisure.   Time free from work or duty that may be spent in recreational activities of one's choice.

libido.   The psychic energy of the sex drive.

life review.   A naturally occurring process of self-review prompted by the realization that life is approaching an end.

lithium.   A natural mineral salt and mood stabilizer that is used to treat people with bipolar disorder.

living will.   An instrument that instructs doctors and family members to stop using life-sustaining procedures in the event of a terminal condition.

locus of control.   The source from which an individual believes control over life events originates—either within the person or with something outside of the person.

logotherapy.   Victor Frankl's approach for dealing with the spiritual aspects of psychopathology, such as confronting clients with their responsibility for finding personal meaning in life. Stresses the importance of clarifying those values that give personal meaning and purpose to one's life.

loneliness.   A subjective state reflecting the fact that the quality of relationships wanted is lower than the quality and quantity of relationships available.

longitudinal studies.   Research in which the same people are studied over a long period of time.

love.   Deep and tender feelings of affection for or attachment to one or more persons.

maintenance activities.   Nonleisure and nonwork time spent in activities necessary for the maintenance of life, such as preparing meals and sleeping.

maladaptive behavior.   Significant impairment in one or more areas of psychological functioning, especially the ability to work and to get along with others.

male impotence disorder.   The inability to experience an erection.

mania.   A disorder in which the individual exhibits such symptoms as an expansive mood, increased social activity, talkativeness, sleeplessness, and reckless behavior.

marital satisfaction.   The sense of gratification and contentment in a marriage, especially in the personal relationship between the partners.

marriage.   The state of being married; usually the legal union between two people.

matching hypothesis.   The tendency to settle for someone like ourselves, at least in regard to the level of physical attractiveness.

mediation.   The intervention in a conflict by a neutral third party who assists the conflicting parties in managing or resolving their dispute.

mediators.   Neutral third parties who intervene in conflict and who help the two disputing parties come to common agreements via communication, creative problem solving, and other techniques.

menopause.   The period in a woman's life that includes the cessation of monthly menstrual cycles.

microexpressions.   Fleeting facial expressions that last only a fraction of a second.

middle adulthood.   The middle stage of adult development, from the late 30s to the mid-60s, characterized by the fulfillment of career and family goals.

midlife transition.   The period of personal evaluation that comes sometimes with the realization that one's life is about half over.

mild cognitive impairment (MCI).   An early form of Alzheimer's disease identified in a subgroup of people who have memory problems during the course of normal aging but are otherwise healthy and functional.

mindguards.   A situation in groupthink in which individuals in the group take it upon themselves to censor dissenters in the group.

minority groups.   Groups that are relatively small in number or that have less power as compared to majority groups. Any ethnic, racial, religious, or political group smaller than and differing from the larger, controlling group in a community or nation.

mistaken impression.   The false or erroneous perception of others, often based on insufficient evidence.

mnemonic neglect.   Poor recall (or forgetting) of negative feedback that is inconsistent with core aspects of the self-concept.

motivation.   A general term referring to the forces that energize and direct our efforts toward a meaningful goal.

motive.   Goal-directed activity that energizes and directs behavior.

motive targets.   The people toward whom our attention or motives are directed.

mourning.   The outward expressions of bereavement and grief, such as the wearing of black.

multiple orgasms.   Experiencing two or more climaxes within a short period of time.

narcissistic personality.   A personality disorder characterized by an undue sense of self-importance, often accompanied by a sense of inferiority.

nature or nurture issue.   The debate over the importance of heredity versus environment.

near-death experience.   The distinctive state of recall associated with being brought back to life from the verge of death.

needs.   Tension states that arouse us to seek gratification.

negotiation.   Making mutual concessions with another person.

networking.   Using personal contacts to establish career opportunities.

neurotransmitter.   Chemical substances that transmit neural impulses.

nicotine addiction.   Difficulty giving up nicotine use, or smoking, when smoking has become habitual.

nominal group technique.   A systematic (round-robin polling) approach to soliciting individual inputs into a group project.

non-age-related changes.   Events and influences that are unique to each of us and may occur at any age or not at all, such as divorce or the decision to change careers.

norm of reciprocity.   An unwritten rule that guides reciprocal behavior related to the granting of favors.

norming (stage).   The third stage of group formation in which the group comes to consensus about the rules under which it will operate.

norms.   Unwritten standards or rules by which groups function and by which groups exert pressure on nonconforming members.

nutrition.   Eating a proper, balanced diet to promote health.

obedience.   Following a direct order or command.

obesity.   An excessive amount of body fat, usually defined as exceeding the desirable weight for one's height, build, and age.

observational learning.   The process in which people learn by observing other people and events without necessarily receiving any direct reward or reinforcement.

obsession.   A thought or image that keeps recurring in the mind, despite the individual's attempts to ignore or resist it.

obsessive–compulsive disorder.   The condition characterized by the involuntary dwelling on an unwelcome thought or the involuntary repetition of an unnecessary act.

occupation.   The activities and responsibilities necessary to perform given work tasks in a particular line of work, such as nursing or marketing.

Oedipus complex.   The sexual attraction of boys to their mothers and envy of their fathers.

oral stage.   According to Freud, the stage that occurs during the first few years of life when the mouth becomes the primary means of gratifying desires of the id.

orgasm (stage in the sexual response cycle).   The climax of sexual excitement that is pleasurable and releases tension.

out-group.   Any group we perceive as being different from (outside of) our own group.

panic disorder and panic attacks.   The type of anxiety disorder characterized by the occurrence of severe panic.

paralinguistics.   Unspoken but important features of spoken communications, such as gestures.

paraprofessionals.   Individuals who have 2- or 4-year degrees (or sometimes no degree at all) and work in the mental health field.

passion.   The emotional or motivational aspect of love that involves physiological arousal and an intense desire to be united with the loved one.

passionate love.   An intense emotional reaction to a potential romantic partner who may not even love you in return.

people- or relationship-oriented leaders.   Leaders who concern themselves with their group members' feelings and relationships.

perceived control.   The belief that we can influence the occurrence of events in our environment that affect our lives.

performing (stage).   The final stage of group development, when the group functions better and performs its business.

personal control.   The achieved amount of control we have over our lives; this term is often synonymous with perceived control.

personal distress.   Intense or chronic negative self-awareness that interferes with one's sense of well-being or functioning.

personal growth.   Personal change or development in a desirable direction, including the fulfillment of one's inborn potential.

personality disorders.   When personality traits are so inflexible and maladaptive that they cause marked impairment in individual's social and occupational life.

personality traits.   Enduring patterns of thinking, feeling, acting, and relating to others that we exhibit in a wide range of situations.

person-centered therapy.   According to Carl Rogers, the view that the helper's genuineness, acceptance, and empathic understanding of the client are necessary and sufficient conditions for producing therapeutic change.

phallic stage.   According to Freud, the stage that extends from the third to the fifth or sixth year, is the period in which the child experiences sensual pleasure through handling of his or her genitals.

phenomenal self.   An individual's overall self-concept available to awareness.

phobic disorders.   The conditions characterized by a persistent and irrational fear of a specific object or activity, accompanied by a compelling desire to avoid it.

physical fitness.   A human's ability to function efficiently and effectively, including both health-related and skill-related fitness components.

pituitary gland.   The master gland of the endocrine, or hormonal, system.

plateau (stage in the sexual response cycle).   The stage just before orgasm; in this phase, sexual arousal becomes more pronounced.

pleasure principle.   The principle by which our actions are guided by the seeking of gratification or pleasure.

positive psychology.   An umbrella term for the study of positive emotions, positive character traits, and enabling institutions.

positive regard.   Acceptance by others.

postdecision regret.   The regret that can be experienced shortly after we have finally made a particularly difficult choice or decision.

posttraumatic stress disorder.   A severe anxiety disorder characterized by symptoms of anxiety and avoidance behavior; resulting from an unusually distressing event such as being assaulted.

power distance.   The idea that people in groups accept the concept that people in an organization rightly have different levels of power and authority. The more status and privileges they ascribe to those in authority, the greater the power distance.

prejudice.   An unfair, often negative attitude toward another person or group based solely on group membership..

premature ejaculation.   Early orgasm in a man.

prevalence (of a disorder).   The total number of active cases that can be identified in a given population at a particular time.

primary control.   Actions directed at attempting to change the world to fit one's needs and desires.

primary drives.   Drives that have a clear physiological basis and that are related to survival.

primary emotions.   The view that basic emotions such as disgust and sadness are frequently combined to form secondary emotions such as remorse, analogous to the mixing of primary colors to form other shades of color.

primary group.   This group is important because it is small, intimate, and interacts face-to-face.

principle of perfection.   A principle that motivates a person to be moral and perfect.

problem-focused coping.   The attempts by the distressed individual to change the environment or find a solution.

propinquity.   Physical closeness.

psychiatric social workers.   Social workers who receive supervised clinical training as part of their master's degree program in the field of social work, and some earn a doctorate as well.

psychiatrists.   Medical doctors who specialize in the treatment of mental illness.

psychoactive substance dependence disorder.   A disorder whereby the individual is dependent on a drug like alcohol or marijuana and exhibits characteristic symptoms.

psychoanalysis.   Psychotherapy aimed at helping the person gain insight and mastery over unconscious conflicts. Also referred to as Freudian theory.

psychoanalysts.   Psychiatrists or other mental health professionals who have received several years of additional training in personality theory and the therapeutic methods of one of the founding analysts.

psychodynamic theory.   A group of related theories that view personality and behavior in terms of the dynamics, or interactions, of driving forces of personality and development such as desires, anxieties, conflicts, and defenses.

psychological disorder.   A clinically significant behavioral or psychological pattern that is associated with (1) present personal distress; (2) disability or impairment in one or more important areas of functioning, e.g., maladaptive behavior; (3)

significantly increased risk of suffering disability, pain, or death; and (4) an important loss of freedom or personal control.

psychological hardiness.   The attitude that allows individuals to make the most of what are often bad situations. A characteristic of individuals who cope successfully with stress.

psychologists.   Professionals who receive clinical training in the methods of psychological assessment and treatment as part of a program in clinical, counseling, or school psychology.

psychosexual stages.   According to Freud, the sequence of critical stages in the developmental process; the way in which individuals handle the conflicts among their pleasure-seeking impulses, inhibitions, and environmental restrictions that becomes decisive for adult personality.

psychosurgery.   Surgery designed to destroy or disconnect brain tissue in an attempt to regulate abnormal behavior.

psychotherapy.   A helping process in which a trained, socially sanctioned therapist performs certain activities that will facilitate a change in the client's attitudes and behaviors.

psychotic symptoms.   Symptoms that are signs of psychosis (e.g., schizophrenia) and that include hallucinations such as hearing voices, marked impairment in self-care and social relationships, and other signs of severe disturbance.

quality care.   Care provided by a warm, supportive adult in a safe, healthy, and stimulating environment.

rape.   Sexual intercourse under conditions of actual or threatened force that overcome the victim's resistance.

rational-emotive therapy.   A therapy in which the central assumption is that emotional and behavioral problems result from an individual's distorted thoughts and reactions to external events rather than from the events themselves. This approach encourages people to think more rationally about themselves and their problems.

reactance.   An oppositional response that occurs when our personal freedom is restricted.

reality principle.   The rational orientation that guides the ego in its attempts to put the individual's well-being above the pleasure seeking of the id or the moralistic control of the superego.

refractory period.   The period of time following an orgasm when added stimulation will not result in orgasm.

reinforcement.   The addition of something that increases the likelihood of a behavior.

relapse.   A return to a previous state; in psychology, the return to a former problematic behavior.

reminiscence.   Thinking about oneself and reconsidering past events and their meaning.

resentment.   The second stage of death and dying, in which dying individuals resent those who are healthy.

resilience.   Positive growth or adaptation following brief periods of stress after some stressful disruption or extreme adversity.

resistance.   In therapy, when an individual hesitates or is reluctant to talk about some painful experiences.

resolution phase (stage in the sexual response cycle).   The stage immediately following orgasm, in which the body returns to its normal, nonexcited phase.

responsibility diffusion.   A phenomenon in which individuals in groups feel less responsible for the risk so are willing to make riskier decisions in groups.

retarded ejaculation.   A delay or absence of orgasm in a man.

right to die.   The legal and ethical view that competent individuals who are able to understand treatment choices and their consequences have the right to decide their own fate, such as the withholding of treatment that would delay death.

risky shift.   A phenomenon in which groups coming to consensus make riskier decisions than individuals.

role.   A set of rules that defines how an individual in a particular post in a group will behave.

romantic love.   Consists of intimacy or closeness and passion. Strong emotional attachment to a person of the opposite or same sex, primarily on the basis of physical, sexual intimacy.

schizophrenia.   A group of related psychotic disorders characterized by severe disorganization of thoughts, perceptions, and emotions; bizarre behavior; and social withdrawal.

seasonal affective disorder (SAD). A depression that is more likely to occur at certain times of the year, usually the winter months.

secondary control. Involves the individual utilizing processes directed at making him- or herself fit into the world better.

secondary erectile inhibition disorder. That is, they've previously experienced erections but are consistently unable to have an erection of sufficient firmness to penetrate the woman's vagina.

secondary group. This group is usually larger than a primary group, has a formal or contractual reason for coming together, often disbands when the reason for their existence disappears, and are less likely to engage in regular face-to-face interaction.

securely attached. An attachment style by which people develop happy and trusting love relationships.

self-actualization/self-actualized. The process of fulfilling our inborn potential, involving a biological growth tendency as well as self-conscious efforts at growth.

self-alienation. The failure to acknowledge or accept certain aspects of ourselves; the feeling these qualities are foreign to us and we project them onto others, whom we then dislike.

self-clarity. The extent to which one's individual self-beliefs are clearly and confidently defined, internally consistent, and stable.

self-complexity. The extent to which one's self-concept is comprised of many differentiated self-aspects.

self-concept. The overall image or awareness we have of ourselves. It includes all those perceptions of "I" and "me," together with the feelings, beliefs, and values associated with them.

self-consistency. The tendency to perceive our experiences in a manner that is consistent with our self-concept; experiences that are not consistent with the self are distorted or denied to awareness.

self-direction. The need to learn more about ourselves and our world as a means of directing our lives more effectively.

self-disclosure. The sharing of intimate or personal information with others.

self-efficacy. The belief in one's capabilities to organize and execute courses of action required to produce give attainments.

self-enhancement theory. The tendency to try to get positive feedback that affirms their own ideas about our positive qualities.

self-esteem. The sense of personal worth associated with one's self-concept.

self-fulfilling prophecy. A prophecy that is fulfilled when people's expectations become a reality by virtue of their own behavior.

self-image. The personal evaluation of ourselves and the resulting feelings of worth associated with our self-concept.

self-immunization. The trivialization of threatening information, such as failure, by making the behavior seem less important.

self-recognition. A child's ability to differentiate him- or herself from others in the social environment.

self-serving attributions. Attributions that glorify the self or conceive of the self as causing the good outcomes that come our way.

self-verification theory. The tendency to want to preserve our own images (both positive and negative) of ourselves and therefore elicit feedback that verifies or confirms our own self-perceptions.

sensation-seeking motive. The tendency to seek out stimulating and novel experiences, partly because of biological factors.

serotonin. A neurotransmitter that has been linked to depression.

sexual dysfunction. A persistent problem that prevents the individual from engaging in or enjoying sexual intercourse.

sexual harassment. Any unwanted attention of a sexual nature occurring in the workplace that interferes with a person's ability to work.

sexual intercourse. The penetration of the vagina by the penis.

sexual orientation. A component of sexuality and is characterized by enduring emotional, romantic, or sexual attraction to a particular gender.

sexual prejudice. Negative attitudes based on sexual orientation, whether the target is homosexual, bisexual, or heterosexual.

sexual response cycle. The basic sexual response patterns of men and women, as in sexual intercourse.

sexual victimization. Being coerced to engage in sexual acts under duress or force, such as rape.

sexually transmitted diseases (STDs). Infections transmitted primarily by sexual intercourse.

shyness. The tendency to avoid contact or familiarity with others.

simple phobia. A most common type of phobia in which individuals are irrationally afraid of common objects such as dogs, snakes, insects, stairs, etc.

skill. The ability to perform a task well. It is usually developed over time through training or experience.

social anxiety/social phobia. An extreme form of shyness that can interfere with an individual's daily life and involves a chronic, irrational fear of and a compelling desire to avoid situations where others may scrutinize the individual.

social change. Changes in the social patterns and institutions in society.

social-cognitive perspective. The view that human learning and behavior necessarily involve higher cognitive abilities as well as environmental influences.

social comparison. The process of using others to compare ourselves to in order to understand who we are relative to them.

social influence. Efforts on the part of one person to alter the behavior or attitudes of one or more others.

social loafing. Contributing less to a group effort than would be contributed to an individual effort.

social norms. The generalized expectations regarding appropriate behavior in a given situation or society.

social phobia. An extreme form of shyness that can interfere with an individual's daily life and involves a chronic, irrational fear of and a compelling desire to avoid situations where others may scrutinize the individual.

social self(selves). The way we feel others see us.

social support. A process whereby one individual or group offers comfort and advice to others who can use it as a means of coping.

stage of exhaustion. Stage of Selye's notion of the general adaptation syndrome response to stress in which the body is unable to continue secreting hormones at an increased rate, so the organism can no longer adapt to chronic stress. Body defenses break down, adaptation energy runs out, and the physical symptoms of the alarm reaction reappear.

stage of resistance. Stage of Selye's notion of the general adaptation syndrome response in which the human organism develops an increased resistance to the stressor.

stereotypes. Widespread generalizations about people (based solely on their group membership) that have little if any basis in fact.

stigma. The use of negative labels to identify a person living with a mental disorder or with another distinguishing feature and who you believe differs from you.

storming. The second stage in group formation in which group members disagree or often openly conflict when they learn about each other's opinions.

stress. The pattern of responses individuals make to stimulus events that disturb their equilibrium or exceed their coping abilities.

stressors. The collective label for the variety of external and internal stimuli that evoke stress.

stress-related illness. Any illness that is affected in an important way by one's emotions, lifestyle, or environment.

stress tolerance. The degree of stress you can handle or how long you can put up with a demanding task without acting in an irrational or disorganized way.

subjective well-being (SWB). A state with a preponderance of positive thoughts and feelings about one's life.

substitution. A conflict resolution strategy whereby we seek alternative goals with another person.

superego. The part of the personality which has been shaped by the moral standards of society as transmitted by the parents.

syphilis. A sexually transmitted and serious disease caused by a spiral-shaped bacterium, or spirochete.

systems theory. A theory stating that human existence is made up of various subsystems and is itself an integral part of larger systems.

tardive dyskinesia. A side effect of antipsychotic drugs, characterized by jerking movements around the neck and face and involuntary protrusions of the tongue.

task-oriented leaders. Leaders who are primarily concerned with getting the job done well and in a timely fashion.

technophobia. A fear of technology.

temperament. An individual's characteristic pattern of emotional response and behavioral reactivity to situations and stressors.

temporal memory. Memory for things related to time.

therapist. A person trained to help people with psychological problems.

third force in psychology.   The view that humanistic psychology is a major alternative to the deterministic outlook of psychodynamic and behavioral psychology.

tobacco abuse.   The abuse of tobacco to such an extent that heart, respiratory, and other health-related problems develop.

transference.   The unconscious tendency of clients to project onto the therapist their feelings and fantasies, both positive and negative, about significant others in their childhood.

transformational leader.   A leader who stimulates interest among colleagues and followers to view their work from a new perspective. The leader does this by generating awareness of the mission or vision of the organization and helps members to look beyond their own interests.

transinstitutionalization.   The revolving-door syndrome in which mental patients find themselves housed in one institution after another, often including jails and prisons.

transition (stage in the sexual response cycle).   The gradual shift from a nonsexual state to a sexual state of being and includes the awakening of sexual desire and a readiness for sexual arousal.

transsexuals.   People who believe that they were born into the body of the wrong sex. They sometimes want to change this situation through hormone therapy and gender reassignment surgery.

transvestites.   Individuals who dress to look like the opposite gender. Some transvestites wear other-gender clothing full-time and successfully pass as the opposite sex.

triangular theory of love.   A theory of love that suggests there are three components to love—intimacy, passion, and commitment.

trust.   People's abstract but positive expectations that they can count on friends and partners to care for them and be responsive to their needs, now and in the future.

Type A individuals.   People who tend to be competitive, argumentative, time-urgent, ambitious, and impatient, and sometimes hostile. They are heart-attack prone.

Type B individuals.   Individuals who are relaxed and easygoing, rather than competitive and impatient.

unconditional leisure.   Any activity freely chosen, excluding work and maintenance activities.

unconditional positive regard.   Unconditional positive acceptance; generally utilized in person-centered therapy.

underemployed.   Working in a job beneath one's abilities or education.

unembodiment.   The sense of not being intimately attached to one's body.

unresolved grief.   A psychological state in which one's emotional reaction to loss remains repressed, often being manifested in unexplained physical or psychological symptoms.

virtual therapy.   A therapy that employs the high-tech tools of virtual reality, which essentially is often a computer-generated fanatasy world that can be controlled by the client.

visualization.   A procedure that helps a person shut off the outside world and bypass the censor we call the brain, enabling the person to see, experience, and learn from an intuitive, feeling, unconscious nature. (See also **guided imagery**.)

voluntary marriage.   The assumption that two people will remain married only as long as they are in love.

wellness.   The positive ideal of health in which one strives to maintain and improve one's health.

withdrawal.   To remove oneself physically or emotionally from an activity, organization, or person. In sexual relationships, a response pattern in which one partner ignores the other.

work values.   Those values that bring you the most enjoyment and satisfaction in a career or job.

workplace.   Place of paid employment outside the home.

References

A very revealing picture: *Psychology Today's* 1997 body image survey find. (1997, January/February). *Psychology Today, 30,* 34–40.

AARP. (2000, September/October). Start the conversation. *Modern Maturity* (Special Section), *43,* 51–68.

AARP. (2002, November/December). Why we work. *Modern Maturity,* 90.

ABLON, J.S., & JONES, E.E. (2002). Validity of controlled clinical trials of psychotherapy: Findings from the NIMH treatment of depression collaborative research program. *The American Journal of Psychiatry, 159,* 775–783.

ABRAMOVITZ, M. (2002, February). Mirror mirror in your head: Your mental picture of your body can have a direct effect on your self-esteem and your behavior. *Current Health, 2,* 26–30.

ABRAMS, D.C., & LAMB, M. (2002, April). Father nature: The making of a modern dad. *Psychology Today,* 38–47.

ACKERMAN, P.L., BEIER, M.E., & BOWEN, K.R. (2002). What we really know about our abilities and our knowledge. *Personality and Individual Differences, 33,* 587–616.

ACKERMAN, S.J., & HILSENROTH, M.J. (2003). A review of therapist characteristics and techniques positively impacting therapeutic alliance. *Clinical Psychology Review, 23,* 1–32.

ACTON, R.G., & DURING, S.M. (1992). Preliminary results of aggression management training for aggressive parents. *Journal of Interpersonal Violence, 7,* 410–417.

ADAMS, J., & ROSCIGNO, V.J. (2005). White supremacists, oppositional culture and the world wide web. *Social Forces, 84,* 759–778.

ADAMS, R.E., BOSCARINO, J.A., & FIGLEY, C.R. (2006). Compassion fatigue and psychological distress among social workers: A validation study. *American Journal of Orthopsychiatry, 76,* 103–108.

ADELMANN, P. (1988, April). Possibly yours. *Psychology Today, 8,* 10.

ADELSON, R. (2005). Hard-hitting hormones: The stress-depression link. *Monitor on Psychology, 36,* 24.

ADLER, J. (1999, June 14). Stress, *Newsweek,* 56–63.

Administration on Aging. (2005). A profile of older Americans—2004. Retrieved August 7, 2006, from aoa.gov/prof/statistics/profile/2004.

Administration on Aging. (2006). Healthy people 2010. Retrieved August 7, 2006, from http://www.aoa.gov/prof/adddiv/healthy/addov_healthy.asp.

ADRIANSON, L. (2001). Gender and computer-mediated communication: Group processes in problem solving. *Computers in Human Behavior, 17,* 71–94.

Aging in America: Trends and projections. (1991). Prepared by U.S. Senate Special Committee on Aging, American Association of Retired Persons, Federal Council on Aging, and U.S. Administration on Aging (DHHS Publ. No. 91-28001 [FCoA]). Washington, DC: U.S. Government Printing Office.

AHLFINGER, N.R., & ESSER, J.K. (2001). Testing the groupthink model: Effects of promotional leadership and conformity predisposition. *Social Behavior and Personality, 29,* 31–41.

AI, A.L., EVANS-CAMPBELL, T., SANTANGELO, L.K., & CASCIO, T. (2006). The traumatic impact of the September 11, 2001, terrorist attacks and the potential protection of optimism. *Journal of Interpersonal Violence, 21,* 689–700.

AIRHIHENBUWA, C.O., KUMANYIKA, S., AGURS, T.D., & LOVE, A. (1995). Perceptions and beliefs about exercise, rest, and health among African Americans. *American Journal of Health Promotion, 9,* 426–429.

AJZEN, I. (2002). Perceived behavioral control, self-efficacy, locus of control, and the theory of planned behavior. *Journal of Applied Social Psychology, 32,* 665–683.

AKKIRMAN, A.D., & HARRIS, D.L. (2005). Organizational communication satisfaction in the virtual workplace. *Journal of Management Development, 24,* 397–409.

ALBANO, A.M., & HAYWARD, C. (2004). *Social anxiety disorder.* New York: Oxford University Press.

ALICKE, M.D., & LARGO, E. (1995). The role of the self in the false consensus effect. *Journal of Experimental Social Psychology, 31,* 28–47.

ALICKE, M.D., BRAUN, J.C., GLOR, J.E., KLOTZ, N.L., NAGEE, J., SEDERHOLD, H., & SIEGEL, R. (1992). Complaining behavior in social interaction. *Personality and Social Psychology Bulletin, 18,* 286–298.

ALIMO-METCALFE, B., & ALBAN-METCALF, R.J. (2001). The development of a new transformational leadership questionnaire. *Journal of Occupational & Organizational Psychology, 74,* 1–27.

ALLEN, B.P. (1997). Personality theories: Development, growth and diversity. Boston: Allyn & Bacon.

ALLOY, L.B., ABRAMSON, L.Y., & FRANCES, E.L. (1999). Do negative cognitive styles confer vulnerability to depression? *Current Directions in Psychological Science, 8,* 128–132.

ALLUMBAUGHT, D.L., & HOYT, W.T. (1999). Effectiveness of grief therapy: A meta-analysis. *Journal of Counseling Psychology, 46,* 370–380.

ALMEDOM, A.M. (2005). Resilience, hardiness, sense of coherence, and posttraumatic growth: All paths leading to "light at the end of the tunnel"? *Journal of Loss & Trauma, 10,* 253–265.

ALMEIDA, D.M. (2005). Resilience and vulnerability to daily stressors assessed via diary methods. *Current Directions in Psychological Science, 14,* 64–68.

ALONI, M., & BERNIERI, F.J. (2004). Is love blind? The effects of experience and infatuation on the perception of love. *Journal of Nonverbal Behavior. Special Issue: Interpersonal Sensitivity, Part II, 28,* 287–295.

ALTERMAN, J. (Speaker). (1999). The social/cultural dimension of the information revolution. Retrieved January 10, 2006, from http://www.cia.gov/nic/pdf_gif_research/html/cf154.chap6.html.

Alzheimers Association. (2006a). Fact sheet: Mild cognitive impairment (MCI). Retrieved August 7, 2006, from http://www.alz.org.resources/topicindex/mci.asp.

Alzheimers Association. (2006b). New data indicate beta-amyloid antibodies may slow cognitive decline in alzheimers disease. Retrieved August 7, 2006, from http://www.alz.org/news/03q2/052203vaccine.asp.

Alzheimers Association. (2006c). Statement of the alzeheimers association on new CDC mortality rates. Retrieved August 7, 2006, from http://www.alz.org/media.newsreleases/2001/062701alzstatement.asp.

465

AMATO, P.R., JOHNSON, D.R., BOOTH, A., & ROGERS, S.J. (2003). Continuity and change in marital quality between 1980 and 2000. *Journal of Marriage & the Family, 65,* 1–22.

AMATO, P.R., & PREVITI, D. (2003). People's reasons for divorcing: Gender, social class, the life course, and adjustment. *Journal of Family Issues, 24,* 602–626.

AMBADY, N., HALLAHAN, M., & ROSENTHAL, R. (1995). On judging and being judged accurately in zero-acquaintance situations. Journal of Personality and Social Psychology, 69, 518–529.

American Academy of Family Physicians. (2003). *Parenting tips.* http://familydoctor .org/handouts/368.html.

American Academy of Pediatrics. (2006). Sexual stereotypes and sexual orientation. Retrieved May 04, 2006, from http://www.medem.com/MedLB/article_ detaillb.cfm?article_ID=ZZZNZ1L6W7C&sub_cat=269.

American Academy of Pediatrics. (n.d.). What media teaches children. Retrieved January 12, 2006, from http://www.medem.com/search/article_display.cfm? path=\\TANQUERAY\M_ContentItem&mstr=/M_ContentItem/ZZZ5F I0XQ7C.html&soc=AAP&srch_typ=NAV_SERCH.

American Cancer Society. (1985). *Cancer facts and figures.* New York: Author.

American Psychiatric Association. (2000). *Diagnostic and statistical manual of mental disorders* (DSM-IV) (4TR). Washington, DC: Author.

American Psychiatric Association. (1994). *Diagnostic and statistical manual of mental disorders* (DSM-IV) (4th ed). Washington, DC: Author.

American Psychoanalytic Association. (1999). *Outcome studies on psychoanalysis.* http:// www://apsa.org/pubinfo/IPAstudy.htm.

American Psychological Association. (1998, October). *How therapy helps.* http:// helping.apa.org/therapy/psychotherapy.htm.

American Psychological Association. (2004a). *Answers to your questions about sexual orientation and homosexuality.* http://www.apa.org/pubinfo/orient.html.

American Psychological Association. (2004b). What lies behind the habit of 'tending and befriending' during stress. *Monitor on Psychology, 35,* 15.

American Psychological Association. (2006). Control over day-to-day tasks can reduce fatigue. *Monitor on Psychology, 37,* 11.

American Psychological Association. (2006a). News release: Americans engage in unhealthy behaviors to manage stress. Retrieved May 30, 2006, from http:// apahelpcenter.mediaroom.com/index.php?s=press_release&item=23.

American Psychological Association. (2006b). News release: Stress and emotions can negatively affect heart health. Retrieved May 30, 2006, from http:// apahelpcenter.mediaroom.com/index.php?s=press_release&item=22.

American Psychological Association. (2007). *Answers to your questions about sexual orientation and homosexuality.* http://www.apa.org/topics/sbehavior1.html.

American Psychological Society. (1999, July/August). Web assessments equally effective as interventions. *APS Observer, 19,* 37.

American Vocational Association (2000). Stressed out on campus. *Techniques, 75,* 9.

AMIRKHAN, J.H., RISINGER, R.T., & SWICKERT, R.J. (1995). Extroversion: A "hidden" personality factor in coping? *Journal of Personality, 63,* 189–212.

ANASTASIO, P.A., ROSE, K.C., & CHAPMAN, J. (1999). Can the media create public opinion? A social-identity approach. *Current Directions in Psychological Science, 8,* 152–155.

ANDERSON, B.L., CYRANOWSKI, J.M., & ESPINDLE, D. (1999). Men's sexual self-schema. *Journal of Personality and Social Psychology, 76,* 645–661.

ANDERSON, C.A., & BUSHMAN, B.J. (2001). Effects of violent video games on aggressive behavior, aggressive cognition, aggressive affect, physiological arousal, and prosocial behavior: A meta-analytic review of the scientific literature. *Psychological Science, 12,* 353–359.

ANDERSON, C.J. (2003). The psychology of doing nothing: Forms of decision avoidance result from reason and emotion. *Psychological Bulletin, 129,* 139–168.

ANDERSON, S.M., & BERK, M.S. (1998). The social-cognitive model of transference: Experiencing past relationships in the present. *Current Directions in Psychological Science, 7,* 109–115.

ANDERSON, T.L. (2005). Relationships among internet attitudes, internet use, romantic beliefs, and perceptions of online romantic relationships. *CyberPsychology & Behavior, 8,* 521–531.

Anonymous. (2002). Small violent acts lead to larger problems, says study. *What Works in Teaching and Learning, 8.*

Anonymous. (2003). Going online for a new job rarely pays. *USA Today, 131,* 4–5.

Anonymous. (2004). Survey results: support for 'first'. *The Quill, 92,* 36.

Anonymous. (2005). Research says living wills won't guarantee patients' wishes: Michigan researchers say Patient Self-Determination Act a failure. *Medical Ethics Advisor, 21,* 1–4.

Anred.com (2000, August). *Anorexia and related eating disorders.* http://anred.com.

ANSFIELD, M.E., DePAULO, B.M., & BELL, K.L. (1995). Familiarity effects in nonverbal understanding: Recognizing our own facial expressions and our friends'. *Journal of Nonverbal Behavior, 19,* 135–149.

ANTONIO, A.L. (2004). When does race matter in college friendships? Exploring men's diverse and homogeneous friendship groups. *Review of Higher Education: Journal of the Association for the Study of Higher Education, 27,* 553—575.

ARCHIBALD, F.S., BARTHOLOMEW, K., & MARX, R. (1995). Loneliness in early adolescence: A test of the cognitive discrepancy model of loneliness. *Personality and Social Psychology Bulletin, 21,* 296–301.

ARKIN, R.C. (2005). Moving up the food chain: Motivation and emotion in behavior-based robots. In J. Fellous, & M. A. Arbib (Eds.), *Who needs emotions?: The brain meets the robot* (pp. 245–269). New York: Oxford University Press.

ARMOUR, S. (1999a, November 2). Net peeves: Bosses police cyber-slackers. *USA Today,* 1B–2B.

ARMOUR, S. (1999b, November 23). The new interview etiquette. *USA Today,* 1B–2B.

ARNOLD, P., FLETCHER, S., & FARROW, R. (2002). Condom use and psychological sensation seeking by college students. *Sexual and Relationship Therapy, 17,* 355–366.

ARON, E.N., ARON, A., & DAVIES, K.M. (2005). Adult shyness: The interaction of temperamental sensitivity and an adverse childhood environment. *Personality and Social Psychology Bulletin, 31,* 181–197.

ARONOFF, J. (2006). How we recognize angry and happy emotion in people, places, and things. *Cross-Cultural Research: The Journal of Comparative Social Science, 40,* 83–105.

ASAI, A., & BARNLUND, D.C. (1998). Boundaries of the unconscious private and public self in Japanese and Americans: A cross-cultural comparison. *International Journal of Intercultural Relations, 22,* 431–452.

ASCH, S.E. (1951). Effects of group pressure upon the modification and distortion of judgments. In H. Guetzkow (Ed.), *Groups, leadership, and men.* Pittsburgh, PA: Carnegie Press.

ASCH, S.E. (1956). Studies of independence and conformity: A minority of one against unanimous majority. *Psychological Monographs, 70* (Whole No. 416).

ASHER, S.R., & PAQUETTE, J.A. (2003). Loneliness and peer relations in childhood. *Current Directions in Psychological Science, 12,* 75–78.

ASHMAN, O., SHIOMURA, K., & LEVY, B.R. (2006). Influence of culture and age on control beliefs: The missing link of interdependence. *International Journal of Aging & Human Development, 62,* 143–157.

ASMUS, C.L., & JAMES, K. (2005). Nominal group technique, social loafing, and group creative project quality. *Creativity Research Journal, 17,* 349–354.

ASPINWALL, L.G., & TAYLOR, S.E. (1992). Modeling cognitive adaptation: A longitudinal investigation of the impact of individual differences and coping on college adjustment and performance. *Journal of Personality and Social Psychology, 63,* 989–1003.

ATTWOOD, F. (2005). What do people do with porn? Qualitative research into the consumption, use, and experience of pornography and other sexually explicit media. *Sexuality & Culture, 9,* 65–86.

ATWATER, E. (1992). *I hear you: A listening skills handbook.* New York: Walker & Company.

AUNE, K.S., & AUNE, R.K. (1996). Cultural differences in the self-reported experience and expression of emotions in relationships. *Journal of Cross-Cultural Psychology, 27,* 67–81.

AUSTENFELD, J.L., & STANTON, A.L. (2004). Coping through emotional approach: A new look at emotion, coping, and health-related outcomes. *Journal of Personality. Special Issue: Emotions, Personality, and Health, 72,* 1335–1363.

AVELLAR, S., & SMOCK, P.J. (2005). The economic consequences of the dissolution of cohabiting unions. *Journal of Marriage and Family, 67,* 315–327.

AZAR, B. (1998, October). Researchers decipher our ability to taste. *APA Monitor,* 24.

AZAR, B. (2000, January). What's in a face. *Monitor on Psychology,* 44–45.

BAARS, B.J. (2003). I.P. Pavlov and the freedom reflex. *Journal of Consciousness Studies, 10,* 19–40.

BACHMAN, G.F., & BIPPUS, A.M. (2005). Evaluations of supportive messages provided by friends and romantic partners: An attachment theory approach. *Communication Reports, 18,* 85–94.

BAER, J.S. (2002). Student factors: Understanding individual variation in college drinking. *Journal of Studies on Alcohol. Special Issue: College drinking, what it is, and what to do about it: Review of the state of the science, 14,* 40–53.

BAGWELL, C.L., BENDER, S.E., ANDREASSI, C.L., KINOSHITA, T.L., MONTARELLO, S.A., & MULLER, J.G. (2005). Friendship quality and perceived relationship changes predict psychosocial adjustment in early adulthood. *Journal of Social and Personal Relationships, 22,* 235–254.

BAKER, C.N. (2005). Images of women's sexuality in advertisements: A content analysis of Black- and White-oriented women's and men's magazines. *Sex Roles, 52,* 13–27.

BAKER, S.R. (2004). Intrinsic, extrinsic, and amotivational orientations: Their role in university adjustment, stress, well-being, and subsequent academic performance. *Current Psychology: Developmental, Learning, Personality, Social, 23,* 189–202.

BALSAM, K.F., BEAUCHAINE, T.P., MICKEY, R.M., & ROTHBLUM, E.D. (2005). Mental health of lesbian, gay, bisexual, and heterosexual siblings: Effects of gender, sexual orientation, and family. *Journal of Abnormal Psychology, 114,* 471–476.

BANDURA, A. (1973). *Aggression.* Englewood Cliffs, NJ: Prentice Hall.

BANDURA, A. (1986). *Social foundations of thought and action.* Englewood Cliffs, NJ: Prentice Hall.

BANDURA, A. (1997). *Self-efficacy: The exercise of control.* New York: W. H. Freeman.

BANDURA, A. (2000). Self-efficacy: The foundation of agency. In W.J. Perrig & A. Grob. (Eds.), *Control of human behavior, mental processes, and consciousness: Essays in honor of the 60th birthday of August Flammer.* Mahwah, NJ: Lawrence Erlbaum.

BANKS, I. (2001). No man's land: Men, illness, and the NHS. *British Medical Journal, 323,* 1058–1060.

BAR, M., & NETA, M. (2006). Humans prefer curved visual objects. *Psychological Science, 17,* 645–648.

BARBER, B.L. (2006). To have loved and lost . . . adolescent romantic relationships and rejection. In A. C. Crouter, & A. Booth (Eds.), *Romance and sex in adolescence and emerging adulthood: Risks and opportunities* (pp. 29–40). Mahwah, NJ: Lawrence Erlbaum.

BARBOUR, K.A., & BLUMENTHAL, J.A. (2005). Exercise training and depression in older adults. *Neurobiology of Aging. Special Issue: Aging, Diabetes, Obesity, Mood and Cognition, 26,* 119–123.

BARBUTO, J.E.J., & BURBACH, M.E. (2006). The emotional intelligence of transformational leaders: A field study of elected officials. *Journal of Social Psychology, 146,* 51–64.

BARGAL, D. (2004). Structure and process in reconciliation-transformation workshops: Encounters between Israeli and Palestinian youth. *Small Group Research, 35,* 596–616.

BARGH, J.A., McKENNA, K.Y.A., & FITZSIMONS, G.M. (2002). Can you see the real me? Activation and expression of the "true self" on the internet. *Journal of Social Issues, 58,* 33–48.

BARNES, B.L., & SRINIVAS, R. (1993). Self-actualization in different sex subgroups. *Journal of Personality and Clinical Studies, 9,* 19–24.

BARNETT, M.M. (2006) Does it hurt to know the worst?—Psychological morbidity, information preferences and understanding of prognosis in patients with advanced cancer. *Psycho-Oncology. 15,* 44–55.

BARON, R.A., & BYRNE, D. (1997). *Social psychology.* Boston: Allyn & Bacon.

BARRY, P. (1999, April). It's no joke: Humor heals. *AARP Newsletter, 14*–17.

BARTHOLOME, A., TEWKSBURY, R., & BRUZZONE, A. (2000). "I want a man": Patterns of attraction in all-male personal ads. *Journal of Men's Studies, 8,* 309–321.

BASOW, S.A., & RUBENFIELD, K. (2003). "Troubles talk": Effects of gender and gendertyping. *Sex Roles, 48,* 183–187.

BASS, B.M., & RIGGIO, R.E. (2006). *Transformational leadership. 2nd edition.* Mahwah, NJ: Lawrence Erlbaum.

BATESON, P. (2002). The corpse of a wearisome debate. *Science, 297,* 2212–2213.

BATTLE, C.L., SHEA, M.T., JOHNSON, D.M., YEN, S., ZLOTNICK, C., & ZANARINI, M.C., et al. (2004). Childhood maltreatment associated with adult personality disorders: Findings from the collaborative longitudinal personality disorders study. *Journal of Personality Disorders, 18,* 193–211.

BAUER, J.J., McADAMS, D.P., & SAKAEDA, A.R. (2005). Interpreting the good life: Growth memories in the lives of mature, happy people. *Journal of Personality and Social Psychology, 88,* 203–217.

BAUM, D. (2004). The price of valor. *The New Yorker, 80,* 44.

BAUMEISTER, R.F., & LEARY, M.R. (1995). The need to belong: Desire for interpersonal attachments as a fundamental human motivation. *Psychological Bulletin, 117,* 497–529.

BAUMEISTER, R.F., CAMPBELL, J.D., KRUEGER, J.I., & VOHS, K.D. (2003). Does high self-esteem cause better performance, interpersonal success, happiness, or healthier lifestyles? *Psychological Science in the Public Interest, 4,* 1–44.

BAUMEISTER, R.F., CAMPBELL, J.D., KRUEGER, J.I., & VOHS, K.D. (2005, December 20). Exploding the self-esteem myth. *Scientific American, 292.*

BAUMEISTER, R.F., DALE, K., & SOMMER, K.L. (1998). Freudian defense mechanisms and empirical findings in modern psychology: Reaction formation, projection, displacement, undoing, isolation, sublimation, and denial. *Journal of Personality. Special Issue: Defense Mechanisms in Contemporary Personality Research, 66,* 108–124.

BEARDSLEY, K.C., QUINN, D.M., BISWAS, B., & WILKENFELD, J. (2006). Mediation style and crisis outcomes. *Journal of Conflict Resolution, 50,* 58–86.

BEAUPRÉ, M.G., & HESS, U. (2005). Cross-cultural emotion recognition among Canadian ethnic groups. *Journal of Cross-Cultural Psychology, 36,* 355–370.

BEBETSOS, E., CHRONI, S., & THEODORAKIS, Y. (2002). Physically active students' intentions and self-efficacy towards health eating. *Psychological Reports, 91,* 485–495.

BECK, A.T. (1979). *Cognitive therapy and emotional disorders.* New York: American Library.

BECK, A.T. (1988). *Love is never enough.* New York: Harper & Row.

BECK, A.T., BROWN, G., STEER, R.A., EIDELSON, J.I., & RISKIND, J.H. (1987). Differentiating anxiety and depression: A test of the cognitive content-specificity hypothesis. *Journal of Abnormal Psychology, 96,* 179–183.

BEILOCK, S.L., KULP, C.A., HOLT, L.E., & CARR, T.H. (2004). More on the fragility of performance: Choking under pressure in mathematical problem solving. *Journal of Experimental Psychology: General, 133,* 584–600.

BEITEL, M., FERRER, E., CECERO, J.J. (2005). Psychological mindedness and awareness of self and others. *Journal of Clinical Psychology, 61,* 739–750.

BENENSON, J.F., & ALAVI, K. (2004). Sex differences in children's investment in same-sex peers. *Evolution and Human Behavior, 25,* 258–266.

BENNETT, M.D.J., & MILLER, D.B. (2006). An exploratory study of the urban hassles index: A contextually relevant measure of chronic multidimensional urban stressors. *Research on Social Work Practice, 16,* 305–314.

BEN-ZE'EV, A. (2004). *Love online: Emotion on the internet.* New York: Cambridge University Press.

BERDAHL, J.L., & MOORE, C. (2006). Workplace harassment: Double jeopardy for minority women. *Journal of Applied Psychology, 91,* 426–436.

BERG, T. (2005). A structural account of phonological paraphasias. *Brain and language, 94,* 104–129.

BERGSTROM, R.L., NEIGHBORS, C., & LEWIS, M.A. (2004). Do men find "bony" women attractive?: Consequences of misperceiving opposite sex perceptions of attractive body image. *Body Image, 1,* 183–191.

BERKLEY, K.J. (1997). Sex differences in pain. *Behavior and Brain Sciences, 20,* 371–380.

BERNDT, T.J. (2002). Friendships quality and social development. *Current Direction in Psychological Science, 11,* 7–10.

BERSCHEID, E. (1994). Interpersonal relationships. *Annual Review of Psychology, 45,* 79–129.

BERTACCO, M., & DEPONTE, A. (2005). Email as a speed-facilitating device: A contribution to the reduced-cues perspective on communication. *Journal of Computer-Mediated Communication, 10,* article 2.

BESTE, S.A., BERGNER, R.M., & NAUTA, M.M. (2003). What keeps love alive? An empirical investigation. *Family Therapy, 30,* 125–141.

BETZ, N.E., & ROTTINGHAUS, P.J. (2006). Current research on parallel measures of interests and confidence for basic dimensions of vocational activity. *Journal of Career Assessment, 14,* 56–76.

BEUTLER, L.E., MOHR, D.C., GRAWE, K., ENGLE, D., & MacDONALD, R. (1991). Looking for differential treatment effects: Cross-cultural predictors of differential psychotherapy efficacy. *Journal of Psychotherapy Integration, 1,* 121–141.

BEUTLER, L.E., MOLEIRO, C., & TALEBI, H. (2002). Resistance in psychotherapy: What conclusions are supported by research. *Journal of Clinical Psychology, 58,* 207–217.

BIGLER, M., NEIMEYER, G., & BROWN, E. (2001). The divided self revisited: Effects of self-concept differentiation on psychological adjustment. *Journal of Social and Clinical Psychology, 20,* 396–415.

BIPPUS, A.M. (2005). Humor usage during recalled conflicts: The effect of form and sex on recipient evaluations. In S.P. Shohov (Ed.), *Advances in psychology research, vol. 34* (pp. 115–126). Hauppauge, NY: Nova Science Publishers.

BISHOP, G.D. (1994). *Health psychology.* Boston: Allyn & Bacon.

BLANCHARD, E., & HICKLING, E.J. (2003). *After the crash: Psychological assessment and treatment of survivors of motor vehicle accidents.* Washington, DC: American Psychological Association.

BLATT, S.J., & SHAHAR, G. (2004). Psychoanalysis—with whom, for what, and how? comparisons with psychotherapy. *Journal of the American Psychoanalytic Association, 52,* 393–447.

BLESKE, A.L., & BUSS, D.M. (2000). Can men and women be just friends? *Personal Relationships, 7,* 131–151.

BLOCK, S.D., & BILLINGS, J.A. (2005). Learning from dying. *New England Journal of Medicine, 353,* 1313–1315.

BLUM, D. (1998, May/June). Finding strength: How to overcome anything. *Psychology Today, 32*–38, 66–73.

BOAKWALA, J., & JACOBS, J. (2004). Age, marital processes, and depressed affect. *Gerontologist, 44,* 328–338.

BOBROW, D., & BAILEY, M.J. (2001). Is male homosexuality maintained via kin selection? *Evolution and Human Behavior, 22,* 361–368.

BODENHAUSEN, G.V. (1990). Stereotypes as judgmental heuristics: Evidence of circadian variations in discrimination. *Psychological Science, 1,* 319–322.

BOERNER, K., WORTMAN, C.B., & BONANNO, G.A. (2005). Resilient or at risk? A 4-year study of older adults who initially showed high or low distress following conjugal losses. *Journals of Gerontology: Series B: Psychological Sciences and Social Sciences, 60B,* 67–73.

BOGART, L.M., BIRD, S.T., WALT, L.C., DELAHANTY, D.L., & FIGLER, J.L. (2004). Association of stereotypes about physicians to health care satisfaction, help-seeking behavior, and adherence to treatment. *Social Science & Medicine, 58,* 1049–1058.

BOHART, A.C., & BYOCK, G. (2005). Experiencing Carl Rogers from the client's point of view: A vicarious ethnographic investigation. I. extraction and perception of meaning. *Humanistic Psychologist, 33,* 187–212.

BONANNO, G.A. (2004). Loss, trauma, and human resilience: Have we underestimated the human capacity to thrive after extremely aversive events? *American Psychologist, 59,* 20–28.

BONANNO, G.A. (2005). Resilience in the face of potential trauma. *Current Directions in Psychological Science, 14,* 135–138.

BONANNO, G.A., & KALTMAN, S. (2001). The varieties of grief experience. *Clinical Psychology Review, 21,* 705–734.

BONANNO, G.A., MOSKOWITZ, J.T., PAPA, A., & FOLKMAN, S. (2005). Resilience to loss in bereaved spouses, bereaved parents, and bereaved gay men. *Journal of Personality and Social Psychology,* 827–843.

BONANNO, G.A., PAPA, A., LALANDE, K., WESTPHAL, M., & COIFMAN, K. (2004). The importance of being flexible: The ability to both enhance and suppress emotional expression predicts long-term adjustment. *Psychological Science, 15,* 482–487.

BONANNO, G.A., PAPA, A., LALANDE, K., ZHANG, N., & NOLL, J.G. (2005). Grief processing and deliberate grief avoidance: A prospective comparison of bereaved spouses and parents in the United States and the People's Republic of China, *Journal of Consulting and Clinical Psychology, 73,* 86–98.

BOND, R. (2005). Group size and conformity. *Group Processes & Intergroup Relations, 8,* 331–354.

BONEY-MCCOY, S., & FINKELHOR, D. (1995). Prior victimization: A risk factor for child sexual abuse and for PTSD-related symptomatology among sexually abused youth. *Child Abuse and Neglect, 19,* 1401–1421.

BOOD, S., ARCHER, T., & NORLANDER, T. (2004). Affective personality in relation to general personality, self-reported stress, coping, and optimism. *Individual Differences Research, 2,* 26–37.

BOUCHARD, T.J., LYKKEN, D.T., MCGUE, M., SEGAL, N.L., & TELLEGEN, A. (1990). Sources of human psychological differences: The Minnesota study of twins reared apart. *Science, 250,* 223–228.

BOWER, B. (2001). Faces of perception. *Science News, 160,* 10–12.

BOWER, B. (2002). The social net: Scientists hope to download some insight into online interactions. *Science, 161,* 282–284.

BRAMLETT, M.D., & MOSHER, W.D. (2003). *Cohabitation, marriage, divorce, and remarriage in the United States: The 1995 national survey of family growth.* Washington, DC: National Center for Health Statistics and the National Institute for Child Health and Human Development.

BRANDSTADTER, J., & ROTHERMUND, K. (1994). Self-percepts of control in middle and later adulthood: Buffering losses by rescaling goals. *Psychology and Aging, 9,* 265–273.

BRAZIL, K. HOWELL, D., BEDARD, M., KRUEGER, P., & HEIDEBRECHT, C. (2005). Preferences for place of care and place of death among informal caregivers of the terminally ill. *Palliative Medicine, 19,* 492–499.

BRAY, J.H., & JOURILES, E.N. (1995). Treatment of marital conflict and prevention of divorce. *Journal of Marital and Family Therapy. Special Issue: The effectiveness of marital and family therapy, 21,* 461–473.

BRAZA, P., BRAZA, F., CARERAS, M.R., & MUÑOZ, J.M. (1993). Measuring the social ability of preschool children. *Social Behavior and Personality, 21,* 145–158.

BRETT, J.M., & STROH, L.K. (2003). Working 61 plus hours a week: Why do managers do it? *Journal of Applied Psychology, 88,* 67–78.

BREWER, P.R., & WILCOX, C. (2005). The polls-trends: Same-sex marriage and civil unions. *Public Opinion Quarterly, 69,* 599–616.

BREWIS, A., & MEYER, M. (2005). Marital coitus across the life course. *Journal of Biosocial Science, 37,* 499–518.

BRINGLE, R.G. (1991). Psychosocial aspects of jealousy: A transactional model. In P. Salovey (Ed.), *The psychology of jealousy and envy* (pp. 103–131). New York: Guilford Press.

BRODY, J.E. (2002, November 19). Adding some heft to the ideal feminine form. *The New York Times,* p. D7.

BRODY, L.R., & HALL, J.A. (1993). Gender and emotion. In M. Lewis & J.M. Haviland (Eds.), *Handbook of emotion* (pp. 447–460). New York: Guilford Press.

BROMAN, C.L. (1995). Leisure-time physical activity in an African American population. *Journal of Behavioral Medicine, 18,* 341–353.

BROWN, A. (1991, December). How old is old? *Current Health, 2,* 4–10.

BROWN, F.W., & MOSHAVI, D. (2005). Transformational leadership and emotional intelligence: A potential pathway for an increased understanding of interpersonal influence. *Journal of Organizational Behavior, 26,* 867–871.

BROWN, K.T. (2004). The power of perception: Skin tone bias and psychological well-being for Black Americans. In G. Philogène (Ed.), *Racial identity in context: The legacy of Kenneth B. Clark* (pp. 111–123). Washington, DC: American Psychological Association.

BROWN, L.M., BRADLEY, M.M., & LANG, P.J. (2006). Affective reactions to pictures of ingroup and outgroup members. *Biological Psychology, 71,* 303–311.

BROWN, P.L. (1985, May 15). Disguised to learn the troubles of age. *Philadelphia Inquirer,* 1.

BROWNE, K.D., & HAMILTON-GIACHRITSIS, C. (2005). The influence of violent media on children and adolescents: A public-health approach. *Lancet, 365,* 702–710.

BRUCH, M.A., & BELKIN, D.K. (2001). Attributional style in shyness and depression: Shared and specific maladaptive patterns. *Cognitive Theory and Research, 25,* 247–259.

BRUCH, M.A., HAMER, R.J., & HEIMBERG, R.G. (1995). Shyness and public consciousness: Additive or interactive relation with social interaction? *Journal of Personality, 63,* 47–63.

BRYSON, J.B. (1991). Modes of response to jealousy-evoking situations. In P. Salovey (Ed.), *The psychology of jealousy and envy* (pp. 178–207). New York: Guilford Press.

BUI, K., & TAKEUCHI, D.T. (1992). Ethnic minority adolescents and the use of community mental health care services. *American Journal of Community Psychology, 20,* 403–417.

BULLER, D.J. (2005). *Adapting minds: Evolutionary psychology and the persistent quest for human nature.* Cambridge, MA: MIT Press.

BULLOCK, J.R. (2002). Bullying among children. *Childhood Education, 3,* 130–133.

Bureau of Labor Statistics. (2003). *Occupational outlook handbook.* http://www.bls.gov.

BURGER, J.M. (1991). Change in attributions over time: The ephemeral fundamental attribution error. *Social Cognition, 9,* 182–193.

BURKE, R.J., MATTHIESEN, S.B., & PALLESEN, S. (2006). Personality correlates of workaholism. *Personality and Individual Differences, 40,* 1223–1233.

BUSHMAN, B.J. (1998). Priming effects of media violence on the accessibility of aggressive constructs in memory. *Personality and Social Psychology Bulletin, 24,* 537–545.

BUSHMAN, B.J. (2002). Does venting anger feed or extinguish the flame? Catharsis, rumination, distraction, anger and aggressive responding. *Personality and Social Psychology Bulletin, 28,* 724–731.

BUTLER, A.C., CHAPMAN, J.E., FORMAN, E.M., & BECK, A.T. (2006). The empirical status of cognitive-behavioral therapy: A review of meta-analyses. *Clinical Psychology Review, 26,* 17–31.

BUTLER, D., & GEIS, F.L. (1990). Nonverbal affect responses to male and female leaders: Implications for leadership evaluations. *Journal of Personality and Social Psychology, 58,* 48–59.

BUYS, L.R. (2001). Life in a retirement village: Implications for contact with community and village friends. *Gerontology, 47,* 55–59.

BUZZI, G., COUPER, R.T.L., BARDY, A.H., & EVANS, J.M. (2002). Near-death experiences (Letter to the editor). *The Lancet, 359,* 2116.

BYBEE, J.A., & WELLS, Y.V. (2003). *The development of possible selves during adulthood.* New York: Kluwer Academic/Plenum Publishers.

BYRNE, D., ERVIN, C.R., & LAMBERTH, J. (2004). *Continuity between the experimental study of attraction and real-life computer dating.* Philadelphia, PA: Taylor & Francis.

CACIOPPO, J.R., HAWKLEY, L.C., & BERNTSON, G.G. (2003). The anatomy of loneliness. *Current Directions in Psychological Science, 12,* 71–74.

CADELL, S., REGEHR, C., & HEMSWORTH, D. (2003). Factors contributing to posttraumatic growth: A proposed structural equation model. *American Journal of Orthopsychiatry, 73,* 279–287.

CAMERON, A.F., & WEBSTER, J. (2004). Unintended consequences of emerging communication technologies: Instant messaging in the workplace. *Computers in Human Behavior, 21,* 85–103.

CAMPBELL, A., CUMMING, S.R., & HUGHES, I. (2006). Internet use by the socially fearful: Addiction or therapy? *CyberPsychology & Behavior, 9,* 69–81.

CAMPBELL, W.K., BAUMEISTER, R.F., DHAVALE, D., & TICE, D.M. (2003). Responding to major threats to self-esteem: A preliminary, narrative study of ego-shock. *Journal of Social and Clinical Psychology, 22,* 79–91.

CAMPBELL-SILLS, L., COHAN, S.L., & STEIN, M.B. (2006). Relationship of resilience to personality, coping, and psychiatric symptoms in young adults. *Behaviour Research and Therapy, 44,* 585–599.

CANLI, T., & GABRIELI, J.D.E. (2004). Imaging gender differences in sexual arousal. *Nature Neuroscience, 7,* 325–326.

CAPISTA, J. (1999, June 2). Do you have an allergy—to people? *The Detroit News.* http://www.detnews.com.

CAPPELLERI, J.C., BELL, S.S., ALTHOF, S.E., SIEGEL, R.L., & STECHER, V.J. (2006). Comparison between sildenafil treated subjects with erectile dysfunction and control subjects on the Self-Esteem And Relationship questionnaire. *The Journal of Sexual Medicine, 3,* 274–282.

CARBONELL, J. (2003). Baby boomers at the gate: Enhancing independence through innovation and technology. United States Department of Health and Human Services. Retrieved January 10, 2006, from http://www.hhs.gov.asl.testify/t030520.html.

CARDONA-COLL, D. (2003). Bargaining and strategic demand commitment. *Theory and Decision, 54,* 357–374.

CARDUCCI, B.J. (1999). *Shyness: A bold new approach.* New York: HarperCollins.

CARDUCCI, B.J., & ZIMBARDO, P.G. (1995, November/December). Are you shy? *Psychology Today,* 34–40.

CAREY, A.R., & WARD, S. (2000, January 1). Thinking of retirement. *USA Today,* 1B.

CARLSON, E., & CHAMBERLAIN, R.M. (2004). Black-White perception gap and health disparities research. *Public Health Nursing, 21,* 372–379.

CARSTENSEN, L.L., & CHARLES, S.T. (1998). Emotion in the second half of life. *Current Directions in Psychological Science, 7,* 144–149.

CARSTENSEN, L.L., & MIKELS, J.A. (2005). At the intersection of emotion and cognition: Aging and the positivity effect. *Current Directions in Psychological Science, 14,* 117–121.

CASERTA, M.S., & LUND, D.A. (1992). Bereavement stress and coping among older adults: Expectations versus the actual experience. *Omega Journal of Death and Dying, 25,* 33–45.

CASPI, A., & HERBENER, E.S. (1990). Continuity and change: Assortative marriage and the consistency of personality in adulthood. *Journal of Personality and Social Psychology, 58,* 250–258.

CASSIDY, C., O'CONNOR, R.C., HOWE, C., & WARDEN, D. (2004). Perceived discrimination and psychological distress: The role of personal and ethnic self-esteem. *Journal of Counseling Psychology, 5,* 329–339.

CASSIDY, G.L., & DAVIES, L. (2003). Explaining gender differences in mastery among married parents. *Social Psychology Quarterly, 66,* 48–61.

CASTEL, A.D. (2005). Memory for grocery prices in younger and older adults: The role of schematic support. *Psychology and Aging. Special Issue: Emotion-Cognition Interactions and the Aging Mind, 20,* 718–721.

CATIPOVIC-VESELICA, K. (2003). Bortner type a scores and basic emotions: Aggression, distrustful, depression, and gregarious. *Psychological Reports, 93,* 132–134.

CEBALLO, R., LANSFORD, J.E., ABBEY, A., & STEWART, A.J. (2004). Gaining a child: Comparing the experiences of biological parents, adoptive parents, and stepparents. *Family Relations: Interdisciplinary Journal of Applied Family Studies, 53,* 38–48.

Center for Mental Health Services. (2003, April). *After a disaster: Self-care tips for dealing with stress.* http://www.mentalhealth.org/publications/allpubs/KEN-01-0097.

Centers for Disease Control and Prevention. (2000). *Most teens not provided STD or pregnancy prevention counseling during check-ups.* http://www.cdc.gov/nchstp/dstd/press_Releases/Teens2000.htm.

Centers for Disease Control and Prevention. (2001). *Youth risk behavior surveillance—United States, 2001.* http://www.cdc.gov/mmwr/preview/mmwrhtml/ss5104a1.htm.

Centers for Disease Control and Prevention. (2002a). *CDC Issues National Report Card on STDs.* http://www.cdec.gov/nchstp/dstd/Press_Releases/National_Report.

Centers for Disease Control and Prevention. (2002b). *43 percent of first marriages break up within 15 years.* http://www.cdc.gov/nchs/releases/01news/firstmarr.htm.

Centers for Disease Control and Prevention. (2002c). *New report sheds light on trends and patterns in marriage, divorce, and cohabitation.* http://www.cdc.gov/nchs/releases/02news/div-mar-cohab.htm.

Centers for Disease Control and Prevention. (2002d). *The burden of tobacco use.* http://www.cdc.gov/tobacco/overview/oshsummary02.htm.

Centers for Disease Control and Prevention. (2002f). *Trends in sexual risk behaviors among high school students—United States, 1991–2001.* http://www.cdc.gov/mmwr/preview/mmwrhtml/mm5138a2.htm.

Centers for Disease Control and Prevention. (2004). Family health and fitness day: USA. Retrieved August 7, 2006, from http://www.cdc.gov/omh/highlights/2004/hsept2504.htm.

Centers for Disease Control and Prevention. (2005). Physical activity for everyone: The importance of physical activity. Retrieved August 7, 2006, from http://www.cdc.gov/nccdphp/dnpa/physical/importance/index.htm.

Centers for Disease Control and Prevention. (2006a, April). Prevention pays. Retrieved May 11, 2006 from http://www.cdc.gov/hiv/resources/reports/comp_hiv_prev/prev_pays.htm.

Centers for Disease Control and Prevention. (2006b, April). STD facts—Chlamydia. Retrieved May 11, 2006, from http://www.cdc.gov/std/Chlamydia/ STDFact-Chlamydia.htm.

CERRATO, P.L. (2001, February). Pollyanna may have been right after all. *Contemporary OB/GYN, 1.*

CHANG, E.C. (1996). Cultural differences in optimism, pessimism, and coping: Predictions of subsequent adjustment. *Journal of Counseling Psychology, 43,* 113–123.

CHANG, E.C., & SANNA, L.J. (2003). Experience of life hassles and psychological adjustment among adolescents: Does it make a difference if one is optimistic or pessimistic? *Journal of Personality and Individual Differences, 34,* 867–879.

CHAPMAN, M.A. (1999, September/October). Bad choices: Why we make them. How to stop. *Psychology Today,* 36–39, 71.

CHATTERJEE, C. (2001, September/October). Can men and women be friends? *Psychology Today,* 60–67.

CHATZISARANTIS, N.L.D., HAGGER, M.S., BIDDLE, S.J., & KARAGEORGHIS, C. (2002). The cognitive processes by which perceived locus of causality predicts participation in physical activity. *Journal of Health Psychology, 7,* 685–699.

CHEN, G.M. (1995). Differences in self-disclosure patterns among Americans versus Chinese: A comparative study. *Journal of Cross-cultural Psychology, 26,* 84–91.

CHEN, X., RUBIN, K.H., & SUN, Y. (1992). Social reputation and peer relationships in Chinese and Canadian children: A cross-cultural study. *Child Development, 63,* 1336–1343.

CHENG, C. (2005). Processes underlying gender-role flexibility: Do androgynous individuals know more or know how to cope? *Journal of Personality, 73,* 645–673.

CHIDAMBARAM, L., & TUNG, L.L. (2005). Is out of sight, out of mind? An empirical study of social loafing in technology-supported groups. *Information Systems Research, 16,* 149–168.

CHIVERS, M.L., RIEGER, G., LATTY, E., & BAILEY, J.M. (2004). A sex difference in the specificity of sexual arousal. *Psychological Science, 15,* 736–744.

CHO, C., & CHEON, H.J. (2005). Cross-cultural comparisons of interactivity on corporate web sites: The United States, the United Kingdom, Japan, and South Korea. *Journal of Advertising, 34,* 99–115.

CHO, H., & WILKE, D.J. (2005). How has the violence against women act affected the response of the criminal justice system to domestic violence? *Journal of Sociology & Social Welfare, 32,* 125–139.

CHOCHINOV, H.M., HACK, T., HASSARD, T., KRISTJANSON, L.J., MCCLEMENT, S., & HARLOS, M. (2002). Dignity in the terminally ill: A cross-sectional, cohort study. *The Lancet, 360,* 2026–2030.

CHOI, I., & CHOI, Y. (2002). Culture and self-concept flexibility. *Personality and Social Psychology Bulletin, 28,* 1508–1517.

CHRISTENSEN, A.J., & JOHNSON, J.A. (2002). Patient adherence with medical treatment regimens: An interactive approach. *Current Directions in Psychological Science, 11,* 94–97.

CHRISTENSEN, T.C., WOOD, J.V., & BARRETT, L.F. (2003). Remembering everyday experience through the prism of self-esteem. *Personality and Social Psychology Bulletin, 29,* 51–62.

CHUNG, D. (2005). Violence, control, romance and gender equality: Young women and heterosexual relationships. *Women's Studies International Forum, 28,* 445–455.

CLAY, D., VIGNOLES, V.L., & DITTMAR, H. (2005). Body image and self-esteem among adolescent girls. Testing the influence of sociocultural factors. *Journal of Research on Adolescence, 15,* 451–477.

Clinical Psychiatry News. (2001, October). Psychiatrists call for overhaul of unwieldy DSM, *29,* 20.

COHAN, C.L., & KLEINBAUM, S. (2002). Toward a greater understanding of the co-habitation effect: Premarital cohabitation and marital communication. *Journal of Marriage and the Family, 64,* 180–192.

COHEN, F., SOLOMON, S., MAXFIELD, M., PYSZCZYNSKI, T., & GREENBERG, J. (2004). Fatal attraction: The effects of mortality salience on evaluations of charismatic, task-oriented, and relationship-oriented leaders. *Psychological Science, 15,* 846–851.

COHEN, S., & PRESSMAN, S.D. (2006). Positive affect and health. *Current Directions in Psychological Science, 15,* 122–125.

COHEN, S., & WILLIAMSON, G.M. (1988). Perceived stress in a probability sample of the United States. In S. Spacapan & S. Oskamp (Eds.), *The social psychology of health.* Newbury Park, CA: Sage.

COHEN, S., & WILLIAMSON, G.M. (1991). Stress and infectious disease in humans. *Psychological Bulletin, 109,* 5–24.

COLLEY, A., & TODD, Z. (2002). Gender-linked differences in the style and content of e-mails to friends. *Journal of Language and Social Psychology, 21,* 380–392.

COLLINS, A.W., MACCOBY, E.E., STEINBERG, L., HETHERINGTON, E.M., & BORNSTEIN, M.H. (2000). Contemporary research on parenting: The case for nature and nurture. *American Psychologist, 55,* 218–232.

COLLINS, W.A., & VAN DULMEN, M. (2006). "The course of true love(s) . . .": Origins and pathways in the development of romantic relationships. In A.C. Crouter, & A. Booth (Eds.), *Romance and sex in adolescence and emerging adulthood: Risks and opportunities* (pp. 63–86). Mahwah, NJ: Lawrence Erlbaum Associates, Publishers.

Committee on the Practice of Psychotherapy. (1996). *Resource document on medical psychotherapy.* http://www.psych.org/pract_of_psych/psychotherapy53000.cfm.

CONE, A.L., & OWENS, S.K. (1991). Academic and locus of control enhancement in a freshman study skills and college adjustment course. *Psychological Reports, 68,* 1211–1217.

CONNOLLY, T., & ZEELENBERG, M. (2002). Regret in decision-making. *Current Directions in Psychological Science, 11,* 212–216.

Consumer Reports. (2004). Drugs vs. talk therapy: 3,079 readers rate their care for depression and anxiety. *Consumer Reports, 69,* 22–29.

CONTRADA, R.J., ASHMORE, R.D., GARY, M.L., COUPS, E., EGETH, J.D., & SEWELL, A., et al. (2000). Ethnicity-related sources of stress and their effects on well-being. *Current Directions in Psychological Science, 9,* 136–139.

CONTRADA, R.S., LEVENTHAL, H., & O'LEARY, A. (1990). Personality and health. In L.A. Pervin (Ed.), *Handbook of personality: Theory and research* (pp. 638–669). New York: Guilford Press.

CONTRERAS, R., HENDRICK, S.S., & HENDRICK, C. (1996). Perspectives on marital love and satisfaction in Mexican American and Anglo American couples. *Journal of Counseling and Development, 74,* 408–415.

CONWAY, L.G., III, & SCHALLER, M. (2005). When authorities' commands backfire: Attributions about consensus and effects on deviant decision making. *Journal of Personality and Social Psychology, 89,* 311–326.

CONWAY, T.L., VICKERS, R.R., & FRENCH, J.R. (1992). An application of person-environment fit theory: Perceived versus desire control. *Journal of Social Issues, 48,* 95–107.

CONWAY-GIUSTRA, F., CROWLEY, A., & GORIN S.H. (2002) Crisis in caregiving: A call to action. *Health and Social Work, 27,* 307–311.

COOPER, H., OKAMURA, L., & MCNEIL, P. (1995). Situation and personality correlates of psychological well-being, social activity, and personal control. *Journal of Research in Personality, 29,* 395–417.

CORNELIUS-WHITE, J.H.D., & CORNELIUS-WHITE, C.F. (2005). Reminiscing and predicting: Rogers's beyond words speech and commentary. *Journal of Humanistic Psychology, 45,* 383–396.

CORR, C.A. (1993). Coping with dying: Lessons that we should and should not learn from the work of Elisabeth Kübler-Ross. *Death Studies, 17,* 69–83.

COSTA, P.T., Jr., ZONDERMAN, A.B., MCCRAE, R.R., COMONI-HUNTLEY, J., LOCK, B.Z., & BARRANO, H.E. (1987). Longitudinal analysis of psychological well-being in a national sample: Stability of mean levels. *Journal of Gerontology, 42,* 50–55.

COULSON, M. (2004). Attributing emotion to static body postures: Recognition accuracy, confusions, and viewpoint dependence. *Journal of Nonverbal Behavior, 28,* 117–139.

COULTAS, J.C. (2004). When in Rome . . . an evolutionary perspective on conformity. *Group Processes & Intergroup Relations, 7,* 317–331.

COURT, A. (2003, September 5–7). Out of Africa. *USA Weekend, 5.*

CRAMER, P. (2003). Defense mechanisms and physiological reactivity to stress. *Journal of Personality, 71,* 221–244.

CRANDALL, C.S. (1994). Prejudice against fat people: Ideology and self-interest. *Journal of Personality and Social Psychology, 66,* 882–894.

CRANE, R.D., SODERQUIST, J.N., & GARDNER, M.D. (1995). Gender differences in cognitive and behavioral steps toward divorce. *American Journal of Family Therapy, 23,* 99–105.

CRAWFORD, C.B. (1994). Effects of sex and sex roles on avoidance of same-and-opposite-sex touch. *Perceptual and Motor Skills, 79,* 107–112.

CRAWFORD, M.T., MCCONNELL, A.R., LEWIS, A.C., & SHERMAN, S.J. (2002). Reactance, compliance, and anticipated regret. *Journal of Experimental Social Psychology, 38,* 56–63.

CREMONA, K. (2004). Getting smart about emotional intelligence. *Keeping Good Companies, 56,* 56–58.

CROCKER, J., & KNIGHT, K.M. (2005). Contingencies of self-worth. *Current Directions in Psychological Science, 14,* 200–203.

CROCKER, J., & MAJOR, B., (1989). Social stigma and self-esteem: The self-protective properties of stigma. *Psychological Review, 96,* 608–630.

CROCKER, J., & PARK, L.E. (2004a). Reaping the benefits of pursuing self-esteem without the costs? Reply to DuBois and Flay (2004), Sheldon (2004), and Pyszczynski and Cox (2004). *Psychological Bulletin, 130,* 430–434.

CROCKER, J., & PARK, L.E. (2004b). The costly pursuit of self-esteem. *Psychological Bulletin, 130,* 392–414.

CROCKER, J., & WOLFE, C.T. (2001). Contingencies of self-worth. *Psychological Review, 108,* 593–623.

CRONE, D., SMITH, A., & GOUGH, B. (2005). 'I feel totally at one, totally alive and to-tally happy': A psycho-social explanation of the physical activity and mental health relationship. *Health Education Research, 20,* 600–611.

CROPLEY, M., & STEPTOE, A. (2005). Social support, life events and physical symptoms: A prospective study of chronic and recent life stress in men and women. *Psychology, Health & Medicine, 10,* 317–325.

CROSBY, F.J. (1991). *Juggling.* New York: Free Press.

CROSNOE, R., & ELDER, G.H. (2002). Successful adaptation in the later years: A life course approach to aging. *Social Psychology Quarterly, 65,* 309–328.

CROWLEY, S.L. (1999, July/August). Live to 100? No thanks. *AARP Bulletin,* 6–7.

CROZIER, W.R. (2005). Measuring shyness: Analysis of the revised cheek and buss shyness scale. *Personality and Individual Differences, 38,* 1947–1956.

CSANK, P., & CONWAY, M. (2004). Engaging in self-reflection changes self-concept clarity: On differences between women and men, and low-and high-clarity individuals. *Sex Roles, 50,* 469–480.

CUMMINGS, S.M. (2002). Predictors of psychological well-being among assisted-living residents. *Health and Social Work, 27,* 293–303.

CUSHNER, K. (2005). Conflict, negotiation, and mediation across cultures: Highlights from the fourth biennial conference of the international academy for intercultural research. *International Journal of Intercultural Relations. Special Issue: Conflict, negotiation, and mediation across cultures: Highlights from the fourth biennial conference of the International Academy for Intercultural Research, 29,* 635–638.

CUTLER, M. (2001, May 26). Whodunit—The media? *The Nation, 272,* 18–20.

D'AUGELLI, A.R., HERSHBERGER, S.L., & PILKINGSTON, N.W. (1998). Lesbian, gay and bisexual youth and their families: Disclosure of sexual orientation and its consequences. *American Journal of Orthopsychiatry, 68,* 361–371.

DAHLEN, E.R., & MARTIN, R.C. (2005). The experience, expression, and control of anger in perceived social support. *Personality and Individual Differences, 39,* 391–401.

DANIELS, C. (2002). The last taboo: It's not sex. It's not drinking. It's stress—and it is soaring. *Fortune, 146,* 136–139.

DAVIDSON, S. (2000, September–October). Jules & Tim. *Modern Maturity,* 64–65, 95–96.

DAVIS, G.F. (2001). Loss and the duration of grief (Letter to the editor). *The Journal of the American Medical Association, 285,* 1152.

DAVIS, K., & NEWSTROM, J.W. (1985). *Human behavior at work: Organizational behavior.* New York: McGraw-Hill.

DAVIS, M., MARKUS, K.A., WALTERS, S.B., VORUS, N., & CONNORS, B. (2005). Behavioral cues to deception vs. topic incriminating potential in criminal confessions. *Law and Human Behavior, 29,* 683–704.

DAVIS, S. (1996, July/August). The enduring power of friendship. *American Health,* 60–63.

DAY, A.L., & CHAMBERLAIN, T.C. (2006). Committing to your work, spouse, and children: Implications for work-family conflict. *Journal of Vocational Behavior, 68,* 116–130.

DAY, J.C., JANUS, A., & DAVIS, J. (2005). Computer and internet use in the United States: 2003. U.S. Census Bureau Computer and Internet Use Supplement to the October 2003 Current Population Survey.

DE DREU, C.K.W. (2005). A PACT against conflict escalation in negotiation and dispute resolution. *Current Directions in Psychological Science, 14,* 149–152.

DEARBORN, K. (2002). Studies in emotional intelligence redefine our approach to leadership development. *Public Personnel Management, 31,* 523–530.

DEBELL, C. (2001). Ninety years in the world of work in America. *Career Development Quarterly, 50,* 77–89.

DEBERARD, M.S., & KLEINKNECHT, R.A. (1995). Loneliness, duration of loneliness and reported stress symptomatology. *Psychological Reports, 76,* 1363–1369.

DECI, E.L., & MOLLER, A.C. (2005). *The concept of competence: A starting place for understanding intrinsic motivation and self-determined extrinsic motivation.* New York: Guilford Publications.

DECI, E.L., & RYAN, R.M. (2000). The "what" and "why" of goal pursuits: Human needs and the self-determination of behavior. *Psychological Inquiry, 11,* 227–268.

DEFFENBACHER, J.L., OETTING, E.R., & DIGIUSEPPE, R.A. (2002). Principles of empirically supported interventions applied to anger management. *Counseling Psychologist, 30,* 262–280.

DEMOREST, A. (2005). *Psychology's grand theorists: How personal experiences shaped professional ideas.* Mahwah, NJ: Lawrence Erlbaum Associates.

DENEVE, K.M. (1999). Happy as an extraverted clam? The role of personality for subjective well-being. *Current Directions in Psychological Science, 8,* 141–144.

DENNERSTEIN, L., & HAYES, R.D. (2005). Confronting the challenges: Epidemiological study of female sexual dysfunction and the menopause. *Journal of Sexual Medicine, 2,* 118–132.

DENRELL, J. (2005). Why most people disapprove of me: Experience sampling in impression formation. *Psychological Review, 112,* 951–978.

DENTINGER, E., & CLARKBERG, M. (2002). Informal caregiving and retirement timing among men and women. *Journal of Family Issues, 25,* 857–879.

DERDEYN, A.P. (1994). Parental separation, adolescent psychopathology, and problem behaviors: Comment. *Journal of the American Academy of Child and Adolescent Psychiatry, 33,* 1131–1133.

DE-SOUZA, G., & KLEIN, H.J. (1995). Emergent leadership in the group goal-setting process. *Small Groups Research, 26,* 475–496.

DESTENO, D., BARTLETT, M.Y., BRAVERMAN, J., & SALOVEY, P. (2002). Sex differences in jealousy: Evolutionary mechanism or artifact of measurement? *Journal of Personality and Social Psychology, 83,* 1103–1116.

DEUTSCH, M., & KRAUSS, R.M. (1960). The effect of threat upon interpersonal bargaining. *Journal of Abnormal and Social Psychology, 61,* 181–189.

DEY, E.L., ASTIN, A.W., & KORN, W.S. (1991, September). *The American freshman: Twenty-five year trends.* Los Angeles: Higher Education Research Institute, University of California.

DEY, E.L., ASTIN, A.W., KORN, W.S., & RIGGS, E.R. (1991, December; 1992, December). *The American freshman: National norms for fall 1991 and 1992.* Los Angeles: Higher Education Research Institute, University of California.

DEYOUNG, R. (2005). Contingency theories of leadership. In N. Borkowski (Ed.), *Organizational behavior in health care* (pp. 187–208). Boston, MA: Jones and Bartlett Publishers.

DIAMOND, L.M. (2003). What does sexual orientation orient? A biobehavioral model distinguishing romantic love and sexual desire. *Psychological Review, 110,* 173–192.

DIAMOND, L.M. (2004). Emerging perspectives on distinctions between romantic love and sexual desire. *Current Directions in Psychological Science, 13,* 116–119.

DICKENSON, A. (2002, May). Dads and daughters: Strengthening this special relationship can strengthen a girl's self-esteem, too. *Time,* F9–F10.

DIENER, E., & BISWAS-DIENER, R. (2002). Will money increase subjective well-being? *Social Indicators Research, 57,* 119–169.

DIENER, E., SANDVIK, E., SEIDLITZ, L., & DIENER, M. (1993). The relationship between income and subjective well-being: Relative or absolute? *Social Indicators Research, 28,* 195–223.

DIENER, E., & SELIGMAN, M.R.P. (2002). Very happy people. *Psychological Science, 13,* 81–84.

DIENER, E., WOLSIC, B., & FUJITA, F. (1995). Physical attractiveness and subjective well-being. *Journal of Personality and Social Psychology, 69,* 120–129.

DILORENO, T.M., BARGMAN, E.P., STUCKY-ROPP, R., BRASSINGTON, G.S., FRENSCH, P.A., & LAFONTAINE, T. (1999). Long-term effects of aerobic exercise on psychological outcomes. *Preventive Medicine, 28,* 75–85.

DIMBERG, U., THUNBERG, M., & ELMEHED, K. (2000). Unconscious facial reactions to emotional facial expressions. *Psychological Science, 11,* 86–89.

DINAN, T.G. (2005). Stress: The shared common component in major mental illnesses. *European Psychiatry, 20,* 326–328.

DION, K.K., & DION, K.L. (1993). Individualistic and collectivistic perspectives on gender and the cultural context of love and intimacy. *Journal of Social Issues, 49,* 53–69.

DION, K.L., & DION, K.K. (2005). *Culture and relationships: The downside of self-contained individualism.* In R.M. Sorrentino, D. Cohen, J.M. Olson, & M.P. Zanna (Eds.), Culture and social behavior: The Ontario symposium: Volume 10 (pp. 77–94). Mahwah, NJ: Lawrence Erlbaum Associates.

Discover. (2003, August). Believe it: Letter from *Discover. Discover,* 3.

DITOMMASO, E., BRANNEN, C., & BURGESS, M. (2005). The universality of relationship characteristics: A cross-cultural comparison of different types of attachment and loneliness in Canadian and visiting Chinese students. *Social Behavior and Personality, 33,* 57–68.

DOKA, L.K. (2005). Ethics, end-of-life decisions and grief. *Mortality. Special Issue: Ethical concerns involving end-of-life issues in the United States—Introduction: Ethics and end-of-life issues, 10,* 83–90.

DOLGIN, K.G., & KIM, S. (1994). Adolescents' disclosure to best and good friends: The effects of gender and topic intimacy. *Social Development, 3,* 146–157.

DOLGIN, K.G., MEYER, L., & SCHWARTZ, J. (1991). Effects of gender, target's gender, topic, and self-esteem on disclosure to best and midling friends. *Sex Roles, 25,* 311–329. http://www.foxnews.com/story/0,2933,87256,00.html.

DONALDSON-EVANS, C. (2003, May 21). *Online dating is net success.* http://www.foxnews.com/story/0,2933,87256,00.html. Page: 1.

DONNAY, D.A.C., & BORGEN, F.H. (1996). Validity, structure, and content of the 1994 Strong Interest Inventory. *Journal of Counseling Psychology, 43,* 275–291.

DONNELL, A.J., THOMAS, A., & BUBOLTZ, W.C. (2001). Psychological reactance: Factor structure and internal consistency of the Questionnaire for the Measurement of Psychological Reactance. *The Journal of Social Psychology, 141,* 679–687.

DONOVAN, R.J., & JALLEH, G. (2000). Positive versus negative framing of a hypothetical infant immunization: The influence of involvement. *Health Education and Behavior, 27,* 82–95.

DOUBLE, J. (2004). Three kinds of control. PsycCRITIQUES,

DOVIDIO, J.F., & GAERTNER, S.L. (1999). Reducing prejudice: Combatting intergroup biases. *Current Directions in Psychological Science, 8,* 101–105.

DOVIDIO, J.F., GLICK, P., & RUDMAN, L.A. (Eds.). (2005). *On the nature of prejudice: Fifty years after Allport.* Malden, MA: Blackwell Publishing.

DOWNEY, L., & VAN WILLIGEN, M. (2005). Environmental stressors: The mental health impacts of living near industrial activity. *Journal of Health and Social Behavior, 46,* 289–305.

DOZOIS, D.J.A., FREWEN, P.A., & COVIN, R. (2006). *Cognitive theories.* Hoboken, NJ: John Wiley & Sons.

DRENTEA, P. (2002). Retirement and mental health. *Journal of Aging and Health, 14,* 167–194.

DRENTEA, P., & MOREN-CROSS, J.L. (2005). Social capital and social support on the web: The case of an internet mother site. *Sociology of Health & Illness, 27,* 920–943.

DUBROVSKY, V.J., KIESLER, S., & SETHNA, B.N. (1991). The equalization phenomenon: Status effects in computer mediated and face-to-face decision-making groups. *Human Computer Interaction, 6,* 119–146.

DUFFY, K. (1991). Introduction to community mediation programs: Past, present, and future. In K.G. Duffy, J.W. Grosch, & P.V. Olczak (Eds.), *Community mediation: A handbook for practitioners and researchers* (pp. 21–34). New York: Guilford Press.

DUFFY, K.G., GROSCH, J., & OLCZAK, P.V. (1991). *Community mediation: A handbook for practitioners and researchers.* New York: Guilford Press.

DUFFY, K.G., & THOMSON, J. (1992). Community mediation centers: Humanistic alternatives to the court system, a pilot study. *Journal of Humanistic Psychology, 32,* 101–114.

DUFFY, K.G., & WONG, F. (2003). *Community psychology.* Boston: Allyn & Bacon.

DUFFY, V.B., PETERSON, J.M., & BARTOSHUK, L.M. (2004). Associations between taste genetics, oral sensation and alcohol intake. *Physiology & Behavior, 82,* 435–445.

DUNN, J., O'CONNOR, T.G., & CHENG, H. (2005). Children's responses to conflict between their different parents: Mothers, stepfathers, nonresident fathers, and nonresident stepmothers. *Journal of Clinical Child and Adolescent Psychology, 34,* 223–234.

DUNNE, G.A. (2000). Lesbians as authentic workers? Institutional heterosexuality and the reproduction of gender inequalities. *Sexualities. Special Issue: Speaking From a Lesbian Position: Opening up Sexuality Studies, 3,* 133–148.

DUNNING, D., HEATH, C., & SULS, J.M. (2004). Flawed self-assessment: Implications for health, education, and the workplace. *Psychological Science in the Public Interest, 5,* 69–106.

DUPRAS, A. (1994). Internalized homophobia and psychosexual adjustment among gay men. *Psychological Reports, 75,* 23–28.

DWECK, C.S. (1999). Caution—praise can be dangerous. *American Educator, 23,* 4–9.

EAGLY, A.H., & JOHANNESEN-SCHMIDT, M.C. (2001). The leadership styles of women and men. *Journal of Social Issues, 57,* 781–797.

EAGLY, A.H., & JOHNSON, B.T. (1990). Gender and leadership style: A meta-analysis. *Psychological Bulletin, 108,* 233–256.

EAGLY, A.H., KARAU, S.J., & MAKHIJANI, M.G. (1995). Gender and the effectiveness of leaders: A meta-analysis. *Psychological Bulletin, 117,* 125–145.

EAGLY, A.H., & MAKHIJANI, M.G. (1991). What is beautiful is good but . . .: A meta-analytic review of research on the physical attractiveness stereotype. *Psychological Bulletin, 110,* 109–128.

EAGLY, A.H., MAKHIJANI, M.G., & KLONSKY, B.G. (1992). Gender and the evaluation of leaders: A meta-analysis. *Psychological Bulletin, 11,* 3–22.

EASTMAN, P. (2000, January). Scientists piecing Alzheimer's puzzle. *AARP Bulletin,* 18–19.

ECKEL, R.H. (2005). Cardiology patient page. *Circulation, 111,* 257–259.

ECKHOLM, E. (1992, June 28). AIDS, fatally steady in the U.S., accelerates worldwide. *The New York Times.*

EDWARDS, R. (1998). The effects of gender, gender role, and values on the interpretation of messages. *Journal of Language and Social Psychology. Special Issue: The Language of Equivocation, 17,* 52–71.

EDWARDS, W.J. (1996a). A sociological analysis of an invisible minority group: Male adolescent homosexuals. *Youth and Society, 27,* 334–355.

EDWARDS, W.J. (1996b). Operating within the mainstream: Coping and adjustment among a sample of homosexual youths. *Deviant Behavior, 17,* 229–251.

EFKLIDES, A. (2005). Motivation and affect in the self-regulation of behavior. *European Psychologist, 10,* 173–174.

EGAN, D. (2005). Magical mystery cure: What would you do if a lobotomy was your only hope for happiness? *This Magazine, 38,* 14–23.

EISENBERG, N., FABES, R.A., GUTHRIE, I.K., & REISER, M. (2000). Dispositional emotionality and regulation: Their role in predicting quality of social functioning. *Journal of Personality and Social Psychology, 78,* 136–157.

EKMAN, P. (1985a). Expression and the nature of emotion. In K.R. Sherer & P. Ekman (Eds.), *Approaches to emotion.* Hillsdale, NJ: Erlbaum.

EKMAN, P. (1985b). *Telling lies.* New York: W. W. Norton.

EKMAN, P. (1993). Facial expression and emotion. *American Psychologist, 48,* 384–392.

ELIAS, M. (1999a, November 23). Culture affects choice on post-menopause estrogen. *USA Today,* D1.

ELIAS, M. (1999b, December 14). Mapping the mental-illness fight. *USA Today,* 7D.

ELIZUR, Y., & ZIV, M. (2001). Family support and acceptance, gay male identity, and psychological adjustment: A path model. *Family Process, 40,* 125–144.

ELLEVEN, R.K., & ALLEN, J. (2004). Applying technology to online counseling: Suggestions for the beginning E-therapist. *Journal of Instructional Psychology, 31,* 223–227.

ELIAS, M., (2002, September 12). Baby boomers' '70s mind-set has changed with the times; Back then, generation gap was greater, *USA Today,* D7.

ELLIOT, A., & DWECK, C. (2005). Competence and motivation: competence as the core of achievement motivation. In A. Elliot & C. Dweck (Eds.), *Handbook of Competence and Motivation.* New York: Guilford.

ELLIOTT, R., & ELLIOTT, C. (2005). Idealized images of the male body in advertising: A reader-response exploration. *Journal of Marketing Communications, 11,* 3–19.

ELLIOTT, V.S. (2002). Stressing health: Physicians have long suspected that high levels of stress can make people sick. Now some practices are incorporating stress management to help patients feel better. *American Medical News, 45,* 25–26.

ELLIS, A., & HARPER, R.A. (1975). *A new guide to rational living.* Englewood Cliffs, NJ: Prentice Hall.

ELLIS, A., & MACLAREN, C. (1998). *Rational emotive behavior: A therapist's guide.* Atascadero, CA: Impact Publishers.

ENSARI, N., & MILLER, N. (2005). Prejudice and intergroup attributions: The role of personalization and performance feedback. *Group Processes and Intergroup Relations, 8,* 391–410.

EPLEY, N., & KRUGER, J. (2005). When what you type isn't what they read: The perseverance of stereotypes and expectancies over e-mail. *Journal of Experimental Social Psychology, 41,* 414–422.

ERBER, R., & THERRIAULT, N. (1993, October). *Sweating to the oldies: The mood-absorbing qualities of exercise.* Paper presented at the annual meeting of the Society for Experimental Social Psychology, San Diego, CA.

EREZ, M., KLEINBECK, U., & THIERRY, H. (Eds.). (2001). *Work motivation in the context of a globalizing economy.* Mahwah, NJ: Lawrence Erlbaum.

ERICKSON, R.J. (2005). Why emotion work matters: Sex, gender, and the division of household labor. *Journal of Marriage and Family, 67,* 337–351.

ERIKSON, E.H. (1963). *Childhood and society* (2nd ed.). New York: W. W. Norton.

ERIKSON, E.H. (1968). *Identity: Youth and crisis.* New York: W. W. Norton.

ERIKSON, E.H. (1974). *Dimensions of a new identity.* New York: W. W. Norton.

EVANS, G.W., & STECKER, R. (2004). Motivational consequences of environmental stress. *Journal of Environmental Psychology, 24,* 143–165.

EYSENCK, H.J. (1966). *The effects of psychotherapy.* New York: International Science Press.

FAWCETT, J. (2004). Denial versus consciousness: Consideration of our own death can result in greater awareness and appreciation for life and all it entails. *Psychiatric Annals, 34,* 659.

FAY, N., GARROD, S., & CARLETTA, J. (2000). Group discussion as interactive dialogue or as serial monologue: The influence of group size. *Psychological Science, 11,* 481–486.

The Federal Executive Institute and Management Development Centers. (2006). From vets to the net: Leading across generations. Retrieved January 10, 2006, from http://www.leadership.opm.gov/printcontent.cfm?cat=fvtn.

FEHR, B. (2004). Intimacy expectations in same-sex friendships: A prototype interaction-pattern model. *Journal of Personality and Social Psychology, 86,* 265–284.

FEINBERG, C. (2002, April 8). Hitting home. *The American Prospect,* 30–34.

FEIST, J. (1985). *Theories of personality.* New York: Holt, Rinehart, & Winston.

FELDMAN, J., MIYAMOTO, J., & LOFTUS, E.F. (1999). Are actions regretted more than inactions? *Organizational Behavior and Human Decision Processes, 78,* 232–255.

FERRARI, J.R., & DOVIDIO, J.F. (2000). Examining behavioral processes in indecision: Decisional procrastination and decision-making style. *Journal of Research in Personality, 34,* 127–137.

FIEDLER, F. (1978). The contingency model and the dynamics of the leadership process. In L. Berkowitz (Ed.), *Advances in experimental social psychology* (Vol. 11). Orlando, FL: Academic Press.

FIELD, D., & COPP, G. (1999). Communication and awareness about dying in the 1990s. *Palliative Medicine, 13,* 459–468.

FINCHAM, F.D. (2003). Marital conflict: Correlates, structure, and context. *Current Directions in Psychological Science, 12,* 23–27.

FINHOLT, T., & SPROULL, L.S. (1990). Electronic groups at work. *Organization Science, 1,* 41–64.

FINKELHOR, D., & JONES, L.M. (2004, January). Explanations for the decline in sexual abuse cases. *OJJDP Crimes Against Children Series: Bulletin,* 1–12.

FINN, M.A., BLACKWELL, B.S., STALANS, L.J., STUDDARD, S., & DUGAN, L. (2004). Dual arrest decisions in domestic violence cases: The influence of departmental policies. *Crime & Delinquency, 50,* 565–589.

FISCHER, A.H., RODRIGUEZ MOSQUERA, P.M., VAN VIANEN, A.E.M., & MANSTEAD, A.S.R. (2004). Gender and culture differences in emotion. *Emotion, 4,* 87–94.

FISCHER, S. (1999, November 8). Stay fit, fend off breast cancer. *U.S. News & World Report,* 91.

FISHER, H.E. (2006). Broken hearts: The nature and risks of romantic rejection. In A.C. Crouter & A. Booth (Eds.), *Romance and sex in adolescence and emerging adulthood: Risks and opportunities* (pp. 3–28). Mahwah, NJ: Lawrence Erlbaum Associates.

FISK, A.D., & ROGERS, W.A. (2002). Psychology and aging: Enhancing the lives of an aging population. *Current Directions in Psychological Science, 11,* 107–110.

FISKE, S.T. (2002). What we know now about bias and intergroup conflict, the problem of the century. *Current Directions in Psychological Science, 11,* 123–128.

FLETT, G.L., HEWITT, P.L., BLANKSTEIN, K.R., & MOSHER, S.W. (1991). Perfectionism, self-actualization, and personal adjustment. *Journal of Social Behavior and Personality. Special Issue: Handbook of Self-Actualization. 6,* 147–160.

FLYNT, S.W., & MORTON, R.C. (2004). Bullying and children with disabilities. *Journal of Instructional Psychology, 31,* 330–333.

FOLKES, V.S. (1982). Forming relationships and the matching hypothesis. *Personality and Social Psychology Bulletin, 82,* 631–636.

FOOTE, D., & SEIBERT, S. (1999, Spring/Summer). The age of anxiety. *Special Issue: Newsweek,* 68–72.

FOSTER, G. (2005). Making friends: A nonexperimental analysis of social pair formation. *Human Relations, 58,* 1443–1465.

FRANKL, V. (1978). *The unheard cry for meaning.* New York: Simon & Schuster.

FRAZIER, P., STEWARD, J., & MORTENSEN, H. (2004). Perceived control and adjustment to trauma: A comparison across events. *Journal of Social & Clinical Psychology, 23,* 303–324.

FREDRICKSON, B.L., TUGADE, M.M., WAUGH, C.E., & LARKIN, G.R. (2003). What good are positive emotions in crisis? A prospective study of resilience and emotions following the terrorist attacks on the United States on September 11th, 2001. *Journal of Personality and Social Psychology, 84,* 365–376.

FREEDMAN, R.E.K., CARTER, M.M., SBROCCO, T., & GRAY, J.J. (2004). Ethnic differences in preferences for female weight and waist-to-hip ratio: A comparison of African-American and White American college and community samples. *Eating Behaviors, 5,* 191–198.

FRENCH, M. (1992). *The war against women.* New York: Summit Books.

FREUD, S. (1965). *New introductory lectures on psychoanalysis.* New York: W. W. Norton. (First German edition, 1933).

FRICK, W.B. (2000). Remembering Maslow: Reflections on a 1968 interview. *Journal of Humanistic Psychology, 40,* 128–147.

FRIEDMAN, M.J. (2005). Introduction: Every crisis is an opportunity. *CNS Spectrums, 10,* 96–98.

FRIEDMAN, M., & ROSENMAN, R.N. (1974). *Type A behavior and your heart.* New York: Knopf.

FRIES, J.F. (2002). Reducing disability in older age. *Journal of the American Medical Association, 288,* 3164–3166.

FROMM, E. (1963). *Escape from freedom.* New York: Holt.

FRONSTIN, P. (1999). Retirement patterns and employee benefits: Do benefits matter? *The Gerontologist, 39,* 37–47.

FUDGE, A.K., KNAPP, M.L., & THEUNE, K.W. (2002). Interaction appearance theory: Changing perceptions of physical attractiveness through social interaction. *Communication Theory, 12,* 8–40.

FULTON, R. (1987). The many faces of grief. *Death Studies, 11,* 243–256.

FURNHAM, A., LAVANCHY, M., & McCLELLAND, A. (2006). Waist to hip ratio and facial attractiveness: A pilot study. *Personality and Individual Differences, 30,* 491–502.

FURSTENBERG, A. (2002). Trajectories of aging: Imagined pathways in later life. *International Journal of Aging and Human Development, 55,* 1–24.

GABBARD, G.O., & LAZAR, S.G. (Accessed March 10, 2004, no other date given). Efficacy and cost effectiveness of psychotherapy. Report prepared for the APA Commission on Psychotherapy by Psychiatrists. http://www.psych.org/psych_pract/ispe_efficacy.cfm.

GABRIEL, S., CARVALLO, M., DEAN, K.K., TIPPIN, B., & RENAUD, J. (2005). How I see me depends on how I see we: The role of attachment style in social comparison. *Personality and Social Psychology Bulletin, 31,* 1561–1572.

GAINES, L.M., DUVALL, J., WEBSTER, J.M., & SMITH, R.H. (2005). Feeling good after praise for a successful performance: The importance of social comparison information. *Self and Identity, 4,* 373–389.

GALDAS, P.M., CHEATER, F., & MARSHALL, P. (2005). Men and health help-seeking behaviour: Literature review. *JAN Journal of Advanced Nursing, 49,* 616–623.

GALLACHER, J.E.J., SWEETNAM, P.M., YARNELL, J.W.G., ELWOOD, P.C., & STANSFELD, S.A. (2003). Is type A behavior really a trigger for coronary heart disease events? *Psychosomatic Medicine, 65,* 339–346.

GAMINO, L.A., & SEWELL, K.W. (2004). Meaning constructs as predictors of bereavement adjustment: A report from the Scott & White grief study. *Death Studies, 28,* 397–421.

GARNER, D.M. (1997, February). The 1997 body image survey results. *Psychology Today,* 30–47.

GARRICK, J. (2006). The humor of trauma survivors: Its application in a therapeutic milieu. *Journal of Aggression, Maltreatment & Trauma, 12,* 169–182.

GARY, F.A. (2005). Stigma: Barrier to mental health care among ethnic minorities. *Issues in Mental Health Nursing, 26,* 979–999.

GAVIN, M. (2005). How tv affects your child. Retrieved January 12, 2006, from http://kidshealth.org.

GAVZER, B. (2000, July 16). How can we help? *Parade,* 4–5.

GEDO, J.E. (2002, Spring). The enduring scientific contributions of Sigmund Freud. *Perspectives in Biology and Medicine,* 200–212.

GENOVA, P. (2003). Dump the DSM! *Psychiatric Times, 20,* 72.

GERBNER, G. (1996). *Violence in cable-originated television programs: A report to the National Cable Television Association.* Philadelphia: Annenberg School for Communication, University of Pennsylvania.

GERDES, E.P. (1995). Women preparing for traditionally male professions: Physical and psychological symptoms associated with work and home stress. *Sex Roles, 32,* 787–807.

GERSHOFF, E.T. (2002). Corporal punishment by parents and associated child behaviors and experiences: A meta-analytic and theoretical review. *Psychological Bulletin, 128,* 539–579.

GIANAKOS, I. (2002). Predictors of coping with work stress: The influences of sex, gender role, social desirability, and locus of control. *Sex Roles, 46,* 149–158.

GIARRUSSO, R., MABRY, B.J., & BENGTSON, V.L. (2001). The aging self in social contexts. In R.H. Binstock (Ed.), *Handbook of aging and the social sciences* (pp. 295–312). San Diego, CA: Academic Press.

GIBBS, J.L., ELLISON, N.B., & HEINO, R.D. (2006). Self-presentation in online personals: The role of anticipated future interaction, self-disclosure, and perceived success in internet dating. *Communication Research, 33,* 152–177.

GIBSON, S. (2005). On judgment and judgmentalism: How counseling can make people better. *Journal of Medical Ethics, 31,* 575–577.

GILBERT, D.T., BROWN, R.P., PINEL, E.C., & WILSON, T.D. (2000). *Journal of Personality and Social Psychology, 79,* 690–700.

GILBERT, D.T., MOREWEDGE, C.K., RISEN, J.L., & WILSON, T.D. (2004). Looking forward to looking backward: The misprediction of regret. *Psychological Science, 15,* 346–350.

GILES, L.C., GLONEK, G.F.V., LUSZCZ, M.A., & ANDREWS, G.R. (2005). Effect of social networks on 10 year survival in very old Australians: The Australian longitudinal study of aging. *Journal of Epidemiology & Community Health, 59,* 574–579.

GILOVICH, T., & MEDVEC, V.H. (1995). The experience of regret: What, when, and why. *Psychological Review, 102,* 379–395.

GILOVICH, T., & SAVITSKY, K. (1999). The spotlight effect and the illusion of transparency: Egocentric assessments of how we are seen by others. *Current Directions in Psychological Science, 8,* 165–168.

GIORGI, A. (2005). Remaining challenges for humanistic psychology. *Journal of Humanistic Psychology, 45,* 204–216.

GLADWELL, M. (2002, August 5). The naked face. *The New Yorker,* 38–49.

GLASER, R. (2005). Stress-associated immune dysregulation and its importance for human health: A personal history of psychoneuroimmunology. *Brain, Behavior and Immunity, 19,* 3–11.

GLICK, D. (1999, Spring/Summer). Sleepy? Keep on dreaming. *Special Issue: Newsweek*, 76–78.

GODFREY, J.R. (2004). Toward optimal health: The experts discuss therapeutic humor. *Journal of Women's Health, 13*, 474–479.

GODOY, R., REYES-GARCÍA, V., HUANCA, T., TANNER, S., LEONARD, W.R., & MCDADE, T., et al. (2005). Do smiles have a face value? Panel evidence from Amazonian Indians. *Journal of Economic Psychology, 26*, 469–490.

GOLDING, J.M. (1990). Division of household labor, strain, and depressive symptoms among Mexican Americans and non-Hispanic Whites. *Psychology of Women Quarterly, 14*, 103–117.

GOLDIN-MEADOW, S. (2006). Talking and thinking with our hands. *Current Directions in Psychological Science, 15*, 34–39.

GOLDMEIER, D., & RICHARDSON, D. (2005). Romantic love and sexually transmitted infection acquisition: Hypothesis and review. *International Journal of STD & AIDS, 16*, 585–587.

GOLEMAN, D. (1995). *Emotional intelligence*. New York: Bantam.

GOLEMAN, D. (1998). What makes a leader? *Harvard Business Review, 76*, 92–102.

GOLEMAN, D. (2005). *Emotional intelligence: 10th Anniversary Edition*. New York: Bantam Books.

GOLOGOR, E. (1977). Group polarization in a non-sick-taking culture. *Journal of Cross-Cultural Psychology, 8*, 331–346.

GOODE, E. (2000, March 14). Human nature: Born or made? *The New York Times*, pp. F1, F9.

GOODWIN, R., & ENGSTRON, G. (2002). Personality and the perception of health in the general population. *Psychological Medicine, 32*, 325–332.

GOODWIN, R., NIZHARADZE, G., LUU, L.A.N., KOSA, E., & EMELYANOVA, T. (1999). Glasnost and the art of conversation: A multilevel analysis of intimate disclosure across three former communist cultures. *Journal of Cross-Cultural Psychology, 30*, 72–90.

GORDON, K.C., FRIEDMAN, M.A., MILLER, I.W., & GAERTNER, L. (2005). Marital attributions as moderators of the marital discord-depression link. *Journal of Social & Clinical Psychology, 24*, 876–893.

GORDON, T., & SANDS, J.S. (1984). *P.E.T. in action*. New York: Bantam.

GORMAN, C. (2002, June 20). The science of anxiety. *Time*, 47–54.

GOTTMAN, J.M. (1994). *Why marriages succeed or fail*. New York: Simon & Schuster.

GOTTMAN, J., & CARRERE, S. (2000, September 23). Welcome to the love lab. *Psychology Today*, 42–47, 87.

GRABHORN, R., KAUFHOLD, J., MICHAL, M., & OVERBECK, G. (2005). The therapeutic relationship as reflected in linguistic interaction: Work on resistance. *Psychotherapy Research, 15*, 470–482.

GRAD, O.T., & ZAVASNIK, A. (1999). Phenomenology of bereavement process after suicide, traffic accident and terminal illness (in spouses). *Archives of Suicide Research, 5*, 157–172.

GRAY, C.A., & GERON, S.M. (1995). The other sorrow of divorce: The effects on grandparents when their adult children divorce. *Journal of Gerontological Social Work, 23*, 139–159.

GRAY-LITTLE, B., BAUCOM, D.H., & HAMBY, S.L. (1996). Marital power, marital adjustment, and therapy outcome. *Journal of Family Psychology, 10*, 292–303.

GRAZIANO, W.G., JENSEN-CAMPBELL, L.A., SHEBILSKE, L.J., & LUNDGREN, S.R. (1993). Social influence, sex differences, and judgment of beauty: Putting the interpersonal back in interpersonal attraction. *Journal of Personality and Social Psychology, 65*, 522–531.

GREAVES, S. (2005). Happy hours: Stress and long hours are key contributors to a demotivated workforce with high levels of absenteeism and staff turnover. *Incentive Today, 20*, 25–28.

GREEN, B.C. (2005). Homosexual signification: A moral construct in social contexts. *Journal of Homosexuality, 49*, 119–134.

GREEN, B.L., & KENRICK, D.T. (1994). The attractiveness of gender-typed traits at different relationship levels: Androgynous characteristics may be desirable after all. *Personality and Social Psychological Bulletin, 20*, 244–253.

GREEN, S.P., & PRITCHARD, M.E. (2003). Predictors of body image dissatisfaction in adult men and women. *Social Behavior and Personality, 31*, 215–222.

GREENBERG, L.S., & WATSON, J.C. (2006). *The therapeutic relationship*. Washington, DC: American Psychological Association.

GREENBERG, S., & SPRINGEN, K. (Fall/Winter 2001 Special Edition). Keeping hope alive. *Newsweek, 138*, 60–63.

GREENE, K., & FAULKNER, S.L. (2005). Gender, belief in the sexual double standard, and sexual talk in heterosexual dating relationships. *Sex Roles, 53*, 239–251.

GREENE, S.M., ANDERSON, E.R., DOYLE, E.A., & RIEDELBACH, H. (2006). Divorce. In G.G. Bear & K.M. Minke (Eds.), *Children's needs III: Development, prevention, and intervention* (pp. 745–757). Washington, DC: National Association of School Psychologists.

GREENHAUS, J.H., PARASURAMAN, S., & WORMLEY, W.M. (1990). Effects of race on organizational experiences, job performance evaluations, and career outcomes. *Academy of Management Journal, 33*, 64–86.

GREVE, W., & WENTURA, D. (2003). Immunizing the self: Self-concept stabilization through reality-adaptive self-definitions. *Personality and Social Psychology Bulletin, 29*, 39–50.

GRIFFIN, J.M., FUHRER, R., STANSFELD, S.A., & MARMOT, M. (2002). The importance of low control at work and home on depression and anxiety: Do these effects vary by gender and social class? *Social Science and Medicine. Special Issue: Social and Economic Patterning of Women's Health in a Changing World, 54*, 783–798.

GROCKE, D. (2005). The role of the therapist in the bonny method of guided imagery and music (BMGIM). *Music Therapy Perspectives, 23*, 45–52.

GROOPMAN, J. (2000, April 10). The doubting disease: When is obsession a sickness? *The New Yorker*, 52–57.

GROTH-MARNAT, G., & SUMMERS, R. (1998). Altered beliefs, attitudes, and behaviors following near-death experiences. *Journal of Humanistic Psychology, 38*, 110–125.

GROUZET, F.M.E., KASSER, T., AHUVIA, A., DOLS, J.M.F., KIM, Y., & LAU, S., et al. (2005). The structure of goal contents across 15 cultures. *Journal of Personality and Social Psychology, 89*, 800–816.

GRÜHN, D., SMITH, J., & BALTES, P.B. (2005). No aging bias favoring memory for positive material: Evidence from a heterogeneity-homogeneity list paradigm using emotionally toned words. *Psychology and Aging. Special Issue: Emotion-Cognition Interactions and the Aging Mind, 20*, 579–588.

GUASTELLO, D.D., & GUASTELLO, S.J. (2003). Androgyny, gender role behavior, and emotional intelligence among college students and their parents. *Sex Roles, 49*, 663–673.

GUERRERO, L.K. (1997). Nonverbal involvement across interactions with same-sex friends, opposite-sex friends and romantic partners: Consistency or change. *Journal of Social and Personal Relationships, 14*, 31–58.

GUERRERO, L.K., & ANDERSEN, P.A. (1998). The dark side of jealousy and envy: Desire, delusion, desperation, and destructive communication. In B.H. Spirtzberg & W.R. Cupach (Eds.), *The dark side of close relationships* (pp. 33–70). Mahwah, NJ: Lawrence Erlbaum.

GUINTO, J. (2005, December). Time bandits. *Southwest Airlines Spirit, 143–144*, 153–154.

GUPTA, S. (2002, December 2). A hurry-up lifestyle can hurt the young: Even if you're only 18, impatience can mean hypertension later on. And that can be bad news for your heart. *Time, 103*.

GUPTA, S. (2006). The consequences of maternal employment during men's childhood for their adult housework performance. *Gender & Society, 20*, 60–86.

Guttmacher Institute. (2004). Contraception in the United States: Current use and continuing challenges. Retrieved May 04, 2006, from http://www.guttmacher.org/presentations/contraception-us.html.

HADDAD, A. (2003). Ethics in action (acute care decisions). *RN, 66*, 27–29.

HAGGERTY, K., KOSTERMAN, R.F., CATALANO, R.F., & HAWKINS, J.D. (1999, July). Preparing for the drug free years. *Juvenile Justice Bulletin*, 1–11.

HAGIHARA, A., ODAMAKI, M., NOBUTOMO, K., & TARUMI, K. (2006). Physician and patient perceptions of the physician explanations in medical encounters. *Journal of Health Psychology, 11*, 91–105.

HAINES, M.P., BARKER, G.P., & RICE, R. (2003). *Using social norms to reduce alcohol and tobacco use in two Midwestern high schools*. San Francisco: Jossey-Bass.

HAJJAR, I., GABLE, S.A., JENKINSON, V.P., KANE, L.T., & RILEY, R.A. (2005). Quality of internet geriatric health information: The GeriatricWeb project. *Journal of the American Geriatrics Society, 53*, 885–890.

HALDEMAN, D.C. (2006). Queer eye on the straight guy: A case of gay male heterophobia. In M. Englar-Carlson & M.A. Stevens (Eds.), *In the room with men: A casebook of therapeutic change* (pp. 301–317). Washington, DC: American Psychological Association.

HALFORD, W.K., O'DONNELL, C., LIZZIO, K., & WILSON, A.L. (2006). Do couples at high risk of relationship problems attend premarriage education? *Journal of Family Psychology, 20*, 160–163.

HALL, C.T. (1999, September 15). Big rise is forecast in mental illness among elderly. *San Francisco Chronicle*. http://www.sfgate.com:80/cgi-bin/article.cgi.

HALL, C., & MOSEMAK, J. (1999, October 11). Making a successful marriage. *USA Today*, 1D.

HALL, R. (1995). The bleaching syndrome: African Americans' response to cultural domination vis-a-vis skin color. *Journal of Black Studies, 26,* 172–184.

HALL, J.A., ROTER, D.L., & MILBURN, M.A. (1999). Illness and satisfaction with medical care. *Current Directions in Psychological Science, 8,* 96–99.

HALPERN-FELSHNER, B.L., & MILLSTEIN, S.G. (2002). The effects of terrorism on teens; perceptions of dying: The new world is riskier than ever. *Journal of Adolescent Health, 30,* 308–311.

HAMARAT, E., THOMPSON, D., STEELE, D., MATHENY, K., & SIMONS, C. (2002). Age differences in coping resources and satisfaction with life among middle-aged, young-old, and oldest-old adults. *The Journal of Genetic Psychology, 163,* 360–367.

HANLEY, S.J., & ABELL, S.C. (2002). Maslow and relatedness: Creating an interpersonal model of self-actualization. *Journal of Humanistic Psychology, 42,* 37–56.

HANNAH, A., & MURACHVER, T. (1999). Gender and conversational style as predictors of conversational behavior. *Journal of Language & Social Psychology, 18,* 153–174.

HANSEN, E.B., & BREIVIK, G. (2001). Sensation seeking as a predictor of positive and negative risk behavior among adolescents. *Personality and Individual Differences, 30,* 627–640.

HANSEN, J.C., & DIK, B.J. (2005). Evidence of 12-year predictive and concurrent validity for SII occupational scale scores. *Journal of Vocational Behavior, 67,* 365–378.

HANSENNE, M., PINTO, E., PITCHOT, W., REGGERS, J., SCANTAMBURIO, G., MOOR, M., & ANSSEAU, M. (2002). Further evidence on the relationship between dopamine and novelty seeking: A neuroendocrine study. *Personality and Individual Differences, 33,* 967–977.

HANSON, M.S., FINK, P., SONDERGAARD, L., & FRYDENBERG, M. (2005). Mental illness and health care: A study among new neurological patients. *General Hospital Psychiatry, 27,* 119–124.

HARDER, B. (2005). Potent medicine: Can Viagra and other lifestyle drugs save lives? *Science News, 168,* 124–126.

HARDEY, M. (2004). Mediated relationships: Authenticity and the possibility of romance. *Information, Communication & Society, 7,* 207–222.

HARPER, G. (2004). *The joy of conflict: Transforming victims, villains, and heroes in the workplace and at home*. British Columbia, CA: New Society Publishers.

HARRELL, S.P. (2000). A multidimensional conceptualization of racism-related stress: Implications for the well-being of people of color. *American Journal of Orthopsychiatry, 70,* 42–57.

HARRIS, A.H.S., & THORESEN, C.E. (2005). Volunteering is associated with delayed mortality in older people: Analysis of the longitudinal study of aging. *Journal of Health Psychology, 10,* 739–752.

HARRIS, C.R. (2002). Sexual and romantic jealousy in heterosexual and homosexual adults. *Psychological Science, 13,* 7–12.

HARRIS, J.R. (1998). *The nature assumption*. New York: Free Press.

HARTMAN, M., & WARREN, L.H. (2005). Explaining age differences in temporal working memory. *Psychology and Aging. Special Issue: Emotion-Cognition Interactions and the Aging Mind, 20,* 645–656.

HARTMANN, E. (1999, March). The nature and uses of dreaming. *USA Today Magazine*, 64–66.

Harvard Health Letter. (2001, May). Doctors from Venus and Mars: How they differ, 4.

Harvard Health Letter. (2002, August). In brief—Heavenly experiences, 2.

Harvard Health Letter. (2004, July). Nine tips for patients, 1.

Harvard Health Letter. (2004, October). Staying the course, 1.

Harvard Health Letter. (2006, January). Patient, protect thyself ? 1–2.

Harvard Mental Health Letter. (1998, November). Obsessive-compulsive disorder, 1–4.

Harvard Mental Health Letter. (2002, April). The mind and the immune system—Part I, 1–4.

Harvard Mental Health Letter. (2002a, January). General review—Disaster and trauma, 1–4.

Harvard Mental Health Letter. (2002b, November). Classifying psychiatric disorders: An alternative approach, 1.

Harvard Mental Health Letter (2005). Dysthymia. Psychotherapists and patients confront the high cost of "low-grade" depression. (2005). *The Harvard Mental Health Letter from Harvard Medical School, 21,* 1–3.

Harvard Women's Health Watch. (2001, June). Three for 2003: Reducing the burden of stress, 1–2.

Harvard Women's Health Watch. (2002, March). Anxiety—When anxiety is overwhelming, 1–2.

Harvard Women's Health Watch. (2003, September). Research reveals biology of harmful stress, 1–2.

Harvard's Women's Health Watch, (2005, March). Not getting over it: Post-traumatic stress disorder, 1–2.

HASELTON, M.G. (2003). The sexual overperception bias: Evidence of a systematic bias in men from a survey of naturally occurring events. *Journal of Research in Personality, 37,* 34–47.

HASELTON, M.G., & BUSS, D.M. (2000). Error management theory: A new perspective on biases in cross-sex mind reading. *Journal of Personality and Social Psychology, 78,* 81–91.

HASSIN, R.R., ULEMAN, J.S., & BARGH, J.A. (Eds.). (2005). *The new unconscious*. New York: Oxford University Press.

HATALA, M.N., BAACK, D.W., & PARMENTER, R. (1998). Dating with HIV: A content analysis of gay male HIV-positive and HIV-negative personal advertisements. *Journal of Social and Personal Relationships, 15,* 268–276.

HATFIELD, E. (1988). Passionate and companionate love. In R.J. Sternberg & M.I. Barnes (Eds.), *The psychology of love* (pp. 191–217). New Haven, CT: Yale University Press.

HATFIELD, E., & RAPSON, R.L. (1993). Historical and cross-cultural perspectives on passionate love and sexual desire. *Annual Review of Sex Research, 4,* 67–97.

HATFIELD, E., & SPRECHER, S. (1995). Men's and women's preferences in marital partners in the United States, Russia, and Japan. *Journal of Cross-Cultural Psychology, 26,* 728–750.

HAVEREN, R.V., HABBEN, C.J., & KUTHER, T.L. (2005). New psychologists online: Changing the face of psychology through technology. In R.D. Morgan, T.L. Kuther & C.J. Habben (Eds.), *Life after graduate school in psychology: Insider's advice from new psychologists* (pp. 321–327). New York: Psychology Press.

HAZAN, C., & SHAVER, P. (1994). Attachment as an organizing framework for research on close relationships. *Psychological Inquiry, 5,* 1–22.

Health & Medicine Week. (2003, June 10). Role of chronic stress clarified, 3.

HEALY, M. (1999, December 28). Sex and the teenage girl: Curiosity wins over love. *USA Today*, 6D.

HEATON, T. (2002). Factors contributing to increasing marital stability in the US. *Journal of Family Issues, 23,* 392–409.

HEBERT, R. (2005). Vacation: Not what you remember. *APS Observer, 18,* 12–19.

HECKER, D.E. (2001, November). Occupational employment projections to 2010. *Monthly Labor Review Online,* 1.

HEDGE, J.W., BORMAN, W.C., & LAMMLEIN, S.E. (2006). *Physical capabilities, cognitive abilities, and job performance*. Washington, DC: American Psychological Association.

HEIFETZ, A., & SEGEV, E. (2005). Escalation and delay in protracted international conflicts. *Mathematical Social Sciences, 49,* 17–37.

HELGESON, V.S. (1990). *The female advantage: Women's ways of leadership*. New York: Doubleday Currency.

HELGESON, V.S. (1994). Long-distance romantic relationships: Sex differences in adjustment and break-up. *Personality and Social Psychology Bulletin, 20,* 254–265.

HELGESON, V.S., & COHEN, S. (1996). Social support and adjustment to cancer: Reconciling descriptive, correlational, and intervention research. *Health Psychology, 15,* 135–148.

HELSON, R., KWAN, V.S.Y., JOHN, O.P., & JONES, C. (2002). The growing evidence for personality change in adulthood: Findings from research with personality inventories. *Journal of Research in Personality, 36,* 287–106.

HELSON, R., & SOTO, C.J. (2005). Up and down in middle age: Monotonic and nonmonotonic changes in roles, status, and personality. *Journal of Personality and Social Psychology, 89,* 194–204.

HENDRICK, C., & HENDRICK, S.S. (2004). *Sex and romantic love: Connects and disconnects*. Mahwah, NJ: Lawrence Erlbaum Associates.

HENDRICK, S.S. (2006). *Love, intimacy, and partners*. New York: Oxford University Press.

HENNINGSEN, D.D., HENNINGSEN, M.L.M., EDEN, J., & CRUZ, M.G. (2006). Examining the symptoms of groupthink and retrospective sensemaking. *Small Group Research, 37,* 36–64.

HENSS, R. (1995). Waist-to-hip ratio and attractiveness: Replication and extension. *Personality and Individual Differences, 19,* 479–488.

HERBERT, W. (1999, July 26). Losing your mind? *U.S. News & World Report*, 44–51.

HEREK, G.M. (1994). Assessing attitudes toward lesbians and gay men: A review of the empirical research with the ATLG scale. In B. Greene & G.M. Herek (Eds.), *Lesbian and gay psychology* (pp. 206–208). Thousand Oaks, CA: Sage.

HEREK, G.M. (2000a). Sexual prejudice and gender: Do heterosexuals' attitudes toward lesbians and gay men differ? *Journal of Social Issues. Special Issue: Women's Sexualities, 56,* 251–266.

HEREK, G.M. (2000b). The psychology of sexual prejudice. *Current Directions in Psychological Science, 9,* 19–22.

HERSHEY, D.A., JACOBS-LAWSON, J.M., & NEUKAM, K.A. (2002). Influences of age and gender on workers' goals for retirement. *Aging and Human Development, 55,* 163–179.

HESS, U., SENECAL, S., KIROUAC, G., HERRERA, P., PHILIPPOT, P., & KLECK, R.E. (2000). Emotional expressivity in men and women: Stereotypes and self-perception, *Cognition and Emotion, 14,* 609–642.

HETH, J.T., & SOMER, E. (2002). Characterizing stress tolerance: "Controllability awareness" and its relationship to perceived stress and reported health. *Personality and Individual Differences, 33,* 883–895.

HEWSTONE, M., RUBIN, M., & WILLIS, H. (2002). Intergroup bias. *Annual Review of Psychology, 53,* 575–604.

HINE, T. (1999). The rise and decline of the teenager. *American Heritage, 50,* 70–81.

HINSZ, V.B., & JUNDT, D.K. (2005). Exploring individual differences in a goal-setting situation using the motivational trait questionnaire. *Journal of Applied Social Psychology, 35,* 551–571.

HOBFOLL, S.E., SCHROEDER, K.E.E., WELLS, M., & MALEK, M. (2002). Communal versus individualistic construction of sense of mastery in facing life challenges. *Journal of Social and Clinical Psychology, 21,* 362–399.

HOFFMAN, K.R. (2002, May 3). Are girls meaner than boys? *Time for Kids,* 4–5.

HOFSTEDE, G. (2001). *Culture's consequences.* Thousand Oaks, CA: Sage.

HOGARTH, R.M. (2005). Deciding analytically or trusting your intuition? The advantages and disadvantages of analytic and intuitive thought. In T. Betsch, & S. Haberstroh (Eds.), *The routines of decision making* (pp. 67–82). Mahwah, NJ: Lawrence Erlbaum Associates.

HOHWY, J. (2004). The experience of mental causation. *Behavior and Philosophy, 32,* 377–400.

HOLLON, S.D., THASE, M.E., & MARKOWITZ, J.C. (2002). Treatment and prevention of depression. *Psychological Science in the Public Interest, 3,* 39–77.

HOLMES, T.H., & RAHE, R.H. (1967). The social readjustment rating scale. *Journal of Psychosomatic Research, 11,* 213–217.

HOLTZWORTH-MUNROE, A. (2000). A typology of men who are violent toward female partners: Making sense of the heterogeneity in husband violence. *Current Directions in Psychological Science, 9,* 140–143.

HOPE, D.A., HOLT, C.S., & HEIMBERG, R.G. (1995). Social phobia. In T.R. Giles (Ed.), *Handbook of effective psychotherapy.* New York: Plenum.

HOPKO, D.R., CRITTENDON, J.A., GRANT, E., & WILSON, S.A. (2005). The impact of anxiety on performance IQ. *Anxiety, Stress & Coping: An International Journal, 18,* 17–35.

HORGEN, K.B. (2005). Big food, big money, big children. In S. Olfman (Ed.), *Childhood lost: How American culture is failing our kids* (pp. 123–135). Westport, CT: Praeger Publishers/Greenwood Publishing Group, Inc.

HORNE, R., & WEINMAN, J. (1999). Patients' beliefs about prescribed medicines and their role in adherence to treatment in chronic physical illness. *Journal of Psychosomatic Research, 47,* 555–567.

HORNSEY, M.J., & JETTEN, J. (2005). Loyalty without conformity: Tailoring self-perception as a means of balancing belonging and differentiation. *Self and Identity, 4,* 81–95.

HOSPICE Foundation of America. (2003). *What is hospice?* http://www.tiospice-foundation.org/what_is.

Hospice Management Advisor. (2003). Innovative programs help stressed-out caregivers cope with problems: Alert systems, community nursing fill gaps, *8,* 73–75.

HOURAN, J., LANGE, R., RENTFROW, P.J., & BRUCKNER, K.H. (2004). Do online matchmaking tests work? An assessment of preliminary evidence for a publicized 'predictive model of marital success.' *North American Journal of Psychology, 6,* 507–526.

HOWE, M.J.A. (2001). Twin research problems, *Psychologist, 14,* 234.

HOWLETT, D. (1999, November 9). Loving a good fright: It's in our nature. *USA Today,* 6D.

HUDD, S.S., DUMLAO, J., ERDMANN-SAGER, D., MURRAY, D., PHAN, E., SOUKAS, M., & YOKOZUKA, N. (2000). Stress at college: Effects on health habits, health status and self-esteem. *College Student Journal, 34,* 217–227.

HUDDY, L., KHATIB, N., & CAPELOS, T. (2002). The polls—trends: Reactions to the terrorist attacks of September 11, 2001. *Public Opinion Quarterly, 66,* 418–451.

HUGICK, L., & LEONARD, J. (1991). Job dissatisfaction grows; "moonlighting" on the rise. *Gallup Poll News Service, 56,* 1–11.

HUGUET, P., CROIZET, J., & RICHETIN, J. (2004). Is "what has been cared for" necessarily good? Further evidence for the negative impact of cosmetics use on impression formation. *Journal of Applied Social Psychology, 34,* 1752–1771.

HUNTER, B.T. (1998). The importance of taste (genetics, physiology, and tasting ability). *Consumers' Research Magazine,* 8–9.

HUNTER, M. (1999, May/June). Work, work, work, work! *Modern Maturity,* 36–49.

HUNTINGTON, S.P. (1999, June/July). When cultures collide. *Civilization,* 76–77.

HYDE, J.S., & DELAMETER, J. (1997). *Understanding human sexuality.* New York: McGraw-Hill.

HYDE, J.S., & JAFFEE, S.R. (2000). Becoming a heterosexual adult: The experiences of young women. *Journal of Social Issues. Special Issue: Women's Sexualities, 58,* 283–296.

IMPETT, E., & PEPLAU, L.A. (2003). Sexual compliance: Gender, motivational, and relationship perspectives. *Journal of Sex Research, 40,* 87–100.

INGRASSIA, M., & BECK, M., (1994, July 4). Patterns of abuse. *Newsweek,* 26–33.

INSKO, C.A., SCHOPLER, J., HOYLE, R.H., DARDIS, G.J., & GRAETZ, K.A. (1990). Individual-group discontinuity as a function of fear and greed. *Journal of Personality and Social Psychology, 58,* 68–79.

IYENGAR, S.S., WELLS, R.E., & SCHWARTZ, B. (2006). Doing better but feeling worse: Looking for the "best" job undermines satisfaction. *Psychological Science, 17,* 143–150.

IZARD, C., FINE, S., SCHULTZ, D., MOSTOW, A., ACKERMAN, B., & YOUNGSTROM, E. (2001). Emotion knowledge as a predictor of social behavior and academic competence in children at risk. *Psychological Science, 12,* 18–23.

JACCOBY, S. (1999, September/October). Great sex: What's age got to do with it? *Modern Maturity,* 41–45.

JACKSON, D., ENGSTROM, E., & HASSENZAHL, D.M. (2005). Effects of sex and seating arrangement on selection of leader. *Perceptual and Motor Skills, 100,* 815–818.

JACKSON, L.A., HUNTER, J., & HODGE, C.N. (1995). Physical attractiveness and intellectual competence: A meta-analytic review. *Social Psychology Quarterly, 58,* 108–122.

JACKSON, L.M., PRATT, M.W., HUNSBERGER, B., & PANCER, S.M. (2005). Optimism as a mediator of the relation between perceived parental authoritativeness and adjustment among adolescents: Finding the sunny side of the street. *Social Development, 14,* 273–304.

JACKSON, M. (2005). The limits of connectivity: Technology and 21st-century life. In D.F. Halpern, & S.E. Murphy (Eds.), *From work-family balance to work-family interaction: Changing the metaphor.* (pp. 135–150). Mahwah, NJ: Lawrence Erlbaum Associates.

JACKSON, T., FLAHERTY, S.R., & KOSUTH, R. (2000). Culture and self-presentation as predictors of shyness among Japanese and American female college students. *Perceptual and Motor Skills, 90,* 475–482.

JACKSON, T., FRITCH, A., NAGASAKA, T., & GUNDERSON, J. (2002). Towards explaining the association between shyness and loneliness: A path analysis with American college students. *Social Behavior and Personality, 30,* 263–270.

JACKSON, T., WEISS, K.E., LUNDQUIST, J.J., & SODERLIND, A. (2002). Perceptions of goal-directed activities of optimists and pessimists: A personal projects analysis. *Journal of Psychology, 136,* 521–532.

JACOBI, J. (1973). *The psychology of C.G. Jung.* New Haven, CT: Yale University Press.

JACOBSEN, C., & HOUSE, R.J. (2001). Dynamics of charismatic leadership: A process theory, simulation model, and tests. *Leadership Quarterly, 12,* 75–112.

JACOBSON, D. (1999). Impression formation in cyberspace: Online expectations and offline experiences in text-based virtual communities. *Journal of Computer-Mediated Communication, 5.* http://www.ascusc.org/jcmc/vol5/issue1/jacobson.html#Abstract.

JAFFE, E. (2006). Empirical science for the spotless mind, *APS Observer, 18,* 13–17.

JAMAL, M. (2005). Short communication: Personal and organizational outcomes related to job stress and type-A behavior: A study of Canadian and Chinese employees. *Stress and Health: Journal of the International Society for the Investigation of Stress, 21,* 129–137.

JAMES, V.H., & OWENS, L.D. (2005). 'They turned around like I wasn't there': An analysis of teenage girls' letters about their peer conflicts. *School Psychology International, 26,* 71–88.

JAMES, W. (1950). *The principles of psychology* (Vols. 1–2). New York: Dover. (Original work published in 1890.)

JANIS, I.L. (1982). *Groupthink* (2nd ed.). Boston: Houghton Mifflin.

JANSSEN, E., CARPENTER, D., & GRAHAM, C.A. (2003). Selecting films for sex research: Gender differences in erotic film preference. *Archives of Sexual Behavior, 32*, 243–251.

JAUHAR, S. (2003, March 16). When doctors slam the door. *The New York Times Magazine*, 32–35.

JEWELL, K.S. (1993). *From Mammy to Miss America and beyond: Cultural images and the shaping of U.S. social policy.* London: Routledge.

JEWELL, R.D., & KIDWELL, B. (2005). The moderating effect of perceived control on motivation to engage in deliberative processing. *Psychology & Marketing, 22*, 751–769.

JOHNSON, C. (2005). Dating in cyberspace: Meeting the right person may be a click away. Retrieved April 02, 2006, from http://dnj.midsouthnews.com/apps/pbcs.dll/article?AID=/20051113/LIFESTYLE/511130301/1024.

JOHNSON, S. (2003, March). Fear. *Discover*, 33–39.

JOHNSON, S.D., PHELPS, D.L., & COTTLER, L.B. (2004). The association of sexual dysfunction and substance use among a community epidemiological sample. *Archives of Sexual Behavior, 33*, 55–63.

JOHNSON, S., & LEBOW, J. (2000). The "coming of age" of couple therapy: A decade review. *Journal of Marriage and Family Counseling, 26*, 23–38.

JOHNSON, S., & PATZ, A. (2003, March/April). Save your relationship. *Psychology Today*, 50–58.

JOHNSON, T., KULESA, P., CHO, Y.I., & SHAVITT, S. (2005). The relation between culture and response styles: Evidence from 19 countries. *Journal of Cross-Cultural Psychology, 36*, 264–277.

JOHNSTONE, B., FRAME, C.L., & BOUMAN, D. (1992). Physical attractiveness and athletic and academic ability in controversial-aggressive and rejected-aggressive children. *Journal of Social and Clinical Psychology, 11*, 71–79.

JOINER, T.E., WONDERLICH, S.A., METALSKY, G., SCHMIDT, N.B. (1995). Body dissatisfaction: A feature of bulimia, depression, or both? *Journal of Social and Clinical Psychology, 14*, 339–355.

JONER, A. (2005). Job satisfaction and job performance: Causal relationship or illusory correlation? *Nordisk Psykologi, 57*, 161–176.

JONES, D. (1995). Sexual selection, physical attractiveness, and facial neoteny: Cross-cultural evidence and implication. *Current Anthropology, 36*, 723–748.

JONES, E. (1953). *The life and work of Sigmund Freud* (Vol. 1). New York: Basic Books.

JONES, S.M., & BURLESON, B.R. (2003). Effects of helper and recipient sex on the experience and outcomes of comforting messages: An experimental investigation. *Sex Roles, 48*, 1–19.

JORM, A.F. (2005). Social networks and health: It's time for an intervention trial. *Journal of Epidemiology & Community Health, 59*, 537–538.

JOSEPHS, R.A., BOSSON, J.K., & JACOBS, C.G. (2003). Self-esteem maintenance processes: Why low self-esteem may be resistant to change. *Personality and Social Psychology Bulletin, 29*, 920–933.

JUDGE, T.A., EREZ, A., BONO, J.E., & THORESON, C.J. (2002). Are measures of self-esteem, neuroticism, locus of control, and generalized self-efficacy indicators of a common core construct? *Journal of Personality and Social Psychology, 83*, 693–710.

JUDGE, T.A., PICCOLO, R.F., & ILIES, R. (2004). The forgotten ones? the validity of consideration and initiating structure in leadership research. *Journal of Applied Psychology, 89*, 36–51.

JUMPER, S.A. (1995). A meta-analysis of the relationship of child sexual abuse to adult psychological adjustment. *Child Abuse and Neglect, 19*, 715–728.

KALMIJN, M. (2005). Attitude alignment in marriage and cohabitation: The case of sex-role attitudes. *Personal Relationships, 12*, 521–535.

KAMINSKI, P.L., CHAPMAN, B.P., HAYNES, S.D., & OWN, L. (2005). Body image, eating behaviors, and attitudes toward exercise among gay and straight men. *Eating Behaviors, 6*, 179–187.

KANEMASA, Y., & DAIBO, I. (2003). Effects of early adult attachment styles on intimate opposite-sex relationships. *Japanese Journal of Social Psychology, 19*, 59–76.

KANTROWITZ, B., & WINGERT, P. (1999, April 19). The science of a good marriage. *Newsweek*, 52–57.

KAPLAN, H.S. (1983). *The evaluation of sexual disorders.* New York: Brunner/Mazel.

KAPLAN, R.E., & KAISER, R.B. (2003). Rethinking a classic distinction in leadership: Implications for the assessment and development of executives. *Consulting Psychology Journal: Practice and Research. Special Issue: Leadership development: New perspectives, 55*, 15–25.

KAPLAN, R., SALLIS, J.F., & PATTERSON, T.L. (1993). *Health and human behavior.* New York: McGraw-Hill.

KARAU, S.J., & WILLIAMS, K.D. (1993). Social loafing: A meta-analytic review and theoretical integration. *Journal of Personality and Social Psychology, 65*, 681–706.

KARAVIDAS, M., LIM, N.K., & KATSIKAS, S.L. (2005). The effects of computers on older adult users. *Computers in Human Behavior, 21*, 697–711.

KARK, R., SHAMIR, B., & CHEN, G. (2003). The two faces of transformational leadership: Empowerment and dependency. *Journal of Applied Psychology, 88*, 246–255.

KASSER, T., & RYAN, R.M. (1996). Further examining the American dream: Differential correlates of intrinsic and extrinsic goals. *Personality and Social Psychology Bulletin, 22*, 280–287.

KATZ, S. (2003). *Physical appearance: The importance of being beautiful.* New York: Free Press.

KAYES, A.B., KAYES, D.C., & KOLB, D.A. (2005). Experiential learning in teams. *Simulation & Gaming, 36*, 330–354.

KAYES, D.C. (2005). The destructive pursuit of idealized goals. *Organizational dynamics, 34*, 391–401.

KAZDIN, A.E., & BENJET, C. (2003). Spanking children: Evidence and issues. *Current Directions in Psychological Science, 12*, 99–103.

KEERY, H., BOUTELLE, K., VAN DEN BERG, P., & THOMPSON, J.K. (2005). The impact of appearance-related teasing by family members. *Journal of Adolescent Health, 37*, 120–127.

KEINAN, G., & KOREN, M. (2002). Teaming up Type As and Bs: The effects of group composition on performance and satisfaction. *Applied Psychology: An International Review, 51*, 425–445.

KELLY, A.E. (1999). Revealing personal secrets. *Current Directions in Psychological Science, 8*, 105–109.

KELSEY, J. (1999, January). Up from depression. *Healthline*, 6–11.

KENSIT, D.A. (2000). Rogerian theory: A critique of the effectiveness of pure client-centered therapy. *Counseling Psychology Quarterly, 13*, 345–351.

KEOGH, E., BOND, F.W., FRENCH, C.C., RICHARDS, A., & DAVIS, R.E. (2004). Test anxiety, susceptibility to distraction and examination performance. *Anxiety, Stress & Coping: An International Journal, 17*, 241–252.

KESSLER, R.C., DEMLER, O., FRANK, R.G., OLFSON, M., PINCUS, H.A., & WALTERS, E.E., et al. (2005). Prevalence and treatment of mental disorders, 1990 to 2003. *New England Journal of Medicine, 352*, 2515–2523.

KESSLER, R.C., MOLNAR, B.E., FEURER, I.D., & APPLEBAUM, M. (2001). Patterns and mental health predictors of domestic violence in the United States: Results from the National Comorbidity Survey. *International Journal of Law and Psychiatry, 24*, 487–509.

KIECOLT-GLASER, J.K., & GLASER, R. (1995). Psychoneuroimmunology and health consequences: Data and shared mechanisms. *Psychosomatic Medicine, 57*, 269–274.

KIEFFER, K.M., CRONIN, C., & GAWET, D.L. (2006). Test and study worry and emotionality in the prediction of college students' reasons for drinking: An exploratory investigation. *Journal of Alcohol and Drug Education, 50*, 57–81.

KIERNAN, K. (2004). Redrawing the boundaries of marriage. *Journal of Marriage and Family, 66*, 980–987.

KIM, H.K., & McKENRY, P.C. (2002). The relationship between marriage and psychological well-being: A longitudinal analysis. *Journal of Family Issues, 23*, 885–911.

KIM, J., & HATFIELD, E. (2004). Love types and subjective well-being: A cross-cultural study. *Social Behavior and Personality, 32*, 173–182.

KIM-PRIETO, C., DIENER, E., TAMIR, M., SCOLLON, C., & DIENER, M. (2005). Integrating the diverse definitions of happiness: A time-sequential framework of subjective well-being. *Journal of Happiness Studies, 6*, 261–300.

KINSEY, A.C., POMEROY, W.B., & MARTIN, C.E. (1948). *Sexual behavior in the human male.* Philadelphia: W. B. Saunders.

KIRK, J., & BELOVICS, R. (2006). Making e-working work. *Journal of Employment Counseling, 43*, 39–46.

KIRCALDY, B., FURNHAM, A., & LEVINE, R. (2001). Attitudinal and personality correlates of a nation's pace of life. *Journal of Managerial Psychology, 16*, 20–34.

KIRKPATRICK, L.A., & DAVIS, K.E. (1994). Attachment style, gender, and relationship stability: A longitudinal analysis. *Journal of Personality and Social Psychology, 66*, 502–512.

KIRSH, S.J. (2006). *Children, adolescents, and media violence: A critical look at the research.* Thousand Oaks, CA: Sage.

KIRSCHENBAUM, H., & JOURDAN, A. (2005). The current status of Carl Rogers and the person-centered approach. *Psychotherapy: Theory, Research, Practice, Training, 42*, 37–51.

KITAYAMA, S., & UCHIDA, Y. (2005). *Interdependent agency: An alternative system for action*. In R.M. Sorrentino, D. Cohen, J.M. Olson, & M.P. Zanna (Eds.), Ontario symposium on personality and social psychology, June 2002, University of Western Ontario, London, Canada; an earlier version of this paper was presented at the aforementioned symposium (pp. 137–164). Mahwah, NJ: Lawrence Erlbaum Associates.

KITO, M. (2005). Self-disclosure in romantic relationships and friendships among American and Japanese college students. *Journal of Social Psychology, 145*, 127–140.

KIVLIGHAN, D.M., MULTON, K.D., & PATTON, M.J. (2000). Insight and symptom reduction in time-limited psychoanalytic counseling. *Journal of Counseling Psychology, 47*, 50–58.

KLEESPIES, P.M. (2004). Life and death decisions: Psychological and ethical considerations in end-of-life care. In P.M. Kleespies (Ed.), *Life and death decisions: Psychological and ethical considerations in end-of-life care.* Washington, D. C.: American Psychological Association.

KLEIBER, D.A., HUTCHINSON, S.I., & WILLIAMS, R. (2002). Leisure as a resource in transcending negative life events: Self-protection, self-restoration, and personal transformation. *Leisure Sciences, 24*, 219–235.

KLEIN, C.T.F., & HELWEG-LARSON, M. (2002). Perceived control and the optimistic bias: A meta-analytic review. *Psychology and Health, 17*, 437–446.

KLOHNEN, E.C. (1996). Conceptual analysis and measurement of the construct of ego-resiliency. *Journal of Personality and Social Psychology, 70*, 1067–1079.

KLONOWICZ, T. (2001). Discontented people: Reactivity and locus of control as determinants of subjective well-being. *European Journal of Personality, 15*, 29–47.

KLUGER, J. (2005). Vitamin sherpa. *Time, 166*, 93–94.

KLUGER, J., BRUNTON, M., & ROBINSON, S. (2005). Motorcycle riders. *Time, 166*, 97.

KNICKMEYER, N., SEXTON, K., & NISHIMURA, N. (2002). The impact of same-sex friendships on the well-being of women: A review of the literature. *Women and Therapy, 25*, 37–59.

KNIGHT, J. (2002). Sexual stereotypes. *Nature, 415*, 254–256.

KNOX, D., & ZUSMAN, M.E. (2001). Marrying a man with "baggage": Implications for second wives. *Journal of Divorce and Remarriage, 35*, 67–79.

KOCH, S.C. (2005). Evaluative affect display toward male and female leaders of task-oriented groups. *Small Group Research, 36*, 678–703.

KOERNER, B.I. (1997, March 31). Life after death? *U. S. News & World Report, 123*, 61–64.

KOGAN, N., & WALLACH, M.A. (1964). *Risk-taking: A study in cognition and personality.* New York: Holt.

KOLATA, G. (2002, November 19). Is frailty inevitable? Some experts say no. *The New York Times*, p. D5.

KOLDEN, G.G., CHISHOLM-STOCKARD, S.M., STRAUMAN, T.J., TIERNEY, S.C., MULLEN, E.A., & SCHNEIDER, K.L. (2006). Universal session-level change processes in an early session of psychotherapy: Path models. *Journal of Counseling and Clinical Psychology*, 74, 327–336.

KOMARRAJU, M., & KARAU, S.J. (2005). The relationship between the big five personality traits and academic motivation. *Personality and Individual Differences, 39*, 557–567.

KORNBLUSH, K. (2003, January–February). The parent trap: Working American parents have twenty-two fewer hours a week to spend with their kids than they did thirty years ago. Here's how to help the new "juggler family." *The Atlantic Monthly*, 111–112.

KORTE, S.M., KOOLHAAS, J.M., WINGFIELD, J.C., & McEWEN, B.S. (2005). The Darwinian concept of stress: Benefits of allostasis and costs of allostatic load and the trade-offs in health and disease. *Neuroscience & Biobehavioral Reviews. Special Issue: Individual differences in behavior and physiology: Causes and consequences, 29*, 3–38.

KRAAIJ, V., PRUYMBOOM, E., & GARNEFSKI, N. (2002). Cognitive coping and depressive symptoms in the elderly: A longitudinal study. *Aging & Mental Health, 6*, 275–281.

KRAUSE, N. (2005). God-mediated control and psychological well-being in late life. *Research on Aging, 27*, 136–164.

KRAUSE, N. (2006). Exploring the stress-buffering effects of church-based and secular social support on self-rated health in late life. *The Journals of Gerontology, 61*, 35–43.

KRAUT, R., PATTERSON, M., LUNDMARK, V., KIESLER, S., MUKOPHADHYAY, T., & SCHERLIS, W. (1998). Internet paradox: A social technology that reduces social involvement and psychological well-being? *American Psychologist, 53*, 1017–1031.

KRESS, V.E.W., ERIKSEN, K.P., RAYLE, A.D., & FORD, S.J.W. (2005). The DSM-IV-TR and culture: Considerations for counselors. *Journal of Counseling & Development, 83*, 97–104.

KRUGER, J., EPLEY, N., PARKER, J., & NG, Z. (2005). Egocentrism over e-mail: Can we communicate as well as we think? *Journal of Personality and Social Psychology, 89*, 925–936.

KÜBLER-ROSS, E. (1975). *Death.* Englewood Cliffs, NJ: Prentice Hall.

KÜBLER-ROSS, E. (1987). *Working it through.* New York: Macmillan.

KÜBLER-ROSS, E. (1993). *On death and dying.* New York: Collier Books.

KÜBLER-ROSS, E. (1997a). *Death: The final stage of growth.* New York: Simon & Schuster.

KÜBLER-ROSS, E. (1997b). *On death and dying.* New York: Simon & Schuster.

KURDEK, L. A. (2005). What do we know about gay and lesbian couples? *Current Directions in Psychological Science, 14*, 251–254.

KUZEMCHAK, S. (2005, November). Feeding a fighting frenzy? *Family Circle*, 21.

LAGERFELD, S. (1999, February). Spending time: Do we have more or less today? *Current*, 10–16.

LAIRD, B. (1991, August 9). How live-in partners fared. *USA Today*, p. 1D.

LAMBERT, A.J., PAYNE, B.K., JACOBY, L.L., SHAFFER, L.M., CHASTEEN, A.L., & KHAN, S. (2003). Stereotypes as dominant responses: On the "social facilitation" of prejudice in anticipated public contexts. *Journal of Personality and Social Psychology, 84*, 277–295.

LANCE, L.M. (1998). Gender differences in heterosexual dating: A content analysis of personal ads. *Journal of Men's Studies, 6*, 297–305.

LANG, F.R., & CARSTENSEN, L.L. (1994). Close emotional relationships in late life: Further support for proactive aging in the social domain. *Psychology and Aging, 9*, 315–324.

LANGLOIS, J.H., KALAKANIS, L., RUBENSTEIN, A.J., LARSON, A., HALLAM, M., & SMOOT, M. (2000). Maxims or myths of beauty: A meta-analytic and theoretical view. *Psychological Bulletin, 126*, 390–423.

LANTZ, A. (2001). Meetings in a distributed group of experts: Comparing face-to-face, chat and collaborative virtual environments. *Behaviour and Information Technology, 20*, 111–117.

LAPINSKI, M.K., & RIMAL, R.N. (2005). An explication of social norms. *Communication Theory, 15*, 127–147.

LASALA, M. (2002). Walls and bridges: How coupled gay men and lesbians manage their intergeneration relationships. *Journal of Marital and Family Therapy, 28*, 327–339.

LASSER, J., THARINGER, D., & CLOTH, A. (2006). Gay, lesbian, and bisexual youth. In G.G. Bear, & K.M. Minke (Eds.), *Children's needs III: Development, prevention, and intervention* (pp. 419–430). Washington, DC: National Association of School Psychologists.

LAUZEN, M.M., & DOZIER, D.M. (2005). Recognition and respect revisited: Portrayals of age and gender in prime-time television. *Mass Communication and Society, 8*, 241–256.

LAVELLE, M. (1999, November 8). Behind the teen birth decline. *U. S. News & World Report*, 22.

LAWRENCE, J.A., GOODNOW, J.J., WOODS, K., & KARANTZAS, G. (2002). Distributions of caregiving tasks among family members: The place of gender and availability. *Journal of Family Psychology, 16*, 493–509.

LAZARUS, A. (1997). *Brief but comprehensive psychotherapy: The multimodal way.* New York: Springer.

LAZARUS, R.S. (1993). From psychological stress to the emotions: A history of changing outlooks. *Annual Review of Psychology, 44*, 1–21.

LEARY, M.R. (1999). Making sense of self-esteem. *Current Directions in Psychological Science, 10*, 32–35.

LEIBLUM, S.R. (2004). Gay marriage: Notes from North America. *Sexual and Relationship Therapy, 19*, 361–362.

LEITENBERG, H., & HENNING, K. (1995). Sexual fantasy. *Psychological Bulletin, 117*, 469–496.

LEMONICK, M.D. (2003, January 20). A frazzled mind, a weakened body. *Time. Special Issue*, 68–69.

LEMONICK, M.D. (2003, January). The power of mood. *Time. Special Issue*, 62–66.

LENDERKING, W.R. (2005). The psychology of quality of life. *Quality of Life Research: An International Journal of Quality of Life Aspects of Treatment, Care & Rehabilitation, 14*, 1439–1441.

LEONARD, F., & LOEB, L. (1992, January). Heading for hardship: The future of older women in America. *USA Today Magazine,* 19–21.

LEPORE, L., & BROWN, R. (2002). The role of awareness: Divergent automatic stereotype activation and implicit judgment correction. *Social Cognition, 20,* 321–351.

LEVENTHAL, E.A. (1994). Gender and aging: Women and their aging. In V.J. Adesso, D.M. Reddy, & R. Fleming (Eds.), *Psychological perspectives on women's health* (pp. 11–35). Washington, DC: Taylor & Francis.

LEVESQUE, M.J., STECIUK, M., & LEDLEY, C. (2002). Self-disclosure patterns among well-acquainted individuals: Disclosers, confidants, and unique relationships. *Social Behavior and Personality, 30,* 579–592.

LEVINE, R.V. (1990, September/October). The pace of life. *American Scientist, 78,* 450–459.

LEVINE, R., SATO, S., HASHIMOTO, T., & VERMA, J. (1995). Love and marriage in eleven cultures. *Journal of Cross-Cultural Psychology, 26,* 554–571.

LEVINSON, D.J., DARROW, C.N., KLEIN, E.B., LEVINSON, M.M., & MCKEE, B. (1978). *The seasons of a man's life.* New York: Knopf.

LEVITON, C.D., & LEVITON, P. (2004). What is guided imagery? The cutting-edge process in mind/body medical procedures. *Annuals of the American Psychotherapy Association, 7,* 22–29.

LEVY, B.R. (2001). Eradication of ageism requires addressing the enemy within. *The Gerontologist, 41,* 578–579.

LEVY, B.R., SLADE, M.D., KUNKEL, S.R., & KASL, S.V. (2002). Longevity increased by positive self-perceptions of aging. *Journal of Personality and Social Psychology, 83,* 261–270.

LI, L.W. (2005). From caregiving to bereavement: Trajectories of depressive symptoms among wife and daughter caregiver. *Journals of Gerontology: Series B: Psychological Sciences and Social Sciences, 60B,* 190–198.

LIBBY, L.K., EIBACH, R.P., & GILOVICH, T. (2005). Here's looking at me: The effect of memory perspective on assessments of personal change. *Journal of Personality and Social Psychology, 88,* 50–62.

LIND, M.R. (2001). An exploration of communication channel usage by gender. *Work Study: A Journal of Productivity Science, 50,* 234–240.

LINDGREN, A. (2002a). Career development strategies for teens, 20-somethings. *Knight Ridder/Tribune News Service,* K4833.

LINDGREN, A. (2002b). Career development strategies for workers in their 60s. *Knight Ridder/Tribune News Service,* K4958.

LINDSTROM, T.C. (1995). Anxiety and adaptation in bereavement. *Anxiety, Stress, and Coping: An International Journal, 8,* 251–261.

LING, K., BEENEN, G., LUDFORD, P., WANG, X., CHANG, K., & LI, X., et al. (2005). Using social psychology to motivate contributions to online communities. *Journal of Computer-Mediated Communication, 10,* (n.p.).

LINLEY, P.A., & JOSEPH, S. (2004). Positive change following trauma and adversity: A review. *Journal of Traumatic Stress, 17,* 11–21.

LIPPKE, S., & ZIEGELMANN, J.P. (2006). Understanding and modeling health behavior: The multi-stage model of health behavior change. *Journal of Health Psychology, 11,* 37–50.

LITTLE, A.C., BURT, D.M., & PERRETT, D.I. (2006). Assortative mating for perceived facial personality traits. *Personality and Individual Differences, 40,* 973–984.

LIU, J.H., CAMPBELL, S.M., & CONDIE, H. (1995). Ethnocentrism in dating preferences for an American sample: The in-group bias in social context. *European Journal of Social Psychology, 25,* 95–115.

LIU, Y., & YUSSEN, S.R. (2005). A comparison of perceived control beliefs between Chinese and American students. *International Journal of Behavioral Development, 29,* 14–23.

LOCKWOOD, P., JORDAN, C.H., & KUNDA, Z. (2002). Motivation by positive or negative role models: Regulatory focus determines who will best inspire us. *Journal of Personality and Social Psychology, 83,* 854–864.

LOFSHULT, D. (2006). Caloric restriction is for the birds. *IDEA Fitness Journal, 3,* 79–80.

LOPES, P.N., BRACKETT, M.A., NEZLEK, J.B., SCHÜTZ, A., SELLIN, I., & SALOVEY, P. (2004). Emotional intelligence and social interaction. *Personality and Social Psychology Bulletin, 30,* 1018–1034.

LUCAS, R.E. (2005). Time does not heal all wounds: A longitudinal study of reaction and adaptation to divorce. *Psychological Science, 16,* 945–950.

LUCAS, T.W., WENDORF, C.A., IMAMOGLU, E.O., SHEN, J., PARKHILL, M.R., & WEISFELD, C.C., et al. (2004). Marital satisfaction in four cultures as a function of homogamy, male dominance and female attractiveness. *Sexualities, Evolution & Gender, 6,* 97–130.

LUCE, M.F. (2005). Decision making as coping. *Health Psychology. Special Issue: Basic and Applied Decision Making in Cancer Control, 24,* S23–S28.

LUM, T.Y., & LIGHTFOOT, E. (2005). The effects of volunteering on the physical and mental health of older people. *Research on Aging, 27,* 31–55.

LUSZCZYNSKA, A., SCHOLZ, U., & SCHWARZER, R. (2005). The general self-efficacy scale: Multicultural validation studies. *Journal of Psychology: Interdisciplinary and Applied, 139,* 439–457.

LYONS, J.B., & SCHNEIDER, T.R. (2005). The influence of emotional intelligence on performance. *Personality and Individual Differences, 39,* 693–703.

LYUBOMIRSKY, S., SHELDON, K.M., & SCHKADE, D. (2005). Pursuing happiness: The architecture of sustainable change. *Review of General Psychology. Special Issue: Positive Psychology, 9,* 111–131.

MACCRAE, C.N., HOOD, B.M., MILNE, A.B., ROWE, A.C., & MASON, M.F. (2002). Are you looking at me? Eye gaze and person perception. *Psychological Science, 13,* 460–464.

MACGEORGE, E.L., SAMTER, W., & GILLIHAN, S.J. (2005). Academic stress, supportive communication, and health. *Communication Education, 54,* 365–372.

MACKAY, K.A., & KUH, G.D. (1994). A comparison of student effort and educational gains of Caucasian and African-American students at predominantly white colleges and universities. *Journal of College Student Development, 35,* 217–223.

MACKIE, D.M., DEVOS, T., & SMITH, E.R. (2000). Intergroup emotions: Explaining offensive action tendencies in an intergroup context. *Journal of Personality and Social Psychology, 79,* 602–616.

MADDI, S.R. (2005). On hardiness and other pathways to resilience. *American Psychologist, 60,* 261–262.

MAHER, B. (2003, January). Patching up the American family. *The World and I, 56–58.*

MAJOR, B., & ECCLESTON, C.P. (2005). Stigma and social exclusion. In D. Abrams, M.A. Hogg, & J.M. Marques (Eds.), *The social psychology of inclusion and exclusion* (pp. 63–87). New York: Psychology Press.

MAJOR, B., KAISER, C.R., & MCCOY, S.K. (2003). It's not my fault: When and why attributions to prejudice protect self-esteem. *Personality and Social Psychology Bulletin, 29,* 772–781.

MALLIKARJUN, P. (2005, February). Understanding seasonal affective disorder. *The Practitioner, 249,* 116–124.

MALMBERG, J., MIILUNPALO, S., PASANEN, M., VUORI, I., & OJA, P. (2005). Characteristics of leisure time physical activity associated with risk of decline in perceived health—A 10-year follow-up of middle-aged and elderly men and women. *Preventive Medicine: An International Journal Devoted to Practice and Theory, 41,* 141–150.

MANDELL, B., & PHERWANI, S. (2003). Relationship between emotional intelligence and transformational leadership style: A gender comparison. *Journal of Business and Psychology, 17,* 387–404.

MANDLER, G. (2001). Apart from genetics: What makes monozygotic twins similar? *Journal of Mind and Behavior, 22,* 147–160.

MANGER, T., EIKELAND, O.J., & ASBJORNSEN, A. (2002). Effects of social-cognitive training on students; locus of control. *School Psychology International, 23,* 342–354.

MANNING, W.D., & SMOCK, P.J. (2002). First comes cohabitation then comes marriage? A research note. *Journal of Family Issues, 23,* 1065–1087.

MANSFIELD, A.K., ADDIS, M.E., & COURTENAY, W. (2005). Measurement of men's help seeking: Development and evaluation of the barriers to help seeking scale. *Psychology of Men & Masculinity, 6,* 95–108.

MARANO, H.E. (1992, January/February). The reinvention of marriage. *Psychology Today, 26,* 48–53.

MARANO, H.E. (2005). What's a shy guy to do? *Psychology Today, 38,* 14.

MARAZZITI, D., Di NASSO, E., MASALA, I., BARONI, S., ABELLI, M., & MENGALI, F., et al. (2003). Normal and obsessional jealousy: A study of a population of young adults. *European Psychiatry, 18,* 106–111.

MARCUS, B. (1999). The efficacy of exercise as an aid for smoking cessation in women: A randomized, controlled study. *Archives of Internal Medicine, 159,* 1229–1234.

MARION, M. (1994). Encouraging the development of responsible anger management in young children. *Early Child Development and Care, 97,* 155–163.

MARKUS, H., & KITAYAMA, S. (1991). Culture and the self: Implications for cognition, emotion, and motivation. *Psychological Review, 98,* 224–253.

MARKUS, H.R., & KITAYAMA, S. (2003). Culture, self, and the reality of the social. *Psychological Inquiry, 14,* 277–283.

MARQUES, J., ABRAMS, D., & SERODIO, R.G. (2001). Being better by being right: Subjective group dynamics and derogation of in-group deviants when generic norms are undermined. *Journal of Personality and Social Psychology, 81,* 436–477.

MARSH, A.A., ELFENBEIN, H.A., & AMBADY, N. (2003). Nonverbal "accents": Cultural differences in facial expressions of emotion. *Psychological Science, 14,* 373–376.

MARTIN, M. (1999). *Work and family: Today's juggling act.* http://www.uwyo.edu/CES/County_Info/Teton/News?feb99.htm.

MARTIN, R.A. (2001). Humor, laughter, and physical health: Methodological issues and research. *Psychological Bulletin, 127,* 504–519.

MARTSCH, M.D. (2005). A comparison of two group interventions for adolescent aggression: High process versus low process. *Research on Social Work Practice, 15,* 8–18.

MARUFF, P., & DARBY, D. (2006). *Age-related memory impairment.* Washington, DC: American Psychological Association.

MARZILLIER, S.L., & DAVEY, G.C.L. (2004). The emotional profiling of disgust-eliciting stimuli: Evidence for primary and complex disgusts. *Cognition & Emotion, 18,* 313–336.

MASLACH, C., SCHAUFELI, W.B., & LEITER, M.P. (2001). Job burnout. *Annual Review of Psychology, 52,* 397–422.

MASLOW, A.H. (1968). *Toward a psychology of being* (2nd ed.). New York: Van Nostrand Reinhold.

MASLOW, A.H. (1970). *Motivation and personality* (2nd ed.). New York: Harper & Row.

MASLOW, A.H. (1971). *The farther reaches of human nature.* New York: Viking.

MASON, J. (2003) Enter the mesh: How small tech and pervasive computing will weave a new world. *Smalltimes.* http://www.smalltimes.com/document_display.cfm? document_id+4391.

MASTERS, W., & JOHNSON, V. (1966). *Human sexual response.* Boston: Little, Brown.

MASTERS, W., & JOHNSON, V. (1979). *Homosexuality in perspective.* Boston: Little, Brown.

MASTERS, W.H., JOHNSON, V.E., & KOLODNY, R.C. (1988a). *Crisis: Heterosexual behavior in the age of AIDS.* New York: Grove Press.

MASTERS, W.H., JOHNSON, V.E., & KOLODNY, R.C. (1988b). *Human sexuality* (3rd ed.). Boston: Little, Brown.

MASTERS, W.H., JOHNSON, V.E., & KOLODNY, R.C. (1995). *Human sexuality.* New York: HarperCollins.

MATHER, M., & CARSTENSEN, L.L. (2005). Aging and motivated cognition: The positivity effect in attention and memory. *Trends in Cognitive Sciences, 9,* 496–502.

MATJASKO, J.L., & FELDMAN, A.F. (2006). Bringing work home: The emotional experiences of mothers and fathers. *Journal of Family Psychology, 20,* 47–55.

MATLIN, M. (1995). *Psychology.* Orlando, FL: Harcourt Brace.

MATLIN, M.W. (1996). *The psychology of women.* Fort Worth, TX: Harcourt Brace.

MATLIN, M.W. (1999). *Psychology.* Fort Worth, TX: Harcourt Brace.

MATOUSEK, M. (2000, September/October). The last taboo. *Modern Maturity,* 48–59.

MATSUMOTO, D. (1992). More evidence for the universality of a contempt expression. *Motivation and Emotion, 16,* 363–368.

MATSUMOTO, D. (1993). Ethnic differences in affect intensity, emotion judgments, display rule attitudes, and self-reported emotional expression in an American sample. *Motivation and Emotion, 17,* 107–123.

MATSUMOTO, D. (1996). *Culture and psychology.* Pacific Grove, CA: Brooks/Cole.

MATSUMOTO, D. (2000). *Culture and psychology.* Pacific Grove, CA: Brooks/Cole.

MATSUMOTO, D. (2002). Methodological requirements to test a possible ingroup advantage in judging emotions across cultures: Comments on Elfenbein and Ambady and evidence. *Psychological Bulletin, 128,* 236–342.

MATSUMOTO, D. (2003). The discrepancy between consensual-level culture and individual-level culture. *Culture & Psychology, 9,* 89–95.

MATSUMOTO, D. (2004). Paul Ekman and the legacy of universals. *Journal of Research in Personality, 38,* 45–51.

MATTHEWS, K.A., RAIKKONEN, K., SUTTON-TYRRELL, K., & KULLER, L.H. (2004). Optimistic attitudes protect against progression of carotid atherosclerosis in healthy middle-aged women. *Psychosomatic Medicine, 66,* 640–644.

MATUD, P.M. (2004). Gender differences in stress and coping styles. *Personality and Individual Differences, 37,* 1401–1415.

MAU, W.C., & KOPISCHKE, A. (2001). Job search methods, job search outcomes, and job satisfaction of college graduates: A comparison of race and sex. *Journal of Employment Counseling, 38,* 141–149.

MAY, R. (1977, April). Freedom, determinism, and the future. *Psychology Today,* 11.

Mayo Clinic. (2002, September 4). *Women and depression: Understanding the gender gap.* http://www.mayoclinic.com.

Mayo Clinic. (2005). Obesity. Retrieved August 7, 2006, from http://www.mayoclinic.com/health/obesity/d500314.

MCCABE, M.P. (2005). Boys want sex, girls want commitment: Does this trade-off still exist? *Sexual and Relationship Therapy, 20,* 139–141.

MCCONATHA, J.T., LIGHTNER, E., & DEANER, S.L. (1994). Culture, age, and gender as variables in expression of emotions. *Journal of Social Behavior and Personality, 9,* 481–488.

MCCONNELL, A.R., RENAUD, J.M., DEAN, K.K., GREEN, S.P., LAMOREAUX, M.J., & HALL, C.E., et al. (2005). Whose self is it anyway? Self-aspect control moderates the relation between self-complexity and well-being. *Journal of Experimental Social Psychology, 41,* 1–18.

MCCRAE, R.R., & COSTA, P.T. (1994). The stability of personality: Observations and evaluations. *Current Directions in Psychological Science, 5,* 173–175.

MCCRAE, R.R., & COSTA, P.T.J. (2003). *Personality in adulthood: A five-factor theory perspective* (2nd ed.). New York: Guilford Press

MCDONALD-MISZCZAK, L., MAKI, S.A., & GOULD, O.N. (2000). Self-reported medication adherence and health status in late adulthood: The role of beliefs. *Experimental Aging Research, 26,* 189–207.

MCDONOUGH, E.M., & MUNZ, D.C. (1994). General well-being and perceived adult friendship behaviors. *Journal of Social Behavior and Personality, 9,* 743–752.

MCEWEN, B.S. (2005). Stressed or stressed out: What is the difference? *Journal of Psychiatry & Neuroscience, 30,* 315–318.

MCFARLAND, B.H. (2005). Introduction: Disaster dangers and decisions. *Community Mental Health Journal, 41,* 631–632.

MCGILLIS, D. (1997). *Community mediation programs: Developments and challenges.* Washington, DC: U.S. Department of Justice.

MCGREW, J.F., BILOTTA, J.G., & DEENEY, J.M. (1999). Software team formation and decay: Extending the standard model for small groups. *Small Group Research, 30,* 209–234.

MCGUE, M. (1999). The behavioral genetics of alcoholism. *Current Directions in Psychological Science, 8,* 109–115.

MCGUIRE, K.M.B., GREENBERG, M.A., & GEVIRTZ, R. (2005). Autonomic effects of expressive writing in individuals with elevated blood pressure. *Journal of Health Psychology. Special Issue: Psychological Interventions in Chronic Illness, 10,* 197–209.

MCNALLY, R.J., BRYANT, R.A., & EHLERS, A. (2003). Does early psychological intervention promote recovery from posttraumatic stress? *Psychological Science in the Public Interest, 4,* 45–79.

MEANA, M., & NUNNINK, S.E. (2006). GENDER differences in the content of cognitive distraction during sex. *Journal of Sex Research. Special Issue: Scientific Abstracts, World Congress of Sexology 2005, 43,* 59–67.

MEESTERS, C., & MURIS, P. (2002). Attachment style and self-reported aggression. *Psychological Reports, 90,* 231–235.

MEHRA, B., MERKEL, C., & BISHOP, A.P. (2004). The internet for empowerment of minority and marginalized users. *New Media & Society, 6,* 781–802.

MEIN, G., MARTIKAINEN, P., HEMINGWAY, H., STANSFELD, S., & MARMOT, M. (2003). Is retirement good or bad for mental and physical health functioning? Whitehall II longitudinal study of civil servants. *Journal of Epidemiology & Community Health, 57,* 46–49.

MENEC, V.H. (2003). The relation between everyday activities and successful aging: A 6-year longitudinal study. *The Journals of Gerontology, Series B, Psychological Sciences and Social Sciences, 58,* 74–83.

Mental Health Weekly. (2002). Caregivers at increased risk for depression, anxiety, 12, 7.

Mentalhelp.net (2000a, August). *Anxiety.* http://anxiety/anxietytoc.htm.

Mentalhelp.net (2000b, August). *Personality disorders.* http://personality disorders.mentalhelp.net.

Mentalhelp.net (2005). *Depression and women.* http://mentalhelp.net/poc/view_doc.php?type=doc&id=7983&cn=5. Accessed April 3, 2007.

MESSMAN, S.J., CANARY, D.J., & HAUSE, K.S. (2000). Motives to remain platonic, equity, and the use of maintenance strategies in opposite-sex friendships. *Journal of Social and Personal Relationships, 17,* 67–94.

MEZULIS, A.H., ABRAMSON, L.Y., HYDE, J.S., & HANKIN, B.L. (2004). Is there a universal positivity bias in attributions? A meta-analytic review of individual, developmental, and cultural differences in the self-serving attributional bias. *Psychological Bulletin, 130,* 711–747.

MICHAEL, S., & SNYDER, C.R. (2005). Getting unstuck: The roles of hope, finding meaning, and rumination in adjustment to bereavement among college students. (2005), *Death Studies, 29,* 435–458.

MICHALOS, A.C. (1991). *Global report on student well-being (Vol. 1): Life satisfaction and happiness.* New York: Springer-Verlag.

MIKULINCER, M., FLORIAN, V., & WELLER, A. (1993). Attachment styles, coping strategies, and posttraumatic psychological distress: The impact of the Gulf War in Israel. *Journal of Personality and Social Psychology, 64,* 817–826.

MILGRAM, S. (1974). Obedience to authority. *Human Relations, 18,* 57–76.

MILLER, J.G. (1999). Cultural psychology: Implications for basic psychological theory. *Psychological Science, 10,* 85–91.

MISRA, R., McKEAN, M., WEST, S., & RUSSO, T. (2000). Academic stress of college students: Comparison of student and faculty perceptions. *College Student Journal, 34,* 236–245.

MISSILDINE, W., PARSONS, J.T., & KNIGHT, K. (2006). Split ends: Masculinity, sexuality and emotional intimacy among HIV-positive heterosexual men. *Men and Masculinities, 8,* 309–320.

MITCHELL, T. (2003, September 5–7). After 9/11. *USA Weekend,* 4.

MSH, P., & ROEHLING, P. (2005). *The career mystique: Cracks in the American dream.* Lanham, MD: Rowman & Littlefield.

MOHAN, J. (2006). Cardiac psychology. *Journal of the Indian Academy of Applied Psychology. Special Issue: Commemoration of the 10th International and 41st National Conference of IAAP, 32,* 214–220.

MOHR, R.D., & ZOGHI, C. (2006). Is job enrichment really enriching? Retrieved August 09, 2006, from bls.gov/ore/pdf/ec060010.pdf.

MONK, T.H., HOUCK, P.R. & SHEAR, M.K. (2006). The daily life of complicated grief patients—What gets missed, what gets added? *Death Studies, 30,* 77–85.

MONTMARQUETTE, C. CANNINGS, K., & MAHSEREDJIAN, S. (2002). How do young people choose college? *Economics of Education Review, 21,* 543–557.

MOODY, E. J. (2001). Internet use and its relationship to loneliness. *CyberPsychology and Behavior, 4,* 393–401.

MOORE, N.B., & DAVIDSON, J.K. (2000). Communicating with new sex partners: College women and questions that make a difference. *Journal of Sex and Marital Therapy, 26,* 215–230.

MOORHEAD, G., FERENCE, R., & NECK, C.P. (1991). Group decision fiascoes continue. Space Shuttle Challenger and a revised groupthink framework. *Human Relations, 44,* 539–550.

MORAHAN-MARTIN, J.M. (2004). How internet users find, evaluate, and use online health information: A cross-cultural review. *CyberPsychology & Behavior, 7,* 497–510.

MOREAU, D. (2002, November). Payday: Sooner or later? *AARP Bulletin,* 26.

MORELAND, R.L., & BEACH, S.R. (1992). Exposure effects in the classroom: The development of affinity among students. *Journal of Experimental Social Psychology, 28,* 255–276.

MORREAL, L.J. (1991). Humor and work. *International Journal of Humor Research, 4,* 359–373.

MORRIS, C.G. (1986). *Psychology: An introduction* (6th ed). Englewood Cliffs, NJ: Prentice Hall.

MORRIS, J.A., BROTHERIDGE, C.M., & URBANSKI, J.C. (2005). Bringing humility to leadership: Antecedents and consequences of leader humility. *Human Relations, 58,* 1323–1350.

MORRIS, J.F., WALDO, C.R., & ROTHBLUM, E.D. (2001). A model of predictors and outcomes of outness among lesbian and bisexual women. *American Journal of Orthopsychiatry, 71,* 61–71.

MORRIS, M., NADLER, J., KURTZBERG, T., & THOMPSON, L. (2002). Schmooze or lose: Social friction and lubrication in e-mail negotiations. *Groups Dynamics. Special Issue: Group and Internet, 6,* 89–100.

MORRY, M.M. (2005). Allocentrism and friendship satisfaction: The mediating roles of disclosure and closeness. *Canadian Journal of Behavioural Science, 37,* 211–222.

MORRY, M.M., & GAINES, S.O. (2005). Relationship satisfaction as a predictor of similarity ratings: A test of the attraction-similarity hypothesis. *Journal of Social and Personal Relationships, 22,* 561–584.

MORSE, J. (2002, October 7). An Rx for teen sex. *Time,* 63–65.

MOXEY, A., O'CONNELL, D., McGETTIGAN, P., & HENRY, D. (2003). Describing treatment effects to patients: How they are expressed makes a difference. *Journal of General Internal Medicine, 18,* 948–959.

MROCZEK, D.K., & SPIRO, A., III. (2005). Change in life satisfaction during adulthood: Findings from the veterans affairs normative aging study. *Journal of Personality and Social Psychology, 88,* 189–202.

MULAK, A., ERLANDSON, K.T., FARRER, J.W., HALLETT, J.S., MOLLOY, J.L., & PRESCOTT, M.E. (1998). "Un-huh. What's that all about?" Differing interpretations of conversational backchannels and questions as sources of miscommunication across gender boundaries. *Communication Research. Special Issue: (Mis)communicating Across Boundaries, 25,* 641–688.

MURPHY, S.M., VALLACHER, R.R., SHACKELFORD, T.K., BJORKLUND, D.F., & YUNGER, J.L. (2006). Relationship experience as a predictor of romantic jealousy. *Personality and Individual Differences. Special Issue: Chat-up Lines as Male Sexual Displays, 40,* 761–769.

MURRAY, S.L. (2005). Regulating the risks of closeness: A relationship-specific sense of felt security. *Current Directions in Psychological Science, 14,* 74–78.

MUSGRAVE, C. (1997). The near-death experience: A study of spiritual transformation. *Journal of Near Death Studies, 15,* 187–201.

MUUSS, R.E. (1986, Summer). Adolescent eating disorders: Bulimia. *Adolescence, 21,* 257–267.

MYERS, D.G. (1993). *The pursuit of happiness.* New York: Avon Books.

MYERS, D.G. (1998). *Social psychology.* New York: McGraw-Hill.

MYERS, D.G., & ARENSON, S.J. (1972). Enhancement of dominant risk tendencies in group discussion. *Psychological Reports, 30,* 615–623.

MYERS, D.G., & DIENER, E. (1995). Who is happy? *Psychological Science, 6,* 10–19.

NAH, K. (1993). Perceived problems and service delivery for Korean immigrants. *Social Work, 38,* 289–296.

NAIL, P.R., MISAK, J.E., & DAVIS, R.M. (2004). Self-affirmation versus self-consistency: A comparison of two competing self-theories of dissonance phenomena. *Personality and Individual Differences, 36,* 1893–1905.

NAIR, E. (2001). The emperor has no clothes, or do you see individualist-collectivist societies? *International Psychology Reporter,* 18–20.

NANSEL, T.R., OVERPECK, M., PILLA, R.S., RUAN, W.J., SIMONS-MORTON, B., & SCHEIDT, P. (2001). Bullying behaviors among US youths: Prevalence and association with psychosocial adjustment. *Journal of the American Medical Association, 285,* 2094–2100.

NAPLES, N.A. (2004). Queer parenting in the new millennium. *Gender & Society, 18,* 679–684.

NASS, C., & MOON, Y. (2000). Machines and mindlessness: Social responses to computers. *Journal of Social Issues, 56,* 81–103.

National Center for Chronic Disease Prevention and Health Promotion. (1996). *You can quit smoking consumer guide.* http://www.cdc.gov/tobacco/quit/canquit.htm.

National Center for Chronic Disease Prevention and Health Promotion. (1999). *Physical activity and health: A report of the Surgeon General.* http://www.cdc.gov/nccdphp/sgr/summary.htm.

National Center for Chronic Disease Prevention and Health Promotion. (2000). *Statistics related to overweight and obesity.* http://www.niddk.nih.gov/health/nutrit/pubs/statobes.htm.

National Center for Chronic Disease Prevention and Health Promotion. (2005). *Adult cigarette smoking in the U.S.: Current estimates.* Washington, DC: Centers for Disease Control.

National Center for Health Statistics. (2002). *Environmental health.* http://www.cdc.gov/nchs/fastats/environ.htm.

National Center for Health Statistics. (2005). National health and nutrition examination survey. Retrieved August 7, 2006, from http://www.cdc.gov/nchs/nhanes.htm.

National Center for Missing and Exploited Children. (2006). Child pornography—What is it? Retrieved May 11, 2006, from http://www.cybertipline.com/missingkids/servlet/pageservlet.

National Coalition Against Domestic Violence. (2005). *The problem.* NCADV.org.learn/the problem-100.html.

National Family Caregivers Association. (2005). *Caregiving statistics.* http://www.Thefamilycaregiver.org (accessed on August 12, 2006).

National Institute of Diabetes and Digestive and Kidney Diseases. (2000). Statistics related to overweight and obesity. http://www.niddk.nih.gov/health/nutritlpubs/statobes.htm.

National Institute of Health. (2000). *Obesity: The practical guide: Identification, evaluation, and treatment of overweight and obesity in adults.* Washington, DC: National Institutes of Health.

National Institute of Mental Health. (2001, January). *When someone has schizophrenia.* http://www.nimh.nih.gov/publicat/schizsoms.cfm.

National Institute of Mental Health. (2001a). *Facts about post-traumatic stress disorder.* Washington, DC: Author.

National Institute of Mental Health. (2001b). *A neuroendocrine model explains gender differences in behavioral responses to stress.* Washington, DC: 1–2.

National Institute of Mental Health. (2002, September). *Depression.* http://www.nimh.nih.gov/publicat/depression.cfm.

National Institute of Mental Health. (2003). *Suicide facts.* http://www.nimh.nih.gov/research/suifact.htm.

National Institute of Mental Health. (2006a). Depression: Diagnostic evaluation and treatment. Retrieved July 06, 2006, from http://www.nimh.nih.gov/publicat.depression.cfm.

National Institute of Mental Health. (2006b). Eating disorders: Facts about eating disorders and the search for solutions. Retrieved July 05, 2006, from http://www.nimh.nih.gov/publicat/eatingdisorders.cfm.

National Institute of Mental Health. (2006c). Medications: Antianxiety medications. Retrieved July 06, 2006, from http://www.nimh.nih.gov/publicat/medicate.cfm.

National Institute of Mental Health. (2006d). Mental disorders in America. Retrieved July 2, 2006, from http://www.nimh.nih.gov/publicat/numbers.cfm.

National Institute of Mental Health. (2006e). Reliving trauma: Post-traumatic stress disorder. Retrieved July 05, 2006, from http://www.nimh.nih.gov/publicat/reliving.cfm.

National Institute of Mental Health. (2006f). When someone has schizophrenia. Retrieved July 05, 2006, from http://www.nimh.nih.gov/publicat/schizosoms.cfm.

National Institute of Mental Health. (2006g). Women hold up half the sky: Women and mental health research. Retrieved July 02, 2006, from http://www.nimh.nih.gov/publicat/womensoms.cfm.

National Institute of Occupational Safety and Health. (1999). *Stress . . . at work.* Washington, DC: Author.

National Mental Health Information Center. (2003). *The myth of the bad parent.* http://www.mentalhealth.org/publications/allpubs/Ca-0035/default.asp.

National Science Foundation. (2003). *Science and technology: Public attitudes and public understanding.* http://www.nsf.gov/sbe/srs/seind02/c7/c7h.htm.

National Victim Center. (1992, April 23). *Rape in America.* Fort Worth, TX: Author.

NECK, C.P., & MOORHEAD, G. (1995). Groupthink remodeled: The importance of leadership, time pressure, and methodological decision-making procedures. *Human Relations, 48,* 537–557.

NEFF, K.D. (2003). Self-compassion: An alternative conceptualization of a healthy attitude toward oneself. *Self and Identity, 2,* 85–101.

NEIMARK, J. (1999, July/August). Night life. *Psychology Today,* 30–33, 66.

NELSON, C.A. (2006). Of eggshells and thin-skulls: A consideration of racism-related mental illness impacting Black women. *International Journal of Law and Psychiatry, 29,* 112–136.

NEMEROFF, C.B., BREMNER, J.D., FOA, E.B., MAYBERG, H.S., NORTH, C.S., & STEIN, M.B. (2006). Posttraumatic stress disorder: A state-of-the-science review. *Journal of Psychiatric Research, 40,* 1–21.

NETO, F. (1992). Loneliness among Portuguese adolescents. *Social Behavior and Personality, 20,* 15–22.

NEUGARTEN, G.L. (1986). The aging society. In A. Pifer & L. Bronte (Eds.), *Our aging society.* New York: W.W. Norton.

The New York Times. (2001, April 30). Those crazy rockin' teenagers. *New York Times Upfront,* pp. 22–23.

NEWMAN, M.G. (2004). Technology in psychotherapy: An introduction. *Journal of Clinical Psychology, 60,* 141–145.

NEWSON, J.T. (1999). Another side to caregiving: Negative reactions to being helped. *Current Directions in Psychological Science, 8,* 183–186.

NICHOLSON, T. (2003, March). Boomers discover age bias. *AARP Bulletin,* 10.

NIETZEL, M.T., BERNSTEIN, D.A., & MILICH, R. (1991). *Introduction to clinical psychology.* Englewood Cliffs, NJ: Prentice Hall.

Nine tips for patients. Few of us like being patients, but there are ways to take charge of the situation and make the best of it. (2004). *Harvard Health Letter from Harvard Medical School, 29,* 1–2.

NISHINA, A., JUVONEN, J., & WITKOW, M.R. (2005). Sticks and stones may break my bones, but names will make me feel sick: The psychosocial, somatic, and scholastic consequences of peer harassment. *Journal of Clinical Child and Adolescent Psychology, 34,* 37–48.

NOLEN-HOEKSEMA, N., PARKER, L.E., & LARSON, J. (1994). Ruminative coping with depressed mood following loss. *Journal of Personality and Social Psychology, 67,* 92–104.

NORUM, D. (2000). The family has the solution. *Journal of Systemic Therapies, 19,* 3–15.

Not getting over it: Post-traumatic stress disorder. For some people, merely recalling a traumatic event feels just like going through it all over again. Psychotherapy and some other strategies can help. (2005). *Harvard Women's Health Watch, 12,* 4–6.

NOVELLI, W.D. (January, 2006). William Novelli on valuing older workers. *AARP Bulletin,* 31.

O'CONNOR, D.B., & SHIMIZU, M. (2002). Sense of personal control, stress and coping style: A cross-cultural study. *Stress and Health, 18,* 173–183.

O'DONOHUE, W., BUCHANAN, J.A., & FISHER, J.E. (2000). Characteristics of empirically supported treatments. *Journal of Psychotherapy Practice and Research, 9,* 69–74.

OETZEL, J.G., & TING-TOOMEY, S. (2003). Face concerns in interpersonal conflict: A cross-cultural empirical test of the face negotiation theory. *Communication Research, 30,* 599–624.

Office of the Surgeon General (1999). *The Surgeon General's call to action to prevent suicide.* Washington, DC: Office of the Surgeon General.

OGGINS, J., VEROFF, J., & LEBER, D. (1993). Perceptions of marital interaction among Black and White newlyweds. *Journal of Personality and Social Psychology, 56,* 219–227.

OHANNESSIAN, C.M., MCCAULEY, C., LERNER, R.M., LERNER, J.V., & VON EYE, A. (1994). A longitudinal study of perceived family adjustment and emotional adjustment in early adolescence. *Journal of Early Adolescence, 14,* 371–390.

OHTAKI, S., OHTAKI, T., & FETTERS, M.D. (2003). Doctor-patient communication: A comparison of the USA and Japan. *Family Practice, 20,* 276–282.

OISHI, S., HAHN, J., SCHIMMACK, U., RADHAKRISHAN, P., DZOKOTO, V., & AHADI, S. (2005). The measurement of values across cultures: A pairwise comparison approach. *Journal of Research in Personality, 39,* 299–305.

OLAH, A. (1995). Coping strategies among adolescents: A cross-cultural study. *Journal of Adolescence. Special Issue: Adolescent Research: A European Perspective, 18,* 491–512.

OLFSON, M., MARCUS, S.C., DRUSS, B., & PINCUS, H.A. (2002). National trends in the use of outpatient psychotherapy. *The American Journal of Psychiatry, 159,* 1914–1920.

OLSON, M.B., KRANTZ, D.S., KELSEY, S.F., PEPINE, C.J., SOPKO, G., & HANDBERG, E., et al. (2005). Hostility scores are associated with increased risk of cardiovascular events in women undergoing coronary angiography: A report from the NHLBI-sponsored WISE study. *Psychosomatic Medicine, 67,* 546–552.

ONG, A.D., BERGEMAN, C.S., & BISCONTI, T.L. (2005). Unique effects of daily perceived control on anxiety symptomatology during conjugal bereavement. *Personality and Individual Differences, 38,* 1057–1067.

Onguard.gov (2006). Social networking sites: Safety tips for tween and teens. Retrieved August 09, 2006, from http://onguardonline.gov/socialnetworking_youth.html.

ORANGE, L.M., & BRODWIN, M.G. (2005). Childhood sexual abuse: What rehabilitation counselors need to know. *The Journal of Rehabilitation, 71,* 5–11.

OSBORNE, L. (2001, May 6). Regional disturbances. *The New York Times Magazine,* 6.

OSGOOD, C.E. (1962). *An alternative to war or surrender.* Urbana, IL: University of Illinois Press.

OSTBYTE, T., & TAYLOR, D.H., Jr. (2004). The effect of smoking on years of healthy life lost among middle-aged and older Americans. *Health Services Research, 39,* 531–551.

OSTERBERG, L., & BLASCHKE, T. (2005). Drug therapy: Adherence to medication. *New England Journal of Medicine, 353,* 487–497.

O'SULLIVAN, M. (2003). The fundamental attribution error in detecting deception: The boy-who-cried-wolf effect. *Personality and Social Psychology Bulletin, 29,* 1316–1327.

O'SULLIVAN, M. (2005). Emotional intelligence and deception detection: Why most people can't "read" others, but a few can. In R.E. Riggio & R.S. Feldman (Eds.), *Applications of nonverbal communication.* Mahwah, NJ: Lawrence Erlbaum.

OSWALD, D.L., & CLARK, E.M. (2003). Best friends forever?: High school best friendships and the transition to college. *Personal Relationships, 10,* 187–196.

OSWALD, R.F. (2000). Family friendship relationships after young women come out as bisexual or lesbian. *Journal of Homosexuality, 38,* 65–83.

OSWALD, R.F. (2002). Inclusion and belonging in the family rituals of gay and lesbian people. *Journal of Family Psychology, 16,* 428–436.

OWEN, S.S. (2004). Corporal punishment experiences and attitudes in a sample of college students. *Psychological Reports, 94,* 348–350.

OXLEY, N.L., DZINDOLET, M.R., & MILLER, J.L. (2002). Sex differences in communication with close friends: Testing Tannen's claims. *Psychological Reports, 91,* 537–544.

OYSERMAN, D., COON, H.M., & KEMMELMEIER, M. (2002). Rethinking individualism and collectivism: Evaluation of theoretical assumptions and meta-analyses. *Psychological Bulletin, 128,* 3–72.

OZER, E.J., & WEISS, D.S. (2004). Who develops posttraumatic stress disorder? *Current Directions in Psychological Science, 13,* 169–172.

ÖZKAN, S., ALATAS, E.S., & ZENCIR, M. (2005). Women's quality of life in the premenopausal and postmenopausal periods. *Quality of Life Research: An International Journal of Quality of Life Aspects of Treatment, Care & Rehabilitation, 14,* 1795–1801.

PACE, B. (2001). Bullying. *Journal of the American Medical Association, 285,* 2156.

PACEY, S. (2005). Step change: The interplay of sexual and parenting problems when couples form stepfamilies. *Sexual and Relationship Therapy, 20,* 359–369.

PANAYIOTOU, G. (2005). Chronic self-consciousness and its effects on cognitive performance, physiology, and self-reported anxiety. *Representative Research in Social Psychology, 28,* 21–34.

PAREKH, R., & BERESIN, E.V. (2001). Looking for love? Take a cross-cultural walk through the personals. *Academic Psychiatry, 25,* 223–233.

PARK, H.S., LEE, H.E., & SONG, J.A. (2005). "I am sorry to send you SPAM": Cross-cultural differences in use of apologies in email advertising in Korea and the U.S. *Human Communication Research, 31,* 365–398.

PARK, L.E., CROCKER, J., & MICKELSON, K.D. (2004). Attachment styles and contingencies of self-worth. *Personality and Social Psychology Bulletin, 30,* 1243–1254.

PARK, S. (2005). The influence of presumed media influence on women's desire to be thin. *Communication Research, 32,* 594–614.

PARKER, S., & DEVRIES, B. (1993). Patterns of friendship for women and men in same and cross-sex relationships. *Journal of Social and Personal Relationships, 10,* 617–626.

PARROTT, W.G., & SMITH, R.H. (1993). Distinguishing the experiences of envy and jealousy. *Journal of Personality and Social Psychology, 64,* 906–920.

Patient, protect thyself? Studies show that you can, as a patient, spot and possibly prevent a medical error from happening to you. (2006). *Harvard Health Letter from Harvard Medical School, 31,* 6.

PAUL, A.M. (1998, May/June). Where bias begins: The truth about stereotypes. *Psychology Today,* 52–56.

PAYNE, D. (2004). Frequent spanking of toddlers may lead to behavioural problems. *Medical Post, 40,* 41.

PECCHIONI, L.L., & CROGHAN, J.M. (2002). Young adults' stereotypes of older adults with their grandparents as the targets. *Journal of Communication, 52,* 715–731.

PEDRO-CARROLL, J.L. (2005). Fostering resilience in the aftermath of divorce: The role of evidence-based programs for children. *Family Court Review. Special Issue on Prevention: Research, Policy, and Evidence-Based Practice, 43,* 52–64.

PELL, M.D. (2005). Nonverbal emotion priming: Evidence from the 'facial affect decision task.' *Journal of Nonverbal Behavior, 29,* 45–73.

PEPLAU, L.A. (2003). Human sexuality: How do men and women differ? *Current Directions in Psychological Science, 12,* 37–40.

PEPPER, J. (2002). Wired and retired: Assisted living: Residents go online. *Nursing Homes, 51,* 60–63.

PERKINS, A.M., & CORR, P.J. (2005). Can worriers be winners? The association between worrying and job performance. *Personality and Individual Differences, 38,* 25–31.

PERLMAN, D. (1991). *Age difference in loneliness: A meta-analysis.* Vancouver: University of British Columbia. (ERIC Document Reproduction Service No. ED 326745.)

PERRIG, W., & GROB, A. (Eds.). (2000). *Control of human behavior, mental processes, and consciousness: Essays in honor of the 60th birthday of August Flammer.* Mahwah, NJ: Lawrence Erlbaum.

PERRY, A. (2005, November 7). The listeners. *Time, 166,* 97.

PERRY, P. (1997, July/August). Personality disorders: Coping with the borderline. *The Saturday Evening Post,* 44–52.

PERRY, P. (2005). New strategy for diagnosing bipolar disorder: Can diagnostic brain scans help identify patients with bipolar disorder? Interview with Dr. John D. Port. *Saturday Evening Post, 277,* 64–68.

PETER, R., HAMMARSTRÖM, A., HALLQVIST, J., SIEGRIST, J., & THEORELL, T. (2006). Does occupational gender segregation influence the association of effort-reward imbalance with myocardial infarction in the SHEEP study? *International Journal of Behavioral Medicine, 13,* 34–43.

PETERSON, C., & SELIGMAN, M.E.P. (2003). Character strength before and after September 11. *Psychological Science, 14,* 381–384.

PETERSON, C., & VAIDYA, R.S. (2001). Explanatory style, expectations, and depressive symptoms. *Personality and Individual Differences, 31,* 1217–1223.

PETERSON, K. (2002, July 8). Cohabiting can make marriage an iffy proposition. *USA Today,* pp. D1–D2.

PETERSON, K.S. (1999a, September 29). A hostile start makes the argument for divorce. *USA Today,* pp. D1.

PETERSON, K.S. (1999b, November 23). Personal ads get back to nature. *USA Today,* pp. 1D.

PFAFFENBERGER, A.H. (2005). Optimal adult development: An inquiry into the dynamics of growth. *Journal of Humanistic Psychology, 45,* 279–301.

PHILLIPS, J.A., & SWEENEY, M.M. (2005). Premarital cohabitation and marital disruption among White, Black, and Mexican American women. *Journal of Marriage and Family, 67,* 296–314.

PHILLIPS, L. (2005). Both specific functions and general ability can be useful: But it depends on what type of research question you ask. *Cortex, 41,* 236–237.

PHUA, V.C. (2002). Sex and sexuality in men's personal advertisements. *Men and Masculinities, 5,* 178–191.

PHUA, V.C., HOPPER, J., & VAZQUEZ, O. (2002). Men's concerns with sex and health in personal advertisements. *Culture, Health and Sexuality, 4,* 355–363.

PIENTA, A.M., & HAYWARD, M.D. (2002). Who expects to continue working after age 62? The retirement plans of couples. *Journal of Gerontology: Series B: Psychological Sciences and Social Sciences, 57,* 199–208.

PIERSON, M.R., & GLAESER, B.C. (2002). Self-concept: Differences among adolescents by gender. *Academic Exchange Quarterly, 6,* 152–157.

PINEL, E.C., LONG, A.E., LANDAU, M.J., ALEXANDER, K., & PYSZCZYNSKI, T. (2006). Seeing I to I: A pathway to interpersonal connectedness. *Journal of Personality and Social Psychology, 90,* 243–257.

PINKER, S. (2002, October). The blank slate. *Discover,* 34–40.

PINQUART, M., & SÖRENSEN, S. (2005). Caregiving distress and psychological health of caregivers. In K.V. Oxington, (Ed.), *Psychology of stress.* Hauppauge, NY: Nova Biomedical.

PIPHER, M. (2002). Society fears the aging process. In L. Egendorl (Ed.), *Opposing viewpoints: An aging population.* San Diego, CA: Greenhaven Press.

PLATOW, M.J., BYRNE, L., & RYAN, M.K. (2005). Experimentally manipulated high in-group status can buffer personal self-esteem against discrimination. *European Journal of Social Psychology. Special Issue: In Honour of Ken Dion, 35,* 599–608.

PLOMIN, R., & RENDE, R. (1991). Human behavioral genetics. *Annual Review of Psychology, 42,* 161–190.

PLONK, W.M., & ARNOLD, R.M. (2005). Terminal care: The last weeks of life. *Journal of Palliative Medicine, 8,* 1042–1054.

PLUTCHIK, R. (2001). The nature of emotions. *American Scientist, 89,* 344–350.

POLIVY, J., & HERMAN, C.P. (2000). The false-hope syndrome: Unfulfilled expectations of self-change. *Current Directions in Psychological Science, 9,* 128–131.

PORAN, M.A. (2002). Denying diversity: Perceptions of beauty and social comparison processes among Latina, Black, and White women. *Sex Roles, 47,* 65–81.

POTTER-EFRON, R.T. (2005). *Handbook of anger management: Individual, couple, family, and group approaches.* Binghamton, NY: Haworth Clinical Practice Press.

POUND, P., BRITTEN, N., MORGAN, M., YARDLEY, L., POPE, C., & DAKER-WHITE, G., et al. (2005). Resisting medicines: A synthesis of qualitative studies of medicine taking. *Social Science & Medicine, 61,* 133–155.

POWELL, A.D., & KAHN, A.S. (1995). Racial differences in women's desires to be thin. *International Journal of Eating Disorders, 17,* 191–195.

POWELL, G.N., BUTTERFIELD, D.A., & PARENT, J.D. (2002). Gender and managerial stereotypes: Have times changed? *Journal of Management, 28,* 177–193.

PRENTKY, R.A., KNIGHT, R.A., & LEE, A.F.S. (2006). Child sexual molestation: Research issues. In C.R. Bartol, & A.M. Bartol (Eds.), *Current perspectives in forensic psychology and criminal justice* (pp. 119–129). Thousand Oaks, CA: Sage Publications.

PRESSMAN, S.D., COHEN, S., MILLER, G.E., BARKIN, A., RABIN, B.S., & TREANOR, J.J. (2005). Loneliness, social network size, and immune response to influenza vaccination in college freshmen. *Health Psychology, 24,* 297–306.

PREVITI, D., & AMATO, P.R. (2004). Is infidelity a cause or a consequence of poor marital quality? *Journal of Social and Personal Relationships, 21,* 217–230.

PRISLIN, R., & WOOD, W. (2005). *Social influence in attitudes and attitude change.* Mahwah, NJ: Lawrence Erlbaum Associates.

PRITCHARD, M.E., & WILSON, G.S. (2006). Do coping styles change during the first semester of college? *Journal of Social Psychology, 146,* 125–127.

PTACEK, J.T., & DODGE, K.L. (1995). Coping strategies and relationship satisfaction in couples. *Personality and Social Psychology Bulletin, 21,* 76–84.

PUGH, D.N. (1993). The effects of problem-solving ability and locus of control on prisoner adjustment. *International Journal of Offender Therapy and Comparative Criminology, 37,* 163–176.

PUTERBAUGH, D. (2005, May). Why newborns cause acrimony and alimony. *USA Today Magazine, 133,* 26–29.

PYSZCZYNSKI, T., & COX, C. (2004). Can we really do without self-esteem? Comment on Crocker and Park (2004). *Psychological Bulletin, 130,* 425–429.

QUIGLEY, D.G., & SCHATZ, M.S. (1999). Men and women and their responses in spousal bereavement. *Hospice Journal, 14,* 65–78.

QUILLIAN, L., & CAMPBELL, M.E. (2003). Beyond Black and White: The present and future of multiracial friendship segregation. *American Sociological Review, 68,* 540–566.

RAIT, D.S. (2000). The therapeutic alliance in couples and family therapy. *Journal of Clinical Psychology, 56,* 211–224.

RALL, M.L., PESKOFF, F.S., & BYRNE, J.J. (1994). The effects of information-giving behavior and gender on perceptions of physicians: An experimental analysis. *Social Behavior and Personality, 22,* 1–16.

Rape, Abuse, & Incest National Network. (2006a). Statistics. Retrieved May 17, 2006, from http://www.rainn.org/statistics.

Rape, Abuse, & Incest National Network. (2006b). Rape trauma syndrome. Retrieved May 17, 2006, from http://www.rainn.org/effects-of-rape/rapetrauma-syndrome .html.

RATELLE, C.F., VALLERAND, R.J., CHANTAL, Y., & PROVENCHER, P. (2004). Cognitive adaptation and mental health: A motivational analysis. *European Journal of Social Psychology, 34,* 459–476.

RAUER, A.J., & VOLLING, B.L. (2005). The role of husbands' and wives' emotional expressivity in the marital relationship. *Sex Roles, 52,* 577–587.

RAYMOND, N. (2000, July/August). Mood: Blues around the world. *Psychology Today,* 12.

RAYNOR, D.A., PHELAN, S., HILL, J.O., & WING, R.R. (in press). Television viewing and weight maintenance: Results from the National Weight Control Registry. *Obesity.*

RAYNOR, D.A., WING, R.R., & PHELAN, S. (in press). Depression and adherence to medical advice. In A. Steptoe (Ed.), *Depression and physical illness.* Cambridge, UK: Cambridge University Press.

READE, N. (2002, February). Love at first sight. *Attache,* 34–37.

REEVE, J. (1992). *Understanding motivation and emotion.* San Diego, CA: Harcourt Brace Jovanovich.

REEVE, J. (2004). *Understanding motivation and emotion.* New York: Wiley.

REGAN, P.C., & ATKINS, L. (2006). Sex differences and similarities in frequency and intensity of sexual desire. *Social Behavior and Personality, 34,* 95–102.

REGAN, P.C., DURVASULA, R., HOWELL, L., UREÑO, O., & REA, M. (2004). Gender, ethnicity, and the developmental timing of first sexual and romantic experiences. *Social Behavior and Personality, 32,* 667–676.

REID, A. (2004). Gender and sources of subjective well-being. *Sex Roles, 51,* 617–629.

REISBURG, L. (2000). Student stress is rising, especially among women. *The Chronicle of Higher Education, 46,* 49–50.

REISS, S., & HAVERCAMP, S.M. (2005). Motivation in developmental context: A new method for studying self-actualization. *Journal of Humanistic Psychology, 45,* 41–53.

REMPEL, J.K., & HOLMES, J.G. (1986, February). How do I trust thee? *Psychology Today, 20,* 28–34.

RENNISON, C.M. (2003). *Intimate partner violence: Crime data brief.* Washington, DC: Bureau of Justice Statistics.

RENNISON, C.M., & WELCHANS, S. (2000, May). *Intimate partner violence: Bureau of Justice Statistics Special* Report. Washington, DC: U.S. Department of Justice.

RENSHAW, D.C. (2002). Rage 2002. *Family Journal—Counseling and Therapy for Couples and Families, 10,* 240–243.

Research on Today's Issues. (1998, October). Improving children's well-being: Understanding, nurturing fatherhood, 1–2.

REYNOLDS, B.M., & REPETTI, R.L. (2006). *Adolescent girls' health in the context of peer and community relationships.* New York: Oxford University Press.

RHODES, G., YOSHIKAWA, S., CLARK, A., LEE, K., MCKAY, R. & AKAMATSU, S. (2001). Attractiveness of facial averageness and symmetry in non-Western cultures: In search of biologically based standards of beauty. *Perception, 30,* 611–625.

RICE, T.W., & STEELE, B.J. (2004). Subjective well-being and culture across time and space. *Journal of Cross-Cultural Psychology, 35,* 633–647.

RICHARDS, J.M. (2004). The cognitive consequences of concealing feelings. *Current Directions in Psychological Science, 13,* 131–134.

RICHARDSON, J.D. (1991). Medical causes of male sexual dysfunction. *The Medical Journal of Australia, 155,* 29–33.

RITTER, B.A., & YODER, J.D. (2004). Gender differences in leader emergence persist even for dominant women: An updated confirmation of role congruity theory. *Psychology of Women Quarterly, 28,* 187–193.

ROBERTI, J.W. (2004). A review of behavioral and biological correlates of sensation seeking. *Journal of Research in Personality, 38,* 256–279.

ROBERTS, S.T., & KENNEDY, B.L. (2006). Why are young college women not using condoms? Their perceived risk, drug use, and developmental vulnerability may provide important clues to sexual risk. *Archives of Psychological Nursing, 20,* 32–40.

ROBINS, R.W., & TRZESNIEWSKI, K.H. (2005). Self-esteem development across the lifespan. *Current Directions in Psychological Science, 14,* 158–162.

ROBINSON, R.V., & JACKSON, E.F. (2001). Is trust in others declining in America? An age-period-cohort analysis. *Social Science Research, 30,* 117–146.

ROBLES, T.F., GLASER, R., & KIECOLT-GLASER, J.K. (2005). Out of balance: A new look at chronic stress, depression, and immunity. *Current Directions in Psychological Science, 14,* 111–115.

Rochford.org. (2000, August). *Suicide.* http://Rochford.org/suicide/resources/ stats/us.

RODRIGUEZ-CALCAGNO, M., & BREWER, E.W. (2005). Job stress among Hispanic professionals. *Hispanic Journal of Behavioral Sciences, 27,* 504–516.

ROESE, N.J., & SUMMERVILLE, A. (2005). What we regret most . . . and why. *Personality and Social Psychology Bulletin, 31,* 1273–1285.

ROFFE, L., SCHMIDT, K., & ERNST, E. (2005). A systematic review of guided imagery as an adjuvant cancer therapy. *Psycho-oncology, 14,* 607–617.

ROGERS, C.R. (1951). *Client-centered therapy.* Boston: Houghton Mifflin.

ROGERS, C.R. (1961). *On becoming a person.* Boston: Houghton Mifflin.

ROGERS, C.R. (1980). *A way of being.* Boston: Houghton Mifflin.

ROGERS, C.R. (1985, March 7). *Toward a more human science of the person.* Paper presented at the conference on A Quarter Century of Humanistic Psychologies, San Francisco.

ROGGE, R.D., BRADBURY, T.N., HAHLWEG, K., ENGL, J., & THURMAIER, F. (2006). Predicting marital distress and dissolution: Refining the two-factor hypothesis. *Journal of Family Psychology, 20,* 156–159.

ROHNER, R.P. (1998). Father love and child development: History and current evidence. *Current Directions in Psychological Science, 7,* 157–161.

ROKACH, A., & NETO, F. (2005). Age, culture, and the antecedents of loneliness. *Social Behavior and Personality, 33,* 477–494.

RORTY, A.O. (2004). Enough already with "theories of the emotions". In R.C. Solomon (Ed.), *Thinking about feeling: Contemporary philosophers on emotions* (pp. 269–278). New York: Oxford University Press.

ROSARIO, M., SCHRIMSHAW, E.W., HUNTER, J., & BRAUN, L. (2006). Sexual identity development among lesbian, gay, and bisexual youths: Consistency and change over time. *Journal of Sex Research. Special Issue: Scientific Abstracts, World Congress of Sexology 2005, 43,* 46–58.

ROSATO, J.L. (2006). Special issue on the evolution of marriage: Preface. *Family Court Review. Special Issue: The Evolution of Marriage, 44,* 31–32.

ROSE, S. (2000, February). A new biology. *Prospect,* 27–32.

ROSEN, R.C., & LEIBLUM, S.R. (1995). Treatment of sexual disorders in the 1990's: An integrated approach. *Journal of Consulting and Clinical Psychology, 63,* 877–890.

ROSEN, R.C., SHABSIGH, R., KURITZKY, L., WANG, W. C., & SIDES, G.D. (2006). The efficacy of tadalafil in improving sexual satisfaction and overall satisfaction in men with mild, moderate, and severe erectile dysfunction: A retrospective pooled analysis of data from randomized, placebo-controlled clinical trials. *Current Medical Research and Opinion, 21,* 1701–1710.

ROSENTHAL, E.C. (2005). *The era of choice: The ability to choose and its transformation of contemporary life.* Cambridge, MA: MIT Press.

ROSS, C.E., & MIROWSKY, J. (2002). Age and the gender gap in the sense of personal control. *Social Psychology Quarterly, 65,* 125–145.

ROSS, M.W. (2002, January/February). Sex in America: Unintended pregnancies. *Psychology Today,* 56–62.

ROSS, M., & WILSON, A.E. (2003). Autobiographical memory and conceptions of self: Getting better all the time. (2003). *Current Directions in Psychological Science, 12,* 66–69.

ROSS, N. (2005). Health, happiness, and higher levels of social organization. *Journal of Epidemiology & Community Health, 59,* 614.

RÖSSLER, W., SALIZE, H.J., VAN OS, J., & RIECHER-RÖSSLER, A. (2005). Size of burden of schizophrenia and psychotic disorders. *European Neuropsychopharmacology. Special Issue: Size and Burden of Mental Disorders in Europe, 15,* 399–409.

ROTHBLUM, E.D., & FACTOR, R. (2001). Lesbians and their sisters as a control group: Demographic and mental health factors. *Psychological Science, 12,* 63–69.

ROTHERAM-BORUS, M.J., WALKER, J.U., & FERNS, W. (1996). Suicidal behavior among middle-class adolescents who seek crisis services. *Journal of Clinical Psychology, 52,* 137–143.

ROTHMAN, A.J., & SALOVEY, P. (1997). Shaping perceptions to motivate healthy behavior: The role of message framing. *Psychological Bulletin, 121,* 3–19.

ROTHMAN, A.J., SALOVEY, P., ANTONE, C., KEOUGH, K., & MARTIN, C.D. (1993). The influence of message framing on intentions to perform health behaviors. *Journal of Experimental Social Psychology, 29,* 408–433.

ROWE, D.C. (1990). As the twig is bent? The myth of child-rearing influences on personality development. *Journal of Counseling and Development, 68,* 606–611.

RUBIN, J.Z., PRUITT, D.G., & KIM, S.H. (1994). *Social conflict: Escalation, stalemate, and settlement.* New York: McGraw-Hill.

RUBIN, L.C. (2004). Merchandising madness: Pills, promises, and better living through chemistry. *Journal of Popular Culture, 38,* 369–383.

RUBIN, R. (1999, November 9). Pregnancy no longer pushes women to wed. *USA Today,* p. 1D.

RUDIN, M.M., ZALEWSKI, C., & BODMER-TURNER, J. (1995). Characteristics of child sexual abuse victims according to perpetrator gender. *Child Abuse and Neglect, 19,* 963–973.

RUDMAN, L.A., & GOODWIN, S.A. (2004). Gender differences in automatic ingroup bias: Why do women like women more than men like men? *Journal of Personality and Social Psychology, 87,* 494–509.

RUSCHER, J.B., CRALLEY, E.L., & O'FARRELL, K.J. (2005). How newly acquainted dyads develop shared stereotypic impressions through conversation. *Group Processes & Intergroup Relations, 8,* 259–270.

RUSHTON, J.P., & BONS, T.A. (2005). Mate choice and friendship in twins: Evidence for genetic similarity. *Psychological Science, 16,* 555–559.

RUSSO, F. (2005). Giving expertise: The new volunteers: More than just envelope stuffers. *Time Bonus Section, 166,* F18–F20.

RÜTER, K., & MUSSWEILER, T. (2005). Bonds of friendship: Comparative self-evaluations evoke the use of routine standards. *Social Cognition, 23,* 137–160.

RUTHERFORD, M. (2001, April). Reconcilable differences. *Time,* F1–F5.

RUTTER, M. (2002). Nature, nurture, and development: From evangelism through science toward policy and practice. *Child Development, 73,* 1–21.

RYAN, M.K., & HASLAM, S.A. (2005). The glass cliff: Evidence that women are over-represented in precarious leadership positions. *British Journal of Management, 16,* 81–90.

SAARDCHOM, N., & LEMAIRE, J. (2005). Causes of increasing ages at marriage: An international regression study. *Marriage & Family Review, 37,* 73–97.

SABINI, J., & SILVER, M. (2005). Ekman's basic emotions: Why not love and jealousy? *Cognition & Emotion, 19,* 693–712.

SACKETT, S.A., & HANSEN, J.I.C. (1995). Vocational outcomes of college freshmen with flat profiles on the Strong Interest Inventory. *Measurement and Evaluation in Counseling and Development, 28,* 9–24.

SAFREN, S.A., & PANTALONE, D.W. (2006). Social anxiety and barriers to resilience among lesbian, gay, and bisexual adolescents. In A.M. Omoto, & H.S. Kurtzman (Eds.), *Sexual orientation and mental health: Examining identity and development in lesbian, gay, and bisexual people* (pp. 55–71). Washington, DC: American Psychological Association.

SAGY, S. (2005). Chronic versus acute stress situations: A comparison of moderating factors. In K.V. Oxington (Ed.), *Psychology of stress* (pp. 101–112). Hauppauge, NY: Nova Biomedical Books.

SAKURAGI, T. (2004). Association of culture with shyness among Japanese and American university students. *Perceptual and Motor Skills, 98,* 803–813.

SALOVEY, P., & GREWAL, D. (2005). The science of emotional intelligence. *Current Directions in Psychological Science, 14,* 281–285.

SALTZBURG, S. (1996). Family therapy and the disclosure of adolescent homosexuality. *Journal of Family Psychotherapy, 7,* 1–18.

SANCHEZ, D.T., & CROCKER, J. (2005). How investment in gender ideals affects well-being: The role of external contingencies of self-worth. *Psychology of Women Quarterly, 29,* 63–77.

SANCHEZ-BERNARDOS, M.L., & SANZ, J. (1992). Effects of the discrepancy between self-concepts on emotional adjustment. *Journal of Research in Personality, 26,* 303–318.

SÁNCHEZ-FRANCO, M.J. (2006). Exploring the influence of gender on the web usage via partial least squares. *Behaviour & Information Technology, 25,* 19–36.

SANDEEP, J. (March 16, 2003). When doctors slam the door. *The New York Times Magazine,* 32–35.

SANGRADOR, J.L., & YELA, C. (2000). "What is beautiful is loved": Physical attractiveness in love relationships in a representative sample. *Social Behavior and Personality, 28,* 207–218.

SANTESSO, D.L., SCHMIDT, L.A., & FOX, N.A. (2004). Are shyness and sociability still a dangerous combination for substance use? Evidence from a U.S. and Canadian sample. *Personality and Individual Differences, 37,* 5–17.

SAPOLSKY, R. (1999, March). Stress and your shrinking brain. *Discover,* 116–122.

SARGENT, J.D., WILLS, T.A., STOOLMILLER, M., GIBSON, J., & GIBBONS, F.X. (2006). Alcohol use in motion pictures and its relation with early-onset teen drinking. *Journal of Studies on Alcohol, 67,* 54–65.

SAUCIER, M.G. (2004). Midlife and beyond: Issues for aging women. *Journal of Counseling & Development, 82,* 420–425.

SAVARD, J., LEDUC, N., LEBEL, P., BÉLAND, F., & BERGMAN, H. (2006). Caregiver satisfaction with support services: Influence of different types of services. *Journal of Aging and Health, 18,* 3–27.

SAVIN-WILLIAMS, R.C. (2006). Who's gay? Does it matter? *Current Directions in Psychological Science, 14,* 40–44.

SAYER, L.C. (2005). Gender, time and inequality: Trends in women's and men's paid work, unpaid work and free time. *Social Forces, 84,* 285–303.

SCARPA, A., HADEN, S.C., & HURLEY, J. (2006). Community violence victimization and symptoms of posttraumatic stress disorder: The moderating effects of coping and social support. *Journal of Interpersonal Violence, 21,* 446–469.

SCARR, S. (1987). Personality and experience: Individual encounters with the world. In J. Aronoff, A.I. Rabin, & R.A. Zucker (Eds.), *The emergence of personality* (pp. 49–78). New York: Springer.

SCARR, S. (1998). American child care today. *American Psychologist, 53,* 95–108.

SCARR, S. (2004). Families and day care: Both matter for children. *PsycCRITIQUES.*

SCEALY, M., PHILLIPS, J.G., & STEVENSON, R. (2002). Shyness and anxiety as predictors of patterns of internet usage. *CyberPsychology and Behavior, 5,* 507–515.

SCHACHNER, D.A., & SHAVER, P.R. (2004). Attachment dimensions and sexual motives. *Personal Relationships, 11,* 179–195.

SCHEIER, M.F., & CARVER, C.S. (1993). On the power of positive thinking: The benefits of being optimistic. *Psychological Science, 4,* 26–30.

SCHINDEHETTE, S., CALANDRA, B., PODESTA, J.S., & WILLIAMS, K. (2004, April 5). Why did Julie take her life? *People,* 58–63.

SCHLEICHER, D.J., WATT, J.D., & GREGURAS, G.J. (2004). Reexamining the job satisfaction-performance relationship: The complexity of attitudes. *Journal of Applied Psychology, 89,* 165–177.

SCHLINGER, H.D. (2002). Not so fast, Mr. Pinker: A behaviorist looks at the blank slate. A review of Steven Pinker's the blank slate: The modern denial of human nature. *Behavior and Social Issues, 12,* 75–79.

SCHMITT, D.P., & ALLIK, J. (2005). Simultaneous administration of the Rosenberg self-esteem scale in 53 nations: Exploring the universal and culture-specific features of global self-esteem. *Journal of Personality and Social Psychology, 89,* 623–642.

SCHOCKETT, E.R., TENO, J.M., MILLER, S.C., & STUART, B. (2005). Late referral to hospice and bereaved family member perception of quality of care. *Journal of Pain and Symptom Management, 30,* 400–407.

SCHOLING, A., & EMMELKAMP, P.M.G. (1990). Social phobia: Nature and treatment. In H. Leitenberg (Ed.), *Handbook of social and evaluation anxiety* (pp. 269–324). New York: Plenum.

SCHOOLER, D., WARD, L.M., MERRIWETHER, A., & CARUTHERS, A. (2004). Who's that girl: Television's role in the body image development of young White and Black women. *Psychology of Women Quarterly, 28,* 38–47.

SCHRAUFHAGEL, T.J., WAGNER, A.W., MIRANDA, J., & ROY-BYRNE, P.P. (2006). Treating minority patients with depression and anxiety: What does the evidence tell us? *General Hospital Psychiatry, 28,* 27–36.

SCHROF, J.M., & SCHULTZ, S. (1999a, March 8). Melancholy nation. *U.S. News & World Report,* 56–63.

SCHROF, J.M., & SCHULTZ, S. (1999b, June 21). Social anxiety. *U.S. News & World Report,* 50–57.

SCHULZ, R., & HECKHAUSEN, J. (1996). A life span model of successful aging. *American Psychologist, 51,* 702–714.

SCHUTTE, N.S., MALOUFF, J.M., BOBIK, C., COSTON, R.D., GREESON, C., JEDLICKA, C., & RHODES, E., et al. (2001). Emotional intelligence and interpersonal relations. *The Journal of Social Psychology, 141,* 523–536.

SCHUTTE, N., TOPPINENE, S., KALIMO, R., & SCHAUFELI, W. (2000). The factorial validity of the Maslach Burnout Inventory–General Survey (MBI-GS) across occupational groups and nations. *Journal of Occupational and Organizational Psychology, 73,* 53–66.

SCHÜTZWOHL, A. (2006). Sex differences in jealousy: Information search and cognitive preoccupation. *Personality and Individual Differences, 40,* 285–292.

SCHWARTZ, B. (2004). *The paradox of choice: Why more is less.* New York: Harper-Collins Publishers.

SCHWARTZ, P. (2002, May/June). Love is all you need. *Psychology Today,* 56–62.

SCHWARTZ, S.H., & RUBEL, T. (2005). Sex differences in value priorities: Cross-cultural and multimethod studies. *Journal of Personality and Social Psychology, 89,* 1010–1028.

SCHWINGHAMMER, S.A., STAPEL, D.A., & BLANTON, H. (2006). Different selves have different effects: Self-activation and defensive social comparison. *Personality and Social Psychology Bulletin, 32,* 27–39.

SCOLLON, C.N., DIENER, E., OISHI, S., & BISWAS-DIENER, R. (2004). Emotions across cultures and methods. *Journal of Cross-Cultural Psychology, 35,* 304–326.

SCZESNY, S., BOSAK, J., NEFF, D., & SCHYNS, B. (2004). Gender stereotypes and the attribution of leadership traits: A cross-cultural comparison. *Sex Roles, 51,* 631–645.

SEDIKIDES, C., GAERTNER, L., & VEVEA, J.L. (2005). Pancultural self-enhancement reloaded: A meta-analytic reply to Heine (2005). *Journal of Personality and Social Psychology, 89,* 539–551.

SEDIKIDES, C., GREEN, J.D., & PINTER, B. (2004). Self-protective memory. In D.R. Beike, J.M. Lampinen & D.A. Behrend (Eds.), *The self and memory* (pp. 161–179). New York: Psychology Press.

SEDIKIDES, C., & KOOLE, S.L. (2004). In defense of the self. *Social Cognition, 22,* 1–3.

SEGELL, M. (1991). The American man in transition. In K.G. Duffy (Ed.), *Personal growth and behavior* (pp. 91–92). Guilford, CT: Dushkin Publishing Group.

SEGERSTROM, S.C., & MILLER, G.E. (2004). Psychological stress and the human immune system: A meta-analytic study of 30 years of inquiry. *Psychological Bulletin, 130,* 601–630.

SELIGMAN, M.E.P. (1981). A learned helplessness point of view. In L.P. Rehm (Ed.), *Behavior therapy for depression.* New York: Academic Press.

SELIGMAN, M.E.P. (1988, October). Boomer blues. *Psychology Today,* 50–55.

SELIGMAN, M.E.P. (1992). *Learned optimism.* New York: Knopf.

SELIGMAN, M.E.P. (1994, May/June). What you can change and what you cannot change. *Psychology Today,* 34–41, 70, 72–74, 84.

SELIGMAN, M.E.P. (1995). *The effectiveness of psychotherapy: The Consumer Reports study. American Psychologist, 50,* 965–974.

SELIGMAN, M.E.P., & CSIKSZENTMIHALY, M. (2000). Positive psychology. *American Psychologist, 55,* 5–14.

SELIGMAN, M.E.P., STEEN, T.A., PARK, N., & PETERSON, C. (2005). Positive psychology progress: Empirical validation of interventions. *American Psychologist, 60,* 410–421.

SELYE, H. (1974). *Stress without distress.* Philadelphia: Lippincott.

SELYE, H. (1980). The stress concept today. In I.L. Kutash, et al. (Eds.), *Handbook on stress and anxiety.* San Francisco: Jossey-Bass.

SELYE, H. (1991). History and present states of the stress concept. In A. Monat & R.S. Lazarus (Eds.), *Stress and coping: An anthology* (3rd ed., pp. 21–35). New York: Columbia University Press.

SENKO, C., & HARACKIEWICZ, J.M. (2005). Regulation of achievement goals: The role of competence feedback. *Journal of Educational Psychology, 97,* 320–336.

SETA, J.J., SETA, C.E., & MCELROY, T. (2006). Better than better-than-average (or not): Elevated and depressed self-evaluations following unfavorable social comparisons. *Self and Identity, 5,* 51–72.

Sex Information and Education Council of the United States. (2001). *Lesbian, gay, bisexual and transgender youth issues.* http://www.siecus.org/pubs/fact/fact0013.html.

Sex Information and Education Council of the United States. (2002). *Sexuality in middle and later life.* http://www.siecus.org/pubs/fact/fact0018.html.

Sex Information and Education Council of the United States. (2003). Why it's important to talk about sexual orientation. *Families Are Talking, 3,* 1–4.

SHACKELFORD, T.K., GOETZ, A.T., BUSS, D.M., EULER, H.A., & HOIER, S. (2005). When we hurt the ones we love: Predicting violence against women from men's mate retention. *Personal Relationships, 12,* 447–463.

SHACKELFORD, T.K., & MOUZOS, J. (2005). Partner killing by men in cohabiting and marital relationships: A comparative, cross-national analysis of data from Australia and the United States. *Journal of Interpersonal Violence, 20,* 1310–1324.

SHAFIRKIN, A.V. (2003). Compensatory reserves of the human body and population health under conditions of exposure to chronic anthropogenic factors and prolonged psychoemotional stress. *Human Physiology, 29,* 12–22.

SHALALA, D. (1999). *Mental health: A report of the surgeon general.* http://www.surgeon general.gov/library/mentalhealth/home.html.

SHARMA, V., & ROSHA, J. (1992). Altruism as a function of self-actualization and locus of control of benefactor. *Psychological Studies, 37,* 26–30.

SHAVER, P., & HAZAN, C. (1993). Adult romantic attachment: Theory and evidence. In D. Perlman & W. Jones (Eds.), *Advances in personal relationships* (Vol. 4, pp. 29–170). London: Jessica Kingsley.

SHEAR, K., FRANK, E., HOUCK, P.R., REYNOLDS, C.F. (2005). Treatment of complicated grief: A randomized controlled trial. *Journal of the American Medical Association, 293,* 2601–2608.

SHEEHY, G. (1995, June 12). New passages. *U.S. News & World Report, 121,* 62, 64, 66, 69.

SHEETS, V.L., & LUGAR, R. (2005). Sources of conflict between friends in Russia and the United States. *Cross-Cultural Research: The Journal of Comparative Social Science, 39,* 380–398.

SHEETS, V.L., & WOLFE, M.D. (2001). Sexual jealousy in heterosexuals, lesbians, and gays. *Sex Roles, 44,* 255–276.

SHEFFIELD, M., CAREY, J., PATENAUDE, W., & LAMBERT, M.J. (1995). An exploration of the relationship between interpersonal problems and psychological health. *Psychological Reports, 76,* 947–956.

SHELDON, K.M., ELLIOT, A.J., RYAN, R.M., CHIRKOV, V., KIM, Y., & WU, C., et al. (2004). Self-concordance and subjective well-being in four cultures. *Journal of Cross-Cultural Psychology, 35,* 209–223.

SHELDON, K.M., KASSER, T., HOUSER-MARKO, L., JONES, T., & TURBAN, D. (2005). Doing one's duty: Chronological age, felt autonomy, and subjective well-being. *European Journal of Personality, 19,* 97–115.

SHER, L. (2004). Light therapy for depressive disorders. *Psychiatric Times, 21,* 68.

SHERMAN, J.W., STROESSNER, S.J., CONREY, F.R., & AZAM, O.A. (2005). Prejudice and stereotype maintenance processes: Attention, attribution, and individuation. *Journal of Personality and Social Psychology, 89,* 607–622.

SHINEW, K.J., FLOYD, M.F., & PARRY, D. (2004). Understanding the relationship between race and leisure activities and constraints: Exploring an alternative framework. *Leisure Sciences, 26,* 181–199.

SHIOZAKI, M., MORITA, T., HIRAI, K., SAKAGUCHI, Y., TSUNETO, S., & SHIMA, Y. (2005). Why are bereaved family members dissatisfied with specialised inpatient palliative care service? A nationwide qualitative study. *Palliative Medicine, 19,* 319–327.

SHMOTKIN, D. (2005). Happiness in the face of adversity: Reformulating the dynamic and modular bases of subjective well-being. *Review of General Psychology, 9,* 291–325.

SIAS, P.M., & CAHILL, D.J. (1998). From coworkers to friends: The development of peer friendships in the workplace. *Western Journal of Communication, 62,* 273–299.

SIEVER, M.D. (1994). Sexual orientation and gender as factors in socio-culturally acquired vulnerability to body dissatisfaction and eating disorders. *Journal of Consulting and Clinical Psychology, 62,* 252–260.

SIMONS, J.S., GAHER, R.M., CORREIA, C.J., & BUSH, J.A. (2005). Club drug use among college students. *Addictive Behaviors, 30,* 1619–1624.

SIMONS, R.L., LIN, K.H., & GORDON, L.C. (1998). Socialization in the family of origin and male dating violence: A prospective study. *Journal of Marriage and the Family, 60,* 467–478.

SIMONTON, D.K. (1987). *Why presidents succeed: A political psychology of leadership.* New Haven, CT: Yale University Press.

SIMPSON, J.A., & GANGESTAD, S.W. (1992). Sociosexuality and romantic partner choice. *Journal of Personality, 60,* 31–51.

SINGH, D. (1995). Female judgment of male attractiveness and desirability for relationships: Role of waist-to-hip ratio and financial status. *Journal of Personality and Social Psychology, 69,* 1089–1101.

SLADE, E.P., & WISSOW, L.S. (2004). Spanking in early childhood and later behavior problems: A prospective study of infants and young toddlers. *Pediatrics, 113,* 1321–1331.

SLATER, A., HOCKING, I., & LOOSE, J. (2003). Theories and issues in child development. In A. Slater & G. Bremmer (Eds.), *An Introduction to developmental psychology* (pp. 34–63). Malden, MA: Blackwell.

SLEEBOS, E., ELLEMERS, N., & DE GILDER, D. (2006). The carrot and the stick: Affective commitment and acceptance anxiety as motives for discretionary group efforts by respected and disrespected group members. *Personality and Social Psychology Bulletin, 32,* 244–255.

SLEEK, S. (1998, November). Better parenting may not be enough for some children. *APA Monitor, 30.*

SMITH, B.N., KERR, N.A., MARKUS, M.J., & STASSON, M.F. (2001). Individual differences in social loafing: Need for cognition as a motivator in collective performance. *Group Dynamics, 5,* 150–158.

SMITH, C.A., & STILLMAN, S. (2002). Butch/femme in the personal advertisements of lesbians. *Journal of Lesbian Studies, 6,* 45–51.

SMITH, D.E., & COGSWELL, C. (1994). A cross-cultural perspective on adolescent girls' body perception. *Perceptual and Motor Skills, 78,* 744–746.

SMITH, P.B., & BOND, M.H. (1993). *Across cultures.* Boston: Allyn & Bacon.

SMITH, P.K., PEPLER, D., & RIGBY, K. (Eds.). (2004). *Bullying in schools: How successful can interventions be?* New York: Cambridge University Press.

SMITH, R.A., & WEBER, A.L. (2005). Applying social psychology in everyday life. In F.W. Schneider, J.A. Gruman & L.M. Coutts (Eds.), *Applied social psychology: Understanding and addressing social and practical problems* (pp. 75–99). Thousand Oaks, CA: Sage Publications.

SMITH, T.W. (2003). *American sexual behavior: Trends, socio-demographic differences, and risk behavior.* Chicago, IL: University of Chicago, National Opinion Research Center.

SMITH, T.W., GLAZER, K., RUIZ, J.M., & GALLO, L.C. (2004). Hostility, anger, aggressiveness, and coronary heart disease: An interpersonal perspective on personality, emotion, and health. *Journal of Personality. Special Issue: Emotions, Personality, and Health, 72,* 1217–1270.

SMOCK, P.J., MANNING, W.D., & PORTER, M. (2005). "Everything's there except money": How money shapes decisions to marry among cohabitors. *Journal of Marriage and Family, 67,* 680–696.

SNIR, R., & HARPAZ, I. (2002). Work-leisure relations: Leisure orientation and the meaning of work. *Journal of Leisure Research, 34,* 178–203.

SOLOMON, R.S. (2005). Name that feeling: Sabini and silver on emotional names. *Psychological Inquiry, 16,* 41–44.

SOMECH, A. (2006). The effects of leadership style and team process on performance and innovation in functionally heterogeneous teams. *Journal of Management, 32,* 132–157.

SOMMER, K.L., & BAUMEISTER, R.F. (2002). Self-evaluation, persistence, and performance following implicit rejection: The role of trait self-esteem. *Personality and Social Psychology Bulletin, 28,* 926–938.

SONNENTAG, S., & ZIJLSTRA, F.R.H. (2006). Job characteristics and off-job activities as predictors of need for recovery, well-being, and fatigue. *Journal of Applied Psychology, 91,* 330–350.

SOOD, A., & TELLIS, G.J. (2005). Technological evolution and radical innovation. *Journal of Marketing, 69,* 152–168.

SOSIK, J.J. (2001). Self-other agreement on charismatic leadership: Relationships with work attitudes and managerial performance. *Group and Organization Management, 26,* 484–511.

SOUSA-POZA, A., & SOUSA-POZA, A. (2000). Well-being at work: A cross-national analysis of the levels and determinants of job satisfaction. *Journal of Socio-Economics, 29,* 517–538.

SOUTHWICK, S.M., VYTHILINGAM, M., & CHARNEY, D.S. (2005). The psychobiology of depression and resilience to stress: Implications for prevention and treatment. *Annual Review of Clinical Psychology, 1,* 255–291.

SPAKE, A. (2006). Stop Dieting! *U.S. News & World Report, 140,* 60–62, 65–66.

SPECTOR, P.E. (1996). *Industrial and organizational psychology: Research and practice.* New York: Wiley.

SPECTOR, P.E. (2002). Employee control and occupational stress. *Current Directions, 11,* 133–136.

SPIELBERGER, C.D. (2000). Cross-cultural assessment of state and trait anxiety and anger. *International Psychology Reporter, 4,* 17–20.

SPINDLER, S.R. (2001). Reversing the negative genomic effects of aging with short-term caloric restriction. *The Scientific World, 1,* 544–546.

SPOTTS, E.L., PEDERSON, N.L., NEIDERHISER, J.M., REISS, D., LICHTENSTEIN, P., & HANSSON, K., et al. (2005). Genetic effects on women's positive mental health: Do marital relationships and social support matter? *Journal of Family Psychology, 19,* 339–349.

SPRECHER, S., & HENDRICK, S.S. (2004). Self-disclosure in intimate relationships: Associations with individual and relationship characteristics over time. *Journal of Social & Clinical Psychology, 23,* 857–877.

SPRECHER, S., & REGAN, P.C. (2002). Liking some things (in some people) more than others: Partner preferences in romantic relationships and friendships. *Journal of Social and Personal Relationships, 19,* 463–481.

SPURGAS, A.K. (2005). Body image and cultural background. *Sociological Inquiry, 75,* 297–316.

SRIVASTAVA, S., & BEER, J.S. (2005). How self-evaluations relate to being liked by others: Integrating sociometer and attachment perspectives. *Journal of Personality and Social Psychology, 89,* 966–977.

STAMBOR, Z. (2006). Stressed out nation. *Monitor on Psychology, 37,* 28.

STANLEY, S.M., AMATO, P.R., JOHNSON, C.A., & MARKMAN, H.J. (2006). Premarital education, marital quality, and marital stability: Findings from a large, random household survey. *Journal of Family Psychology, 20,* 117–126.

Staying the course. Getting the right medication is only half the battle (2004). *Harvard Health Letter from Harvard Medical School, 29,* 4–5.

STEELE, C.M. (1992). Race and the shooting of Black Americans. *Atlantic Monthly, 69,* 68–78.

STEELE, K.M., & SIMONS, C. (2002). Age differences in coping resources and satisfaction with life among middle-aged, young-old, and oldest-old adults. *The Journal of Genetic Psychology, 163,* 360–367.

STEINER, A. (2002). Got time for friends? *Utne Reader,* 67–71.

STEINHAUER, S. (1995, April 10). Big benefits in marriage, studies say. *The New York Times,* p. A10.

STEPHENS, M.A.P., & FRANKS, M.M. (1999). Parent care in the context of women's multiple roles. *Current Directions in Psychological Science, 8,* 149–151.

STEPNISKY, J. (2005). Global memory and the rhythm of life. *American Behavioral Scientist, 48,* 1383–1402.

STERN, J. (2006). A short introduction to psychoanalysis. *Psychoanalytic Psychotherapy, 20,* 65–68.

STERNBERG, R.J. (2004). *A triangular theory of love.* Philadelphia, PA: Taylor & Francis.

STERNBERG, R.J., & GRAJEK, S. (1984). The nature of love. *Journal of Personality and Social Psychology, 47,* 312–329.

STERNBERG, S. (2005, June 6) New use for Viagra: Treating lung disease. *USA Today,* p. 8D.

STERNGLANZ, R.W., & DEPAULO, B.M. (2004). Reading nonverbal cues to emotions: The advantages and liabilities of relationship closeness. *Journal of Nonverbal Behavior. Special Issue: Interpersonal Sensitivity, Part II, 28,* 245–266.

STEWART, G.L. (2006). A meta-analytic review of relationships between team design features and team performance. *Journal of Management, 32,* 29–55.

STILES, W.B., BARKHAM, M., TWIGG, E., MELLOR-CLARK, J., & COOPER, M. (2006). Effectiveness of cognitive-behavioural, person-centred and psychodynamic therapies as practised in UK national health service settings. *Psychological medicine, 36,* 555–566.

STOCK, R. (1999, September). Lost and found. *Modern Maturity,* 50–53.

STODOLSKA, M. (2005). A conditioned attitude model of individual discriminatory behavior. *Leisure Sciences, 27,* 1–20.

STOLZ, H.E., BARBER, B.K., & OLSEN, J.A. (2005). Toward disentangling fathering and mothering: An assessment of relative importance. *Journal of Marriage and Family, 67,* 1076–1092.

STONE, J. (2003). Self-consistency for low self-esteem in dissonance processes: The role of self-standards. *Personality and Social Psychology Bulletin, 29,* 846–858.

STRAUS, M.A. (2001, September/October). New evidence for the benefits of never spanking. *Society,* 52–60.

STRAUS, M.A., & STEWART, J.H. (1999). Corporal punishment by American parents: National data on prevalence, chronicity, severity, and duration, in relation to child and family characteristics. *Clinical Child and Family Psychology Review, 2,* 55–70.

STREETER, S.A., & McBURNEY, D.H. (2003). Waist-hip ratio and attractiveness: New evidence and a critique of a "critical test." *Evolution and Human Behavior, 24,* 88–98.

STROEBE, W., SCHUT, H., & STROEBE, M.S. (2005). Grief work, disclosure and counseling: Do they help the bereaved? *Clinical Psychology Review, 25,* 395–414.

STROEBE, W., ZECH, E., STROEBE, M.S., & ABAKOUMKIN, G. (2005). Does social support help in bereavement. *Journal of Social and Clinical Psychology, 24,* 1030–1050.

STROM, P., & STROM R. (2005). Parent-child relationships in early adulthood: College students living at home. *Community Journal of Research and Practice, 29,* 517–529.

SUE, S., FUJINO, D., HU, L., TAKEUCHI, D., & ZANE, N. (1991). Community mental health services for ethnic minority groups: A test of the cultural responsiveness hypothesis. *Journal of Consulting and Clinical Psychology, 59,* 533–540.

SUH, E.J., MOSKOWITZ, D.S., FOURNIER, M.A., & ZUROFF, D.C. (2004). Gender and relationships: Influences on agentic and communal behaviors. *Personal Relationships, 11,* 41–59.

SUHAIL, K., & CHAUDHRY, H.R. (2004). Predictors of subjective well-being in Eastern Muslim culture. *Journal of Social & Clinical Psychology, 23,* 359–376.

SULLIVAN, A. (2003, August 11). Beware the straight backlash. *Time,* 35.

SULS, J., MARTIN, R., & WHEELER, L. (2002). Social comparison: Why, with whom, and with what effect. *Current Directions in Psychological Science, 11,* 159–163.

SUNNAFRANK, M., RAMIREZ, A.J., & METTS, S. (2004). At first sight: Persistent relational effects of get-acquainted conversations. *Journal of Social and Personal Relationships, 21,* 361–379.

SWANN, W.B., Jr., DE LARONDE, C., & HIXON, J.G. (1994). Authenticity and positive strivings in marriage and courtship. *Journal of Personality and Social Psychology, 52,* 881–889.

SWINGLE, C. (1999, November 4). When parents stop talking down. *Democrat and Chronicle,* pp. 1–2C.

SZABO, A., AINSWORTH, S.E., & DANKS, P.K. (2005). Experimental comparison of the psychological benefits of aerobic exercise, humor, and music. *Humor: International Journal of Humor Research, 18,* 235–246.

TALBOT, L.A., FLEG, J.L., & METTER, E.J. (2003). Secular trends in leisure-time physical activity in men and women across four decades. *Preventive Medicine: An International Journal Devoted to Practice and Theory, 37,* 52–60.

TALLIS, F. (2005). Crazy for you. *Psychologist, 18,* 72–74.

TANGRI, S.S., THOMAS, V.G., MEDNICK, M.T., & LEE, K.S. (2003). Predictors of satisfaction among college-educated African American women in midlife. *Journal of Adult Development, 10,* 113–125.

TAYLOR, S.E., & BROWN, J.D. (1994). Positive illusions and well-being revisited: Separating fact from fiction. *Psychological Bulletin, 116,* 21–27.

Techniques. (2000, March). Stressed out on campus. *Techniques, 9.*

TEICHERT, N.W. (2002). *Nation faces inadequate care for seniors as baby boomers age.* Knight Ridder/Tribune Business News, Item 02333003.

THASE, M.E., GREENHOUSE, J.B., FRANK, E., REYNOLDS, C.F., PILKONIS, P.A., & HURLEY, K., et al. (1997). Treatment of major depression with psychotherapy or psychotherapy-pharmacotherapy combination. *Archives of General Psychiatry, 54,* 1009–1015.

THOBABEN, M. (2005). Defense mechanisms and defense levels. *Home Health Care Management & Practice, 17,* 330–332.

THOMAS, J.L., PATTEN, C.A., DECKER, P.A., CROGHAN, I.T., COWLES, M.L., & BRONARS, C.A., et al. (2005). Development and preliminary evaluation of a measure of support provided to a smoker among young adults. *Addictive Behaviors, 30,* 1351.

THOMAS, K. (2000, October 29). Blacks post net gains. *USA Today,* p. 10D.

THOMPSON, K.M. (2005). Addicted media: Substances on screen. *Child and Adolescent Psychiatric Clinics of North America, 14,* 473–489.

THOMPSON, L. (1991). Information exchange in negotiation. *Journal of Experimental Social Psychology, 27,* 161–179.

THOMPSON, M.S., JUDD, C.M., & PARK, B. (2000). The consequences of communicating social stereotypes. *Journal of Experimental Social Psychology, 36,* 567–599.

THOMPSON, S.C. (1999). Illusions of control: How we overestimate our personal influence. *Current Directions in Psychological Science, 8,* 187–190.

THOMPSON, T.D.B., BARBOUR, R.S., & SCHWARTZ, L. (2003). Health professionals' views on advance directives: A qualitative interdisciplinary study. *Palliative Medicine, 17,* 403–409.

THOMPSON, V.S.S. (2002). Racism: Perceptions of distress among African Americans. *Community Mental Health Journal, 38,* 111–118.

TIEFER, L. (1991). Historical scientific, clinical, and feminist criticisms of "the human sexual response cycle" model. *Annual Review of Sex Research, 2,* 1–23.

TIGGEMANN, M. (2004). Body image across the adult life span: Stability and change. *Body Image, 1,* 29–41.

TIGGEMANN, M. (2005). Television and adolescent body image: The role of program content and viewing motivation. *Journal of Social & Clinical Psychology, 24,* 361–381.

TING-TOOMEY, S., GAO, G., TRUBISKY, P., YANG, Z., KIM, H.S., LIN, S.L., & NISHIDA, T. (1991). Culture, face maintenance, and styles of handling interpersonal conflict: A study in five cultures. *International Journal of Conflict Management, 2,* 275–296.

TKACHUK, G.A., & MARTIN, G.L. (1999). Exercise therapy for patients with psychiatric disorders: Research and clinical implications. *Professional Psychology: Research and Practice, 30,* 275–282.

Today's Issues. (1998, October). Improving children's well-being: Understanding, nurturing fatherhood. *Today's Issues, 9,* 1–2.

TOKER, S., SHIROM, A., SHAPIRA, I., BERLINER, S., & MELAMED, S. (2005). The association between burnout, depression, anxiety, and inflammation biomarkers: C-reactive protein and fibrinogen in men and women. *Journal of Occupational Health Psychology, 10,* 344–362.

TOMBERG, T., TOOMELA, A., PULVER, A., & TIKK, A. (2005). Coping strategies, social support, life orientation and health-related quality of life following traumatic brain injury. *Brain Injury, 19,* 1181–1190.

TOSEVSKI, D.L., & MILOVANCEVIC, M.P. (2006). Stressful life events and physical health. *Current Opinion in Psychiatry, 19,* 184–189.

TREAS, J., & GIESEN, D. (2000). Sexual infidelity among married and cohabiting Americans. *Journal of Marriage & the Family, 62,* 48–60.

TRIANDIS, H.C. (2004). Extending social psychology. *PsycCRITIQUES.*

TRIERWEILER, L.I., ELD, M., & LISCHETZKE, L. (2002). The structure of emotional expressivity: Each emotion counts. *Journal of Personality and Social Psychology, 82,* 1023–1040.

TRUCHOT, D., MAURE, G., & PATTE, S. (2003). Do attributions change over time when the actor's behavior is hedonically relevant to the perceiver? *Journal of Social Psychology, 143,* 202–208.

TSAI, J.L., KNUTSON, B., & FUNG, H.H. (2006). Cultural variation in affect valuation. *Journal of Personality and Social Psychology, 90,* 288–307.

TUCKER, P., & ARON, A. (1993). Passionate love and marital satisfaction at key transition points in the family life cycle. *Journal of Social and Clinical Psychology, 12,* 135–147.

TUCKMAN, B.W. (1965). Development sequences in small groups. *Psychological Bulletin, 63,* 384–399.

TUGADE, M.M., & FREDRICKSON, B.L. (2004). Resilient individuals use positive emotions to bounce back from negative emotional experiences. *Journal of Personality and Social Psychology, 86,* 320–333.

TURK, D.C. (1994). Perspectives on chronic pain: The role of psychological factors. *Current Directions in Psychological Science, 3,* 45–48.

TWENGE, J.M., & CROCKER, J. (2002). Race and self-esteem: Meta-analyses comparing Whites, Blacks, Hispanics, Asians, and American Indians and comment on Gray-Little and Hafdahl (2002). *Psychological Bulletin, 128,* 371–408.

U.S. Bureau of the Census. (1990). *Statistical abstract of the United States, 1990* (110th ed.). Washington, DC: U.S. Government Printing Office.

U.S. Bureau of the Census. (1991). *Statistical abstract of the United States, 1991* (111th ed.). Washington, DC: U.S. Government Printing Office.

U.S. Bureau of the Census. (1992). *Statistical abstract of the United States, 1992* (112th ed.). Washington, DC: U.S. Government Printing Office.

U.S. Bureau of the Census. (2001). America's families and living arrangements. *Current Populations Reports.* Washington, DC: Author.

U.S. Census Bureau. (2003, February). Married-couple and unmarried-partner households: 2000. *Census 2000 Special Reports,* 1–14.

U.S. Department of Agriculture. (2005). Johanna reveals USDA's steps to a healthier you. Retrieved August 7, 2006, from http://www.mypyramid.gov/global_nav/meida_press_release.html.

U.S. Department of Commerce. (1992). *1990 census of population and housing: Summary population and housing characteristics.* Washington, DC: U.S. Government Printing Office.

U.S. Department of Commerce. (2002). A nation online: Executive summary. http://www.esa.doc.gov/508/esa/ANationOnlineEXSFeb02.htm.

U.S. Department of Labor, Bureau of Labor Statistics. (1990). *Occupational outlook handbook, 1990–1991.* Washington, DC: U.S. Government Printing Office.

U.S. Department of Labor, Bureau of Labor Statistics. (1996). *Occupational outlook handbook, 1996–1997.* Washington, DC: U.S. Government Printing Office.

U.S. Department of Labor, Bureau of Labor Statistics. (2000). *Tomorrow's jobs.* http://www.bls.gov/oco/oco2003.htm.

U.S. Department of Labor, Bureau of Labor Statistics. (2003). Occupational outlook handbook. http://www.bls.gov.

U.S. Department of Labor, Bureau of Labor Statistics. (2004). Job search methods. Retrieved April 06, 2006, from http://www.bls.gov/oco/oco20042.htm.

U.S. Department of Labor, Bureau of Labor Statistice. (2005a). The 10 detailed industries with the largest wage and salary employment growth, 2004–14. Retrieved December 07, 2005, from http://www.stats.bls.gov/news.release/ecopro.to3.htm.

U.S. Department of Labor, Bureau of Labor Statistics. (2005b). Volunteering in the United States, 2005. Retrieved April 06, 2006, from http://www.bls.gov/news.release/volun.nr0.htm.

U.S. Department of Labor, Bureau of Labor Statistics. (2006a). Futurework: Trends and challenges for work in the 21st century. Retrieved April 06, 2006, from http://www.dol.gov/oasam/programs/history/herman/reports/futurework/report/chapter4/main.htm.

U.S. Department of Labor, Bureau of Labor Statistics. (2006b). Women's share of labor force to edge higher by 2008. Retrieved April 26, 2006, from http://www.bls.gov/opud/ted/2000/feb/wk3/art01.htm.

U.S. Department of Labor, Bureau of Labor Statistics. (2006c, March). Women still underrepresented among highest earners. *Issues in Labor Statistics,* 1–2.

U.S. Environmental Protection Agency. (2004). Municipal solid waste. Retrieved January 10, 2006, from http://www.epa.gov/epaoswer/non-hw/muncpl/facts.htm.

U.S. Merit Systems Protection Board. (2005). Understanding job satisfaction. Issues of merit. Retrieved April 26, 2006, from http://www.mspb.gov/studies/newsletters/05septnws/05Septembernws.htm.

UCHINO, B.N., UNO, D., & HOLT-LUNDSTAD, J. (1999). Social support, physiological processes, and health. *Current Directions in Psychological Science, 8,* 145–148.

ULIJN, J., RUTKOWSKI, A.F., KUMAR, R., & ZHU, Y. (2005). Patterns of feelings in face-to-face negotiation: A Sino-Dutch pilot study. *Cross Cultural Management, 12,* 103–118.

UNDERWOOD, M.K. (2004). III. Glares of contempt, eye rolls of disgust and turning away to exclude: Non-verbal forms of social aggression among girls. *Feminism & Psychology, 14,* 371–375.

UNDERWOOD, N. (2002b, January 21). Marital fixes. *McLean's,* 30–31.

UNDERWOOD, N. (2002a, January 21). The happy divorce. *McLean's,* 25–29.

VACCARO, J. (2004). The forgotten illness: Stigma still keeping many Americans from crucial mental-health treatment. (Opinions). *Modern Healthcare, 34,* 18.

VALLACHER, R.R., NOWAK, A., FROEHLICH, M., & ROCKLOFF, M. (2002). The dynamics of self-evaluation. *Personality and Social Psychology Review, 6,* 370–379.

VALLERAND, A.H., HASENAU, S., TEMPLIN, T., & COLLINS-BOHLER, D. (2005). Disparities between Black and White patients with cancer pain: The effect of perception of control over pain. *Pain Medicine, 6,* 242–250.

van ASSEMA, P., MARTENS, M., RUITER, A.C., & BRUG, J. (2001). Framing of nutrition education messages in persuading consumers of the advantages of a healthy diet. *Journal of Human Nutrition and Dietetics, 14,* 435–442.

van DIJK, E., & ZEELENBERG, M. (2005). On the psychology of 'if only': Regret and the comparison between factual and counterfactual outcomes. *Organizational Behavior and Human Decision Processes, 97,* 152–160.

van ENGEN, M.L., van DER LEEDEN, R., & WILLEMSEN, T. M. (2001). Gender, context and leadership styles: A field study. *Journal of Occupational and Organizational Psychology, 74,* 581–598.

van ENGEN, M.L., & WILLEMSEN, T.M. (2004). Sex and leadership styles: A meta-analysis of research published in the 1990s. *Psychological Reports, 94,* 3–18.

van LOMMEL, P., van WEES, R., MEYERS, V., & ELFFERICH, I. (2001). Near-death experience in survivors of cardiac arrest: A prospective study in the Netherlands. *The Lancet, 358,* 2039–2045.

VANGELISTI, A.L., & GERSTENBERGER, M. (2004). Communication and marital infidelity. In J. Duncombe, K. Harrison, G. Allan, & D. Marsden (Eds.), *The state of affairs: Explorations in infidelity and commitment.* (pp. 59–78). Mahwah, NJ: Lawrence Erlbaum Associates.

VANGELISTI, A.L., & YOUNG, S.L. (2000). When words hurt: The effects of perceived intentionality on interpersonal relationships. *Journal of Social and Personal Relationships, 17,* 393–424.

VASTAG, B. (2001). Easing the elderly online in search of health information. *Journal of the American Medical Association, 285,* 1563.

VECCHIO, R.P. (2002). Leadership and gender advantage. *Leadership Quarterly, 13,* 643–671.

VEGG, P.R., SPIELBERGER, C.D., & WASSALA, C.F. (2002). Effects of organizational level and gender on stress in the workplace. *International Journal of Stress Management, 9,* 243–261.

VITTENGL, J.R., & HOLT, C.S. (2000). Getting acquainted: The relationship of self-disclosure and social attraction to positive affect. *Journal of Social and Personal Relationships, 17,* 53–66.

VODANOVICH, S.J., & KASS, S.J. (1990). Age and gender differences in boredom proneness. *Journal of Social Behavior and Personality, 5,* 297–307.

VOGEL, D.L., WESTER, S.R., WEI, M., & BOYSEN, G.A. (2005). The role of outcome expectations and attitudes on decisions to seek professional help. *Journal of Counseling Psychology, 52,* 459–470.

WALLERSTEIN, J.S., & LEWIS, J.M. (2004). The unexpected legacy of divorce: Report of a 25-year study. *Psychoanalytic Psychology, 21,* 353–370.

WALLERSTEIN, J.S., & LEWIS, J.M. (2005). The reality of divorce. Reply to Gordon (2005). *Psychoanalytic Psychology, 22,* 452–454.

WALSH, J. (2002). Shyness and social phobia: A social work perspective on a problem in living. *Health and Social Work, 27,* 137–144.

WAMPOLD, B.E., MINAMI, T., TIERNEY, S.C., BASKIN, T.W., BHATI, K.S. (2005). The placebo is powerful: Estimating placebo effects in medicine and psychotherapy from randomized clinical trials. *Journal of Clinical Psychology, 61,* 835–854.

WARD, C., & SEARLE, W. (1991). The impact of value discrepancies and cultural identity on psychological and sociocultural adjustment of sojourners. *International Journal of Intercultural Relations, 15,* 209–225.

WARD, S. (2003, February 27). 1 in 4 have at least 2 computers. *USA Today,* p. 1A.

WARGO, E. (2006). Nature, nurture, nuance. *APS Observer,* 19, 11–12.

WARREN, N.A., (1997). Bereavement care in the critical care setting. *Critical Care Nursing Quarterly, 20,* 42–47.

WASSERMAN, I.M., & RICHMOND-ABBOTT, M. (2005). Gender and the Internet: Causes of variation in access, level, and scope of use. *Social Science Quarterly, 86,* 252–270.

WATKINS, E.C. (1993). What have surveys taught us about the teaching and practice of vocational assessment? *Counseling Psychologist, 21,* 109–117.

WATT, D.F. (2004). The blank slate: The modern denial of human nature. *Neuropsychoanalysis, 6,* 116–118.

WEINER, B., PANTON, S., & WEBER, M. (1999, April 28). *New study first to quantify illicit drug and substance use in movies and music popular among youth.* http://www.mediacampaign.org/inthenews/mediascope.html.

WEISS, M.G., & RAMAKRISHNA, J. (2006). Stigma interventions and research for international health. *Lancet, 367,* 536–538.

WESTERHOF, G.J., & BARRETT, A.E. (2005). Age identity and subjective well-being: A comparison of the United States and Germany. *Journals of Gerontology: Series B: Psychological Sciences and Social Sciences, 60B,* 129–136.

WESTMAN, A., HUNT, E., CICILLINI, V., & LEWANDOWSKI, L. (1999). Relationships among assisted suicide and religiousness, resources available, denial of dying, and autonomy. *Psychological Reports, 85,* 1070–1076.

WHARTON, A.S., ROTOLO, T., & BIRD, S.R. (2000). Social context at work: A multilevel analysis of job satisfaction. *Sociological Forum, 15,* 65–90.

WHEELAN, S.A., & VERDI, A.F. (1992). Differences in male and female patterns of communication in groups: A methodological artifact? *Sex Roles, 27,* 1–15.

WHITBECK, L.B., & HOYT, D.R. (1994). Social prestige and assortive mating: A comparison of students from 1956 and 1988. *Journal of Social and Personal Relationships, 11,* 137–145.

WHITE, J.L., & PARHAM, T.A. (1990). *The psychology of Blacks: An African-American perspective* (2nd ed.). Englewood Cliffs, NJ: Prentice Hall.

WHITTY, M.T., & CARR, A.N. (2006). New rules in the workplace: Applying object-relations theory to explain problem internet and email behaviour in the workplace. *Computers in Human Behavior, 22,* 235–250.

WIEDENFELD, S.A., O'LEARY, A., BANDURA, A., BROWN, S., LEVINE S., & RASKA K. (1990). Impact of perceived self-efficacy in coping with stressors on components of the immune system. *Journal of Personality & Social Psychology, 59,* 1082–109.

WILBURN, C. (2006). Mediation: a possible asset for EAPs: Though mediation is not always a good fit for workplace disputes, mediation services can provide EAPs with another tool to add to their repertoire of skills. *The Journal of Employee Assistance, 36,* 7–8.

WILCOX, D., & DOWRICK, P.W. (1992). Anger management with adolescents. *Residential Treatment for Children and Youth, 9,* 29–39.

WILDE, A., & DIEKMAN, A.B. (2005). Cross-cultural similarities and differences in dynamic stereotypes: A comparison between Germany and the United States. *Psychology of Women Quarterly, 29,* 188–196.

WILKINSON, S., & KITZINGER, C. (2005). Same-sex marriage and equality. *Psychologist, 18,* 290–293.

WILLIAMS, J.M.G., CRANE, C., BARNHOFER, T., VAN DER DOES, A.J.W., & SEGAL, Z.V. (2006). Recurrence of suicidal ideation across depressive episodes. *Journal of Affective Disorders, 91,* 189–194.

WILLIAMS, K.E., & BOND, M.J. (2002). The roles of self-efficacy, outcome expectancies and social support in the self-care behaviours of diabetics. *Psychology, Health, and Medicine, 7,* 127–141.

WILLIAMS, T.L., CLARKE, V., & BORLAND, R. (2001). Effects of message framing on breast-cancer-related beliefs and behaviors: The role of mediating factors. *Journal of Applied Social Psychology, 31,* 925–950.

WILLOUGHBY, B.L.B., MALIK, N.M., & LINDAHL, K.M. (2006). Parental reactions to their sons' sexual orientation disclosures: The roles of family cohesion, adaptability, and parenting style. *Psychology of Men & Masculinity, 7,* 14–26.

WILLS, T.A., VACARO, D., & MCNAMARA, G. (1994). Novelty seeking, risk taking, and related constructs as predictors of adolescent substance use: An application of Cloninger's theory. *Journal of Substance Abuse, 6,* 1–20.

WILSON, J.M., STRAUS, S.G., & MCEVILY, B. (2006). All in due time: The development of trust in computer-mediated and face-to-face teams. *Organizational Behavior and Human Decision Processes, 99,* 16–33.

WILSON, R.S., BARNES, L.L., KREUGER, K.R., HOGANSON, G., BIENAS, J.L., & BENNETT, D.A. (2005). Early and late cognitive activity and cognitive systems in old age. *Journal of the International Neurological Society, 11,* 400–407.

WILSON, T.D., & GILBERT, D.T. (2005). Affective forecasting: Knowing what to want. *Current Directions in Psychological Science, 14,* 131–134.

WING, R.R., & RAYNOR, D.A. (2006). Lifestyle modifications in the obese patient with cardiovascular disease. In M.K. Robinson & A. Thomas (Eds.). *Obesity and cardiovascular disease.* New York: Taylor & Francis.

WINGFIELD, A., TUN, P.A., & MCCOY, S.L. (2005). Hearing loss in older adults: What is it and how it interacts with cognitive performance. *Current Directions in Psychological Science, 14,* 144–148.

WISEMAN, H., MAYSELESS, O., & SHARABANY, R. (2006). Why are they lonely? Perceived quality of early relationships with parents, attachment, personality predispositions and loneliness in first-year university students. *Personality and Individual Differences, 40,* 237–248.

WOLFE, C., & CROCKER, J. (2003). What does the self want? Contingencies of self-worth and goals. In S.J. Spencer, S. Fein, M.P. Zanna, & J.M. Olson (Eds.), Ontario symposium on personality and social psychology, May 2000, University of Waterloo, Waterloo, Canada; this book consists of the expanded and updated versions of articles initially presented at the aforementioned conference, and two additional related articles (pp. 147–170). Mahwah, NJ: Lawrence Erlbaum Associates.

WOLPE, J. (1973). *The practice of behavior therapy.* New York: Pergamon.

Women's Way. (2006). Power skills: How volunteering shapes professional success. Retrieved August 9, 2006, from http://www.volunteermatch.org/volunteers/resources/surveyfnl.pdf.

WOOD, N.D., CRANE, D.R., SCHAALJE, G.B., & LAW, D.D. (2005). What works for whom: A meta-analytic review of marital and couples therapy in reference to marital distress. *American Journal of Family Therapy, 33,* 273–287.

WOODHILL, B.M., & SAMUELS, C.A. (2003). Positive and negative androgyny and their relationship with psychological health and well-being. *Sex Roles, 48,* 555–565.

WOODHILL, B.M., & SAMUELS, C.A. (2004). Desirable and undesirable androgyny: A prescription for the twenty-first century. *Journal of Gender Studies, 13,* 15–28.

WOODS, S., & WHITE, E. (2005). The association between bullying behaviour, arousal levels and behaviour problems. *Journal of Adolescence, 28,* 381–395.

World Health Organization. (2006). Women and mental health. Retrieved July 2, 2006, from http://www.who.int/mediacentre/factsheets/fs248/en/.

WRIGHT, C.E., KUNZ-EBRECHT, S.R., ILIFFE, S., FOESE, O., & STEPTOE, A. (2005). Physiological correlates of cognitive functioning in an elderly population. *Psychoneuroendocrinology, 30,* 826–838.

WRIGHT, K. (2002, June). Six degrees of speculation. *Discover,* 19–21.

WRIGHT, K. (2003). Relationships with death: The terminally ill talk about dying. *Journal of Marital and Family Therapy, 29,* 439–453.

XIAO-PING, W. (2004). A comparison study of persons found not criminally responsible by reason of mental disorder between British Columbia, Canada and Hunan, China. *Chinese Journal of Clinical Psychology, 12,* 405–407.

XIRASAGAR, S., SAMUELS, M.E., & STOSKOPF, C.H. (2005). Physician leadership styles and effectiveness: An empirical study. *Medical Care Research and Review, 62,* 720–740.

YAMAGUCHI, S., GELFAND, M., OHASHI, M.M., & ZEMBA, Y. (2005). The cultural psychology of control: Illusions of personal versus collective control in the United States and Japan. *Journal of Cross-Cultural Psychology, 36,* 750–761.

YANCEY, G., & YANCEY, S. (1998). Interracial dating: Evidence from personal advertisements. *Journal of Family Issues, 19,* 334–348.

YANG, K. (2003). Beyond Maslow's culture-bound linear theory: A preliminary statement of the double-y model of basic human needs. In V. Murphy-Berman, & J.J. Berman (Eds.), *Cross-cultural differences in perspectives on the self* (pp. 192–272). Lincoln, NE: University of Nebraska Press.

YARAB, P.E., & ALLGEIER, E.R. (1997, April). *Just don't have sex! Acceptability, disclosure, and forgiveness of extradyadic relationships.* Paper presented at the annual meeting of the Eastern Psychological Association, Washington, DC.

YBARRA, O. (2001). When first impressions don't last: The role of isolation and adaptation processes in the revision of evaluative impressions. *Social Cognition, 19,* 491–520.

YODANIS, C. (2005). Divorce culture and marital gender equality: A cross-national study. *Gender & Society, 19,* 644–659.

YOSHIMURA, S.M. (2004). Emotional and behavioral responses to romantic jealousy expressions. *Communication Reports, 17,* 85–101.

YOVETICH, N.A., DALE, J.A., & HUDAK, M.A. (1990). Benefits of humor in reduction of threat-induced anxiety. *Psychological Reports, 66,* 51–58.

YUEN, C.N., & LAVIN, M.J. (2004). Internet dependence in the collegiate population: The role of shyness. *CyberPsychology & Behavior, 7,* 379–383.

YURCHISIN, J., WATCHRAVESRINGKAN, K., & MCCABE, D.B. (2005). An exploration of identity re-creation in the context of internet dating. *Social Behavior and Personality, 33,* 735–750.

ZABRISKIE, P. (2004). Wounds that don't bleed: How severe stress is taking a toll on U.S. troops in Iraq. *Time, 164,* 40–42.

ZAMPELLI, S.O. (2000). *From sabotage to success: How to overcome self-defeating behavior and reach your true inner potential.* Oakland, CA: New Harbinger Publications.

ZARIT, S.H., PEARLIN, L.I., & SCHAIE, K.W. (Eds.) (2003). *Personal control in social and life course contexts.* New York: Springer Publishing Co.

ZAUTRA, A.J., AFFLECK, G.G., TENNEN, H., REICH, J.W., & DAVIS, M.C. (2005). Dynamic approaches to emotions and stress in everyday life: Bolger and Zuckerman reloaded with positive as well as negative affects. *Journal of Personality. Special Issue: Advances in Personality and Daily Experience, 73,* 1–28.

ZEA, M.C., REISEN, C.A., POPPEN, P.J., BIANCHI, F.T., & ECHEVERRY, J.J. (2005). Disclosure of HIV status and psychological well-being among Latino gay and bisexual men. *AIDS and Behavior, 9,* 15–26.

ZEIDNER, M. (1995). Adaptive coping with test situations: A review of the literature. *Educational Psychologist, 30,* 123–133.

ZEIDNER, M., & MATTHEWS, G. (2005). Evaluation anxiety: Current theory and research. In A. Elliot & C. Dweck (Eds.), *Handbook of competence and motivation* (pp. 141–163). New York: Guilford.

ZHENG, H., LIU, Y., LI, W., YANG, B., CHEN, D., & WANG, X., et al. (2006). Beneficial effects of exercise and its molecular mechanisms on depression in rats. *Behavioural Brain Research, 168,* 47–55.

ZIEBLAND, S., ROBERTSON, J., JAY, J., NEIL, A. (2002). Body image and weight change in middle age: A qualitative study. *International Journal of Obesity & Related Metabolic Disorders, 26,* 1083–1091.

ZIMBARDO, P.G. (1986). The Stanford shyness project. In W.H. Jones, J.M. Cheek, & S.R. Briggs (Eds.), *Shyness: Perspectives on research and treatment* (pp. 17–25). New York: Plenum.

ZIMMERMAN, B.J., & SCHUNK, D.H. (2003). *Albert Bandura: The scholar and his contributions to educational psychology.* Mahwah, NJ: Lawrence Erlbaum Associates.

ZIMMERMAN, C. (2004). Denial of impending death: A discourse analysis of the palliative care literature. *Social Science & Medicine, 59,* 1769–1780.

ZUCKERMAN, M. (1990a). The psychophysiology of sensation-seeking. *Journal of Personality, 58,* 313–345.

ZUCKERMAN, M. (1990b). Some dubious premises in research and theory on racial differences: Scientific, social, and ethical issues. *American Psychologist, 45,* 1297–1303.

ZUCKERMAN, M. (2005). The neurobiology of impulsive sensation seeking: Genetics, brain physiology, biochemistry, and neurology. In C. Stough (Ed.), *Neurobiology of exceptionality* (pp. 31–52). New York: Kluwer Academic/Plenum Publishers.

ZUCKERMAN, M., KNEE, C.R., KIEFFER, S.C., & GAGNE, M. (2004). What individuals believe they can and cannot do: Explorations of realistic and unrealistic control beliefs. *Journal of Personality Assessment, 82,* 215–232.

ZUCKERMAN, M., & KUHLMAN, D.M. (2000). Personality and risk-taking: Common biosocial factors. *Journal of Personality: Special Issue: Personality Processes and Problem Behavior, 68,* 999–1029.

ZUMMUNER, V.L., & FISCHER, A.H. (1995). The social regulation of emotions in jealousy situations: A comparison between Italy and the Netherlands. *Journal of Cross-Cultural Psychology, 26,* 189–208.

ZURBRIGGEN, E.L., & YOST, M.R. (2004). Power, desire, and pleasure in sexual fantasies. *Journal of Sex Research, 41,* 288–300.

Photo Acknowledgments

Chapter 1 Page 1, Jessica Shuman; p. 7, Jessica Shuman; p. 9, Karen Duffy; p. 19, Karen Duffy.

Chapter 2 Page 25, Jessica Shuman; p. 29, Jessica Shuman; p. 42, Jessica Shuman; p. 47, Jessica Shuman.

Chapter 3 Page 57, Karen Duffy; p. 62, Jessica Shuman; p. 64, Jessica Shuman; p. 74, Karen Duffy.

Chapter 4 Page 82, Karen Duffy; p. 86, Karen Duffy; p. 91, Karen Duffy; p. 96, Jessica Shuman.

Chapter 5 Page 105, Jessica Shuman; p. 112, Karen Duffy; p. 121, Jessica Shuman; p. 128, Jessica Shuman.

Chapter 6 Pages 139, 143, 151, 154, Jessica Shuman.

Chapter 7 Page 163, Karen Duffy; p. 166, Jessica Shuman; p. 169, Jessica Shuman; p. 176, Karen Duffy.

Chapter 8 Pages 193, 203, 210, 215, Jessica Shuman.

Chapter 9 Page 221, Karen Duffy; p. 223, Karen Duffy; p. 229, Jessica Shuman; p. 232, Karen Duffy.

Chapter 10 Page 252, Jessica Shuman; p. 257, Jessica Shuman; p. 267, Karen Duffy; p. 273, Jessica Shuman.

Chapter 11 Page 280, Jessica Shuman; p. 282, Jessica Shuman; p. 289, Pacific Stock; p. 305, AP Wide World Photos.

Chapter 12 Page 312, Jessica Shuman; p. 320, Karen Duffy; p. 325, Jessica Shuman; p. 335, Jessica Shuman.

Chapter 13 Page 343, Jessica Shuman; p. 346, Jessica Shuman; p. 356, Jessica Shuman; p. 362, Karen Duffy.

Chapter 14 Pages 369, 380, 390, 394, Jessica Shuman.

Chapter 15 Page 401, Karen Duffy; p. 405, AP Wide World Photos; p. 414, Karen Duffy; p. 416, PhotoEdit Inc.

Chapter 16 Pages 430, 435, 439, 444, Jessica Shuman.

Name Index

AARP, 265
Abakoumikin, G., 442
Abbey, A., 330
Abell, S.C., 43
Abelli, M., 183, 185
Abramo-Vitz, M., 107
Abrams, D., 33, 225
Abramson, L.Y., 84, 88, 385
Ackerman, B., 178
Ackerman, S.J., 421
Acton, R.G., 183
Adams, J., 228
Adams, R.E., 264
Addis, M.E., 123, 124
Adler, J., 351
Administration on Aging, 59,
        74, 124, 438
Adrianson, L., 228
Affleck, G.G., 348
Ahadi, S., 10
Ahlfinger, N.R., 242
Ahuvia, A., 166, 168
Ai, A.L., 355
Ainsworth, M., 50
Ainsworth, S.E., 363
Ajzen, I., 141
Akamatsu, S., 197
Akkirman, A.D., 267
Alatas, E.S., 68
Alavi, K., 212
Alban-Metcalf, R.J., 240
Albano, A.M., 205
Alexander, K., 203
Alicke, M.D., 203
Alimo-Metcalf, B., 240
Allen, J., 424
Allgeier, E.R., 330
Allik, J., 88
Alloy, L.B., 385
Allumbaught, D.L., 442
Almedon, A.M., 357

Almeida, D.M., 346, 347, 353
Aloni, M., 316
Alterman, J., 4, 5
Althof, S.E., 69
Alzheimer's Association, 68
Amato, P.R., 329, 330, 332, 334
Ambady, N., 201
Amen, D.G., 400
American Academy of Pediatrics, 107, 283
American Medical Association, 137
American Psychiatric Association, 372, 393
American Psychoanalytic Association, 406
American Psychological Association, 264, 293,
        315, 344, 355, 420
American Psychological Society, 120
Amerkhan, J.H., 147
Anastasio, P.A., 150, 151
Andersen, P.A., 185
Anderson, B.L., 282
Anderson, C.J., 149, 155, 156, 157
Anderson, E.R., 333
Anderson, S.M., 201
Anderson, T.L., 317
Andreassi, C.L., 213
Andrews, G.R., 75
Anred.com, 389, 390
Ansfield, M.E., 200
Ansseau, M., 170
Antonio, A.L., 225
Applebaum, M., 321
Archer, T., 148
Archibald, F.S., 214
Arenson, S.J., 235
Aristotle, 272
Arkin, R.C., 165
Armour, S., 267
Arnold, P., 170
Arnold, R.M., 447
Aron, A., 207
Aron, E.N., 207
Aronoff, J., 201

Asai, A., 211
Asbjornsen, A., 143
Asch, Solomon, 232
Asher, S.R., 208, 214
Ashman, O., 142
Ashmore, R.D., 225
Asmus, C.L., 235
Aspinwall, L.G., 146, 148
Astin, A.W., 62
Atkins, L., 282
Atkinson, 50
Atwater, E., 202
Atwood, F., 288
Aune, K.S., 178
Aune, R.K., 178
Austenfeld, J.L., 356
Avellar, S., 334
Azam, O.A., 204
Azar, B., 167, 178

Báland, F., 448
Baack, D.W., 198
Baars, B.J., 37, 41
Bagwell, C.J., 213
Bailey, J.M., 289
Bailey, M.J., 315
Baker, C.N., 287
Baker, S.R., 13
Balsam, K.F., 294
Baltes, P.B., 72
Bandura, A., 37, 38, 39, 40, 52, 111,
        142, 161, 172
Banks, I., 123
Bar, M., 201
Barber, B.K., 33
Barber, B.L., 334
Barbour, K.A., 418
Barbour, R.S., 446
Barbuto, J.E.J., 239
Bardy, A.H., 437
Bargal, D., 244

Bargh, J.A., 86
Bargman, E.P., 418
Barker, G.P., 120
Barkin, S., 214
Barnes, B.L., 14
Barnes, L.L., 67
Barnett, M.M., 437
Barnhofer, T., 384, 386
Barnlund, D.C., 211
Baron, R.A., 178
Baroni, S., 183, 185
Barrett, A.E., 186
Barrett, L.F., 88
Bartholome, A., 198
Bartholomew, K., 214
Bartlett, M.Y., 185
Bartoshuk, L.M., 168
Basow, S.A., 202
Bass, B.M., 239, 240
Battle, C.L., 391
Baucom, D.H., 331
Bauer, J.J., 66
Bauer, K., 310
Baum, D., 355
Baumeister, R.F., 88, 91, 92,
    208, 353
Beach, S.R., 200
Beardsley, K.C., 247
Beauchaine, T.P., 294
Beaupré, M.G., 177, 201
Bebetsos, E., 111
Beck, A.T., 409, 421
Bedard, M., 447–448
Beenen, G., 235
Beer, J.S., 97
Beilock, S.L., 182
Beitel, M., 174
Belkin, D.K., 205, 207
Bell, K.L., 200
Bell, S.S., 69
Belovics, R., 267, 272
Bender, S.E., 213
Beneson, J.F., 212
Bengston, V.L., 59
Benjet, C., 38
Bennett, D.A., 67
Bennett, M.D.J., 347
Ben-Ze'ev, A., 317
Berdahl, J.L., 270
Beresin, E.V., 198
Bergeman, C.S., 142
Bergman, H., 448
Bergner, R.M., 315, 318
Bergstron, R.L., 109
Berk, L., 55
Berk, M.S., 201
Berliner, S., 264
Berndt, T.J., 208
Bernieri, F.J., 316
Bernstein, D.A., 421

Berntson, G.G., 214
Berscheid, E., 213
Bertacco, M., 202
Beste, S.A., 315
Beste, S.E., 318
Betz, N.E., 258
Beutler, L.E., 406
Bianchi, F.T., 208, 209
Biddle, S.J., 142
Bienas, J.L., 67
Bigler, M., 84, 86, 88
Billings, J.A., 437
Bilotta, J.G., 226, 227
bin Laden, Osama, 243
Bippus, A.M., 243
Birch, 46
Bird, S.R., 269
Bird, S.T., 125
Bisconti, T.L., 142
Bishop, A.P., 5
Biswas, B., 247
Biswas-Diener, R., 178, 187
Bjorklund, D.F., 185
Blackwell, B.S., 322
Blair, G.R., 191
Blanchard, E., 355
Blankstein, K.R., 14
Blanton, H., 227
Blashke, T., 125
Blatt, S.J., 406, 420
Bleske, A.L., 212
Block, S.D., 437
Blum, D., 155
Blumenthal, J.A., 418
Boakwala, J., 70
Bobik, C., 216
Bobrow, D., 315
Bodenhausen, G.V., 225
Bodmer-Turner, J., 303
Boerner, K., 440
Bogart, L.M., 125
Bohart, A.C., 407
Bolles, R.N., 279
Bonanno, G.A., 174, 175, 178, 356,
    440, 441, 442
Bond, F.W., 181
Bond, M.H., 233
Bond, R., 233
Bono, J.E., 141
Bons, T.A., 199
Bood, S., 148
Booth, A., 329
Borgen, F.H., 257
Borman, W.C., 67
Bornstein, M.H., 33
Boscarino, J.A., 264
Bosnak, J., 240
Bouchard, T.J., 29
Bouman, D., 197
Bourne, E.J., 400

Boutelle, K., 85
Bowlby,, 50
Boyatzis, R.E., 250
Boysen, G.A., 421
Brackett, M.A., 215
Bradbury, T.N., 316
Bradley, M.M., 225
Bramlett, M.D., 328
Brandstadter, J., 73
Brannen, C., 216
Brassington, G.S., 418
Braun, L., 292, 294
Braverman, J., 185
Bray, J.H., 331
Braza, F., 215
Braza, P., 215
Brazil, K., 447–448
Breivik, G., 170
Bremner, J.D., 383
Brett, J.M., 272
Brewer, E.W., 269
Brewer, P.R., 324
Brewis, A., 332
Bringle, R.G., 185
Britten, N., 125
Brodwin, M.G., 303
Brody, L.R., 177
Bronars, C.A., 117
Brooks-Gunn, J., 49
Brotheridge, C.M., 237
Brown, A., 71
Brown, E., 84, 86, 88
Brown, F.W., 239
Brown, J.D., 93
Brown, K.D., 39
Brown, K.T., 225
Brown, L.M., 225
Brown, P., 70
Brown, R.P., 146
Brown, S., 40
Brownell, K.D., 400
Bruch, M.A., 205, 207
Bruckner, K.H., 317
Brug, J., 125
Brunton, M., 124
Bruzzone, A., 198
Bryant, R.A., 355, 383
Bryne, D., 178
Bryson, J.B., 185
Buboltz, W.C., 152
Buchanan, J.A., 420, 421
Buffone, G., 24
Bui, K., 421
Buller, D.J., 29
Bullock, J.R., 184
Burbach, M.E., 239
Bureau of Labor Statistics,
    260, 275
Burgess, M., 216
Burke, R.J., 264

Burleson, B.R., 202
Burt, D.M., 197
Bush, G.W., 243
Bush, J.A., 170
Bushman, B.J., 182
Buss, D.M., 185, 202, 212
Butler, A.C., 409, 421
Butler, D., 240
Butterfield, D.A., 240
Buys, L.R., 210
Buzzi, G., 437
Bybee, J.A., 84
Byock, G., 407
Byrne, D., 196, 199
Byrne, J.J., 125
Byrne, L., 225

Cacioppo, J.R., 214
Cadell, S., 442
Cahill, D.J., 200
Cameron, A.F., 267
Campbell, A., 207, 208
Campbell, J.D., 91, 92
Campbell, M.E., 225
Campbell, S.M., 197
Campbell-Sills, L., 357
Canary, D.J., 212
Canli, T., 288, 289, 290
Cannings, K., 62
Capelos, T., 5
Capista, J., 205
Cappelleri, J.C., 69
Carbonell, J., 65
Cardona-Coll, D., 244
Carducci, B.J., 205, 207
Careeras, M.R., 215
Carey, A.R., 76
Carey, J., 13
Carletta, J., 227
Carlson, E., 124
Carpenter, D., 288
Carr, A.N., 228, 267, 272
Carr, T.H., 182
Carrere, S., 286, 326, 327
Carstensen, L.L., 66, 72, 75, 177
Carter, M.M., 197
Caruthers, A., 197
Carvallo, M., 196
Carver, C.S., 148
Cascio, T., 355
Caserta, M.S., 442
Caspi, A., 16, 48
Cassidy, C., 94, 346–347, 349
Cassidy, G.L., 49, 142
Castel, A.D., 72
Catalano, R.F., 120
Catipovic-Veselica, K., 182
CDC Office on Smoking Health, 114, 115
Ceballo, R., 330

Center for Mental Health Services, 383
Centers for Disease Control, 132
Centers for Disease Control and Prevention, 109, 116, 299–302, 323, 325, 333, 335–336
Cerrato, P.L., 148
Chamberlain, R.M., 124
Chamberlain, T.C., 270
Chang, E.C., 148
Chang, K., 235
Chantal, Y., 147
Chapman, B.P., 109
Chapman, J., 150, 151
Chapman, J.E., 409, 421
Chapman, M.A., 147, 157
Charles, S.T., 177
Charlesworth, E.A., 367
Charney, D.S., 357
Chasse, V., 225
Chasteen, A.L., 204
Chatterjee, C., 212
Chatzisarantis, N.L.D., 142
Cheater, F., 123
Chen, D., 418
Chen, G.M., 211, 240
Chen, X., 207
Cheng, H., 335
Cheon, H.J., 241
Chess, 46, 47
Chidambaram, L., 235
Chirkov, V., 187
Chisholm-Stockard, S.M., 420, 421
Chivers, M.L., 289
Cho, C., 241
Cho, H., 322
Cho, Y.I., 226, 233, 241, 245
Chochinov, H.M., 444
Choi, I., 88
Choi, Y., 88
Christensen, A.J., 125
Christensen, T.C., 88
Chroni, S., 111
Chung, D., 282
Cicillini, V., 444
Clark, A., 197
Clark, E.M., 208, 213
Clarkberg, M., 76
Clay, D., 107
Clinical Psychiatry News, 372
Clinton, H., 240
Cloth, A., 315
Cogswell, C., 109
Cohan, C.L., 323
Cohan, S.L., 357
Cohen, F., 240
Cohen, S., 110, 214, 227, 434
Coifman, K., 174, 175, 178
Colley, A., 211
Collins, A.W., 33
Collins, W.A., 212

Collins-Bohler, D., 142
Comfort, A., 310
Condie, H., 197
Cone, A.L., 142–143
Connolly, T., 151, 152
Connors, B., 202
Conrey, F.R., 204
Consumer Reports, 420
Contrada, R.J., 225
Contrada, R.S., 182
Contreras, R., 319
Conway, L.G., III, 225
Conway, M., 94
Conway, T.L., 142
Conway-Giustra, F., 65
Coon, H.M., 10
Cooper, H., 146
Copeland, M.E., 219
Copp, G., 437
Corey, G., 428
Cornelius-White, C.F., 406
Cornelius-White, J.H.D., 406
Corr, C.A., 438
Corr, P.J., 181
Correia, C.J., 170
Costa, P.T.J., 16, 59
Coston, R.D., 216
Cottler, L.B., 295
Coultas, J.C., 233
Couper, R.T.L., 437
Coups, E., 225
Court, A., 10
Courtenay, W., 123, 124
Covin, R., 411
Cowles, M.L., 117
Cox, C., 93
Crain, W., 56
Cralley, E.L., 204
Cramer, P., 353
Crandall, C.S., 199
Crane, C., 384, 386
Crane, D.R., 330–331
Crane, R.D., 334
Crawford, C.B., 283
Crawford, M.T., 152
Cremona, K., 216
Crittendon, J.A., 181
Crocker, J., 88, 91, 92, 93, 94, 95
Croghan, I.T., 117
Croghan, J.M., 70
Croizet, J., 204
Crone, D., 131
Cronin, C., 347, 348
Crooks, R.L., 310
Cropley, M., 347
Crosby, F.J., 240
Crosnoe, R., 66
Crowley, A., 65
Crowley, S.L., 67
Crozier, W.R., 205

Cruz, M.G., 242
Csank, P., 94
Cumming, S.R., 207, 208
Cushner, K., 244
Cyranowski, J.M., 282

Dahlen, E.R., 183
Daibo, I., 319
Daker-White, G., 125
Dale, K., 353
Damon, 49
Daniels, C., 345, 346
Danks, P.K., 363
Darby, D., 72
Dardis, G.J., 246
Darrow, C.N., 61
D'Augelli, A.R., 94
Davey, G.C.L., 175
Davidson, J.K., 287
Davidson, S., 444
Davies, K.M., 207
Davies, L., 142
Davis, G.F., 440
Davis, K., 227
Davis, M.C., 202, 348
Davis, R.E., 181
Davis, R.M., 84, 88
Dawes, R.M., 161
Day, A.L., 270
De Dreu, C.K.W., 243
de Gilder, D., 199
De LaRonde, C., 314
Dean, K.K., 86
Deaner, S.L., 177
Dearborn, K., 239
DeBell, C., 272
DeBerard, M.S., 214
Deci, E.L., 166, 168
Decker, P.A., 117
Declaire, J., 341
Deeney, J.M., 226, 227
Deffenbacher, J.L., 182
Delahanty, D.L., 125
DeLameter, J., 288, 291
Dement, W.C., 137
Demier, O., 420
Demorest, A., 405
Dench, J., 72
DeNeve, K.M., 186
Dennerstein, L., 296
Denrell, J., 196, 200
Dentinger, E., 76
Department of Health and Human
    Services, 133
DePaulo, B.M., 200
Deponte, A., 202
Derdeyn, A.P., 335
deSchonen, 49
De-Souza, G., 236
DeSteno, D., 185

Deutsch, M., 244
Devos, T., 225
deVries, B., 211
Dey, E.L., 62
DeYoung, R., 237
Di Nasso, E., 183, 185
Diamond, L.M., 282, 292
Dickinson, A., 33
Diekman, A.B., 287
Diener, E., 178, 186, 187, 197
Diener, M., 186, 187
DiGiuseppe, R.A., 182
Dik, B.J., 257, 258
DiLoreno, T.M., 418
Dimberg, U., 178
Dinan, T.G., 347
Dinkmeyer, D., 191
Dion, K.K., 318
Dion, K.L., 318
Discover, 4
Ditommaso, E., 216
Dittmar, H., 107
Dodge, K.L., 331
Doka, L.K., 444, 446
Dolgin, K.G., 211
Dols, J.M.F., 166, 168
Domitrz, M., 310
Donaldson-Evans, 198
Donnay, D.A.C., 257
Donnell, A.J., 152
Donovan, R.G., 125
Double, R., 141
Dovidio, J.F., 150, 225
Dowrick, P.W., 183
Doyle, E.A., 333
Dozier, D.M., 240
Dozois, D.J.A., 411
Drentea, P., 76, 228
Druss, B., 413, 416, 417, 420
Dubrovsky, V.J., 228
Duffy, K.G., 3, 4, 5, 209, 227, 246,
    247, 271, 322, 331, 364, 376,
    413, 417, 419, 420
Duffy, V.B., 168
Dugan, L., 322
Dumlao, J., 348
Dunlap, L.L., 56
Dunn, J., 335
Dunne, G.A., 329
Dunning, D., 88, 91
Dupras, A., 294
During, S.M., 183
Durvasula, R., 282, 283
Duvall, J., 196
Dweck, C.S., 88
Dzindolet, M.R., 211
Dzokoto, V., 10

Eagly, A.H., 197, 240
Echeverry, J.J., 208, 209

Eckel, R.H., 113
Eden, J., 242
Edison, T., 14
Edwards, W.J., 294
Efklides, A., 165
Efran, J.S., 137
Egan, D., 418
Egeth, J.D., 225
Eglund, 50
Ehlers, A., 355, 383
Eibach, R.P., 96
Eikeland, O.J., 143
Eisenberg, N., 178
Ekman, P., 177, 178
Eld, M., 175
Elder, G.H., 66
Elfenbein, H.A., 201
Elfferich, I., 436
Elias, M., 65, 69, 184
Elizur, Y., 294, 315
Ellemers, N., 199
Elleven, R.K., 424
Elliot, A.J., 187
Elliot, C., 108
Elliot, R., 108
Ellis, A., 411
Ellison, N.B., 198, 209, 317
Elmehed, K., 178
Elmwood, P.C., 182
Emelyanova, T., 211
Emmelkamp, P.M.G., 207
Engl, J., 316
Engstrom, E., 237
Engstron, G., 111
Ensari, N., 225
Epley, N., 202, 228
Epstein, R., 367
Erdmann-Sager, D., 348
Erez, A., 141
Erez, M., 241
Eriksen, K.P., 421
Erikson, E.H., 35, 36, 62, 66, 73,
    76, 270
Erlandson, K.T., 202
Erman, P., 191
Ernst, E., 95
Ervin, C.R., 196, 199
Espindle, D., 282
Esser, J.K., 242
Euler, H.A., 185
Evans, G.W., 121, 122
Evans, J.M., 437
Evans-Campbell, T., 355
Ewell, K., 225
Eysenck, H., 420

Fabes, R.A., 178
Factor, R., 293
Fairburn, C.G., 400
Fanning, P., 104

Farrar, J.W., 202
Farrow, R., 170
Faulkner, S.L., 283, 284, 287
Fawcett, J., 435
Fay, N., 227
(The) Federal Executive Institute and Management Development Centers, 60
Fehr, B., 211
Feinberg, C., 316
Feldman, A.F., 271
Feldman, J., 152
Felson, R.B., 104
Ferns, W., 386
Ferrari, J.R., 150
Fetters, M.D., 124
Feurer, I.D., 321
Fiedler, F., 237
Field, D., 437
Figler, J.L., 125
Figley, C.R., 264
Fincham, F.D., 326
Finchman, F.D., 329, 330, 331
Fine, S., 178
Finholt, T., 228
Finkelhor, D., 303
Finn, M.A., 322
Fischer, A.H., 177, 185
Fischer, S., 132
Fisher, J.E., 420, 421
Fisk, A.D., 70
Fiske, S.T., 225
Fitzsimmons, G.M., 86
Flaherty, S.R., 205
Fleg, J.L., 273
Fletcher, S., 170
Flett, G.L., 14
Floyd, M.F., 273
Flynt, S.W., 184
Foa, E.B., 383
Foese, O., 71
Fogg, N.P., 80
Folkman, 449
Folkman, S., 442
Foote, D., 385
Ford, 49
Ford, S.J.W., 421
Forman, E.M., 409, 421
Foster, G., 196
Fournier, M.A., 211
Fox, N.A., 205
Frame, C.L., 197
Frances, E.L., 385
Frank, E., 416, 441, 442
Frank, R.G., 420
Frankl, V., 14
Franklin, B., 72, 73
Franks, M.M., 330
Frazier, P., 142
Fredrickson, B.L., 356, 357
Freeman, C., 80–81

Freeman, R.E.K., 197
French, C.C., 181
French, J.R., 142
French, M., 241
Frensch, P.A., 418
Freud, A., 35
Freud, S., 31, 32, 34, 35, 36, 50, 52, 115, 405
Frewen, P.A., 411
Friedman, M., 182
Friedman, M.A., 332, 333
Friedman, M.J., 126
Friel, J.C., 341
Friel, L.D., 341
Fries, J.F., 71
Fritch, A., 205
Froehlich, M., 84
Fromm, E., 10
Fudge, A.K., 197
Fuhrer, R., 142
Fujino, D., 421
Fujita, F., 197
Fulton, R., 442
Fung, H.H., 177
Furnham, A., 197
Furstenberg, A., 65, 75

Gabbard, G.O., 420
Gable, S.A., 150
Gabriel, S., 196
Gabrieli, J.D.E., 288, 289, 290
Gaertner, L., 88, 332, 333
Gaertner, S.L., 225
Gagne, M., 142, 143, 145, 146
Gaher, R.M., 170
Gaines, L.M., 196
Gaines, S.O., 199
Galdas, P.M., 123
Gallacher, J.E.J., 182
Gamino, L.A., 442, 449
Gandhi, M., 73
Gangestad, S.W., 315
Garbarino, J., 56
Gardner, M.D., 334
Garnefski, N., 76
Garrick, J., 363
Garrod, S., 227
Gary, F.A., 373, 375, 402
Gary, M.L., 225
Gates, B., 14
Gavin, M., 39
Gavzer, B., 71, 448
Gawet, D.L., 347, 348
Gedo, J.E., 406
Geis, F.L., 240
Gelfand, M., 142
Genova, P., 372
Geron, S.M., 335
Gershoff, E.T., 38
Gerstenberger, M., 284, 332

Gervirtz, R., 182
Gianakos, I., 354
Giarrusso, R., 59
Gibbons, F.X., 121
Gibbs, J.L., 198, 209, 317
Gibson, J., 121
Gibson, S., 407
Giesen, D., 332
Gilbert, D.T., 146, 152, 175
Giles, L.C., 75
Gillihan, S.J., 347, 348
Gilovich, T., 93, 96, 152
Giorgi, A., 41
Gladwell, M., 201
Glaeser, B.C., 94
Glaser, R., 110, 351
Glick, P., 225
Glonek, G.F.V., 75
Godfrey, J.R., 363
Godoy, R., 204
Goetz, A.T., 185
Goldin-Meadow, S., 202
Goldmeier, D., 287
Goleman, D., 219, 239
Gologor, E., 236
Goode, E., 30
Goodnow, J.J., 330, 448
Goodwin, R., 211
Goodwin, S.A., 94
Gorbachev, M., 14
Gordon, K.C., 332, 333
Gordon, L.C., 38
Gordon, T., 179
Gorin, S.H., 65
Gorman, C., 180
Gottman, J., 286, 326, 327, 341
Gottman, J.S., 341
Gough, B., 131
Gould, O.N., 129
Goyal, T.M., 225
Grühn, D., 72
Grabhorn, R., 406
Grad, O.T., 440
Graetz, K.A., 246
Graham, C.A., 288
Grajek, Susan, 318
Grant, E., 181
Gray, C.A., 335
Gray, J.J., 197
Gray-Little, B., 331
Graziano, W.G., 199
Greaves, S., 272
Green, B.L., 283
Green, S.M., 333
Green, S.P., 86
Greenberg, J., 240
Greenberg, L.S., 407
Greenberg, M.A., 182
Greenberg, S., 75
Greene, K., 283, 284, 287

Greenhaus, J.H., 269
Greenhouse, J.B., 416
Greeson, C., 216
Gregson, D., 137
Greguras, G.J., 265
Greve, W., 84, 88
Grewal, D., 215
Griffin, J.M., 142
Grochocinski, V., 416
Grocke, D., 95
Groopman, J., 381
Grosch, J., 246, 247
Groth-Marnat, G., 436
Grouzet, F.M.E., 166, 168
Guastello, D.D., 283
Guastello, S.J., 283
Guerrero, L.K., 185, 202
Guinto, J., 271, 345
Gunderson, J., 205
Gupta, S., 330, 362
Guthrie, I.K., 178
Guttmacher Institute, 298

Hébert, R., 273, 274
Habben, C.J., 424
Hack, T., 444
Haddad, A., 443
Haden, S.C., 363
Hagerty, K., 120
Hagger, M.S., 142
Hagihara, A., 124
Hahlweg, K., 316
Hahn, J., 10
Haines, M.P., 150
Hajjar, I., 150
Halderman, D.C., 292
Haldt, J., 24
Halford, W.K., 330
Hall, B.J., 24
Hall, C., 323
Hall, C.E., 86
Hall, J.A., 124, 125, 128, 177
Hall, R., 197
Hallahan, M., 201
Hallam, M., 197
Hallett, J.S., 202
Hallqvist, J., 354
Halpern-Felshner, B.L., 436
Hamarat, E., 59
Hamby, S.L., 331
Hamer, R.J., 205
Hamilton-Giachritsis, C., 39
Hammarström, A., 354
Handberg, E., 182
Hani, T., 406
Hankin, B.L., 84, 88
Hanley, S.J., 43
Hannah, A., 202
Hansen, E.B., 170
Hansen, J.C., 257, 258

Hansen, J.I.C., 258
Hansenne, M., 170
Hanson, M.S., 384
Hansson, K., 70
Harackiewicz, J.M., 171, 172
Harder, B., 69
Hardey, M., 317
Harlos, M., 444
Harpaz, I., 272
Harper, G., 243, 250
Harrell, S.P., 349
Harrington, P., 80
Harrington, T., 80
Harris, A.H.S., 275
Harris, C.R., 185
Harris, D.L., 267
Harris, J.R., 29
Harris, L., 271
Hart, 49
Hartman, M., 72
Hartmann, E., 131
Harvard Health Letter, 71, 110, 124,
    125, 128, 129
Harvard Mental Health Letter, 372, 382, 383,
    385, 436
Harvard Women's Health Watch, 352, 378,
    382, 448
Harvey, J.H., 81
Haselton, M.G., 202
Hasenau, S., 142
Hashimoto, T., 318
Haslam, S.A., 270
Hassard, T., 444
Hassenzahl, D.M., 237
Hastie, R., 161
Hatala, M.N., 198
Hatfield, E., 197, 316, 318, 319
Hause, K.S., 212
Havercamp, S.M., 43, 46
Haveren, R.V., 424
Hawkins, J.D., 120
Hawkley, L.C., 214
Hayes, R.D., 296
Haynes, S.D., 109
Hayward, C., 205, 207
Hayward, M.D., 76
Hazan, C., 50, 319
Health & Medicine Week, 448
Healy, D., 428
Heath, C., 88, 91
Heaton, T., 328
Heckhausen, J., 73
Hedge, J.W., 67
Heidebrecht, C., 447–448
Heifetz, A., 243
Heimberg, R.G., 205, 216
Heino, R.D., 198, 209, 317
Helgeson, V.S., 227, 240, 334
Helson, R., 59, 66
Helwig-Larson, M., 147

Hemingway, H., 76
Hemsworth, D., 442
Henderson, D.R., 161
Hendrick, C., 319, 323
Hendrick, S.S., 319, 323, 326, 334
Henning, K., 289
Henningsen, D.D., 242
Henningsen, M.L.M., 242
Henry, D., 125
Henss, 197
Herbener, E.S., 16
Herbert, W., 67
Herek, G.M., 292, 293
Herman, C.P., 95
Herrera, P., 177
Hershberger, S.L., 94
Hershey, D.A., 75
Hess, U., 177, 201
Heth, J.T., 146
Hetherington, E.M., 33
Hewitt, P.L., 14
Hewstone, M., 224
Hickling, E.J., 355
Hill, J.O., 49, 114, 137
Hilliard E.B., 219
Hilsenroth, M.J., 421
Hinsz, V.B., 167
Hirai, K., 447
Hirkowitz, M., 137
Hirsch, G., 191
Hixon, J.G., 314
Hocking, I., 27, 35, 37, 41, 43, 51
Hodge, C.N., 196, 197
Hoeger, S.A., 137
Hoeger, W.W.K., 137
Hoffman, K.R., 184
Hofstede, G., 241, 244
Hoganson, G., 67
Hogarth, R.M., 150
Hohwy, J., 37, 40, 41
Hoier, S., 185
Hollon, S.D., 421
Holmes, T.H., 346
Holt, C.S., 200, 216
Holt, L.E., 182
Holtzworth-Munroe, A., 321
Hooper, C.L., 161
Hope, D.A., 216
Hopko, D.R., 181
Hopper, J., 198
Horgen, K.B., 112
Horne, R., 125
Hornsby, M.J., 225, 226
Hospice Foundation of America, 447
Hospice Management Advisor, 448
Houck, P.R., 440, 441, 442
Houran, J., 317
House, R.J., 239
Houser-Marko, L., 66
Howe, C., 94, 346–347, 349

Howe, M.J.A., 30
Howell, D., 447–448
Howell, L., 282, 283
Howlett, D., 174
Hoyle, R.H., 246
Hoyt, D.R., 314
Hoyt, W.T., 442
Hu, L., 421
Huanca, T., 204
Hudd, S.S., 348
Huddy, L., 5
Hughes, I., 207, 208
Huguet, P., 204
Hunsberger, B., 148
Hunt, E., 444
Hunter, J., 196, 197, 292, 294
Hunter, M., 168, 272
Huntington, S.P., 243
Hurley, J., 363
Hurley, K., 416
Husted, 152
Hutchinson, S.I., 273
Hyde, J.S., 84, 88, 287, 288, 294

Ibarra, H., 279
Ilies, R., 237
Iliffe, S., 71
Ingrassia, M., 322
Imamoglu, E.O., 314, 315
Impett, E., 282
Insko, C.A., 246
Izard, C., 178

Jaccoby, S., 70
Jackson, D., 237
Jackson, E.F., 213
Jackson, L.A., 196, 197
Jackson, L.M., 148
Jackson, M., 4
Jackson, T., 140, 143, 205
Jacobs, J., 70
Jacobsen, C., 239
Jacobs-Lawson, J.M., 75
Jacobson, D., 200
Jacoby, L.L., 204
Jaffee, S.R., 287
Jalleh, G., 125
Jamal, M., 349
James, K., 235
James, V.H., 184
James, W., 95
Janis, I., 242
Janssen, E., 288
Jauhar, 444, 446
Jay, J., 66
Jedlicka, C., 216
Jenkinson, V.P., 150
Jenson-Campbell, L.A., 199
Jetten, J., 225, 226
Jewell, K.S., 240

Jewell, R.D., 141, 143
Johannesen-Schmidt, M.C., 240
John, O.P., 59
Johnson, C., 198
Johnson, C.A., 330
Johnson, D.M., 391
Johnson, D.R., 329
Johnson, D.W., 24
Johnson, J.A., 125
Johnson, S., 331, 352, 414
Johnson, S.D., 295
Johnson, T., 226, 233, 241, 245
Johnson, V.E., 283, 287–290, 291, 293, 294, 296, 297, 332
Johnstone, B., 197
Joiner, T.E., 390
Joner, A., 265
Jones, C., 59
Jones, D., 197
Jones, E., 35, 115
Jones, L.M., 303
Jones, S.M., 202
Jones, T., 66
Jordan, C.H., 167
Jorm, A.F., 133
Joseph, S., 346
Jourdan, A., 407
Jouriles, E.N., 331
Judd, C.M., 204
Judge, T.A., 141, 237
Jumper, S.A., 303
Jundt, D.K., 167
Jung, C., 35
Juvoven, J., 184

Kübler-Ross, E., 437, 438, 449, 450, 453
Kahn, A.S., 390
Kaiser, C.R., 94
Kaiser, R.B., 237
Kalakanis, L., 197
Kalimo, R., 264
Kalmijn, M., 326
Kaltman, S., 441
Kaminski, P.L., 109
Kaminsky, N., 310
Kane, L.T., 150
Kanemasa, Y., 319
Kantrowitz, B., 330, 331, 333, 334
Kaplan, R.E., 237, 291
Karageorghis, C., 142
Karantzas, G., 330, 448
Karau, S.J., 171, 235
Karavidas, M., 5
Kark, R., 240
Karney, 316
Kasl, S.V., 73
Kass, S.J., 170
Kasser, T., 13, 66
Kasser T., 166, 168

Katsikas, S.L., 5
Katz, S., 196
Kaufhold, J., 406
Kayes, D.C., 173
Kazdin, A.E., 38
Keery, H., 85
Keinan, G., 182
Keller, 49
Kelly, A.E., 209
Kelsey, J., 385, 386
Kelsey, S.F., 182
Kemmelmeier, M., 10
Kennedy, B.L., 303
Kenrick, D.T., 283
Kensit, D.A., 412
Keogh, E., 181
Kerr, N.A., 235
Kessler, D., 453
Kessler, R.C., 321, 420
Keyes, C.L.M., 24
Khan, S., 204
Khatib, N., 5
Kidwell, B., 141, 143
Kiecolt-Glaser, J.K., 110
Kieffer, K.M., 39, 347, 348
Kieffer, S.C., 142, 143, 145, 146
Kierkegaard, S., 16
Kiesler, S., 208, 228
Kim, J., 316, 318, 328
Kim, S., 211
Kim, S.H., 243
Kim, Y., 166, 168, 187
Kim-Prieto, C., 186
King, C.S., 240
King, M.L., 93
Kinoshita, T.L., 213
Kinsey, A.C., 292
Kircaldy, B., 362
Kirk, J., 267, 272
Kirouac, G., 177
Kirschenbaum, H., 407
Kirsh, 39, 183
Kitayama, S., 10, 88, 172
Kito, M., 211
Kitzinger, C., 324
Kivlighan, D.M., 405
Kleck, R.E., 177
Kleespies, P.M., 442, 443, 444, 446
Kleiber, D.A., 273
Klein, C.T.F., 147
Klein, E.B., 61
Klein, H.J., 236
Kleinbaum, S., 323
Kleinbeck, U., 241
Kleinknecht, R.A., 214
Klohnen, E.C., 147
Klonsky, B.G., 240
Kluger, J., 124
Knapp, M.L., 197
Knee, C.R., 142, 143, 145, 146

Knickmeyer, N., 208
Knight, J., 282
Knight, K., 282
Knight, K.M., 93
Knight, R.A., 303
Knox, D., 336
Knutson, B., 177
Koch, S.C., 240
Kochanska, 50
Koerner, B.I., 436, 437
Kogan, N., 235
Kohn, A., 56
Kolata, G., 71
Kolden, G.G., 420, 421
Kolodny, R.C., 283, 291, 294,
    296, 297, 332
Komarraju, M., 171
Konowicz, 146
Koole, S.L., 84, 88
Koolhaas, J.M., 352
Kopischke, A., 269
Koren, M., 182
Korn, W.S., 62
Kornblush, K., 64
Korte, S.M., 352
Kosa, E., 211
Kosterman, R.F., 120
Kosuth, R., 205
Kouzes, J.M., 250
Kraaij, V., 76
Krantz, D.S., 182
Krause, N., 133, 436
Krauss, R., 244
Kraut, R., 208
Kress, V.E.W., 421
Kreuger, K.R., 67
Kristjanson, L.J., 444
Krueger, J.I., 91, 92
Krueger, P., 447–448
Kruger, J., 202, 228
Kuh, G.D., 14
Kuhlman, D.M., 169
Kulesa, P., 226, 233, 241, 245
Kuller, L.H., 148
Kulp, C.A., 182
Kumar, R., 245
Kunda, Z., 167
Kunkel, S.R., 73
Kunz-Ebrecht, S.R., 71
Kupfer, D.J., 416
Kurdek, L.A., 292, 294, 323,
    324, 329
Kuritzky, L., 69
Kurtzberg, T., 228
Kuther, T.L., 424
Kwan, V.S.Y., 59

LaFontaine, T., 418
Lagerfeld, S., 271
Lalande, K., 174, 175, 178, 441

Lamb, M., 33
Lambert, A.J., 204
Lambert, M.J., 13
Lamberth, J., 196, 199
Lammlein, S.E., 67
Lamoreaux, M.J., 86
Landau, M.J., 203
Lang, F.R., 75
Lang, P.J., 225
Lange, R., 317
Langlois, J.H., 197
Lansford, J.E., 330
Lapinski, M.K., 203
Largo, E., 203
Larkin, G.R., 356
Larson, A., 197
Larson, J., 441, 442
LaSala, M., 315
Lasley, E.N., 368
Lasser, J., 315
Latty, E., 289
Lau, S., 166, 168
Lauzen, M.M., 240
Lavanchy, M., 197
Lavin, M.J., 207
Law, D.D., 330–331
Lawrence, J.A., 330, 448
Lazar, S.G., 420
Lazarus, R.S., 347
Leary, M.R., 93, 208
Lebel, P., 448
Lebow, J., 414
Ledley, C., 209
Leduc, N., 448
Lee, A.F.S., 303
Lee, H.E., 9
Lee, K., 197
Lee, K.S., 269
Leiblum, S.R., 295, 296, 324
Leitenberg, H., 289
Leiter, M.P., 264, 279
Lekuton, J.L., 10
Lemaire, J., 324, 325
Lemme, B.H., 81
Lemonick, M.D., 110, 352
Lenderking, W.R., 37, 41
Leonard, W.R., 204
Leventhal, E.A., 123
Leventhal, H., 182
Levesque, M.J., 209
Levine, M., 279, 318
Levinson, D.J., 61
Levinson, M.M., 61
Leviton, C.D., 95
Leviton, P., 95
Levy, B.R., 70, 73, 142
Lewandowski, L., 444
Lewis, 49, 152
Lewis, J.M., 334, 335
Lewis, M., 49

Lewis, M.A., 109
Li, L.W., 448
Li, W., 418
Li, X., 235
Libby, L.K., 96
Lichtenstein, P., 70
Lightfoot, E., 275
Lightner, E., 177
Lim, N.K., 5
Lin, K.H., 38
Lind, M.R., 228
Lindahl, K.M., 315
Lindgren, A., 66
Lindstrom, T.C., 440
Ling, K., 235
Linley, P.A., 346
Lippke, S., 111
Lischetzke, L., 175
Little, A.C., 197
Littlefield, 24
Liu, J.H., 197
Liu, Y., 418
Lizzio, K., 330
Lockwood, P., 167
Lofshut, D., 129
Loftus, E.F., 152
Long, A.E., 203
Loose, J., 27, 35, 37, 41, 43, 51
Lopes, P.N., 215
Love, P., 341
Lucas, R.E., 334
Lucas, T.W., 314, 315
Luce, M.F., 149, 150, 152
Ludford, P., 235
Lugar, R., 213
Lum, T.Y., 275
Lund, D.A., 442
Lundgren, S.R., 199
Lundmark, V., 208
Lundquist, J.J., 140, 143, 145, 147
Luszcz, M.A., 75
Luszczynska, A., 112
Luu, L.A.N., 111
Lykken, D.T., 29
Lyons, J.B., 215, 216
Lyubomirsky, S., 186

Mabry, B.J., 59
Maccoby, E.E., 33
MacGeorge, E.L., 347, 348
MacKay, K.A., 14
Mackie, D.M., 225
MacLaren, C., 411
Maddi, S.R., 356
Maher, B., 326, 334, 335
Mahseredjian, S., 62
Major, B., 94
Makhijani, M.G., 197, 240
Maki, S.A., 129
Malik, N.M., 315

Mallikarjun, P., 385
Malmberg, J., 67
Malouff, J.M., 216
Mandell, B., 239, 240
Mandler, G., 30
Manger, T., 143
Manning, W.D., 323, 325
Mansfield, A.K., 123, 124
Manstead, A.S.R., 177
Marano, H.E., 205
Marazziti, D., 183, 185
Marcus, B., 117
Marcus, S.C., 413, 416, 417, 420
Marion, M., 182
Markman, H.J., 330
Markowitz, J.C., 421
Markus, H., 88, 172
Markus, H.R., 88
Markus, K.A., 202
Markus, M.J., 235
Marmot, M., 76, 142
Marques, J., 225
Marsh, A.A., 201
Marshall, P., 123
Martens, M., 125
Martikainen, P., 76
Martin, C.E., 292
Martin, G.L., 418
Martin, M., 329
Martin, R., 227
Martin, R.A., 363
Martin, R.C., 183
Martsch, M.D., 183
Maruff, P., 72
Marx, R., 214
Marzillier, S.L., 175
Masala, I., 183, 185
Maslach, C., 264, 279
Maslow, A., 14, 43–44, 45, 46, 91
Maslow, A.H., 52, 165
Masters, W.H., 283, 287–290, 291,
        293, 294, 296, 297, 332
Matheny, K., 59
Mather, M., 66
Matjasko, J.L., 271
Matlin, M.W., 303
Matousek, M., 436
Matsumoto, D., 10, 142, 172, 177, 201,
        225, 226, 245, 269, 318,
        319, 325
Matthews, G., 5, 180, 181
Matthews, K.A., 148
Matthiesen, S.B., 264
Matud, P.M., 123, 355, 356
Mau, W.C, 269
Maure, G., 204
Maxfield, M., 240
Mayberg, H.S., 383
Mayo Clinic, 113, 385
Mayseless, O., 214

McAdams, D.P., 66
McBurney, D.H., 197
McCabe, D.B., 317
McCabe, M.P., 282, 283
McClelland, A., 197
McClement, S., 444
McConatha, J.T., 177
McConnell, A.R., 86, 152
McCoy, S.K., 94
McCoy, S.L., 71
McCrae, R., 16
McCrae, R.R., 59
McDade, T., 204
McDonald-Miszczak, L., 129
McDonough, E.M., 209
McElroy, T., 196
McEvily, B., 228
McEwen, B.S., 346, 352–353, 368
McFarland, B.H., 355
McGettigan, P., 125
McGillis, D., 246, 331
McGraw, P., 104
McGrew, J.F., 226, 227
McGue, M., 29, 117
McGuire, K.M.B., 182
McKay, G., 191
McKay, M., 104
McKay, R., 197
McKean, M., 348
McKee, A., 250
McKee, B., 61
McKenna, K.Y.A., 86
McKenry, P.C., 328
McNally, R.J., 355, 383
McNamara, G., 170
McNeil, P., 146
Meacham, 49
Meana, M., 289, 290
Mednick, M.T., 269
Medvec, V.H., 152
Meesters, C., 182
Mehra, B., 5
Mein, G., 76
Meins, G., 50
Meir, G., 73
Melamed, S., 264
Menec, V.H., 67
Mengali, F., 183, 185
Mental Health Weekly, 448
Mentalhelp.net, 378, 382, 385
Mercer, D., 341
Merkel, C., 5
Merriwether, A., 197
Messman, S.J., 212
Metalsky, G., 390
Metter, E.J., 273
Metts, S., 196
Meyer, L., 211
Meyer, M., 332
Meyers, V., 436

Mezulis, A.H., 84, 88
Michael, S., 441
Michal, M., 406
Michalos, A.C., 186
Michelangelo, 73
Mickelson, K.D., 88
Mickey, R.M., 294
Miilunpalo, S., 67
Mikels, J.A., 72
Milburn, M.A., 124, 125, 128
Milgram, S., 234
Milich, R., 421
Miller, D.B., 347
Miller, G.E., 110, 214, 345, 351
Miller, I.W., 332, 333
Miller, J.G., 88, 97
Miller, J.L., 211
Millon, T., 429
Millstein, S.G., 436
Milovancevic, M.P., 347
Miranda, J., 375
Mirowsky, J., 142
Misak, J.E., 84, 88
Mishina, A., 184
Misra, R., 348
Misseldine, W., 282
Mitchell, T., 165
Mitford, J., 453
Miyamoto, J., 152
Moen, P., 5, 15, 24
Moffitt,, 48
Mohr, R.D., 265
Moleiro, C., 406
Moller, A.C., 166
Molloy, J.L., 202
Molnar, B.E., 321
Monk, T.H., 440
Montarello, S.A., 213
Montmarquette, C., 62
Moody, E.J., 208
Moon, Y., 267
Moor, M., 170
Moore, C., 270
Moore, N.B., 287
Morahan-Martin, J.M., 150
Moreau, D., 75
Moreland, R.L., 200
Moren-Cross, J.L., 228
Morewedge, C.K., 152
Morgan, M., 125
Morita, T., 447
Morris, J.A., 237
Morris, J.F., 315
Morris, M., 228
Morry, M.M., 199, 209
Mortensen, H., 142
Morton, R.C., 184
Mosemak, J., 323
Moses, A.M.R. ("Grandma"), 73
Moshavi, D., 239

Mosher, S.W., 14
Mosher, W.D., 328
Moskowitz, D.S., 211
Moskowitz, J.T., 442, 449
Mosquera, P.M., 177
Mostow, A., 178
Mouzos, J., 322
Moxey, A., 125
Mroczek, D.K., 66
Muñoz, J.M., 215
Mukophadhyay, T., 208
Mulak, A., 202
Mullen, E.A., 420, 421
Muller, J.G., 213
Multon, K.D., 405
Munz, D.C., 209
Murachver, T., 202
Muris, P., 182
Murphy, S.M., 185
Murray, D., 348
Murray, S.L., 85, 327
Musgrave, C., 436
Mussweiler, T., 196
Myers, D.G., 186, 187, 200, 235
Myss, C., 104

Nadler, J., 228
Nagasaka, T., 205
Nah, K., 216
Nair, E., 10
Nall, P.R., 84, 88
Nansel, T.R., 184
Naples, N.A., 324
Nass, C, 267
Nathan, R.G., 367
National Center for Chronic Disease
    Prevention and Health Promotion,
    114, 115, 132, 133
National Center for Health Statistics, 121
National Center for Missing and Exploited
    Children, 304, 305
National Coaliton Against Domestic
    Violence, 321, 322
National Family Caregivers Association, 448
National Health and Nutrition Examination
    Survey, 113
National Institute of Diabetes and Digestive
    and Kidney Diseases, 114
National Institute of Mental Health, 355,
    374, 376, 383, 384, 385, 386, 389,
    390, 392, 393, 394, 396, 417
National Institutes of Health, 113
National Science Foundation, 5
Nauta, M.M., 315, 318
Neff, D., 240
Neff, K.D., 43, 316
Neiderhiser, J.M., 70
Neighbors, C., 109
Neil, A., 66
Neimark, J., 131

Neimeyer, G., 84, 86, 88
Nelson, C.A., 375
Nemeroff, C.B., 383
Neta, M., 201
Neto, F., 214, 216
Neugarten, B., 76
Neukam, K.A., 75
Newman, M.G., 48, 424
Newstrom, J.W., 227
Nezlek, J.B., 215
Ng, Z., 202, 228
Nicholson, T., 70
Nielsen, 49
Nietzel, M.T., 421
NIMH, 352
Nishimura, N., 208
Nizharadze, G., 111
Nobutomo, K., 124
Nolen-Hoeksema, N., 441, 442
Noll, J.G., 441
Norcross, J.C., 429
Norlander T., 148
North, C.S., 383
Norum, D., 405
Novak, M., 81
Novelli, W.D., 75
Nowak, A., 84
Nunnink, S.E., 289, 290

O'Connell, D., 125
O'Connor, D.B., 142
O'Connor, R.C., 94, 346–347, 349
O'Connor, T.G., 335
Odamaki, M., 124
O'Donohue, W., 420, 421
Oetting, E.R., 182
Oetzel, J.G., 245
O'Farrell, K.J., 204
Office of the Surgeon General, 377
Ohashi, M.M., 142
Ohtaki, S., 124
Ohtaki, T., 124
Oishi, S., 10, 178
Oja, P., 67
Okamura, L., 146
Olczak, P.V., 246, 247
O'Leary, A., 40, 182
Olfson, M., 413, 416, 417, 420
Olsen, J.A., 33
Olson, M.B., 182
Ong, A.D., 142
Onguard.gov, 317
Orange, L.M., 303
Osborne, L., 374
Osgood, Charles, 246
Ostbyte, T., 114, 115
Osterberg, L., 125
O'Sullivan, M., 202, 204
Oswald, D.L., 208, 213
Oswald, R.F., 315

O'Toole, P., 72
Overbeck, G., 406
Overpeck, M., 184
Owen, S.S., 38
Owens, L.D., 184
Owens, S.K., 142–143
Own, L., 109
Oxington, K.V., 110, 346
Oxley, N.L., 211, 212
Oyserman, D., 10
Ozer, E.J., 355
Ozkan, S., 68

Pace, B., 184
Pacey, S., 336
Palladino Green, S., 108
Pallesen, S., 264
Pancer, S.M., 148
Pantalone, D.W., 94, 294
Panton, S., 121
Papa, A., 174, 175, 178, 441,
    442, 449
Paquette, J.A., 208, 214
Parasuraman, S., 269
Parekh, R., 198
Parent, J.D., 240
Park, B., 204
Park, H.S., 9
Park, L.E., 88, 92, 93
Park, N., 41
Park, S., 107
Parker, J., 202, 228
Parker, L.E., 441, 442
Parker, S., 211
Parkhill, M.R., 314, 315
Parmenter, R., 198
Parrott, W.G., 183
Parsons, J.T., 282
Pasanen, M., 67
Patenaude, W., 13
Patte, S., 204
Patten, C.A., 117
Patterson, M., 208
Patton, M.J., 405
Patz, A., 331
Paul, A.M., 204
Paul, M., 219
Pavlov, Ivan, 37
Payne, B.K., 204
Payne, D., 38
Pearlin, L.I., 73
Pecchioni, L.L., 70
Pederson, N.L., 70
Pedro-Carroll, J.L., 334, 336
Pell, M.D., 178
Pepine, C.J., 182
Peplau, L.A., 282, 283, 289
Perkins, A.M., 181
Perlman, D., 214
Perlow, L.A., 250–251

Perrett, D.I., 197
Perry, A., 124
Perry, D., 273
Perry, P., 388, 392
Peskoff, F.S., 125
Peter, R., 354
Peterson, C., 41, 148
Peterson, J.M., 168
Peterson, K., 323, 324
Peterson, K.S., 326
Pfaffenberger, A.H., 16, 59, 60, 66
Phan, E., 348
Phelan, S., 111, 114, 125, 137
Phelps, D.L., 295
Pherwani, S., 239, 240
Philippot, P., 177
Phillips, J.A., 323
Phillips, J.G., 207
Phillips, L., 71
Phua, V.C., 198
Picasso, P., 73
Piccolo, R.F., 237
Pienta, A.M., 76
Pierson, M.R., 94
Pilkingston, N.W., 94
Pilkonis, P.A., 416
Pilla, R.S., 184
Pincus, H.A., 413, 416, 417, 420
Pinel, E.C., 146, 203
Pinquart, M., 448
Pinto, E., 170
Pitchot, W., 170
Platow, M.J., 225
Plomin, R., 29
Plonk, W.M., 447
Plutchik, R., 174–175
Polivy, J., 95
Pollan, S.M., 279
Pomeroy, W.B., 292
Pope, C., 125
Poppen, P.J., 208, 209
Poran, M.A., 197
Porter, M., 323, 325
Potter-Efron, R., 191
Potter-Efron, R.T., 182
Pound, P., 125
Powell, A.D., 390
Powell, G.N., 240
Pozner, B.C., 250
Pratt, M.W., 148
Prentky, R.A., 303
Prescott, M.E., 202
Pressman, S.D., 110, 214, 434
Preston, J., 368
Previti, D., 332
Priel,, 49
Prislin, R., 236
Pritchard, M.E., 108, 348
Provencher, P., 147
Pruett, M., 341

Pruitt, D.G., 243
Pruymboom, E., 76
Ptacek, J.T., 331
Pulver, A., 133
Puterbaugh, D., 330
Puterbaught, D., 64
Pyszczynski, T., 203, 240
Pyszcynski, T., 93

Quigley, D.G., 438
Quillian, L., 225
Quinn, D.M., 247

Rössler, W., 374
Rúter, K., 196
Rabin, B.S., 214
Rachlin, H., 161
Radhakrishan, P., 10
Rahe, R.H., 346
Raikkonen, K., 148
Rait, D.S., 414
Rall, M.L., 125
Ramakrishna, J., 373, 402
Ramirez, A.J., 196
Ramsay, 49
Rape, Abuse, and Incest National
    Network, 305
Rapson, R.L., 319
Ratelle, C.F., 147
Rauer, A.J., 328
Rayle, A.D., 421
Raymond, N., 385
Raynor, D.A., 111, 112, 114,
    125, 137
Rea, M., 282, 283
Reade, N., 316
Reeve, J., 165
Regan, P.C., 282, 283
Regehr, C., 442
Reggers, J., 170
Reich, J.W., 348
Reicher-Rössler, A., 374
Reid, A., 186
Reisberg, L., 348
Reisen, C.A., 208, 209
Reiser, M., 178
Reiss, D., 70
Reiss, S., 43, 46
Renaud, J., 196
Renaud, J.M., 86
Rende, R., 29
Rennison, C.M., 321
Renshaw, D.C., 183
Rentfrow, P.J., 317
Repetti, R.L., 209
Reyes-Garcia V., 204
Reynolds, B.M., 209
Reynolds, C.F., 416, 441, 442
Rhodes, E., 216
Rhodes, G., 197

Rice, R., 120
Rice, T.W., 187
Richards, A., 181
Richards, J.M., 174
Richardson, D., 287
Richardson, J.D., 297
Richetin, J., 204
Richmond-Abbott, M., 5
Ridwan, S., 69
Riedelbach, H., 333
Rieger, G., 289
Riggio, R.E., 239, 240
Riley, R.A., 150
Rimal, R.N., 203
Risen, J.L., 152
Risinger, R.T., 147
Ritter, B.A., 240
Roberti, J.W., 170
Roberts, S.T., 303
Robertson, J., 66
Robins, R.W., 94
Robinson, R.V., 213
Robinson, S., 124
Robles, T.F., 110
Rochford.org, 384, 386
Rockloff, M., 84
Rodriguez Mosquera, P.M., 177
Rodriguez-Calcagno, M., 269
Roehling, P., 5, 15, 24
Roese, N.J., 151, 152
Roffe, L., 95
Rogers, C., 41, 50, 59, 86, 88, 91, 98,
    100, 406
Rogers, C.R., 52, 407
Rogers, S.J., 329
Rogers, W.A., 70
Rogge, R.D., 316
Rohner, R.P., 32
Rokach, A., 214, 216
Rorty, A.O., 165
Rosario, M., 292, 294
Rosato, J.L., 324
Roscigno, V.J., 228
Rose, K.C., 150, 151
Rose, S., 29
Rosen, R.C., 69, 295, 296
Rosenblum, K.E., 341
Rosenman, R.N., 182
Rosenthal, E.C., 149
Rosenthal, R., 201
Rosha, J., 14
Ross, C.E., 142
Ross, M., 93
Ross, M.W., 290
Ross, N., 66
Roter, D.L., 124, 125, 128
Rothblum, E.D., 293, 294, 315
Rotheram-Borus, M.J., 386
Rothermund, K., 73
Rothman, A.J., 125

Rotolo, T., 269
Rottinghaus, P.J., 258
Routh, L.C., 400
Roy-Byrne, P.P., 375
Ruan, W.J., 184
Rubel, T., 233
Rubenfield, K., 202
Rubenstein, A.J., 197
Rubin, J.Z., 243
Rubin, K.H., 207
Rubin, M., 224
Rubin, R., 335, 416
Rubinstein, A., 73
Rudin, M.M., 303
Rudman, L.A., 94, 225
Ruiter, A.C., 125
Ruscher, J.B., 204
Rushton, J.P., 199
Russo, F., 275
Russo, T., 348
Rutherford, M., 334
Rutkowski, A.F., 245
Rutter, M., 30
Ryan, M.K., 225, 270
Ryan, R.M., 13, 168, 187
Rychlak, J.E., 24

Sörensen, S., 448
Sánchez-Franco, M.J., 228
Saardchom, N., 324, 325
Sabini, J., 177
Sackett, S.A., 258
Safren, S.A., 94, 294
Sagy, S., 347
Sakaeda, A.R., 66
Sakaguchi, Y., 447
Sakuragi, T., 207
Salize, H.J., 374
Salovey, P., 125, 185, 215
Saltzburg, S., 294
Samter, W., 347, 348
Samuels, C.A., 283
Samuels, M.E., 240
Sanchez, D.T., 94
Sanchez-Bernardos, M.L., 85
Sands, J.S., 179
Sandvik, E., 187
Sangrador, J.L., 196
Santangelo, L.K., 355
Santesso, D.L., 205
Sanz, J., 85
Sarafino, E.P., 137
Sargent, J.D., 121
Sato, S., 318
Savard, J., 448
Savin-Williams, R.C., 292
Savitsky, K., 93, 96
Sayer, L.C., 329
Sbrocco, T., 197
Scaer, R.C., 368

Scantamburio, G., 170
Scarpa, A., 363
Scarr, S., 64
Scealy, M., 207
Schützwohl, A., 185
Schaalje, G.B., 330–331
Schachner, D.A., 322–323
Schaie, K.W., 73
Schaller, M., 225
Schatz, M.S., 438
Schaufeli, W.B., 264
Scheier, M.F., 148
Schein, E.H., 279
Scherlis, W., 208
Schimmack, U., 10
Schindehette, 384, 386
Schiraldi, G., 104
Schkade, D., 186
Schleicher, D.J., 265
Schmidt, J.J., 104
Schmidt, K., 95
Schmidt, L.A., 205
Schmidt, N.B., 390
Schmitt, D.P., 88
Schneider, K.L., 420, 421
Schneider, T.R., 50, 215, 219
Scholing, A., 207
Scholz, U., 112
Schooler, D., 197
Schopler, J., 246
Schraufhagle, T.J., 375
Schrimshaw, E.W., 292, 294
Schrof, J.M., 205, 207, 384, 386
Schultz, D., 178
Schultz, S., 205, 207, 384, 386
Schulz, R., 73
Schunk, D.H., 37, 40
Schut, H., 440
Schutte, N., 264
Schutte, N.S., 216
Schutz, A., 215
Schwartz, B., 149, 150
Schwartz, J., 211
Schwartz, L., 446
Schwartz, P., 328
Schwartz, S.H., 233
Schwarzer, R., 112
Schwinghammer, S.A., 227
Schyns, B., 240
Scollon, C., 186
Scollon, C.N., 178
Sczesny, S., 240
Searle, W., 216
Sedikides, C., 84, 88
Segal, N.L., 29
Segal, Z.V., 384, 386
Segerstrom, S.C., 110, 345, 351
Segev, E., 243
Seibert, S., 385
Seidlitz, L., 187

Seligman, M., 147
Seligman, M.E.P., 41, 149, 186, 421
Sellin, I., 215
Selye, H., 346, 351, 352
Senecal, S., 177
Senko, C., 171, 172
Serodio, R.G., 225
Seta, C.E., 196
Seta, J.J., 196
Sethna, B.N., 228
Sewell, A., 225
Sewell, K.W., 442, 449
Sexton, K., 208
Shackelford, T.K., 185, 322
Shaffer, L.M., 204
Shafirkin, A.V., 352
Shahar, G., 406, 420
Shalala, D., 374, 402
Shamir, B., 240
Shapira, I., 264
Sharabany, R., 214
Sharma, V., 14
Shaver, P., 50, 319
Shaver, P.R., 322–323
Shavitt, S., 226, 233, 241, 245
Shea, M.T., 391
Shear, K., 441, 442
Shear, M.K., 440
Shebilske, L.J., 199
Sheets, V.L., 185, 213
Sheffield, M., 13
Sheldon, K.M., 66, 186, 187
Shen, J., 314, 315
Sher, L., 110
Sherman, J.W., 204
Sherman, S.J., 152
Shima, Y., 447
Shimizu, M., 142
Shinew, K.J., 273
Shiomura, K., 142
Shiozaki, M., 447
Shirom, A., 264
Shmotkin, D., 186, 187
Sias, P.M., 200
Sides, G.D., 69
SIECUS, 291, 292, 293
Siegel, R.L., 69
Siegrist, J., 354
Siever, M.D., 390
Silva,, 48
Silver, M., 177
Simons, C., 59
Simons, J.S., 170
Simons, R.L., 38
Simonton, D.K., 236
Simpson, J.A., 315
Skinner, B.F., 37
Slade, E.P., 38
Slade, M.D., 73
Slater, A., 27, 35, 37, 41, 43, 51

Slaughter, 49
Sleebos, E., 199
Sleek, S., 335
Smith, A., 131
Smith, B.N., 235
Smith, C.A., 198
Smith, D.E., 109
Smith, E.R., 225
Smith, H.W., 161
Smith, J., 72
Smith, P.B., 137, 233
Smith, R.A., 196, 200
Smith, R.H., 183, 196
Smith, T.W., 323, 332
Smock, P.J., 323, 325, 334
Smoot, M., 197
Snir, R., 272
Snyder, C.R., 441
Soderlind, A., 140, 143, 145, 147
Soderquist, J.N., 334
Solomon, A., 400
Solomon, R.S., 175
Solomon, S., 240
Solzhenitsyn, A., 11
Somech, A., 237
Somer, E., 146
Sommer, K.L., 88, 353
Song, J.A., 9
Sonnentag, S., 264
Sophocles, 73
Sopko, G., 182
Soto, C.J., 66
Soukas, M., 348
Sousa-Poza, A., 265
Southwick, S.M., 357
Spector, P.E., 266
Spielberger, C.D., 177, 354
Spindler, S.R., 129
Spiro, A., III, 66
Spotts, E.L., 70
Sprecher, S., 197, 326
Springen, K., 75
Sproull, L.S., 228
Spurgas, A.K., 108
Srinivas, R., 14
Srivastava, S., 97
Sroufe, 50
Stalans, L.J., 322
Stambor, Z., 345
Stanley, S.M., 330
Stansfeld, S., 76
Stansfeld, S.A., 142, 182
Stanton, A.L., 356
Stapel, D.A., 227
Stasson, M.F., 235
Stecher, V.J., 69
Steciuk, M., 209
Stecker, R., 121, 122
Steele, B.J., 187
Steele, C.M., 172

Steele, D., 59
Steen, T.A., 41
Stein, M.B., 357, 383
Steinberg, L., 33
Steiner, A., 195, 210
Stephens, M.A.P., 330
Stepinsky, J., 4
Steptoe, A., 71, 347
Stern, J., 405
Sternberg, R., 318
Sternberg, R.J., 69
Sternglanz, R.W., 200
Stevenson, R., 207
Steward, J., 142
Stewart, A.J., 330
Stewart, G.L., 240
Stewart, J.H., 38
Stillman, S., 198
Stodolska, M., 273
Stolz, H.E., 33
Stone, J., 88
Stoolmiller, M., 121
Stoskopf, C.H., 240
Strauman, T.J., 420, 421
Straus, M.A., 38
Straus, S.G., 228
Streeter, S.A., 197
Stroebe, M.S., 440, 442
Stroebe, W., 440, 442
Stroessner, S.J., 204
Stroh, L.K., 272
Strom, P., 61, 62
Strom, R., 61, 62
Stucky-Ropp, R., 418
Studdard, S., 322
Suddendorf, 49
Sue, S., 421
Suh, E.J., 211
Suhail, K., 187
Sullivan, Andrew, 324
Suls, J., 227
Suls, J.M., 88, 91, 104
Summers, R., 436
Summerville, A., 151
Sun, Y., 207
Sunnafrank, M., 196
Sutton-Tyrell, K., 148
Swann, W.B., Jr., 314
Sweeney, M.M., 323
Sweetnam, P.M., 182
Swickert, R.J., 147
Szabo, A., 363

Takeuchi, D.T., 421
Talbot, L.A., 273
Tallis, F., 183
Tamir, M., 186
Tandy, J., 72
Tangri, S.S., 269
Tanner, S., 204

Tardif, 50
Tarumi, K., 124
Taylor, D.H., Jr., 114, 115
Taylor, S.E., 93, 146, 148
Techniques, 348
Teichert, N.W., 70
Tellegen, A., 29
Templin, T., 142
Tennen, H., 348
Tesser, A., 104
Tharinger, D., 315
Thase, M.E., 416, 421
Theodorakis, Y., 111
Theorell, T., 354
Theune, K.W., 197
Thierry, H., 241
Thobaben, M., 353
Thomas, 46, 47
Thomas, A., 152
Thomas, J.L., 117
Thomas, V.G., 269
Thompson, D., 59
Thompson, J.K., 85
Thompson, K.M., 121
Thompson, L., 228, 246
Thompson, M.S., 204
Thompson, S.C., 147
Thompson, T.D.B., 446
Thompson, V.S.S., 349
Thomson, J., 247
Thoresen, C.E., 275
Thoreson, C.J., 141
Thunberg, M., 178
Thurmaier, F., 316
Tierney, S.C., 420, 421
Tiggerman, M., 107, 108, 109
Tikk, A., 133
Ting-Toomey, S., 245
Tippin, B., 196
Tkachuk, G.A., 418
Today's Issues, 32, 33
Todd, Z., 211
Toker, S., 264
Tomberg, T., 133
Tomlin, 49
Toomela, A., 133
Toppinene, S., 264
Torrey, E.F., 400
Tosevski, D.L., 347
Travis, T.C., 341
Treanor, J.J., 214
Treas, J., 332
Triandis, H.C., 235
Trierweiler, L.I., 175
Truchot, D., 204
Trzesniewski, K.H., 94
Tsai, J.L., 177
Tsunet, S., 447
Tuckman, B.J., 226, 227
Tugade, M.M., 356, 357

Tun, P.A., 71
Tung, L.L., 235
Turban, D., 66
Turk, D.C., 123
Tweksbury, R., 198
Twenge, J.M., 94

Uchida, Y., 10
Ufema, J., 453
Ulijn, J., 245
Underwood, M.K., 184
Underwood, N., 331
Urbanski, J.C., 237
Ureño, O., 282, 283
U.S. Bureau of Labor Statistics, 270
U.S. Bureau of the Census, 61–62
U.S. Census Bureau, 8
U.S. Census Bureau American
    Community Survey Data Profile
    Highlights, 8
U.S. Department of Agriculture, 130
U.S. Department of Commerce, 11
U.S. Department of Labor, 262,
    268, 269
U.S. Merit Systems Protections Board, 265

Vacaro, D., 170
Vaccaro, J., 373, 402
Vaidya, R.S., 148
Vallacher, R.R., 84, 185
Vallerand, A.H., 142
Vallerand, R.J., 147
van Assema, P., 125
van den Berg, P., 85
Van der Does, A.J.W., 384, 386
van der Leeden, R., 240
van Dijk, E., 152
van Dulmen, M., 212
van Engen, M.L., 240
van Lommel, P., 436
van Os, J., 374
van Vianen, A.E.M., 177
van Wees, R., 436
Vangelisti, A.L., 284, 332, 333
Vazquez, O., 198
Vecchio, R.P., 241
Vegg, P.R., 354
Verma, J., 318
Vevea, J.L., 88
Vickers, R.R., 142
Vignoles, V.L., 107
Vittengl, J.R., 200
Vodanovoch, S.J., 170
Vogel, D.L., 421
Vohs, K.D., 91, 92
Volling, B.L., 328
Vorus, N., 202
Vuori, I., 67
Vythilingam, M., 357

Wagner, A.W., 375
Waldo, C.R., 315
Walker, J.U., 386
Wallach, M.A., 235
Wallerstein, J.S., 334, 335
Walsh, J., 205, 207
Walt, L.C., 125
Walters, E.E., 420
Walters, S.B., 202
Wampold, B.E., 421
Wang, X., 235, 418
Ward, C., 216
Ward, L.M., 197
Ward, S., 76
Warden, D., 94, 346–347, 349
Warren, L.H., 72
Warren, N.A., 441
Wassala, C.F., 354
Wasserman, I.M., 5
Watchravesringkan, K., 317
Watkins, E.C., 257
Watson, J., 37
Watson, J.C., 407
Watt, D.F., 30
Watt, J.D., 265
Waugh, C.E., 356
Weber, A.L., 81, 196, 200
Weber, M., 121
Webster, J., 267
Webster, J.M., 196
Wei, M., 421
Wei Wang, C., 69
Weiner, B., 121
Weinman, J., 125
Weisfeld, C.C., 314, 315
Weiss, D.S., 355
Weiss, K.E., 140, 143, 145, 147
Weiss, M.G., 373, 402
Welchans, S., 321
Wells, Y.V., 84
Wendorf, C.A., 314, 315
Wendorf, G., 216
Wentura, D., 84, 88
West, S., 348
Wester, S.R., 421
Westerhof, G.J., 186
Westman, A., 444
Westphal, M., 174, 175, 178
Wharton, A.S., 269
Wheelen, S., 251
Wheeler, L., 227
Whitbeck, L.B., 314
Whitty, M.T., 228, 267, 272
Wiedenfeld, S.A., 40
Wilburn, C., 246
Wilcox, C., 324
Wilcox, D., 183
Wilde, A., 287
Wilke, D.J., 322
Wilkenfeld, J., 247

Wilkinson, S., 324
Willemsen, T.M., 240
Williams, J.M.G., 384, 386
Williams, K.D., 235
Williams, R., 273
Willis, H., 224
Willoughby, B.L.B., 315
Wills, T.A., 121, 170
Wilson, A.E., 93
Wilson, A.L., 330
Wilson, G.S., 348
Wilson, J.M., 228
Wilson, R.S., 67
Wilson, S.A., 181
Wilson, T.D., 146, 152, 175
Wing, R.R., 111, 112, 114, 125, 137
Wingert, P., 330, 331, 333, 334
Wingfield, A., 71
Wingfield, J.C., 352
Wiseman, H., 214
Wissow, L.S., 38
Witkow, M.R., 184
Wolfe, C.T., 91, 95
Wolfe, M.D., 185
Wolpe, J., 409
Wolsic, B., 197
Women's Way, 275
Wonderlich, S.A., 390
Wong, F., 3, 4, 5, 209, 227, 246, 247, 271, 322,
    364, 376, 413, 417, 419, 420
Wood, J.V., 88
Wood, N.D., 330–331
Wood, W., 236
Woodhill, B.M., 283
Woods, K., 330, 448
Woods, S., 184
Woods, S.G., 310
Woods, T., 167
Woodward, J., 453
World Health Organization, 376, 377
Wormley, W.M., 269
Wortman, C.B., 440
Wright, C.E., 71
Wright, F.L., 73
Wright, K., 4, 438
Wu, C., 187

Xiao-Ping, W., 374
Xirasager, S., 240

Yager, J., 219
Yalom, I.D., 429
Yamaguchi, S., 142, 147
Yancey, G., 198
Yancey, S., 198
Yang, B., 418
Yarab, P.E., 330
Yardley, L., 125
Yarnell, J.W.G., 182
Ybarra, O., 196

Yela, C., 196
Yen, S., 391
Yoder, J.D., 240
Yokozuka, N., 348
Yoshikawa, S., 197
Yoshimura, S.M., 185
Yost, M.R., 289
Young, S.L., 333
Youngstrom, E., 178
Yuen, C.N., 207
Yunger, J.L., 185
Yurchisin, J., 317

Zabriskie, P., 355
Zalewski, C., 303

Zampelli, S.O., 95
Zanarini, M.C., 391
Zane, N., 421
Zarit, S.H., 73
Zautra, A.J., 348
Zavasnik, A., 440
Zea, M.C., 208, 209
Zech, E., 442
Zeelenberg, M., 151, 152
Zeidner, M., 5, 180, 181
Zemba, Y., 142
Zencir, M., 68
Zhang, N., 441
Zheng, H., 418
Zhu, Y., 245

Ziebland, S., 66
Ziegelmann, J.P., 111
Zijlstra, F.R.H., 264
Zimbardo, P.G., 205, 207
Zimmerman, B.J., 37, 40
Zimmerman, C., 437
Ziv, M., 294, 315
Zlotnick, C., 391
Zoghi, C., 265
Zuckerman, M., 142, 143, 145, 146, 169, 170
Zummuner, V.L., 185
Zurbriggen, E.L., 289
Zuroff, D.C., 211
Zusman, M.E., 336

Subject Index

abstract reasoning, 67
abusers, 321–322
acceptance, 438
achievement motivation, 167, 169, 171–172
achievements, 90, 171–172, 254, 256
activity level and genetic factors, 29–30
activity theory of aging, 76
actualization therapy, 408
acute stress, 347
addictive behavior, 413
adjustment, importance of self-concept to, 48
adolescents
 identity exploration, 63
 major transitions, 120
 sexuality, 291
 smoking, 115
 suicide, 386
adult development, 58–60
adulthood, 59
 medial violence, 39
 obesity, 113
 sexual abuse, 304
 smoking, 115
 well being, 66
affective affirmation, 328
affiliate, 228
African Americans, 268–269
 ideal body, 109
 leisure-time activity, 273
 suicide, 386
after-the-fact couples therapy, 330
age
 awareness of death, 436
 leisure, 273
 stress, 348
ageism, 70
age-related changes, 59
aggressive behavior, 37–38
aging, 66, 71, 76
AIDS (acquired immune deficiency
 syndrome), 301–304

alarm reaction, 351
alcohol abuse, 117–120
alcohol and smokers, 115
allostatic load, 353
all-purpose friend, 212
altruism, 14
Alzheimer's disease, 67–68
ambiguity, 122
American Association for Retired Persons, 65
American Medical Association, 444
American Psychiatric Association, 292, 372,
 417, 420
American Psychological Association, 420
American Self-Help Clearing House
 web site, 413
anal stage, 32
androgyny, 283
anger, 182–183, 185–186, 438
anniversary reaction, 350–351
anorexia nervosa, 389
antianxiety drugs, 416
antidepressants, 416–417
antipsychotic drugs, 417
antisocial personality, 391–392
anxiety, 16, 180–182, 353, 378
 behaviors to avoid, 382
 exercise and, 132, 418
 free-floating, 378
 loneliness, 214
 self-esteem, 92
anxiety disorders, 378–383, 416, 421
anxiety-reducing strategies, 181
anxious-ambivalent, 50, 320
arbitrators, 246
archival method, 20
Aristotle, 272
arousal and erotic fantasies, 289
artistic skills, 255
Asch, Solomon, 232–233
Asians, 207, 268
aspirations, 85

assertiveness, 15, 359–360
attachment style, 319–320, 322–323
attachments, 49–50
attention, 37
attributions, 84, 207, 332
atypical antipsychotics, 417
autobiographical memory, 93
autonomy, 36, 166
avoidance, 123
avoidant attachments, 50, 319–320
avoidant personality, 392
awareness of death, 435–436

baby boomers, 68
backchannels, 202
bargaining for time, 438
basal ganglia, 382
basic decisions, 155–156
basic needs, 165–168
battering, 321–322
Beck, Aaron, 411
behavior rehearsal, 410
behavioral reactions, 174
behavioral therapies, 409–411
behaviorism, 37
behaviors, 39–41
 androgyny, 283
 breaking down into components, 41
 detection, 125
 extrinsically and intrinsically motivated,
  168
 negative, 156–157
 preventive, 125
 procrastinating, 156
 self-defeating, 155, 157
 stress, 354
being in a process of becoming, 99–100
bereavement, 438
binge eating, 389–391
biological perspective, 27–31, 47
biological processes, 111

biology, 28–29
biomedical therapies, 415–418
bipolar disorder, 375, 387–388, 417
birth control, 298–299
bisexuality, 292–293, 314–315
blended families, 336
body, 107–109, 132
body image, 84, 107–109
body leakage, 178
Body Mass Index (BMI), 108, 112–114
borderline personality disorder, 392
brain, 27, 109, 382
bulimia nervosa, 389–390
bullying, 92, 183–184
burnout, 264–265
Bush, George W., 243

careers
    achievements, 254, 256
    apprenticeship, 259
    burnout, 264–265
    changing, 263
    child rearing and, 64
    choosing, 62–63, 254–264
    education, 259–260
    identifying compatible, 256–258
    internships, 259
    job interview, 260–262
    middle adulthood changes, 67
    outlook, 262–263
    personality, 256
    planning assistance, 257
    preparing for, 259–260
    psychological inventories for, 257–258
    résumé, 260
    skills, 254–256
    work values, 256
caregivers, 65, 68, 448
catharsis, 182
change, 16–17, 59, 155–156
characteristics, 29–30
charismatic leader, 239
child care, 64, 270
child pornography, 304–305
child rearing, 64
childhood
    developmental challenges, 46–51
    friendships, 208
    importance of, 42
children, 224
    affecting marriage, 64–65
    anger management, 182
    confidence, 48
    divorce, 334–335
    drug abuse, 120
    education, 28
    health, 28
    Inhibited style, 48
    joint or shared custody, 334
    major transitions, 120

medial violence, 39
    obesity, 113
    parents, 32
    reserved, 48
    self-appraisal skills, 172
    self-worth, 42
    sexual abuse, 303–304
    smoking, 115
    social and personality development, 28
    spanking, 38
    stress, 335, 336
    Undercontrolled style, 48
    Well-Adjusted style, 48
Children of Divorce Intervention Program, 336
chlamydia, 298–300
chronic stress, 347
climacteric, 69
clinical depression, 384
Clinton, Hillary, 240
clitoral stimulation, 297
close relationships, 63, 195, 319–320,
        322–323
cognition and behavior, 39–40
cognitive changes
    late adulthood, 71–73
    middle adulthood, 66–67
cognitive dissonance, 152
cognitive distortions, 384
cognitive processes, 174
cognitive psychology, 37
cognitive therapies, 409, 411
cognitive variables, 40
cognitive-behavioral therapies, 409, 421
cohabitation, 323–324
collectivistic societies, 172, 226, 245, 269, 318
college students, 214, 348
coming out, 315
commitment, 20, 314, 318, 323–328
common-law marriages, 324
communication, 328–331
    sexual, 284–287
    skills, 255
Community Mental Health Centers Act, 419
community-based services, 418–419
companionate love, 295, 316, 326
compatibility, 200, 328
compatible careers, 256–258
competence, 166
compliance, 233–234
complicated grief, 440
compromise, 246, 360–361
compulsion, 382
compulsive overeaters, 390–391
computers, 4, 267
confederates, 232
confident children, 48
conflicts, 44, 329–331
    groups, 243–247
    lifelong learning, 44
    marriage, 326

mediators, 246–247
    positive social change, 243
conformity, 232–233, 360
conscientiousness, 111
consensual-level cultures, 10
consummate love, 295, 328
contempt, 286
contingency planning, 258
contingency theory of leadership, 237
continuity, 16–17, 59
contraception, 298
contradictions, 15–16, 19
cooperative relationships, 200
cost of failure, 149
counselors, 423
couple adjustment, 63–64, 329
couples therapy, 331
creativity and late adulthood, 71–72
crisis, 18–19
crisis intervention, 419
criticism, 97–98, 286
crossdressers, 293
crystallized intelligence, 71
cults and social influence, 231
cultural clashes, 9
cultural diversity, 7, 10
culture-bound syndromes, 376
cultures, 10, 241
    collectivistic, 226
    conflicts, 245
    eating, 168
    emotions, 177–178
    happiness, 187
    health care, 124
    health professionals, 376
    ideal body, 109
    individualistic, 10, 225–226
    in-groups and out-groups, 225
    interdependence, 233
    loneliness, 216
    mental disorders, 373
    motives, 167
    pain, 123
    physical attractiveness, 197
    professional groups, 376
    self-disclosure, 211
    self-efficacy, 112
    self-promotion, 172
    shyness, 205, 207
    social loafing, 235
    social norms, 373
Current Directions in Psychological Science, 110
cyberslacking, 267
cybertherapy, 424

date rape, 305
dating, 38, 198–199
death, 431
    awareness of, 435–436
    denial of, 432

growth and, 449–450
late adulthood, 71
leading causes of, 434
memories and, 440
mourning customs, 438–439
natural, 446–448
negative emotions, 440
perspective, 442–450
death instinct, 33
decentralized communication networks, 229–230
decision by default, 157
decision making, 13, 258, 329
assessing, 150
balance sheet, 153
basic, 155–156
better decisions, 153–155
clarifying values and objectives, 153–154
cognitive dissonance, 152
commitments, 150, 157–158
decision by default, 157
faulty decisions, 154–155
group, 158
media and, 150–151
negative and positive outcomes, 155
new decisions, 156–157
personal growth, 155–158
personal resolve and, 149–155
postdecisional regret, 151–152
process of, 150–152
putting off, 149, 157
reactance, 152
role of, 140
shortcuts, 150–151
defensiveness, 286
depersonalization, 107, 264
depression, 16, 374–375
antidepressants, 416–417
brain and, 385–386
causes, 385
cognitive distortions, 384
cognitive-behavior therapies, 421
commonness of, 384
dying, 438
electroconvulsive therapy, 417
exercise and, 132, 418
loneliness, 214
major and severe, 384
SAD (seasonal affective disorder), 384–385
shyness, 205
suicide, 384, 386–387
desensitization, 409
desire for approval, 167
desire for success, 171–172
detection behaviors, 125
development, 58
biological perspective, 27–31
goals, 35
heredity, 29

humanistic perspective, 41–46
psychodynamic theory, 31–33
self-actualization, 43–44
self-directed aspects, 35
social-cognitive perspective, 37–41
stages, 31–33
developmental challenges, 46–50
developmental changes, 51
devil effect, 204
Diagnostic and Statistical Manual of Mental Disorders, Fourth Edition (DSM-IV-TR), 372
diathesis-stress hypothesis, 394–395
diet, 129
dieting, 113–114
direct bullying, 184
direct guarding, 186
disaster, 382–383
discrimination, 225
minority women, 385
physical attractiveness, 199
self-esteem, 94
disengagement theory of aging, 76
disgust, 175
dissatisfaction, 17–18
dissonance, 17–18
distinction between us and them, 224–226
distorted beliefs, 393
distress, 346
distress-enhancing attributions, 332–333
distressful thoughts, 363
diversity
marriage, 325
mental disorders, 375
population, 7
workplace, 268–271
divorce, 326, 333–336
doctors, 123–125, 129
domestic violence, 321–322
door-in-the-face effect, 234
dreams, 131, 406
drug abuse, 117–120
drug therapies, 416
dying, risks of, 432, 434–435

early adulthood, 61–65, 376
early life temperament, 46–47
early old age and happiness, 66
eating, 167–168
sensibly, 129–130
well, 72
eating disorders, 388–391
ecounseling, 424
education, 28, 270
EFT (Emotion Focused Therapy), 331
ego, 34
elderly
grown children and, 62
volunteering, 275
women and poverty, 74

electroconvulsive therapy, 417
electronic communication, 230–231
Ellis, Albert, 411
e-mail, 202
emotional arousal, 98
emotional balance, 177
emotional disorders, 413
emotional exhaustion, 264
emotional intelligence (EI), 215–216, 239–240
emotional intimacy, 323
emotional stability, 111
emotion-focused coping, 356
emotion-focused therapy, 331
emotions, 165
age-related differences, 66
anger, 182–183
anxiety, 180–182
behavioral reactions, 174
body leakage, 178
cognitive factors and, 174–175
cultures, 177–178
deceptions, 178
describing, 173–175
disgust, 175
experiencing, 175, 177
expressing, 177–178
facial expressions, 177–178
genetic factors, 29–30
hand gestures, 178
happiness, 186–187
lives affected by, 175
managing, 178–180
microexpressions, 178
misinterpreting, 175
physiological arousal, 174
potential control over, 174–175
primary, 175
recognizing and interpreting, 177
secondary, 175
self-control, 178
sharing, 179
special, 180–187
universal, 177
empathy, 407
employee alienation, 6
employment, 5, 329
entrapment, 245
environment, 28–29
health issues, 121–122
health of, 6–7
interaction with, 31
modifying and stress, 359–361
envy, 183
Equal Employment Opportunity Commission (EEOC), 270, 271
e-recruiting, 267–268
erectile dysfunction, 69
erectile inhibition, 69
Erikson, Erik, 36, 66
erotic fantasies, 289

escalation or tension building stage, 322

esteem needs, 165–166

etherapy, 424

ethnic minorities, 124, 375

eustress, 346

excessive stress, 346

excitement phase, 288–289

exercise, 113–114, 132–133

    depression, 418

    late adulthood, 72

    smoking, 117

exhaustion stage, 352

existential therapy, 408

experience of dying, 437–438

explanatory style, 148–149

expressive therapies, 408

external attributions, 84

external locus of control, 142–143

extramarital sex, 332

extrinsic motivation, 168

extroversion, 111

extroverts, 122–123

face-to-face groups, 231

facial expressions, 201

false consensus effect, 203

families, 28, 63–65, 223–224

    blended, 336

    self-agency, 172

family caregivers, 68

family mediation, 331

Family Medical Guide, 128

family therapy, 415

fathers, importance of, 33

fear of failure, 171–172

fears and desensitization, 409

feedback, 93, 100

feelings

    complexity of, 99

    sharing, 177, 179

female orgasmic disorder, 297

female-headed homes, 335

fight or flight response, 344, 352

first impressions, 196–197, 199–202

firstborn children, 167

fixation, 31–32

flattery, 234

fluid intelligence, 71

food guide pyramid Web site, 129–130

forming, 226

Frankl, Viktor, 408

Franklin, Ben, 432

free association, 406

free-floating anxiety, 378

Freud, Sigmund, 31–35

    nicotine addiction, 115

    psychological disturbances, 405

    psychosexual stages, 31–33

    structure of personality, 33–35

friends, 208–213, 314–315

friendships

    childhood, 208

    late adulthood, 75

    marriages, 327–328

    men and women, 211–212

    quality of relationship, 208

Fromm, Erich, 10–11

fundamental attribution error, 204, 245

funerals, 449

gays, 292

    AIDS (acquired immune deficiency
        syndrome), 198, 301–303

    dissatisfaction with bodies, 109

    domestic duties, 329

    eating disorders, 390

    erotic fantasies, 289

    estrangement, 315

    jealousy, 185

    long-term relationships, 334

    marriage, 324

    personal ads, 198

gender differences

    erotic fantasies, 289

    Internet, 231

    leadership, 240–241

    leisure, 273

    life-expectancy, 434

    sexual responsiveness, 290–295

    stress, 348, 354–355

gender roles

    changing, 283, 328–329

    self-esteem, 93–94

general adaptation syndrome, 351–353

general therapies, 408

generalized anxiety disorder, 378–379

generativity, 36, 66

genes, 27, 109

genetic factors, 29–30

genital herpes, 300–301

genital stage, 32–33

gestalt therapy, 408

glass ceiling, 270

goals, 15, 172–173

gonorrhea, 300

good events, 148

good grief, 441–442

good stress, 346

Gottman, John, 326

graduated and reciprocated initiatives
    in tension reduction (GRIT), 246

grandparents, 61, 335

Great Man Theory, 236–237, 240

grief, 438–442

group therapies, 413

group-level cultures, 10

groups, 223, 228

    collectives, 224

    communication patterns, 229–231

    compliance, 233–234

    conflict, 243–247

    conformity, 232–233

    decisions, 158, 235–236

    dynamics, 225

    electronic communication, 230–231

    formation of, 226–227

    groupthink, 242–243

    in-groups, 224–226

    intergroup contact, 225

    joining, 227–228, 242

    leaders, 236–241

    networks, 229–230

    norming, 227

    obedience, 234–235

    out-groups, 224–226

    perceptions of, 224–225

    polarization, 235–236

    primary, 223–224

    problems with, 241–247

    responsibility diffusion, 235

    roles, 227

    secondary, 224

    size, 230

    social comparison, 228

    social influence, 231–235

    social loafing, 235

    social support, 228

    storming, 226–227

groupthink, 242–243

growth

    choices enhancing, 46

    death and, 449–450

    needs motivation, 166

    potential for, 43

The Guide to Job Opportunities, 257

guided imagery, 95

halfway house, 419

hallucinations, 393

halo effect, 204

happiness, 92, 186–187

happy couples attributions, 332–333

Hazan, Cindy, 319

health, 111

    children, 28

    copying styles, 123

    daily hassles, 347

    late adulthood, 71

    loneliness, 214

    minor problems, 122

    optimum, 126

    stress, 345

    taking charge of, 128–129

health care, 124

health insurance, 124

health professionals, 376

health psychology, 107

heredity, 29–30

hermaphrodites, 293

heterosexuality, 293, 315

heterosexuals, 292
   dissatisfaction with bodies, 109
   jealousy, 185
   sexual responses, 293–294
heuristics, 203
hierarchy of motives, 167
hierarchy of needs (Maslow), 43, 165–166
high control situation, 237
high self-esteem, 90–92, 211
higher-level needs, 165–166
Hispanics, 109, 268–269, 319
histrionic personality, 392
hoarders, 382
homophobic, 292
homosexuals, 292–294, 315–315
hospice, 447
hostility, 16
human growth, 28
human service workers, 264
humanistic perspective, 41–46
humanistic psychology, 41
humor and stress, 363
hunger, 167–168
husbands, 224
hyperstress, 346
hypoactive sexual desire, 295–296
hypochondriacs, 122–123
hypostress, 346
hypothalamus, 167

"I" messages, 179–180, 286
id, 33–34
ideal body, 109–110
ideal self, 84–87
identity *versus* role confusion, 36
illness, 122–125
illnesses, 110, 122–125, 348–349
illusion of control, 147
illusion of invulnerability, 242
immigrants, 269
immune system, 110, 345, 351
in vivo desensitization, 410–411
inaction and regret, 152
incidence, 376
incompatibilities, 200
independent cultures, 10
individualism, 18–20
individualistic societies, 14–15, 225–226,
   318–319
   collectivist societies, 10
   conflicts, 245
   work and social activities, 269
individual-level culture, 10
individuals, 15–16, 43–44
industrialized societies, 142
industry *versus* inferiority, 36
infidelity, 332
ingratiation, 234
in-groups, 224–226
inhibited sexual desire, 295–296

Inhibited style, 48
inhibited vaginal lubrication, 296–297
initiative *versus* guilt, 36
insight therapies, 405–408
insomniacs, 119
insufficient stress, 346
integrative solutions, 246
integrity, 36, 73, 76
intelligence, 29–30
intercourse, frequency of, 331–332
interdependence, 233
interdependent societies, 10
intergroup conflict, 243
intergroup contact, 225
internal attributions, 84
internal locus of control, 73, 142–143, 168
internationalization, 269
Internet, 198, 207–208
   access in United States, 4
   gender differences, 231
   paralinguistic cues, 202
   romance, 316–317
interpersonal relationships, 91–92
interpersonal skills, 255
interracial marriage, 324
intersexed persons, 293
intimacy, 36, 318
intimate relationships, 195, 314–315,
   328–333
intragroup communication, 229
intrinsic motivation, 168
introversion-extroversion, 16
invulnerability, illusion of, 242

jealousy, 183, 185–186
job burnout, 264–265
job interview, 260–262
job satisfaction, 265–266, 269
jobs, 254, 263–266, 268–269
Johnson, Virginia, 284, 287–290
joint or shared custody, 334
joint problem-solving ability, 328

Kübler-Ross, Elisabeth, 437
King, Coretta Scott, 240
Kinsey, Alfred, 292
knowledge, rate of growth, 4–5

labor unions, 228
lack of control, 48
late adulthood, 70–76, 214, 386
latency period, 32
leaders, 236–237, 239–241
leadership, 237, 239–241
learned helplessness, 147
learned optimism, 147–149
learning, 37
learning from criticism, 97–98
learning theory, 37
leisure, 271–274

lesbians, 292
   erotic fantasies, 289
   jealousy, 185
   personal ads, 198
   relationships with parents, 315
libido, 31
life
   changing pace and stress,
      362–363
   freedom and control over, 11–12
   perspective, 442–450
   taking charge of, 11–14
life events, 148, 346–347
life instinct, 33
life review, 76
life satisfaction, 66
life-expectancy, 432, 434–435,
   442–443
liking, 199–200
living wills, 444–446
lobotomies, 418
locus of control, 141, 168
logotherapy, 408
loneliness, 213–216
long-range goals, 173
long-term friendships, 195
long-term marriages, 328
love
   belongingness needs, 165–166
   close relationships and, 319–320,
      322–323
   companionate love, 295
   consummate love, 295
   individualistic societies, 318–319
   ingredients of, 314–316, 318–319
   relationships, 315–316
   sex and, 294–295
lovers, 314–315
low or medium control situations, 237
low self-esteem, 90, 92, 211, 214
low sexual desire, 296

maintenance activities, 272
major depression, 110
maladaptive behavior, 40, 146, 372
maladjustment, 42–44, 146–147
managerial skills, 255
mania, 387–388
manic depression (bipolar disorder), 110.
   See also bipolar disorder
marital happiness, 295
marital partners, 197
marital satisfaction, 326
marriage
   attitudinally similar people, 326
   children affecting, 64–65
   cohabitation, 323–324
   communication, 328
   conflict, 326
   couples therapy, 331

diversity, 325
divorce, 333–336
duration, 326
friendship, 327–328
having fun together, 328
joint problem-solving ability, 328
long-term, 328
median age, 324–325
new, 326–328
partners, 325
primary goal, 333
quality of relationships, 326
reasons for, 325
self-disclosure, 326–327
stress, 64
success in, 326
voluntary, 325–326
Maslow, Abraham, 43, 45, 165–166
mass tragedies, 350–351
Masters, William, 284, 287–290
mastery, 140–149
masturbation, 297
Match.com, 198
matching hypothesis, 197
math and computer anxiety, 180
mathematics skills, 255
May, Rollo, 408
MCI (mild cognitive impairment), 68
mechanical skills, 255
media, 38–39, 150–151
mediation, 331
mediators, 246–247
medication, 125
medium-range goals, 173
meeting people
    first impressions, 196–197, 199–202
    mistaken impressions, 202–204
    negative and positive information, 196
    personal ads, 198
    shyness, 205–208
memory, 72–73
men
    backchannels, 202
    body image, 108
    casual sex, 283
    climacteric, 69
    death and illness rates, 123
    depression, 385
    doctors and, 123–124
    erection, 288
    friendship, 211–212
    gender ideals, 94
    happiness, 186
    housework performance, 329–330
    ideal body, 109
    impotence, 69
    internal control, 142
    leadership, 240–241
    lifetime changes in sexuality, 291
    midlife transitions, 67

nonverbal communication, 202
orgasm, 290
pay, 270
polar opposites, 283
problem-focused coping, 356
psychological disorders patterns,
    376–377
rape, 305
refractory period, 290
roles defined, 240
self-disclosure, 211
self-reflection, 94
sensation seekers, 170
sex and, 282, 295
sexual arousal, 290–291
shyness, 205
stress, 354–355
suicide, 386
task-oriented, 240
violence against partners, 321
women friends, 212
workforce, 269–270
menopause, 68–69
mental disorders, 373–376. See also
    psychological disorders, 402
mental health
    cultures, 375–376
    polluting industries, 121
mental health centers, 419, 422
mental health services, 375–376, 419
microexpressions, 178
micro-goals, 173
middle adulthood, 65–70
midlife crisis, 65–66
midlife transition, 65–66
mindguards, 242
mini-goals, 173
minorities, 94, 269, 375
minority women and discrimination, 385
misperception, 146–147
mistaken impressions, 203–204
mixed-motive conflicts, 246
mnemonic neglect, 90
mobility limitations, 72
mood disorders, 383–388
moods, 347
motivation, 37, 165, 167–168, 172–173, 180
motives, 165, 167–172
mourning, 438
multiple orgasms, 292
multiple selves, 86, 88
mutual-help groups, 413

narcissistic personality, 391
National Center for Complementary and
    Alternative Medicine, 408
National Coalition Against Domestic
    Violence, 321
The National Domestic Violence Hotline, 321
National Family Caregivers Association, 448

National Household Survey on Drug
    Abuse, 120
National Institutes of Health, 408
National Mental Health Information
    Center, 33
National Survey on Drug Use and
    Health, 120
National Victim Center, 321
natural death, 446–448
nature versus nurture, 27–30, 207
nature via (through) nurture, 30
nature wedded to nurture, 30
near-death experiences, 436–437
needs, basic, 165–168
negative behaviors, 156
negative events, 148, 347
negative inducement, 186
negative role models, 167
negotiation, 360–361
nesters, 61
networking, 260
networks, 229–230
neuroticism, 16
neurotransmitters, 109, 415
new marriages, 326–328
nicotine addiction, 117
nominal group technique, 235
non-age-related changes, 60
nonverbal signals, 201
norm of reciprocity, 198, 233–234, 246
norming, 227
nuclear family, 223–224
nursing homes, 74
nutrition, 130

obedience, 234–235
Obedience to Authority (Milgram), 234–235
obesity, 112–114, 390
objectives, clarifying, 153–154
objects, irrational avoidance, 380–381
observational learning, 37
obsession, 382
obsessive-compulsive personality, 392
Occupational Outlook Handbook (OOH), 256
occupations, 256
OCD (obsessive-compulsive disorder),
    381–382
Oedipal (or Electra) complex, 32, 50
old elderly, 71
on-line matchmaking, 317
opinion conformity, 234
opposite-sex friends, 211–213
optimism, 147–148
optimistic explanatory style, 149
optimists, 7
oral stage, 31–32
orderers, 382
orgasms, 290–292, 297
osteoarthritis, 72
other-directedness, 93

out-groups, 224–226
out-of-wedlock births, 335
outpatient services, 419

pain, 123
panic attacks, 378–379
paralinguistic cues, 202
paranoid personality, 392
paraprofessionals, 423
parental acceptance, 42
parents, 33, 38, 224, 334
Parents Without Partners, 336
partner abuse, 316, 321–322
partners, sharing responsibilities, 329–330
passionate love, 183, 316, 318
pathological (obsessional) jealousy, 185
pathological obsessions, 382
PDE5 inhibitors, 69
people- or relationship-oriented leaders, 237
perceived control, 142–146
perceived mastery and personal adjustment,
    145–146
performance, 181
performing, 227
Perls, Fritz, 408
permanence, 148
personal adjustment
    late adulthood, 73–75
    self-control and, 145–146
personal ads, 198–199
personal attributes, 30
personal control, 258
    diminished sense of, 146
    importance, 141
    learned optimism, 147–149
    maladjustment and misperception, 146–147
    overestimates of, 147
    perceived control, 141–146
personal crisis, 209
personal development, 30
personal distress, 372
personal freedom, 10–11
personal fulfillment, 19
personal goals, 172–173
personal growth, 15–20, 44, 58, 317
    accepting criticism, 97
    decisions, 155–158
    divorce, 334
    leisure, 274
    memories of, 66
    process of becoming, 99–100
    self-concept and, 48, 94–100
    stress, 364
personal identity, 84, 88
personal information, 211
personal motivation, 172–173
personal needs, preoccupation with, 19
personal resolve and decision making,
    149–155
personal satisfaction, 76

personal secrets, 209
personal support system, 210
personality, 33–36, 111
    adulthood, 59
    alternating between, 88
    career, 256
    psychological factors and physical health,
        110–112
    stability throughout lifetime, 16
    temperament, 46–48
personality disorders, 391–392
personality traits, 391
personalization, 148
person-centered approach, 406–407
pervasiveness, 148
pessimists, 7
phallic stage, 32
phenomenal self, 41–44
phobias, 409
phobic disorders, 380–381
physical appearance, 107
physical attractiveness, 196–197, 199
physical changes, 66–67, 71–73
physical environment, 14
physical fitness, 132–133
physical health, 121
physical illnesses, 110
physical punishment, 38
physician-assisted suicide, 444
physiological arousal, 174
physiological needs, 165–166
physiological stress reactions, 351–353
plateau phase, 289
pleasure principle, 34
Plutchik's theory, 175
pollution, 8, 121
population, 6–8
positive behaviors, 38
positive feedback, 93
positive inducement, 186
positive life events, 347
positive potential, 44
positive psychology, 41
positive regard, 42
positive role models, 167
possible selves, 95
post-decisional regret, 151–152, 156
potential, 14, 46
poverty, 6, 74, 335
power distance, 241
pregnancy, 69
preindividualistic society, 11
prejudices, 225, 349
premarital education, 330
preventive behaviors, 125
primary caregiver, 50
primary control, 142
primary drives, 167–168
primary emotions, 175
primary groups, 223–224, 228

principle of perfection, 34
problem-focused coping, 356
professional groups, 376
professional help, 422
promoting wellness, 126–134
propinquity, 200–201
proximity, 200–201
psychiatric social workers, 423
psychiatrists, 423
psychoactive drugs, 415–416
psychoactive substance dependence
    disorder, 119
psychoanalysis, 405–406
psychoanalysts, 423
psychodynamic perspective, 35–36
psychodynamic theory, 31–35
psychological disorders, 109–110, 371–374,
    376–377
    See also mental disorders
psychological factors and physical health,
    110–122
psychological hardiness, 356
psychological stress reactions, 353–354
psychologists, 423
psychology, 44
psychopathic personality, 391
psychosocial motives, 168–172
psychosurgery, 418
psychotherapists, 424
psychotherapy, 99, 403, 411–413, 416
psychotic symptoms, 393
PTSD (posttraumatic stress disorder), 354–355,
    382–383
purges, 389

Al Qaeda, 243

racial minorities, 124, 198, 273, 375
racism, 6
rape, 305–307
rational-emotive therapy, 411
Raynaud's syndrome, 69
reactance, 152
reality principle, 34
reciprocal determinism, 40
refractory period, 290
reinforcement, 37
relapse, 119
relational bullying, 184
relationship therapy, 414
relationship-enhancing attributions, 332–333
relationships, 63, 92, 195, 200
relaxation and stress-reduction
    techniques, 408
remarriage, 335–336
reminiscence, 76
repeaters, 382
repression, 89
reputations, 199
resentment, 438

reserved children, 48
resilience, 357
resistance, 406
resolution phase, 290
responsibilities, 329–330
responsibility diffusion, 235
résumé, 260
retention, 37
retirement, 75–76, 274
right to die, 443–446
risks of dying, 432, 434–435
risk-taking, 432
risky shift, 235
Rogers, Carl, 406–407
roles, 227
romance and Internet, 317
romantic jealousy, 183, 185–186
romantic love, 294–295, 316
romantic partners, 199
    attachment style, 319–320, 322–323
    Internet, 316
    physical attractiveness, 197
rouge test, 49

SAD (seasonal affective disorder), 384–385
same-sex friends, 211–213
schizoid personality, 392
schizophrenia, 109, 374–375, 392–395, 417
schmoozing, 231
schools and bullying, 184
science skills, 256
secondary control, 142
secondary emotions, 175
secondary groups, 224
secure attachments, 50
securely attached people, 319
self complexity, 86, 88
self concept, 88–94
self image, 84–85, 87
self you'd like to be, 95
self-acceptance, 44, 76, 99
self-actualization, 11, 13–14, 43–46
self-actualizing needs, 165–166
self-agency, 172
self-alienation, 99
self-awareness, 100
self-change, 95
self-clarity, 88, 94–95
self-concept, 42, 48–49, 83
    body image, 107
    changes, 94
    fragmented, incoherent view, 88
    greater self-direction, 98–100
    how others view us, 95
    ideal self, 84–86
    learning from criticism, 97–98
    multiple selves, 86, 88
    personal growth and, 94–100
    self image, 84–85
    self you'd like to be, 95

self-enhancement, 93–94
self-verification, 93–94
    social and cultural influences, 97
    social self, 95–97
self-consistency, 89–90
self-control, 145–146, 178
self-created standards, 93
self-defeating behaviors, 155
self-determination, 166
self-determined, 93
self-directedness, 93
self-direction, 9–10, 11–15, 44, 98–100
self-disclosure, 209–211, 326–327
self-efficacy, 40, 111–112, 114, 142, 172
self-enhancement, 88, 93–94
self-esteem, 90–94, 186
self-fulfilling prophecy, 245
self-growth pattern, 98–99
self-help groups, 413
self-image, 42, 84, 94, 96–97
self-immunization, 90
self-improvement, 95
self-interest, 391
self-mastery, 143, 146
self-perceptions, 85, 94, 98–99
self-promotion, 172
self-realization, 14
self-recognition, 48–49
self-reflection, 94
self-revision stages, 98–99
self-serving attributions, 84
self-sufficiency, 61, 403
self-understanding, 364, 405
self-verification, 93–94
self-worth, 42, 94
Seligman, Martin, 147
sensation-seeking motive, 169–170
sense of identity, 84
sensory stimulation, 169
sex, 167
    cultural differences, 290–291
    discrimination, 293
    double standard, 290–291, 332
    gender stereotypes, 281–284
    initiating, 287
    love and, 294–295
    occasional problems, 295
    quality of, 332
    refusing, 287
    reluctance to talk about, 284
    romantic love, 294–295
sex drive, 34
sex partners, 292
sexual abuse of children, 303–304
sexual arousal, 288–291
sexual assault myths, 306
sexual behavior, 287
sexual changes, 68–70
sexual communication, 284–287
sexual desire, 288

sexual dysfunctions, 295–297
sexual experience, 284
sexual fulfillment, 295
sexual harassment, 270–271
sexual histories, 287
sexual intercourse, 288
sexual monogamy, 332
sexual orientation, 292–293, 314–315
sexual prejudice, 292–293
sexual response cycle, 288–290
sexual responses, 293–307
sexual victimization, 295, 303–307
sexuality, 281–284, 331–332
Shalala, Donna, 374
sharing responsibilities, 329–330
Shaver, Phillip, 319
Shostrom, Everett, 408
shyness, 205–208, 214
SIECUS (Sex Information and Education
    Council of the United States), 293
similarity, 199–200
simple phobias, 380
single-mother adoptions, 67
single-parent families, 334–336
situational factors, 349
skills, 254–256
sleep, 130–131
smoking, 72, 114–117, 146
sociability, 29–30
social adjustment, 73–75
social and economic inequality, 6
social anxiety, 85, 180, 205
social changes, 3–9, 14
social comparison, 90–91, 196, 228
social environment, 14
social influence, 231–235
social interactions, 35
social learning theories, 37–39
social loafing, 235
social norms, 373–374
social phobia, 205, 381
social selves, 84, 95–97
social skills training, 183
social stimulation, 169
social support, 72, 133–134, 209, 228, 264
social withdrawal, 394
social workers, 264
social-cognitive perspective, 37–41
sociopathic personality, 391
solitude, 214
SPAM, 9–10
spanking, 38
spatial relationships, 67
special emotions, 180–187
speech disorders, 393
split personality, 393
spotlight effect, 96
stagnation, 36
starting family, 63–65
STDs (sexually transmitted diseases), 298–303

stepparents, 335–336
stereotypes, 203–204, 225
stigmas and mental disorders, 373, 374, 402
stimulation, 169–171
storming, 226–227
Strange Situation, 50
stress, 351–352
　acute, 347
　age, 348
　alarm reaction, 351
　altering lifestyle, 361–365
　anxiety, 353
　assertiveness, 359
　behavior, 346, 354
　beneficial effects, 346
　burnout, 264
　children, 335, 336
　chronic, 347
　college students, 348
　common reactions, 350
　compromise, 360–361
　conceptualizing, 345–347
　conformity, 360
　defense mechanisms, 353–354
　difficulty defining, 345
　distress, 346, 363
　emotion-focused coping, 356
　eustress, 346
　fight or flight response, 352
　gender, 348, 354–355
　health, 110, 345
　humor, 363
　hyperstress, 346
　hypostress, 346
　jobs, 266
　late adulthood, 72
　levels, 354
　life events, 346–347
　managing, 359–364
　marriage, 64
　miscommunication, 330
　modifying environment, 359–361
　multifaceted, 346
　negotiation, 360–361
　perceiving, 346, 348–349
　personal growth, 364
　physiological reactions, 346, 351–353
　powers of mind and, 110
　prejudice, 349
　problem-focused coping, 356
　problem-solving skills, 363–364
　psychological hardiness, 356
　psychological reactions, 353–354
　reactions to, 349–358
　remarriage, 335
　resilience, 357
　self-understanding, 364
　situational factors, 349
　stages, 351–352
　statistics on, 345

　strategies for coping with, 146
　substitution, 361
　symptoms of, 349, 351
　terrorism, 349
　tolerance for, 361–362
　ways to ease, 350–351
　withdrawal, 359–360
stress-coping style, 357–358
stress-related disorders, 416
stress-related illnesses, 110, 348–349
Strong Interest Inventory, 257–258, 262
subjective feelings, 174
Subjective Well-Being (SWB), 186
substance abuse, 117–121, 146
Substance Abuse and Mental Health Services
　Administration, 120
substitution, 361
successes, 90, 167
suicide, 384, 386–387
superego, 34
surprise-mark test, 49
survival motives, 167–168
symptoms, 122–124
syphilis, 301
systems theory, 110

tardive dyskinesia, 417
task-oriented leaders, 237
tasks, 143
teachers, 264
technology, 4–6, 41, 266–268
technophobia, 5
telecommuters, 267
telecounseling, 424
television, 183, 273–274
temperament, 46–48
temporal memory, 72
terrorism, 349–351
test anxiety, 180–182
therapists, 403, 405, 407, 411–412
therapy, 403, 408, 420–425
thinness, 112
third force in psychology, 41
tobacco abuse, 114–117
toddlers, 49
transference, 405
transformational leaders, 239
transinstitutionalization, 419
transition (or desire) phase, 288
transsexuals, 293
transvestites, 293
trauma, 382–383
treatment plans, 125
treatments, other approaches to,
　413–418
triangular theory of love, 316, 318
trust, 36, 100, 213
tunnel vision, 386
Type A personality, 182, 348–349
Type B personality, 182, 349

Undercontrolled style, 48
underemployed, 254
unembodiment, 107
unemployment, 254
unhappiness, 214
unhappy couples attributions, 332–333
United States Department of Agriculture, 129
universal emotions, 177
unpredictability, 122
unresolvable, 122
unresolved grief, 440–441
U.S. Food and Drug Administration (FDA), 116

vacations, 271–272, 274
values, clarifying, 153–154
vasodilators, 69
verbal signals, 201–202
violence and romantic jealousy, 185–186
virtual office workers, 267
virtual therapy, 424
visualization, 95–96
vocational-technical school, 259
voluntary childlessness, 63
voluntary marriage, 325–326
volunteering, 274–275
volunteermatch.org, 275

wealth and happiness, 186–187
Well-Adjusted behavioral style, 48
wellness, promoting, 126–134
when to seek help, 403
Whites
　ideal body, 109
　job satisfaction, 269
　leisure-time activity, 273
　seeking help from doctors, 124
　suicide, 386
widowers and widows, 75
wish-fulfillment theory, 131
withdrawal, 286, 359–360, 416
Wolpe, Joseph, 409
women
　arousal, 288
　biochemical differences, 385
　child care, 270
　clitoral stimulation, 297
　committed relationship, 283
　communicating with men, 202
　conflicts between home and work,
　　270–271, 329
　death and illness rates, 123
　defining roles, 240
　depression, 385
　divorce, 334
　domestic violence, 321–322
　education, 270
　emotional intelligence (EI), 240
　emotion-focused coping, 356
　facilitative style, 202
　friendship, 75, 211–212

gender ideals, 94
glass ceiling, 270
happiness, 186
hormone supplements, 69
ideal body, 109
leadership, 240–241
lifetime changes in sexuality, 291
masturbation, 297
menopause, 68–69
midlife transitions, 67
nonverbal communication, 202
orgasm, 290
plateau phase, 290
psychological disorders patterns,
    376–377

rape, 305–307
self-disclosure, 211
self-reflection, 94
sex and, 282, 290–291, 295
sexual harassment, 270
shyness, 205
stress, 354–355
suicide, 386
thinness, 107–108
transformational leaders, 240
unequal power and status, 385
workforce, 269–270
work
    contemporary issues, 265–274
    job satisfaction, 265–266

leisure and, 272–273
technology and, 266–268
values, 256
workers, 272
workforce, 269–270
working from home, 272
workplace, 254, 268–272
World Wide Web, 4

young elderly, 71

zero acquaintanceship, 196